The School Counselor's Guide to Multi-Tiered Systems of Support

The School Counselor's Guide to Multi-Tiered Systems of Support is the first book to provide school counseling practitioners, students, and faculty with information and resources regarding the alignment and implementation of Comprehensive School Counseling Programs (CSCPs) such as the ASCA National Model and Multi-Tiered Systems of Support (MTSS).

This innovative text provides a strong theoretical and research base, as well as practical examples from the field, case studies, and relevant hands-on resources and tools to assist school counselors in comprehending, facilitating, and strengthening the implementation of CSCPs, particularly through MTSS alignment. Furthermore, chapters include pertinent information from the CACREP standards and the ASCA National Model.

This book is an essential resource for pre-service and practicing school counselors, as well as their leaders, supervisors, and faculty looking to better understand and utilize the overlap between CSCPs and MTSS, to strengthen school counseling programs to better serve students, schools, and communities.

Emily Goodman-Scott, PhD, LPC, NCC, NCSC, ACS, is an Associate Professor, School Counseling Coordinator, and Graduate Program Director in counselor education at Old Dominion University, Virginia. She lives in Norfolk, VA with her family.

Jennifer Betters-Bubon, PhD, LPC, is an Associate Professor and Program Coordinator in counselor education at the University of Wisconsin-Whitewater. She lives in Stoughton, WI with her family.

Peg Donohue, PhD, is an Assistant Professor and School Counseling Coordinator at Central Connecticut State University. She lives in Old Saybrook, CT with her family.

The School Counselor's Guide to Multi-Tiered Systems of Support

Edited by Emily Goodman-Scott,
Jennifer Betters-Bubon, and Peg Donohue

Routledge
Taylor & Francis Group

NEW YORK AND LONDON

First published 2019
by Routledge
52 Vanderbilt Avenue, New York, NY 10017

and by Routledge
2 Park Square, Milton Park, Abingdon, Oxon, OX14 4RN

Routledge is an imprint of the Taylor & Francis Group, an informa business

© 2019 Taylor & Francis

Library of Congress Cataloging-in-Publication Data
A catalog record for this title has been requested

ISBN: 978-1-138-50087-7 (hbk)
ISBN: 978-1-138-50161-4 (pbk)
ISBN: 978-1-315-14446-7 (ebk)

Typeset in Baskerville
by Swales & Willis Ltd, Exeter, Devon, UK

Visit the eResources: www.routledge.com/9781138501614

Contents

List of Figures   vii
List of Tables   ix
About the Editors   xi
List of Contributors   xiii
Preface   xvii
CACREP Standards Addressed by Chapter   xx
Acknowledgments   xxiii

1 Multi-Tiered Systems of Support: The What, Why, and How for
   School Counselors   1
   GEORGE SUGAI, TAMIKA P. LA SALLE, SUSANNAH EVERETT, AND
   ADAM B. FEINBERG

2 Integrating School Counseling and MTSS   29
   EMILY GOODMAN-SCOTT AND MELISSA S. OCKERMAN

3 Tier 1: Creating Strong Universal Systems of Support and
   Facilitating Systemic Change   62
   CHRISTOPHER SINK

4 Tier 1: School Counseling Core Curriculum and Classroom
   Management for Every Student   99
   ERIN MASON AND CAROLINE LOPEZ-PERRY

5 Tier 2: Providing Supports for Students with Elevated Needs   133
   JACOB OLSEN

6 Tier 3: Specialized Services for Students with Intensive Needs   163
   JOLIE ZIOMEK-DAIGLE, JASON CAVIN, JENNIFER DIAZ, BRENT HENDERSON,
   AND ALEXANDRA HUGUELET

7 Universal Screening to Support MTSS   189
   PEG DONOHUE

8   School Counselors Consulting and Collaborating Within MTSS   222
    BLAIRE CHOLEWA AND KATHLEEN C. LAUNDY

9   Using Data in MTSS to Demonstrate How School Counselors
    Make a Difference   246
    JULIA V. TAYLOR AND MELANIE BURGESS

10 Evidence-Based Practices Across MTSS   267
    MELISSA MARIANI AND SUMMER PERHAY KUBA

11 Culturally Responsive MTSS: Advocating for Equity for
    Every Student   298
    JENNIFER BETTERS-BUBON, HOLLY KORTEMEIER, AND STEPHANIE SMITH-DURKIN

12 Voices from the Field   330

    Concluding Thoughts   352
    Index   356

Figures

1.1	Three-tiered prevention continuum logic	6
1.2	Example of continuum of behavior need and responsiveness	7
1.3	Example of continuum of classroom behavior management practices	7
1.4	Example of school-wide continuum of practices and systems	8
1.5	Example of the front page of a teaching matrix	10
1.6	Example of a back page of guidelines for encouraging, teaching, and recognizing displays of expected behavior	10
1.7	Dynamic MTSS implementation phases	11
1.8	MTSS implementation blueprint	16
2.1	The ASCA National Model	32
2.2	The MTSS framework, including three tiers of support	35
2.3	Missouri Comprehensive Guidance Program: linking school success with life success	42
2.4	Overlap and similarities between a Multi-Tiered System of Support and Comprehensive School Counseling Programs	43
2.5	Triangle teaching activity	56
3.1	Depiction of Bronfenbrenner's (1979) Social-Ecological Model of Human Development	66
3.2	Lerner's Systems Model	70
3.3	Accountability cycle for MTSS Tier 1 practices	89
4.1	Sample needs assessment from Capistrano Unified school district	104
4.2	ASCA lesson plan template	108
4.3	Sample elementary-school-wide expectations	110
4.4	Sample middle-school-wide expectations	111
4.5	Sample school-wide expectations, modified for a specific school setting: the cafeteria	112
4.6	Sample school-wide expectations, modified for the school counselor	113
4.7	Continuum of classroom-level behavior management supports	118
5.1	Tier 2 decision-making process	137
5.2	ODR data analysis for Tier 2	140
5.3	Tier 2 request for assistance template	141
5.4	Daily progress report	147
6.1	Tiers of support	166
6.2	Sample FBA	168
6.3	Sample Behavior Intervention Plan	172
6.4	Daily Progress Report (DPR)	173
6.5	Progress monitoring tool	181
7.1	Sample universal screening plan	200

7.2	Three-year depression screening comparison data	206
7.3	Three-year anxiety screening comparison data	207
7.4	District BASC2 data by school	207
7.5	Data-based decision making to allocate mental health services	208
7.6	The ASCA National Model	209
7.7	Stand up to stigma	214
8.1	Triadic process of consultation	224
8.2	School-based mental health professionals	232
9.1	Individual student outcome data for behavior-related office visits	251
9.2	Grade level outcome data for behavior-related office visits for all students	252
9.3	Sample high school completion rate by gender	253
9.4	Sample high school completion rate by disability status	254
9.5	Sample high school completion rate by economic disadvantage	254
9.6	Sample high school completion rate by ethnicity	255
9.7	Sample SWIS report	260
10.1	Evidence-Based Practice model	268
10.2	MTSS Tier alignment with school counselor approach to direct services	269
10.3	Data-based decision making and EBP process	271
10.4	Process for building evidence-based school counseling programs	274
11.1	Academic achievement across student groups	299
11.2	Four-year graduation rates across student groups	299
11.3	Discipline data	300
11.4	Multicultural and Social Justice Counseling Competencies	304
11.5	Integrating school-wide positive behavior support and culturally responsive practices	306
11.6	Equity and equality	308
11.7	Culturally responsive school expectations	314
11.8	Risk Ratio for office discipline referrals	318
11.9	Graduation rates	318
11.10	Sample Risk Ratio data for student suspension	323
11.11	Sample Risk Ratio data for student reading assessment	324
12.1	Elementary school behavior outcome data	333
12.2	Elementary school academic outcome data	333
12.3	Elementary school SPARCS group attendance data	334
12.4	Elementary school academic outcome data	334
12.5	Sample elementary behavior tracking form	337
12.6	Sample Check-in/Check-out (CICO) point sheet	342

Tables

1.1   MTSS core operating characteristics, descriptions, and PBIS examples   13
1.2   Leadership team implementation guiding questions   20
1.3   School counselor role and MTSS implementation driver   21
1.4   School counseling and MTSS self-assessment   23
2.1   Comparing CSCPs and MTSS   40
2.2   School counselor role: supporter and intervener   46
2.3   Examples of school counseling supports at each tier and domain   47
3.1   Sample matrix of expected behaviors for elementary-age students   75
3.2   Sample matrix of expected behaviors for high school students   76
3.3   Sample school- to classroom-wide Tier 1 supports   82
3.4   Sample CSCP foundational statements incorporating MTSS language   86
4.1   Tier 1 supports: aligning MTSS supports and school counseling core curriculum   101
4.2   Sample month from annual school counselor department calendar: aligning school counseling Tier 1 supports (classroom lessons, large-group and school-wide activities) with MTSS school-wide expectations. Sample from the first month of the school year   117
4.3   Recommended school counseling classroom management strategies   119
5.1   Functions of student behavior   144
5.2   CICO data-based decision-making guidelines   151
5.3   Intervention checklist   155
6.1   Tier 3 evidence-based practices   176
6.2   CBITS lessons   178
7.1   Students in grades 9–12 identified with clinical levels of anxiety prior to universal screening   194
7.2   Commonly used behavioral and mental health universal screeners   197
7.3   Optimal procedural timeline for initial universal screening program in schools   201
7.4   Review of middle school students' academic, social/emotional, behavioral, and attendance data   203
7.5   RCADS average grades 5–8   206
8.1   Six stages of consultation   225
8.2   MTSS leadership teams   231
9.1   Examples of process data   247
9.2   Examples of perception data   248
9.3   Examples of outcome data   248
9.4   RCA in a high school setting   256
9.5   Current PBIS assessments   261

9.6	SMART or not?	264
10.1	Resource sites used for compiling school counseling EBP Tier 1, 2, 3 lists	276
10.2	Tier 1 evidence-based programs	280
10.3	Tier 2 evidence-based programs	285
10.4	Tier 3 evidence-based programs	289
11.1	Culturally responsive MTSS elements	309
11.2	Additional factors that influence learning or behavioral problems in school	316
12.1	Behavior matrix for core school counseling lessons	341

About the Editors

Emily Goodman-Scott, PhD, LPC, NCC, NCSC, ACS, is an Associate Professor, School Counseling Coordinator, and the Counseling Master's Graduate Program Director at Old Dominion University, in Norfolk, Virginia. She completed a PhD at Virginia Tech and previously worked as a school counselor and special education teacher, and in several mental health settings serving youth. She has published over 20 articles in national peer-reviewed journals, including *Professional School Counseling, Counselor Education and Supervision,* and the *Journal of Counseling and Development.* She serves as a reviewer for two national journals, *Professional School Counseling* and *The Journal for Child and Adolescent Counseling.* Other professional service includes nearly ten years as a member of the Virginia School Counselor Association, and co-coordinator of the School Counseling Interest Network of the Association for Counselor Education and Supervision. She enjoys living in Norfolk with her family, including her spouse and their three young children.

Jennifer Betters-Bubon, PhD, LPC, is an Associate Professor and Program Coordinator in the Counselor Education department at the University of Wisconsin-Whitewater. She received her PhD in Educational Psychology from the University of Wisconsin-Madison, and a MEd in counseling from Boston University. Dr. Betters-Bubon is a licensed school counselor in Wisconsin and worked as an elementary school counselor for 11 years. In her current work she focuses on the role of data-driven and culturally responsive leadership practices in transforming the role of the school counselor. She has published extensively in journals including *Professional School Counseling, The Professional Counselor, The Journal of School Counseling* and *Education and Urban Society,* examining the role and voice school counselors have within Multi-Tiered Systems of Support (MTSS) as well as on topics such as social justice and disproportionality. She has previously served on the Wisconsin School Counseling Association board of directors and presents regularly at state and national conferences.

Peg Donohue, PhD, is an Assistant Professor and School Counseling Program Coordinator at Central Connecticut State University. Before joining the CCSU faculty, Dr. Donohue spent 16 years working as a school counselor in both Connecticut and California. She taught elementary, middle, and high school in both comprehensive and alternative settings. She completed her PhD at the University of Connecticut. Her primary research, publication, and presentation topics of interest include: aligning school counselor preparation with Multi-Tiered Systems of Support (MTSS), universal screening for mental health concerns in schools, the impact of school counselor ratios on student outcomes, and fostering social emotional learning for adults and children. She has published in several peer-reviewed journals including *Professional School Counseling, The Professional Counselor,* and *The Journal of Counselor Preparation and Supervision.* She is a research fellow at the Center for School Counseling Outcome Research and Evaluation at the University of Massachusetts, Amherst. She currently serves on the board of the Connecticut School Counseling Association and the Connecticut Association of Counselor Educators and Supervisors. Most importantly, she is mom to two teenagers, Isabella and Joey.

Contributors

Melanie Burgess, PhD, is an Assistant Professor in Counseling, University of Memphis, Tennessee. She earned her MSEd in Counseling with a concentration in School Counseling. Her research interests include school counselor preparation, school counselor supervision, and data-driven evidence-based school counseling practices. She has presented at state and national conferences, and has published articles in peer-reviewed journals, including *Professional School Counseling, Journal of Counseling and Development, The Clinical Supervisor,* and *Journal of Child and Adolescent Counseling.*

Jason Cavin, MS, MA, LPC, BCBA, serves as the Clinical Director at Comprehensive Behavioral Solutions. Jason works with individuals, families, agencies, and school systems to assist with individualized positive behavior support initiatives, behavior support consultation, staff training, and organizational development. Jason's research interests include functional behavior assessment, community-based interventions, parent training and education programs, and training and staff development practices. Jason has served in many roles in the behavioral health field, including both developmental disabilities and mental health. In addition, Jason is a licensed professional counselor and a board-certified assistant behavior analyst.

Blaire Cholewa, PhD, NCC, is an Assistant Professor in the Counselor Education Program in the Department of Human Services at the University of Virginia. She completed her master's and doctoral degrees at the University of Florida. Her research is grounded in exploring ways counselors and educators can improve educational equity so all students have the opportunity to succeed. She is particularly interested in school counselor consultation and school counselors' work with marginalized populations.

Jennifer Diaz, EdS, LPC, is a doctoral candidate in the Department of Counseling and Human Development Services at the University of Georgia and has been a school counselor in Gwinnett County Public Schools for 17 years. She was named Georgia School Counselor of the Year by the Georgia School Counselor Association in 2013 and was a top five finalist for the American School Counselor Association School Counselor of the Year award in 2015. Throughout her career, her counseling departments have earned the Recognized ASCA Model Program distinction at four separate schools. Her research interests include advocacy efforts for comprehensive school counseling programs on state and national levels as well as the effect the implicit bias of educators has on achievement gaps. She currently serves on the board of the Georgia School Counselor Association as Advocacy Chairperson.

Susannah Everett received her PhD in Clinical and School Psychology from the University of Virginia and completed her internship and postdoctoral fellowship at Dartmouth Hitchcock Medical Center. She is a Research Associate at the Center for Behavioral Education and Research (CBER) at the University of Connecticut (UConn). After several years of clinical work with children and families in community mental health settings, she transitioned to work as a school psychologist in Oregon and then in Connecticut. Prior to joining CBER, she was the school psychologist for eight years at Ashford School and an adjunct professor for the school psychology program at UConn.

Adam B. Feinberg, PhD, BCBA-D, is an Assistant Research Professor at the University of Connecticut and the Director of the Northeast PBIS Network. He earned his PhD in School Psychology from Lehigh University, and currently is a licensed psychologist in Massachusetts. His research and clinical interests include the development and implementation of Multi-Tiered Systems of Support in schools and districts, with a focus on developing and supporting coaching knowledge, skills, and networks.

Brent Henderson, EdS, NCC, NCSC, is a doctoral candidate in the Department of Counseling and Human Development Services at the University of Georgia and a Coordinator of School Counseling for Gwinnett County Public Schools. He was a practicing school counselor for 13 years and taught at the elementary school level for eight years. He is an active member of the Georgia School Counselor Association where he has held many leadership positions including president. His research interests include the impact a collaborative relationship between school counselors and school administrators has on student success, as well as issues surrounding LGBTQ public school students.

Alexandra Huguelet, EdS, NCC, is a doctoral candidate in the Department of Counseling and Human Development Services at the University of Georgia and the School Counseling Consultant for the Cobb County School District. She was named the 2016 School Counselor of the Year by the Georgia School Counselor Association (GSCA) for her leadership and work promoting equity and access to opportunities for all students.

Holly Kortemeier, MS, NCC, is a school counselor at Community Elementary School in Edgerton, Wisconsin. She received her MS in Counseling from the University of Wisconsin-Whitewater. Her work titled "Pupils to Peers: Socializing Graduate Students to the Counseling Profession" was previously published in the academic journal *Sociological Imagination*. She has served as a Coordinator for the Wisconsin School Counseling Association and has presented at state and regional conferences.

Tamika P. La Salle, PhD, is an Assistant Professor of School Psychology at the University of Connecticut. Dr. La Salle studies culturally responsive educational practices and school climate. She is particularly interested in the impact of culture on students' educational experiences, and in developing and maintaining culturally responsive school environments that are equitable, safe, and positive for students, teachers, and families. She is currently involved in national and international research projects related to cross-cultural perceptions of school climate. Currently, Dr. La Salle serves as a member of the National Association of School Psychology Minority Scholarship Board, co-chair of the International School Psychology Association research committee, and as an ex-officio on the Association of Positive Behavior Support Board in the Equity seat.

Kathleen C. Laundy, PsyD, LMFT, MSW, is a Professor in the Counselor Education and Family Department at Central Connecticut State University. She is a licensed psychologist and family therapist who has treated children, adolescents, adults and families who experience chronic illness for over 40 years. As a strong believer in "medical and educational home," she collaborates with medical and educational teams when appropriate to build, support, and maintain the health of her patients. She consults regularly with schools, agencies, and other groups serving children and families.

Caroline Lopez-Perry, PhD, PPS, is an Assistant Professor in the Department of Advanced Studies in Education and Counseling at California State University, Long Beach. She received her PhD from Ohio University and her MS and PPS Credential in School Counseling from California State University, Long Beach. Prior to this, Dr. Lopez-Perry served as Assistant Professor at Chapman University. She has worked as a school counselor in both the K-8 and middle school setting. Her research interests include school counselor leadership and advocacy, group work in schools, school counselor training, and college and career readiness.

Melissa Mariani, PhD, is an Assistant Professor in the Department of Counselor Education at Florida Atlantic University (FAU), where she also received her PhD in Counseling. She has a wealth of experience in the field of school counseling, having worked as a school counselor and guidance program/testing coordinator for close to a decade. She coauthored the book *Facilitating Evidence-Based, Data-Driven School Counseling: A Manual for Practice* with Dr. Brett Zyromski (Ohio State University). In 2016, Dr. Mariani was recognized by FAU as both the University and College of Education's Scholar of the Year (Assistant Professor level). She has presented regionally, nationally, and internationally on the subjects of student success skills, school counseling interventions and outcome research, evidence-based guidance programs, higher education and K-12 collaboration, and cultural sensitivity in school counselor education.

Erin Mason, PhD, is an Assistant Professor in the Department of Counseling and Psychological Services at Georgia State University in Atlanta. After 13 years in the field as a school counselor, and earning her PhD, she spent nine years as a faculty member in the Counseling program at DePaul University in Chicago. Throughout her career, she has been actively involved in both state and national school counseling organizations, frequently serving in leadership roles. Dr. Mason's primary research focuses on school counselor professional identity, social justice, and technology and innovation. She is also the co-founder of the original Twitter hashtag for school counselors, #scchat, and can be followed @ecmmason. Dr. Mason is a regular conference presenter, keynote speaker, and a co-author of *101 Solutions for School Counselors and Leaders in Challenging Times.*

Melissa S. Ockerman, PhD, is an Associate Professor in the Counseling Program at DePaul University, Chicago. She has established a strong research agenda focusing on the efficacy of school counselor preparation, Multi-Tiered Systems of Support (MTSS), and systemic anti-bullying strategies. She is on the Board of Directors for the Illinois Safe Schools Alliance and has served in leadership positions for both state and national professional organizations. She is co-author of a text entitled *101 Solutions for School Counselors and Leaders in Challenging Times.* Dr. Ockerman's passion for educating the next generation of school counselors is matched only by her desire to dismantle the achievement gap in schools through transformative evidence-based school counseling interventions.

Jacob Olsen, PhD, is an Assistant Professor in Advanced Studies in Education and Counseling at California State University, Long Beach. He received his PhD in Counseling from the University of North Carolina, Charlotte, and his MEd in School Counseling from Seattle Pacific University. His research interests include the school counselor's role in and use of Multi-Tiered Systems of Support (MTSS), comprehensive school counseling program implementation, and the school counselor's role in supporting students' career and college readiness.

Summer Perhay Kuba, PhD, is a faculty member in the Department of Counselor Education and Family Studies at Liberty University, Virginia. She earned her Master of Social Work degree from the University of Central Florida and her Master of Elementary Education degree from the University of Phoenix. After earning her Education Specialist Degree in School Counseling she went on to earn her PhD in Counseling also from Florida Atlantic University. She has diverse counseling experience and has worked with children/students ranging from toddlerhood to the college level. In addition, Dr. Perhay Kuba is active in the Florida School Counselor Association and actively presents at state and national conferences.

Christopher Sink, PhD, NCC, LMHC (WA Inactive), is a Professor and Batten Endowed Chair of Counseling and Human Services at Old Dominion University, Virginia. Earlier, he spent 21 years as a Professor of Counselor Education at Seattle Pacific University and five years at Northwest Missouri State University. Prior to serving in the professoriate, he worked as a secondary and post-secondary counselor. He is a strong advocate for systemic and strengths-based school-based counseling. Currently, his research agenda includes topics examining social-emotional learning program evaluation, outcomes of comprehensive school counseling programs, research methods in counselor education, positive psychology, and spirituality as an important feature of adolescent resiliency.

Stephanie Smith-Durkin received her MSEd from Old Dominion University, Virginia, with a concentration in School Counseling. Prior to earning her Master's degree, she worked in multiple public school districts with low income students and their families. Stephanie currently works as a high school counselor in Virginia Beach City Public Schools. She is also enrolled in Old Dominion University's PhD program in Counselor Education and Supervision, with her research interests including multicultural competent school counseling practices, Multi-Tiered Systems of Support and restorative justice practices in schools. Stephanie is also a nationally certified counselor (NCC).

George Sugai received his MEd in 1974 and PhD in 1980 at the University of Washington, Seattle. Currently at the University of Connecticut, Dr. Sugai is the Carole J. Neag Endowed Chair in Behavior Disorders and Professor with tenure. His primary areas of interest are positive behavior support (PBS), systems change, personnel preparation, behavioral disorders, social skills instruction, behavioral consultation, behavioral assessment procedures, applied behavior analysis (ABA), and strategies for effective school-wide, classroom, and individual behavior management. He has taught graduate level special education courses in applied behavior analysis, emotional or behavioral disorders, behavioral consultation, social skills instruction, and classroom/behavior management.

Julia V. Taylor, PhD, is an Assistant Professor of Counselor Education in the Curry School of Education at the University of Virginia in Charlottesville. Prior to academia, she spent a decade in the field as a school counselor and dean of student services. Her research interests include girls' leadership, yoga and contemplative practices in schools, and the development, implementation, and evaluation of comprehensive school counseling programs.

Jolie Ziomek-Daigle, PhD, LPC, is a Professor in the Department of Counseling and Human Development Services (Counseling and Student Personnel Services) at the University of Georgia in Athens. Her research interests include service learning in counseling training programs, dropout prevention, clinical preparation of school counselors, social/emotional development of children, Multi-Tiered Systems of Support, and work/life balance.

Preface

School counselors are busy. We typically face large student caseloads and see students with a host of needs: anxiety, depression, family challenges, feelings of isolation, trauma, and school violence. Due to technology, especially social media, our society is becoming faster-paced and constantly connected. We also have greater diversity: our students, families, and communities represent cultures and countries throughout the world. In addition, we are often asked to complete a range of non-school counseling tasks (e.g., scheduling, testing, and 504 coordination) as well as our primary responsibilities. We need strategies to be effective and efficient with our time, and to meet our students' complex and diverse needs. We need to work smarter.

As practicing school counselors, we (the three editors) implemented Comprehensive School Counseling Programs (CSCPs). While the school counseling profession recommends implementing CSCPs, we also know that school counselors across the country struggle to communicate their purpose and roles to influential stakeholders. Building principals, teachers, parents, and school-district administrators are not always aware of CSCPs and our recommended roles. As school counselors, we need to weave ourselves into the fabric of our schools, demonstrating that our CSCPs reflect the goals and mission of our school. We must align our CSCPs with prioritized school-wide initiatives, thus speaking to our stakeholders' priorities.

We did just that through our own school counseling work with Multi-Tiered Systems of Support, or MTSS. Over the last 20 years, we've seen the rise of MTSS across the country. Multi-Tiered Systems of Support is often used as an overarching descriptor for Positive Behavior Intervention and Supports (PBIS) and Response to Intervention (RTI), which are both three-tiered continuums of school-wide supports, particularly academic and behavioral prevention and intervention. Further, MTSS is recommended by a wealth of professional organizations, such as the U.S. Department of Education. In particular, RTI is federally mandated as part of the *Individuals with Disabilities Education Act*, and PBIS is implemented in all 50 states and nearly 26,000 schools throughout the country, a number that is continually growing.

We know that MTSS is implemented throughout the country, which means that many school counselors are working in schools with MTSS. If our schools are facilitating MTSS, we need to show stakeholders how school counseling programs fit within the MTSS framework. Luckily, we know that CSCPs and MTSS share overlapping goals, and can be aligned or integrated. Comprehensive school counseling programs and MTSS share similar goals: culturally responsiveness, equitable systemic change, focusing on the whole child, using data-driven evidence-based practices to proactively and preventatively serve all students, and providing small group and individual services to students with greater needs. Aligning our school counseling work with MTSS makes sense as an efficient and effective strategy to address our large caseloads and meet our students' complex and diverse needs. Aligning CSCPs and MTSS helps us to work smarter and to advocate for our roles, weaving our school counseling program into the fabric of our schools.

We have seen this alignment first-hand. Our own experiences as school counselors and now as counselor educators prompted us to begin championing the alignment between CSCPs and MTSS, in an effort to advocate for the school counseling profession and as a strategy to best serve students and schools. We started collaborating with public schools in our home states of Virginia, Wisconsin, and Connecticut, which led to conversations in other states and even nationally.

At the same time, through our work we have realized that the school counseling profession has only recently begun discussing this CSCP–MTSS alignment. Our profession needs a roadmap to guide us in this alignment. This book provides just that. This book is the first of its kind, providing school counselors with information and practical resources regarding strengthening a CSCP through aligning CSCPs and MTSS across three tiers of support.

As such, in the first chapter of this book, Dr. George Sugai and colleagues provide historical background and key features of MTSS, and an introduction to the alignment between CSCPs and MTSS. This alignment is described in greater detail in the second chapter by Drs. Emily Goodman-Scott and Melissa Ockerman, including how school counselors can utilize MTSS in their CSCP to more efficiently and effectively serve students, acting as leaders, collaborators, advocates, and systemic change agents. Next, in Chapter 3, Dr. Christopher Sink examines the school counselor's role in school-wide Tier 1 efforts, applying tenets of systems theory and whole-school systemic change. Tier 1 is discussed further in Chapter 4 by Drs. Erin Mason and Caroline Lopez-Perry, specifically the school counseling core curriculum and classroom management strategies.

Dr. Jacob Olsen presents content on Tier 2 supports for students with elevated needs (Chapter 5), while Dr. Jolie Ziomek-Daigle and colleagues discuss Tier 3 specialized services (Chapter 6); authors in both these chapters relay school counselors' roles as *interveners* to directly serve students, as well as *supporters*, providing indirect services. In Chapter 7, universal mental health screening is introduced by Dr. Peg Donohue as a comprehensive strategy to preventatively identify and serve students through MTSS, highlighting the school counselor's role as a member of the related multidisciplinary team. Drs. Blaire Cholewa and Kathleen Laundy portray school counselors as collaborators and consultants when implementing CSCPs and MTSS, in Chapter 8. The use of data is discussed in Chapter 9 by Dr. Julia Taylor and Ms. Melanie Burgess, as a crucial aspect of both frameworks.

In Chapter 10, Drs. Melissa Mariani and Summer Perhay Kuba outline evidence-based practices school counselors can use across the three tiers as part of a CSCP and MTSS. Then, in Chapter 11, Dr. Jennifer Betters-Bubon and colleagues highlight culturally responsive practices in the alignment of CSCPs and MTSS, in order to create effective learning environments. The last chapter in the book includes voices from the field, or vignettes from practicing school counselors, relaying their perspective on the benefits and challenges to implementing MTSS in elementary, middle, and high schools, within urban, suburban, and rural school districts in the U.S. The book concludes with a reflection on next steps and future directions.

The chapters in our book provide a strong theoretical and research base, as well as practical examples from the field, case studies, and relevant hands-on resources and tools to assist school counselors comprehend, facilitate, and strengthen the implementation of CSCPs, particularly through MTSS alignment. To assist readers to utilize this book, 2016 CACREP (Council for Accreditation of Counseling & Related Educational Programs) accreditation standards as well as the 2016 ASCA Ethical Codes are listed according to the content in each chapter. Related teaching activities and multiple choice questions are also provided for each chapter. Lastly, infused through-out every chapter is content foundational to school counseling: cultural responsiveness, evidence-based practices, and the use of data, including assessment and evaluation. The chapters in this book can be read individually or as a collection.

Overall, our book is written for pre-service and practicing school counselors, as well as their leaders, supervisors, and faculty. We hope to assist you to better understand the overlap between CSCPs and MTSS, with the overarching goal of strengthening school counseling programs to serve students, schools, and communities. We hope this book can improve your knowledge, implementation, and evaluation of CSCPs. Our inspiration for this book was initially the work we did in K-12 schools surrounding CSCPs and MTSS, and more recently from the school counselors we collaborate with currently in the schools. We know that you work hard, desire to serve your students, and can struggle under the tremendous responsibilities of your job. We see you, and we hear you.

We hope this book is helpful to readers in the following ways:

- We hope school counselors acknowledge that aligning MTSS and CSCPs isn't nec-essarily "one more thing to do," but rather reframes much of their current work in schools.
- We hope school counselors view themselves as change agents, recognizing the interconnected systemic factors influencing students, schools, and communities; understanding that improving student behaviors and academics is best facilitated by changing the system.
- We hope this book can empower school counselors to view the child as a whole. Rather than addressing students' academic, behavior, and social/emotional func-tioning separately, we hope school counselors see these domains as intertwined.
- We hope this book increases school counselors' comfort with data, utilizing practi-cal strategies to apply MTSS data collection and analysis to strengthen a CSCP, and vice versa.
- We hope the three-tiered MTSS framework can be utilized within CSCPs, understand-ing how school counselors meet students' needs in each tier, and utilizing related evidence-based practices to do so.
- We hope that school counselors can view themselves as leaders and facilitate this very important work listed above through a culturally responsive lens that promotes equity and lessens students' opportunity and achievement gaps.

As school counselors, we are in the business of serving students, schools, and communities. Aligning CSCP and MTSS has assisted us, Emily, Jen, and Peg, to best serve our students, and we hope for the same for you. We hope this book helps you to enter your school building with more knowledge, courage, passion, and strategies than you did before. We hope you feel empowered to serve your students, school, and community as effectively and efficiently as possible, armed with a new perspective. We hope you see yourselves as systemic change agents, leaders, collaborators, and advocates, knowing you make a dif-ference each day. And we hope that you continue learning, growing, and improving, not only for yourself, but also for your students.

CACREP Standards Addressed by Chapter

Chapters	1	2	3	4	5	6	7	8	9	10	11
Professional Counseling Identity **F Counseling Curriculum Core Areas**											
1. Professional Counseling Orientation and Ethical Practice											
b The multiple professional roles and functions of counselors across specialty areas, and their relationship with human service and integrated behavioral health care systems, including interagency and inter-organizational collaboration and consultation	X	X			X	X		X			
e Advocacy process needed to address institutional and social barriers that impede access, equity, and success for clients	X		X	X					X	X	X
k Strategies for personal and professional self-evaluation and implications for practice	X						X		X	X	
2. Social and Cultural Diversity											
h Strategies for identifying and eliminating barriers, prejudices, and processes of intentional and unintentional oppression and discrimination	X		X	X			X	X			X
3. Human Growth and Development											
f Systemic and environmental factors that affect human development, functioning, and behavior	X		X	X			X			X	X
h A general framework for understanding differing abilities and strategies for differentiated interventions	X		X	X	X	X	X			X	X
i Ethical and culturally relevant strategies for promoting resilience and optimum development and wellness across the lifespan	X		X	X	X	X	X			X	X
5. Counseling and Helping Relationships											
a A systems approach to conceptualizing clients			X	X	X	X	X			X	X
c Theories, models, and strategies for understanding and practicing consultation	X				X	X		X			
h Developmentally relevant counseling treatment or intervention plans					X	X				X	X

	1	2	3	4	5	6	7	8	9	10	11
i Development of measurable outcomes for clients	X							X	X		
j Evidence-based counseling strategies and techniques for prevention and intervention	X				X	X	X	X	X	X	

7. Assessment and Testing

	1	2	3	4	5	6	7	8	9	10	11
e Use of assessments for diagnostic and intervention planning purposes						X		X			
h Reliability and validity in the use of assessments						X					
i Use of assessments relevant to academic/ educational, career, personal, and social development	X					X					X
j Use of environmental assessments and systematic behavioral observations	X				X	X					
m Ethical and culturally relevant strategies for selecting, administering, and interpreting assessment and test results						X			X		

8. Research and Program Evaluation

	1	2	3	4	5	6	7	8	9	10	11
a The importance of research in advancing the counseling profession, including how to critique research to inform counseling practice								X			
b Identification of evidence-based counseling practices								X			
c Needs assessments				X				X			
d Development of outcome measures for counseling programs								X			
e Evaluation of counseling interventions and programs	X			X	X	X	X	X	X	X	X
g Designs used in research and program evaluation				X	X			X			
i Analysis and use of data in counseling	X					X		X			X

Section 5: Entry-Level Specialty Area
G School Counseling

1. Foundation

	1	2	3	4	5	6	7	8	9	10	11
a History and development of school counseling		X	X								
b Models of school counseling programs		X									
d Models of school-based collaboration and consultation	X		X				X				
e Assessments specific to P-12 education						X		X			

2. Contextual Dimensions

	1	2	3	4	5	6	7	8	9	10	11
a School counselors as leaders, advocates, and systems change agents in P-12 schools	X	X				X		X			X
b School counselor roles in consultation with families, P-12 and postsecondary school personnel, and community agencies				X	X	X	X				
c School counselors as leaders, advocates, and systems change agents in P-12 schools	X	X			X	X					
d School counselor roles in school counselor leadership and multidisciplinary teams	X	X	X	X				X	X	X	X
f Competencies to advocate for school counseling roles		X									

(continued)

Chapters	1	2	3	4	5	6	7	8	9	10	11
g Characteristics, risk factors, and warning signs of students at risk for mental health and behavioral disorders							X				
j Qualities and styles of effective leadership in schools		X									
k Community resources and referral sources						X		X			
n Legal and ethical considerations specific to school counseling	X	X	X	X	X	X	X	X	X	X	X

3. Practice

	1	2	3	4	5	6	7	8	9	10	11
a Development of school counseling program mission statements and objectives			X								
b Design and evaluation of school counseling programs		X									
c Core curriculum design, lesson plan development, classroom management strategies, and differentiated instructional strategies				X							
d Interventions to promote academic achievement	X	X			X						
f Techniques for personal/social counseling in school settings						X	X				
h Skills to critically examine the connections between social, familial, emotional, and behavior problems and academic achievement	X		X			X	X				X
i Approaches to increase promotion and graduation rates				X	X	X	X	X	X	X	X
j Interventions to promote college and career readiness										X	
k Strategies to promote equity in student achievement and college access	X	X									X
l Techniques to foster collaboration and teamwork within schools	X	X	X			X		X			X
n Use of accountability data to inform decision making	X	X		X						X	X
o Use of data to advocate for programs and students	X	X				X	X		X	X	X

Acknowledgments

Collectively, we would like to recognize and thank those who made this textbook possible. First, we are indebted to each chapter author and contributor for their unique and innovative contribution. You demonstrated passion for and expertise in making positive, systemic, school-based change. Your experiences are varied, rich, and expertly told. We are eternally grateful for your willingness to join this essential conversation, putting your thoughts into words, and bringing this project to life.

We would also like to thank the key organizations that lead and support innovation in the field of school counseling: the American School Counselor Association (ASCA), the Association for Counselor Education and Supervision (ACES), and the Ronald H. Fredrickson Center for School Counseling Outcome Research & Evaluation (CSCORE). Your leadership continues to promote professional collaboration focused on equity, social justice, positive school climate, and improving our capacity through professional best practice, research, and data.

We'd also like to acknowledge the importance of our own K-12 school counseling and MTSS experiences. Thank you to our previous schools, students, colleagues, and friends. Thank you for continuing this important work in the schools, and for being our first direct teachers. And thank you to our current students at our respective universities for being our current and constant teachers.

Dr. Emily Goodman-Scott: I would like to thank my family. Especially my partner, Tim: thank you for your unwavering support, love, and confidence in me; you are my sunshine. To my three darling children: you inspire me to improve K-12 education for you, and your generation; I'm grateful for your laughter, play, curiosity, and wisdom. To my parents: showing me from a young age the importance of hard work, passion, determination, and service to others, and to take "one bite at a time." And a special thank you to my co-editors Jen and Peg: I'm eternally grateful our paths crossed, and our friendship and partnership has blossomed. Thank you for the vision, hard work, perspective, and the laughs. I'm proud of and grateful for our work. Cheers to future projects together!

Dr. Jennifer Betters-Bubon: I would like to thank my partner Tim: you have served as my support, my sounding board, and my comic relief during so many moments within this process. To Mary Estelle and Mathew: I have appreciated your patience and understanding as I sat behind my laptop for hours on end—you help me see the purpose behind everything. Without my parents and sisters, and students and colleagues—both past and present—I would not be the person and professional I am today. Finally, to my co-editors Emily and Peg: thanks for walking alongside me during this process. I am thankful that we met at those fateful conferences years ago and made this dream come alive.

Dr. Peg Donohue: I would like to thank my co-editors Emily and Jen for their friendship, shared vision, and tenacity. I have no doubt that our collaboration has made me a better educator. I am immensely proud of and grateful for the love, support, and patience of the three most important people in my life—my husband and best friend, John, and my children, Isabella and Joey. I am indebted to my parents, Sandy and Mike Dowley, and my siblings, Mark, Ann, and Ellen, for their unwavering encouragement. To my two closest friends, Lisa Sherman and Karen Evans, I am so grateful for your lifetime service as educators and your friendship which sustains me always. To my mentors, Kathie Laundy and Cherie King, thanks for believing in me. Finally, I wish to thank my students at CCSU who make an enormous difference in the lives of their students, and in mine as well.

1   Multi-Tiered Systems of Support

The What, Why, and How for School Counselors

George Sugai, Tamika P. La Salle, Susannah Everett,
and Adam B. Feinberg

Introduction

Schools represent one of our most important systems for the social, emotional, academic, and behavioral development of our children and youth. More than 98,000 school buildings are distributed across the United States, and provide free public education to more than 50 million students for approximately six hours a day and 180 days a year. For at least 12 years of their lives, children and youth spend more structured learning time with educators in schools than with their families.

Educators are responsible for preparing students for college and career experiences by establishing basic academic competencies (e.g., literacy, numeracy), foundational knowledge (e.g., physical and social sciences, technology, literature), and specialized electives (e.g., music, art, sports). Schools provide equally important opportunities for the development and shaping of the social, emotional, and behavioral competencies of children and youth, often in the context of ever-changing and diverse learning environments (e.g., culture, race, gender, language, disability, socio-economic background).

Schools also provide opportunities for students of all ages to understand and respond to images, experiences, and events occurring around them, both prosocial (e.g., friendships, clubs, athletics) and antisocial (e.g., violence, disrespect, irresponsibility, bullying), often displayed by individuals in influential positions (e.g., politicians, entertainers, athletes). Similarly, economic, political, and environmental tragedies directly and indirectly create significant personal challenges for many family and community members. In sum, schools can serve as important positive, predictable, and safe places for all students, especially for those who may be traumatized, injured, and/or socially isolated (Sugai, Freeman, Simonsen, La Salle, & Fixsen, 2017).

Given these incredible academic, social, emotional, and behavioral responsibilities, educators, including school counselors, must use every minute of the school day wisely to ensure that all students can experience maximum success. As such, school counselors and other staff members must (a) select and become experts in the use of the best interventions and practices available, (b) work as a team to maximize the impact of their collective strengths, and (c) explicitly and actively participate across classroom and non-classroom settings to ensure that every student has opportunities to maximize their academic and social development.

Thus, the overarching purpose of this chapter is to highlight the important role that school counselors, in particular, contribute to the success of every student in every classroom within and across schools. Specifically, new and veteran school counseling professionals are provided with information and resources regarding the alignment and implementation of Comprehensive School Counseling Programs (CSCPs) (e.g., the

American School Counselor Association [ASCA] National Model, 2012) within a Multi-Tiered Systems of Support (MTSS) approach.

In this chapter, we describe how a MTSS approach provides a working structure for maximizing the individual and collective competencies of educators and, in particular, school counselors. We specifically address five questions:

1 What is MTSS?
2 What influenced the development of MTSS?
3 What are the operating characteristics of MTSS?
4 What is considered when implementing MTSS within CSCP?
5 What is the role of school counselors in MTSS and CSCP implementation?

What Is MTSS?

The conditions and challenges of contemporary schools have become more diverse, complex, and demanding, for example, widening gaps in socio-economic status, lower levels of student school readiness, contemporary workforce demands, and shifts in family structure and functioning (Weist, Garbacz, Lane, & Kincaid, 2017). Today's students and school staff members also must maintain high levels of academic engagement and prosocial interpersonal exchanges while also experiencing daily and real social pressures (e.g., substance use, discrimination, antisocial and violent models, crime, natural and human-made disasters and acts).

Multi-Tiered Systems of Support have been encouraged as a framework for effectively and efficiently organizing and delivering academic, social, emotional, and behavioral resources and supports, and MTSS is generally described as a *prevention-based framework (process, approach, organization) for enhancing the development and implementation of a continuum of evidence-based practices and achieving academically and behaviorally important outcomes for all students* (McIntosh & Goodman, 2016). Overall, MTSS is best described as an overarching approach or "umbrella" for a range of tiered systems of support. For instance, Positive Behavioral Interventions and Supports (PBIS) is an MTSS application that specifically focuses on maximizing social, emotional, and behavioral outcomes and supports CSCPs (Goodman-Scott, Betters-Bubon, & Donohue, 2016; Positive Behavioral Interventions and Supports, 2018).

School counselors are assuming collaborative and leadership roles through CSCP and within MTSS to effectively and efficiently support all students (ASCA, 2018). School counselors who engage in MTSS expand their influence at the individual level through enhanced universal screening, progress monitoring, and selection and use of evidence-based counseling practices. At the systems level, school counselors become more involved in whole classroom and school-wide improvement efforts through, for example, evaluating implementation fidelity, using data to monitor student responsiveness, and participating in multidisciplinary teams. In fact, school counselors appreciate that MTSS implementation expands their professional capacity to work collaboratively on positive systemic reform and enhances their roles as advocates and change agents (Goodman-Scott & Grothaus, 2017).

What Influenced the Development of MTSS?

Many influences have shaped the evolution and contemporary descriptions of MTSS. In this section, we describe nine key MTSS influences. We recommend that school counselors pay particular attention to the important historical practices and support systems (*italicized*) that are still essential to MTSS, CSCP, and the success of school counseling.

1 Disabilities and Special Education

One of the biggest MTSS influences is legislation related to the education of individuals with disabilities. Beginning in the 1960s, children and youth with disabilities and their families were afforded due process rights and safeguards to ensure access to individualized educational experiences that specifically considered the influence of their disabilities on learning. Public Law 94-142 (National Education Association of United States, 1978) and the Individuals with Disabilities Education Act (IDEA) and its reauthorizations codified educational principles related to, for example, free and public education, individualized education plans, least restrictive environment, child find, early intervention, and data-based decision making. Special education focused attention on students who, because of their disability, did not have access to or were not benefiting from the general education curriculum.

A number of special education derived procedures are reflected in MTSS. For example, the *individual education program planning* (IEP) process includes a number of MTSS-related elements: (a) planning must be *team based*, (b) long- and short-term *objectives and goals* must be based on current level of functioning and consideration of disability, (c) *intervention decisions and instructional adjustments* must be aligned with pre-determined goals and objectives and be evidence-based, and (d) *student progress and responsiveness to intervention* must be monitored continuously. In addition, a requirement called "child find" established a routine and expectation for regular screening for students who may have a disability that affects their academic achievement.

2 Curriculum-Based Measurement and Precision Teaching

In the 1960s, Stan Deno and Phyllis Mirikin led researchers and practitioners in the development and use of data assessment and measurement procedures, known as *curriculum-based measurement* (CBM), for improving the quality of progress monitoring and instructional decisions for all students, with a particular focus on students with disabilities (Deno, 2003; Deno & Mirikin, 1977). Focused on literacy and numeracy, CBM highlighted the importance of using *brief precise measures* based on the local (school and district) academic curriculum (Deno, 1985). Application of these measures occurred regularly (e.g., weekly, monthly) to provide timely graphic indications of the student's responsiveness to intervention and to enhance decision making (Deno, Fuchs, Marston, & Shin, 2001).

Similar to CBM, an approach called precision teaching (PT) was developed to further the applications of *formative or continuous decision making*, especially for a broader range of academic and behavioral targets for young children, youth, and adults in both general and special education (i.e., mild, moderate, and severe disabilities). Precision teaching researchers and practitioners (e.g., Norris Haring, Owen White, Ogden Lindsley, Kathleen Liberty) developed a number of instructional enhancements for (a) estimating *trend lines* (e.g., split middle technique), (b) *extending predictions* based on current trend, (c) using rate (response per minute) as the primary measure of learning and responding, (d) making instructional decisions based on *patterns of correct and error responses*, (e) establishing *graphing norms* (standard behavior charts) that would enable comparisons among different measures and students and over a full academic year, and (f) operationalizing *learning into phases* that are related to specific instructional or treatment emphases

(White, 1986; White & Haring, 1980). Curriculum-based measurement and PT provide practitioners with organizational guidelines to improve their decision making related to what data to collect, how to collect information, and how to enhance decision making, especially for students who display the greatest difficulty in responding to instruction and interventions.

3 Teacher Consultation and Inclusionary Resource Room

Beginning in the 1970s, classroom-based and school-wide instructional approaches increased the attention on *teacher-based consultation*, and *resource-room-based delivery systems* became the preferred means for educating students with disabilities (Bergan & Kratochwill, 1990; Chalfant, Pysh, & Moultrie, 1979; Colarusso, 1987; Graden, 1989; Idol, 1983; Pugach & Johnson, 1989; Zins, Graden, & Ponti, 1988). As a result, general and special education faculty and staff members, including school counselors and psychologists, *worked as teams* to provide a common and inclusive experience for all students and a collaborative process for developing and delivering specialized educational supports for students with learning and behavior difficulties.

This focus on *all students and differentiated instruction for some students* resulted in greater emphasis on general classroom instruction and behavior management (Darch & Kame'enui, 2004) and attention specifically on the mutually beneficial inter-relationship between *academic achievement and behavioral competence*. With respect to classroom management, carefully considering the physical characteristics of the classroom, explicitly teaching and encouraging classroom routines, delivering high rates of specific praise, and actively supervising student activities became important in supporting academic success (Myers, Simonsen, & Sugai, 2011; Scott, 2017; Scott, Hirn, & Cooper, 2017). Similarly, effective academic instruction emphasized direct instructional approaches, maximum opportunities to respond, and continuous progress monitoring (Simonsen & Myers, 2015).

These advances in teaching consultation and resource room approaches aided the development of the MTSS emphasis on *integrating academic and behavior instruction, explicit teaching of academic skills and social behavior, delivering differentiated instruction in general classroom contexts and settings*, and *teacher-based teaming and consultation*. In particular, the roles and responsibilities of specialists, such as school counselors and psychologists and special educators, created opportunities for more collaborative, comprehensive, and efficient opportunities within the general education context for all students.

4 Response to Intervention

In the 1990s, emphasis increased on the use of data to monitor the progress and improve the evaluation of students with learning disabilities and decision making relative to their responsiveness to instruction. Although initiated in special education, principles of Response to Intervention (RTI) (Brown-Chadsey & Steege, 2005; Bradley, Danielson, & Doolittle, 2007; Caplan & Grunebaum, 1967; Fuchs & Fuchs, 2007; Gresham et al., 2005; Gresham, 2005; Kame'enui, 2007; Sugai & Horner, 2009) were adapted to general education across academic content areas (e.g., early literacy, numeracy), enhanced the roles and responsibilities of specialists (e.g., school counselors and psychologists, speech and language pathologists), and included a number of important elements that shaped the current MTSS approach.

First, *universal screening* procedures were used regularly to identify students with potential risk for academic and/or behavior difficulties. Rather than wait for a student to fail or demonstrate a lack of responding, the intent is to screen regularly for students who display characteristics (e.g., disability, language, sensory, behavior) that present a clear risk to their ability to benefit from instruction.

Second, RTI increased the emphasis on the selection of *evidence-based practices and their alignment* with the current level of functioning for the student. The attention was on ensuring that an accurate assessment of student functioning was used to select instructional and/or behavioral practices that had research evidence of their effectiveness for achieving the desired learning outcome.

Third, RTI emphasized the importance of monitoring and evaluating the *accuracy and fluency of practice implementation (fidelity)*. Although educators typically examine how well required instructions and procedures for a practice are being followed, they also must consider a number of other implementation aspects. For example, aspects of an evidence-based practice may need to be modified to accommodate differences in language, cultural backgrounds, disability, etc. In addition, if students are not making adequate progress, educators might decide to (a) modify the practice based on learners' response patterns, (b) continue to use the practice while carefully monitoring learner responsiveness, or (c) replace the practice with a more appropriate one.

Finally, one of the most important contributions of RTI to MTSS is the emphasis on *continuous monitoring of student progress and careful consideration of student responsiveness to intervention*. Rather than waiting until the end of a grading period or academic year, learner progress is checked on a daily, weekly, and/or monthly basis so that educators can make timely adjustments and decisions.

Although RTI was initiated in the context of special education, the basic principles have relevance to the instructional and behavioral programming of all students and became an important developmental precursor to MTSS.

5 Three-Tiered Prevention Logic

Multi-Tiered Systems of Support emphasizes *prevention* to reduce the likelihood of problem development (incidence) and intensity, frequency, duration, etc., of existing problems (prevalence) (Biglan, 1995, 2015). A prevention perspective means all students should be equipped with the useful and effective academic and social skills. For students who display risk factors (e.g., disability, anxious or withdrawn behavior, attention), the prevention focus is on strengthening protective factors (e.g., social skills, peer supports). For individual students who display high-risk behaviors (e.g., aggression, elopement, depressed behaviors), the focus is on improving environments so triggers of problem behavior are removed and desired behaviors are promoted. An important prevention priority is to remove the excessive use of reactive, non-educative consequence responses (e.g., removal, seclusion, restraint, reprimands) that can promote rather than reduce the likelihood of problem behaviors, especially for students whose behaviors require additional (e.g., Tiers 2/3) supports. The focus on incidence and prevalence de-emphasizes the development and use of reactive responses (e.g., suspension) to presenting problems and serves as the base for many school-based disciplines, like school counseling, to emphasize *prevention*.

Hill Walker extended the prevention logic to educational service delivery for students with behavior disorders and was particularly influential in conceptualizing a *continuum-based approach* that is foundational to MTSS. Walker et al. (1996) developed a three-tiered logic (Figure 1.1): (a) *universal or primary prevention* (Tier 1) that focused on strengthening the social, emotional, and learning competence of students who presented little to no risk for behavior disorders (incidence); (b) *indicated or secondary prevention* (Tier 2) that emphasized solidifying protective factors and minimizing influential risk factors for students who present indicators of problem behavior (prevalence); and (c) *intensive or tertiary prevention* (Tier 3) that addressed the existence of significant risk and absence of protective factors for students whose challenges require specialized and individualized supports.

The "triangle" or continuum logic has become one of the most important defining elements of any tiered approach. Although usually presented in a three-tiered configuration, the continuum is best represented as an integrated continuum that organizes behavior, practices, and systems with careful consideration of cultural factors and contexts. For example, in Figure 1.2, a continuum of behavior responsiveness is illustrated for "Caesar." Whereas "anger management," "problem solving," "punctuality," and "work submission" require more intensive (Tiers 2/3) support, a number of other behaviors (e.g., "goal setting," "self-assessment," and "responding to adult requests") are acceptably responsive to general classroom practices and routines (Tier 1).

An example of a continuum of classroom management practices is illustrated in Figure 1.3. "Ms. Antonette" has selected and implemented a range of intervention options in her classroom. In addition to the most "effective instruction" available, her students also experience "continuous active supervision," "frequent positive active engagement," and "contingent and specific positive reinforcement." A small group of students participates in a peer-mentoring program to improve their bystander

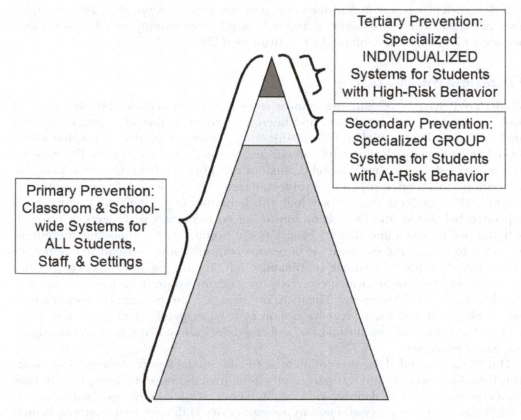

Figure 1.1 Three-tiered prevention continuum logic.

(Source: the Authors.)

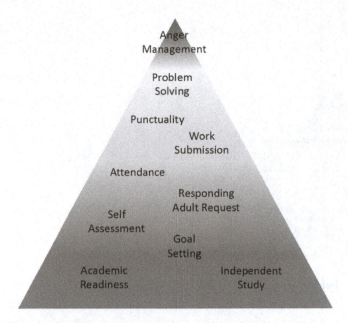

Figure 1.2 Example of continuum of behavior need and responsiveness.

(Source: the Authors.)

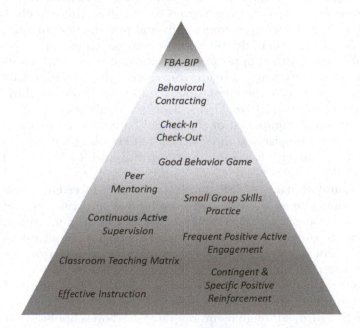

Figure 1.3 Example of continuum of classroom behavior management practices.

(Source: the Authors.)

response to teasing and bullying. A few of her students, like Caesar, have individualized behavioral contracts that use a function-based intervention to address particularly challenging behaviors.

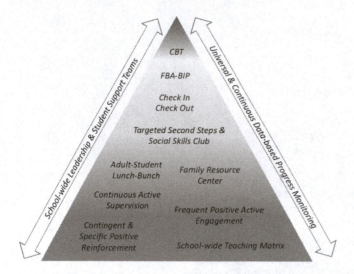

Figure 1.4 Example of school-wide continuum of practices and systems.

(Source: the Authors.)

School-wide practices and systems at Ms. Antonette's school are also organized using the same continuum logic (Figure 1.4). At South Maori School, all students are taught a small set of school-wide behavioral expectations across all settings (including the classroom) by all staff and faculty members throughout the school year. In addition, all staff and faculty members deliver specific and contingent positive acknowledgments when observing setting-appropriate displays of expected behaviors. To support this school-wide continuum, a leadership team (which includes the school counselor) coordinates practice implementation. Data are reviewed regularly (e.g., monthly for Tier 1 decision making, weekly for Tier 2/3 student responsiveness), and a student support team (comprised of the school counselor and special educator and district school psychologist and nurse) meet weekly to screen for students with high-risk behaviors and monitor students on group and/or individual behavior plans.

The continuum logic is foundational to MTSS, and has a number of essential features that are particularly important to the roles, responsibilities, and functions of school counselors. First, students are not "placed" and labelled within the continuum. Instead, practices and systems of support are aligned and organized based on student responsiveness and cultural context and influences. Second, Tier 1 or universal supports are available and delivered to all students. Students whose behaviors require a more specialized assistance (Tiers 2/3) still participate within the classroom and school-wide systems (Tier 1); however, they require additional supports to address their academic and behavior needs. Third, although teams operate based on school-wide or individual student responsiveness, team members participate in delivery of practices across the full continuum. Finally, the development, implementation, evaluation, and adjustment of these continua are based on data collected on student responsiveness and practice or systems implementation fidelity (accuracy and fluency). School counselors participate in and make significant prevention and intervention contributions across all tiers for all students.

6 Behavioral Sciences

Multi-Tiered Systems of Support is grounded in the *behavioral sciences*, which aligns well with a prevention approach and an emphasis on empirically-based practices and strategies. A behavioral perspective acknowledges the influence of biology and prior learning history; however, the implementation of tiered systems of support (e.g., PBIS) emphasises three important behavioral tenets: (a) behavior (academic and social) is learned, (b) behavior is predictably lawful, and (c) behavior can be taught and/or occurrences influenced through manipulation of environmental antecedent and consequence events (i.e., direct instruction and intervention) (Alberto & Troutman, 2013; Cooper, Heron, & Heward, 2007; Sidman, 1960; Wolery, Bailey, & Sugai, 1988).

7 Evidence-Based Practices

Given the importance of and opportunity to promote academic achievement and behavior success, MTSS emphasizes the selection, adoption, and high fidelity *use of evidence-based practices*, strategies, and interventions. At Tier 1, the goal is to ensure that most students (e.g., >80%) are maximally engaged, have high rates of academic engagement, and progress at rates that prevent falling behind. At Tiers 2/3, greater precision in practice selection and alignment with desired outcomes is needed because these students have risk factors and/or a failure to benefit from Tier 1 supports. That is, school counselors and educators must have high confidence in the effectiveness of their practice selection. Evidence-based practices are discussed in greater detail in Chapter 10.

8 Direct Instruction

Another key influence on the development of MTSS has been the emphasis on a more explicit approach to teaching social skills, providing professional development, and developing practice and systems materials. First, *teaching and supporting social, emotional, and behavioral skills are approached in the same manner as academic skills* (Becker, 1992; Colvin, Kame'enui, & Sugai, 1993; Colvin & Sugai, 1988; Engelmann & Carnine, 1991; Engelmann, Becker, Carnine, & Gersten, 1988). For example, rather than assuming social skills are acquired through indirect and chance experiences at home, with peers, or by watching adult models, MTSS approaches develop specific and daily classroom and school-wide social skills lesson plans that have a specific year-long delivery schedule, carefully selected setting and culturally appropriate teaching examples, structured practice to raise fluency, and specific feedback about correct skill use and corrective practice when errors are observed.

Similar to the direct approach for teaching social skills for students, an MTSS approach to professional development for school staff acknowledges that one-time (e.g., an in-service day) or episodic (e.g., quarterly communities of practice) professional development events are associated with limited change in classroom practice (Joyce & Showers, 2002; Latham, 1988; Showers & Joyce, 1996). Similar to learning any new and/or complex skill (e.g., new social skills curriculum, multi-step problem solving system), efforts to change or *improve classroom and school-wide practices involves a direct instruction approach*: (a) rationale and knowledge, (b) models and positive and negative examples, (c) supervised fluency-building practice, (d) systematic implementation prompts, (e) positive error corrections, and (f) regular positive feedback on appropriate use.

Within MTSS, the direct instruction emphasis is also applied to the development of the materials and instruction experienced by students and the implementation of practices and systems used and experienced by all staff members, including school counselors. In general,

TEACHING MATRIX		Setting			
		Classroom	Entering, In, & Exiting Hallways	Cafeteria	Assembles & Sports Events
Expectations	Respect Ourselves	Be on task. Give your best effort. Be prepared.	Walk. Have a plan.	Eat all your food. Select healthy foods.	Sit in one spot.
	Respect Others	Be kind. Hands/feet to self. Help/share with others.	Use normal voice volume. Walk to right.	Practice good table manners.	Listen & watch. Use appropriate applause.
	Respect Environment	Recycle. Clean up after self.	Pick up litter. Maintain physical space.	Replace trays & utensils. Clean up eating area.	Pick up. Push in & use chairs appropriately.

Figure 1.5 Example of the front page of a teaching matrix.

(Source: the Authors.)

General Guidelines

When teaching, encouraging, recognizing, and/or correcting, interact in manner that is

1. Developmentally appropriate
2. Culturally relevant
3. Objective & professional
4. Individually appropriate to history of responsiveness

Encouragement & Recognition

At every opportunity across all school settings, when an appropriate display of a behavior expectation is observed,

1. Personally recognize student
2. Describe observed behavior
3. Acknowledge the setting
4. Provide appropriate social positive acknowledgement

Error Correction

When an inappropriate behavior display of expectation is observed

1. Personally recognize student
2. State relevant school-wide expectation
3. State example of desired expected behavior
4. Ask student to restate or show desired expectation & desired behavior
5. Ask student to state or show what s/he will do next time in this setting

Figure 1.6 Example of a back page of guidelines for encouraging, teaching, and recognizing displays of expected behavior.

(Source: the Authors.)

MTSS materials and instruction (e.g., reminders, lesson plans, scripts) are designed to initiate and promote sustained use of desired or expected actions. For example, within PBIS, a one-page lesson plan (teaching matrix) is used to teach school-wide social skills. The example in Figure 1.5 includes (a) three school-wide expectations (respect self, others, and environment), (b) a range of relevant settings (classroom, entering/exiting school and hallways, cafeteria, assemblies and sporting events), and (c) two positive behavior examples for each expectation and setting. General instructions for using the teaching matrix, correcting errors, and providing positive feedback for appropriate displays of the behavior examples are found on the back of the teaching matrix (Figure 1.6).

9 Innovation Implementation Research

Last, but not least, influence that has shaped our current conceptualization and application of MTSS is the inclusion of innovation implementation research (Fixsen, Naoom, Blasé, Friedman, & Wallace, 2005). As indicated above, MTSS is not an intervention, practice, or curriculum, but instead MTSS is a *framework or approach* for how any innovation, practice, system, etc., is implemented. First, classrooms, schools, districts, or any educational unit are characterized as an "organization." Instead of assuming that classrooms and schools, for example, change, MTSS frameworks consider the *organization as comprised of individuals* (students, teachers, specialists, administrators) whose individual behavior changes (Skinner, 1938). When the collective behaviors are similar in that they are directed toward a common end, goal, or objective, and represent an agreed upon approach, practice, or routine, then the organization is more likely to be effective, efficient, and relevant (Daniels & Bailey, 2014; Gilbert, 1978; Gilbert & Gilbert, 1992; Horner & Sugai, 2018; Horner, Sugai, & Fixsen, 2017).

Another important operating principle is that activities must consider the *implementation phase*. A general phase sequence is described in Figure 1.7. Because implementation

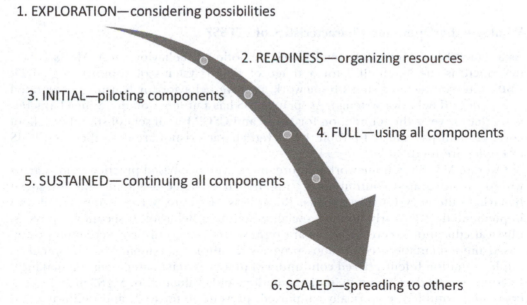

1. EXPLORATION—considering possibilities

2. READINESS—organizing resources

3. INITIAL—piloting components

4. FULL—using all components

5. SUSTAINED—continuing all components

6. SCALED—spreading to others

Figure 1.7 Dynamic MTSS implementation phases.

(Source: the Authors.)

is continuously changing, these phases are used as general process guidelines for organizing and restructuring operations (Fixsen, Naoom, Blasé, Friedman, & Wallace, 2005). In other words, practice implementation is never done. During any hour, day, month, or year, priority levels may change, practice effectiveness may wane, implementation fidelity may decrease, new innovations may be identified, implementation resources may need to be shifted, etc.

In Sum

The purpose of reviewing these foundational influences, or *basics*, is to describe the evolutionary path and coming together of many best practices and systems that now represent and are still associated with MTSS. We learned that MTSS is the outcome of many conceptually sound, empirically grounded, and applied practices and processes. The guiding principles of the MTSS framework can be applied to many different practices, innovations, and initiatives across academic, social, emotional, and behavioral domains. In addition, we learned that no one discipline is responsible for developing and implementing MTSS. Instead, school counseling and psychology, general and special education, mental and public health, etc., work together to improve implementation fidelity of MTSS systems and practices and in achieving important student outcomes.

This section described the nine key MTSS influences.

Which of these influences were you already familiar with?

Which of these influences were new for you?

How does this information relate to school counseling?

What Are the Operating Characteristics of MTSS?

As a general framework (academic, social, emotional, behavior, etc.), MTSS is best described as the "umbrella" for a range of tiered systems of support (e.g., RTI, PBIS, interconnected systems framework, positive behavior for learning, integrated academic and behavior systems). As such, MTSS has a number of operating characteristics that serve as the foundation for MTSS and CSCP for all school staff, but school counselors in particular. In Table 1.1, seven characteristics are described and PBIS examples are used.

Overall, MTSS is a framework that organizes evidence-based practices and systems within an integrated continuum of supports to enhance academic and/or social behavior outcomes for all students. Regardless of where MTSS is developed and implemented (e.g., early literacy; social, emotional, behavioral; secondary physics, physical education), core elements are represented (i.e., universal screening, team-based implementation, continuous progress monitoring, evidence-based practices, implementation fidelity, tiered continuum of practices, data-based decision making). In addition, the development, implementation, and evaluation of MTSS must be conceptually grounded, empirically supported, prevention-focused, and culturally and contextually relevant.

Table 1.1 MTSS core operating characteristics, descriptions, and PBIS examples

Characteristic	Description	PBIS Example
Team-Based	School teams comprised of faculty, students, family members, administrators, etc., are formed to develop, guide, monitor, and adjust an implementation action plan. These teams meet on a regular schedule and have representation from faculty and staff.	School-wide leadership teams (Tier 1) develop lesson plans for all staff to teach all students a common and small set of behavioral expectations (see Teaching Matrix, Figures 1.5 and 1.6). Specialized teams (Tiers 2/3) that support development, implementation, and evaluation of small group and individual behavior intervention plans.
Decision-Based Data System	Specific data are collected and used by teams to make equitable decisions about practice selection, student progress or responsiveness to intervention, and practice implementation fidelity.	Six main school-wide PBIS questions are considered on a monthly basis: 1 How often are behavioral incidents being referred and recorded? 2 What behaviors are being referred and recorded? 3 Where are behaviors being referred from and recorded? 4 When are behaviors being referred and recorded? 5 Which students are associated with referred and recorded behaviors? Simultaneously, PBIS schools annually assess the fidelity or accuracy of their practices implementation at all three tiers by using the Tiered Fidelity Inventory (Algozzine et al., 2014). If fidelity is >70% and student responsiveness is adequate, interventions are continued. If fidelity is <70%, a plan is developed to improve staff member implementation.

(*continued*)

Table 1.1 (continued)

Characteristic	Description	PBIS Example
Universal Screening	On a regular schedule (e.g., monthly, quarterly, semester) student status is systematically reviewed to provide an initial identification of students who present existing, early, or at-risk indicators of academic and/or social behavior difficulties.	In school-wide PBIS, all teachers review (step 1) their class lists to identify students who display unusual or noticeable changes in one or more of the following behavioral concerns or risk factors over the current grading period: 1 Academic engagement and/or progress 2 Self-management 3 Attendance 4 Peer interactions 5 Adult interactions 6 Major office discipline referrals 7 Visits to counselor, nurse, or other school staff 8 Verbal statements (e.g., self-injury, violence) 9 Self-regulation (e.g., anxiety, withdrawal, sleeping, crying). If an identified student is determined to be a possible priority, additional available information is collected and reviewed (step 2) to clarify need. If a student is determined to be a high priority, a team (Tier 2/3) is formed (step 3) to develop an intervention plan.
Continuous Progress Monitoring	Student responsiveness to specific academic instruction and/or social behavior practices and interventions is collected and analyzed on a frequent and regular (e.g., lesson, daily, weekly) basis to make, if indicated, timely and informed adjustments, for example: 1 Make instruction or intervention less/more difficult 2 Increase/decrease learning outcome 3 Provide professional development 4 Modify instruction or intervention 5 Transition to new learning or behavioral objective	Continuous progress monitoring by teams occurs at all levels in a school implementing PBIS practices. At Tier 1, school-wide data (e.g., attendance, office discipline referrals) are reviewed on a monthly basis by PBIS leadership team. If a specific intervention plan (e.g., cafeteria, hallways, entering/exiting the building) is being implemented, data relevant to specific behavior indicators (e.g., noise level, inappropriate language in hallway after last bell) are reviewed weekly. If a group of students (Tier 2) or an individual student (Tier 3) are involved in more targeted interventions, student-specific behavior indicators are collected and reviewed on a weekly, daily, and sometimes hourly basis. Fidelity of intervention implementation is assessed more frequently at Tiers 2/3 (e.g., daily, weekly) than Tier 1 (e.g., annually).

Evidence-Based Practices	Practices must be empirically sound, that is, sufficient replicated scientific support giving users confidence that the desired outcome can be produced.	The PBIS framework is populated with evidence-based practices, for example: • targeted social skills instruction; • cognitive behavior therapy (CBT); • functional behavioral assessment; • behavioral contracting; • positive reinforcement; • active supervision • Check-in/Check-out.
Tiered Continuum of Practices and Systems	All students experience prevention-based and school-wide practices and systems that promote academic and behavior success by all staff members across all school settings (Tier 1). Additional practices, interventions, instruction, etc. (Tier 2/3) are aligned and integrated with Tier 1 to address the needs of students who require additional supports in groups (Tier 2) or individually (Tier 3).	Practices and supports within a PBIS continuum of supports have core elements or characteristics that, when aligned and integrated, support all students based on their risk factors and responsiveness to intervention: • Tier 1: (a) common positively stated school-wide purpose or vision, (b) coordinating leadership team, (c) small number (3–5) of positively stated behavioral expectations, (d) procedures for teaching and practicing these expectations across typical classroom and school settings, (e) hourly/daily positive and specific acknowledgments and feedback on displays of expected behavior, (f) continuum of corrective and reteaching consequences for norm-violating behaviors, and (g) regular review of data for implementation decision making. • Tier 2: increase in intensity, frequency, duration, etc., of Tier 1 core elements for small groups of students with similar support needs. Addition of evidence-based group-based practices (e.g., Check-in/Check-out, targeted social skills and behavioral counseling). • Tier 3: increase in intensity, frequency, duration, etc., of Tier 1 and 2 core elements; however, individualized for specific student challenges and strengths. Addition of specialized individualized evidence-based practices (e.g., function-based supports, behavioral contracts, cognitive behavior therapy, intensive social skills training, school-based mental health).
Implementation Fidelity	Collection, analysis, and decision making of data related to accuracy, fluency, and appropriateness of implementation of an intervention, practice, curriculum, etc., in the context of student responsiveness to intervention. Implementation decisions may include one or more of the following: (a) discontinue, (b) replace, (c) continue, or (d) modify (+/–).	Validated instruments are available to assess PBIS implementation fidelity (e.g., Tiered Fidelity Inventory – TFI, Benchmarks of Quality – BoQ, School-wide Evaluation Tool (SET)). The TFI, for example, allows for review of practices and systems annually for Tier 1, monthly/weekly for Tier 2 (e.g., BAT, MATT), and weekly/daily for Tier 3 (e.g., ISSET, individualized BIP fidelity checklists). PBIS teams examine both practice implementation fidelity data and student data on responsiveness to intervention to make action planning decisions.

What Is Considered When Implementing MTSS?

School counselors and most educators appreciate the importance of defining a problem, need, or concern, selecting a practice or intervention that directly aligns with that definition, and implementing that practice. However, less attention is given to the implementation fidelity, sustainability, and scaled or extended use of the selected practice (see implementation phases in Figure 1.7) (Center on Positive Behavioral Interventions and Supports, 2017). In this section, we summarize considerations and guidelines for implementing MTSS.

MTSS Implementation Considerations

Moving from exploration to scaled MTSS implementation is enhanced if school team members and leadership carefully operate from and consider the main drivers of an effective and efficient implementation plan or blueprint (Figure 1.8). Four main driver areas should be considered: (a) leadership teaming, (b) foundations, (c) implementation, and (d) demonstrations.

Leadership Teaming

Central to all implementation is having a group of individuals who have the authority, schedule, resources, and incentives to develop, implement, and monitor MTSS.

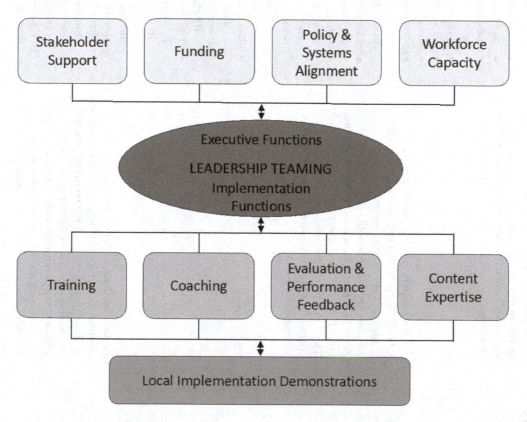

Figure 1.8 MTSS implementation blueprint.

(Source: the Authors.)

This multidisciplinary team should have representation from key stakeholder groups across the school, for example, school administrators, grade level teacher, department representative, special support staff (e.g., school counselors and/or psychologists, special educators, nurses, speech language therapists), classified staff (e.g., paraprofessionals, office assistants, bus drivers), family members, and students.

This team has two categories of responsibilities. *Executive functions* include responsibilities related to securing and encouraging stakeholder support, developing policy, maintaining funding, and establishing local implementation capacity. *Implementation functions* involve organizing and providing personnel training, coordinating coaching supports, and ensuring local specialized behavior capacity.

School administrators (e.g., principals, vice/assistant principals, deans) are particularly important participants on leadership teams for four main reasons, First, they have the *decision-making authority* related to policy, calendar, curriculum, action planning, professional development, etc. School teams are unable to implement MTSS practices and systems if faculty members do not see that the team has the authority and support from leadership to engage in MTSS practices and systems. Second, school leaders are important prompters, *models*, and encouragers for student and staff member participation. If school leaders are actively and visibly engaged in the same expected behaviors, practices, and professional development activities, students and staff members are more likely to see the importance of their own participation and engagement.

Third, not only are school leaders responsible for encouraging and securing most (>80%) staff member participation in MTSS implementation, they are also responsible for *supervising* and *supporting* staff members who oppose or do not understand why they should be involved in MTSS. Analogous to the tiered support logic for students, the school leadership team works with, educates, and encourages all staff and faculty members with the goal of achieving >80% participation in implementation. The school leaders' responsibility is increasing participation by those who need additional encouragement to join the school-wide effort.

Finally, one of the most important functions of school leaders and members of the leadership team is providing frequent *positive recognition and acknowledgment* for staff participation and contributions to MTSS implementation activities. Like positive reinforcement for student expected behaviors, staff recognition should be authentic, socially and culturally relevant (privately in classrooms and publicly when appropriate in meetings and activities), and frequent (e.g., daily, weekly). In usual MTSS fashion, school leaders and team members are responsible for recognition and acknowledgment for all (Tier 1) faculty, staff, and students; however, this responsibility is even more important for those who are unsure, reluctant, and/or resistant to participate in MTSS activities.

Executive Functions

The leadership team has four main *executive or administrative* responsibilities, which are portrayed in Figure 1.8. First, support for MTSS implementation goes beyond the classroom and school, but includes *stakeholders*. For example, parents and family members are particularly important in prompting and reinforcing classroom and school-wide expectations at home and in the community. In addition to having a family member on the leadership team, securing participation by parent–teacher associations, parent volunteers and tutors, and special interest parent groups (e.g., clubs, special events) can be helpful. Stakeholders also include local businesses, non-profit agencies, and community service providers (e.g., law enforcement, mental and public health, medical services). Examples of stakeholder support include "walkthroughs" (i.e., regular classroom and non-classroom visits), data review, fundraisers, dissemination and visibility, as well as alignment with important priorities of the identified stakeholder.

Second, the leadership team should have access to adequate recurring *funding* to establish and maintain MTSS implementation for three to five years. Although temporary funding (e.g., grants, budget supplements) is useful for establishing readiness and initial implementation, having a recurring budget line increases possibilities of MTSS implementation and supports integration and institutionalization in classroom and school-wide routines and operations. Similarly, initial implementation should emphasize development of internal and local expertise (i.e., sustained implementation capacity) rather than temporary hiring of personnel who are not supportable after external funding ceases.

Third, development, implementation, and modification of MTSS *policy* are important leadership team functions that promote institutionalization and sustainability. In particular, established policy facilitates transitions in leadership, teaching faculty, and support staff, and continued practice and systems implementation fidelity. Policy development should accommodate data-based decision making that integrates and aligns new student, classroom, or school-wide needs with existing policy areas, operating procedures, and district/school improvement plan outcomes.

Finally, to maximize practice implementation, fidelity, and sustainability, leadership teams have a continuous responsibility to establish and maintain expert *workforce capacity*. Procedural guides, new personnel orientation activities, regularly scheduled professional development events, and guided practice and implementation fine-tuning are examples of structures and opportunities for establishing and maintaining a competent and expert implementation staff and faculty.

Implementation Functions

In addition to executive functions or drivers, leadership teams are responsible for MTSS activities and procedures that relate to (a) training, (b) coaching, (c) evaluation and performance feedback, and (d) content expertise (Figure 1.8).

The *training* driver is focused on developing leadership team fluency on MTSS concepts, practices, leadership functions, data-based decision making, and all staff training activities. Rather than presenting content to faculty in typical one-time professional development events, the leadership team develops a two–three-year training action plan that emphasizes explicit lesson plans, a calendar for regular training and implementation, supervised practice, continuous prompting and coaching, regular data sharing, and regular monitoring of practice implementation fidelity. Although outside trainers and/or consultants are often utilized during readiness and initial implementation, the goal is to develop internal and local expert training capacity during later implementation phases.

The *coaching* driver is established to bridge and facilitate practice use between training and actual classroom and school-wide implementation. Generally, all leadership team members engage in coaching activities, for example: (a) providing prompts and reminders (e.g., practice use, data collection and decision making, team meetings); (b) reinforcing appropriate and correcting inappropriate practice use; (c) finding information and resources; and (d) team-teaching implementation activities. When feasible, both external and internal coaching capacity is established. Internal coaching is supported by members of the school leadership team, and external coaching is provided by members of district (regional, county) leadership teams or of neighboring school leadership teams. Individuals engaged in external coaching have responsibilities that bridge school and district supports, for example, training opportunities, demonstrations, and exemplars in other classrooms and schools, communications between district and school leadership, specialized behavior supports (e.g., mental health, medical), dissemination and visibility, etc. Because of their flexible scheduling, school counselors, for example, can participate in classroom activities, observe and provide feedback on implementation of individualized practices, and demonstrate and model use of newly adopted strategies.

One of the main responsibilities of school and district leadership teams is providing *evaluation and performance feedback* using local data to guide decision making regarding implementation and executive functions. Focusing on both student progress and responsiveness to intervention and implementation fidelity, leadership teams base feedback on (a) identifying and prioritizing needs, questions, and decisions; (b) developing data collection procedures and schedules that directly address needs, questions, and decisions; (c) analyzing data and providing actionable recommendations; and (d) establishing communication and dissemination routines for sharing and providing feedback. The objective is focused on improving implementation fidelity and student progress. Additionally, leadership teams must share and interpret data with their staff and stakeholders (McIntosh, Mercer, Nese, Strickland-Cohen, & Hoselton, 2016).

The final leadership team implementation driver is related to ensuring that *content expertise* is identified, established, and sustained within and across classrooms and schools. Content expertise ensures that one or more individuals have knowledge of the specific domain, and is linked directly to the implementation practice and its core features, essential implementation steps, fidelity tools and measures, and progress monitoring procedures. Although one or two individuals may have oversight responsibility for a specific practice, ownership and responsibility for content expertise is shared across the leadership team to maximize durable and accurate implementation across all faculty and staff members. Personnel, like school counselors, are important for providing universal prevention-based practices for all students (i.e., Tier 1) and targeted and intensive practices and interventions for students who require additional supports to be academically and behaviorally successful.

Implementation Demonstrations

The final MTSS implementation driver in Figure 1.8 is the development and use of implementation examples or demonstrations. As classroom and school-wide practices are fully implemented, leadership teams identify, support, make visible, and disseminate examples of sustained high-fidelity implementation. Demonstrations can range from individual student interventions to school-wide practices, from one tier to full continuum, from on classroom to whole grade levels, etc. Support for these examples is bolstered by data regarding student responsiveness and practice implementation fidelity. Leadership teams use and disseminate these examples to (a) enhance confidence in new implementers about pertinence, effectiveness, and relevance; (b) model implementation of core features for professional development; and (c) increase system-wide practice sustainability and scaling.

In conclusion, the MTSS blueprint serves as a general implementation roadmap for focusing the attention and priorities of leadership team action planning, which includes leadership team operations, executive and implementation functions, and implementation demonstrations. Leadership teams must ensure that action plan elements are appropriately adapted to local developmental, cultural, setting, and regional characteristics. To maximize individualized use, leadership teams should consider the guidelines included in Table 1.2.

Table 1.2 Leadership team implementation guiding questions

Question	Decision-Making Guidelines
Will students benefit directly?	Shorten and straighten the pathway between practice implementation and student success.
Are you willing to bet your next month's salary on that decision?	Give priority to practice decisions that have empirical evidence supporting effectiveness.
Is this the smallest thing we can do that will be associated with the biggest effect?	Select the most efficient, actionable, doable, etc., practice that has the highest probability of producing the largest effect.
Is this decision fair and equitable?	Consider culture, context, and learning history of student, school, family, and community when making practice selections, adaptations, and evaluations.
What two things can we replace or stop doing to enhance what we expect to do?	Evaluate and prioritize current practices when considering adoption of a practice with higher priority.
Are we doing this the right way every day?	Check regularly implementation fidelity and fluency when evaluating student progress.
Are all students getting what they need to succeed individually?	Ensure that most students are benefiting from classroom and school-wide supports (Tier 1) so that more specialized supports (Tier 2/3) can be provided for students with risk and/or difficulty in responding and learning.

Please see Table 1.2: there are many questions that guide MTSS implementation.

In a similar vein, please ask these questions regarding CSCP implementation.

What do you notice?

What Is the Role of School Counselors in MTSS Implementation?

Thus far, we have described the essential or core features of an MTSS approach with a general emphasis on classroom and school-wide implementation. A common misconception is that the primary role of school counselors is to provide direct supports to students outside the classroom context, for example, individual and small group counseling, grade and school transitions, college and career readiness, and attendance monitoring. School counselors actually are prepared to work with the whole child directly and indirectly, that is academic, social, emotional, and behavior success (ASCA, 2012, 2014).

Within an MTSS approach, the actual roles and responsibilities of school counselors align and integrate well with the focus on prevention, educating and supporting all students, and supporting entire school communities. These include active involvement within and across a continuum of evidence-based practices, coaching and collaborating with all school staff, and collecting and using data to guide decision making (ASCA, 2018; Betters-Bubon, Brunner, & Kansteiner, 2016; Goodman-Scott et al., 2016; Sink, 2016; Sink & Ockerman, 2016; Ziomek-Daigle, Goodman-Scott, Cavin, & Donohue, 2016).

In Table 1.3, the general role of school counseling is summarized with examples in the context of the features of the MTSS implementation blueprint. Further, the next chapter provides elaboration on the alignment between school counseling and MTSS (see Chapter 2).

Table 1.3 School counselor role and MTSS implementation driver

MTSS Implementation Driver	School Counseling Role
Leadership Teaming	• Participating as active and equal member of school-wide leadership team. • Facilitating and providing specialized group and individual supports. • Incorporating school-wide leadership team members onto school counseling advisory council.
Stakeholder Support	• Directly engaging and collaborating with key stakeholder groups (e.g., families, mental health, medical, juvenile justice).
Funding	• Coordinating and implementing specialized CSCP services with general school supports to ensure blended and balanced funding throughout both CSCPs and MTSS frameworks.
Policy and Systems Alignment	• Aligning and integrating CSCP procedures, systems, and practices within MTSS continuum. • Incorporating MTSS practices and systems into CSCP routines, procedures, and protocols.
Workforce Capacity	• Participating in and contributing to counseling-specific school and district professional development events and with other related specialized disciplines (e.g., school psychology, nursing, special education).
Training	• Providing training to staff and faculty members on CSCP practices that are merged within and across training of full MTSS curriculum. • Participating in leadership team, staff, and faculty member training activities.
Coaching	• Prompting, reminding, modeling, and reteaching staff and faculty members' practice implementation. • Acknowledging and positively reinforcing staff and faculty members' practice implementation. • Providing specialized technical assistance (e.g., consultation and collaboration) to staff and faculty members who have been unresponsive to general professional development activities and opportunities.
Evaluation and Performance Feedback	• Gathering and sharing CSCP student and school-wide data (process, perception, outcome) with MTSS leadership and specialty teams, staff and faculty members, students, and family members. • Conducting regular CSCP program evaluations and using those data to guide practice and system decision making and ensure equitable outcomes for all students.
Content Expertise	• Demonstrating general knowledge practices for academic, career, social, emotional, and behavioral supports for all students (Tier 1). • Demonstrating specialized knowledge and practices (Tier 2/3) for students with risk factors or who are unresponsive to general supports (Tier 1).
Demonstrations	• Preparing and disseminating examples or models of CSCP practice implementation. • Participating in classroom and school-wide displays or presentations. • Identifying exemplars or models in other schools and/or districts.

Please see Table 1.3, where the school counselor's role is summarized within the context of the MTSS implementation blueprint.

What are your reactions to this conceptualization of the school counselor's role?

What questions do you have about the school counselor's roles listed in Table 1.3?

In sum, the role of school counselors in MTSS implementation focuses on integrating and aligning CSCP practices, procedures, and systems into MTSS and vice versa, so the two frameworks are complementary and collaborative. School counselors support all students across all tiers and within and across all classroom and school settings. Through such alignment and integration, *all* students have increased opportunities for academic and behavior success.

Conclusion

The purpose of this chapter is to provide school counselors with an overview of MTSS practices and systems with an emphasis on highlighting the benefit of aligning and integrating CSCP and MTSS. We highlight five main summary points.

1   MTSS is a prevention-based framework for enhancing the development and implementation of a continuum of evidence-based practices to achieve academically and behaviorally important outcomes for all students.
2   MTSS is grounded in and shaped by a number of foundational influences: (a) disabilities and special education, (b) curriculum-based measurement and precision teaching, (c) teacher consultation and resource rooms, (d) response to intervention, (e) prevention, (f) behavioral sciences, (f) evidence-based practices, (g) direct instruction, and (h) innovation implementation research.
3   MTSS has seven core operating characteristics: (a) team-based, (b) decision-based data systems, (c) universal screening, (d) continuous progress monitoring, (e) evidence-based practices, (f) tiered continuum of practices and systems, and (g) implementation fidelity.
4   MTSS implementation considers (a) leadership teaming, (b) executive teaming functions (stakeholders, funding, policy, workforce capacity), (c) implementation teaming functions (training, coaching, evaluation and performance feedback, content expertise), (d) implementation demonstrations or examples, and (e) guidelines for implementation effectiveness and efficiency.
5   MTSS aligns and integrates with the roles and responsibilities of school counseling, such as implementing a CSCP, and vice versa to maximize school counselors' impact.

We conclude with an MTSS self-assessment (Table 1.4) that can be used by school counselors and leadership teams to examine the alignment and integration of CSCPs and MTSS. Results from this examination can be the basis for action planning.

Please see Table 1.4 and complete this MTSS self-assessment. As a result, please answer the following questions:

What are your reactions?

What are your strengths?

Which areas can you further develop?

For more information and a school counselor's perspective on *MTSS: The What, Why, and How for School Counselors*, please see Chapter 12 "Voices from the Field," Voices 1 and 6.

Table 1.4 School counseling and MTSS self-assessment

School Counseling and MTSS Self-Assessment	Self-Rating 5 high . . . 1 low				
1 I am a member and active participant in a school-wide *MTSS leadership team* (Tier 1).	5	4	3	2	1
2 I am a member and active participant in *targeted or indicated MTSS teams* (Tier 2/3).	5	4	3	2	1
3 My *CSCP/counseling practices and systems* are aligned with and integrated into MTSS practices and systems.	5	4	3	2	1
4 *MTSS practices and systems* are aligned with and integrated into my *CSCP/ counseling practices and systems.*	5	4	3	2	1
5 I am an active participant in MTSS *professional development* activities.	5	4	3	2	1
6 I directly *train and coach* others in becoming fluent users of CSCP and MTSS practices and systems.	5	4	3	2	1
7 I collect and develop descriptions, displays, and *demonstrate* examples of effective CSCP and MTSS practices and systems.	5	4	3	2	1
8 I align and integrate CSCP and MTSS school-wide *funding and policies.*	5	4	3	2	1
9 I collect and disseminate CSCP *data* within MTSS decision making.	5	4	3	2	1
10 I consider MTSS *data* (e.g., universal screening and progress monitoring) when collecting and analyzing CSCP data.	5	4	3	2	1
11 I regularly assess the *implementation fidelity* of my counseling practices and systems.	5	4	3	2	1
12 My decision making emphasizes the use of *evidenced practices and data-based decision making.*	5	4	3	2	1
13 I actively recruit and prepare others on *CSCP/counseling practices and systems* within MTSS.	5	4	3	2	1

ASCA Ethical Standards

School counselors play an integral role in the creation of Multi-Tiered Systems of Support in school systems. As noted throughout this chapter, the role of the school counselor aligns with the focus on prevention and intervention efforts across all tiers of support. With training in systemic change, school counselors can utilize data and evidence-based practices to provide needed interventions for students. Further, school counselors have an ethical imperative to collaborate with stakeholders to support student academic, social/ emotional and career development. In doing so, school counselors are called to use their knowledge on coaching and collaboration in their work with staff to best support students and to support school improvement goals. All of these imperatives are made easier within the context of MTSS. While many ethical standards relate to these efforts, we highlight those that relate most specifically to MTSS below. Specifically, school counselors:

A   **Responsibility to Students**

   A.1   Supporting Student Development

   - A.1.e. Are concerned with students' academic, career and social/emotional needs and encourage each student's maximum development.
   - A.1.h. Provide effective, responsive interventions to address student needs.

   A.3   Comprehensive Data-Informed Program

   - A.3.a. Collaborate with administration, teachers, and staff and decision makers around school-improvement goals.

- A.3.c. Review school and student data to assess needs including, but not limited to, data on disparities that may exist related to gender, race, ethnicity, socio-economic status, and/or other relevant classifications.
- A.3.d. Use data to determine needed interventions, which are then delivered to help close the information, attainment, achievement and opportunity gaps.

A.10 Underserved and At-Risk Populations

- A.10.g. Recognize the strengths of students with disabilities as well as their challenges and provide best practices and current research in supporting their academic, career, and social/emotional needs.

B   Responsibility to Parents/Guardians, School and the Self

B.2   Responsibilities to the School

- B.2.a. Develop and maintain professional relationships and systems of communication with faculty, staff, and administrators to support students.
- B.2.d. Provide leadership to create systemic change to enhance the school.
- B.2.e. Collaborate with appropriate officials to remove barriers that may impede the effectiveness of the school or the school counseling program.
- B.2.k. Affirm the abilities of and advocate for the learning needs of all students. School counselors support the provision of appropriate accommodations and accessibility.
- B.2.q. Collaborate as needed to provide optimum services with other professionals such as special educators, school nurses, school social workers, school psychologists, college counselors/admissions officers, physical therapists, occupational therapists, speech pathologists, administrators.

Resources

Websites

Links to the following can be found on our eresource at www.routledge.com/9781138501614.

- PBIS implementation networks.
- State PBIS and MTSS examples.
- PBIS state coordinators' network ("Find a PBIS contact in your state").
- Data-based decision making.
- Implementation:
  - National Implementation Research Network;
  - State Implementation and Scaling-up Evidence-Based Practices.

Teaching Activity

Directions: The goal of this activity is for students to learn, first hand, about the challenges and rewards of implementing MTSS from a school counselor's perspective. Interview a school counselor about their MTSS implementation process. Invite them to take the MTSS self-assessment for school counselors (Table 1.4). Review their responses and discuss what hurdles they have cleared and what they are hoping to accomplish this school year. Discuss the use of this assessment as a helpful tool while planning for effective MTSS.

Multiple Choice Questions

1   MTSS is best described as:

    a   An evidence-based practice.
    b   A systems framework for improving student outcomes and implementation fidelity.
    c   A curriculum for aligning and integrating school counseling with classroom and school-wide systems.
    d   a and c.
    e   a and b.

2   CSCPs should be:

    a   Aligned within and integrated across MTSS.
    b   Considered primarily as a specialized resource for students requiring Tier 2 or 3 supports.
    c   Implemented as a supplement to academic and social behavior instruction.
    d   Placed in a shared leadership position with the school principal.
    e   None of the above.

3   Students receiving specialized counseling supports should be:

    a   Excluded from Tier 1 school-wide behavior supports.
    b   Included to the greatest degree possible in Tier 1 classroom and school-wide activities and practices.
    c   Be receiving special education services.
    d   Used as a demonstration of the integration of MTSS and school counseling.
    e   Funded by community and mental health resources.

4   An integrated approach to school counseling and MTSS does NOT emphasize:

    a   Prevention.
    b   Special education.
    c   Practice implementation fidelity.
    d   Evidence-based practices.
    e   Behavioral sciences.

5   School teams leading the implementation of MTSS should include representation from:

    a   Classroom teachers and administrators.
    b   Support staff including school counselors and psychologists and special education teachers.
    c   Family members.
    d   Community service providers.
    e   All of the above.

Answers: Q1 e, Q2 a, Q3 b, Q4 b, Q5 e.

Disclaimer

The development of this chapter was supported in part by a grant from the Office of Special Education Programs, U.S. Department of Education (H029D40055). Opinions expressed herein are the authors' and do not reflect necessarily the position of the US Department of Education, and such endorsements should not be inferred. Contact: George Sugai (george.sugai@uconn.edu), OSEP Center on Positive Behavioral Interventions and Supports (www.pbis.org), Center for Behavioral Education and Research (www.cber.org), Neag School of Education, University of Connecticut, Storrs.

References

Alberto, P. A., & Troutman, A. C. (2013). *Applied behavior analysis for teachers* (9th Ed.). Columbus, OH: Prentice-Hall-Merrill.

Algozzine, R. F., Barrett, S., Eber, L., George, H., Horner, R. H., Lewis, T. J., . . . Sugai, G. (2014). *SWPBIS tiered fidelity inventory.* Eugene, OR: OSEP Technical Assistance Center on Positive Behavioral Interventions and Supports. Available from: www.pbis.org.

American School Counselor Association (ASCA) (2012). *The ASCA National Model: A framework for school counseling programs* (3rd Ed.). Alexandria, VA: Author.

American School Counselor Association (ASCA) (2014). *Mindsets and behaviors for student success: K-12 college- and career-readiness standards for every student.* Alexandria, VA: Author.

American School Counselor Association (ASCA) (2018). The school counselor and multitiered systems of support. *American School Counselor Association Position Statement.* Alexandria, VA: Author. Retrieved from: www.schoolcounselor.org/asca/media/asca/PositionStatements/PS_MultitieredSupportSystem.pdf.

Becker, W. C. (1992). Direct instruction: A twenty year review. In R. P. West and L. A. Hamerlynck (Eds), *Designs for excellence in education: The legacy of B. F. Skinner* (pp. 71–112). Longmont, CO: Sopris West, Inc.

Bergan, J. R., & Kratochwill, T. R. (1990). *Behavioral consultation and therapy.* New York: Plenum Press.

Betters-Bubon, J., Brunner, T., & Kansteiner, A. (2016). Success for all? The role of the school counselor in creating and sustaining culturally responsive positive behavior interventions and supports programs. *The Professional Counselor, 6,* 263–277.

Biglan, A. (1995). Translating what we know about the context of antisocial behavior in to a lower prevalence of such behavior. *Journal of Applied Behavior Analysis, 28,* 479–492.

Biglan, A. (2015). *The nurture effect: How the science of human behavior can improve our lives and our world.* Oakland, CA: New Harbinger Publications.

Bradley, R., Danielson, L., & Doolittle, J. (2007). Responsiveness to intervention: 1997–2007. *Teaching Exceptional Children, 39*(5), 8–12.

Brown-Chadsey, R., & Steege, M. W. (2005). *Response to intervention: Principles and strategies for effective practice.* New York: Guildford Press.

Caplan, G., & Grunebaum, H. (1967). Perspective on primary prevention. A review. *Archives of General Psychiatry, 17,* 331–346.

Center on Positive Behavioral Interventions and Supports (2017). *SWPBS implementation blueprint* (revised). Eugene, OR: University of Oregon, Author. Available at: www.pbis.org.

Chalfant, J. C., Pysh, M. V., & Moultrie, R. (1979). Teacher assistance teams: A model for within-building problem solving. *Learning Disabilities Quarterly, 2,* 85–96.

Colarusso, R. P. (1987). Diagnostic-prescriptive teaching. In M. C. Wang, M. C. Reynolds, & H. J. Walberg (Eds), *Handbook of special education: Research and practice* (pp. 155–166). Elmsford, NY: Pergamon Press.

Colvin, G., Kame'enui, E. J., & Sugai, G. (1993). Reconceptualizing behavior management and school-wide discipline management in general education. *Education and Treatment of Children, 16,* 361–381.

Colvin, G., & Sugai, G. (1988). Proactive strategies for managing social behavior problems: An instructional approach. *Education and Treatment of Children, 11,* 341–348.

Cooper, J. O., Heron, T. E., & Heward, W. L. (2007). *Applied behavior analysis* (2nd Ed.). Upper Saddle River, NJ: Pearson Prentice Hall.

Daniels, A. C., & Bailey, J. S. (2014). *Performance management: Changing behavior that drives organizational effectiveness* (5th Ed.). Atlanta, GA: Aubrey Daniels International.

Darch, C. B., & Kame'enui, E. J. (2004). *Instructional classroom management: A proactive approach to behavior management* (2nd Ed.). Upper Saddle River, NJ: Prentice Hall.

Deno, S. L. (1985). Curriculum-based measurement: The emerging alternative. *Exceptional Children, 52*, 219–232.

Deno, S. L. (2003). Developments in curriculum-based measurement. *Journal of Special Education, 37*, 184–192.

Deno, S. L., Fuchs, L. S., Marston, D., & Shin, J. (2001). Using curriculum based measurement to establish growth standards for students with learning disabilities. *School Psychology Review, 30*, 507–524.

Deno S. L., & Mirikin, P. K. (1977). *Data-based program modification: A manual.* Reston, VA: Council for Exceptional Children.

Engelmann, S., Becker, W. C., Carnine, D., & Gersten, R. (1988). The direct instruction follow through model: Design and outcomes. *Education and Treatment of Children, 11*, 303–317.

Engelmann, S., & Carnine, D. (1991). *Theory of instruction: Principles and applications.* Eugene, OR: ADI Press.

Fixsen, D. L., Naoom, S. F., Blasé, K. A., Friedman, R. M., & Wallace, F. (2005). *Implementation research: A synthesis of the literature.* Tampa, FL: University of South Florida, Louis de la Parte Florida Mental Health Institute, The National Implementation Research Network (FMHI Publication #231).

Fuchs, D., & Fuchs, L. S. (Eds) (2007). Responsiveness to intervention [Special issue]. *Teaching Exceptional Children, 39*(5), 14–20.

Gilbert, T. F. (1978). *Human competence: Engineering worthy performance.* New York: McGraw Hill.

Gilbert, T. F., & Gilbert, M. B. (1992). Potential contributions of performance science to education. *Journal of Applied Behavior Analysis, 25*(1), 43–49.

Goodman-Scott, E., Betters-Bubon, J., & Donohue, P. (2016). Aligning Comprehensive School Counseling Programs and Positive Behavioral Interventions and Supports to maximize school counseling efforts. *Professional School Counseling, 19*(1), 57–67, doi: 10.5330/1096-2409-19.1.57.

Goodman-Scott, E., & Grothaus, T. (2017). School counselors' roles in RAMP and PBIS: A phenomenological investigation. *Professional School Counseling, 21*(1), 130–141, doi: 10.5330/1096-2409-21.1.130.

Graden, J. L. (1989). Redefining "prereferral" intervention as intervention assistance: Collaboration between general and special education. *Exceptional Children, 56*, 227–231.

Gresham, F. M., Reschly, D. J., Tilly, W. D., Fletcher, J., Burns, M., Prasse, D., et al. (2005). A response to intervention perspective. *The School Psychologist, 59*(1), 26–33.

Gresham, R. M. (2005). Response to intervention: An alternative means of identifying students as emotionally disturbed. *Education and Treatment of Children, 28*, 328–344.

Horner, R. H., & Sugai, G. (2018). Future directions for positive behavior support: A commentary. *Journal of Positive Behavior Interventions, 20*, 19–22, doi:10.1177/1098300717733977.

Horner, R., Sugai, G., & Fixsen, D. (2017). Implementing effective educational practices at scales of social importance. *Clinical Child and Family Psychology Review, 20*, 25–30, doi: 10.1007/s1056701702247.

Idol, L. (1983). *Special educator's consultation handbook.* Austin, TX: Pro-Ed.

Joyce, B., & Showers, B. (2002). *Student achievement through staff development* (3rd Ed.). Alexandria, VA: Association for Supervision and Curriculum Development.

Kame'enui, E. J. (2007). A new paradigm: Responsiveness to intervention. *Teaching Exceptional Children, 39*(5), 6–7.

Latham, G. (1988). The birth and death cycles of educational innovations. *Principal, 68*(1), 41–43.

McIntosh, K., & Goodman, S. (2016). *Integrated multi-tiered systems of support: Blending RTI and PBIS.* New York: Guilford.

McIntosh, K., Mercer, S. H., Nese, R. N. T., Strickland-Cohen, M. K., & Hoselton, R. (2016). Predictors of sustained implementation of school-wide behavioral interventions and supports. *Journal of Positive Behavior Interventions, 18*, 209–218.

Myers, D., Simonsen, B., & Sugai, G. (2011). Increasing teachers' use of praise with a response to intervention approach. *Education and Treatment of Children, 34*, 35–59.

National Education Association of the United States (1978). *P.L. 94–142: Related federal legislation for handicapped children and implications for coordination.* Washington, DC: The Association.

Positive Behavioral Interventions and Supports (2018). *SWPBS for School Counselors*. Retrieved from: www.pbis.org/resource/881.

Pugach, M. C., & Johnson, L. J. (1989). Prereferral interventions: Progress, problems, and challenges. *Exceptional Children, 56,* 217–226.

Scott, T. M. (2017). *Teaching behavior: Managing classrooms through effective instruction.* Thousand Oaks, CA: Corwin.

Scott, T. M., Hirn, R. G., & Cooper, J. T. (2017). *Teacher and student behaviors: Keys to success in classroom instruction.* Lanham, MD: Rowan and Littlefield Publishing.

Showers, B., & Joyce, B. (1996). The evolution of peer coaching. *Educational Leadership, 53*(6), 12–16.

Sidman, M. (1960). *Tactics of scientific research.* New York: Basic Books.

Simonsen, B., & Myers, D. (2015). *Classwide positive behavior interventions and supports: A guide to proactive classroom management.* New York: Guilford Press.

Sink, C. A. (2016). Incorporating multi-tiered systems of supports into school counselor preparation. *The Professional Counselor, 6,* 203–219.

Sink, C. A., & Ockerman, M. S. (Eds) (2016). Introduction to the special issue: School counselors and a multi-tiered system of supports. *The Professional Counselor, 6,* v–ix.

Skinner, B. F. (1938). *The behavior of organisms: An experimental analysis.* New York: Appleton-Century.

Sugai, G., Freeman, J., Simonsen, B., La Salle, T., & Fixsen, D. (2017). National climate change: Doubling down on our precision and emphasis on prevention and behavioral sciences. *Report on Emotional Behavioral Disorders in Youth, 17*(3), 58–63.

Sugai, G., & Horner, R. H. (2009). Responsiveness-to-intervention and school-wide positive behavior supports: Integration of multi-tiered system approaches. *Exceptionality, 17,* 223–237.

Walker, H. M., Horner, R. H., Sugai, G., Bullis, M., Sprague, J. R., Bricker, D., & Kaufman, M. J. (1996). Integrated approaches to preventing antisocial behavior patterns among school-age children and youth. *Journal of Emotional and Behavioral Disorders, 4,* 194–209.

Weist, M. D., Garbacz, S. A., Lane, K. L., & Kincaid, D. (2017). *Aligning and integrating family engagement in Positive Behavioral Interventions and Supports (PBIS): Concepts and strategies for families and schools in key contexts.* Center for Positive Behavioral Interventions and Supports (funded by the Office of Special Education Programs, U.S. Department of Education). Eugene, OR: University of Oregon Press.

White, O. R. (1986). Precision teaching – precision learning. *Exceptional Children, 52,* 522–534.

White, O. R., & Haring, N. G. (1980). *Exceptional Teaching* (2nd Ed.). Columbus, OH: Charles E. Merrill.

Wolery, M. R., Bailey, D. B. Jr., & Sugai, G. M. (1988). *Effective teaching: Principles and procedures of applied behavior analysis with exceptional students.* Boston, MA: Allyn and Bacon.

Zins, J. E., Graden, J. L., & Ponti, C. R. (1988). Prereferral interventions to improve special services delivery. *Special Services in the Schools, 4,* 109–130.

Ziomek-Daigle, J., Goodman-Scott, E., Cavin, J., & Donohue, P. (2016). Integrating a multi-tiered system of supports with Comprehensive School Counseling Programs. *The Professional Counselor, 6,* 220–232, doi:10.15241/jzd.6.3.220.

2 Integrating School Counseling and MTSS

Emily Goodman-Scott and Melissa S. Ockerman

Introduction

Imagine if you woke up tomorrow and all the challenges and flaws in K-12 education had disappeared. What would you see? How would things be different?

While we know there is no magic antidote to solve obstacles in K-12 education and to help students and schools succeed, we also know there are many promising programs, concepts, and frameworks that can help. In this chapter, we'll discuss two frameworks that are considered to be gold standards or best practices in K-12 education. First, we'll discuss one well-known school counseling framework: Comprehensive School Counseling Programs (CSCPs), specifically the American School Counselor Association (ASCA) National Model. Then we'll delve into another widely used K-12 framework: Multi-Tiered Systems of Support (MTSS), including Response to Intervention (RTI) and Positive Behavioral Interventions and Supports (PBIS). Then finally, in the last section of this chapter, we will outline how these two frameworks are aligned and can work hand-in-hand to support students and schools, and, most importantly, how school counselors can be integral in this process and alignment.

While most school counselors are familiar with school counseling programs, and may likely be in schools implementing MTSS, they may not always see the natural alignment between the two frameworks. We believe aligning these two approaches assists us to better serve more students, be efficient with our time, and helps us collaborate with the greater school community. Our goal for this chapter, and the remainder of the book, is to provide a roadmap for aligning school counseling and MTSS, to best help you in your current or future school counseling job. Let's begin!

What's a School Counselor, Anyway?

When I (the first author) was an elementary school counselor, the first month of school I visited each classroom to introduce myself and talk about the role of the school counselor. I asked students: "What is the school counselor's job?" And they often responded with some variation of the following—school counselors:

"Help students do their best in school."

"Teach students to get along with friends."

"Show students different careers and schools after high school."

"Help teachers and parents to help students learn."

"Bring puppets to class."

(I must admit, nothing kept the attention of a class of five year olds like an enthusiastic puppet demonstration and a song!). Overall, my young students understood a large part of my role as a professional school counselor. Similarly, according to ASCA, the flagship professional school counseling organization:

> School counselors are certified/licensed educators with a minimum of a master's degree in school counseling, making them uniquely qualified to address all students' academic, career and social/emotional development needs by designing, implementing, evaluating and enhancing a Comprehensive School Counseling Program that promotes and enhances student success. School counselors are employed in elementary, middle/junior high and high schools; in district supervisory positions; and counselor education positions." (ASCA, para. 1, n.d.)

While my students grasped the key tenets of school counseling, what they may not have known is that the role of the school counselor has ebbed and flowed over the last century, changing with the educational, political, and cultural tides. You may ask: how has the school counselor's role changed over the years? And what the heck is a Comprehensive School Counseling Program (CSCP)? Let's take closer look in the next section.

Not Your Grandmother's Guidance Counselor: School Counseling Through the Years

During the late 1800s and early 1900s, the United States transitioned from an agricultural to an industrial economy, and, as a result, needed to fill new jobs. Thus, vocational counseling bloomed. Initially, school counselors were called "guidance officers" or "guidance counselors." They were staff in the schools who placed or guided students to post-school employment based on their interests, abilities, intelligence, and professional aspirations (Gysbers & Henderson, 2012). But these school counselors of yesterday didn't have nearly the training of today's school counselors. Often, they were teachers given extra responsibilities, with little or no training or resources. While school counseling started with vocational counseling and little formal training, the profession has expanded and evolved drastically in the resulting years. Since the inception of vocational guidance over a century ago, school counseling has gone through phases, which included: directive vocational counseling; clinical diagnosis and assessment; student development; humanistic, person-centered counseling; scheduling and administrative tasks; multiculturalism, social justice and equity; career and technology education; consultation and collaboration; prevention; and the use of data and accountability (Gysbers, 2010). One turning point in particular was the Space Race and the National Defense Education Act, in which the number of school counselors increased, as they were asked to guide students toward careers in science and technology.

For the last several decades and even today, school counselors have wrestled with professional identity. What do we do? What is our professional orientation? Do we identify more with psychological mental health or education? Can we be both counselors and educators? What is the role of the professional school counselor? These changes in professional roles have led to confusion and questions for those within our profession, as well as for those outside of the school counseling profession. For instance, school administrators' lack of understanding of the school counselor role can lead to assigning non-school counseling duties. Within the evolution of the school counseling identity, the concept of a Comprehensive School Counseling Program (CSCP) was first developed in the 1960s and 1970s and helped provide role clarity. Through a CSCP, school counselors provide a school counseling program with a range of purposeful, developmentally appropriate tasks to serve *all* students and the school community through direct and indirect services, and data-driven decisions (ASCA, 2012; Gysbers & Henderson, 2012).

In order to create a more uniform school counselor identity, and to assist school counselors serve *all* students, organizations like ASCA have striven to uphold their motto: *One Vision, One Voice*. They've helped give consistency and legitimacy to the field, enabling school counseling to have a concrete professional definition, so we can best serve our students, schools, and communities, and also successfully communicate our role to stakeholders, such as administrators. As such, ASCA created a host of resources, including a definition of school counseling, professional standards, an ethical code, and even a CSCP called the ASCA National Model. These tools helped transition the profession from "guidance" to "school" counselors. Thus, the term "school counselor" reflects this recent paradigm shift in our professional identity. The National Model was created in 2003, updated in both 2005 and 2012, and is the most common type of CSCP (ASCA, 2012). Want to know more about CSCPs? Hold on to your hats: there is more to come. Next we'll focus on CSCPs, followed by the ASCA National Model.

Comprehensive School Counseling Programs are commonly known today as school counseling best practice. According to researchers, CSCP implementation has been related to many positive school and student outcomes, such as higher student attendance, graduation, and retention rates; greater student math and reading achievement scores; increased college and career readiness; as well as lower suspension, discipline, and truancy rates (Burkard, Gillen, Martinez, & Skytte, 2012; Carey, Harrington, Martin, & Hoffman, 2012a; Carey, Harrington, Martin, & Stevenson, 2012b). There's been a lot of positive feedback regarding school counselors implementing CSCPs!

While CSCPs share a common framework, there are various CSCP models. For instance, some states, such as Virginia, have created their own state-specific version of a CSCP based on the ASCA National Model, integrating their state standards and related documents accordingly. As mentioned above, the ASCA National Model is an especially prevalent CSCP, implemented throughout the U.S., and the framework on which many state CSCPs are based. In fact, there are over 700 schools throughout the country that have been awarded ASCA's national designation for exceptionally implementing the ASCA National Model (Cook, 2017).

As a result of CSCPs, no longer are school counselors encouraged to spend most of their time providing individual counseling to students with the highest needs, or reactively completing miscellaneous tasks determined by their school or district. Gone are the years when school counselors' primary task was pushing administrative paperwork. *The school counselors of today are not your grandmother's guidance counselors.* Today we are school counselors, with a concrete and purposeful identity and mission. We have a better understanding of our role and we strive to share that role with our stakeholders, so they can understand how we can best serve students, schools, and communities. Next, we will explore more about school counseling today, specifically describing the ASCA National Model (ASCA, 2012).

School Counseling Today: The ASCA National Model

The ASCA National Model (see Figure 2.1) is a purposeful, preventative, data-driven, developmentally-appropriate, systematic framework that can be tailored to each school to best serve their unique needs and culture (ASCA, 2012). At the same time, the model has standard components that are part of the flexible framework, including three domains (academic, career, and social/emotional), four themes (leadership, collaboration,

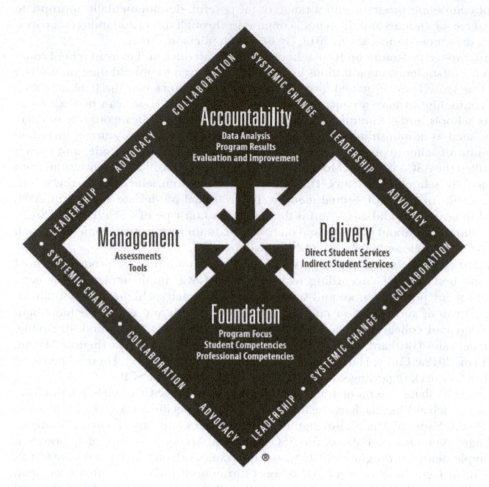

Figure 2.1 The ASCA National Model.

Reprinted from *ASCA National Model: A framework for school counseling programs* (3rd Ed.), by the American School Counselor Association, 2012, Alexandria, VA: Author. Copyright 2012, used with permission.

advocacy, and systemic change), and, lastly, four components (foundation, delivery, management, and accountability). Let's break it down a little further, explaining each of these in more depth.

Domains: Academic, Career, and Social/Emotional

Through implementing the ASCA National Model, school counselors serve *all* students' school-based needs, focusing on three interconnected domains: *academic, career,* and *social/emotional* (ASCA, 2012; ASCA, 2014). School counselors coordinate prevention for all students and intervention for students with the highest needs. For instance, school counselors may address academic concerns both directly and indirectly. Direct assistance can include providing students with related counseling and education, such as study skills and organization. Indirect services could include examining student and school-wide student achievement gaps, tracking student academic data, and assisting to remove systemic barriers to students' academic success. Next, there has recently been renewed emphasis on K-12 college and career readiness (United States Department of Education,

2017). For instance, school counselors expose students to post-secondary options and help facilitate their creation of Academic and Career Plans. Last, but certainly not least, is social and emotional development. Today's school counselors acknowledge the impact of social and emotional competencies on students' school and home functioning, as well as on their future. Social and emotional competence has a substantial influence on academic and career success; students' personal well-being and mental health impact all areas of their functioning (Collaborative for Academic, Social, and Emotional Learning, n.d.). Examples of social and emotional competencies include self-awareness, self-management, social awareness, relationship skills, and decision-making skills.

Four Themes: Leadership, Collaboration, Advocacy, and Systemic Change

According to the ASCA National Model, the themes of leadership, collaboration, advocacy, and systemic change guide the school counselors' work (see Figure 2.1). In a nutshell, school counselors are *leaders* in their school who *collaborate* with a range of stakeholders to *advocate* for student success, close the achievement and opportunity gaps between groups of students, remove barriers to student success through recommending and providing individual and small group interventions (e.g., counseling), as well as creating *systemic change* throughout the school (ASCA, 2012). To break this down a little further, we use an ecological or systems model of development (e.g., Bronfenbrenner & Morris, 2006). Thus, school counselors are trained to approach schools as systems, proposing that learning is impacted by several intersecting systems within the student (e.g., level of motivation and engagement, personality, learning experiences, etc.) and outside the student (e.g., quality of schooling, familial relationships, support for learning, socioeconomic status and other cultural factors, etc.). Relatedly, we view the school as a system made up of smaller interconnected systems: students, classes, grade-levels, teams, staff, families, the greater community, society as a whole, national cultural trends, and so forth (see Chapter 3 for more information on systems theory). In addition to school administrators, school counselors are some of the few school staff who prescribe to a broad systemic perspective of the school, acknowledging the school as a system or whole (McMahon, Mason, Daluga-Guenther & Ruiz, 2014). As such, school counselors are leaders who collaborate with members throughout the school or system (e.g., administrators, families, staff, community members) to advocate for systemic change, or change throughout the entire system, ensuring equitable practices and cultural responsivity to remove students' academic, career, and social/emotional barriers (Grothaus & Johnson, 2012). Rather than working in isolation, school counselors are central to the heart of their school. They collaborate and team with a range of stakeholders to serve students directly and indirectly, including serving on school-wide leadership teams and student intervention teams; inviting a range of stakeholders onto the school counseling advisory committee; and serving on committees affiliated with the school community. Further, from a systems perspective, school counselors are members of teams that assess school and student-level data; recommend and provide interventions; and monitor the progress and outcomes of interventions. While this may sound like a lot of responsibility (and it is!), rest assured that, as a school counselor, you are part of a multidisciplinary student support team, and often a team of school counselors.

Four Components: Foundation, Delivery, Management, and Accountability

The ASCA National Model includes of four components or sections (please see Figure 2.1; ASCA, 2012). The Foundation is the basis for the model, and literally sets the foundation or tone. To start with, the Foundation includes the program's vision, mission, and goals. As school counselors, we strive to show that our purpose is directly aligned with that of the school and district; as such, the school counseling vision, mission, and goals should be closely related to the school's and district's strategic plan. Housed in the Foundation section are key documents such as school counseling competencies, standards, ethical codes, and the like.

Next, the Delivery System describes how school counselors deliver their services to students: directly and indirectly. Examples of direct student services include: (a) core curriculum, such as school counseling-specific classroom lessons based on related standards (e.g., the ASCA Mindsets and Behaviors) (ASCA, 2014); (b) individual and small group counseling, which is short-term and provided for students with elevated needs; (c) individual student planning, such as meeting with students and family members to assist them in creating individualized academic and career plans; and (d) crisis response, assisting with student and school-level crises as needed. The individual and group counseling services offered by school counselors is time-bound, allowing them to tend to their multitude of other responsibilities in running a CSCP. As such, students with severe mental health needs and chronic counseling concerns should be referred out to mental health providers in the community, such as Licensed Professional Counselors, while the school counselors liaise with the outside provider, with needed permission. This relates specifically to indirect services. According to the ASCA National Model, examples of indirect student services are referrals, consultation, and collaboration, which are a tremendous aspect of school counseling. For instance, in a large national study, school counselors reported that their most frequent job activity was consultation (Goodman-Scott, 2015). Thus, with large caseloads and many responsibilities, it seems fitting that school counselors can reach the most students through consulting and collaborating with school staff, parents/family members, and community members, using their expertise to assist these important stakeholders to serve students. Overall, while 80% of a school counselor's time should be spent directly or indirectly serving students, the ASCA Model is a framework that allows each school to decide how school counselors spend that time allocated to direct and indirect services.

The Management and Accountability systems aid school counselors to organize, implement, and evaluate the ASCA model. Specific tools include self-assessments examining school counselors' time (Use-of-Time-Assessment), performance evaluations conducted by supervisors (School Counselor Performance Appraisal), determining the level of CSCP implementation (School Counseling Program Assessment), recruiting and running an Advisory Council, and preparing for classroom lessons (Lesson Plans). Further, plans for the year are documented through an Annual Agreement between the school counselor and building administrator, which are further delineated through the school counselors' Calendars.

As previously mentioned, data are an important part of any CSCP. School counselors must answer the question "how are students different, as a result of a Comprehensive School Counseling Program" (ASCA, 2012). Tools from the Accountability and Management systems assist in answering this question. School counselors, both individually and as part of a school-wide team, collect and analyze data at various levels (e.g., by student, class, grade, school, special populations, etc.), such as organizing the data in their annual School Data Report. Student outcome data is especially valued, including student attendance, behavior (e.g., discipline referrals), and achievement (e.g., course enrollment, grades, standardized tests) (Kaffenberger & Young, 2013). After determining needs (e.g., achievement gaps, disproportionality in discipline referrals, etc.) school counselors create Action Plans and goals to drive services and plans, then report their findings through Results Reports, which they communicate to the school community. Gathering and analyzing data, and making data-driven decisions, are iterative processes, continually informing school counselors' time, goals, and CSCP services.

As mentioned previously, school counselors are leaders in their school, central to the school's mission and efforts. Thus, rather than working in isolation, school counselors are embedded into the very fabric of the school and must work within other important school initiatives and frameworks. One such initiative is MTSS, a popular framework implemented throughout the United States. And, as luck would have it, MTSS also aligns well with the role of school counselors implementing a CSCP. As such, let's take a closer look at MTSS.

> What interactions did you have with your school counselor when you were a K-12 student?
>
> Compare the role of your childhood school counselors with the school counselors of today. How are they alike and different?

MTSS: More than Alphabet Soup

Overall, Multi-Tiered Systems of Support, or MTSS, is an overarching or umbrella term to describe a variety of prevention and intervention frameworks to serve students academically and behaviorally across three tiers of prevention (Brown-Chidsey & Bickford, 2016; McIntosh & Goodman, 2016). Multi-Tiered Systems of Support is often comprised of Academic Response to Intervention (RTI) and School-Wide Positive Behavioral Intervention and Supports (PBIS) (please see Chapter 1 for more information)—MTSS, RTI, PBIS . . . more acronyms and alphabet soup? Before we go any further, let's take a closer look at the meaning of these terms.

Academic RTI

Academic Response to Intervention, or RTI, is a "preventative systems approach to improving school-wide and individual achievement through high-quality universal instruction and additional tiered supports provided in response to student need" (McIntosh & Goodman, 2016, p. 6). In other words, RTI is a type of MTSS framework for addressing

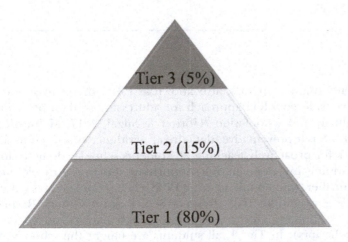

Figure 2.2 The MTSS framework, including three tiers of support.

student academics across tiers of prevention, providing increased supports or interventions depending on students' needs, then monitoring student progress to determine success of the interventions and the need for more supports.

The RTI framework includes three tiers of academic supports; each tier provides students with greater supports, based on their needs (please see Figure 2.2). First, in Tier 1, all students proactively receive universal curriculum and instruction (e.g., general education literacy instruction). For students who still need greater support, they also receive additional small group interventions in Tier 2 (e.g., small group literacy support). Tier 3, or targeted supports, are the most intensive services and are provided to students who continue to struggle after receiving Tier 1 and 2 services (e.g., literacy support in very small groups or individual settings). Thus, by utilizing a RTI framework, both general education and special education teachers work together to provide a range or continuum of services to students, based on student needs, using data to continually monitor students' progress. In addition to school staff, family involvement is encouraged and beneficial.

Academic RTI is a common framework found in schools throughout the nation. Currently, forty-five states have guidelines related to the implementation of RTI and seventeen states require it for the identification of specific learning disabilities (Patrikakou, Ockerman, & Hollenbeck, 2016). Academic RTI is most commonly practiced in reading at the elementary level (McIntosh & Goodman, 2016) and is used as a way for teachers to reduce the stigma often associated with learning disabilities (Johnston, 2010). Some research related to RTI is promising, as special education classes are now more representative of socioeconomic and ethnic diversity (Speece, Case, & Eddy, 2001). Additionally, "when Tier 2 reading interventions are implemented in primary grades with fidelity and ample support for interventionists, they tend to result in improved outcomes for students at risk for or with reading difficulties" (Gersten, Jayanthi, & Dimino, 2017, p. 249). However, these researchers also noted that students who score on the cusp of screenings (at or below the 40th percentile) are not yet benefiting from RTI. Additional studies reviewing the efficacy of RTI and the fidelity of its implementation are merited.

Students who struggle with academics may also display behavioral challenges in the classroom.

Consider: why would a child who struggles with reading or math also display challenging behaviors in school?

School-Wide PBIS

Positive Behavioral Intervention and Supports, also known as PBIS, shares many overlaps with RTI and is often considered a RTI approach for addressing student behaviors and emotions both individually and school-wide (Horner & Sugai, 2017; McIntosh & Goodman, 2016). Overall PBIS is a preventative, data-driven, evidence-based, culturally responsive MTSS framework for proactively teaching all students school-wide behaviors and expectations, and providing increased tiered supports to students with elevated needs. To break this down further, when implementing PBIS, each school creates culturally appropriate school-wide expectations (e.g., Respect Self, Respect Others, Respect Property) and procedures (e.g., processes for re-teaching student behaviors and acknowledging students' desired behaviors). In Tier 1, all students are taught the school-wide expectations (e.g., school rules) and procedures (e.g., how to walk outside for a fire drill) (see Figure 2.2). Students who need greater behavioral support receive Tier 2 (small group) or Tier 3 (targeted) services, such as a behavioral chart, individual or small-group counseling, or wraparound comprehensive services from a variety of school and community professionals. Students across all tiers receive acknowledgments or positive reinforcement for engaging in the desired behaviors (e.g., school expectations). These acknowledgments are specific to a school context and based on what is desired or popular for students in that school (e.g., tickets toward a school-wide skating party, positive words, sitting with friends during lunch, being a special teacher helper, etc.). Through PBIS, the school is viewed as a system, and school climate and school-wide procedures are analyzed and adjusted to meet students' needs. As such, staff are taught uniform procedures, such as the processes for student acknowledgments, student referrals, and collecting related data. Staff collaboration and support for PBIS are crucial, as the school staff must work together to implement the PBIS framework across the entire school, and to implement with fidelity, or faithfully.

Positive Behavioral Intervention and Supports is implemented throughout the country in nearly 26,000 schools (PBIS, 2018) and supported by a number of studies. For instance, researchers found that fully implementing PBIS is related to fewer student suspensions, greater academic performance, higher perceptions of student safety and school organizational health (Bradshaw, Koth, Bevans, Ialongo, & Leaf, 2008; Bradshaw, Koth, Thornton, & Leaf, 2009; Bradshaw, Mitchell, & Leaf, 2010; Bradshaw, Waasdorp & Leaf, 2012; Horner et al., 2009; Kim, McIntosh, Mercer, & Nese, 2018). Also, Curtis, Van Horne, Robertson, and Karvonen (2010) found that PBIS implementation resulted in decreasing losses in instructional time. Overall, students and schools can gain major benefits due to a fully functioning PBIS framework.

MTSS

We've discussed RTI, with a primary focus on student academics, and PBIS, with a main focus on student behaviors. However, we don't view students *only* in regard to their academics. Nor do we view students *only* in regard to their behaviors. Rather, growing research indicates the importance of viewing academic, behavior, and emotional functioning as intertwining, impacting each other (McIntosh & Goodman, 2016). Thus, in recent years, educators have begun merging RTI and PBIS under one larger, overarching, integrative framework to address students' academic and behavioral needs comprehensively: Multi-Tiered Systems of Support, or MTSS (Brown-Chidsey & Bickford, 2016; McIntosh & Goodman, 2016).

According to McIntosh and Goodman (2016), Multi-Tiered Systems of Support, also known as MTSS:

> Provides all students with the best opportunities to succeed both academically *and* behaviorally in school . . . focuses on providing high-quality instruction and interventions matched to student need across domains [e.g., academic and behavioral] . . . monitoring progress frequently to make decisions about changes in instruction or goals. It is not simply the implementation of both academic RTI and PBIS systems. There is a careful integration of these systems to enhance the efficiency and effectiveness of all school systems. (p. 6)

To unpack this further, the MTSS framework demonstrates the overlap between RTI and PBIS (Brown-Chidsey & Bickford, 2016; McIntosh & Goodman, 2016), which is described below:

- **Prevention**: all students are taught academics and behavioral expectations preventatively, rather than waiting for student failure or challenges (see Chapter 4).
- **Tiered Supports** (see Figure 2.2):
  - All students receive **Tier 1** supports, or academic and behavioral prevention geared toward every student, such as general education curriculum or school-wide expectations. On average, 80% of students will be successful when receiving only primary, or universal, Tier 1 supports (please see Chapters 3 and 4 for more information on Tier 1).
  - Students with elevated academic and behavioral needs, beyond Tier I, receive **Tier 2** small-group supports, such as academic instruction, group counseling, Check-in/Check-out (a goal-directed behavior chart which will be described later in this chapter). Tier 2 will be discussed in greater detail in Chapter 5.
  - In **Tier 3**, students with the highest needs receive individualized supports in order to meet their academic and behavioral needs. Providers in and out of the schools provide supports (e.g., individualized instruction, long-term individualized counseling, wraparound services) to comprehensively address chronic student concerns. It is important to note that students in the advanced tiers continue to receive supports from less intensive tiers such as Tier 1 services. Further, student needs are often fluid, and the intensity of services typically change over time rather than students continuing to receive advanced tiered supports indefinitely. Lastly, students may have differing needs across tiers. For instance, a student could require Tier 2 supports in some areas (e.g., math and anger management) and yet require Tier 1 supports in most other areas (e.g., social skills and literacy). (Please see Chapter 6 for more information on Tier 3 supports.)

Ramón was a school counselor for several years at a school with strong MTSS implementation. He recently started a different school counseling position at a school that also claims to implement MTSS. He learns the following about his new school. They hold RTI meetings on Mondays to discuss student academics and related interventions. Then a separate PBIS team meets on Tuesdays to discuss student behaviors and corresponding interventions. There is also a leadership team that makes and monitors school-wide improvement goals and last, a school-counselor-run CSCP, but without an Advisory Council nor staff input or buy-in. Thus, all four of these faculty committees/programs meet in isolation.

What are your reactions to Ramón's new school structure?

What next steps can you recommend to Ramón?

- **Cultural Responsivity and Collaboration**: MTSS implementation can be modified based on the needs of each unique school community. Relatedly, schools implementing MTSS should include high levels of collaboration with and feedback from community members and stakeholders in order to develop and guide cultural responsivity. Overall, aspects of MTSS implementation should be based on the population, and the MTSS team should include stakeholders from the school and community such as school teachers and classified staff, family members, students, and community leaders/liaisons. Thus, in order for MTSS to be successful, school professionals

as well as families must collaborate. Further, school personnel must buy into the benefits of MTSS for implementation to be successful. In fact, it is recommended that 80% of staff support PBIS implementation in order to effectively implement it (OSEP Technical Assistance Center on Positive Behavioral Interventions and Supports [OSEP Center on PBIS], 2015). (Please see Chapter 8 for more information on collaboration and consultation, and Chapter 11 for more information on cultural responsiveness.)

Think of the following two schools with different demographics.

School 1: primarily comprised of Caucasian students in a rural, farming, middle school with high poverty.

School 2: predominantly African-American elementary students in a gifted, middle-class, suburban magnet school.

How could you ensure MTSS implementation would be culturally responsive to the needs of each school?

Do your students and families speak languages other than English? Consider posting school-wide expectations in your community's primary language.

For example, we recently saw school-wide behavioral expectations written in Crow, the language of the local Native American tribe, who were the majority of the school's student population. (See p. 314, Chapter 11.)

- **Data-Driven Evidence-Based Practices**: MTSS is guided by data, such as determining students' academic and behavioral needs. For example, MTSS teams use academic benchmark tests, grades, attendance, and office discipline referrals (to name a few) to determine students' academic and behavioral needs. Interventions put in place to meet these needs (e.g., general education curriculum, small group counseling) should be evidence-based, meaning their effectiveness has been tested and proven. With the growing emphasis on accountability and the use of data in schools, MTSS provides a framework to assist school staff to become increasingly familiar and comfortable using data (additional content on data and evidence-based practices is covered in Chapters 9 and 10, respectively).
- **Systemic Approach**: MTSS uses a systems approach, viewing schools and students as interconnected systems, i.e., as a whole. Thus, rather than only looking at student academics or behaviors in isolation, best practice recommends that we, counselors and educators, consider both in combination, as well as the influence of classrooms, school procedures, family culture, and so forth, on that student's development. Similarly, we strive to make systemic changes across the school as a whole (e.g., school climate and culture) based on school-wide data, teaching school-wide procedures to all staff members. (Please see Chapter 3 for more information on systems theory.)

To summarize, MTSS is an intentional, systemic, preventative integration of the RTI and PBIS frameworks to address student academics and behaviors comprehensively. When utilizing MTSS, we (a) view students and schools as a whole, or a system, (b) integrate academics

Table 2.1 Comparing CSCPs and MTSS

We described **CSCPs such as the ASCA National Model** as:	We described **MTSS, including RTI and PBIS** as:
• Preventative	• Preventative
• Data-driven	• Data-driven, utilizing evidence-based practices
• Culturally-responsive	• Culturally responsive
• Utilizing a system's approach	• Utilizing a systems approach
• Serving all students through direct and indirect services	• Serving all students through a tiered continuum of supports
• Focusing on students' academic, career and social/emotional domains, and the interconnectedness of these domains	• Integrating academic and behavioral student domains, and the interconnectedness of these domains
• Developmentally-appropriate	• Collaborative
• School counselor roles as leaders, collaborators, advocates, and systemic change agents	

and behaviors, and (c) utilize MTSS implementation to assist school staff work more effectively and efficiently, combining school-wide efforts and resources toward a common goal.

You are a school counselor and want to begin MTSS implementation in your school. You are preparing a presentation to inform your school administration on the benefits of MTSS implementation. What points would you include in your presentation?

What potential concerns could your administrators have about MTSS implementation? How would you respond to these concerns?

MTSS and School Counseling: A Perfect Union

To recap these first two sections of the chapter please see Table 2.1.

In looking at the table above, do you notice any similarities or overlaps between CSCPs and MTSS in the two columns? So do we. And so have many others.

When I (the first author) was a brand new school counselor, fresh out of my master's program, I was asked to lead my school's PBIS team. In my eagerness to be a team player I willingly agreed, despite the fact that I had no knowledge of PBIS or MTSS. In those days, PBIS was emerging in my region and was not yet present in the school counseling literature. However, I had a strong grasp of the ASCA Model. As I attended my first of many PBIS trainings, I learned the basic premise of PBIS/MTSS and a lightbulb went off in my head. I realized that PBIS (and MTSS) have the same key goals as CSCPs such as the ASCA National Model. As luck would have it, I found MTSS can align seamlessly with CSCPs.

Thus, I pondered: (a) if the school is implementing PBIS/MTSS, (b) I'm implementing a CSCP, and (c) PBIS/MTSS are aligned with CSCPs:

How can we integrate these two frameworks?

Specifically:

> How could a school counselor be involved in PBIS/MTSS?
>
> How could PBIS/MTSS be used as a vehicle to strengthen CSCPs?

CSCP–MTSS Alignment

In the last several years, a host of scholars have proposed the alignment between CSCPs and MTSS, which has also been increasingly supported by research. Several scholars have conceptualized an alignment between CSCPs such as the ASCA Model and RTI (Ockerman, Mason, & Hollenbeck, 2012), and more recently PBIS (Goodman-Scott, Betters-Bubon, & Donohue, 2016), and MTSS (Ziomek-Daigle et al., 2016). Experts realized this alignment early on when RTI was first introduced state-wide (Gruman & Hoelzen, 2011; Ockerman et al., 2012) and when it became commonly implemented throughout the nation (Patrikakou et al., 2016). Specifically, Ockerman et al. (2012) noted both RTI and CSCPs are proactive data-driven tiered frameworks grounded in social justice reform. Moreover, they encouraged school counselors to align their interventions within the RTI framework (see Figure 2.3) while seeking a balanced role between an *intervener* and *supporter* as an RTI team member. We'll discuss this balancing act more later.

In a similar vein, Goodman-Scott and colleagues (2016) proposed the alignment between CSCPs and PBIS, suggesting that (a) both CSCP and PBIS frameworks are preventative, evidence-based, data-driven, systems' approaches for providing student services, (b) that they also centered on the four themes of the ASCA National Model: collaboration, systemic change, advocacy, and leadership. Further, the authors proposed that school counselors' CSCP roles could be viewed through the three tiers of prevention. Thus, the authors looked at school counselors' job activities recommended by ASCA and placed them within the PBIS three-tiered model, showing that the majority of school counselors' job activities can be viewed within the lens of MTSS (see Figure 2.3 for a similar example). Moreover, ASCA developed a position statement summarizing the alignment between MTSS and the ASCA National Model (ASCA, 2018). Similarly, Ziomek-Daigle et al. (2016) noted several overlapping features of MTSS and CSCPs, as displayed in the Venn diagram in Figure 2.4 below.

These features include:

> collaboration and coordinated services; effectively using the school counselors' time through tiered supports; collecting and reviewing student and school data; using evidence-based practices; developing culturally responsive interventions that close achievement gaps; promoting prevention and intervention through a tiered continuum; and facilitating school-wide systemic change and positive school climate. (Ziomek-Daigle et al. 2016, pp. 226–227)

Not only has the alignment between CSCPs and MTSS been theorized, it has also been backed by research. First, several researchers have found the alignment or positive relationship between CSCPs and MTSS. As such, Bookard (2015) reported school counselors experienced increased self-efficacy in performing counseling duties related to their involvement in RTI. Similarly, Olsen, Parikh-Foxx, Flowers and Algozzine (2016) surveyed over 4,000 school counselors and found the more time school counselors spent on ASCA-aligned activities, the higher their levels of competency in MTSS knowledge and

Integrated School-Wide Systems Promoting Mental Health

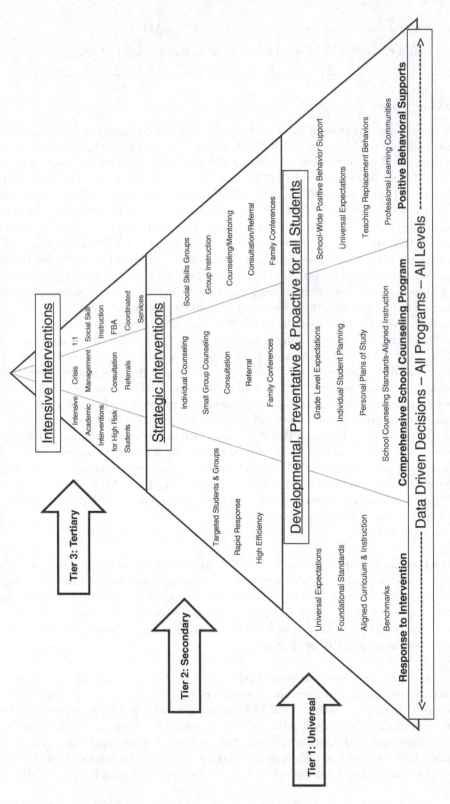

Figure 2.3 Missouri Comprehensive Guidance Program: linking school success with life success.

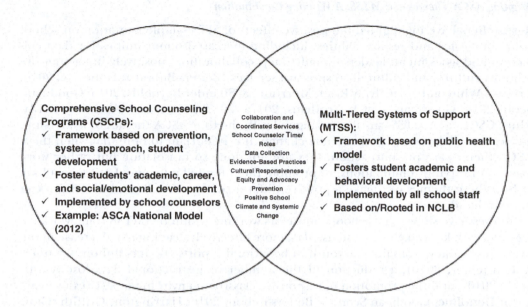

Figure 2.4 Overlap and similarities between a Multi-Tiered System of Support and Comprehensive School Counseling Programs.

Reprinted from J. Ziomek-Daigle, E. Goodman-Scott, J. Cavin, & P. Donohue, 2016, Integrating a Multi-Tiered System of Supports with Comprehensive School Counseling Programs, *The Professional Counselor*, 6(3), p. 225. Copyright 2016 *The Professional Counselor*. Used with permission.

skills. Thus, implementing aspects of the ASCA model improved their abilities to implement MTSS. School counselors in both of these studies reported benefits to implementing MTSS.

Relatedly, Goodman-Scott and Grothaus (2017a) interviewed school counselors at Recognized ASCA Model Programs (RAMP) schools regarding their schools' high levels of PBIS implementation. According to the majority of these school counselors, the integration of their CSCP and PBIS often informed and supported each other, or were intertwined. Similarly, as a school counselor, Goodman-Scott (2014) found that aligning her CSCP and PBIS implementation maximized her time and efficiency to do both well. In addition, school counselors who took on leadership roles in MTSS implementation described increased professional capacity in addressing student behavior and making positive systemic change in schools (Betters-Bubon & Donohue, 2016).

Lastly, according to a school counselor in a different study, implementing PBIS helped make school counselors central to the mission of the school, saying

> It's not like school counselors are over here [pointing in one direction] and we have our own agenda, and the rest of the school is doing their own thing [gesturing to another direction]. We're supporting the mission of the school. (Goodman-Scott, Hays, & Cholewa, 2018, p. 115)

Overall, several researchers found empirical backing to support the alignment between MTSS and school counseling, providing compelling evidence to implement the two frameworks together.

Aligning ASCA Themes and MTSS: A Winning Combination

Researchers have highlighted the positive effects of MTSS implementation on school counselor roles and responsibilities, including increased opportunities for data collection and assessment, leadership, advocacy, collaboration, positively impacting the school's culture, and culturally responsive services (Betters-Bubon & Donohue, 2016; Cressey, Whitcomb, McGilvray-Rivet, Morrison, & Shander-Reynolds, 2015; Goodman-Scott, 2014; Goodman-Scott & Grothaus, 2017a, 2017b; Martens & Andreen, 2013). Thus, CSCPs and MTSS can also be aligned with the four ASCA themes of leadership, advocacy, collaboration, and systemic change. It is important to note that when these ASCA themes are put into action, they are not done so in isolation but rather work *together*, in varying combinations, to promote the intended outcome. Let's take a look at how these themes can make a positive difference when CSCPs and MTSS work in hand in hand.

Studies have shown that school counselors working within the MTSS framework *collaborated* with key stakeholders to use *data* more effectively, leading to a decrease in the overrepresentation of minority youth in behavioral reports (Betters-Bubon, Brunner, & Kansteiner, 2016), a reduction of the number of instructional days lost (Curtis et al., 2010), and the promotion of responsive classroom environments (Cressey et al., 2015; Donohue, Goodman-Scott, & Betters-Bubon, 2016; Harrington, Griffith, Gray, & Greenspan, 2016). Thus, these skill sets created more *culturally relevant practices* that led to *systemic change* within their schools. Similarly, Donohue (2014) found school counselors implementing PBIS with high fidelity had an increased capacity for preventing challenging student behavior, as well as greater competency in *data* analysis and *systemic* thinking. According to Goodman-Scott and Grothaus (2017a), the school counselors in their study found using *data* in both their CSCP and PBIS implementation helped them to become more effective in all aspects of their work. Moreover, these researchers aptly noted, "*advocacy* and *systemic change* efforts require school counselor *leadership*" (Goodman-Scott & Grothaus, 2017b, p. 138). Indeed, numerous studies have shown that school counselors who take *leadership* roles in MTSS implementation foster *systemic change* throughout their school (Cressey et al., 2015; Curtis et al., 2010; Goodman-Scott, 2014).

Challenges in CSCP–MTSS Alignment

While the research on aligning CSCPs and MTSS is promising, there are, however, some noted challenges. Researchers found discrepancies between school counselors' perceptions of their training for roles related to MTSS and the time necessary to complete them. For example, when examining the school counselor's role implementing RTI at the state and national levels, school counselors believed they were unprepared for the key skills of data collection, management, and the collaboration necessary to make RTI an efficient and effective framework (Ockerman, Patrikakou, & Hollenbeck, 2015; Patrikakou et al., 2016). Similarly, some of the school counselors in Goodman-Scott and Grothaus' studies also reported a lack of preparation and training regarding PBIS implementation (2017a; 2017b). Additionally, a few school counselors reported decreased time to complete counseling-related tasks and increased demands to coordinate and organize logistics related to RTI (Bookard, 2015). According to Olsen and colleagues (2016), school counselors who indicated they spent less time on ASCA-related activities also expressed a greater need for MTSS training. Thus, there may be a greater need for additional MTSS preparation in graduate programs and school district in-services.

> Can you make a list of the benefits and challenges in aligning and implementing both a CSCP and MTSS?

So What? CSCP–MTSS Alignment in Action

At this point, you might think "Okay this sounds great, but how does it work?" We're glad you asked. While it's essential to know the research behind aligning CSCPs and MTSS, we must know how to put the two into cohesive practice. To start with, due to the school counselor's unique skill set in prevention and remediation, their background in academic, career, and social/emotional development, and their training with the use and management of data, school counselors should be an integral part of their school's MTSS team, offering their expertise on students and families, school climate, and data collection (see Cressey et al., 2015; Goodman-Scott, 2014; Patrikakou et al., 2016). Similarly, as school counselors, we can also ask members of the MTSS committee to join the school counseling Advisory Council, to provide input and act as liaisons between the two initiatives. Relatedly, school counselors' MTSS-specific responsibilities should be reflected in the Annual Agreement and the school counselors' Calendar within the Management System of a CSCP. Further, the school counseling Belief, Vision, and Mission Statements as well as Program Goals should also be aligned with school-wide MTSS efforts.

Intervener and Supporter

As we discussed earlier, school counselors provide evidence-based counseling interventions through direct services (e.g., classroom instruction, small-group counseling, individual counseling) and indirect services (e.g., consultation, collaboration, referrals, data collection, and analysis). Therefore, as integral members of the MTSS team, school counselors play both the role of *intervener* when directly providing student services, and *supporter* when providing those services indirectly (Ockerman et al., 2012). These roles of *supporter* and *intervener* are vital to student success, and are helpful ways to understand how school counselors contribute to the implementation of MTSS (described in Table 2.2).

> In your own words: what does it mean for a school counselor to be an *Intervener* and a *Supporter*?
>
> How can these roles be utilized in not only MTSS implementation, but also in facilitating a CSCP?

School Counseling Activities Across the Three Tiers

All, Some, Few

As we discuss the three tiers, it may be helpful to think of how these services are delivered based on the ASCA domains (academic, career, social/emotional) and by the number of students served by them. Thus, at Tier 1, *all* students receive services, at Tier 2, *some* students receive the services, and at Tier 3, *few* students are in need of these services (Hatch, Duarte, & De Gregorio, 2018). Chicago Public Schools, the third largest school district

Table 2.2 School counselor role: supporter and intervener

School Counseling Program Element		School Counselor Role in MTSS	
		Supporter (Indirect Services)	*Intervener (Direct Services)*
	Tiered Model	Serve on MTSS team: • Provide background information on students, families, and school climate • Suggest evidence-based curriculum and interventions • Assist in creating school-wide procedures and expectations • Collaborate and consult with stakeholders • Provide referrals to internal and external providers	Address academic and/or behavioral concerns through core curriculum: • School-wide activities • Classroom lessons • Small group and individual counseling • Crisis response
	Data	Provide the MTSS team with data collected from counseling interventions that are used to meet MTSS team goals and to serve students identified by the team. Collect and analyze data as a part of all interventions used to meet the goals of the MTSS team and to serve students identified by the team.	Deliver evidence-based core curriculum lessons and universal screenings to all students in Tier 1. Provide data-driven small-group and individual counseling interventions at Tier 2 and Tier 3 (only as appropriate).
	Social Advocacy	Highlight specific data in relation to disciplinary and academic policies that may disproportionally impact minority students. Bring to the team's attention issues of social justice and the needs of marginalized populations while connecting these issues to MTSS team goals.	Create and deliver specific counseling interventions based upon the needs of underserved populations.

Modified from Ockerman et al., 2012. Used with permission.

Table 2.3 Examples of school counseling supports at each tier and domain

	Academic	Career	Social/Emotional
Tier 3 **(FEW)**	• Referrals for tutoring, academic supports, or re-engagement centers • Academic support plans/contracts • Intensive, short-term, solution-focused individual academic planning for students identified as at-risk • Transition plans for incarcerated, expelled, and hospitalized students • Intensive attendance-related supports (i.e., home visits)	• Referrals as appropriate (i.e., Student Outreach And Reengagement (SOAR) Centers, Job Corp) • Intensive, short-term, solution-focused individual counseling for students identified as at-risk • Individual student/family advising around postsecondary issues • Postsecondary advocacy (i.e., financial aid appeals; arranging one-on-one admissions interviews with college reps) • Coordinating one-on-one postsecondary supports (i.e., college essay-writing supports, drawing out students who are interested in non-traditional pathways) • Transition plans for incarcerated, expelled, and hospitalized students • Summer melt advocacy/planning • Postsecondary reengagement	• Collaboration with crisis team/Screening, Assessment, and Supportive Services (SASS) • Referrals (i.e., Department of Children & Family Services (DCFS), mental health services, shelters, other community services) • Consultation with a student's outside therapist • Consultation with or reports to Department of Children & Family Services (DCFS) • Behavior Support Plans • Intensive, short-term, solution-focused individual counseling for students identified as at-risk • Transition plans for incarcerated, expelled, hospitalized, and/or homebound students • Behavioral Health Team; Interventionist Entity of Culture and Climate Team • Wraparound Services • Student/family behavior conferences

Table 2.3 (continued)

	Academic	Career	Social/Emotional
Tier 2 (SOME)	• Short-term, solution-focused small group counseling (i.e., study skills, executive functioning skills) • Closing the gap activities and equity, access, and systemic change activities • DREAMer and Deferred Action for Childhood Arrivals (DACA) support • Brokering credit recovery options for students with credit deficiencies • Check-in/Check-out • Supports for students in temporary living situations • Coordination of mentoring supports • Consultancy/collaboration • Participation on IEP/504 teams • Individual academic planning for students identified as at-risk • Small groups for students identified as at-risk • Diverse Learner/English Language Learner (ELL) Progress Monitoring • Collaboration with Grade Level Teams/House Teacher Teams	• Short-term, solution-focused small group counseling (i.e., Posse, Gates) • Closing the gap activities and equity, access, and systemic change activities • DREAMer and Deferred Action for Childhood Arrivals (DACA) support • Check-in/Check-out • Supports for students in temporary living situations • FAFSA workshops for families of first-generation students • College tours for special populations • Coordination of mentoring supports • College essay-writing supports • Supporting Posse applicants • Consultancy, collaboration • Small groups for students identified as at-risk • Recognition and awards ceremonies • College and career fairs for special populations • Summer melt work	• Short-term, solution-focused small group counseling (i.e., children of divorce, grief, relationships, social skills) • Closing the gap activities and equity, access, and systemic change activities • DREAMer and Deferred Action for Childhood Arrivals (DACA) support • Trauma-focused interventions (e.g., Cognitive Behavioral Intervention for Trauma in Schools (CBITS), Bounce Back, Structured Psychotherapy for Adolescents Responding to Chronic Stress (SPARCS) • Aggression prevention interventions (e.g., Anger Coping, Think First) • Social skills interventions (e.g., Social Skills Group Intervention (S.S. GRIN) • Peace Circles, Peer Jury, Peer Conference • Check-in/Check-out • Restorative Conversations • Supports for students in temporary living situations • Coordination of mentoring supports • Consultancy, collaboration, teaming • Recognition and awards ceremonies • Community Business Organization consultation and supports (Step Up, Becoming A Man (BAM), ENLACE, Teen Parenting Initiative) • School Behavioral Health Team referrals

Tier 1 (ALL)

- Teaching standards-based, developmental classroom lessons focused on the academic domain (i.e., transcript review, high school applications)
- Facilitating completion of the Individual Learning Plan for all students
- Collaboration with Grade Level Teams/House Teacher Teams
- High school fairs and informational sessions for students and families
- Advisory lessons on academic domain content
- Student/parent orientations
- Marketing of enrichment and extracurricular opportunities
- High School Investigation Day
- Freshman Connection
- Service Learning supports
- Academic Progress Monitoring of ALL students (i.e., Dashboard, D/F Gradebook Report, Grade Level/Dept. discussions)
- Culture and Climate Team: (inclusive of admin., school staff and clinicians)

- Teaching standards-based, developmental classroom lessons focused on the career domain
- Facilitating completion of the Individual Learning Plan for all students
- College tours, business tours, or other postsecondary site visits for all students in a particular grade level
- FAFSA workshops, open to all students
- Fairs (college, career, scholarship)
- Career day/guest speakers
- Senior Seminar courses
- Advisory lessons on career domain
- Student/parent orientations
- Career domain workshops for families
- Marketing of enrichment and extracurricular opportunities (i.e., job shadowing, internships)
- Decision Day activities
- Resume and interviewing workshops (i.e., "What Not to Wear" fashion show)
- Summer melt preventative supports

- Teaching Social Emotional Learning (SEL) standards-based, developmental classroom lessons
- Training appropriate school staff to deliver standards-based curriculum/coordinating school-wide Social Emotional Learning (SEL) curricula (i.e., Second Step)
- Co-teaching Social Emotional Learning (SEL) standards with content-area teachers
- School-wide expectations about behavior (i.e., BRAVE, ACHIEVE)
- Advisory lessons on Social Emotional Learning (SEL) domain content
- Coordination of Sexual Health Curriculum
- Marketing of enrichment and extracurricular opportunities
- School-wide or grade-level-wide team building, leadership workshops
- Social/emotional workshops for families
- Coordinating school-wide responsive services to address an emergency, disaster, or other crisis situation
- Coordination of school-wide awareness events (i.e., Day of Silence)
- Adolescent depression prevention in health class

in the country, has adopted this model and offers examples of how this content can be put into practice (see Table 2.3). It is important to note that these services must be determined based on school data and through collaboration with administration and staff, as appropriate to each school's population.

What are *general* school-based activities that are performed for All, Some, and Few students?

What are *school-counseling-specific* activities performed for All, Some, and Few students?

What overlap do you notice in your responses to these two questions?

Now, let's take a closer look at how school counselors act in both of these roles across the three tiers. Please note that supporting information can be found in Figure 2.3 and Table 2.3.

Tier 1

For Tier 1 supports, school counselors act as *interveners* when providing direct services, which can occur through classroom lessons and school-wide events; school counselors act as *supporters* as members of a multidisciplinary team that consults and collaborates on school-wide Tier 1 implementation. The process begins with the MTSS team selecting evidence-based core academic curriculum for the general population, ensuring *all* students receive scientifically-based, high quality instruction. Additionally, staff determine and teach school-wide student academic and behavioral expectations (e.g., Be Responsible, Be Professional, Be Respectful, etc.). School counselors offer Tier 1 services that include research-based core curriculum lessons aligned with MTSS goals and objectives. For example, school counselors can offer lessons on character education and executive functioning, such as *Student Success Skills* (Brigman & Webb, 2007), *Second Step* (Committee for Children, 2010), *Why Try* (Bird, 2010) and *Expect Respect* (Nese, Horner, Dickey, Stiller, & Tomlanovich, 2014). School counselors, serving as advocates, must consider integrating culturally responsive strategies such as *Sheltered Instruction Observation Protocol* (SIOP) to ensure English language learners have the requisite background information to understand the core curriculum lessons they are delivering (Betters-Bubon et al, 2016). Relatedly, when implementing aspects of their *School Counseling Core Curriculum*, such as classroom lessons and school-wide initiatives, school counselors can teach and reinforce the MTSS school-wide behavioral expectations.

School-wide data gathered from annual student and staff needs assessments (Kaffenberger & Young, 2013) allow MTSS teams to make relevant decisions about Tier 1 school-wide programming addressing all ASCA domains. Examples include conflict resolution and anti-bullying policies, positive behavior and academic incentive programs, and college/career fairs (Belser, Shillingford & Joe, 2016; Ockerman et al., 2012). Additionally, other disaggregated baseline data, such as student office discipline referrals (ODRs), attendance, and achievement (Belser et al., 2016; Harrington et al., 2016; Losen, Gillespie, & University of California, 2012; Ziomek-Daigle et al., 2016), provide direction for relevant classroom lessons and school-wide initiatives at Tier 1. For example, as a leader and advocate effecting systemic change, school counselors can note demographic trends in ODRs, particularly for historically overrepresented students. If disproportionality exists, school counselors should create psychoeducational programs aimed at creating prosocial behavior, including restorative justice practices (e.g., peace circles, peer mediations), and advocate for alternatives to punitive discipline polices (Belser et al., 2016; Betters-Bubon et al., 2016; Donohue et al., 2016; Losen et al., 2012). Historically, school counselors have struggled to gather and analyze student and school outcome data. However, utilizing existing PBIS student outcome data within the CSCP can assist school counselors in completing their School Data Profile, as well as creating Program Goals, Closing the Gap Action Plans and Results Reports (see the ASCA website).

Moreover, at Tier 1, the MTSS team selects evidence-based universal screenings normed for children and youth, such as the *Behavior Assessment System for Children, Second Edition Behavioral and Emotional Screening System* (BASC-2 BESS), the *Student Risk Screening Scale* (SRSS) and/or the *John Hopkins Depression Scale*. These instruments are then administered routinely to *all* children to assess their mental health and well-being. The team should look for screening assessments that have been normed with their specific school population (e.g., the SRSS has been normed in urban elementary schools) (Belser et al., 2016; Betters-Bubon, et al., 2016; Donohue et al., 2016; Ennis, Lane, & Oakes, 2012; Gruman & Hoelzen, 2011; Ockerman et al., 2012; Ziomek-Daigle et al., 2016). Some students will not respond to Tier 1 interventions as expected or, based upon results from universal screening, will warrant additional academic, personal/social, or behavioral interventions (see Chapter 7 for more information on universal screening). Thus, collectively, the MTSS team may recommend moving the student to the next tier of services. Let's look at the pivotal ways in which school counselors can serve these students best.

Tae is a school counselor and implements a variety of Tier 1 strategies within his school counseling program. His first classroom lesson of the year is based on the MTSS-generated school-wide expectations and teaching matrix; thus, during his lessons, he explicitly teaches the school-wide expectations using the MTSS tools. When interacting with students during his lessons and at other times during the school day, he passes out MTSS tickets to acknowledge students' positive behaviors. Due to increased bullying-related ODRs across the school, Tae and the MTSS team suggest the evidence-based program *Bully Prevention in PBS* to be implemented school-wide. He incorporates this program in his classroom lessons and collaborates with the school MTSS team to host a pep rally at which they introduce this initiative to all students and staff at once.

Tier 2

As a rule of thumb for the average school, approximately 15% of students will need Tier 2 services comprised of targeted interventions with increased intensity and frequency. Academic and behavioral interventions at this tier are often synonymous with small-group interventions for six–eight students with similar needs. School counselors can act as *interveners*, providing direct services to these students. For example, school counselors can facilitate weekly anger management small-group interventions for students with ongoing discipline problems (Gruman & Hoelzen, 2011; Ockerman et al., 2012). However, inherent within the school counselor's role is time-limited individual counseling. Thus, whether one-to-one counseling falls under Tier 2 or Tier 3 is determined by the nature of the concern (i.e., common vs rare; moderate vs severe) and/or the number of sessions needed (brief vs chronic). For example, a student in need of intensive college/career advising addressed in four to six individual school counseling sessions would fall into Tier 2, while a student demonstrating extreme psychological distress or ongoing familial discord would be referred to Tier 3 supports. School counselors can use the PBIS-generated outcome data to determine students for small-group and individual counseling, as well as to monitor their related progress.

As members of the interdisciplinary MTSS team, school counselors can act as *supporters*, recommending and monitoring services and interventions for students with elevated needs. In this way, school counselors can be involved with Tier 2 services through consulting and collaborating, as well as directly providing services. One example is the individualized evidence-based program Check-in/Check-out (CICO) (Crone, Hawken, & Horner, 2010). Check-in/Check-out pairs students with trusted adults in the school building; students obtain teacher feedback throughout the day via a behavior report card and "check in" and "check out" daily with their designated faculty to review progress towards reaching their behavioral goals (Belser et al., 2016; Betters-Bubon et al., 2016; Goodman-Scott et al., 2016). Check-in/Check-out is effective in reducing disciplinary problems (Martens & Andreen, 2013) and helps cultivate positive relationships between students and staff (Belser et al., 2016) thereby promoting positive school climates. With this Tier 2 intervention, school counselors can help coordinate the process (e.g., examining data to determine student participation) and collaborate with school faculty who serve as CICO partners, thereby acting in a supportive role. School counselors may also be the trusted adult within CICO, thereby acting in a more direct role. See Chapter 5 for additional information on CICO.

School Counseling Director Nykki and her team of counselors attend their school's MTSS team meetings. The MTSS team has a system for tracking students in need of Tier 2 and 3 supports, based on elevated needs in academics, behaviors, attendance, and social/emotional concerns. Together, the MTSS team and school counseling team decide on students who could benefit from small-group counseling provided by Nykki and the other school counselors. Then, the school counselors implement an evidence-based small-group curriculum based on students' needs. The school counselors continue attending the MTSS team meetings and reviewing the MTSS-gathered data, which is used to monitor students' progress in the group counseling.

Tier 3

While your grandmother's "guidance counselor" may have spent much of her/his time delivering long-term individual counseling, we now believe school counselors should typically render this service in the short term, making referrals to allied professionals to conduct long-term counseling. Further, long-term individual counseling should typically be provided when the evidence-based practices provided in Tier 1 and Tier 2 have been proven to be ineffective (for the average school, this is approximately 5% of the student population). Thus, a large part of the school counselor's role in Tier 3 is as a *supporter*: consulting and collaborating with the MTSS team, teachers, family members, and outside providers, to provide wraparound services, assist students to secure resources (e.g., counseling outside of the school), and continue to advocate for students receiving services in the most appropriate educational setting. Moreover, in Tier 3, school counselors also provide crisis response for critical and immediate student concerns, as a direct service or *intervener*. Thus, Tier 3 services are highly individualized and can include long-term counseling with school personnel such as the school psychologist or other school-based mental health professionals, as well as staff providing outside referrals for more intensive psychotherapy and wraparound services. In Tier 3, school counselors and the interdisciplinary school-based team also engage in ongoing consultation and collaboration with community partners as well as with parents/guardians. School staff may conduct Functional Behavior Assessments (FBAs), Behavior Intervention Plans (BIP) and academic plans for students with persistent academic and behavioral challenges. The MTSS team, including the school counselor, may decide, based on a student's inadequate response to academic interventions across all three tiers, to refer the student for a comprehensive evaluation for special education eligibility at this stage (NASP, 2016). (See Chapter 6 for additional information on Tier 3 supports.)

> As a school counselor, overall, Lydia spends most of her time engaged in Tier 1 and Tier 2 activities. When engaging in Tier 3 services, she primarily engages in consultation and collaboration. For example, she is a member of her school's multidisciplinary MTSS leadership team, using her expertise to recommend student interventions and monitor students' progress. She also gives referrals to community-based mental health professionals and provides teachers and family with strategies for best serving their students.

Conclusion: The Bottom Line

In this chapter, we've covered a lot of ground regarding CSCPs, MTSS, and their alignment. A few final points. First, it's important to remember that CSCPs and MTSS are flexible frameworks, not static ones. Thus, as with all counseling modalities, integrating MTSS and CSCPs should be viewed as dynamic and fluid. Ongoing assessment and evaluative data will make this an iterative process whereby interventions and protocols will routinely change to address existing and emerging needs. Moreover, students will naturally move between tiers, requiring more intensive services during periods of transition (e.g., from elementary to middle school, during the college search, etc.) and should need only Tier 1 services once they have acclimated (McIntosh & Goodman, 2016; Ockerman et al., 2012). Lastly, as change agents we, as school counselors, don't *solely* examine a class or a grade or a student. Rather, we investigate how all aspects of the school community create a greater whole. Thus, by aligning our CSCP with MTSS, we can advocate for systemic change throughout the micro and macro systems inherent within our building and community.

While it is important to advocate for our students, we must also advocate for ourselves and for the importance of our job. One way to advocate for our profession is to work smarter and more efficiently. Integrating or aligning CSCPs and MTSS can help us to maximize our time and energy, and also provide a common language between us and our colleagues. If the rest of our school community is talking about three tiers, we also want to conceptualize school counseling in similar terms that are meaningful and familiar to our stakeholders.

In summary, while there is no magical cure-all for the challenges inherent to K-12 schools, there are widely-used practices backed by evidence. We hope this chapter has provided you with insight into how, by aligning your CSCP with MTSS, you can ultimately best serve your students and school, save time, and work more efficiently. And, while we as school counselors don't have magic wands, seeing students improve and schools function with greater organizational health and overall effectiveness can sometimes feel almost like . . . well, magic.

One school counselor explained that after three years of successfully implementing MTSS, their discipline data had changed so dramatically that the State Department of Education called their principal to find out what they had been doing.

Think about yourself as a school counselor in three to five years. What success stories could you have regarding MTSS implementation? And what will you do to find this success?

For more information and a school counselor's perspective on *Integrating School Counseling and MTSS*, please see Chapter 12 "Voices from the Field," Voices 1, 2, 5, 7, and 8.

ASCA Ethical Standards

As noted, at the core of MTSS is the foundational ASCA component of using data ethically to ensure all students, regardless of their race/ethnicity, culture, religion, gender identity, sexual orientation, social class and/or socio-economic status, achieve equitable educational outcomes. As such, MTSS propels school counselors into advocacy and leadership roles by ensuring the assessments and services offered at each tier are unbiased, accessible, and culturally relevant. Moreover, implementing MTSS necessitates that school counselors work collaboratively with all stakeholders (i.e., administration, parents, teachers, students, and community members) to cultivate a culture of shared responsibility and ownership within the process. Working as a team member, school counselors can bolster the strengths of others while becoming more efficient and effective themselves. The ability to do so is not just fundamental to the success of MTSS, it is the ethical obligation of school counselors, as noted below.

While many standards from the ASCA Ethical Standards for School Counselors (2016) are relevant to this chapter, we highlight below those that most relate to the content in Chapter 2. Specifically, school counselors:

A   **Responsibility to Students**

    A.1   Supporting Student Development

- A.1.e. Are concerned with students' academic, career, and social/emotional needs and encourage each student's maximum development.
- A.1.h. Provide effective, responsive interventions to address student needs.

    A.3   Comprehensive Data-Informed Program

- A.3.a. Collaborate with administration, teachers, staff, and decision makers around school-improvement goals.

- A.3.b. Provide students with a Comprehensive School Counseling Program that ensures equitable academic, career, and social/emotional development opportunities for all students.
- A.3.d. Use data to determine needed interventions, which are then delivered to help close the information, attainment, achievement, and opportunity gaps.
- A.3.e. Collect process, perception, and outcome data and analyze the data to determine the progress and effectiveness of the school counseling program. School counselors ensure the school counseling program's goals and action plans are aligned with district's school improvement goals.
- A.3.g. Share data outcomes with stakeholders.

B   Responsibility to Parents/Guardians, School and the Self

B.2   Responsibilities to the School

- B.2.b. Design and deliver Comprehensive School Counseling Programs that are integral to the school's academic mission; driven by student data; based on standards for academic, career, and social/emotional development; and promote and enhance the learning process for all students.
- B.2.c. Advocate for a school counseling program free of non-school-counseling assignments identified by *The ASCA National Model: A Framework for School Counseling Programs* as inappropriate to the school counselor's role.
- B.2.d. Provide leadership to create systemic change to enhance the school.
- B.2.e. Collaborate with appropriate officials to remove barriers that may impede the effectiveness of the school or the school counseling program.

B.3   Responsibilities to Self

- B.3.k. Work toward a school climate that embraces diversity and promotes academic, career and social/emotional development for all students.

Resources

Websites

Links to the following can be found on our eresource at www.routledge.com/9781138501614.

ASCA National Model

- American School Counselor Association.
- American School Counselor Association Position Statement: The School Counselor and Multitiered System of Supports.
- Center for Excellence in School Counseling and Leadership.

Intervention Planning

- Center on Response to Intervention.
- CSCORE: The Ronald H. Frederickson Center for School Counseling Outcome Research & Evaluation.

- IES What Works Clearinghouse.
- Intervention Central: RTI resources.

Positive Behavior Interventions and Supports

- Behavior Interventions and Supports. U.S. Department of Education's Office of Special Education Programs.
- PBIS World.

Response to Intervention

- RTI Action Network.

Teaching Activity

Directions: The goal is that school counselors will apply the three-tiered prevention model to a Comprehensive School Counseling Program. Please list school counseling activities by tier in the image below (Figure 2.5). How do school counseling activities fit into the MTSS three tiers? Which tiers were easier to complete than others?

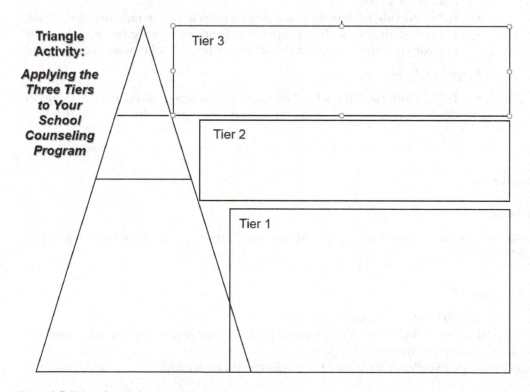

Figure 2.5 Triangle teaching activity.

Reprinted from *The Role of School Counselors in Multitier Models of Support (e.g., RTI, PBIS): Ideas and Implementation Strategies* [webinar], by J. Betters-Bubon, 2014, in the American School Counselor Association webinar series. Reprinted with permission.

Multiple Choice Questions

1   **What's a school counselor anyway?**

    a   Someone who guides students by offering advice.
    b   A therapist in the school who provides long-term counseling.
    c   A certified/licensed master level professional who addresses students' academic, career and social/emotional development.
    d   The person in the school responsible for administering standardized tests.

2   **According to the American School Counselor Association (ASCA), the four themes that guide school counselors' work are**:

    a   Consultation, leadership, testing, and teaming.
    b   Leadership, collaboration, advocacy, and systemic change.
    c   Testing, collaboration, counseling, and accountability.
    d   Crisis counseling, responsive services, community outreach, and staff development.

3   **When a school counselor delivers an evidence-based core academic curriculum for the general school population, s/he is offering services at which MTSS tier?**

    a   Tier 1.
    b   Tier 2.
    c   Tier 3.
    d   Tiers 2 and 3.

4   **Components of a CSCP and MTSS overlap in which of the following ways**:

    a   Both are data-driven.
    b   Both are culturally-responsive.
    c   Both are preventative.
    d   All of the above.

5   **The Delivery System of the ASCA National Model includes**:

    a   Core curriculum, individual and group counseling, individual student planning, and crisis response.
    b   An advisory council, a mission statement, and guiding beliefs.
    c   Test coordination, lunchroom duty, and small group counseling.
    d   Program assessments, an annual agreement, and a detailed calendar.

Answers: Q1 c, Q2 b, Q3 a, Q4 d, Q5 a.

References

American School Counselor Association (ASCA) (2012). *The ASCA National Model: A framework for school counseling programs* (3rd Ed.). Alexandria, VA: Author.

American School Counselor Association (ASCA) (2014). *ASCA Mindsets & Behaviors for Student Success: K-12 college- and career-readiness standards for every student.* Alexandria, VA: Author.

American School Counselor Association (ASCA) (2016). *ASCA ethical standards for school counselors.* Retrieved from: www.schoolcounselor.org/asca/media/asca/Ethics/EthicalStandards2016.pdf.

American School Counselor Association (ASCA) (2018). The school counselor and multitiered systems of support. *American School Counselor Association Position Statement.* Retrieved from: www.schoolcounselor.org/asca/media/asca/PositionStatements/PS_MultitieredSupportSystem.pdf.

American School Counselor Association (ASCA) (n.d.). *The role of the school counselor.* Retrieved from: www.schoolcounselor.org/asca/media/asca/home/RoleStatement.pdf.

Belser, C. T., Shillingford, M. A., & Joe, J. R. (2016). The ASCA model and a multi-tiered system of supports: A framework to support students of color with problem behavior. *The Professional Counselor, 6*(3), 251–262, doi:10.15241/cb.6.3.251.

Betters-Bubon, J. (2014, March). *The role of school counselors in multitier models of support (e.g., RTI, PBIS): Ideas and implementation strategies* [webinar]. In American School Counselor Association (ASCA) webinar series.

Betters-Bubon, J., Brunner, T., & Kansteiner, A. (2016). Success for all? The role of the school counselor in creating and sustaining culturally responsive positive behavior interventions and supports programs. *The Professional Counselor, 6*(3), 263–277, doi:10.15241/jbb.6.3.263.

Betters-Bubon, J., & Donohue, P. (2016). Professional capacity building for school counselors through school-wide positive behavior interventions and supports implementation. *Journal of School Counseling, 14*(3). Retrieved from: http://jsc.montana.edu/articles/v14n3.pdf.

Bird, B. (2010). *Why try research summaries: Why try program implementation and interventions.* Retrieved from: www.whytry.org/images/stories/Marketing%20PDFs/ResearchSummaries_Extended. pdf.

Bookard, K. L. (2015). Perceived effects of North Carolina's response to intervention process on school counselor's professional duties and responsibilities: A correlational study. *Dissertation Abstracts International Section A, 75.*

Bradshaw, C. P., Koth, C. W., Bevans, K. B., Ialongo, N., & Leaf, P. J. (2008). The impact of school-wide Positive Behavioral Interventions and Supports (PBIS) on the organizational health of elementary schools. *School Psychology Quarterly, 23*(4), 462–473.

Bradshaw, C. P., Koth, C. W., Thornton, L. A., & Leaf, P. J. (2009). Altering school climate through school-wide Positive Behavioral Interventions and Supports: Findings from a group-randomized effectiveness trial. *Prevention Science, 10*(2), 100–115.

Bradshaw, C. P., Mitchell, M. M., & Leaf, P. J. (2010). Examining the effects of school-wide Positive Behavioral Interventions and Supports on student outcomes: Results from a randomized controlled effectiveness trial in elementary schools. *Journal of Positive Behavior Interventions, 12*(3), 133–148.

Bradshaw, C. P., Waasdorp, T. E., & Leaf, P. J. (2012). Effects of school-wide Positive Behavioral Interventions and Supports on child behavior problems. *Pediatrics, 130*(5), 1136–1145.

Brigman, G., & Webb, L. (2007). Student success skills: Impacting achievement through large and small group work. *Journal of Group Dynamics: Theory, Practice and Research, 11*(4), 283–292.

Bronfenbrenner, U., & Morris, P. A. (2006). The bioecological model of human development. In W. Damon & R. M. Lerner (Eds), *Handbook of child psychology.* New York: John Wiley & Sons.

Brown-Chidsey, R., & Bickford, R. (2016). *Practical handbook of Multi-Tiered Systems of Support: Building academic and behavioral success in schools.* New York: Guilford Press.

Burkard, A. W., Gillen, M., Martinez, M. J., & Skytte, S. L. (2012). Implementation challenges and training needs for Comprehensive School Counseling Programs in Wisconsin high schools. *Professional School Counseling, 16*(2), 136–145, doi: 10.5330/PSC.n.2012-16.136.

Carey, J., Harrington, K., Martin, I., & Hoffman, D. (2012a). A statewide evaluation of the outcomes of the implementation of ASCA national model school counseling programs in rural and suburban Nebraska high schools. *Professional School Counseling, 16*(2), 100–107, doi: 10.5330/PSC.n.2012-16.100.

Carey, J., Harrington, K., Martin, I., & Stevenson, D. (2012b). A statewide evaluation of the outcomes of the implementation of ASCA national model school counseling programs in Utah high schools. *Professional School Counseling, 16*(2), 89–99, doi: 10.5330/PSC.n.2012-16.89.

Collaborative for Academic, Social, and Emotional Learning (n.d.). *What is social and emotional learning?* Retrieved from: www.casel.org/social-and-emotional-learning.

Committee for Children (2010). *Second step program and SEL research.* Retrieved from: www.cfchildren. org/second-step/research.

Cook, J. (2017). *RAMP and graduate programs.* Presentation at the annual American School Counselor Association conference, Denver, CO.

Cressey, J. M., Whitcomb, S. A., McGilvray-Rivet, S. J., Morrison, R. J., & Shander-Reynolds, K. J. (2015). Handling PBIS with care: Scaling up to school-wide implementation. *Professional School Counseling, 18*(1), 90–99, doi: 10.5330/prsc.18.1.g1307kql2457q668.

Crone, D. A., Hawken, L. S., & Horner, R. H. (2010). *Responding to problem behavior in schools: The behavior education program* (2nd Ed.). New York: Guilford Press.

Curtis, R., Van Horne, J. W., Robertson, P., & Karvonen, M. (2010). Outcomes of a school-wide positive behavioral support program. *Professional School Counseling, 13*, 159–164, doi: 10.5330/PSC.n.2010-13.159.

Donohue, M. D. (2014). Implementing school-wide positive behavioral interventions and supports (SWPBIS): School counselors' perceptions of student outcomes, school climate, and professional effectiveness. *Doctoral Dissertations*, 436.

Donohue, P., Goodman-Scott, E., & Betters-Bubon, J. (2016). Using universal screening for early identification of students at risk: A case example from the field. *Professional School Counseling, 19*(1), 133–143, doi: 10.5330/1096-2409-19.1.133.

Ennis, R. P., Lane, K. L., & Oakes, W. P. (2012). Score reliability and validity of the student risk screening scale. *Journal of Emotional and Behavioral Disorders, 20*(4), 241–259, doi:10.1177/1063 426611400082.

Gersten, R., Jayanthi, M., & Dimino, J. (2017). Too much, too soon? Unanswered questions from national response to interventions evaluation. *Exceptional Children, 83*(3), 244–254, doi: 10.1177/0014402917692847.

Goodman-Scott, E. (2014). Maximizing school counselors' efforts by implementing school-wide positive behavioral interventions and supports: A case study from the field. *Professional School Counseling, 17*(1), 111–119, doi: 10.5330/prsc.17.1.518021r2x6821660.

Goodman-Scott, E. (2015). School counselors' perceptions of their academic preparedness and job activities. *Counselor Education and Supervision, 54*, 57–67.

Goodman-Scott, E., Betters-Bubon, J., & Donohue, P. (2016). Aligning Comprehensive School Counseling Programs and Positive Behavioral Interventions and Supports to maximize school counselors' efforts. *Professional School Counseling, 19*(1), 57–67.

Goodman-Scott, E., & Grothaus, T. (2017a). RAMP and PBIS: "They definitely support one another." A phenomenological study. *Professional School Counseling, 21*(1), 119–129, doi: 10.5330/1096-2409-21.1.119.

Goodman-Scott, E., & Grothaus, T. (2017b). School counselors' roles in RAMP and PBIS: A phenomenological investigation. *Professional School Counseling, 21*(1), 130–141, doi: 10.5330/1096-2409-21.1.130.

Goodman-Scott, E., Hays, D. G., & Cholewa, B. (2018). "It takes a village:" A case study of Positive Behavioral Interventions and Supports implementation in an exemplary middle school. *The Urban Review, 50*(1), 97–122, doi: 10.1007/s11256-017-0431-z.

Grothaus, T., & Johnson, K. F. (2012). *Making diversity work: Creating culturally competent school counseling programs.* Alexandria, VA: American School Counselor Association.

Gruman, D. H., & Hoelzen, B. (2011). Determining responsiveness to school counseling interventions using behavioral observation. *Professional School Counseling, 14*(3), 183–190, doi: 10.5330/PSC.n.2011-14.183.

Gysbers, N. C. (2010). *School counseling principles: Remembering the past, shaping the future: A history of school counseling.* Alexandria, VA: American School Counselor Association.

Gysbers, N. C., & Henderson, P. (2012). *Developing and managing your school guidance and counseling program* (5th Ed.). Alexandria, VA: American Counseling Association.

Gysbers, N. C., Stanley, J. B., Kosteck-Bunch, L., Magnuson, C. S., & Starr, M. F. (2011). *Missouri comprehensive guidance and counseling program: A manual for program development, implementation, evaluation, and enhancement.* Warrensburg, MO: Missouri Center for Career Education, University of Central Missouri. Retrieved from: www.missouricareereeducation.org/doc/guidemanual/Manual.pdf.

Harrington, K., Griffith, C., Gray, K., & Greenspan, S. (2016). A grant project to initiate school counselors' development of a Multi-Tiered System of Supports based on social-emotional data. *The Professional Counselor, 6*(3), 278–294, doi: 10.15241/kh.6.3.278.

Hatch, T., Duarte, D., & De Gregorio, L. K. (2018). *Hatching results for elementary school counseling: Implementing core curriculum and other tier one activities.* Thousand Oaks, CA: Corwin Press.

Horner, R. H., & Sugai, G. (2017). Future directions for positive behavior support: A commentary. *Journal of Positive Behavior Interventions, 20*(1), 19–22, doi: 10.1177/1098300717733977.

Horner, R., Sugai, G., Smolkowski, K., Eber, L., Nakasato, J., Todd, A., & Esperanza, J. (2009). A randomized, wait-list controlled effectiveness trial assessing school-wide positive behavior support in elementary schools. *Journal of Positive Behavior Interventions, 11*(3), 133–145.

Johnston, P. (2010). An instruction frame for RTI. *The Reading Teacher, 63*(7), 602–604, doi: 10.1598/RT.63.7.8.

Kaffenberger, C., & Young, A. (2013). *Making DATA work.* Alexandria, VA: American School Counselor Association.

Kim, J., McIntosh, K., Mercer, S. H., & Nese, R. N. T. (2018). Longitudinal associations between SWPBIS fidelity of implementation and behavior and academic outcomes. *Behavioral Disorders, 43*(3), 357–369, doi: 10.1177/0198742917747589.

Losen, D. J., Gillespie, J., & University of California (2012). *Opportunities suspended: The disparate impact of disciplinary exclusion from school.* Executive Summary. Center for Civil Rights Remedies at the Civil Right Project.

Martens, K., & Andreen, K. (2013). School counselors' involvement with a school-wide positive behavior support intervention: Addressing student behavior issues in a proactive and positive manner. *Professional School Counseling, 16*(5), 313–322.

McIntosh, K., & Goodman, S. (2016). *Integrated Multi-Tiered Systems of Support: Blending RTI and PBIS.* New York: Guilford.

McMahon, H. G., Mason, E. C. M., Daluga-Guenther, N., & Ruiz, A. (2014). An ecological model of professional school counseling. *Journal of Counseling & Development, 92*(4), 459–471, doi:10.1002/j.1556-6676.2014.00172.x.

National Association for School Psychologists (NASP) (2016). Position statement: *Integrated model of academic and behavior supports.* Retrieved from: www.nasponline.org/research-and-policy/professional-positions/position-statements.

Nese, R. N. T., Horner, R. H., Dickey, C. R., Stiller, B. & Tomlanovich, A. (2014). Decreasing bullying behaviors in middle school: Expect Respect. *School Psychology Quarterly, 29*(4), 272–286.

Ockerman, M. S., Mason, E. C. M., & Hollenbeck, A. F. (2012). Integrating RTI with school counseling programs: Being a proactive professional school counselor. *Journal of School Counseling, 10*(15), 1–37. Retrieved from: http://jsc.montana.edu/articles/v10n15.pdf.

Ockerman, M. S., Patrikakou, E., & Hollenbeck, A. F. (2015). Preparation of school counselors and response to intervention: A profession at the crossroads. *The Journal of Counselor Preparation and Supervision, 7*(3), dx.doi.org/10.7729/73.1106.

Olsen, J., Parikh-Foxx, S., Flowers, C., and Algozzine, B. (2016). An examination of factors that relate to school counselors' knowledge and skills in Multi-Tiered Systems of Support. *Professional School Counselor, 20*(1), 159–171.

OSEP Technical Assistance Center on Positive Behavioral Interventions and Supports (2015). *Positive Behavioral Interventions and Supports implementation blueprint: Part 1 – foundations and supporting information.* Eugene, OR: University of Oregon. Retrieved from: www.pbis.org/blueprint/implementation-blueprint.

Patrikakou, E., Ockerman, M. S., & Hollenbeck, A. F. (2016). Needs and contradictions of a changing field: Evidence from a national response to intervention implementation study. *The Professional Counselor, 6*(3), 233–250, doi: 10.15241/ep.6.3.233.

Positive Behavioral Interventions and Supports (PBIS) (2018). *Implementing PBIS.* Retrieved from: www.pbis.org.

Speece, D. L., Case, L. P., & Eddy, D. M. (2001). Classification in context: An alternative approach to identifying early reading disability. *Journal of Educational Psychology, 93*(4), 735–749, doi: 10.1037/0022-0663.93.4.735.

United States Department of Education (2017). *Reach higher progress report.* Retrieved from: www2.ed.gov/documents/press-releases/reach-higher-progress-report.pdf.

Ziomek-Daigle, J., Goodman-Scott, E., Cavin, J., & Donohue, P. (2016). Integrating a Multi-Tiered System of Supports with Comprehensive School Counseling Programs. *The Professional Counselor, 6*(3), 220–232, doi: 10.15241/jzd.6.3.220.

3 Tier 1

Creating Strong Universal Systems of Support and Facilitating Systemic Change

Christopher Sink

Introduction

Even casual visitors to K-12 schools during lunch periods observe an almost dizzying array of activity, similar to what one might find at airports. Schools operate within a complex ecology of activity, processes, and procedures. To loosely extend the metaphor, both institutions have an essential aim, transporting people to their destination in a safe, effective, and efficient manner. Building administrators, like air traffic controllers, oversee, support, and manage the "big picture," assuring that all the systems are in place and operational. Teachers, like pilots and flight attendants, are focused on everyone in their charge. They facilitate onboarding, takeoff, in-process activities, and landing at the chosen terminus. There are a variety of other airport support staff (e.g., baggage handlers, gate agents) who, like the school bus drivers, lunchroom staff, custodians, security officer, and assistants, are indispensable to maintaining equilibrium among all the interconnected systems. As a highly-trained professional who holistically attends to the various constituents of airport life, the airport manager is central to well-performing airport operations. Professional school counselors function, in part, as managers, facilitating the effective implementation of their counseling program and services (American School Counselor Association [ASCA], 2012). Their accountability responsibilities transcend individual student and school needs to the concerns of families, the broader community, and to the profession itself (Bemak, Williams, & Chung, 2014).

More recently, as we have seen from a previous chapter in this text (Chapter 2) and the work of Goodman-Scott and colleagues (Goodman-Scott, Betters-Bubon, & Donohue, 2016; Ziomek-Daigle, Goodman-Scott, Cavin, & Donohue, 2016), school counselors have an additional obligation to integrate their Comprehensive School Counseling Programs (CSCP; e.g., ASCA, 2012) into their school's Multi-Tiered Systems of Support (MTSS; e.g., Positive Behavioral Interventions and Supports [PBIS] and Response to Intervention [RTI]; Sugai & Horner, 2009). To be effective in assisting staff with the implementation and management of such frameworks, school counselors must consider the systems influencing student behavior and learning. In short, school counselors are facilitators of systems change and student support, collaborating with the multifaceted and multi-tiered school community to positively influence school life, and, ultimately, to improve student learning (Green & Keys, 2001; Mason & McMahon, 2009; McMahon, Mason, Daluga-Guenther, & Ruiz, 2014; Sink, 2016).

Within the context of CSCPs (e.g., ASCA National Model, 2012) and MTSS organizational structures, this chapter focuses primarily on counselor school-wide (universal) prevention and intervention practices. In the first part I cover ecological systems theories (Bronfenbrenner, 1992; Lerner, Agans, DeSouza, & Gasca, 2013). This conceptual foundation will assist school counselors to better focus their (a) systems consultation and collaboration and (b) evidence-based practices to enhance students' resilience and positive development (Galassi, Griffin, & Akos, 2008; Pattoni, 2012).

The second half of the chapter will further describe and provide examples of the systems theories in action, as applied to the alignment of MTSS and CSCP. Specifically, I review Tier 1 MTSS evidence-based strategies for establishing a healthy preventative school climate. Then I address three of five general school-based MTSS areas identified by Sugai and Horner (2009): (1) school-wide (all students and staff), (2) classroom (e.g., behavior management, instructional practices), and (3) non-classroom (common, non-instructional contexts involving supervision, positive reinforcement, teaching of setting-explicit schedules). Interventions associated with Tiers 2 and 3 are considered in subsequent chapters. Related to Tier 1 practices, CSCP belief, vision, and mission statements, and program philosophy/goals are reviewed. For school counselors to maintain role accountability, examples of user-friendly data collection approaches and tools are also described. Before the closing remarks, I review pertinent ethical and cultural/diversity issues that affect prevention and intervention practices.

Definitional Considerations

Multi-Tiered Systems of Support is a general label for a three-tiered continuum of evidence-based school-wide supports (primary, secondary, and tertiary levels of prevention and intervention) that include PBIS and RTI (ASCA, 2014; Sugai & Horner, 2009). At the primary level (Tier 1), schools create prevention-oriented systems of support (e.g., designing and initiating school-wide behavioral expectations; Horner et al., 2004; Sugai & Horner, 2009) and a research-based academic curriculum (Ockerman, Mason, & Hollenbeck, 2012). The next tier involves more structured and focused behavior and/or academic interventions (e.g., individual counseling and small-group supports for students at risk for school failure). Tier 3 includes high intensity wraparound interventions for students who need supplementary assistance that extends beyond the already-tried interventions (Eber, Breen, Rose, Unizyck, & London, 2008). Specifically, the tertiary level attempts to bring families, peers, and other natural support persons together with teachers, behavior specialists, and other professionals involved to create extensive interventions.

From Reactivity to Proactive Systems and Ecologically-Based Practice

To reiterate what school counseling researchers have expressed for many years, namely, proactive strengths-based prevention and intervention models, like CSCPs and MTSS, are associated with positive change in student functioning and school climate (e.g., Bryan & Henry, 2008; Galassi, Griffin, & Akos, 2008; Goodman-Scott et al., 2016; Hernández & Seem, 2004; Wilkerson, Pérusse, & Hughes, 2013). To complement these publications, ASCA (2014) released a document stipulating the positive Mindsets and Behaviors that school counselors should seek to nurture in students. Regrettably, even as the prevention-oriented CSCP movement has been in place since at least the early 1980s and available resources are plentiful, anecdotal evidence suggests that many school counselors find the switch from a reactive-deficits orientation to a proactive agenda to be challenging (Galassi & Akos, 2007). Targeting students' shortcomings with "quick-fix" solutions are the interventions of expediency often used by school counselors. As a result, widespread prevention remains an elusive goal for most school counselors. Overwhelmed by the myriad of responsibilities, school counselors often anecdotally mention being inundated with non-counseling responsibilities. When visiting a high school counselor a few years ago, she reiterated this refrain:

Although I'd really like to, I just don't have the time to really do the National Model; I'm swamped with all those 'other duties as assigned.' My principal thinks I am super-counselor—that I can do it all. I'm afraid to admit it to her, but I can't!

In my response to the discouraged counselor, I validated her concerns and reiterated that counselors are indeed wrestling with the pesky "not enough hours in the school day" problem. I then gently posed this question:

What if most of the building staff, including administrators, teachers, etc., really partnered as a coordinated team, sharing responsibilities, and counselors were able to effectively delegate non-counseling duties to other staff, could you then be more proactive and strengths-based?

"Well, in that case," she recounted, "of course I could do it, but that isn't going to happen any time soon in my building."

In this section, I attempt to provide a meaningful response to this professional's concern by introducing systems thinking and ecological systems theories that ground CSCP and MTSS implementation, management, and accountability practices. Specifically, the seminal approaches of Bronfenbrenner (1992) and Lerner (1991) are explained. Following this conceptual discussion, I present a range of sample Tier 1 CSCPs and MTSS practices that school counselors can plan and implement across the school and within classroom lessons.

Systems Theory and Thinking

Common experience and research suggest that students are an integral part of multiple intersecting systems (families, classrooms, schools, communities) that both directly and indirectly impact their lives, including their progress in school (Anyon, Nicotera, & Veeh, 2016; Hess, Magnuson, & Beeler, 2012). To better grasp the nuances of systems theory and how it is foundational to CSCPs and MTSS practices, let's start with a common point of reference for most school counselors. School counselors during their academic training are often exposed to family systems theory (Berryhill, Soloski, Durtschi, & Adams, 2016; Winek, 2010). Therapists with this conceptual lens view families as units, that is, as one dynamic interconnected web of people. Each family member mutually affects others in healthy and not-so-healthy ways. Systems therapists "treat" the family holistically rather than the so-called "problematic" member (the labeled client). To isolate and only support the client is counterproductive and fails to respect the contextual nature of the problems.

Taking our cue from family therapists, school counselors benefit from thinking about students, classrooms, and school issues from a systems perspective. As "systems thinkers" (or, more colloquially, "big picture" thinkers), prevention and intervention methods require the consideration of the complex functionally related components of different systems (Hess et al., 2012). Technically speaking, effective school counselors are cognizant of the multiple direct (proximal) and indirect (distal) factors which affect a child's life. For instance, when an elementary school counselor's intervention only targets a negative student behavior (e.g., pushing in the hallways) without regarding the various contributing aspects that are related to the action (e.g., the child was yelled at by his mother before school or badly teased on the school bus), it is unlikely that the desired positive change (no pushing) will be sustained over time. In fact, research on systemic interventions that are based within ecological models of human development support this contention (e.g., Darling, 2007).

It makes sense that counselors operating from an ecological systems perspective avoid making causal attributions (e.g., "She pushed him because he was bullying her") without first assessing the issue from several angles. Thus, systems counselors should be slow to judgment and open-minded about student behavior and classroom events. Rather than waiting for problems to arise and then intervening (operating method of a reactive counselor), the effective (proactive) systems counselor anticipates emerging issues and attempts to prevent them from becoming full-scale crises. Systems-oriented staff also avoid dualistic thinking; that is, they try not to see children, caregivers, teachers, incidents, and so on, as either "right" or "wrong," "appropriate" or "inappropriate". Instead, these counselors view most human interactions on a malleable continuum that requires adaptability to the demands of circumstances and the people involved.

> How can you move reactivity to proactivity in your MTSS and CSCP practices? Think of three examples of each.

Ecological Systems Theories of Bronfenbrenner and Lerner

As suggested above, systems thinking is required for successful CSCP and MTSS implementation. School counselors with this skill demonstrate a holistic view of student development and functioning. Obviously, it is not enough to say, "I think systemically." Counselors must not only understand the specific components and processes implicated within the interconnected systems influencing the student, but also, they should be able to operationalize these within systemic prevention and intervention practices. In their writings, school counseling scholars generally speak only to the systems components associated with Bronfenbrenner's (1979) theory (e.g., McMahon et al., 2014). To supplement this literature, I include here Lerner's (1991, 1996) approach as well. His model is beneficial for school counselors for it extends Bronfenbrenner's work to educational systems and practice.

Bronfenbrenner's Systems Theory

After studying the environments involved in human development and functioning, Urie Bronfenbrenner (1979, 1992) proposed an all-encompassing view of human development. He referred to his approach as a bioecological or ecological systems theory. The labels largely reflect the same content and can thus be used interchangeably (Bronfenbrenner & Morris, 2006). In a more "simplified" format, he described his systems orientation as a "person-process-context-time model" (PPCTM; Bronfenbrenner & Crouter, 1983; Bronfenbrenner & Morris, 2006). The PPCTM suggests that child (person) development is influenced over time by the complex interrelationships among human processes and the settings these processes operate. While this interpretation of development reflects the daily experience of school counselors, the finer points of his model need to be grasped as well.

Essentially, Bronfenbrenner postulated that there are five interconnected systems (micro, meso, exo, macro, and chrono) or settings/contexts that have a major role in shaping child development. In his words, "development is a function of the forces emanating from the multiple settings and from the relations among these settings" (Bronfenbrenner & Morris, 2006, p. 817). As depicted in almost all human development textbooks (e.g., Kail & Cavanaugh, 2016) and in Figure 3.1, the systems are represented or mapped as three-dimensional concentric circles around the child, ranging from the most proximal or "close-in" influences (microsystem) to the most distance system (chronosystem). Humans interact within the first four systems but are affected by the passage of time as well.

At the heart of Bronfenbrenner's model is the *person* or student and her individual features (e.g., age, physiognomy, phylogenetic history, gender, race, faith tradition, cultural background, temperament). For counselors working in CSCP or MTSS schools, this is where *systems* prevention and intervention planning and implementation begins. While planning for Tier 1 interventions, say within a school implementing MTSS, school counselors will look to tailor classroom lessons and small-group lessons to specific backgrounds (e.g., culture or ethnicity, gender) and learning needs (e.g., social-cognitive skills, motivation, readiness to learning, previous knowledge of the lesson content) of individual children. Said differently, counselors conducting Tier 1 activities must consider all the *intra*-personal factors that may influence student behavior, thinking, and emotions. For instance, as they deliver a classroom lesson on improving student psychological well-being, instruction should be emotionally engaging (e.g., use humor, storytelling, artistic), speak to actual behavior change (address specifically what students can do differently to achieve well-being), and ways to monitor their negative and positive self-talk (e.g., use a well-being recording notebook; see Well-Being Therapy below, p. 84). As discussed in the next section, differentiating instruction is a tall order for most teachers, let alone school counselors, but it can be achieved with some extra training (Tomlinson, 2014). It stands to reason that these personal characteristics are impacted by the various *inter*-personal and contextual factors the child grows and lives in.

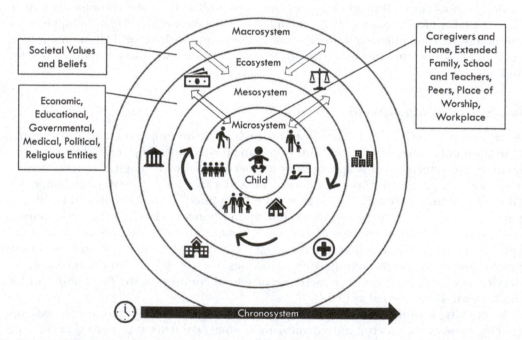

Figure 3.1 Depiction of Bronfenbrenner's (1979) Social-Ecological Model of Human Development.

Adapted from *The ecology of human development* by U. Bronfenbrenner, 1979, Cambridge, MA: Harvard University Press.

Surrounding the child is the microsystem involving the dynamic relationships between the person and the various individuals or groups in her immediate world. Bronfenbrenner (1992) explained the microsystem as

> a pattern of activities, roles, and interpersonal relations experienced by the developing person in a given face-to-face setting with particular psychical and material features and containing other persons with distinctive characteristics of temperament, personality, and systems of belief. (p. 227)

In other words, the microsystem is the layer in which the children have relationships and interactions with their immediate surroundings and key figures. There are numerous examples of micro-settings that directly impact a student's development and functioning, including the home, school, peer groups, and workplace. Every relationship within each of these contexts is generally impactful. However, given children spend the most time with their parents/caregivers and school teachers, they largely have the greatest influence on student development. Thus, counselors' Tier 1 focus should be on these relationships. To reinforce this point, I quote one educator's view concerning the importance of parents in children's microsystem:

> I have witnessed two children develop differently because of the different environment that they were exposed to. One of the children lived with his single mother that constantly had a different man coming in and out of their home. There was always someone different coming to pick him up from childcare. We would see the mother not very often . . . He would see with his own eyes, violent behavior between his mother and these male figures. I would say that the type of environment that he was in was not the best and it did influence him. He would come to the daycare and act up for no apparent reason; he would hit on the little girls in his class and say mean things to them. (Coney, 2013)

It is important to note that the microsystem can include the student's extracurricular activities, afterschool programs, and daycare activities. Thus, if relevant, systems prevention and intervention planning and implementation must include them. At the microsystemic level, school counselors are in direct proximity to three key interrelationships (children, parents/caregivers, and school staff). It then follows that most MTSS Tier 1 interventions will likely occur here. Although counselors' interactions with students' broader systems outlined below will be far less influential, they remain central to understanding children in context.

The next system closest to the person is called the mesosystem (or the middle). It is comprised of the *processes* and *connections/relations* occurring between two or more settings (e.g., family, school, peers, community) where the developing student is active. Bronfenbrenner (1992) proposed that the mesosystem is a system of interacting microsystems that may influence development. The mesosystem encompasses those exchanges between a child's caregivers and the school staff, or, perhaps, the grandfather's racial stereotyping of the neighborhood's "foreigners." While the student may not realize these dynamics affect her development and functioning, school counselors must acknowledge them. Using a parent–teacher conference as the backdrop, Davey (2013) provided a useful school-based example of the mesosystem.

> Individually, the parent and the teacher are a part of the student's microsystem. They are each examples of the student's immediate relationships. When these two

relationships interact with each other in a parent teacher conference, this interaction is a mesosystem. The parent teacher conference helps to insure that the child is getting the same interventions at home and at school. (n.p.)

As another practical illustration of the middle system, Oswald (2015), a social worker, suggested that

if a child's caregivers take an active role in a child's school, such as watching their child's soccer games, this will help ensure the child's overall growth. In contrast, if the child's two sets of caretakers, mom with step-dad and dad with step-mom, disagree how to best raise the child and give the child conflicting lessons when they see him, this will hinder the child's growth in different channels. (n.p.)

Therefore, the mesosystem describes how the various elements of a child's microsystem function together, hopefully for the benefit of the child.

To make development even more complicated, Bronfenbrenner's (1992) exosystem (external) involves the relationships and processes occurring between at least two settings (e.g., home, community, neighborhood, religious center, parent's workplace) that may indirectly influence a child's functioning. In other words, this layer reflects the greater social network in which the child does not directly participate and yet perhaps is still influenced by. For example, counselors recognize that a child's growth can be impacted by the caregivers' workplace relations as parents often take out their work stress at home. Oswald (2015) elaborated on this scenario, indicating that when a student's parent becomes laid off from work, this situation tends to have negative effects on the child, particularly if her caregivers are unable to pay rent or to buy groceries. On the other hand, if the child's parent earns a promotion or a raise at work, this may have a positive influence on the child as her parents will be better able to provide for her physical needs. In short, the exosystem generally includes the larger community in which the child lives, the socioeconomic status of the area, and so on. School counselors' MTSS Tier 1 prevention strategies should consider, at least remotely, the realities of the students' exosystems.

Far beyond the reach of school counselors, but nevertheless important, are students' macrosystems. This system is the most distal and expansive region of the environment influencing the child and family life (Bronfenbrenner, 1992). More abstractly, this system subsumes the previous ones and reflects the "societal blueprint for a particular culture, subculture, or other broader social context" (p. 228). It includes cultural and subcultural belief systems, resources, challenges, life styles, opportunity structures, life course options, and patterns of social discourse. School counselors may assume all students attending a neighborhood school may indirectly "experience" these large-scale influences through, for example, cultural and subcultural values, societal norms, governmental laws, and religious ethics.

Lerner's Systems Theory

To augment Bronfenbrenner's bioecological systems theory, I attempt to familiarize counselors with perhaps a lesser known, but no less important, multi-level ecological model of human development. Even as Richard Lerner's (Lerner, 1991, 1996, 2015; Lerner et al., 2013; Lerner, Brennan, Noh, & Wilson, 1998) developmental contextualism theory continues to evolve (currently also referred to as relational developmental systems theory), its key features have remained consistent. As mentioned above, his work is especially useful for educators like school counselors for his paradigm explicitly addresses child–teacher–classroom–school dynamics and how they influence development and functioning.

Moreover, Lerner's approach fits nicely within the themes of this book and chapter, for it is also optimistic and strengths-oriented, aligned with positive human development (Lerner, 2015). Applications for MTSS Tier 1 programming are wide-ranging and are presented in the following section.

To help explain how contexts, processes, and the relations among these variables affect child development, several defining tenets of Lerner's (2015) model should be acknowledged. First, though viewing human development from its wider lens (i.e., holistic, systemic, organized, and ecological in nature), the theory also narrows its focus to the actions of persons in relationship within various contexts or environments. Consistent with most other contemporary developmental models, children are perceived not as static, passive recipients of environmental inputs (as in strict behaviorism), but rather intrinsically vigorous and engaged. Development in a relational ecology occurs at and across different and integrated levels (e.g., biological, physiological, cultural, historical). Lerner puts a finer point on child development, accentuating children's relative plasticity (modifiability) within their contexts and positive change is not only possible, but most probable, particularly if they learn, live, and play in healthy and nurturing environments. He argues that students are self-creating, organizing, and regulating, adaptive to their various sociocultural milieus (Lerner, 2015, p. xviii). Children and their associations within various environmental contexts have obvious mutual benefit and disadvantage, for they shape current and future student behavior. In brief, context undeniably matters for healthy and, conversely, for less than optimal child development.

To gain a better sense of developmental contextualism, its underlying components or systems are considered next. Because it is not commonly reproduced in general lifespan development textbooks and is highly sophisticated, a simplified depiction of his model (Lerner et al., 1998) is provided (see Figure 3.2). In the center of the diagram, the intrapersonal factors the child and her caregivers (parent) function with are represented. Both share common characteristics which influence their behavior, including intellect, personality/temperament, values, personal strengths, and physiology. As a "development-in-relation-to-context" orientation, one can readily identify the various networks (school, social, or familial composed of parental, marital, and occupational contexts) or microsystems (see Figure 3.2) that the student directly or indirectly interacts with. Of the highest priority to school counselors is the child's relationships within the school network. These generally include caregivers, educational personnel, and peers. Counselors must recognize, for instance, that a child's behavior is nested in these relations, such that if a student picks a fight with a classmate, the entire context of the altercation must be considered, and interventions planned accordingly. Teachers, administration, and parents must all be included in the plan.

Depicted next in the center of Figure 3.2 is the *social network* (parents' and children's broader peer groups), where the school, child, marriage, and parent networks meet. Suppose, for instance, a teenager's parent has a highly flirtatious friend and this friend extends unwanted advances to the youth. The teen reports this situation to her school counselor, who then must act on the potentially harmful information. Since there are multiple intersecting players in this scenario, the counselor must be strategic in her deliberation and support of the student. Again, the wider context is considered when planning and implementing any counseling services.

Lerner's *marriage network* includes the child's non-nuclear family, other parent/spouse, other children, and so on. Here, the child, while growing up in her nuclear family, must navigate indirect familial relations and understand how they influence her functioning. Counselors in support of a troubled student who claims to "hate her aunt" will take note of the closeness or distance between the parent(s) and their sibling(s). These sample

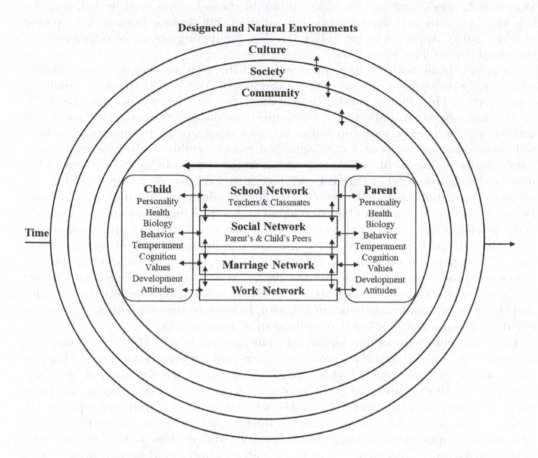

Figure 3.2 Lerner's Systems Model.

Adapted from *The parenting of adolescents and adolescents as parents: A developmental contextual perspective* by R. M. Lerner, A. Brennan, E. R. Noh, & C. Wilson, 1998. Retrieved from Parenthood in America: http://parenthood.library.wisc.edu/Lerner/Lerner.html.

questions may help the counselor to unpack the marriage dynamics affecting the child's life: What are the communication patterns among the actors and how do they affect the student? Is the marriage or partnership network strong and resilient or are the bonds between them fragile? How does the child's nuclear family members interact with the extended family members? A grasp of this marriage system will aid the counselor to design and execute a support plan for the struggling student.

Somewhat further from the daily life of students, yet potentially impactful, is the immediate and indirect associates related to the caregivers' *work network*. This system reflects the influence of the parents' work relationships on their child's development. As discussed above, when there is stress in mom's workplace affecting her psychological well-being, the negativity is likely to be extended to the home environment. Short tempers and increased tension may emerge, harming the child's daily life at school. Counselors, as such, need to be aware of the parental work dynamics and how they may play out in their child's school experiences. They deliberately create their counseling services with this network in mind.

Finally, surrounding the child, parents, and these other networks, are community, societal, and cultural contexts that Bronfenbrenner addresses in his macro and exosystems.

Unlike the mesosystem (i.e., interconnected set of networks such as the home, classroom, neighborhood) within which the person develops, these latter systems include "cultural and public policy components, textures social commerce and influences all other systems embedded within it" (Lerner et al., 1998, n.p.). These distal influences on the child are largely beyond the influence of school counselor activities and services. Finally, the time or historical dimension runs through all the systems, reminding counselors that, as with the people within various social systems, change is continuously taking place.

What makes developmental contextualism so valuable for practitioners is its emphasis on the child's relationships with parents, peers, school personnel, and other extended personal connections (e.g., youth leaders, clerics, neighbors). For instance, it provides insight into child-rearing styles, socialization processes, and parent–child dynamics (Lerner, Castellino, Terry, Villarruel, & McKinney, 1995). Since in Lerner's model children and parents have similar intrapersonal characteristics and social structures (see Figure 3.2), counselors can identify parent–child resemblances (e.g., in behavior, personality, cognition, values) as well as emerging differences (problematic or not) between them. Tier 1 interventions can thus speak to student–parent relationships and coping with family change, ethnic-cultural differences, appropriate ways to socialize, and so on. One might also address the process of acculturation of minority ethnicities in the classroom for this process is clearly impacted by children's sociocultural contexts and reflects, for example, in learning preferences, behavior, and vernacular. An example might be to conduct a "diversity night" celebration and ask families of various backgrounds to share their stories and history. Another way to address this is to have diversity panels during classroom guidance lessons. Individuals from various types of family configurations would share and provide insight into their lives, how they coped with problems and change, and ways to improve interpersonal/intercultural communication.

Other ways Lerner's model can be informative for school counselors relates to systems not normally considered in intervention planning. Custodial issues, effects of parental employment on the child, and social–school relations could be explored in Tier 1 activities (PBIS World, 2018). For example, across the school, children can learn about effective coping skills. These can be role-played and then assessed for accountability purposes to determine whether children, after instruction, are becoming more resilient to significant transitions in the family–child interactions and changes. Moreover, should the school and the family social networks be in conflict, negatively affecting student life and progress, appropriate interventions could be designed and facilitated during large group or classroom guidance periods. The case study below offers additional detail in how the intervention planning might work on the part of the school counselor.

A group of Latino families (e.g., primarily comprised of Mexican and Ecuadorian families) banded together in support of their children's insufficient education. They believe their children are systematically excluded from Highly Capable (Gifted) programming (elementary school) or Honors or International Baccalaureate classwork (high school). After conducting a needs assessment (see ASCA, 2012) looking for school-wide concerns (Carey, 2014; Lee & Burkam, 2002) with these families and the children, the school counselor found that there was a definite perception among the respondents that minority children were not receiving the essential study strategies, test-taking skills, and social/emotional enrichment to prepare them for more challenging school programs and curricula. She followed up with an

(continued)

(continued)

academic-ethnicity group gap analysis to confirm this tentative finding. This action research project focused on determining whether the academic achievement levels of students from minority groups varied substantially from those of students from the majority culture. Certainly, this issue requires school counselors providing Tier 1 supports at several levels. For instance, the school counselor can collaborate with the classroom teaching staff and parents by holding joint meetings to address mutual concerns and creating more focused family–student–teacher–student conferences to develop a meaningful learning plan.

If the counselor wanted to probe a bit deeper into these issues, she might find an unintended result of this academic "segregation," namely the social circles of the Latino parents are limited by children's academic placements. Their children generally do not interact with the mostly white and Asian-American children (and their families) who predominately populate the advanced classes. To perhaps remedy the situation, the counselor could utilize the school's MTSS-CSCP joint framework and create targeted classroom lessons to develop cross-cultural relationship skills. They could, for instance, implement the evidence-based Student Success Skills program in the school setting (Brigman et al., 2018) in order to develop learning and social skills. At another level, to address in part the social–school segregation issue mentioned above, a multicultural celebration night could be held, where all families are invited to participate. Cross-class activities could also be planned, so children of all ethnicities are invited to share and interact on meaningful activities.

Summary

To improve the efficacy of their support services to students and their families, *school counselors are encouraged to utilize systems thinking.* This type of metacognition requires a sound grasp of ecological systems theories, including the impactful approaches of Bronfenbrenner and Lerner. Extrapolating from these largely compatible theories, these basic principles of child development are worth underscoring.

- Development is a shared function of four dynamic elements: the children themselves, the contexts in which they function and evolve, the processes involved within these environments, and time.
- Development is multidetermined and probabilistic.
- Development is multifaceted, multidimensional, and structurally organized. That is to say, children and their networks are inextricably linked.
- Developmental exchanges among children and their environments/systems/contexts are continual and normative (Bornstein & Leventhal, 2015).

On a practical level, school counselors must consider the unique but cooperating systems that affect a student's life, starting with those contiguous to learners (i.e., families, friends, peers, classroom teachers, and neighbors) and extending outward to their cultures and the broader society itself. When serving others within CSCP and MTSS frameworks, school counselors need to consider all student problems or issues in light of the various intersecting systems that may influence the concerns. Counselors must also consider students' intra- and interpersonal factors when designing and initiating school-wide prevention and intervention activities.

> When you think about a student's previous and future developmental trajectory, how can you view it in a broader, systems context?
>
> Consider naming three–five factors that can impact a student's previous and future development.

Implications for Tier 1 MTSS and CSCP Practice

The quality of CSCP service delivery and Tier 1 MTSS activities can be enhanced by situating them within students' social ecologies (McMahon et al., 2014). In this part of the chapter, the focus of the discussion moves from the conceptual to the practical. I offer sample overarching and particular recommendations for school-wide/classroom or Tier 1 CSCP and MTSS practices. I address the importance of placing prevention activities within students' protective factors and strengths (developmental assets), particularly those that foster resilience. Subsequently, best practices in CSCP and Tier 1 pedagogy (e.g., differentiating instruction) and systems consultation are reviewed together with sample evidence-based CSCP and MTSS applications.

Because these systemic frameworks have overlapping purposes, principles, and practices, especially related to counselor school-wide prevention work (Goodman-Scott et al., 2016; Ziomek-Daigle et al., 2016), the following cross-platform large- and small-scale procedures, processes, and practices are suggested.

1   Use systems consultation and collaboration to help formulate Tier 1 prevention and low intensity intervention plans as well as for accountability purposes.

As they design their Tier 1 supports for all students, school counselors should initially place meaningful consultation and collaboration as top priorities (Forman & Chana, 2015; Kaffenberger & O'Rorke-Trigiani, 2013). Just as school counselors use these skills to fully establish components of their CSCPs (e.g., implementing the ASCA [2014] Mindsets and Behaviors, running an advisory or steering committee, participating in multidisciplinary team meetings), MTSS requires these cornerstone actions. Essentially, they are utilized to (a) effectively communicate and work with other stakeholders; (b) increase staff acceptance of the school-wide support system; and (c) promote consistent implementation procedures and processes throughout the school.

To elaborate on these points, effective communication of emerging plans is indispensable to gain "buy in" from teachers, educational leaders, and families. Moreover, interdisciplinary and shared responsibility for the MTSS prevention and intervention work involves close and sensitive collaboration among these system representatives. Without their support and assistance, limited progress will be made in accomplishing Tier 1 goals. One way to enhance the lines of communication is to gather together for focus groups members of the systems that most influence student life and schooling. School counselors can survey key stakeholders (students, families, staff, community leaders) about their needs, concerns, and ideas to improve the school. Request honest feedback from these groups and encourage the participants to aid with logistical problem solving. Finally, systems consultation and collaboration involve the use of evidence-based decision making as well as prevention and intervention activities. These topics will be explored later in the accountability section of the chapter.

2   To enhance school climate and student learning, set clear and measurable school-wide behavior expectations, goals, and procedures.

Positive behavior support systems require coherent and measurable school-wide behavior expectations to be in place (Sugai & Horner, 2009). Behavioral expectations are clearly defined and agreed upon parameters of acceptable school and classroom conduct that are standardized into a school-wide behavior expectations plan. All students and staff are required to comply with expectations in the hope that, by doing so, school climate and student outcomes improve. Generally, schools with these expectations desire to maintain a positive environment founded on the idea of mutual respect. Typically, there are overriding behavioral principles that the school community adopts. It is important to note that the common and consistent school procedures related to the implementation of behavioral expectations are taught to all staff. Doing so will help the school operate more effectively and efficiently, increasing consistency across staff. For instance, a common principle might be: all students have the potential for making good choices and behaving in a positive manner. Another real-world example includes the following statement: "Be Respectful. Be Responsible. Be Ready to Succeed. Be a HORNET!"

Members of the MTSS team typically design and institute a matrix of expected behaviors (see Tables 3.1 and 3.2 for examples from two actual school districts). The matrix rows are the environments (contexts) where the children interact and within the cells are the behavior expectations for each setting. The left column lists the behavioral categories. The number of environments that expectations can be written for is not limited to just these. Counselors meeting with other staff and parent leaders are free to add others, such as the gymnasium, sports field, library, entering and leaving the school, assembly/event hall, and even the school counselor's office. Sample expectations matrices are easily found by searching the web.

The process of expectations matrix implementation is relatively straightforward, involving these essential steps. First, as summarized above, the MTSS team identify the expected Tier 1 behaviors and create a chart or matrix. These expectations should be based on each school's unique culture and include feedback from a variety of stakeholders, including instructional, administrative, and support staff, community and family members, and students. Expectation matrices should also be developmentally appropriate, namely, tailored to the age and functioning level of the students. Second, school staff, such as classroom teachers, teach, model, and practice the ways these behaviors are expressed (how they look, sound, and feel). School counselors can reinforce these school-wide expectations during their classroom lessons and school-wide activities. Next, the staff specifically praise or acknowledge appropriate or expected behavior; schools often have a reinforcement system in place at the individual, class, and school level. Fourth, the MTSS team, including the school counselor, measures outcome data to ascertain whether students were able to meet the behavioral expectations and to identify the existing obstacles that keep students from reaching them. Fifth, counselors and other staff can refine the expectations as needed and remove the barriers to expectation attainment (Positive Behavioral Interventions & Supports, 2018). It is also important to note that these expectations should be retaught in booster sessions at various times throughout the school year, especially after a lengthy school break.

Overall, both school staff and students have described appreciating the consistency inherent in MTSS implementation (Goodman-Scott, Hays, & Cholewa, 2018). Particularly the use of common behavioral expectations taught across the school, used by all school staff, as well as standardized procedures, such as discipline processes, classroom management strategies, data collection and analysis, acknowledgments/reinforcement, and interventions (e.g., Tier 2 and 3 supports).

Table 3.1 Sample matrix of expected behaviors for elementary-age students

Expectation Category	Environment					
Students will be:	Schoolwide	Lunchroom	Playground	Hallway	Bathrooms/Water Fountains	Bus
Respectful	• Use quiet voices • Give others personal space • Listen to others • Use kind words • Use your manners	• Use quiet voices • Follow supervisors' directions	• Listen to and follow supervisors' directions • Agree on game rules before you play • Take turns • Include others • Keep things from the ground on the ground	• Give others personal space • Smile and wave as a greeting • Pick things up off the floor	• Give people privacy • Use quiet voices • Put paper towels in trash can • Take a quick drink	• Listen to the bus driver • Take your seat quickly • Keep bus clean • Slide in to let others sit
Responsible	• Be on time • Have what you need • Keep school clean • Do your best	• Leave no trace • Stay seated unless given permission to get up • Keep your place in line	• Dress for the weather • Line up when called • Stay on assigned play areas • Get permission from supervisor to leave the area	• Keep your things by your hook • Stay with class	• Use two pumps of soap and one paper towel • Report to teacher if towels, soap, or toilet paper are empty • Flush the toilet • Return to your room quickly • Use water fountains only with permission	• Be at your bus line on time • Stand only in your line • Take all your belongings with you
Safe	• Walk • Take turns • Keep hands and feet to yourself	• Eat your own food • Walk into lunchroom • Keep your place in line	• No play fighting or contact sports • Watch for people around you • Use equipment only how it is meant to be used • Let an adult know of a problem	• Face forward • Stay on the right side • Walk in a straight line	• Keep water in the sink • Keep feet on the floor • Use soap and water only for washing hands	• Buckle and tighten seat belt • Use quiet voices • Keep your legs in front of you and your bottom on your seat • Keep belongings out of the aisle • Seated until bus stops • Exit and enter carefully

Adapted from Peoria Public Schools (n.d.).

Table 3.2 Sample matrix of expected behaviors for high school students

Expectation Category	Environment				
Students will be:	Classrooms/ Academic Areas	Common Areas, Hallways, Restrooms, Media Center, Flex Labs, Locker Bays.	Off Campus	School Activities/ Events	Parking Lot/ Outside Areas
Respectful (Be considerate of our community)	• Be an active listener and participant • Follow instructions • Use positive language • Honor and value all property • Foster healthy relationships with others • Look for the best in others	• Value diversity and differences • Honor and value personal boundaries • Use positive language • Maintain proper hygiene • Clean up after yourself • Allow others to pass	• Be considerate of our community • Foster healthy relationships with others • Use kind words and actions • Use social media for positive interactions	• Be an active listener and participant • Follow instructions • Foster healthy relationships with students from other schools • Display positive sportsmanship	• Yield to pedestrians • Obey all traffic laws
Integrity (Do the right thing when nobody is looking)	• Fulfill all commitments • Be truthful and honest • Uphold academic honesty • Take responsibility for your actions • Follow instructions	• Pick up trash • Dress appropriately • Honor and value all property and equipment • Report harassment and bullying • Be honest • Stand up for others	• Represent our school well at community events • Be considerate of our world and community • Be helpful to others • Choose positive influences • Respond to people in need	• Demonstrate positive school spirit • Remind others to keep the area clean	• Take responsibility for your actions • Report any problems to an adult • Pick up trash

Value					
Determination (Persevere through challenges)	• Attend every class, on time, every day • Learn every day • Set goals and strive for your personal best • Manage your time well • Seek help when needed • Turn work in on time	• Be courteous • Get to your destination on time • Maximize classroom attendance	• Reach out to our feeder schools to include them in the high school community • Reach out to our community through service learning • Build positive relationships in the community	• Attend school activities and events • Cheer for our teams • Get involved	• Plan to arrive in a timely manner
Gratitude (Display an attitude of appreciation)	• Appreciate others • Leave surroundings nicer than they were when you found them • Appreciate educational opportunities	• Thank those who keep our school clean and maintained	• Show appreciation for community support of our high school • Forgive yourself • Forgive others	• Appreciate the efforts of the individuals performing • Support and encourage each other • Contribute to a positive atmosphere	• Treat equipment and facilities with care
Excellence (Go beyond the expectation)	• Complete school work to the best of your ability • Be prepared • Plan for your future	• Make healthy choices • Have positive and encouraging social interactions • Reduce and recycle	• Display a quality image of the school • Be a positive role model for peers and others	• Extend and apply your learning • Represent yourself and your school with respect	• Uphold a high standard of conduct • Be a positive role model, leading by example and action

Adapted and modified from Fossil Ridge High School (n.d.).

Note: The expectations can apply in all areas of the matrix. To avoid repetition, bulleted items may not appear in all boxes.

> How do you model positive characteristics and behaviors for students and other staff?

3   Use evidence-based pedagogy that maximizes student learning.

Effective within- and cross-classroom teaching and lesson facilitation, whether they be related to CSCP and/or Tier 1 MTSS curriculum, should be facilitated utilizing a variety of proven teaching or group facilitation strategies. All counselors should use differentiated instruction (DI), a best teaching practice (Algozzine & Anderson, 2007; Tomlinson, 2014). Tomlinson (2014), a leading expert and advocate for the use of DI, noted that educators must understand the multifaceted nature of learning, reflecting the principles underlying ecological systems theory summarized earlier. In more basic terms, Entwistle (2012) reminded educators that since students have such rich and varied backgrounds, lesson content, instructional processes, student products, and learning environments must be arranged, within reason, to account for these differences. To accomplish this goal, school counselors are encouraged to plan and facilitate classroom or large-group lessons and interventions based on these sample recommendations:

- match students' learning preferences (styles and approaches) with learning facilitation practices;
- group students by common interest and topic for assignments;
- manage the classroom to establish a positive, safe, and supportive environment.
- assess students' learning using formative, hands-on assessments;
- periodically measure and, if need be, fine-tune lesson content to meet students' needs (Tomlinson, 2014).

Each of these suggestions also fall under the category of diagnostic/prescriptive teaching, a favored method of MTSS experts (Sugai & Horner, 2009).

Other useful pedagogical methods that school counselors should combine with their didactic instruction are open-ended questioning and discussion, technology, cooperative learning, real-world and hands-on/engaging activities, mindfulness activities, role-playing, simulations, project-based learning, and so on (Smith, Sheppard, Johnson, & Johnson, 2005). Of course, effective instruction requires substantial consultation and collaboration with classroom teachers, who can serve as instructional mentors and co-lesson facilitators. Vanderbilt University's Center for Teaching (2018) should be consulted for descriptions and examples of these strategies and many others (see Chapter 4 for additional strategies as well).

4   Develop and initiate a strengths-based orientation to promote student resilience and draw on students' protective factors.

Whichever operational framework or ecological systems theory school counselors are working from, another important goal is to promote resilience in students by building on their strengths and helping them to access the protective factors present in their microsystems (Ungar, Ghazinour, & Richter, 2013). In other words, whether student networks are supportive, maladaptive, or indifferent, counselors are encouraged to bolster students' specific developmental assets that can lead to improved overall functioning and psychological adaptability. Research suggests that positive-oriented educational programs assist students to achieve greater awareness and application of their personal assets, which in turn often generates higher levels of personal growth (Passarelli et al., 2010). Moreover, a strengths-based orientation supports the enrichment of student metacognition, particularly as it relates to differentiating various intra- and extra-personal factors that contribute to their problems and those which foster positive resolutions (Hammond & Zimmerman, 2012).

All strengths-based prevention activities are predicated on the fact that students are inherently resourceful and resilient. To be clear, resilience is

> the process of adapting well in the face of adversity, trauma, tragedy, threats or even significant sources of stress — such as family and relationship problems, serious health problems or workplace and financial stressors. It means 'bouncing back' from difficult experiences. (American Psychological Association, 2018, para. 4)

Resilience involves cognitions, behaviors, and emotions that are learned and developed by all students. This characteristic is enriched when protective factors are in place, namely those "conditions or attributes in individuals, families, communities, or the larger society that, when present, mitigate or eliminate risk in families and communities that, when present, increase the health and well-being of children and families" (U.S. Department of Health and Human Services, n.d., para. 1). In most cases, the family is the best protective factor for students (Benzies & Mychasiuk, 2009). Caring peers and friends can also serve as a protective screen for struggling learners; therefore, school counselors might consider involving peer and family support systems within Tier 1 services. For example, school counselors could introduce an intervention process to help to assist all students with attendance/tardiness issues, one that involves both responsible family members and peer mentors. The activity might include all students engaging in a daily check-in process with an involved caregiver and a somewhat older responsible peer mentor.

Undoubtedly, on the practical level, a strengths-based approach as applied to Tier 1 prevention preparation and implementation is a challenging process and, again, requires school counselors to think systemically. Many school-counseling-based suggestions are provided in reputable sources (e.g., Galassi & Akos, 2007; Galassi et al., 2008). For instance, activities should at some level aid students to reflect on their positive characteristics and life experiences (Park & Peterson, 2008; Passarelli, Hall, & Anderson, 2010). By engaging students' natural or developmental assets in the lessons, a collaborative link between students (the ones being supported) and those supporting them (e.g., teachers, administration, school counselors) is more likely to be established. Put differently, establishing a bridge between students and their supportive or protective microsystems aids in drawing out strengths.

One important way to undertake this goal is for school counselors to access the developmental assets of students and their families. School counselors can incorporate the research-based 40 Developmental Assets Framework (Search Institute, 2017) into the creation of classroom core curriculum lessons objectives and related practices to support student growth (Sesma, Mannes, & Scales, 2013). For those unfamiliar with the framework, the developmental assets are organized within two dimensions spanning four grade (and age) levels (early childhood, grades K–3, middle childhood, and adolescence). It includes external assets that are embedded in students' microsystems (i.e., the relationships and opportunities learners require in their families, schools, and communities). The extrinsic asset category includes support, empowerment, boundaries and expectations, and constructive use of time. The intrinsic or intrapersonal asset grouping comprises students' commitment to learning, positive values, social competencies, and positive identity. Using this structure, CSCP and Tier 1 activities can be developed for cross-classroom deployment. Counselor-led activities would assist students to identify and apply current and emerging assets (Park & Peterson, 2008).

After reading this section, how would you describe your preventions and interventions?

How are they focused on student asset development?

Counselors can also integrate these assets into their CSCP practice, mapping them onto ASCA's (2014) Mindsets and Behaviors and then devising salient learning (SMART) goals. Several standards, in fact, address the nurturance of student resilience. For example, one ASCA behavioral self-management standard indicates that students should "Demonstrate effective coping skills when faced with a problem" (B-SMS 7). This standard is aligned with various developmental assets (Search Institute, 2017), including number 39, Sense of Purpose ("Young person reports that 'my life has a purpose'."). In other words, if students possess a strong sense of purpose-in-life (Asset 39), they tend to be more psychologically robust, coping (ASCA standard B-SMS 7) better with trauma and more quickly bouncing back to mental health (Lightsey Jr., 2006). Counselors could write SMART goals for prevention activities related to coping and resiliency development, such as "Students will identify at least two coping methods that help them deal with a bullying incident."

How are the Mindsets and Behavior standards implemented in your school?

How are they assessed?

Sample Tier 1 Practices

To further apply the preceding discussion to actual Tier 1 practice, quality strengths-based prevention activities, as well as school-wide positive programming, are described here. The alternatives range from broad-based practices and programs to more narrowly focused applications, such as large-group guidance and psychoeducational groups for all students (see, e.g., Bryan & Henry, 2008; Galassi et al., 2008; Park & Peterson, 2008; Pattoni, 2012; Smith, 2006). Evidence-based practices are well documented in the MTSS and CSCP literature, and common examples are presented in Table 3.3. Several of these were addressed to some extent in prior recommendations. The practice type is described and referenced. If the action is primarily focused on prevention or intervention, the table indicates this. The target grade level(s) (elementary, middle, or high school) is identified as well.

At the most "basic" school-wide level, as shown in Table 3.3, school counselors and other educators should acknowledge positive and prosocial behaviors exhibited by students in whatever context they arise. This is especially relevant when students meet the school-wide and classroom behavior expectations. The common adage that five positive comments/recognitions to every one correction is apropos here. School counselors and staff are wise to spend a substantial amount of time modeling desired behaviors and praising/recognizing these behaviors, versus correcting behaviors. It is also necessary for school counselors and other staff to consistently demonstrate the best ways reinforcement strategies can be applied. Supportive comments should therefore be plentiful when children follow the school's behavioral expectations (e.g., "Be respectful of self, others, and property," "Be responsible and prepared for learning," "Be prepared to follow directions"). The verbal reinforcement should be specific to the learner's action (e.g., "I appreciate Juan that you allowed Kenisha to go first to lunch."). Nonverbal positive feedback can take the form of a smile, nodding, thumbs-up, and so on.

Other essential practices to use school-wide include basic listening skills (feeling-focused responses) demonstrating empathy, care, and warmth. For instance, the counselor teaches the staff to reflect students' emotions ("You seem very frustrated about not making the team."). Furthermore, as mentioned above, strengths-based language should be common practice among students, staff, and families. Emphasis should be on communicating to students that they can be successful in school and in life. Negative deficits-focused information sharing and shaming (e.g., "William, you're failing to meet your responsibilities. What are you going to do about it?") should be avoided. Rather than saying in a serious manner to a struggling student, "You know Tran your grades should be improving by now. We've given you a lot of extra tutoring," try communicating care and support in a gentle voice tone. The positive message to send to Tran is,

> We're here for you and will continue to support you. The staff are proud to see you working more on your class assignments and hope to see you reach the learning goal you set for yourself—at least Cs in all classes. You're on your way. In what ways can we further lend a hand?

Together with the evidence-based programs listed in Table 3.3 (e.g., Second Step and Student Success Skills), I mention several other strength-based prevention options based on the research of positive psychologists (Park & Peterson, 2008; Seligman, Ernst, Gillham, Reivich, & Linkins, 2009; Terjesen, Jacofsky, & Froh, 2004). These do not require implementation school-wide, although they certainly are appropriate for Tier 1 supports. In general, they are used in a more focused manner, perhaps during classroom guidance.

Embedding Positive Education Practices Within Core Academic Curriculum and Instruction

Here, as Seligman et al. (2009) described, classroom teachers infuse positive, strengths-based activities into typical classroom work and presentations. This is a good place for school counselors to co-facilitate lessons with the classroom teacher, for most activities can be readily linked with ASCA's (2014) Mindsets and Behaviors. These standards emphasize the development of social and emotional skills (e.g., positive emotions, resiliency, psychological well-being, signature strengths), the building blocks of academic attainment. Over time, as teachers are more familiar with classroom curriculum, school counselors can reduce their involvement in the classroom. They can transition away from co-teaching lessons to serving more as a classroom consultant. For example, counselors can assist teachers with planning activities that incorporate the pertinent curriculum and Mindsets and Behaviors. We describe specific examples below.

VALUES-IN-ACTION

One well-researched practice that can be implemented across classrooms and grade levels is called Values-in-Action (VIA; Park & Peterson, 2008). This prevention strategy

Table 3.3 Sample school- to classroom-wide Tier 1 supports

Type	Description	Prevention	Intervention	Level	Source
School-wide					
Provide positive reinforcement—verbal and nonverbal	Reinforces positive behaviors and attitudes through praise	√		ES, MS, HS	PBIS World (2018)
Provide positive reinforcement—tokens	Reinforces positive behaviors and attitudes utilizing a token system	√		ES, MS, HS	
Model appropriate language & behaviors	Provides example of appropriate language and behavior for students	√	√	ES, MS, HS	
Reflective listening/ empathy	Listen non-judgmentally and reflect back genuine concern	√	√	ES, MS, HS	
Use strengths-based language	Focus on positive aspects of student	√		ES, MS, HS	
Offer safe-space/redirection space	Provide space for students to redirect behavior		√	ES, MS, HS	
Reflection sheets	Used to redirect inappropriate behaviors & reinforce appropriate behaviors		√	ES, MS, HS	
Develop developmentally appropriate behavior expectations	Assist MTSS team in creation of PBIS behavior expectations	√		ES, MS, HS	Goodman-Scott, Betters-Bubon, and Donohue (2016)
Develop developmentally appropriate consequences	Assist MTSS team in creation of PBIS consequences	√		ES, MS, HS	
Develop developmentally appropriate routines	Assist MTSS team in creation of PBIS routines	√		ES, MS, HS	
Support & reinforce staff via appropriate data	Creates and reinforces a positive climate	√		ES, MS, HS	
Reinforce behavior expectations via classroom lessons	Provide classroom lessons teaching prosocial behavior expectations	√	√	ES, MS, HS	

Program	Description	Level			References
Expect Respect program classroom lessons	Classroom lessons focus on teaching respect and a "stop" method when observing or experiencing bullying	ES, MS	√	√	Nese, Horner, Dickey, Stiller, and Tomlanovich (2014)
Classroom-focused					
Class-wide function-related intervention teams (CW-FIT)	Teaches appropriate social skills using a group contingency program	ES	√	√	Kamps et al. (2011)
Mystery Motivator	Group-contingency, variable-ratio, class-wide behavioral intervention	ES	√	√	Kowalewicz, Coffee, and Jimerson (2014); Robichaux and Gresham (2014)
Student Success Skills	Five classroom curriculum lessons covering cognitive, social, and self-management skills	ES, MS, HS	√	√	Brigman, Villares, & Webb (2018); Lemberger, Selig, Bowers, and Rogers (2015); Villares, Lemberger, Brigman, & Webb (2011)
Bully prevention in positive behavioral support (BP-PBS)	Emphasizes students withholding social rewards associated with bullying	ES	√	√	Ross and Horner (2014)
Safe Date	Classroom lessons about healthy relationships and dating violence	MS, HS (Grades 8–9)	√	√	Cascardi and Avery-Leaf (2014); Edwards and Hinsz (2014)
Steps to Respect	Classroom lessons focus on teaching socially responsible (prosocial) behaviors among students to promote positive climate	ES	√	√	Brown, Low, Smith, and Haggerty (2011); Low, Ryzin, Brown, Smith, and Haggerty (2014)
Second Step	Classroom intervention focusing on violence prevention	MS	√	√	Sullivan, Sutherland, Farrell, and Taylor (2015)

Note: ES = elementary school; MS = middle/junior school; HS = high school.

or program introduces students to the language of character strengths, allowing them to identify signature strengths as well as to use them in new ways at school and at home. For instance, as part of their MTSS/CSCP implementation activities, school counselors and teachers can incorporate the VIA into their classroom lessons as well as in school-wide activities, such as in the school's character education programming. Perhaps key values would be explored with students at the "Value-Of-The-Month" whole-school assemblies.

WELL-BEING THERAPY (WBT)

Well-Being Therapy has been adapted to school-based counseling and general prevention and intervention practices (e.g., Fava, 2016; Sink & Lemich, 2017). The primary goal of this approach is improved psychological well-being and social climate. Its methods are well-structured, easy to follow, and can be implemented in large- or small-group settings with both high functioning students and those with emerging mental health concerns. For example, suppose a counselor is interested in improving the well-being of students. The counselor rightly knows that if student well-being goes up, it is often accompanied by higher educational outcomes. There are many WBT activities that she could deploy across classrooms. Children could be taught to monitor and change their negative automatic thoughts (e.g., "I am not good at essay tests." "My school teachers are all out to get me.") to more positive ones ("I can do essay tests with practice." "I need to better understand teachers' views of me."). Students are asked to regularly think about questions like, "What thoughts are stopping me experiencing more good stuff?" and "How do I do more good things to help me do better in school?" Relatedly, lessons can teach students to monitor their psychological well-being using a "track the good stuff diary."

GRATITUDE JOURNALING

Similar to the "good stuff diary," this "count your blessings" exercise fosters student resilience and psychological well-being. Park and Peterson (2008, pp. 90–91) outlined the gratitude "assignment," recommending that students do some positive journaling on at least a weekly basis. A variation on this approach is the "Three Good Things" exercise that can be conducted in almost any school setting (Seligman et al., 2009). Counselors introduce the activity as a voluntary experiment:

> Every night, before you go to bed, write down three things that went really well on that day and why they went well. You may use a journal or your computer to write about the events. It is not enough to do this exercise in your head. The three things you list can be relatively small in importance or relatively large in importance. Next to each positive event in your list, answer the question, "Why did this good thing happen?"

Which of the above practices are most feasible for your school?

How might you implement them in partnership with other school staff?

How might you deal with resistance to these ideas?

CSCP and MTSS Integration

The components and practices of CSCP can also be incorporated into MTSS Tier 1 work (ASCA, 2014; Goodman-Scott et al., 2016; Ockerman et al., 2012). In fact, many of the practices listed above could be integrated into both. Therefore, school counselors can revisit key aspects of their program to determine which dovetail with the universal core instructional practices and interventions for all students discussed previously. First, the Mindsets and Behaviors (ASCA, 2014) should be aligned with the behavior expectations and used for student outcomes and school counselor accountability. Next, key foundational elements of the National Model (ASCA, 2012) need to be integrated with MTSS language. For example, the program mission, philosophy, and vision statements should include MTSS language and goals. In Table 3.4 a couple of samples are provided. Each statement was modified to include PBIS and RTI terminology, respectively.

Other key areas in which CSCPs can integrate Tier 1 practices fall under the other three components of the ASCA (2012) National Model. First, within the Delivery System, school counselors should align the school counseling core curriculum and individual student planning with MTSS goals and prevention and intervention practices. Examples of how this is accomplished can be found in school counseling/MTSS publications (e.g., Betters-Bubon & Donohue, 2016; Goodman-Scott et al., 2016; Ziomek-Daigle et al., 2016). Essentially, the process should include consultation and collaboration with classroom teachers to ensure the goals, student objectives, and practices of Tier 1 and CSCP classroom curriculum and services are aligned (see Chapter 2 for suggestions).

School-wide data shows that males across ethnicities have lower grades in Algebra II compared with female students. The school counselor consults with the Algebra II teachers and provides class-level supports. Specifically, he develops a flexible plan that includes improving teacher–student communication, in-class help, family encouragement, and weekly check-ins with the Algebra II teachers. The teachers will try to monitor male students' progress and homework completion in a more sensitive way. A reminder chart for all assignments is also created that the teachers review periodically.

Individual planning, a key activity of CSCPs, can serve as a Tier 1 intervention when, for example, school counselors assist students with their schooling in general and academic progress in particular.

In two other areas of CSCP practice (ASCA, 2012), it was suggested that curriculum action planning (Management) and curriculum results reporting alongside school data profiling (Accountability) are appropriate Tier 1 services (ASCA, 2014). Action planning requires school counselors to be in consultation and coordination with classroom teachers. Together they design appropriate lessons that can be delivered to all students in response to a particular need. Should a needs assessment conducted with teachers, students, and caregivers indicate that increased attention on learning and test-taking strategy instruction would be helpful, school counselors can partner with teachers to develop and implement germane curriculum. For example, as mentioned in Table 3.3, a quality evidence-based option, Student Success Skills (Brigman et al., 2018; Lemberger et al., 2015; Villares et al., 2011), is available for this purpose. Finally, to better plan prevention and intervention activities for school-wide implementation, school counselors

Table 3.4 Sample CSCP foundational statements incorporating MTSS language

Mission	Vision	Philosophy
The mission of the Elementary School Counseling Program, aligned to the Positive Behavioral Interventions and Supports system, is to contribute positively and successfully to the educational, social-emotional, and career development of all students. Our collaborative team of counselors, staff, parents, and community members work together to create a supportive, safe, and caring atmosphere to promote high academic achievement. Our goal is to help children develop skills to work to their fullest potential and prepare all students to be lifelong learners.	The vision of the Elementary School Counseling Program, aligned with the Positive Behavioral Interventions and Supports system, is for every student to acquire the academic, career, and social-emotional skills to be successful students and become responsible and productive citizens.	The school counseling staff believe all children: • can learn, • deserve to be well-educated and exhibit psychological well-being, • should be provided a safe, positive, and supportive educational environment, • should receive needed prevention and intervention supports (Positive Behavioral Interventions and Supports), • and their families are essential to the learning process and should take an active role.
Our school district's counseling program's mission is aligned to the goals of Response to Intervention, namely to improve the success of all students, preparing them to develop personal skills and dispositions of wellness, responsibility, cultural awareness, self-direction, ethical character, and good citizenship in an environment that is caring and safe.	The school district vision for the school counseling program, in coordination with Response to Intervention, is for all students to obtain the knowledge, skills, and attitudes to reach their highest potential and positively manage their lives as healthy, responsible, competent, and productive citizens who respect themselves and others.	The most effective way to reach all students with positive, supportive, and inclusive schooling is to ensure the following: all students (preK-12) have equal access to quality, evidence-based educational practices, the school counseling program closely resembles the American School Counselor Association National Model, all student-focused prevention and intervention practices are linked with each school's Response to Intervention program, the Comprehensive School Counseling Program and Response to Intervention should work together to promote student learning, well-being, and long-term life success.

Note. These are adapted and modified from existing school or school district documents. Identifying information was removed.

are encouraged to assess whether their existing curriculum is generating positive student results (for additional details, see the next section) and conduct a school profile that summarizes the student characteristics (e.g., gender, family status, ethnicity, GPA, test scores, attendance, disciplinary issues). With these data points, Tier 1 practices can be more targeted. Tools to accomplish these accountability practices are plentiful (see the Resources at the end of the chapter).

Use of Data and Evidence-Based Practices

Keeping in mind ecological systems theory as suggested earlier, school counselors implementing CSCP/MTSS Tier 1 interventions have a number of preliminary tasks to accomplish prior to initiating relevant activities with students. For instance, they must locate, select, and evaluate those practices they implement in groups and classrooms (Brigman et al., 2018). To help guide this work, I have depicted the circular decision-making/action-planning process involved in the use of data and Tier 1 Evidence-Based Practices (see Figure 3.3). At step 1, counselors in coordination and consultation with other key school personnel (e.g., teachers, principal) devise meaningful Tier 1 intervention objectives or goals. A beneficial starting point in this effort is to refer to ASCA's (2014) Mindsets and Behaviors. To ensure they are more teacher-friendly, it is useful to rephrase them into SMART (Specific, Measurable, Achievable, Realistic/Relevant, and Tangible/Time-bound) goals (Bjerke & Renger, 2017). Because counselors also want to integrate MTSS and the ASCA (2012) National Model, more expansive Tier 1 goals should speak to the improvement of the classroom and school climates and school counselor efficacy. For instance, the school counselor in consultation with the staff attempt to implement these school-wide goals: all students will (1) have equal access to high quality educational and support services; (2) be provided with yearly updates on their academic progress beyond the report card information; (3) meet with their counselor and advising teacher once a semester to discuss academic, social-emotional, and work-related goals.

Step 2 involves scrutinizing reputable educational websites and research literature for evidence-based Tier 1 interventions appropriate for school counselor implementation. However, this work and decision-making can be made by a committee of relevant staff. The most trusted place to look online is the governmental What Works Clearinghouse (listed in the Resources section). This website, managed by the National Center for Educational Evaluation and Regional Assistance, conducts unbiased scientific evaluations of school-based intervention programs and reports on their efficacy. There are a number of general domains to search within (e.g., "Children and Youth with Disabilities," "Early Childhood," "Kindergarten to 12th grade," "Behavior") and it is best to peruse them all. Quality practices can be located by clicking on the "Behavior" link. Here, counselors will find a host of programs and interventions that could serve, at least in part, as meaningful Tier 1 evidence-based practices. It is beyond the scope of the chapter to summarize the multiple alternatives and argue for certain options over others. Nevertheless, sample quality interventions include developing "caring school communities" (the goal is to improve school climate), building decision-making skills in students, anti-bullying, character education, and social skills training. Under the "Path to Graduation" link, one finds an excellent dropout prevention strategy called "Check and Connect." Several other good interventions and programs are highlighted above, in Table 3.3, and in Chapter 10 of this text.

If the Clearinghouse is not sufficient, the educational research literature continues to publish viable Tier 1 interventions that school counselors can readily implement or manage. Google Scholar is a powerful search engine to use to locate relevant publications. Even better, use a university's online search capabilities and obtain copies of the articles from the library. By inputting search phrases such as "multi-tiered system of supports", "evidence-based practice," and "Tier 1," multiple alternatives will be generated. One promising classroom-based intervention method is called Numbered Heads Together (NHT), an alternative student questioning strategy. Reflecting the aims of appropriate Tier 1 interventions, NHT's overarching goal is to improve student performance in general education classrooms (Hunter et al., 2015).

At step 3, the best practices identified above are implemented on a school-wide basis (e.g., in classrooms) with rigor and fidelity. School counselors should deploy well-established instructional and group facilitation methods. In a previous section I highlighted a number of these. I recommend that school counselors emulate the pedagogies utilized by highly effective teachers in their buildings. These "model" teachers may even be willing to serve as Tier 1 instructional mentors. Of course, teaching methods and intervention facilitation should be multiculturally sensitive (i.e., consider diversity issues) and differentiated as much as possible.

With the push for accountability within MTSS and CSCPs, school counselors will want to document the outcomes of their school-wide and classroom interventions (step 4). In fact, like CSCPs, MTSS are data-driven frameworks (e.g., PBIS and RTI). School counselors can utilize MTSS-gathered data, such as school climate measures, and student data, including office discipline referrals, attendance, achievement, and so forth, to reinforce the efficacy of their CSCPs. They can deploy a pretest and posttest action research design with valid assessment tools to obtain pertinent data from participating students. Valuable school counseling resources to consult in this regard are Stone and Dahir's (2011) text and evaluation tools available through the Ronald H. Fredrickson Center for School Counseling Outcome Research and Evaluation (CSCORE; University of Massachusetts, Amherst). Other resources are readily available. For example, Sugai and Horner (2009) developed a versatile qualitative self-assessment protocol for school and leadership implementation teams to improve behavioral interventions and practices. A quantitative option is the School-Wide Evaluation Tool (SET; Horner et al., 2004), a measure designed to be a rigorous assessment of primary prevention practices within MTSS schools. According to its authors, the SET is a valid reliable measure to appraise the impact of school-wide training and technical assistance endeavors as well as formal analyses of the relationship between deployment of school-wide PBIS and changes in social and academic outcomes (Horner et al., 2004). Both are adaptable for school counseling purposes.

Step 5 involves analyzing patterns in the data across time and between student groups (e.g., gender, ethnicity, grade level, resource usage) while also collecting relevant information to demonstrate the efficacy of prevention and intervention practices with all students. This type of data analysis is called "results assessment," where counselors attempt to show tangible evidence to stakeholders that students are demonstrating the standards set in the ASCA (2014) Mindsets and Behaviors. Research questions may include: are students in all classrooms improving their attendance and lowering disciplinary referrals? What are the academic outcomes of minority student groups in comparison with majority students? What social-emotional skills do students need to learn to be successful on the job?

At step 6, data collected is compared with more recent information to determine whether student outcomes are improving over time. If so, the data tend to confirm that the Tier 1 prevention and intervention activities are working. If the findings are less than favorable, counselors transition to step 7 and revisit their objectives and practices. They may adjust and refine them to be more in line with actual classroom and student needs, events, and activities. In any case, these last two steps, among others, suggest the recursive nature of accountability practices and need for continual assessment of Tier 1 services. For more information on accountability and the use of data, please see Chapter 9.

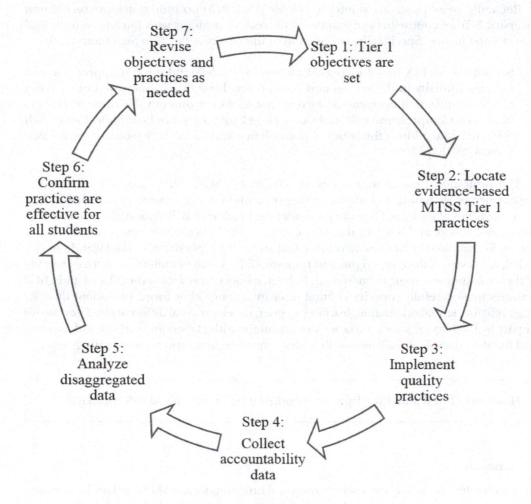

Figure 3.3 Accountability cycle for MTSS Tier 1 practices.

How might you begin implementing the accountability process as depicted in Figure 3.3?

Cultural and Diversity Implications

Ecological systems theories provide counselors with a contextual understanding of children's systems. This includes counselors' level of multicultural sensitivity and competence (see ASCA, 2016, for standards). Similarly, systems thinking helps counselors attend to the culturally diverse contexts influencing groups of students attending the same school. Culture and ethnicity are clearly affected by larger contexts that counselors must acknowledge. The notions of privilege, social justice, and opportunity gaps between cultures/ethnicities related to student macrosystems must be considered with CSCP and MTSS implementation (Avant, 2016).

Relatedly, these points are reinforced by ASCA's (2015) position statement on cultural diversity. School counselors are mandated to treat all students with fairness, equity, and educational justice. Specifically, one section of the Diversity Position Statement reads:

> School counselors foster increased awareness, understanding and appreciation of cultural diversity in the school and community through advocacy, networking and resource utilization to ensure a welcoming school environment. Through the curriculum of a Comprehensive School Counseling Program, school counselors can teach tolerance and address the issues of nonviolence and social justice on a regular basis. (ASCA, 2015, p. 19)

The professional organization's ethical standards (ASCA, 2016) also fully endorse the importance of designing and implementing prevention and intervention supports to best serve all groups of students. For example, under the heading of B. Responsibilities to Parents/Guardians, School and Self (B.1.d.), school counselors "Are culturally competent and sensitive to diversity among families. Recognize that all parents/guardians, custodial and noncustodial, are vested with certain rights and responsibilities for their children's welfare by virtue of their role and according to law" (n.p.). In brief, school counselors in their Tier 1 and CSCP activities must carefully consider cultural diversity among other forms of student diversity (e.g., religion, sexual orientation, learning, gender, developmental differences). They do this in part by their social justice advocacy work, teaming with classroom teachers and families, and building meaningful alliances with leaders who represent various community groups.

How are cultural and diversity issues handled in your school's MTSS approach?

Conclusion

In this chapter, the school counselor's roles and functions within MTSS at Tier 1 (primary/universal level) were discussed. Because Comprehensive School Counseling Programs, such as the ASCA (2012) National Model, are also multi-level and systemic in nature, this framework was integrated into the narrative. The supportive practices discussed herein were situated within the ecological systems theories of Bronfenbrenner and Lerner. These paradigms suggest that school counselors must look beyond simple solutions and short-term decision making. I suggest that counselors need to use systems thinking to best support students and their families. With the larger picture in mind, innovative yet evidence-based practices can be contextualized to achieve better student outcomes. Systems thinking also includes consultation with all school constituents as well as a strengths-based orientation. In other words, counselors deploy positive-focused prevention activities and interventions, while also tapping students' developmental assets and their protective factors. Finally, this chapter provides a multiplicity of evidence-based Tier 1 and CSCP-related practices for school counselors to implement. It encourages counselors to be ethical, responsive to cultural and diversity issues, and accountable for their services within these frameworks.

For more information and a school counselor's perspective on *Tier 1: Creating Strong Universal Systems of Support and Facilitating Systemic Change* please see Chapter 12 "Voices from the Field," Voices 1, 4, 6, 8, and 10.

ASCA Ethical Standards

As indicated above, school counselors are ethically obligated to speak to diversity issues within their practice (ASCA, 2016; Gibbon & Spurgeon, 2015). However, there are other ethical standards that need to be followed in relation to Tier 1 and CSCP practices. As an example, ASCA standards reinforce that school counselors should be strengths-oriented, accountable for their practices, and concerned about all students' academic, social/emotional, and career needs. Moreover, in terms of ethics, individual planning for all students can be a Tier 1 activity for counselors. Clearly, when considering Tier 1 activities that involve many staff, counselors must avoid dual relationships and manage boundaries. Overall, many of the ethical codes of the profession apply to counselors' work within CSCP and MTSS services. Specifically, school counselors:

A   Responsibility to Students

A.1   Supporting Student Development

- A.1.e. Are concerned with students' academic, career, and social/emotional needs and encourage each student's maximum development.

A.4   Academic, Career and Social/Emotional Plans

- A.4.a. Collaborate with administration, teachers, staff, and decision makers to create a culture of postsecondary readiness.
- A.4.b. Provide and advocate for individual students' pre K–postsecondary college and career awareness, exploration and postsecondary planning and decision making, which supports the students' right to choose from the wide array of options when students complete secondary education.
- A.4.c. Identify gaps in college and career access and the implications of such data for addressing both intentional and unintentional biases related to college and career counseling.
- A.4.d. Provide opportunities for all students to develop the Mindsets and Behaviors necessary to learn work-related skills, resilience, perseverance, an understanding of lifelong learning as a part of long-term career success, a positive attitude toward learning and a strong work ethic.

A.5   Dual Relationships and Managing Boundaries

- A.5.a. Avoid dual relationships that might impair their objectivity and increase the risk of harm to students.
- A.5.b. Establish and maintain appropriate professional relationships with students at all times.

A.13 Evaluation, Assessment, and Interpretation

- A.13.i. Conduct school counseling program evaluations to determine the effectiveness of activities supporting students' academic, career, and social/emotional development through accountability measures, especially examining efforts to close information, opportunity and attainment gaps.

B   Responsibility to Parents/Guardians, School, and the Self

B.2   Responsibilities to the School

- B.2.b. Design and deliver comprehensive school counseling programs that are integral to the school's academic mission; driven by student data; based on standards for academic, career, and social/emotional development; and promote and enhance the learning process for all students.

- B.2.d. Provide leadership to create systemic change to enhance the school.
- B.2.e. Collaborate with appropriate officials to remove barriers that may impede the effectiveness of the school or the school counseling program.

B.3   Responsibilities to Self

- B.3.k. Work toward a school climate that embraces diversity and promotes academic, career, and social/emotional development for all students.

Resources

Further Reading

Systems Thinking and Systems Theories as Applied to Counseling

Cigrand, D. L., Havlik, S. G., Malott, K. M., & Jones, S. G. (2015). School counselors united in professional advocacy: A systems model. *Journal of School Counseling, 13*(8), 1–49.

McMahon, H. G., Mason, E., Daluga-Guenther, N., & Ruiz, A. (2014). An ecological model of professional school counseling. *Journal of Counseling & Development, 92*(4), 459–471.

Patton, W., & McMahon, M. (2006). The systems theory framework of career development and counseling: Connecting theory and practice. *International Journal for the Advancement of Counselling, 28*(2), 153–166.

Best Practices and Accountability for Comprehensive School Counseling Programs

ASCA NATIONAL MODEL (ASCA, 2012)

Gysbers, N. C., & Henderson, P. (2012). *Developing and managing your school guidance and counseling program* (5th Ed.). Alexandria, VA: America Counseling Association.

MTSS (PBIS and RTI) Components, Goals, and Processes

Brown-Chidsey, R., & Bickford, R. (2016). *Practical handbook of Multi-Tiered Systems of Support: Building academic and behavioral success in schools.* New York: Guilford.

Horner, R. H., Sugai, G., Lewis-Palmer, T., & Todd, A. (2001). Teaching school-wide behavioral expectations. *Report on Emotional and Behavioral Disorders in Youth, 1*(4), 77–79.

McIntosh, K., & Goodman, S. (2016). *Integrated Multi-Tiered Systems of Support: Blending RTI and PBIS.* New York: Guilford Press.

Sugai, G., & Horner, R. H. (2009). Responsiveness-to-Intervention and School-Wide Positive Behavior Supports: Integration of multi-tiered system approaches. *Exceptionality, 17*(4), 223–237, doi:10.1080/09362830903235375.

School Counselors' Roles and Functions within MTSS (RTI and PBIS)

Belser, C. T., Shillingford, M., & Joe, J. R. (2016). The ASCA Model and a Multi-Tiered System of Supports: A framework to support students of color with problem behavior. *The Professional Counselor, 6*(3), 251–262.

Betters-Bubon, J., & Donohue, P. (2016). Professional capacity building for school counselors through School-Wide Positive Behavior Interventions and Supports Implementation. *Journal of School Counseling, 14*(3), 1–35.

Sink, C. A. (2016). Incorporating Multi-Tiered System of Supports into school counselor preparation. *The Professional Counselor, 6*(3), 203–219.

Evidence-Based Pedagogy

Evidence-Based Education, published by Johns Hopkins School of Education's Center for Research and Reform in Education and the University of York's Institute for Effective Education. Available at: www.betterevidence.org.

Vanderbilt University's Center for Teaching. Available at: https://cft.vanderbilt.edu/teaching-guides/pedagogies-and-strategies.

School Counselor Accountability Practices

The ASCA National Model implementation guide: Foundation, management and accountability (2016).

Kaffenberger, C. & Young, A. (2013). *Making data work.* Alexandria, VA: American School Counselor Association.

Stone, C. B., & Dahir, C. A. (2011). *School counselor accountability: A MEASURE of student success* (3rd Ed.). New York: Pearson.

Ethical Practice with Multi-Tiered System of Supports and Comprehensive School Counseling Programs

Brown-Chidsey, R., & Steege, M. W. (2011). *Response to intervention: Principles and strategies for effective practice.* New York: Guilford Press.

Coffee, G., Ray-Subramanian, C. E., Schanding Jr., G. T., & Feeney-Kettler, K. A. (2013). The law, ethical standards, and guidelines for MTSS in early childhood education. In G. Coffee, C. E. Ray-Subramanian, G. T. Schanding Jr., & K. A. Feeney-Kettler (Eds), *Early childhood education* (Chapter 2; pp. 18–27). New York: Routledge.

Corey, G., Corey, M. S., Corey, C., & Callanan, P. (2014). *Issues and ethics in the helping professions* (9th Ed.). Boston, MA: Brooks Cole.

Stone, C. (2006). *School counseling principles: Ethics and law.* Alexandria, VA: American School Counselor Association.

What Works Clearinghouse. Available at: https://ies.ed.gov/ncee/wwc/WhatWeDo.

Teaching Activity

Directions: The goal is that students will understand more about systems thinking from a personal point of view. Using Bronfenbrenner's systems-ecological model as a guide, have students create a map of their own systems, beginning by putting themselves in the center of the diagram. Ask them to insert about five–eight key intrapersonal characteristics they possess. Ask them to identify the major microsystem influences on their development and current functioning. Which ones are most important? Which ones would they like to minimize? If there are macro- or exosystem influences, ask them to add these to the diagram.

After they finish, have the students share their diagrams with a partner. Have them process this question in the dyad: suppose the high school you attended actually understood the larger context from which you grew up, how might this information help the staff better assist you with learning?

Ask the entire class to volunteer to share what they learned about systems thinking and the importance of understanding students in a wider context.

Multiple Choice Questions

1   **Which of the following is not a Tier 1 practice?**

   a   Classroom-wide academic assistance.
   b   Academic focused individual planning for all students.
   c   Mental health therapy.
   d   Conducting a school profile.
   e   Systems consultation.

2   **Systems work probably does not include which of the following options?**

   a   Seeing the big picture and doing intervention planning accordingly.
   b   Making puppets for teachers.
   c   Talking to parents about their child's strengths.
   d   Visiting a local mental health clinic to see if it is appropriate for students.
   e   Consulting with the school psychologist.

3   **Ecological systems theories are best described as?**

   a   Ways counselors can understand the various student contexts.
   b   Approaches to curriculum development.
   c   Perspectives on teaching.
   d   Orientations to fixing leadership problems.
   e   Organizational frameworks used with school construction.

4   **School climate assessment**

   a   Looks at ways to better regulate classroom temperatures.
   b   Tries to locate the best teachers for awards.
   c   Analyzes classroom computer resources.
   d   Collects data on student and parent perceptions of the learning environments.
   e   Confirms what counselors already know about the quality of their services.

5   **School counselors working within a MTSS approach are most likely to do which of the following?**

   a   Address the healthiness of the cafeteria.
   b   Address concerns about the quality of audio-visual equipment.
   c   Address the needs of all students.
   d   Address the concerns of only at-risk students.
   e   Address the effective implementation of a cross-classroom spelling contest.

Answers: Q1 c, Q2 b, Q3 a, Q4 d, Q5 c.

References

Algozzine, B., & Anderson, K. M. (2007). Tips for teaching: Differentiating instruction to include all students. *Preventing School Failure: Alternative Education for Children and Youth, 51*(3), 49–54.

American Psychological Association (APA) (2018). *What is resilience?* Washington, DC: Author. Retrieved from: www.apa.org/helpcenter/road-resilience.aspx.

American School Counselor Association (ASCA) (2012). *ASCA National Model: A framework for school counseling programs.* Alexandria, VA: Author.

American School Counselor Association (ASCA) (2014). *The ASCA mindsets & behaviors for student success: K-12 college- and career readiness for every student*. Alexandra, VA: Author. Retrieved from: www.schoolcounselor.org/asca/media/asca/home/MindsetsBehaviors.pdf.

American School Counselor Association (ASCA) (2015). *The school counselor and cultural diversity*. Alexandra, VA: Author. Retrieved from: www.schoolcounselor.org/asca/media/asca/PositionStatements/PS_CulturalDiversity.pdf.

American School Counselor Association (ASCA) (2016). *ASCA ethical standards for school counselors*. Alexandra, VA: Author.

Anyon, Y., Nicotera, N., & Veeh, C. (2016). Contextual influences on the implementation of a schoolwide intervention to promote students' social, emotional, and academic learning. *Children & Schools, 38*(2), 81–88.

Avant, D. W. (2016). Using response to intervention/Multi-Tiered Systems of Supports to promote social justice in schools. *Journal for Multicultural Education, 10*(4), 507–520, doi.org/10.1108/JME-06-2015-0019.

Bemak, F., Williams, J., & Chung, R. C.-Y. (2014). Four critical domains of accountability for school counselors. *Professional School Counseling, 18*(1), 100–110.

Benzies, K., & Mychasiuk, R. (2009). Fostering family resiliency: A review of the key protective factors. *Child & Family Social Work, 14*(1), 103–114.

Berryhill, M. B., Soloski, K. L., Durtschi, J. A., & Adams, R. R. (2016). Family process: Early child emotionality, parenting stress, and couple relationship quality. *Personal Relationships, 23*(1), 23–41, doi:doi.org/10.1111/pere.12109.

Betters-Bubon, J., & Donohue, P. (2016). Professional capacity building for school counselors through School-Wide Positive Behavior Interventions and Supports Implementation. *Journal of School Counseling, 14*(3), 1–35. Retrieved from: https://docs.google.com/viewer?url=https%3A%2F%2Ffiles.eric.ed.gov%2Ffulltext%2FEJ1092710.pdf.

Bjerke, M. B., & Renger, R. (2017). Being smart about writing SMART objectives. *Evaluation and Program Planning, 61*, 125–127.

Bornstein, M. C., & Leventhal, T. (2015). Children in bioecological landscapes of development. In M. H. Bornstein, T. Leventhal, & R. M. Lerner (Eds), *Handbook of child psychology and developmental science: Ecological settings and processes* (Vol. 4, pp. 1–5). Hoboken, NJ: John Wiley.

Brigman, G., Villares, E., & Webb, L. (2018). *Evidence-based school counseling: A student success approach*. New York: Routledge/Taylor & Francis Group.

Bronfenbrenner, U. (1979). *The ecology of human development*. Cambridge, MA: Harvard University Press.

Bronfenbrenner, U. (1992). Ecological systems theory. In R. Vasta (Ed.), *Six theories of child development: Revised formulations and current issues* (pp. 187–249). London: Jessica Kingsley.

Bronfenbrenner, U., & Crouter, A. C. (1983). The evolution of environmental models in developmental research. In P. H. Mussen (Ed.), *Handbook of child psychology: Vol. 1. History, theory* (4th Ed., pp. 357–414). New York: Wiley.

Bronfenbrenner, U., & Morris, P. A. (2006). The bioecological model of human development. In W. Damon, & R. M. Lerner (Eds), *Handbook of child psychology* (pp. 793–828). New York: John Wiley.

Brown, E. C., Low, S., Smith, B. H., & Haggerty, K. P. (2011). Outcomes from a school-randomized controlled trial of Steps to Respect: A bullying prevention program. *School Psychology Review, 40*(3), 423–433.

Bryan, J., & Henry, J. (2008). Strengths-based partnerships: A school-family-community partnership approach to empowering students. *Professional School Counseling, 12*(2), 149–156.

Carey, R. L. (2014). Challenging the language and labels used in the work of school reform. *Urban Education, 49*(4), 440–468.

Cascardi, M., & Avery-Leaf, S. (2014). Case study of a school-based universal dating violence prevention program. *SAGE Open, 4*(3), 1–9, doi:10.1177/2158244014551716.

Coney, S. (2013). *Bronfenbrenner's bioecological system: Real life examples*. Retrieved from: https://bronfenbrennerproject.wordpress.com/2013/10/26/bronfenbrenners-bioecological-system.

Darling, N. (2007). Ecological systems theory: The person in the center of the circles. *Research in Human Development, 4*(3), 203–217, doi.org/10.1080/15427600701663023.

Davey, M. (2013). *Bronfenbrenner's bioecological system: Real life examples.* Retrieved from: https://bron fenbrennerproject.wordpress.com/category/reflections.

Eber, L., Breen, K., Rose, J., Unizyck, R., & London, T. H. (2008). Wraparound: As a tertiary level intervention for students with emotional/behavioral needs. *Teaching Exceptional Children, 40*(6), 16–22.

Edwards, S., & Hinsz, V. (2014). A meta-analysis of empirically tested school-based dating violence prevention programs. *SAGE Open, 4*(2), 1–8, doi:10.1177/2158244014535787.

Entwistle, N. (2012). *Styles of learning and teaching.* New York: Routledge.

Fava, G. (2016). *Well-Being Therapy (WBT).* New York: Krager.

Forman, S. G., & Chana, D. (2015). Systems consultation for Multitiered Systems Of Supports (MTSS): Implementation issues. *Journal of Educational and Psychological Consultation, 25*(2–3), 276–285, doi.org/10.1080/10474412.2014.963226.

Fossil Ridge High School (n.d.). *Positive Behavior Intervention Support Matrix.* Retrieved from: https://frh.psdschools.org/webfm/77.

Galassi, J., & Akos, P. (2007). *Strengths-based school counseling: Promoting student development and achievement.* New York: Routledge, Taylor & Francis Group.

Galassi, J., Griffin, D., & Akos, P. (2008). Strengths-based school counseling and the ASCA National Model. *Professional School Counseling, 12*(2), 176–181.

Gibbon, M. M., & Spurgeon, S. L. (2015). Applying the American School Counselor Association (ASCA) Ethical Standards to clinical experiences. In J. R. Studer (Ed.), *A guide to practicum and internship for school counselors-in-training* (pp. 183–195). New York: Routledge.

Goodman-Scott, E., Betters-Bubon, J., & Donohue, P. (2016). Aligning Comprehensive School Counseling Programs and Positive Behavioral Interventions and Supports to maximize school counselors' efforts. *Professional School Counseling, 19*(1), 57–67.

Goodman-Scott, E., Hays, D. G., & Cholewa, B. E. (2018). "It takes a village": A case study of Positive Behavioral Interventions and Supports implementation in an exemplary urban middle school. *Urban Review, 50,* 97–122, doi.org/10.1007/s11256-017-0431-z.

Green, A., & Keys, S. (2001). Expanding the developmental school counseling paradigm: Meeting the needs of the 21st century student. *Professional School Counseling, 5*(2), 84–96.

Hammond, W., & Zimmerman, R. (2012). *A strengths-based perspective: A report for resiliency initiatives.* Retrieved from: www.esd.ca/Programs/Resiliency/Documents/RSL_STRENGTH_BASED_PERSPECTIVE.pdf.

Hernández, T. J., & Seem, S. R. (2004). A safe school climate: A systemic approach and the school counselor. *Professional School Counseling, 7*(4), 256–262.

Hess, R. S., Magnuson, S., & Beeler, L. (2012). *Counseling children and adolescents in schools.* Thousand Oaks, CA: Sage.

Horner, R. H., Todd, A. W., Lewis-Palmer, T., Irvin, L. K., Sugai, G., & Boland, J. B. (2004). The School-Wide Evaluation Tool (SET): A research instrument for assessing school-wide positive behavior support. *Journal of Positive Behavior Interventions, 6*(1), 3–12.

Hunter, W. C., Maheady, L., Jasper, A. D., Williamson, R. L., Murley, R. C., & Stratton, E. (2015). Numbered heads together as a Tier 1 instructional strategy in multitiered systems of support. *Education and Treatment of Children, 38*(3), 345–362.

Kaffenberger, C. J., & O'Rorke-Trigiani, J. (2013). Addressing student mental health needs by providing direct and indirect services and building alliances in the community. *Professional School Counseling, 16*(5), 323–332.

Kail, R. V., & Cavanaugh, J. C. (2016). *Human development: A life-span view.* Boston, MA: Cengage Learning.

Kamps, D., Wills, H. P., Heitzman-Powell, L., Laylin, J., Szoke, C., Petrillo, T., & Culey, A. (2011). Class-Wide Function-Related Intervention Teams: Effects of group contingency programs in urban classrooms. *Journal of Positive Behavior Interventions, 13,* 154–167, doi:10.1177/109 8300711398935.

Kowalewicz, E., Coffee, G., & Jimerson, S. (2014). Mystery Motivator: A Tier 1 classroom behavioral intervention. *School Psychology Quarterly, 29*(2), 138–156, doi: 10.1037/spq0000030.

Lee, V. E., & Burkam, D. T. (2002). *Inequality at the starting gate: Social background differences in achievement as children begin school.* Washington, DC: Economic Policy Institute.

Lemberger, M., Selig, J., Bowers, H., & Rogers, J. (2015). Effects of the Student Success Skills Program on executive functioning skills, feelings of connectedness, and academic achievement in a predominantly Hispanic, low-income middle school district. *Journal of Counseling & Development, 93*(1), 25–37, doi: 10.1002/j.1556-6676.2015.00178.x.

Lerner, R. M. (1991). Changing organism-context relations as the basic process of development: A developmental contextual perspective. *Developmental Psychology, 27*(1), 27–32.

Lerner, R. M. (1996). Relative plasticity, integration, temporality, and diversity in human development: A developmental contextual perspective about theory, process, and method. *Developmental Psychology, 32*(4), 781–786.

Lerner, R. M. (2015). Preface. In R. M. Lerner, M. H. Bornstein, T. Leventhal, & R. M. Lerner (Eds), *Handbook of child psychology and developmental science: Ecological settings and processes* (7th Ed., Vol. *4*, pp. xv–xx). Hoboken, NJ: John Wiley.

Lerner, R. M., Agans, J. P., DeSouza, L. M., & Gasca, S. (2013). Describing, explaining, and optimizing within-individual change across the life span: A relational developmental systems perspective. *Review of General Psychology, 17*(2), 179–183, doi.org/10.1037/a0032931.

Lerner, R. M., Brennan, A., Noh, E. R., & Wilson, C. (1998). *The Parenting of adolescents and adolescents as parents: A developmental contextual perspective.* Retrieved from Parenthood in America: http://parenthood.library.wisc.edu/Lerner/Lerner.html.

Lerner, R. M., Castellino, D. R., Terry, P. A., Villarruel, F. A., & McKinney, M. H. (1995). A developmental contextual perspective on parenting. In M. H. Bornstein (Ed.), *Handbook of parenting: Biology and ecology of parenting* (pp. 285–309). Hillsdale, NJ: L. Erlbaum.

Lightsey Jr., O. R. (2006). Resilience, meaning, and well-being. *The Counseling Psychologist, 34*(1), 96–107.

Low, S., Ryzin, M., Brown, J., Smith, E., & Haggerty, C. (2014). Engagement Matters: Lessons from assessing classroom implementation of Steps to Respect: A bullying prevention program over a one-year period. *Prevention Science, 15*(2), 165–176, doi: 10.1007/s11121-012-0359-1.

Mason, E., & McMahon, H. (2009). Leadership practices of school counselors. *Professional School Counseling, 13*(2), 107–115.

McMahon, H. G., Mason, E., Daluga-Guenther, N., & Ruiz, A. (2014). An ecological model of professional school counseling. *Journal of Counseling & Development, 92*(4), 459–471.

Nese, R. N. T., Horner, R. H., Dickey, C. R., Stiller, B., & Tomlanovich, A. (2014). Decreasing bullying behaviors in middle school: Expect Respect. *School Psychology Quarterly, 29*(3), 272–286, doi: 10.1037/spq0000070.

Ockerman, M. S., Mason, E., & Hollenbeck, A. F. (2012). Integrating RTI with school counseling programs: Being a proactive professional school counselor. *Journal of School Counseling, 10*(15), 1–37. Retrieved from: https://docs.google.com/viewer?url=http%3A%2F%2Ffiles.eric.ed.gov%2Ffulltext%2FEJ978870.pdf.

Oswald, A. (2015). *Urie Bronfenbrenner and child development. The mesosystem.* Retrieved from: www.mentalhelp.net/articles/urie-bronfenbrenner-and-child-development.

Park, N., & Peterson, C. (2008). Positive psychology and character strengths: Application to strengths-based school counseling. *Professional School Counseling, 12*(2), 85–92.

Passarelli, A., Hall, E., & Anderson, M. (2010). A strengths-based approach to outdoor and adventure education: Possibilities for personal growth. *Journal of Experiential Education, 33*(2), 120–135.

Pattoni, L. (2012). *Strengths-based approach for working with individuals.* Retrieved from Insights— The Institute for Research and Innovation in Social Services: https://docs.google.com/viewer?url=https%3A%2F%2Fwww.iriss.org.uk%2Fsites%2Fdefault%2Ffiles%2Firiss-insight-16.pdf.

PBIS World (2018). *Tier 1 interventions.* Retrieved from: www.pbisworld.com/tier-1.

Peoria Public Schools (n.d.). *PBIS Expectation Matrix.* Retrieved from Tier 1 SEL— MTSS Framework: www.peoriapublicschools.org/cms/lib/IL01001530/Centricity/Domain/24/PBIS%20Sample%20Matrix.dotx.

Positive Behavioral Interventions & Supports (PBIS) (2018). *Tier 1 FAQs.* Retrieved from PBIS: www.pbis.org/school/tier1supports/tier1faqs.

Robichaux, N. M., & Gresham, F. M. (2014). Differential effects of the Mystery Motivator intervention using student-selected and mystery rewards. *School Psychology Review, 43*(3), 286–298.

Ross, S. W., & Horner, R. H. (2014). Bully prevention in positive behavior support: Preliminary evaluation of third-, fourth-, and fifth-grade attitudes toward bullying. *Journal of Emotional and Behavioral Disorders, 22*(4), 225–236, doi:10.1177/1063426613491429.

Search Institute (2017). *40 developmental assets.* Retrieved from Search Institute: http://page.search-institute.org/dev-assets-download_1212-17?submission=409727297.

Seligman, M. P., Ernst, R. M., Gillham, J., Reivich, K., & Linkins, M. (2009). Positive education: Positive psychology and classroom interventions. *Oxford Review of Education, 35*(3), 293–311, doi:10.1080/03054980902934563.

Sesma, A., Mannes, M., & Scales, P. C. (2013). Positive adaptation, resilience and the developmental assets framework. In S. Goldstein & R. Brooks (Eds), *Handbook of resilience in children* (pp. 427–442). Boston, MA: Springer, doi.org/10.1007/978-1-4614-3661-4_25.

Sink, C. A. (2016). Incorporating Multi-Tiered System of Supports into school counselor preparation. *The Professional Counselor, 6*(3), 203–219.

Sink, C. A., & Lemich, G. (2017). Well-being therapy in schools: Implications for supporting students with spirituality-related issues. *Counselling and Spirituality, 36*(1–2), 121–143.

Smith, E. J. (2006). The strength-based counseling model. *The Counseling Psychologist, 34*(1), 13–79.

Smith, K. A., Sheppard, S. D., Johnson, D., & Johnson, R. T. (2005). Pedagogies of engagement: Classroom-based practices. *Journal of Engineering Education, 94*(1), 87–101.

Stone, C. B., & Dahir, C. A. (2011). *School counselor accountability: A MEASURE of student success* (3rd Ed.). New York: Pearson.

Sugai, G., & Horner, R. H. (2009). Responsiveness-to-Intervention and School-Wide Positive Behavior Supports: Integration of multi-tiered system approaches. *Exceptionality, 17*(4), 223–237, doi:10.1080/09362830903235375.

Sullivan, T., Sutherland, K., Farrell, A., & Taylor, K. (2015). An evaluation of Second Step. *Remedial and Special Education, 36*(5), 286–298, doi: 10.1177/0741932515575616.

Terjesen, M. D., Jacofsky, M., & Froh, J. (2004). Integrating positive psychology into schools: Implications for practice. *Psychology in the Schools, 41*(1), 163–172, doi:10.1002/pits.10148.

Tomlinson, C. A. (2014). *The differentiated classroom: Responding to the needs of all learners.* Alexandria, VA: ASCD.

Ungar, M., Ghazinour, M., & Richter, J. (2013). Annual research review: What is resilience within the social ecology of human development? *Journal of Child Psychology and Psychiatry, 54*(4), 348–366.

U.S. Department of Health and Human Services (n.d.). *Protective factors promote well-being.* Retrieved from Child Welfare Information Gateway: www.childwelfare.gov/topics/preventing/promoting/protectfactors.

Vanderbilt Center for Teaching (2018). *Pedagogies and strategies.* Retrieved from: https://cft.vanderbilt.edu/teaching-guides/pedagogies-and-strategies.

Villares, E., Lemberger, M., Brigman, G., & Webb, L. (2011). Student Success Skills: An evidence-based school counseling program grounded in humanistic theory. *Journal of Humanistic Counseling, 50*(1), 42–55.

Wilkerson, K., Pérusse, R., & Hughes, A. (2013). Comprehensive school counseling programs and student achievement outcomes: A comparative analysis of RAMP versus non-RAMP schools. *Professional School Counseling, 16*(3), 172–184.

Winek, J. L. (2010). *Systemic family therapy: From theory to practice.* Thousand Oaks, CA: Sage.

Zhu, P. (2018, May 22). *The new book "Problem-Solving Master".* Retrieved from: http://futureofcio.blogspot.com/2018/02/the-new-book-problem-solving-master_24.html.

Ziomek-Daigle, J., Goodman-Scott, E., Cavin, J., & Donohue, P. (2016). Integrating a Multi-Tiered System of Supports with Comprehensive School Counseling Program. *The Professional Counselor, 6*(3), 220–232.

4 Tier 1

School Counseling Core Curriculum and Classroom Management for Every Student

Erin Mason and Caroline Lopez-Perry

Introduction

As school counselors, our role is to serve *every* student.

> I firmly believe that the men and women on this stage – our counselors and educators – have a far bigger impact on our kids' lives than any President or First Lady . . . it doesn't even come close. Just think about who our students are exposed to nearly every single day – all of you, counselors and educators. They watch how you dress . . . they watch how you carry yourselves . . . they watch how you treat others . . . Hour after hour, you all serve as living, breathing examples of the kind of people they should aspire to be. (Michelle Obama, 2018 ASCA School Counselor of the Year event, Kennedy Center, Washington, DC)

As mentioned in this quote, we can have an enormous impact on the students we serve. One strategy for doing this is through facilitating the school counseling core curriculum, a universal, or Tier 1 support for every student. In this chapter, we explore important aspects of Tier 1 supports within Multi-Tiered Systems of Supports (MTSS), including designing and implementing the school counseling core curriculum. First, we will provide an overview of Tier 1 supports, followed by the school counselor's corresponding role. Second, we will describe three strategies for planning these Tier 1 supports, specifically, the use of data, and determining content and format. Third, we will outline approaches for implementing Tier 1 supports, including specific classroom management strategies, followed by consulting and collaborating with teachers, and the use of assessment and evaluation.

Overview of Tier 1 Supports

As discussed in previous chapters, MTSS is an overarching framework for Response to Intervention (RTI) and Positive Behavioral Interventions and Supports (PBIS), and is typically comprised of three tiers of support. Universal, or Tier 1 supports comprise the foundational tier geared toward all students. Specifically, Tier 1 supports help all students succeed both academically and behaviorally through school-wide prevention consisting of high-quality instruction and positive behavioral supports. Academic and behavioral supports are provided to every student through the general education curriculum, the establishment and teaching of school-wide expectations, systematic positive reinforcement for desired behaviors, and proactive school-wide discipline procedures. Ideally, at Tier 1, all students are assessed both academically and behaviorally, in a process referred to as universal screening (Belser, Shillingford & Joe, 2016; Donohue, Goodman-Scott, & Betters-Bubon, 2016; Splett, Trainor, Raborn, Halliday-Boykins, Garzona, Dongo, & Weist, 2018; see also Chapter 7). Students who demonstrate elevated needs on universal screeners, as well as students who struggle to master concepts or strategies, are then given more supports,

> Sample MTSS Tier 1 supports:
>
> Teaching all students the general education curriculum (academics and behavior).
>
> Establishing and teaching school-wide behavioral expectations to all students.
>
> Creating procedures across all staff (e.g., how to reteach student behaviors, when to refer a student to the office, etc.).

such as group interventions in Tier 2 (see Chapter 5), or individual supports in Tier 3 (see Chapter 6). Please see the box above, which provides a sample of MTSS Tier 1 supports.

Overall, Tier 1 supports should be proactive, preventative, and provided to every student in a school. As a result of universal Tier 1 supports, generally speaking, approximately 80% of students tend to have academic and behavioral success. Examples of Tier 1 supports may include teaching all students the general education curriculum, providing a school-wide assembly on a conflict resolution initiative, or providing all eighth-grade students with a lesson about transitioning to high school. Next we will outline the school counselor's role in this universal tier, as well as their related cultural competence.

The Role of the School Counselors in Tier 1 Supports

School counselors provide academic, career, and social/emotional services to *all* students, which means that they inherently provide Tier 1 supports. As described by the American School Counselor Association (ASCA) National Model, the school counseling core curriculum helps students develop the attitudes, knowledge, and skills for their developmental level (ASCA, 2012). This content is defined by the ASCA Mindsets & Behaviors for Student Success: K-12 College and Career-Readiness for Every Student (ASCA, 2014), which consists of 35 standards that identify what students should be able to demonstrate as a result of the counseling program (please see the corresponding link in the chapter Resources section). Delivery of the core curriculum generally includes classroom lessons, and large-group and school-wide activities for all students, portrayed in the box below.

School counseling core curriculum is an important aspect of a Comprehensive School Counseling Program (CSCP), such as the ASCA National Model (ASCA, 2012), as it is a strategy for school counselors to proactively and preventatively serve all students. Further, the school counseling core curriculum is a particularly salient aspect of school counseling programs that aligns CSCPs and MTSS (Ziomek-Daigle, Goodman-Scott, Cavin, & Donohue, 2016; Ockerman, Mason, & Hollenbeck, 2012; see also Chapter 2). Hence, the school counseling core curriculum is considered a Tier 1 support that serves every student (ASCA, 2012, 2018). As such, school counselors are encouraged to purposefully align their school counseling activities with their school's MTSS activities (ASCA, 2018; Goodman-Scott et al., 2016). In summary, Tier 1 supports, provided to every student, are overarching activities that include the school counseling core curriculum. Please see Table 4.1 for a visual of this alignment of MTSS supports and school counseling core curriculum.

> Sample school counseling core curriculum activities:
>
> Classroom lessons
>
> Large-group lessons
>
> School-wide assemblies and initiatives

Table 4.1 Tier 1 supports: aligning MTSS supports and school counseling core curriculum

MTSS Tier 1 Support	School Counseling Core Curriculum	Incorporating MTSS and School Counseling Core Curriculum
Teach general education curriculum to all students, based on academic standards	Facilitate classroom lessons to all students, based on ASCA Mindsets and Behavior standards	School counselors provide a classroom lesson on citizenship, using both grade-level academic standards and ASCA Mindsets and Behavior standards
Create and teach school-wide behavioral expectations to all students	Facilitate school-wide activities to all students based on ASCA Mindsets and Behavior standards	School counselors provide a school-wide assembly highlighting the school's behavioral expectation (Respect Self, Respect Others, Respect Property), aligning content with the ASCA Mindsets and Behavior standards

To describe this alignment further, school counselors act as *supporters* who provide indirect services to students. Thus, school counselors can be leaders in MTSS planning, evaluation, and recommending student and school services. For instance, schools implementing MTSS typically have a leadership team made up of a group of school stakeholders that represents the school community. This team is responsible for coordinating and communicating the school's MTSS implementation. As a member of the MTSS team, school counselors can consult and collaborate to help with MTSS efforts. Specifically, in conjunction with the MTSS team, school counselors can provide suggestions on teachers' evidence-based curriculum, assist in developing school-wide procedures and behavioral expectations, and contribute to the universal screening process (Donohue et al., 2016; Ockerman et al., 2012). Further, as part of the MTSS team, school counselors can collect and analyze data from needs assessments, school-wide outcome data, and universal screening. School counselors can also consult with teachers on matters such as instructional design.

As *interveners* who provide direct services to students, school counselors can provide classroom lessons, large-group activities, and school-wide programs such as college and career activities, LGBTQ+ support/awareness events, and assemblies that highlight expected student behaviors. Also, school counselors can design and deliver school counseling Tier 1 supports that incorporate, reinforce, and expand upon the academic and behavioral supports provided by the MTSS team. For the duration of this chapter we will use the term Tier 1 supports to include the school counseling core curriculum.

Cultural Competence

Within all aspects of MTSS and CSCP, and when implementing Tier 1 supports in particular, school counselors should have an intentional focus on cultural competence for themselves and when collaborating with the MTSS team. School counselors have the knowledge and skills to help the MTSS school teams consider as many cultural variables as possible, taking into account the ecological context of students and schools when planning school-wide activities and lessons (McMahon, Mason, Daluga-Guenther & Ruiz, 2014; see also Chapter 3). Not only should school counselors attend to race, ethnicity, gender, socio-economic status, class, and disability, but also learning style. While it may seem overwhelming to remember all of these factors, acknowledging and celebrating them is what will give the school counselor credibility with students, as well as with families and staff (McMahon et al., 2014). Culturally responsive Tier 1 supports will incorporate culturally relevant materials into lessons. For example, when selecting books to use in classroom lessons, or selecting images for parent newsletters or presentations, school counselors can prioritize content that is representative of the students and community. School counselors can also offer a variety of accommodations in their Tier 1 lessons and activities to meet students' diverse needs, such as offering translation services for English Language Learners/English Speakers of Other Languages (ELL/ESOL), differentiating instruction, and offering specific accommodations to serve varied learning styles and ability levels. For gender diverse or fluid students, school counselors can use non-binary or preferred pronouns, and inclusive terms such as *partner* and *caregiver* rather boyfriend, wife, mom, or dad. In all of these cases, making an effort to be inclusive is at the heart of Tier 1 supports. Students and families who feel included, respected, and celebrated are more likely to be engaged.

Now that we've outlined the overarching tenets of Tier 1 and school counselors' corresponding roles, we will describe how school counselors can prepare for Tier 1 supports, followed by implementing Tier 1 supports.

Planning Tier 1 Supports

To be effective, Tier 1 supports (e.g., the school counseling core curriculum) require significant planning and preparation. We believe that adequate preparation and thoughtful planning are, in and of themselves, a strategy that strengthens Tier 1 supports. In other words, the work done before delivering Tier 1 supports is critical to both the students and school counselors having a successful experience (Hatch, Duarte & DeGregorio, 2018; Lopez & Mason, 2018). The following section explores four strategies for planning Tier 1 supports, including the use of data, how to determine Tier 1 content and format within a CSCP, and, lastly, strategies for communicating with and involving stakeholders.

Using Data

Within Tier 1, data collection, interpretation, and decision-making focus on examining the needs of the entire student population and measuring progress. To plan and prepare for Tier 1 services, school counselors must collect and interpret various types of school-wide data (ASCA, 2012; Dimmitt, Carey, & Hatch, 2007; Young & Kaffenberger, 2013; Zyromski & Mariani, 2016). Specifically, school counselors utilize process, perception, and outcome data, as part of a CSCP (ASCA, 2012; please see Chapter 9 for more information on the use of data in CSCPs and MTSS). Next we'll outline different types of school-wide data, then discuss how these types of data can inform Tier 1 planning.

Needs Assessments

Needs assessments are surveys or questionnaires distributed to stakeholders (e.g., students, parents, staff, families, community members, etc.) that seek to solicit information about school or student needs, such as identifying needed academic and behavioral supports (Dimmitt et al., 2007; Zyromski & Mariani, 2016). For example, a needs assessment might ask teachers to comment on the social/emotional needs of students in their classrooms, or ask parents to rank in order their greatest concerns for their high school junior (e.g., anxiety, college application process, GPA, etc.). Some school counselors may have had training on developing and administering needs assessments in their graduate program, while others may wonder how and when to approach the process. School counselors can develop their own needs assessments or use existing surveys such as those developed by the Center for School Counseling Outcome Research and Evaluation (CSCORE) at the University of Massachusetts at Amherst (see the link in the Resources section). Needs assessments can be conducted at different times of the school year and help school counselors prioritize areas of focus. For instance, needs assessments can be implemented at the end of a school year in preparation for the subsequent school year, or at the beginning of the new school year (Hatch et al., 2018). School counselors can use the data from needs assessments to inform their program goals and measure the effects of their programs.

Needs assessments can be distributed in paper-and-pencil or digital form, in person, or via the internet. School counselors should consider which distribution method will result in the greatest return rate for the intended audience and perhaps even use multiple methods. The suite of Google tools, including Google Forms, are commonly used by school counselors for tasks like developing and distributing needs assessments (Mason, Griffith, & Belser, 2017). School counselors can hand tally the results of paper-and-pencil versions of needs assessments, or use tools like Excel or Google Sheets, which can generate graphs of needs assessment data for easy report writing and sharing. Further, needs assessments should use developmentally appropriate language so that the questions asked are accessible to students. A sample needs assessment from Capistrano Unified school district in California (Figure 4.1) demonstrates questions designed for high school students about their personal, school, and postsecondary needs, with a final section that asks about specific stressors. The directions are clear and easy to understand and explain how the survey will be used. The questions are written with brief phrases and wording that is appropriate for typical 9th through 12th graders. Students can indicate their level of need for information or support on a four-point scale.

Needs assessments are an avenue for gathering stakeholders' voices, in an effort to guide the focus of the school counseling Tier 1 supports. We find using needs assessments is particularly meaningful when used in combination with outcome data, which is described next.

Outcome Data

In addition to evaluating needs assessments, school counselors should also examine school-wide outcome data to influence their Tier 1 supports (Dimmitt, et al., 2007; Hatch et al., 2018; Zyromski & Mariani, 2016). Examples of school-wide outcome data include absentee and tardy patterns, office discipline referrals, citizenship markings, state or national college and career indicators, core social-emotional learning competencies, and universal screening data. This data is often gathered by school leadership teams, such as the MTSS team.

One type of data that is often outcome data is universal screening. Universal screening is a strategy for collecting data to inform the selection and implementation of Tier 1 curriculum, programs, and initiatives (Belser et al., 2016; Donohue et al., 2016; Erickson & Abel, 2013). Specifically, universal screening is the systematic screening of every student in a given school or grade, for specific criteria such as academics, internalizing or externalizing behaviors, mental health, social-emotional competencies, and so forth. As a result of universal screening, school stakeholders gain a better understanding of their school needs across all tiers. School counselors are often one member of the multidisciplinary team assisting with the universal screening process, as it falls within the academic and social/emotional domain of the ASCA National Model and within the Mindsets and Behaviors (ASCA 2012, 2014). Chapter 7 provides an in-depth description of the universal screening process.

> Think about your school, or a school you know well: what does data tell us about their students' needs?

After gathering and analyzing school-wide outcome data, schools typically develop school improvement plans. Specifically, school improvement plans outline schools' yearly goals and can often drive school-wide initiatives; these improvement plans can also serve as a foundation for determining Tier 1 supports (Hatch et al., 2018; Splett et al., 2018). School counselors can examine the overlap between the Mindsets and Behaviors (ASCA,

---

High School Student Needs Assessment; Student Version

The school counseling department wants to ensure we develop and provide programs that meet your needs. Please be honest with your responses. No individual student identifying information will be provided and your answers will be anonymous. This survey will help us learn how many students need programs and activities on certain topics. Thank you for helping us meet your needs.

What grade are you in?
9th
10th
11th
12th

Please read each statement and mark the most appropriate answer choice for you.

I need more information regarding the following PERSONAL concerns:

	Strongly Agree	Agree	Disagree	Strongly Disagree
Making better decisions	☐	☐	☐	☐
Improving communication	☐	☐	☐	☐
Transitioning to a new school	☐	☐	☐	☐
Pregnancy/teen parenting	☐	☐	☐	☐
Getting involved in school activities	☐	☐	☐	☐
Dating or relationship issues	☐	☐	☐	☐
Concerns about alcohol and/or drug use	☐	☐	☐	☐
Helping myself (gaining more self-confidence, feeling better about myself, expressing my feelings and thoughts)	☐	☐	☐	☐
Being more assertive	☐	☐	☐	☐
Handling teasing or being bullied	☐	☐	☐	☐
Getting along with other students better	☐	☐	☐	☐
Getting along with family members	☐	☐	☐	☐
Feeling sad or depressed	☐	☐	☐	☐
Feeling suicidal	☐	☐	☐	☐
Grief over the loss of a loved one	☐	☐	☐	☐
Parental divorce or separation	☐	☐	☐	☐
Dealing with anger	☐	☐	☐	☐
Feeling stressed	☐	☐	☐	☐
Feeling anxious	☐	☐	☐	☐
Skills for resolving conflict	☐	☐	☐	☐
Understanding sexual orientation/gender identity	☐	☐	☐	☐

Figure 4.1 Sample needs assessment from Capistrano Unified school district.

Reprinted from Capistrano United School District, by R. Pianta. Reprinted with permission.

I need more information regarding the following SCHOOL concerns:

	Strongly Agree	Agree	Disagree	Strongly Disagree
Being more organized	☐	☐	☐	☐
Managing my time better	☐	☐	☐	☐
Improving my study skills	☐	☐	☐	☐
Improving test taking skills	☐	☐	☐	☐
Understanding the best career options for me	☐	☐	☐	☐
Planning my options after high school	☐	☐	☐	☐
Understanding my learning style to improve how I learn	☐	☐	☐	☐
Knowing about and applying for scholarships and financial aid	☐	☐	☐	☐
Knowing what educational options are available to me when I graduate	☐	☐	☐	☐
Getting along with teachers	☐	☐	☐	☐
Making responsible decisions towards independent living (budgeting etc.)	☐	☐	☐	☐
Understanding graduation requirements	☐	☐	☐	☐

I need more information regarding the following COLLEGE & CAREER concerns:

	Strongly Agree	Agree	Disagree	Strongly Disagree
College application process				
Paying for college - Financial Aid & Scholarships	☐	☐	☐	☐
Resumes	☐	☐	☐	☐
Ivy League and selective colleges	☐	☐	☐	☐
Planning college visits	☐	☐	☐	☐
Creating a college list	☐	☐	☐	☐
College admittance requirements	☐	☐	☐	☐
Community College	☐	☐	☐	☐
Dream Act & DACA (Undocumented status)	☐	☐	☐	☐
Athletic recruiting process & NCAA eligibility	☐	☐	☐	☐
SAT & ACT test scores/prep	☐	☐	☐	☐
Writing college application essays	☐	☐	☐	☐

The following cause me to feel stressed:

	Strongly Agree	Agree	Disagree	Strongly Disagree
College admission process	☐	☐	☐	☐
Parent expectations	☐	☐	☐	☐
Uncertainty about my future	☐	☐	☐	☐
Not having enough time	☐	☐	☐	☐
Finding a job	☐	☐	☐	☐
Social pressure	☐	☐	☐	☐
Teacher expectations	☐	☐	☐	☐
Social media	☐	☐	☐	☐
Academic pressure	☐	☐	☐	☐
Financial pressure	☐	☐	☐	☐

Figure 4.1 (continued)

2014) and the school improvement goals when determining Tier 1 supports and goals each year (Hatch et al., 2018). For example, a school might examine attendance data and determine that decreasing tardies is a school-wide goal. The school counselor, as a member of the MTSS leadership team, can highlight several Mindsets and Behaviors that align with this goal such as: M 6. *Positive attitude toward work and learning* and B-SMS 1. *Demonstrate ability to assume responsibility* (ASCA, 2014). Then, as part of the school counseling program, the school counselor can create Tier 1 supports (e.g., classroom lessons) to address tardies, based on these Mindsets and Behaviors and the school improvement goals. Overall, by focusing on existing school-wide data, school counselors can identify students' current performance and have a baseline from which to develop and prioritize the goals and objectives of their CSCP, such as their Tier 1 supports (Belser et al., 2016; Ziomek-Daigle et al., 2016). The following case study highlights a school counseling team that used both needs assessments and school-wide outcome data.

The school counselors at Highline Middle School conduct an annual needs assessment at the mid-point of the school year. Recently, they found that many students, staff, and families were concerned about bullying on the school bus. The school counselors shared their findings with the MTSS team and asked to look at the related outcome data. The MTSS team-gathered outcome data also revealed a high rate of student discipline referrals on the school bus, particularly in the afternoon. Using these two data points, school-wide needs assessments and outcome data, the MTSS team, including the school counselors, gathered more specific information through staff and student interviews and by analyzing referral patterns (e.g., specific busses, specific students, time of day, etc.) to determine the root cause. They noted that students had a difficult time handling conflict and emotions, especially after a long school day. After understanding the root cause of the bullying, the school counselors and the MTSS team decided to select an evidence-based program to address bullying school-wide that focused on emotional regulation. The school counselors implemented aspects of the curriculum through their regular classroom lessons, and consulted with teachers and bus drivers, who reinforced key points of the curriculum with the students between school counseling lessons. Further, the MTSS team designed and facilitated school-wide procedures to support the bullying prevention, such as a positive acknowledgment system that allowed school staff to reinforce students who were demonstrating positive (non-bullying) behaviors. Teachers, bus drivers, and other staff acknowledged these behaviors by giving students a Hawk ticket (school mascot). Students could use these tickets during lunch to buy a variety of treats/snacks, as well as to attend the school dance each quarter. The MTSS team also brought in local high school students as guest speakers to talk with students during their advisory about bullying, respectful behavior, and how to stay calm when frustrated.

What types of data collection procedures currently exist in your school?

What types of data collection methods are missing and need to be established?

How can these data impact your Tier 1 supports?

In reflecting on the case study above, rather than selecting lesson topics haphazardly, utilizing needs-assessment and school-wide outcome data allowed the school counselors to make intentional and informed decisions about the topic of their Tier 1 supports, shaping the topic of their lessons. When selecting curriculum, schools can investigate evidence-based programs such as those listed by the *Collaborative for Academic, Social, and Emotional Learning* (CASEL) or the *What Works Clearinghouse* (for more information, please see Chapter 10 for evidence-based practices, as well as the Resources section at the end of this chapter). Further, when school stakeholders collaborate to plan and implement school-wide programs and classroom lessons, students receive consistency across classrooms, teachers, and areas of the school building. For instance, in the case study, the bus driver used the same bullying prevention approach and language as other school staff, such as physical education teachers, language arts teachers, and even the school principal.

Determining Content

Once school counselors collect data and determine school needs, the next step is determining the content of Tier 1 supports and considering the final desired outcome: how will the content be delivered? In the next section, we discuss how to determine content specific for the Tier 1 supports (e.g., the school counseling core curriculum) through developing objectives and lesson plans, as well as academic and behavioral content.

Learning Objectives

Developing objectives is the first and foremost task of designing effective supports. Objectives give Tier 1 supports a clear purpose and direction, and then can be aligned with ASCA's Mindsets and Behaviors (ASCA, 2014). For example, in Apple Elementary, needs assessments and outcome data highlighted that 5th grade students were experiencing cyberbullying. From this data the MTSS team developed the following learning objective: *All 5th grade students will gain knowledge about digital citizenship, including the potential positive and negative impact of their interactions with classmates online.* This objective aligns with the following ASCA Mindsets and Behaviors (2014): B-LS 5: *Apply media and technology skills*; B-SS 1: *Use effective oral and written communication skills and listening skills*; B-SS 9: *Demonstrate social maturity and behaviors appropriate to the situation and environment.* After a review of curricula and lessons on the topic of digital citizenship, the Apple Elementary MTSS team (including the school counselor) decided the school counselor would implement lessons from the Common Sense Media Digital Citizenship curriculum in each 5th grade classroom, in order to meet the given objectives by providing Tier 1 supports aligned with both the MTSS team and the school counseling program. Objectives should be tied directly to activities and assessment. As such, the Apple Elementary school counselor determined how they would assess the success of the lessons. Did students meet the intended objectives?

Lesson Plans

Not only do objectives guide Tier 1 supports, lesson plans do as well. Lesson plans are frequently used in K-12 education, particularly by teachers. However, over the years, fewer states require school counselors to have prior teaching experience. Thus, many school

Lesson Plan Template

School Counselor:_____Date: _____

Activity:_____

Grade(s): _____

ASCA Mindsets & Behaviors (Domain/Standard):

_____

_____

Learning Objective(s) (aligns with competency):

1._____

2._____

3._____

Materials: _____

_____

Procedure:_____

_____

_____

Plan for Evaluation: How will each of the following be collected?

Process Data: _____

_____

Perception Data:_____

_____

Outcome Data: _____

_____

Follow-Up: _____

_____

Figure 4.2 ASCA lesson plan template.

Reprinted from *ASCA National Model: A framework for school counseling programs* (3rd Ed.) by the American School Counselor Association, 2012, Alexandria, VA. Reprinted with permission.

counselors enter the profession without a teaching background (Smith, 2009) and may lack adequate knowledge and skills in constructing effective lesson plans. Creating engaging lessons is one strategy for minimizing classroom disruptions. The ASCA lesson plan template is a helpful tool that school counselors can use to write a detailed plan to guide class learning (see Figure 4.2).

Academic Content

Although they might not be academic subject matter experts (unless they were previously teachers), school counselors should be familiar with their school's academic standards and content as they can assist in strengthening these academic supports in several ways. For instance, school counselors, as part of a team, can share their expertise by giving feedback on academic content, processes, and curriculum. Thus, it is common practice for the school leadership team, including school counselors, to regularly review and suggest changes to academic curriculum and delivery. In a similar vein, MTSS leadership teams can help strengthen academic Tier 1 supports, common in RTI, such as suggesting strategies to provide reputable evidence-based academic curriculum and interventions for all students (Ockerman et al., 2012; Ziomek-Daigle et al., 2016). As part of the multidisciplinary MTSS team that discusses the results of academic universal screening for all students, school counselors can help distinguish students in need of small-group and individual academic supports (Ockerman et al., 2012). Last, school counselors can align their school counseling standards with academic standards, which will be discussed subsequently.

Aligning school counseling program standards (e.g., Mindsets and Behaviors) with subject-area standards (e.g., High School World History) can be a strategic way to connect curriculum, secure teacher buy-in, and gain greater access to the classroom for delivering lessons (Mason, 2010; Schellenberg, 2007). Please see the case study below, which demonstrates this alignment.

The first author discovered that many of her 8th-grade students did not know how to calculate a GPA or why it was important to their future as high school students. Thus, she set out to develop a school counseling classroom lesson on this topic that tied into 8th grade math standards. In consultation with the 8th grade math teachers, she implemented an 8th-grade-wide lesson that taught students how to calculate a GPA and how to understand weighted grades based on the conversions between fractions, decimals, and percentages (Mason, 2010). This practice became a universal Tier 1 intervention that all students received. Other subject area teachers quickly learned about the school counselor's math-related classroom lesson, and this trend expanded across the grade level. The school counselor started creating and delivering school counseling content that simultaneously addressed challenging science and social studies concepts. Family and consumer sciences, P.E., and health are some of the more logical subject areas that align with the ASCA Mindsets and Behaviors (2014), but, with some critical and creative thinking, school counselors and teachers can find connections with most any subject.

In sum, school counselors can provide classroom lessons that address academic content while simultaneously addressing school counseling standards.

Behavioral Content

In addition to supporting students' academics, the school counselor plays an active part in developing and reinforcing their school's behavioral expectations (e.g., school rules).

Thus, the school counselor can assist the MTSS team plan and implement behavioral supports at the school and classroom level, then also reinforce the behavioral expectations and processes when delivering their school counseling classroom lessons (Goodman-Scott et al., 2016). For instance, developing school-wide behavioral expectations is a common tenet of MTSS and PBIS specifically; these behavioral expectations are developed by the MTSS team and taught throughout the school (Goodman-Scott et al., 2016). (See Figures 4.3 and 4.4 for examples of school-wide expectations at an elementary and a middle school).

As a member of the MTSS team, the school counselor can be instrumental in helping to create and implement these school-wide expectations. Specifically, school counselors can use their schools' behavioral expectations to anchor their Tier 1 supports (e.g., classroom lessons, large-group activities, and school-wide activities) and identify the specific attitudes, knowledge, and skills that should be taught. For example, if the school-wide expectations are "Respect Self, Respect Others, Respect Property" (Figure 4.3), the school counselor could focus on developing and implementing classroom lessons that focus on the attitudes, knowledge, and skills related to respecting self, respecting others, and respecting property. Also, school counselors can select ASCA Mindsets and Behaviors that align with their school's school-wide behavioral expectations when designing their classroom lessons. In this way, school counselors' Tier 1 supports (e.g., the school counseling core curriculum) reinforce the behavioral content students hear from other staff members, so all staff throughout the school are speaking a common language (Goodman-Scott, Hays, & Cholewa, 2018).

In fact, school counselors have appreciated this shared responsibility: that they are no longer the primary school staff teaching social skills and positive character traits, as teaching and reinforcing the school-wide behavioral expectations is the task of every

Give me THREE

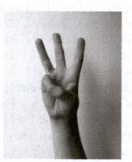

1. Respect **Self**
2. Respect **Others**
3. Respect **Property**

Figure 4.3 Sample elementary-school-wide expectations.

Reprinted with permission from E. Goodman-Scott.

TEACHING MATRIX
C. Alton Lindsay Middle School
SCHOOL-WIDE BEHAVIOR EXPECTATIONS

	Arrival & Dismissal	Hallway & Transitions	Bathroom	Cafeteria	Classroom
Safety First	• Walk directly to my designated area • Stay in my area • Talk softly • Keep hands, feet, and belongings to myself	• Walk directly to my designated area	• Keep hands, feet, and belongings to myself • Allow for the privacy of others	• Enter and exit with a pass or my teacher • Throw away my trash and tray • Clean up after myself	• Listen • Follow directions the first time given • Ask appropriately for help • Clean up after myself • Follow lab rules and procedures
Work Together Respectfully	• Respect the space of others	• Walk quietly to the right side of the hallway so that others can continue learning and working	• Conserve supplies: - 2 squirts of soap - 2 pushes/turns on the paper towel dispenser - Dispose of trash in the trash can	• Move away from conflict or distractions • Ask for help when needed • Be patient • Stay in line	• Accept feedback and discipline from staff by listening, asking questions, and following directions the first time. • Be ready to learn • Be present and focused • Encourage others
Accept Responsibility	• Keep to your own business	• Remain quiet in QUIET ZONES • Carry my own belongings • Keep lockers locked • Walk directly to my designated area	• Flush • Wash my hands • Use appropriate fixtures • Go	• Maintain a clean space and conversation • Keep food on my tray or in my mouth	• Attend class daily and on time • Clean up after myself • Be prepared for instruction with all necessary materials
Guide Me	• Teachers will supervise groups of students at all times • Teachers will ensure that they know the location of all students	• Teachers will enforce safety • Teachers will monitor students by being at their doors and in the hallways	• Teachers will stand by bathrooms to monitor the noise and behavior from the hallway	• Teachers will arrive on time and pick up students on time • Teachers will walk students directly into the cafeteria	• Teachers will supervise groups of students at all times • Teachers will be prepared for class - Lesson plans posted - Engaged and present - Observable outcomes

HAMPTON
City Schools
Every Child, Every Day,
Whatever it Takes!

Figure 4.4 Sample middle-school-wide expectations.

Reprinted from Hampton City Schools. Reprinted with permission.

staff member in the school building (Goodman-Scott & Grothaus, 2017). Please see the example below.

The first editor of this book was an elementary school counselor and the PBIS coach at her school. During the school's first year of PBIS implementation, together with the PBIS team, she helped create their school-wide expectations (see Figure 4.3). At the beginning of the school year, school staff taught these school-wide expectations to the students in their classes, and then taught and practiced the school-wide expectations in settings throughout the school, such as the cafeteria (see Figure 4.5). Similarly, the school counselor's first lesson of the year was on the school-wide expectations and taught students how to follow these expectations during their school counseling classroom lessons (see Figure 4.6). In fact, during the first school counseling lesson of the year, each class completed their own set of school counseling behavioral expectations unique to their class (Figure 4.6). These were revisited throughout the school year.

Respect
in the
Cafeteria

Respect Self

- Stay in your seat
- Raise your hand for help
- Eat only your food

Respect Others

- Use inside voices
- Use school manners
- Listen to the cafeteria staff
- Include other students

Respect Property

- Clean up after your meal
- Line-up quietly
- Be ready to return to the classroom

Figure 4.5 Sample school-wide expectations, modified for a specific school setting: the cafeteria.

Reprinted with permission from E. Goodman-Scott.

How do we show
Respect
during School Counseling Classroom
Lessons?

Respect Self

Respect Others

Respect Property

Figure 4.6 Sample school-wide expectations, modified for the school counselor.

Reprinted with permission from E. Goodman-Scott.

Note. This framework is purposefully left blank for each class to fill out during their first lesson of the year.

Similar practices can be used when teaching behavioral expectations at the middle and high school level and should be modified to be developmentally appropriate. For instance, we've seen the following behavioral expectation at a local high school: "Be Professional," which encourages professionalism as a means to support students' successful post-secondary transition. Also, please see Figure 4.4 for an example of a middle school teaching matrix, which was anchored to their three student expectations (the first three rows), as well as a staff expectations (the fourth row).

Determining Format

After school counselors decide on the objectives and content of their Tier 1 supports (e.g., core curriculum), they must decide on the most appropriate format in which to present the material. Are they presenting this content school-wide, in a large group or through classroom lessons? Are they providing one lesson or a series of lessons? Is the content delivered face-to-face, or could some of the content be flipped (e.g., partially offered in an online format)? How can the content be differentiated to meet the needs of diverse learners? Can stakeholders be involved? These are some of the questions that must be taken into account as school counselors plan their Tier 1 supports. Other factors that impact the format of the school counseling Tier 1 supports include: the size of a school counselor's caseload, the physical space and resources available for delivering the content, the school's daily schedule, available technology, type of content being delivered, and available time.

School-Wide

While classroom lessons may be the first activity that comes to mind when considering a school counselor's involvement in Tier 1 supports, school-wide initiatives and events are truly the most universal intervention of all because they are the most likely to reach all students. Overall, MTSS teams often choose school-wide Tier 1 supports for the purpose of prevention, and to address persistent school climate concerns that often occur across student populations and grade levels (e.g., lingering concerns about recent violence in the local community). For instance, many schools implement school-wide initiatives and programs through an all-school assembly or pep rally that orients students to expectations and builds a sense of community around achieving a common goal. Examples include suicide prevention initiatives, kindness challenges, a multicultural/international fair, Gay-Straight Alliances, Mix It Up at Lunch Day, etc. School counselors, in collaboration with the MTSS team, can assist in planning and implementing these school-wide Tier 1 initiatives as part of their school counseling program. Further, through a pep rally or school-wide event, school counselors can help communicate aspects of MTSS such as the school-wide behavioral expectations common in PBIS (e.g., Betters-Bubon & Donohue, 2016; Goodman-Scott, Doyle, & Brott, 2014).

Large Group

Large group is another frequently used format to deliver Tier 1 supports. In this format, students are gathered by grade-level, house, team, or other designations larger than a typical class to gain content such as a school counseling lesson or school-directed information. Examples include fifth grade students gathering for an orientation to middle school, third grade students meeting for a reteaching of playground expectations, or tenth grade students gathering to watch the movie *Screenagers* and then engaging in small-group facilitated discussions on hate crimes/speech. This large-group format likely necessitates moving into a space such as an auditorium, gym, hallway, or outdoor venue. While the large-group format can provide the efficiency of delivering content to many students at once, the school counselor needs to consider the use of space, supplies, technology, partnering with additional staff, and orchestrating the schedules of several stakeholders across the population (e.g., grade-level, team, etc.). Also, school counselors may need to employ unique classroom management strategies due to students in a larger and different space, especially if students are unaccustomed to meeting in this format. Large-group lessons lend themselves best to lecture-based lessons in which school counselors need to ensure all students have consistent information. The nature of the large-group setting makes it more difficult to facilitate experiential activities or to have a substantive discussion.

Classroom

The classroom format enables school counselors to meet with students in a group setting within their established classes and schedules. The classroom format is the most traditional and likely the most popular for delivering school-counseling-specific Tier 1 supports, because it mimics the classroom experience that students have daily with their teachers (Lopez & Mason, 2018; Ziomek-Daigle, 2015). When delivered through established classes, there is minimal disruption to the school day and to the routine to which students have become accustomed. The room offers familiarity and often the supplies needed to deliver lessons, and teachers should be present during the school counselor's lesson to reinforce the content. Classrooms are generally small enough to allow for a variety of activities including lecture, experiential activities, and discussion, and there are usually established norms and expectations for behavior. Generally, school counselors prepare for their large group and classroom lessons to fit within a 30- to 50-minute time block or class period. It's also helpful for the school counselor to leave a visual reminder of the lesson in the classroom, so students and teachers can refer back to it. For example, after teaching students about conflict resolution, school counselors can leave a poster showing the five essential steps to resolving conflict. These steps can give students a reference outside of the school counseling lesson, as they practice the steps to resolve conflicts that arise.

Individual Lesson vs Lesson Unit

Another consideration is whether or not a topic or standard requires an individual lesson or a unit made up of multiple lessons. Here again, data from school-wide reports and needs assessments can provide direction about how much time and how many lessons are needed in a particular area. For example, a single psychoeducational lesson on digital citizenship may meet immediate needs of addressing a surge in issues related to negative student interactions on social media. However, a four-lesson unit on conflict resolution allows for skills practice and deeper reinforcement of school-wide behavior expectations. Similarly, school counselors may also consider spiraled curriculum: revisiting a given topic (e.g., career exploration) in each grade level, in a way that is different, developmentally appropriate, and builds off the content they received on the topic in the previous grade. For instance, when learning about careers, kindergarten students may learn about basic helping professions, whereas fourth grade students may explore a variety of careers based on their interests.

Flipped Classroom

The rise of flipped teaching and learning presents yet another format option for school counselors to consider in delivering Tier 1 supports (Lopez & Mason, 2018; Zainuddin & Halili, 2016). In a flipped format, students watch a video component prior to the classroom or large-group lesson (e.g., lecture, screencast, film clip, performance, etc.), and then apply knowledge learned in the video during the face-to-face lesson (Bergmann & Sams, 2012). A primary benefit of the flipped format is that students can engage in higher-order cognitive skills (i.e., analysis, application, etc.) within the classroom because they have already engaged in lower-order skills (i.e., being introduced to fundamental concepts) while watching the video. In the flipped format, classroom time is used for the application of concepts rather than for the teaching of concepts. While the flipped and traditional formats both involve school counselor preparation, flipping often involves technology, which can be highly engaging for students. For example, many educators use Kahoot, an interactive quizzing tool, in which students engage via a cell phone, tablet, or computer with a unique participant code. High levels of student engagement, which can be increased by technology, can mitigate some classroom management issues.

Differentiated Instruction

Choosing a format for the school counseling Tier 1 supports also necessitates considering how to differentiate lessons for a variety of learners. When designing a lesson, school counselors should become familiar with students' needs and current knowledge of the topic, their interests surrounding the topic, and the learning profile of the classroom such as preferred style of learning, gender, culture, and abilities (Akos, Cockman, & Strickland, 2007). In particular, school counselors should plan for students with disabilities, gifted students, and ELL/ESOL, as well as students with a range of social, emotional, behavioral, and academic needs. School counselors also must take into account their students' many cultural identities.

To start with, making accommodations will assist students' access to and participation in the lessons. When preparing to deliver lessons, school counselors should become familiar with the needs of the students in the classroom and observe the classroom, if possible. Teachers are also a helpful source for differentiation strategies, whether they are general education, special education, or ELL/ESOL teachers. School counselors should consider integrating project-based learning, in which students work in collaborative teams, contributing a variety of skills and knowledge, which can increase interest over independent seat work for a diverse range of learners.

Students and families for whom English is not their primary language may appreciate materials translated into their native language, the use of a translator, and/or opportunities to ask additional questions. Similarly, if a school has self-contained special education classes, the school counselor may work with the special education teacher to provide school-counseling-specific Tier 1 supports. For example, it may be helpful to provide materials to special educators prior to the classroom lesson so that they can provide ample pre-teaching. This encourages a higher level of engagement for students with special needs. As such, the school counselor can determine classroom lesson topics and format while in close collaboration with the teacher. In some instances, the teacher may assist in co-teaching the lesson. For example, a school counselor learned that the students in a self-contained autism class were working on personal space. To reinforce this content, the school counselor created a related classroom lesson on the appropriateness of giving hugs; this lesson was taught in collaboration with the special education teacher. Further, the school counselor created a social story on giving hugs and sent the content to parents, to reinforce at home.

As mentioned previously, it is imperative that school counselors consider students' and families' cultures. Behavioral norms for classrooms and schools are still often based largely on white, Western, middle- or upper-class social expectations (e.g., being quiet, sitting still, waiting to be called on). If the school staff is primarily representative of this majority demographic, and the students and families are not, power and privilege may also be a force in further embedding such privileged norms. Thus, the school counselor must advocate for Tier 1 supports to be culturally representative of the student and community populations.

Communicating with and Involving Stakeholders

After determining the content and format of their Tier 1 supports, school counselors should consider how they will communicate these services to stakeholders. For instance, Hatch and colleagues (2018) recommended that school counselors publish a calendar of agreed-upon Tier 1 supports (e.g., classroom lessons) for the entire school year, while maintaining the flexibility to modify the calendar and content based on needs that arise. Calendaring the Tier 1 supports ahead of time allows teachers and administration to plan in advance, and to incorporate the school counseling program. School counselors also can provide parents and families with their Tier 1 calendar at the start of the school year, maintain a copy on the school's website, and in a common area such as on a bulletin board outside of their office.

Using a calendar is another way to demonstrate the alignment between school counseling activities and MTSS supports, showing how the two are integrated. For example, Table 4.2 displays an example of the first month of a sixth-grade annual calendar, aligning the sixth

Table 4.2 Sample month from annual school counselor department calendar: aligning school counseling Tier 1 supports (classroom lessons, large-group and school-wide activities) with MTSS school-wide expectations. Sample from the first month of the school year

Grade 6 School Counseling Calendar

MTSS School-Wide Expectations	Be Safe	Be Respectful	Be Responsible
September	School counselors review the MTSS behavior matrix in a large-group lesson, focusing on **safety**, across a sixth grade team (e.g., 100 students). ASCA Standard: Demonstrate personal safety skills (B-SMS 9).	School counselors facilitate a school-wide assembly to address bullying by teaching **respectful** expected behaviors towards peers. ASCA Standard: Create positive and supportive relationships with others (B-SS 2).	School counselors conduct a classroom lesson on **responsibility**, reviewing the use of student planners to track assignments and assessments. ASCA Standard: Demonstrate ability to assume responsibility (B-SMS 1).

grade school counselor's Tier 1 activities (classroom lessons, large-group lessons, and school-wide activities) with their school's MTSS behavioral expectations (Be Safe, Be Respectful, Be Responsible). You can see how the ASCA Mindsets and Behaviors correspond with the MTSS-created school-wide behavioral expectations. While only the first month is shown here, school counselors can expand on a similar calendar for the duration of the year.

Relatedly, school counselors can consider strategies for involving stakeholders such as parents/guardians and community members. Perhaps school counselors send home parent/guardian newsletters on the content of their classroom lessons, along with related guiding questions parents/guardians can ask their children at home. Additionally, community members can be utilized within school counselors' Tier 1 supports, such as inviting the local LGBTQ+ community center to the school-wide roll out of a Gay-Straight Alliance at a high school.

Implementing Classroom-Level Tier 1 Supports

Implementing Tier 1 supports (e.g., the school counseling core curriculum) requires creativity, confidence, flexibility, and valuing relationships with students and teachers, while maintaining focus on the curriculum objectives. The following section explores strategies for implementing Tier 1 supports, including the use of classroom management strategies to engage a variety of learners, the importance of consulting and collaborating with teachers, and the use of evaluation to guide implementation.

Classroom Management Strategies

Recently, the U.S. Department of Education published a report describing a myriad of evidence-based preventative classroom management strategies for teachers to implement across the three tiers (Simonsen et al., 2015). Similarly, Adamson, McKenna, and Mitchell (2016) developed a related graphic to portray how these evidence-based classroom management strategies can be viewed within the MTSS tiered approach (see Figure 4.7; Mitchell, Hirn, & Lewis, 2017, p. 149).

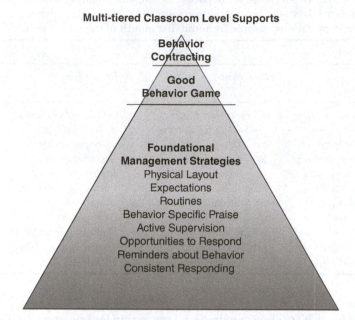

Figure 4.7 Continuum of classroom-level behavior management supports.

Reprinted from "Kicking it up a notch: Spicing up classroom level behavior supports, bam!" by R. A. Adamson, J. McKenna, & B. S. Mitchell, 2016. Presented at the 94th Annual Council for Exceptional Children Convention, St. Louis, Missouri. Reprinted with permission.

For the purpose of this section of the chapter, we will describe the classroom management strategies pertaining to Tier 1. While the Department of Education strategies were geared toward teachers, we believe that school counselors can similarly utilize many of these classroom management strategies, with the exception of disciplinary practices, when conducting their Tier 1 supports, particularly in classroom lessons.

Relatedly, school counselors have reported using a host of classroom management strategies when conducting classroom lessons (Goodman-Scott, in press, anticipated 2019). These strategies included: acting proactively, engaging students, implementing positive reinforcement, using varied modalities (e.g., nonverbal, vocal, proximity, etc.), and utilizing consequences. Further, the school counselors in this national study also described factors that influenced their classroom management, such as personal characteristics (e.g., being calm, confident, consistent, and genuine), knowing students and prioritizing their relationships, collaborating with teachers, and appreciating their previous classroom management experiences.

Table 4.3 summarizes content from the U.S. Department of Education report (Simonsen et al., 2015) and the Goodman-Scott study (Goodman-Scott, in press, anticipated 2019), to provide examples of school-counseling-specific classroom management strategies. It is important to note that classroom management strategies should be purposefully implemented at the start of the school year, during the initial school counseling lesson, and briefly reinforced during each subsequent lesson.

In addition to the evidence-based classroom management strategies listed above, we've gathered here other classroom management strategies school counselors can consider when implementing their Tier 1 supports.

Table 4.3 Recommended school counseling classroom management strategies

Classroom Management Strategy	Description	Examples
Purposefully design the physical layout of the room	Is the room well-organized and physically conducive to learning? Can the students move around comfortably? Depending on the students' ages, school counselors may consider having students move around the room at different points during the lesson to maintain momentum and engagement.	School counselor, to a class of second grade students: "First, we are going to read a story on the carpet, then we'll move back to your chairs to complete an activity."
Create and proactively teach students behavioral expectations	At the start of the year, school counselors can describe how students should behave during school counseling classroom lessons. School counselors can remind students of the MTSS school-wide expectations (Figure 4.1 and Figure 4.4), and adapt these expectations to the school counseling lessons (Figure 4.3). At the start of each lesson, school counselors can provide students with a quick refresher, reminding students of the expectations.	During their first lesson of the year: "Our school-wide expectations are Respect Self, Respect Others, Respect Property. How can we Respect Self, Others, and Property during school counseling classroom lessons? Let's make a list." Then post each class-generated list in the respective classroom and refer back to the expectations at the start of each lesson.
Develop and teach predictable routines	School counselors develop and teach students specific predictable routines associated with their lessons. This can include routines for starting and ending the lessons, routines for administering positive reinforcement, and so forth.	"When my lessons start, I want to see students in 'ready' position. 'Ready' position means desks are clear and . . ." "Remember, if the class earns three tickets for good listening during today's lesson, we can play a game at the end of our lesson."
Give behavior-specific praise	School counselors provide positive verbal feedback, recognizing desired student behavior. This feedback specifically identifies the desired behavior.	"Kiera, I like how you wrote your Language Arts homework in your agenda. You wrote down the page numbers for your reading, and the upcoming quiz on Thursday. Great organization!"

(continued)

Table 4.3 (continued)

Classroom Management Strategy	Description	Examples
Supervise students, including scanning and proximity	While conducting lessons, school counselors actively monitor the room, physically moving around, supervising students. They may scan the room and check-in with students.	While students are engaging in small-group work at tables, the school counselor supervises, walking around the perimeter and the middle of the room, quietly checking-in with student groups on the status of their group work. The school counselor may make observations and provide feedback, as appropriate.
Provide many opportunities to respond	School counselors provide students with a variety of opportunities to respond to questions, such as verbal, written, choral, small group, and/or nonverbal.	School counselor: "On a scale of 1–5, 1 being little knowledge and 5 being a lot of knowledge, raise your hand and show me on your fingers, how much you know about . . ." Call and response: School counselor: "One, two, three . . ." Students: "Eyes on me!" School counselor: "Please get out your reflection journal and answer the prompt on the board . . ."
Acting consistently	When engaging in classroom management, school counselors act consistently, including routinely following-through with classroom procedures; teaching and reteaching school-wide and/or class-specific behavioral expectations; recognizing desired student behaviors; providing error correction, and so forth.	A student is off-task during the journal writing activity in the lesson. The school counselor will remind all students of the "Care for Self" expectation that they taught previously and provide a specific reminder to the student who is off-task. The counselor will acknowledge the student when they respond and return to their work. The school counselor will continue to highlight the school-wide expectations in subsequent lessons.

Used and modified with permission from Goodman-Scott (in press, anticipated 2019; *Professional School Counseling*).

Presenting

If school counselors haven't previously been teachers, they may or may not have experience or training in presentation skills. However, those who come to the profession with degrees or experience in communications, marketing, sales, or non-profit work, may be at an advantage if they have successfully facilitated professional presentations. The delivery of any Tier 1 supports: classroom, large-group, school-wide, and so forth, necessitates, first and foremost, presentation skills. Without a strong grounding in public speaking and presenting, stepping into a classroom for the first time, or even stepping into certain classrooms, can be anxiety-inducing. Presenting takes planning and energy. Even if a school counselor is not initially proficient in this area, one can become more skilled with time and practice. As previously mentioned, teachers can be valuable consultants in this area. If school counselors develop a strong relationship with a teacher, they can ask for specific feedback regarding their presentation skills.

Facilitating

Facilitation skills are, fortunately, something that many school counselors have been trained in, especially through courses like Basic Counseling Skills and Group Counseling (Ziomek-Daigle, 2015). While school counseling lessons may contain a formal presentation, activities are common, including facilitating student interactions and discussions. Aspects of facilitation when providing Tier 1 supports include active listening, paraphrasing and summarizing, expanding, and connecting. School counselors may use facilitation skills to ask students to elaborate on their responses and link student comments to others' responses.

Flexibility

The act of "thinking on your feet" is often associated with the unpredictable nature of the classroom setting, or any setting with a lot of students. When working at the Tier 1 level, those working in education, such as school counselors, must be ready to respond quickly, shifting gears as needed (Konen, 2018). Challenges to conducting student lessons may include students attempting to derail lessons with attention-seeking behaviors or power struggles (McDonald, n.d.). When student behaviors interfere with lessons, the school counselor must maintain flexibility to navigate the given situation. Observing teachers with strong classroom management and who utilize various styles may be especially helpful for new school counselors or for those who need visual examples of responding in the moment (Goodman-Scott, in press, anticipated 2019). Overall, being prepared with additional and alternate activities may be a useful strategy to respond to unpredictable student behaviors and situations (Konen, 2018).

Technology

As mentioned earlier, using technology is one way to engage today's school-aged learner. Because today's students are digital natives, they are accustomed to using technology for a variety of purposes. Technology has also become a staple in schools, though schools with greater resources may have greater access to technology, comparatively. When considering implementing technology in their Tier 1 supports, school counselors can evaluate the technological trends and resources currently used in the school and by students, and utilize that technology (as long as it is appropriate in an educational context). If students are engaged, they are less likely to misbehave during lessons. The pool of tools available to educators is immense and constantly growing; there are options for presentation, design, games, movement, interactive quizzes, and much more. Sources like Common Sense Education provide reviews and rating of educational technology tools at all levels and on a wide variety of subjects and topics. In addition, SCOPE is a website maintained by the first author of the chapter that seeks to support school counselors' use of technology (please see the Resources section at the end of this chapter). In choosing tools, school counselors should use those they are already familiar with or pilot one new tool at a time. One downfall of the attractiveness of technology is that it can overshadow the purpose of the lesson and educators can become too dependent on its "wow" factor. When used intentionally, technology should reinforce the lesson content, engage the student, and support, not replace, the value of the school counselor.

Overall, for some school counselors, classroom management strategies can be implicit and subtle, while other school counselors utilize explicit and obvious strategies. Some school counselors may use visual or auditory signals or proximity control while others verbally offer students choices or rely on teachers' disciplining. Overall, just as school counselors have a plethora of preferences for theoretical orientation and techniques, school counselors also may have different tendencies and preferences in regards to classroom management strategies.

Consulting and Collaborating with Teachers

While consulting and collaborating with teachers could be part of the Tier 1 planning process, we suggest that a different, perhaps deeper and more experiential level of consultation and collaboration can occur when school counselors specifically seek out teachers' expertise, visit their classrooms, and work together to implement school-counseling-guided Tier 1 supports (Brigman, Webb, Mullis, & White, 2005). Thus, next we will discuss several strategies for school counselors to consult and collaborate with classroom teachers, as part of implementing their Tier 1 supports.

Gaining Buy-In

Schools are frequently launching new initiatives that are either mandated by federal, state, or local entities, which can often lead to intervention "fatigue" and can create resistance to change. The Law of Initiative Fatigue states that when the number of initiatives increases, and time, resources, and emotional energy are constant, each new initiative will receive fewer minutes, dollars, and ounces of emotional energy than its predecessors (Reeves, 2012). To prevent initiative fatigue, Reeves (2012) recommends involving teachers in planning, and guiding them through implementation. Therefore, we suggest (a) school counselors develop and nurture strong relationships with teachers, and (b) play a leadership role in implementing Tier 1 services that simultaneously support the school-wide and school counseling program goals. Thus, buy-in from school stakeholders, such as teachers, can provide school counselors with much needed social capital to strengthen the delivery and possible success of Tier 1 supports.

Observing and Seeking Feedback

Observing teachers in their classrooms is time well spent for school counselors, especially those who are new, lack teaching experience, or who need more strategies for improving their classroom management skills. For example, school counselors may consider seeking out a teacher particularly skilled in classroom management, sitting in the back of their class, and observing their classroom management strategies (Goodman-Scott, in press, anticipated 2019). Experienced teachers may also be willing to recommend classroom management strategies, and to observe and provide feedback on school counselors' classroom management during lessons.

Learning Unique Class Dynamics

Observing classrooms before delivering lessons may give school counselors the opportunity to watch teachers in action and also to observe student dynamics. This can be a valuable strategy for classroom management because it allows school counselors to plan lessons and activities for specific classrooms. For example, a school counselor who observes a classroom with a quiet dynamic, in which few students speak, can adjust a lesson to include creative opportunities for students to voice their opinions and share ideas through verbal means, writing, or role play. Likewise, a school counselor who observes a classroom with a loud or energetic dynamic might decrease a movement-oriented lesson, and also include additional time for transitions and calming activities.

Deciding on Classroom Management Strategies

Because school counselors visit all classrooms, they must make intentional choices about whether or not to adopt their own unique classroom management practices that follow them from room to room, or to adopt the classroom management practices of each teacher. Alternatively, one benefit of MTSS is the use of school-wide expectations. Thus, since the universal expectations are utilized across the school, school counselors have a built-in framework of classroom expectations to use in all classrooms.

Including Subject Content

In order to increase efficiency and teacher buy-in, school counselors can strategically include content from academic subject areas (Mason, 2010; Schellenberg, 2007), as we discussed earlier in the chapter. Though it may not seem intuitive for school counselors to learn about academic subject areas when they often have long to-do lists, taking an interest in academic content can win points with teachers and open the door to aligning academic and school counseling standards, as well as co-teaching.

Co-Teaching

Co-teaching is a valuable arrangement for managing a classroom. Consider the messages that students may receive about collaboration, respect, interdisciplinary work, and creativity when they observe a teacher and counselor present a lesson together, integrating both academic and school counseling content. Further, instructional time is valuable, and school counselors may find it challenging to gain access to students and deliver lessons during instructional time. However, co-teaching a lesson that interweaves both academic and school counseling content is efficient, and could strengthen the relationship between teacher and school counselor. Utilizing classroom teachers' expertise and requesting their involvement may strengthen both academic instruction and the school counseling program, making for a stronger and more dynamic learning experience.

Reinforcing Content

School counselors may present classroom lessons as often as twice a month, or as infrequently as two to three times during an academic year. Thus, school counselors possess limited opportunities to deliver classroom content to students. However, collaborating and consulting with classroom teachers can provide opportunities for teachers to not only participate in the school counseling lesson, but to reinforce the school counseling concepts in the classroom after the lesson (Cholewa, Goodman-Scott, Thomas, & Cook, 2017). For example, if a school counselor facilitates a lesson on coping strategies for testing anxiety, they can leave behind a graphic depicting strategies. The teacher can then hang the graphic in the classroom and refer back to the content as a teaching tool when addressing test-taking anxiety. Thus, the classroom teacher can reinforce Tier 1 school counseling content long after the end of the lesson.

It is important to note that teaching styles and classroom management practices vary greatly, and school counselors may need to engage in trial and error to find strategies that work best for them, and for their students and collaborating teachers.

Assessment

A final step critical to understanding the effectiveness of implementing Tier 1 supports is assessment. Although the word "assessment" may seem intimidating, it is simply the practice of asking the audience well-designed questions to understand their knowledge, skills, or attitudes about particular content. For school counseling Tier 1 supports, this is often done through pre-tests, post-tests, or both. Sometimes these assessments have other names to sound more engaging such as bell-ringers, do-nows, or exit tickets. For example, a school counselor might start a lesson with a "do-now," a short activity that is written on the board as students enter the classroom. It is a simple activity that students can begin without any direction from the school counselor, it takes only a few minutes to complete, and can be used to review a recent lesson or preview the day's lesson. An exit ticket can be used to allow students to synthesize or apply the day's content. For example, students' written response to the prompt "Name one thing you learned today" might be their ticket out the door. These types of assessments, as well as informal surveys or short questionnaires, can also be used by school counselors in delivering other Tier 1 activities such as parent education workshops or staff development and training. A critical and sometimes overlooked aspect in the process of assessment is ensuring the development of valid questions. In other words, questions must truly measure what they are intended to measure. Students should be asked questions that align with the given curriculum and with the chosen objectives, and instructions should be clear enough for students to understand how to complete the assessment (Hatch et al., 2018). Hatch and colleagues (2018) recommend designing questions based on the model of "ASK" or attitudes, skills, or knowledge (p. 173). For example, a school counselor might utilize the anger management language in a lesson (e.g., a PowerPoint slide depicting what happens in the body when a person is angry) and match it to a knowledge question on an assessment (e.g., Please name three physical responses to anger). This provides validity and ensures that what is being taught is also being assessed (see Hatch et al., 2018). One way to bolster this part of the assessment process is to develop questions based on lesson objectives with developmentally appropriate language. For example, an objective of a lesson on empathy is "Students will be able to identify facial expressions of happiness, sadness, anger, and surprise." In assessing this objective with first grade students, we might use images of faces (photographs or drawings) that display these emotions. A sample item on a post-test might read, "Circle the face you think is angry." Using more cognitively concrete measures at the early-elementary level is developmentally appropriate. On the other hand, middle school students who have developed greater cognitive complexity can be asked about the same objective in a different way. Thus, a sample item on a post-test might read, "You see a friend in the hallway and notice her eyebrows are scrunched together, her lips are pursed, her shoulders are tight as she clenches her books in her arms, and she is glaring at you with a deep, focused stare. What emotion is she displaying?" In addition to modifying assessment questions by students' development, we must also consider other factors such as students with disabilities, students for whom English is not their primary language, and so forth.

Next, data and assessment are interconnected with classroom management. When school counselors use data to focus the content of their lesson and assessments to evaluate their lessons, they engage students in a way similar to teachers. In other words, students come to understand that learning the skills of conflict resolution or school-wide behavioral expectations are similar to learning the historical events of the Civil War, or the steps to using the quadratic formula. The use of assessment provides an expected structure to a Tier 1 lesson and gives the school counseling content credibility, much like any other subject area.

School Counseling Tier 1 Evaluation

School counselors not only use data to plan and design Tier 1 supports, but also to evaluate the effectiveness of their activities and monitor student progress. Tier 1 focuses on providing quality instruction to prevent gaps in student learning and behavior. By evaluating Tier 1 supports, school counselors can ensure that quality instruction is being delivered. Effective Tier 1 delivery occurs when approximately 80% of a grade level's needs are being met in Tier 1. When examining the impact of the curriculum on students, school counselors should identify when less than 75% of a grade level's needs are being met via Tier 1 and develop a plan for strengthening the curriculum. According to the ASCA National Model (ASCA, 2012), school counselors should focus on answering the question, "How are students different as a result of what we do?" This can include reevaluating the content, scope, and sequence of the curriculum.

Conclusion

In the beginning of this chapter, First Lady Michelle Obama reminded us of the significance school counselors have for the students we serve. Tier 1 activities, such as classroom lessons, small-group activities, and school-wide initiatives are exceptionally important because they are opportunities to connect with all students and to maximize their learning of important academic, career, and social/emotional skills. Dr. Harry Wong also suggested that we must enter the classroom space with great intention and purpose, and that students will be most successful when we set clear expectations.

Throughout this chapter we highlighted the primary elements of preparing, implementing, and evaluating Tier 1 activities as part of a Comprehensive School Counseling Program. We also addressed multicultural considerations and the importance of modifying activities to reach a variety of learners. This chapter also provided evidence-based management strategies to assist school counselors in meeting the demands of the classroom environment. Further, we emphasized the important role of collaboration, specifically with teachers, in helping school counselors be successful in Tier 1 supports.

We end the chapter by acknowledging ethical issues and opportunities that are relevant to lesson plan development, sharing, and dissemination.

For more information and a school counselor's perspective on *Tier 1: School Counseling Core Curriculum and Classroom Management for Every Student* please see Chapter 12 "Voices from the Field," Voices 1, 4, 5, 6, 8, and 10.

ASCA Ethical Standards

The ASCA Ethical Standards (2016) are necessary to guide the planning, implementation, and assessment of Tier 1 activities. In this section we discuss the importance of using Tier 1 supports to make the school community aware of school counselor ethics, along with some specific yet not frequently addressed issues related to the ethics of appropriate use of lesson plans and curricular materials. In particular, we highlight issues of copyright and plagiarism as they might arise in the preparation of Tier 1 activities.

To support ethical practice, we recommend that all stakeholders receive information about the school counselor's role, including basic developmentally appropriate information about ethical standards. The beginning of the new school year is the most optimal time for efforts focused in this area so that stakeholders are reminded of the school counseling program and the responsibilities of school counselors. We especially believe the definition of, and limitations to confidentiality are important for students, staff, and families to understand. When utilizing Tier 1 supports, this information can be presented to all students as part of the counseling classroom lessons or large-group formats. Many school counselors conduct classroom lessons in the beginning of the year to introduce themselves to students and to explain their role. These introductions are the ideal time to include information about ethics such as confidentiality. Staff and families can receive similar information through open house nights, workshops, newsletters, video recordings or other phone or email communications.

School counselors must be aware of how to coordinate, use data, and evaluate their comprehensive programming, which includes Tier 1 curriculum. When implementing Tier 1 activities, school counselors must be aware of issues related to copyright and plagiarism.

For example, it is common among school counselors to use existing materials when implementing Tier 1 supports, as there is little time, opportunity, or need to reinvent the wheel. With the prolific availability of programs, curricula, and readily available lessons, however, come several ethical traps to avoid. Many curricula, especially commercial ones that are published and mass-produced, have copyright restrictions. School counselors are responsible for inspecting these materials to understand what and how much they can copy, and where and for what purpose it can be distributed (Ciszek, 2017).

When following copyright guidelines, even the use of a portion of materials must include proper attribution of the source so that others may locate it for their own use if desired (ASCA, 2016; Ciszek, 2017). Thus, a related issue is that of plagiarism, which is any attempt to pass off the work of another as one's own. Given the regularity of sharing materials in school counseling circles, this is a particularly common pitfall because there is no standard of practice. Some school counselors are reluctant to share materials while others give more freely. It is wise for school counselors to clearly indicate the following on work that is theirs if they intend to share it: the date of creation, and any directions regarding requests to use the work (e.g., "must be used with permission" or "provide proper credit when using this lesson plan," etc.). On the flip side, if a school counselor finds materials from a school counselor (or teacher, administrator, professor, etc.) that they wish to use, adapt, or modify, they should seek permission from the author or creator. Freedman (2004) suggests that with the plethora of resources available through the internet, we must accept that the ability to locate relevant content and material is a valuable skill. However, in preparing and training educators, they should also know how to analyze material for restrictions and learn how to generate new ideas or adapt material while giving credit to the original source (Freedman, 2004).

Thus, there are many ethical standards to consider in the implementation of Tier 1 activities. Additional standards are found below.

A   Responsibility to Students

A.1   Supporting Student Development

- A.1.a. Have a primary obligation to the students, who are to be treated with dignity and respect as unique individuals.

A.3   Comprehensive Data-Informed Program

- A.3.a. Collaborate with administration, teachers, staff, and decision makers around school-improvement goals.
- A.3.b. Provide students with a comprehensive school counseling program that ensures equitable academic, career, and social/ emotional development opportunities for all students.
- A.3.e. Collect process, perception, and outcome data and analyze the data to determine the progress and effectiveness of the school counseling program. School counselors ensure the school counseling program's goals and action plans are aligned with district's school improvement goals.

A.4   Academic, Career, and Social/Emotional Plans

- A.4.a. Collaborate with administration, teachers, staff, and decision makers to create a culture of postsecondary readiness.
- A.4.b. Provide and advocate for individual students' preK– postsecondary college and career awareness, exploration, and postsecondary planning and decision making, which supports the students' right to choose from the wide array of options when students complete secondary education.
- A.4.d. Provide opportunities for all students to develop the mindsets and behaviors necessary to learn work-related skills, resilience, perseverance, an understanding of lifelong learning as a part of long-term career success, a positive attitude toward learning and a strong work ethic.

A.13 Evaluation, Assessment, and Interpretation

- A.13.i. Conduct school counseling program evaluations to determine the effectiveness of activities supporting students' academic, career, and social/emotional development through accountability measures, especially examining efforts to close information, opportunity, and attainment gaps.

A.14 Technical and Digital Citizenship

- A.14.a. Demonstrate appropriate selection and use of technology and software applications to enhance students' academic, career, and social/ emotional development. Attention is given to the ethical and legal considerations of technological applications, including confidentiality concerns, security issues, potential limitations, and benefits and communication practices in electronic media.

B   **Responsibilities to the Parents/Guardians, School, and Self**

B.1   Responsibilities to Parents/Guardians

- B.1e. Inform parents of the mission of the school counseling program and program standards in academic, career, and social/emotional domains that promote and enhance the learning process for all students.
- B.1f. Inform parents/guardians of the confidential nature of the school counseling relationship between the school counselor and student.

B.2   Responsibilities to the School

- B.2.b. Design and deliver comprehensive school counseling programs that are integral to the school's academic mission; driven by student data; based on standards for academic, career, and social/emotional development; and promote and enhance the learning process for all students.
- B.2.k. Affirm the abilities of and advocate for the learning needs of all students. School counselors support the provision of appropriate accommodations and accessibility.

B.3   Responsibilities to Self

- B.3.m. Respect the intellectual property of others and adhere to copyright laws and correctly cite others' work when using it.

Resources

For Further Reading

Cline, F. and Fay, J. (2006). *Parenting with love and logic: teaching children responsibility.* Colorado Springs, CO: Piñon Press.

Dinkmeyer, D., McKay, G., & Dinkmeyer, D. (2008). *Systematic training for effective parenting.* Fredericksburg, VA: STEP Publishers.

Hatch, T., Duarte, D., & De Gregorio, L. K. (2018). *Hatching results for elementary school counseling: Implementing core curriculum and other tier one activities.* Thousand Oaks, CA: Corwin Press.

Hatch, T., Triplett, W., Duarte, D., & Gomez, V. (2019). *Hatching results for secondary school counseling: Implementing core curriculum, individualized student planning, and other tier one activities.* Thousand Oaks, CA: Corwin Press.

Websites

Links to the following can be found on our eresource at www.routledge.com/9781138501614.

- Active Parenting.
- *Collaborative for Academic, Social, and Emotional Learning* (CASEL) program guides.
- ASCA Lesson Plan Template.
- ASCA Mindsets and Behavior Program Planning Tool.
- Center for School Counseling Outcome Research and Evaluation (CSCORE): Survey for program evaluation and review.
- Common Sense Education.
- Common Sense Education. *Digital Citizenship curriculum.*
- Mix It Up at Lunch.

- PBIS.
- SCOPE.
- What Works Clearinghouse.

Teaching Activity

Directions: Divide students into dyads or triads. Give each dyad or triad a set of two to four sample school counseling lesson plans (e.g., those in the ASCA Resource Center or the ASCA Scene). Ask students to work together to critique the lesson plans and to identify strengths and areas for improvement. Use the following questions to guide students' work and then share general findings and themes as a whole class:

1 How well written are the learning objectives? Is the purpose of the lesson clear to you? If not, how would you revise the objectives? What data might have been used to determine the need for the lesson?
2 How well does this lesson address diverse learners? Is there evidence of multicultural considerations and differentiation? If not, how would you modify the lesson?
3 What delivery methods are being used? How does it engage the students? Would you do anything differently if delivering the lesson?
4 What challenges with classroom management might you anticipate in delivering this lesson? How would you plan for and address such challenges?
5 Is there an evaluation component to the lesson? Does it clearly tie back to the learning objectives? How would you add or modify the evaluation component to better assess the effectiveness of the lesson?
6 Does the lesson appropriately cite sources and/or give attribution? Would you be able to find the original materials used in the lesson based on its references? How would you edit the lesson to clarify any copyright or authorship?

Multiple Choice Questions

1 **In what ways can school counselors ensure their Tier 1 supports (e.g., core curriculum) are culturally relevant for their students?**

    a Incorporate images representative of student demographics into class presentation material.
    b Utilize diverse and multicultural books within lessons.
    c Model the use of gender non-specific pronouns when teaching.
    d All of the above.

2 **Universal screening is an example of which type of data?**

    a Process data.
    b Perception data.
    c Outcome data.
    d None of the above.

3 **All but which of the following are considered typical formats for delivering Tier 1 activities:**

    a Schoolwide.
    b Large group.

c   Small group.
d   Classroom.

4   **Starting the first school counseling lesson by joining with students in developing a set of rules or guidelines for future lessons is which of the following classroom management strategies:**

a   Giving behavior-specific praise.
b   Attending to the physical layout of the room.
c   Acting consistently.
d   Proactively creating and teaching students expectations.

5   **The ASCA Ethical Standards (2016) specifically includes an item related to the need for school counselors to observe copyright laws.**

a   True.
b   False.

Answers: Q1 d, Q2 c, Q3 c, Q4 d, Q5 a.

References

Adamson, R. A., McKenna, J., & Mitchell, B. S. (2016, April). Kicking it up a notch: Spicing up classroom level behavior supports, bam! Presentation at the 94th Annual Council for Exceptional Children Convention, St. Louis, Missouri.

Akos, P., Cockman, C., & Strickland, C. (2007). Differentiating classroom guidance. *Professional School Counseling, 10*(5), 455–463, doi.org/10.5330/prsc.10.5.yj92524400355127.

American School Counselor Association (ASCA) (2012). *The ASCA National Model: A framework for school counseling programs* (3rd Ed.). Alexandria, VA: Author.

American School Counselor Association (ASCA) (2014). *ASCA Mindsets & Behaviors for Student Success: K-12 college- and career-readiness standards for every student.* Alexandria, VA: Author. Retrieved from: www.schoolcounselor.org/asca/media/asca/home/MindsetsBehaviors.pdf.

American School Counselor Association (ASCA) (2016). *ASCA ethical standards for school counselors.* Retrieved from: www.schoolcounselor.org/asca/media/asca/Ethics/EthicalStandards 2016.pdf.

American School Counselor Association (ASCA) (2018). *The school counselor and multitiered systems of support. American School Counselor Association Position Statement.* Retrieved from: www.schoolcounselor.org/asca/media/asca/PositionStatements/PS_MultitieredSupportSystem.pdf.

American School Counselor Association (ASCA) (n.d.). *The role of the school counselor.* Retrieved from: www.schoolcounselor.org/asca/media/asca/home/RoleStatement.pdf.

Belser, C. T., Shillingford, M. A., & Joe, J. R. (2016). The ASCA Model and a multi-tiered system of supports: A framework to support students of color with problem behavior. *The Professional Counselor, 6*(3), 251–262, doi:10.15241/cb.6.3.251.

Bergmann, J. and Sams, A. (2012). *Flip your classroom: Reach every student in every class every day.* International Society for Technology in Education. Available at: www.iste.org/resources/product?ID=2285 (Accessed: 5 October 2017).

Betters-Bubon, J., & Donohue, P. (2016). Professional capacity building for school counselors through school-wide positive behavior interventions and supports implementation. *Journal of School Counseling, 14*(3), 1–35.

Brigman, G., Webb, L., Mullis, F., & White, J. (2005). *School counselor consultation: Developing skills for working effectively with parents, teachers, and other school personnel.* Hoboken, NJ: J. Wiley & Sons.

Cholewa, B., Goodman-Scott, E., Thomas, A., & Cook, J. (2017). Teachers' perceptions and experiences consulting with school counselors: A qualitative study (featured research). *Professional School Counseling, 20*(1), 77–88, doi:10.5330/1096-2409-20.1.77.

Ciszek, M. C. (2017). Copyright, fair use, and free use for US K-12 educators: A legal perspective. *The Clearing House: A Journal of Educational Strategies, Issues and Ideas, 90*(5–6), 214–217, doi: 10.1080/00098655.2017.1366791.

Dimmitt, C., Carey, J. C., & Hatch, T. (2007). *Evidence-based school counseling: Making a difference with data-driven practices.* Thousand Oaks, CA: Corwin Press.

Donohue, P., Goodman-Scott, E., & Betters-Bubon, J. (2016). Using universal screening for early identification of students at risk: A case example from the field. *Professional School Counseling, 19*(1), 133–143, doi.org/10.5330/1096-2409-19.1.133.

Erickson, A., & Abel, N. (2013). A high school counselor's leadership in providing school-wide screenings for depression and enhancing suicide awareness. *Professional School Counseling, 16*(5), 283–289.

Freedman, M. P. (2004). A tale of plagiarism and a new paradigm. *Phi Delta Kappan, 85*(7), 545–548, doi.org/10.1177/003172170408500714.

Goodman-Scott, E. (in press, anticipated 2019). Trends in school counseling classroom management strategies: Results from a qualitative study. *Professional School Counseling.*

Goodman-Scott, E., Betters-Bubon, J., & Donohue, P. (2016). Aligning Comprehensive School Counseling Programs and Positive Behavioral Interventions and Supports to maximize school counselors' efforts. *Professional School Counseling, 19*(1), 57–67, doi.org/10.5330/1096-2409-19.1.57.

Goodman-Scott, E., Doyle, B., & Brott, P. (2014). An action research project to determine the utility of bully prevention in positive behavior support for elementary school bullying prevention. *Professional School Counseling, 17*(1), 120–129.

Goodman-Scott, E., & Grothaus, T. (2017). RAMP and PBIS: "They definitely support one another." A phenomenological study. *Professional School Counseling, 21*(1), 119–129, doi:10.5330/1096-2409-21.1.119.

Goodman-Scott, E., Hays, D. G., & Cholewa, B. (2018). "It takes a village:" A case study of Positive Behavioral Interventions and Supports implementation in an exemplary middle school. *The Urban Review, 50*(1), 97–122, doi:10.1007/s11256-017-0431-z.

Hatch, T., Duarte, D., & De Gregorio, L. K. (2018). *Hatching results for elementary school counseling: Implementing core curriculum and other tier one activities.* Thousand Oaks, CA: Corwin Press.

Konen, J. (2018). 6 questions to tackle when demonstrating flexibility and responsiveness in the classroom. *Teacher.org.* Retrieved from: www.teacher.org/daily/demonstrating-flexibility-responsiveness-classroom.

Lopez, C. J., & Mason, E. C. M. (2018). School counselors as curricular leaders: A content analysis of ASCA lesson plans. *Professional School Counseling, 21*(1b), 1–12, doi:10.1177/2156759x18773277.

Mason, E. C. M. (2010). Leveraging classroom time. *ASCA School Counselor,* July/August, pp. 27–29.

Mason, E. C. M., Griffith, C., & Belser, C. (2017). *School counselors' use of technology for program management.* Presented at the Association for Counselor Educators and Supervisors, October, Chicago, IL.

McDonald, E. (n.d.). Freedoms and responsibilities. *Education World.* Retrieved from: www.educationworld.com/a_curr/columnists/mcdonald/mcdonald029.shtml

McMahon, H. G., Mason, E. M., Daluga-Guenther, N., & Ruiz, A. (2014). An ecological model of professional school counseling. *Journal of Counseling & Development, 92*(4), 459–471, doi:10.1002/j.1556-6676.2014.00172.x.

Mitchell, B. S., Hirn, R. G., & Lewis, T. J. (2017). Enhancing effective classroom management in schools: Structures for changing teacher behavior. *Teacher Education and Special Education, 40*(2), 140–153, doi.org/10.1177/0888406417700961.

Ockerman, M. S., Mason, E. C. M., & Hollenbeck, A. F. (2012). Integrating RTI with school counseling programs: Being a proactive professional school counselor. *Journal of School Counseling, 10*(15), 1–37.

Reeves, D. B. (2012). *Transforming professional development into student results.* Association for Supervision and Curriculum Development: Alexandria, VA.

Schellenberg, R.C. (2007). *Standards blending: Aligning school counseling programs with school academic achievement missions.* Faculty Publications and Presentations, 155. Retrieved from: http://digital commons.liberty.edu/educ_fac_pubs/155.

Simonsen, B., Freeman, J., Goodman, S., Mitchell, B., Swain-Bradway, J., Flannery, B., . . . Putnam, B. (2015). *Supporting and responding to behavior: Evidence-based classroom strategies for teachers.* Office of Special Education Programs. Retrieved from: www2.ed.gov/policy/gen/guid/school-discipline/index.html.

Smith, D. F. (2009). *A study of school counselor effectiveness and its relation to prior teaching experience and school achievement.* Orangeburg, SC: South Carolina State University, UMI Number: 3421345 All.

Splett, J. W., Trainor, K. M., Raborn, A., Halliday-Boykins, C. A., Garzona, M. E., Dongo, M. D., & Weist, M. D. (2018). Comparison of universal mental health screening to students already receiving intervention in a Multitiered System of Support. *Behavioral Disorders, 43*(3), 344–356, doi:10.1177/0198742918761339.

Young, A., & Kaffenberger, C. (2013). Making DATA work: A process for conducting action research. *Journal of School Counseling, 11*(2). Retrieved from: http://jsc.montana.edu/articles/v11n2.pdf.

Zainuddin, Z., & Halili, S. H. (2016). Flipped classroom research and trends from different fields of study. *International Review of Research in Open and Distance Learning, 17*(3), doi:10.19173/irrodl.v17i3.2274.

Ziomek-Daigle, J. (2015). *School counseling classroom guidance: prevention, accountability, and outcomes.* Thousand Oaks, CA: Sage Publications.

Ziomek-Daigle, J., Goodman-Scott, E., Cavin, J., & Donohue, P. (2016). Integrating a Multi-Tiered System of Supports with Comprehensive School Counseling Programs. *Professional Counselor, 6*(3), 220–232, doi:10.15241/jzd.6.3.220.

Zyromski, B., & Mariani, M. A. (2016). *Facilitating evidence-based, data-driven school counseling: A manual for practice.* Thousand Oaks, CA: Corwin Press.

5 Tier 2

Providing Supports for Students with Elevated Needs

Jacob Olsen

Introduction

Providing all students with effective core academic instruction and establishing a positive school-wide social culture at Tier 1 are essential to creating a strong foundation for MTSS implementation. However, some students will need additional academic or behavioral support beyond the school-wide supports characteristic of Tier 1. In response to student needs for Tier 2 supports, the immediate questions from school counselors and others involved in supporting students are often, "How do I identify students who need academic or behavioral supports beyond what is already provided at Tier 1?" and "How do I provide those supports?" Increasingly, school counselors I talk to about MTSS are also asking, "What is my role in MTSS?" This chapter seeks to answer these questions.

I have two primary goals for this chapter. First, to highlight the core concepts and practical tools school counselors and key stakeholders need to develop and implement Tier 2 supports in the context of a MTSS framework. To accomplish this goal, I will introduce core concepts and defining features of Tier 2, Tier 2 team functions and roles, strategies to identify students in need of Tier 2 supports, and the process of selecting and implementing Tier 2-specific evidence-based practices. Second, I will also explore strategies to align Comprehensive School Counseling Programs (CSCPs) school counseling with Tier 2 implementation, including cultural implications and ethical considerations. I provide examples and reflection questions to further connect concepts introduced in this chapter to the day-to-day practices of school counselors and key stakeholders.

Core Concepts and Defining Features of Tier 2

The MTSS framework includes a continuum of prevention and intervention practices which can be systematically designed, implemented, monitored and refined. In schools implementing MTSS effectively, 80% or more of students respond to Tier 1 preventative supports (Gerzel-Short & Wilkins, 2009; Ross, Romer, & Horner, 2012). Tier 2 systems and practices are then developed and implemented for the 10–15% of students who need additional intervention while they continue to participate in Tier 1 supports (Horner, Sugai, & Anderson, 2010). For Tier 2 systems and practices to be effective, a Tier 2 team is designated to coordinate a process that includes (a) identifying students in need of Tier 2 supports, (b) aligning interventions to meet student needs, and (c) making data-based decisions once interventions are in place. Given its significance, I will highlight fundamental Tier 2 team functions and roles. Next, I will describe the process involved in Tier 2 implementation.

As you read the following section, think about how your knowledge and skills as a school counselor align with the Tier 2 team functions and roles. Make note of how your training and focus on leadership, collaboration, advocacy, and systemic change can contribute to and enhance the effectiveness of Tier 2 team processes, practices, and out-comes. To add to this, I will also point out some ways school counselors have effectively aligned their CSCP and their school counseling role with Tier 2 teams.

Tier 2 Team Function and Roles

The Tier 2 team focuses on identifying students in need of Tier 2 supports, determin-ing appropriate Tier 2 interventions based on students' needs, and making data-based decisions. Teams meet on a regular basis (i.e., weekly or bi-weekly) to monitor student progress and make data-based decisions about interventions. Tier 2 teams meet more frequently than a Tier 1 or school-wide team to closely monitor student interventions, review data, and make intervention adjustments if needed. Within effective MTSS, as students' needs for academic or behavioral supports increase, the frequency with which student progress is monitored increases to ensure that students receive interventions to meet their needs in a timely manner.

The composition of a Tier 2 team depends on the local context of the school and the availability of school staff with experience and training needed to develop, monitor, or implement Tier 2 interventions. However, fulfilling critical roles and including key personnel on the Tier 2 team, including the school counselor, is essential (Algozzine et al., 2014; Hawken et al., 2015). First, it is important for an administrator to be a part of the Tier 2 team because administrators are involved in making school-wide decisions, often determine the focus of staff professional development and meetings, and can allo-cate resources needed to coordinate and implement Tier 2 interventions. Second, an intervention coordinator is identified. This person ensures the decision-making process is followed, staff are trained to implement interventions, intervention data is collected, and the necessary resources for intervention implementation are available (Anderson & Borgmeier, 2010). In addition, the coordinator provides technical assistance and prob-lem solving to staff involved in intervention implementation, and may meet with students, caretakers, and school staff at various points in the intervention process, particularly when a student begins the intervention (Scott & Martinek, 2006).

Beyond the administrator and intervention coordinator, Tier 2 teams should also include school staff with expertise, training, and experience with academic and behavior assessment and intervention such as school psychologists, school social workers, literacy specialists, numeracy specialists, behavioral specialists, and administrators. This expertise is particularly critical when interpreting academic and behavioral data, and determining evidence-based interventions best suited for students' needs. Key staff from general edu-cation and special education should be represented (Anderson & Borgmeier, 2010) as they bring unique as well as complimentary knowledge and skills about student learning and behavior to the team process.

Tier 2 team membership should reflect the diversity of perspectives and experiences of the school community to ensure the Tier 2 process is culturally responsive (Garbacz et al., 2016). There are two additional ways to increase the cultural responsiveness of the Tier 2 team and the process the team coordinates. First, an advisory group separate from the Tier 2 team and comprised of representative students, parents/caregivers, and com-munity members can be formed to discuss and reflect on the cultural responsiveness of the Tier 2 interventions in which students participate (Leverson, Smith, McIntosh, Rose, & Pinkelman, 2016). Second, Tier 2 teams should involve parents/caregivers of students participating in Tier 2 interventions in the decision-making process regarding appro-priate interventions, implementation strategies, and school–home communication. This is particularly important for families from cultures that consider family involvement in all aspects of school-based services to be critical (Goforth, Nichols, Stanick, Shindorf, & Holter, 2017). Given our rapport with students and parents/guardians and our connections with community stakeholders, school counselors can be instrumental in developing a Tier 2 advisory group and ensuring parent/caregivers' voices are heard throughout the Tier 2 process.

Tier 2 teams generally consist of six or fewer individuals to keep the team process efficient (Anderson & Borgmeier, 2010). For example, at my former elementary school, the Tier 2 team consisted of an assistant principal (administrator), school counselor (intervention coordinator), special education teacher (who had expertise in academic instruction and student behavior), an academic and behavior interventionist (who had expertise in academic instruction and student behavior), and a paraeducator who implemented the Check-in/Check-out intervention. At the high school level, our team consisted of an administrator representative (i.e., principal or dean of students), school counselor representative, school psychologist, graduation coach (intervention coordinator), and the special education teacher (who has expertise in academic instruction and student behavior). These examples highlight how Tier 2 teams may vary slightly depending on the local school context and available personnel.

Tier 2 Meetings

To conduct effective and efficient Tier 2 team meetings, specific functions must be carried out before, during, and after meetings. Prior to Tier 2 team meetings, an agenda is established to increase the efficiency and focus of the meeting time. Agenda items are based on previous meeting action items, new staff requests for assistance, and other issues brought to the attention of the intervention coordinator. A Tier 2 team member with access and proficient technical skills is assigned to preparing intervention data and other relevant information to be shared during the meeting. This role is important given the Tier 2 team's focus on making data-based decisions about student interventions. During meetings, a facilitator ensures the agenda is followed, student data is reviewed, and the decision-making process is used to modify, continue, or transition out of interventions. While the facilitator ensures the agenda is followed and everyone in the meeting has a proportionate time to contribute to the meeting, a note taker records information on the Tier 2 meeting template that displays the agenda, action items assigned to team members and school staff, and any additional notes. Following the meeting, action items and those responsible for carrying out tasks need to be notified and meeting notes shared with appropriate school staff. As action items are completed, the meeting template is updated.

The Role of the School Counselor on Tier 2 Teams

The Tier 2 meeting functions and roles summarized in the previous section are guidelines. Many of these functions and roles can be shared or distributed based on personnel and what works for the local context. The intervention coordinator role is particularly well suited for school counselors in that many of the necessary skills and responsibilities are already incorporated into our training and role (ASCA, 2011; Goodman-Scott, 2014). The intervention coordinator role gives school counselors the opportunity for leadership, advocacy, for fostering effective collaboration among staff, and for increasing our capacity to serve all students (Barrett, Eber, & Weist, 2013; Betters-Bubon & Donohue, 2016; Cressey et al., 2015; Curtis et al., 2010; Ockerman, Mason, & Hollenbeck, 2012; Ryan, Kaffenberger, & Carroll, 2011; Sink & Ockerman, 2016; Sugai & Horner, 2006). In fact, this role extends the reach of what we as school counselors are typically asked to do on our own. At the same time, school counselors must recognize potential limitations to being in a coordinator role, especially when the student caseload is high.

From my experience, I think the facilitator and data collection roles align well with the school counselor skillset. For example, in my former elementary school, I was the Tier 2 meeting facilitator. As a meeting facilitator, I used my leadership and collaboration skills to keep the meeting on track and make sure data was used to make decisions. I also used my group counseling skills to connect team members' ideas and make sure all voices were heard. At the high school level, the team already had a strong facilitator in place, however I fulfilled the role of gathering, organizing, and presenting intervention data during the team meeting. This role was also beneficial because it provided me with an opportunity to use my data skills and show others on the team that school counselors use data to identify student needs, track student progress, and document outcomes. Whether in the role of coordinator or team member, school counselors contribute to creating sustainable and school-wide systems and practices that are available for all students, rather than developing interventions, collecting data, and collaborating with school staff in a silo.

At the beginning of this section you were asked to think about how your knowledge and skills as a school counselor align with the Tier 2 team functions and roles. As you may have noticed, our training and focus on leadership, collaboration, advocacy, and systemic change can contribute to and enhance the effectiveness of Tier 2 team processes, practices, and outcomes. Using the questions below, take some time to reflect on the various Tier 2 team roles and determine how you might align your role as a school counselor with a Tier 2 team role.

What Tier 2 team role aligns with your knowledge, skills, and training?

What knowledge, skills, and training do you bring to this role?

How will participation in this role enhance school counseling program outcomes? How will it enhance the Tier 2 team and intervention process?

As described in the previous section, the Tier 2 team includes key members of the school staff with expertise, training, and experience with academic and behavior assessment and intervention. Given our knowledge, skills, and role in supporting all students' academic, social/emotional, and career success, school counselors are well positioned to play a key role on the Tier 2 team. Now that we have a strong understanding of the Tier 2 team functions and roles, we can now discuss other core concepts and strategies that are important to the success of Tier 2 implementation. This process includes identifying students in need of Tier 2 supports, determining appropriate Tier 2 interventions based on students' needs, and making data-based decisions.

Tier 2 Process

To support students in need of Tier 2 intervention, a process is embedded into the school-wide MTSS framework. This process, illustrated in Figure 5.1, includes systems for identifying students who are not responding to Tier 1 supports, determining appropriate Tier 2 interventions based on student needs, and making data-based decisions. The key components of this process can be adapted by Tier 2 teams to guide their work and communicate the Tier 2 process to school staff. As part of the Tier 2 team, school counselors can also use their leadership, advocacy, collaboration, and data analysis skills to ensure this process is followed with fidelity and that student success is the primary focus. In addition, systematizing the Tier 2 process allows school staff to quickly and efficiently respond to student needs, ensure evidence-based interventions matched to students' needs are used, and use data-based decision making to determine intervention effectiveness. The components of the Tier 2 process are further described in the sections below.

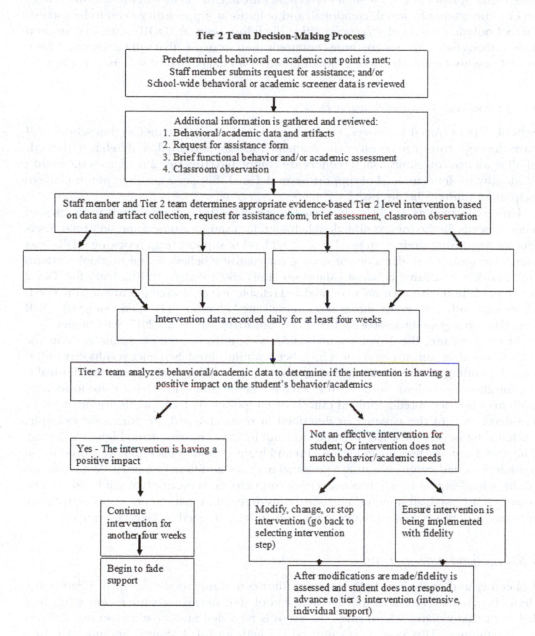

Figure 5.1 Tier 2 decision-making process.

(Source: the Author.)

Identifying Students in Need of Support

Identifying students in need of Tier 2 support is a critical component of effective MTSS and CSCP implementation. We know that when schools implement MTSS effectively, 80% or more of students are expected to respond to the foundational features of Tier 1 MTSS such as the core academic curriculum, school-wide expectations, and the reinforcement system (Gerzel-Short & Wilkins, 2009; Ross, Romer, & Horner, 2012; see Chapters 3 and 4). This means up to 20% of students may need additional support, and a systematic and thorough way to identify these students increases the likelihood that all students in a school receive the academic, social/emotional, and behavioral support they need to be success-ful. School-wide universal screeners, office discipline referral (ODR) data analysis, and staff requests for assistance are three commonly used strategies that will be discussed next, as well as school counselors' corresponding roles with data and data-specific advocacy.

Using School-Wide Universal Screening Data

School-wide universal screeners are given to all students in a school so that school staff have the opportunity to consider the academic, social/emotional, and behavioral needs of all students. After universal screeners are completed, the Tier 2 team uses the results to identify students in need of support beyond Tier 1. Supports are then put in place to help these students be successful.

Universal screeners should be chosen to target specific student populations and a range of student needs. In the context of student behavior, for example, some commonly used strate-gies for identifying students in need of a Tier 2 level of support (e.g., reviewing ODR data) may focus more on students demonstrating externalizing behaviors and overlook students with at-risk internalizing behavior (Marchant et al., 2009; Walker, 2010). Thus, the Tier 2 team could choose from a number of valid and reliable universal screeners to assess the needs of students with both externalizing and internalizing behaviors to be used along with ODR data (Donohue, Goodman-Scott, & Betters-Bubon, 2016; Lane et al., 2017; see Chapter 7).

In terms of use, the Tier 2 team should review universal screener data early in the school year after universal screeners have been administered. Screener results vary in for-mat, depending on the academic, social/emotional, or behavioral screener used. Ideally, organization of student scores on the screener would allow the Tier 2 team to identify students who meet predetermined criteria or cut points. The cut points are provided by the developers of the screener or described in research-based literature. For example, students' names can be listed by grade level and by screener score from highest to lowest. The Tier 2 team reviews the grade level list and highlights students who have scores within a predetermined range indicating a potential need for additional supports. As a facilitator of the school-wide screener process, school counselors can ensure that valid and reliable screeners are used, all students' needs are considered, and that screener results and com-plimentary data are used equitably to identify students in need of Tier 2 supports.

Office Discipline Referrals (ODR)

Collecting and analyzing ODR data is another commonly used strategy to identify stu-dents in need of Tier 2 support. When school staff observe a student engaging in a behavior that violates school rules, the event is recorded and an administrator delivers a consequence. This process is captured through an ODR (Sugai, Sprague, Horner, & Walker, 2000). Research indicates that ODRs are accurate indicators of school-wide behavior climate (Irvin et al., 2004) and using ODR data is a valid and efficient strategy to make decisions about student behavior (Irvin et al., 2006; Pas, Bradshaw, & Mitchell, 2011). With that said, school teams should consider how culture impacts adult interpretation of student behavior, and in turn, how ODRs are distributed. Before focusing on ODR data analysis, school staff need to ensure that acceptable and unacceptable student behaviors are defined for all students and staff. As mentioned elsewhere in this book, students, families, and community members should be included in this process given that acceptable and unacceptable behaviors in the home and community may differ from the school environment (Leverson et al., 2016). For example, students, families, and community stakeholders can be actively sought out to provide input on defining problem behaviors; with the end goal of school staff, students, and families coming to consensus about how to interpret student behavior in a more culturally responsive way. A result of this process is the increased potential for ODRs to be more equitably distributed; an important concept for Tier 2 teams analyzing ODR data to identify students in need of Tier 2 supports.

Tier 2 teams routinely (i.e., weekly or bi-weekly) review ODR data to determine students who may be in need of Tier 2 supports (Bradley, Danielson, & Doolittle, 2007). This data review process is guided by cut points, or established numbers of ODRs, that indicate the level of support a student may need to prevent increased academic decline or increased problem behavior. Students receiving between two and five ODRs are considered at risk or in need of more targeted supports beyond Tier 1 (McIntosh, Campbell, Carter, & Zumbo, 2009b; Sugai et al., 2000). However, relying solely on total ODR counts to determine a student's need for Tier 2 intervention can mean some students are not identified until the middle or end of the school year. At this point, interventions become less effective because students are not accessing the supports they need. Therefore, Tier 2 teams can use an intermediate cut point early in the school year to determine students in need of Tier 2 support. For example, it is recommended that Tier 2 teams identify students with two or more ODRs by the end of October so students receive early intervention and to prevent further academic decline or increased problem behavior later in the school year. These guidelines are based on research showing that two or more ODRs in the fall predicted a high rate (i.e., six or more) of ODRs later in the year (McIntosh, Frank, & Spaulding, 2010; Tobin, Sugai, & Colvin, 1996; Tobin & Sugai, 1999).

In addition to using cut points, Tier 2 teams should regularly disaggregate discipline data by ethnicity, disability status, socioeconomic status, and ELL status to assess and monitor the equity of student outcomes (McIntosh, Barnes, Eliason, & Morris, 2014). Disaggregated data can then be used in decision making related to improving discipline processes and identifying students in need of Tier 2 interventions, as well as informing the planning of culturally responsive interventions. To illustrate the use of ODR data to identify students in need of Tier 2 interventions, an example is provided in Figure 5.2.

Using a Request for Assistance System

A third commonly used strategy for identifying students in need of Tier 2 supports is the implementation of a staff request for assistance system (Anderson & Borgmeier, 2010). The request for assistance system allows a staff member to document a student's problem behavior or academic concern, providing this information about the concern to the Tier 2 team so the student is considered for Tier 2 supports (Sailor, Dunlap, Sugai, & Horner, 2009). The data gleaned from the request for assistance form is used to determine the needs of the student and subsequent Tier 2 intervention. Within this process, the Tier 2 team must confirm that the problem behavior is a result of a skill deficit or individual need

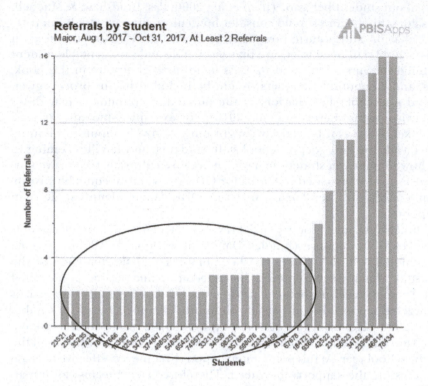

Figure 5.2 ODR data analysis for Tier 2.

At the end of October, the Tier 2 team disaggregates ODR data by individual student. Using the graph above, the Tier 2 team identifies students with 2 to 5 ODRs (circled on graph). ODR data is then compared with universal screener data and teacher referrals for these students. Students identified as needing Tier 2 level interventions are then considered for an appropriate Tier 2 intervention.

From SWIS (www.pbisapps.org). Reprinted with permission from Educational and Community Supports, University of Oregon.

rather than an ineffective Tier 1 intervention (e.g., ineffective classroom management plan, expectations not defined, taught, and reinforced; McIntosh & Goodman, 2016).

Request for assistance forms often include (1) a definition of the problem in specific, observable, and measurable terms; (2) the perceived function of the student's behavior; (3) the time and setting the problem most frequently occurs; (4) academic progress and behavioral data; and (5) interventions that have already been attempted to decrease the problem (Anderson & Borgmeier, 2010; Sailor et al., 2009). An example of how this information is organized on a request for assistance template is illustrated in Figure 5.3. All school staff need to know the process for accessing and completing a request for assistance form, delivering the form to the Tier 2 team, and meeting with the Tier 2 team to determine student needs and appropriate Tier 2 interventions. Tier 2 team members can share this through staff-wide training in which the process is fully described to increase the efficiency for students and staff. The teaching activity at the end of this chapter outlines a process to assess the form used at your school or internship site.

Tier 2 Request for Assistance

Referring Teacher's Name:	Name of Student:
Student Grade:	Date:

Define the area of concern (check all that apply):

	Defiance/Non-Compliance		Attendance
	Physical Aggression		Bullying/Harassment
	Disruption		Plagiarism
	Disrespect		Property Damage
	Inappropriate Language		Student is below grade level in math
	Student is below grade level in reading		Student is below grade level in science
	Student is below grade level in writing		Other

Additional description:_____
_____
_____

Perceived function of student behavior:

	Obtain adult or peer attention		Avoid adult or peer attention
	Obtain access to task or activity		Avoid task or activity

Academic/behavior interventions attempted	Results
1.	1.
2. →	2.
3.	3.

Time and setting where problem most frequently occurs (check all that apply):

Time:	

Setting:	Classroom	Hallway	Common Area	Cafeteria
	Bathroom	Library	Gym	Other

Additional description:_____
_____
_____

Additional comments related to the area of concern_____
_____
_____
_____

Figure 5.3 Tier 2 request for assistance template.

(Source: the Author.)

Taken together, conducting school-wide screeners, reviewing ODR data, and developing and using a request for assistance system are three commonly used, valid, and established strategies to identify students in need of Tier 2 supports. Using these strategies gives school counselors and Tier 2 teams practical approaches for early identification of students who may need support beyond Tier 1 or who may be at risk for further academic or behavioral difficulties. An example from one of my previous schools helps illustrate this process.

The Role of the School Counselor in Identification of Tier 2 Supports

Using data to determine student need in the ways described in the preceding sections aligns with our work as school counselors as described in the ASCA Ethical Standards (2016), the ASCA National Model (2012), and multiple ASCA position statements focused on prevention, intervention, and MTSS implementation (ASCA, 2011; ASCA, 2018). School counselors use data and assessment tools to plan, implement, and evaluate their school counseling programs. In addition, school counselors disaggregate data (e.g., by gender, race, course enrollment) to determine if particular groups of students are underperforming academically or receiving disproportionate amounts of ODRs or suspensions (ASCA, 2012). School counselors also conduct needs assessments to guide program implementation and collect process, perception, and outcome data to evaluate the effectiveness of school counseling practices (ASCA, 2012). Once interventions are implemented, the results can be documented and reported out to stakeholders using the ASCA Closing the Gap Results Report (ASCA, 2012). Assessing school counseling program outcomes and analyzing student data allows school counselors to demonstrate accountability, communicate outcomes to school staff, and guide services (Sink, 2009). The training, experience, and mindset school counselors have when it comes to using data to make decisions demonstrates again how school counselors can enhance Tier 2 implementation.

The following example illustrates how Tier 2 teams can use universal screeners, office discipline referral data, staff requests for assistance, and other relevant data in unison when systematically identifying students in need of Tier 2 supports (OSEP, 2015). Using diverse data better informs the Tier 2 team of the nature and intensity of student need and the intervention that will best help the student be successful. In addition, using multiple sources of data to identify students in need of Tier 2 support lessens the limitations inherent in relying on one indicator of student academic or behavioral needs (McIntosh et al., 2010).

Each year, the principal designated one of the October staff meetings for completion of a school-wide universal behavior screener (i.e., Student Risk Screening Scale; Drummond, 1994). This allowed classroom teachers to complete the screeners without interrupting instruction time and allowed staff time to collaborate and more fully understand the screener procedures. To increase efficiency, our office staff preloaded the list of student names onto each screener form. In this case, each teacher completed a screener for the students in his/her homeroom class. Other schools in our district had each teacher complete a screener for the students in a particular period (e.g., 3rd period). Regardless of the strategy, all students should be considered and rated using the selected universal screener.

Within one week after screeners were completed, the Tier 2 team scheduled a meeting to review results. During this meeting, the Tier 2 team collaborated to

develop a spreadsheet to keep track of students who met or exceeded a predetermined cut off score indicating a possible need for Tier 2 supports. Our team
analyzed the screener results and compiled a master list of students who might need
Tier 2 supports. We compared this with a list of students who received two or more
ODRs at that point in the school year and to the students listed on a request for assistance form. Students who appeared on one of these lists were added to the Tier 2
spreadsheet. In the end, the Tier 2 team had a list of students who may be at risk
of further academic decline or increased problem behavior and in need of Tier 2
supports. As a school counselor, I used this list in collaboration with the Tier 2 team
to form my Tier 2 targeted small-group interventions.

As you can see from the example above, using data to determine student need
within the Tier 2 process is a form of advocacy. Data is used to advocate for student
groups who are underserved or in need of additional supports (Boneshefski & Runge,
2014). As school counselors, we use the direct and indirect student services components of the ASCA National Model (2012) to ensure all students receive the academic,
personal, social, and career supports they need to succeed in school and to access
postsecondary opportunities.

Identifying students in need of support using a variety of data is an important first
step in the Tier 2 process and school counselors play an important role in this process.
However, deciding what to do with this information is often most challenging for school
teams. The next section describes a systematic process for aligning evidence-based
interventions with students' needs so that students have the best chance of benefitting
from intervention.

Aligning Interventions with Students' Needs

Once students in need of Tier 2 support are identified, the Tier 2 team coordinates a
process to determine the function of student behavior and the evidence-based interventions that are most likely to lead to behavior change. This process includes two
key components. First, examining the function of students' behavior allows the Tier 2
team to more effectively align interventions with student needs. Second, identifying
evidence-based intervention strategies, and resources and personnel to implement these
strategies, ensures that students receive effective and timely interventions. School counselors can use their knowledge of student behavior and social environments to ensure
that the Tier 2 team is accurately identifying the function of student behavior and consistently aligning interventions to the function of behavior.

Brief Functional Behavioral Assessment (FBA)

In the context of Tier 2 interventions, Tier 2 teams use efficient strategies to develop a
basic understanding of the function of students' behavior. In general, comprehensive
functional behavioral assessments (FBAs) are typically reserved for students in need of
Tier 3 interventions as they thoroughly define behavior in observable and measurable
terms, predict the behavior, and develop interventions that address the particular function of behavior (March & Horner, 2002; Scott, Alter, Rosenberg, & Borgmeier, 2010).
Comprehensive FBAs can be too time consuming to conduct for all students needing
Tier 2 interventions. Instead, there are brief functional assessment strategies that can be
used within the Tier 2 process to align interventions to students' needs.

Table 5.1 Functions of student behavior

Obtain/Access	Escape/Avoid
Peer or adult attention	Social interaction or attention
Preferred activity	Task or activity
Object, tangible material	Object, tangible material

At the very least, it is useful for Tier 2 teams to think about student behavior in terms of the function or purpose of the behavior. Generally, the function of students' behavior is to obtain or access something, or to escape or avoid something (see Table 5.1; March & Horner, 2002; McIntosh, Brown, & Borgmeier, 2008). When determining the function of a student's behavior, it is useful to ask the questions, "What is the student trying to get, or get away from by demonstrating their behavior?" or, "What is the student getting as a result of their behavior?" Answering these questions and conceptualizing students' behavior using the categories in Table 5.1 increases the likelihood that the Tier 2 team will provide students with an intervention that is designed to address the function of students' behavior.

When Tier 2 teams and school staff attempt to determine the function of students' behavior, information about the frequency of behavior, the setting the behavior takes place in, and the factors that maintain or reinforce the behavior are needed. In these cases, a brief functional behavior assessment, such as the Functional Assessment Checklist: Teachers and Staff (FACTS; March et al., 2000; McIntosh et al., 2008) can be used. The FACTS is a semi-structured interview designed to allow school staff to develop a hypothesis statement describing the function of a student's behavior (March & Horner, 2002) and, depending on how it is utilized, it could be considered brief or more intensive. The FACTS takes approximately 20 minutes to complete depending on the interviewer and interviewee's experience with the measure, knowledge of the interviewee, and complexity of the student behavior (March & Horner, 2002; March et al., 2000). Once completed, the Tier 2 team uses the resulting hypothesis statement to inform the development or selection of an intervention that meets the student's needs and addresses the function of the student's behavior. It is also recommended that a classroom observation is conducted to compliment the FACTS and to further confirm the accuracy of the hypothesis statement describing the function of the student's behavior (Turnbull et al., 2002).

- In Part A of the FACTS, the interviewee (e.g., teacher) identifies the problem behaviors and analyzes the student's daily schedule to determine when the problem behavior occurs (McIntosh et al., 2008).
- In Part B, the interviewee elaborates on the student behavior in an open-ended portion of the FACTS and the problem behavior identified in Part A is operationally defined; the settings and situations in which the problem behaviors are most likely to occur are determined; the events occurring before (i.e., antecedents) and after (i.e., maintaining consequence or function) are identified (Preciado, Horner, & Baker, 2009).

With some basic training, school counselors have been shown to effectively conduct brief functional behavior assessments using the FACTS. In a recent study, Loman and

Horner (2014) found that school counselors could operationally define behavior, identify functions of problem behavior, and conduct technically adequate functional behavior assessments. Equally important, school counselors reported that brief functional assessment using the FACTS was beneficial, practical, and efficient to use in the context of their school (Loman & Horner, 2014). By developing the skills to conduct brief functional behavior assessment, school counselors contribute significant data to the Tier 2 team and grow the capacity of school-based personnel who can conduct brief functional behavior assessment to inform intervention implementation.

Up to this point, I have outlined the first two steps of the Tier 2 team decision-making process (see Figure 5.1), as well as the related role of the school counselor. The next step in the Tier 2 team decision-making process is to implement an evidence-based intervention that is quickly accessible and aligned with the function of the student's behavior. In this step, school counselors may have multiple roles as: (a) interveners, directly implementing Tier 2 interventions; and (b) supporters, working as part of the Tier 2 team to recommend interventions and providers. These roles directly align with what we already do as school counselors to implement our CSCPs through direct and indirect student services. We deliver targeted interventions such as small groups focused on academic, social-emotional, and career success skills, and collaborate and consult to develop systems to organize the interventions (i.e., who is receiving interventions, what's working and what's not).

Identifying Evidence-Based Interventions

A key component of Tier 2 systems and practices is employing evidence-based targeted interventions. Defining features of Tier 2 interventions include (1) explicit instruction of academic or social skills, (2) opportunities to practice these skills, and (3) frequent feedback for students (Anderson & Borgmeier, 2010; Crone, Hawken, & Horner, 2010). These interventions are typically designed to help students develop particular skills (e.g., learning skills, social skills) and replace problem behaviors with more socially acceptable and productive behaviors (Debnam, Pas, & Bradshaw, 2013). In the context of Tier 2, targeted interventions are often provided to groups of students who are not adequately responding to Tier 1 school-wide supports (Hoyle, Marshall, & Yell, 2011).

Evidence-Based Tier 2 Interventions

- Check-in/Check-out
- Social Academic Intervention Groups
- Coping Power
- Peer Tutoring
- Student Success Skills Small Groups
- Summer Melt Transition to College Interventions

All interventions should be aligned with Tier 1 school-wide interventions (e.g., school-wide expectations, core academic curriculum) while having the flexibility to address a variety of student needs. Because of the increased intensity of Tier 2 interventions, parents/caregivers and multiple school staff, including one or more of the student's teachers, school counselors, support staff, and academic interventionists, are typically involved. Whether the intervention is provided by the school counselor or another staff member, it is important for students who are not responding to Tier 1 school-wide supports to have quick access to Tier 2 interventions (i.e., within one week) and their progress monitored throughout the duration of the intervention (Crone, Hawken, & Horner, 2010; Yong & Cheney, 2013).

In the context of both school counseling and MTSS, evidence-based practices are the cornerstone of effective academic, social/emotional, and behavioral supports for all students. With multiple roles, increasingly challenging student needs, and high student ratios, school counselors have little time to waste on implementing practices because "We have always done it this way", or "The kids seem to really like it". In other words, if school counselors and other school staff are going to take the time to plan and implement an intervention, they might as well spend that time doing what is proven to work. To advance our roles as school counselors and demonstrate our value to students' education, we have to be able to show how students are different as a result of what we do. Identifying and implementing evidence-based practices is foundational to making this happen. Luckily for us, there are a growing number of evidence-based interventions that are designed to meet the needs of students not responding to Tier 1 interventions (see Chapter 10 for additional information).

In addition to being evidence-based, the MTSS team, which includes the school counselor, needs to consider the extent to which our interventions are culturally responsive. A few guidelines can help in the selection and implemention of culturally responsive evidence-based interventions. First, the team must review the research to determine if the students that participated in the interventions match your targeted student population (Bal, 2015). Second, the team should choose Tier 2 interventions that are designed to focus specifically on cultural issues that impact students' academic success, social/emotional well-being, or career readiness (Bal & Perzigian, 2013). For example, after analyzing disaggregated data, school counselors have implemented small-group interventions to support diverse students with accessing advanced placement courses (Ohrt, Lambie, & Ieva, 2009); increasing GPAs (Wyatt, 2009); developing ethnic identity (Malott, Paone, Humphreys, & Martinez, 2010); enhancing emotional and psychological wellness (White & Dixon-Rayle, 2007); increasing academic and school counseling curriculum competencies (Schellenberg & Grothaus, 2011); and improving self-esteem (Shi & Steen, 2012). Finally, school counselors and other interveners can integrate culturally responsive practices, making instruction reflect the experiences of diverse learners, including students' language and communication style, and involving family input into Tier 2 interventions (Cartledge & Kourea, 2008; Grothaus, 2013; Uehara, 2005). A few of the most widely researched, commonly used, and relevant Tier 2 interventions for school counselors are described in the following section.

CHECK-IN/CHECK-OUT

Check-in/Check-out (CICO) is a widely used Tier 2 intervention in schools implementing MTSS, primarily because of the efficiency and effectiveness of the intervention (Bruhn, Lane, & Hirsch, 2014; Cheney et al., 2009; Maggin, Zurheide, Pickett, & Baillie, 2015). The CICO intervention has been effectively used to reduce students' problem behaviors (Cheney et al., 2009; Filter et al., 2007; Todd, Campbell, Meyer, & Horner, 2008); improve social skills (Cheney et al., 2010; Hunter, Chenier, & Gresham, 2014; McIntosh, Campbell, Carter, & Dickey, 2009a); teach students goal behaviors (Hawken et al., 2015; Lane, Capizzi, Fisher, & Ennis, 2012; Miller, Dufrene, Joe, Tingstrom, & Filce, 2015a);

increase academic engagement (Campbell, Rodriguez, Anderson, & Barnes, 2013; Miller, Dufrene, Sterling, Olmi, & Bachmayer, 2015b); and improve academic skills (Simonsen, Myers, & Briere, 2011; Turtura, Anderson, & Boyd, 2014).

Students participating in the CICO intervention set specific goals addressing problem behaviors in collaboration with school staff, and these goals are written on a daily progress report (DPR; see Figure 5.4; Stage, Cheney, Lynass, Mielenz, & Flower, 2012). Students meet with a designated school staff member (e.g., CICO coach, school counselor, paraprofessional) at the beginning of the school day to review and rehearse goal behaviors. Students receive verbal feedback from classroom teachers and school staff throughout the day, and feedback is reflected by point totals on the student's DPR. To increase the likelihood of student success with the intervention, verbal feedback and DPR comments should be specific, aligned with the goal behaviors, and focused on what the student is doing well and areas in need of improvement for the following class (Smith, Evans-McCleon, Urbanski, & Justice, 2015). In addition, the point values (e.g., 1 = did not demonstrate goal behavior and needed multiple reminders, 4 = demonstrated goal behavior without reminders) used to reflect student behavior should be clearly defined and described on the DPR. This increases clarity for staff who provide students with DPR scores and for students who interpret DPR scores to gauge progress. At the end of the school day, students check out with the same designated school staff member they checked in with at the beginning of the day (e.g., CICO coach, school counselor, paraprofessional) by reviewing their DPR and reflecting on behavioral progress and areas in need of improvement. Students then discuss their daily progress with parents or caretakers at home.

Daily Progress Report

Name:		Date:		Incentive:	
Goal Behavior(s):					
Goal Points:					
Points Received/Points Possible:	/				
Period	Rating	Comments			Teacher initials
Subject: Teacher:	4 3 2 1				
Subject: Teacher:	4 3 2 1				
Subject: Teacher:	4 3 2 1				
Subject: Teacher:	4 3 2 1				
Subject: Teacher:	4 3 2 1				
Subject: Teacher:	4 3 2 1				

Guide for ratings:

4	3	2	1

Figure 5.4 Daily progress report.

(Source: the Author.)

Check-in/Check-out Procedures

1 Student checks in with designated adult before school day, goals are reviewed.
2 Student receives feedback from teachers throughout day using daily progress report (DPR).
3 Student checks out with designated adult at end of school day, and performance and DPR are reviewed.
4 Student takes DPR home to review with parent/caregivers and returns signed DPR to school.

Research has documented the experiences of school counselors coordinating and directly implementing CICO effectively, resulting in decreased problem behavior and increased academic engagement for students participating in the intervention (Campbell, Rodriguez, Anderson, & Barnes, 2013; Goodman-Scott, 2014; Martens & Andreen, 2013; Smith, Evans-McCleon, Urbanski, & Justice, 2015). Thus, it makes sense for school counselors to incorporate coordination or implementation of CICO into their school counseling role (Goodman-Scott, Betters-Bubon, & Donohue, 2016; Ziomek-Daigle, Goodman-Scott, Cavin, & Donohue, 2016).

As a coordinator, school counselors may assist with training school staff and facilitating Tier 2 meetings focused on reviewing data for students in the CICO intervention. In addition, coordination may include simply ensuring that the CICO implementation process runs smoothly (e.g., evaluate fidelity of implementation, ensure necessary materials are available, problem solve logistical issues). When directly implementing CICO with a small number of students, school counselors meet with students to review and rehearse goal behaviors. This role may also include collecting DPR data and organizing data to present at Tier 2 meetings. To learn more about CICO, see the Resources section at the end of the chapter.

SMALL-GROUP INTERVENTIONS

When a student is struggling in reading or math, often that student needs to further develop their skills in the context of a more targeted approach. This may mean the classroom teacher modifies instruction, or support staff provide a targeted small-group intervention to address a specific deficit or give the student supported opportunities to practice skills needed for mastery. The same approach can be used to support students with social and academic Tier 2 needs. School counselors can use their skills in data analysis, group counseling, and collaboration to develop, implement, and monitor targeted small-group interventions for students (Gruman & Hoelzen, 2011). These interventions fall under the direct services component of a CSCP such as the ASCA National Model, and align nicely with core features of Tier 2 MTSS interventions (Campbell et al., 2013; Martens & Andreen, 2013; Ryan, Kaffenberger, & Carroll, 2011; Sherrod, Getch, & Ziomek-Daigle, 2009; Smith et al., 2015). Two examples of small-group interventions are Social Academic Intervention Groups (SAIG) and psychoeducational groups which are designed to teach students social and/or academic skills.

Both SAIG and psychoeducational group frameworks include identifying student needs by collecting data, forming the group, facilitating the group, and measuring outcomes by collecting data aligned with group goals. Psychoeducational or content-focused groups, typically delivered by student services members (e.g., school counselors, school psychologists, and school social workers), are grounded in supporting students to develop skills or gaining support in certain areas (e.g., changing families, healthy relationships, anxiety/stress). Conversely, SAIGs are structured and centered around a curriculum designed to teach, practice, and reinforce identified behavioral, social, or academic learning skills (Sink, Edwards, & Eppler, 2012), and can be delivered by others in the building (e.g., educational assistants). Each can be used to assist students within a tiered system of support.

Social Academic Intervention Groups

1   Use data to determine skills students need.
2   Teach, model, and practice skills in context where skills are used.
3   Provide students with specific feedback on use of skills.
4   Use data to determine effectiveness of group.

Milwaukee Public Schools developed a comprehensive SAIG curriculum that includes lesson plans, activities, and handouts for elementary, middle, and high school students (a link to the curriculum can be found in the Resources section). Within this curriculum are many activities and strategies, and the skills taught draw from the evidence-based prosocial skills training program Skillstreaming (McGinnis & Goldstein, 2003; Sheridan, MacDonald, Donlon, McGovern, & Friedman, 2011). Other curricula that have been successfully incorporated into both SAIGs and psychoeducational groups include Second Step (Duarte & Hatch, 2015), Skill-Builders (see Falco, Crethar, & Bauman, 2008), and Student Success Skills (Lemberger & Clemens, 2012; Ohrt, Webster, & De La Garza, 2014).

Recommended group size for Tier 2 small-group interventions is four to six students for elementary students, and eight to 10 students for late elementary, middle, and high school students (Sink, Edwards, & Eppler, 2012). When determining group size, it is important to consider the developmental level of the students, the focus of the group, and the intensity of behavioral or academic needs of the students involved. The length of Tier 2 small-group interventions is another important consideration. The SAIGs curriculum outlined by Milwaukee Public Schools spans across nine weeks, which is in line with school-counselor-led content groups that typically last six to eight weeks.

Research demonstrates that small-group interventions led by school counselors contribute to important student outcomes such as increased organizational, time management, and motivation skills (Berger, 2013); strengthened study behaviors (Kayler & Sherman, 2009); increased GPA (Rose & Steen, 2015; Steen, 2011); improved social skills (Gerrity & DeLucia-Waack, 2007; Mitchell, Stormont, & Gage, 2011); and reduced bullying (McCormac, 2015). To highlight the impact of a Tier 2 small-group intervention focused on social and academic learning skills, we examine a study by Miller, Fenty, Scott, & Park (2011). In the study, staff collected data (i.e., via a behavior checklist and structured observation) to identify students who needed behavioral support during reading instruction. Data revealed that off-task behaviors were the most prominent problem behaviors. Once students in need of support and the function of their behavior were identified, students received direct instruction to teach on-task behaviors (e.g., asking and waiting for help appropriately, completing independent work at desks, cooperative learning with peers) during reading instruction. As a result of the direct instruction, all students who received the intervention showed improvement in on-task behaviors during reading (Miller et al., 2011).

Organizing Interventions

A key to effective Tier 2 support is identifying interventions and developing the capacity and resources to implement those interventions. Establishing structures to organize and evaluate interventions that address a variety of student behaviors is equally important. To be efficient, Tier 2 teams need to be able to quickly assess the function of students' behavior and determine a readily accessible intervention that aligns with the function of the students' problem behavior. Tier 2 teams utilize the Tier 2 team decision-making process illustrated in Figure 5.1 as a template to make this happen. Selected evidence-based interventions can be added to the boxes under the third step of the process. This allows Tier 2 teams following the decision-making process to develop a "menu" of evidence-based interventions that students can easily access. For example, the CICO intervention could be one intervention entered into a box on the template. A second box might have a SAIG entered into the box, and so on. The purpose of this is to establish a structure for organizing evidence-based interventions and embedding the interventions into the Tier 2 decision-making process. The key, however, is to identify interventions that are evidence-based and intended for a small number of students, and to give students access to a variety of interventions depending on the function of their behavior. The Teaching Activity 2, found at the end of this chapter, provides an opportunity to assess the interventions in your school.

Previous sections discussed identifying students in need of support and aligning interventions with student needs. Once the evidence-based interventions are in place, we can't stop there. As we know, it is increasingly important for school counselors to show how students are different as a result of our work. This notion is also true for the Tier 2 process. We have to collect and analyze data to determine if Tier 2 interventions are effective, and make decisions about modifying, continuing, or fading interventions in which students are participating. The next section gives us a road map to making this happen.

Tier 2 Data-Based Decision Making

Data-based decision making is a hallmark of effective Tier 2 intervention implementation (Bruhn, Woods-Groves, Fernando, Taehoon, & Troughton, 2017; Cheney et al., 2010; OSEP, 2015; Yong & Cheney, 2013). The Tier 2 team and the school staff directly involved in implementing the interventions review data and make decisions based on student progress and predetermined criteria. For the CICO intervention, several data-based decision-making guidelines (see Table 5.2) are provided in documents and literature describing the intervention.

For SAIGs, as outlined by Milwaukee Public Schools, it is recommended that student progress is monitored on an ongoing basis and that data be used to determine if the intervention is meeting student needs or needs to be adjusted. For example, elementary students should be monitored daily and middle and high school students at least weekly using a daily or weekly progress report. There are more generalized guidelines for data-based decision making for school-counselor-led content groups, as the length, duration, goals, and outcome measures differ depending on the focus of the skills being taught in the group. However, a review of school-counselor-led small-group interventions reveals that interventions are typically implemented on a weekly basis, for 30 minutes to one hour at a time, and are implemented for anywhere between four and 10 weeks (Bruce, Getch, & Ziomek-Daigle, 2009; Schellenberg & Grothaus, 2011; Sherrod et al., 2009; Shi & Steen, 2012). Please see Chapter 9 for more information on using data within your CSCP and MTSS.

Table 5.2 CICO data-based decision-making guidelines

	Guideline	Source
Baseline Data	Collected three to five days before intervention while parent permission is obtained, etc.	Everett et al., 2011
Begin Implementation	Within one week of identification/referral	Crone, Horner, & Hawken, 2010; Yong & Cheney, 2013
Individual Progress	Data reviewed weekly; daily goal is 75% of possible points for more than 80% of the days in eight-week period	Cheney et al., 2010; Everett et al., 2011; Yong & Cheney, 2013
Group Progress	Data reviewed weekly; approximately 70% of students participating should respond to intervention	Everett et al., 2011
Self-Monitoring	After meeting daily goal of 75% of possible points for more than 80% of the days in eight-week period, students self-monitor until student and teacher reach agreement on at least 10 of 15 days	Cheney et al., 2010

The Role of the School Counselor in Data-Based Decision Making

School counselors already use data and ASCA National Model assessment tools to plan, implement, evaluate, and make decisions about their school counselor programs (ASCA, 2012; Sink, 2009). These same skills can be used to play a critical role in data-based decision making in the context of the Tier 2 process. In one study, a school counselor was a member of Tier 2 team targeting students in need of Tier 2 reading intervention (Ryan et al., 2011). The school counselor collaborated with the Tier 2 team and classroom teachers to review students' academic data, place students in appropriate intervention groups, and monitor progress on grade-level reading performance. Notable outcomes included an increase in the percentage of kindergarten and first grade students reading at grade level and high staff ratings of the school counselor in the areas of collaboration, advocacy, intervention implementation, coordination, and communication skills (Ryan et al., 2011). In another study, a school counselor developed a targeted behavior intervention for students who received three or more discipline referrals during the fall semester of school (Sherrod et al., 2009). The targeted intervention consisted of eight weekly counselor-led small-group lessons. Over the course of the intervention, the students learned problem solving, emotion management, and learning skills (Sherrod et al., 2009). Weekly pre- and posttest data, teacher ratings, and office discipline referral data showed an overall improvement of student behavior and a statistically significant decrease in office discipline referrals received by students participating in the intervention (Sherrod et al., 2009).

Data-Based Decision Making and Advocacy

Regardless of intervention, data-based decision-making at Tier 2 should focus on equity and advocacy. At Tier 2, data can be used to advocate for student groups who are underserved or in need of additional supports and to advocate for resource allocation to key stakeholders (Boneshefski & Runge, 2014). In order to expand advocacy efforts within the context of Tier 2, school counselors can also use the American Counseling

Association Advocacy Competencies as a framework to implement advocacy strategies with students or on behalf of students (Ratts & Hutchins, 2009). In addition, school counselors can advocate for students in the context of the Multicultural and Social Justice Counseling Competencies Guidelines by using training and professional judgment to determine when to help students develop self-advocacy skills and when to advocate for students among school staff, students' families, and in the community setting (Ratts, Singh, Nassar-McMillan, Butler, & McCullough, 2016). Perhaps most importantly, Tier 2 teams and school counselors should be accountable for student outcomes, regardless of the students' ethnicity, gender, disability, language spoken, socioeconomic status, or circumstance (Leverson et al., 2016). Implementation of Tier 2 interventions is a way for school counselors to advocate for students to get the academic and social/emotional support needed to succeed and provides equitable supports for all students.

Conclusion

It is clear that CSCP aligned with the ASCA National Model (2012) and the MTSS framework are powerful vehicles school counselors can use to support the academic, social/emotional, and career success for all students. Because of our training as school counselors, we are uniquely positioned to play an especially critical leadership role on the Tier 2 team and in the development, implementation, and evaluation of the Tier 2 processes. This process includes:

- identifying students in need of support,
- aligning interventions with students' needs, and
- utilizing data-based decision making.

Several practical tools were embedded in this chapter so that school counselors in training and practicing school counselors can conceptualize their role in Tier 2, but, more importantly, take action steps to align the work they are currently doing with the process outlined in this chapter.

The alignment of CSCPs with MTSS has the potential to address issues of equity and to contribute to closing opportunity and achievement gaps for students (Belser, Shillingford, & Joe, 2016). However, to make CSCPs and MTSS alignment and implementation culturally responsive, intentional efforts need to be made. For example, Betters-Bubon, Brunner, and Kansteiner (2016) provide a case example of how school counselors can contribute to creating and sustaining culturally responsive MTSS practices. As the diversity of our student populations continues to increase, so does the importance of seeking out professional development opportunities to increase our cultural competence and knowledge of culturally responsive Tier 2 interventions (Bain, 2012; Debnam et al., 2012; Warren & Robinson, 2015; for more on culturally responsive MTSS please see Chapter 11). Because of the nature of the Tier 2 process (i.e., interpretation of student behavior, perceptions of student needs, implementation of interventions), it is critical that we continuously reflect on how our cultural lens impacts the processes and practices we put in place for our students. In the end, we need to have the knowledge and skills to respond to all our students' needs.

For more information and a school counselor's perspective on *Tier 2: Providing Supports for Students with Elevated Needs* please see Chapter 12 "Voices from the Field," Voices 1, 3, 6, 9, and 10.

ASCA Ethical Standards

As school counselors work to intervene with students in need of Tier 2 interventions, they must consider how best to support student development utilizing data and evidence-based interventions. In addition, school counselors must consider how best to identify students in need of interventions and monitor progress for groups and individuals who receive Tier 2 supports. This necessarily requires that they pay attention to the responsibilities to students, families, and parents outlined in the ASCA Ethical Standards (2016). Specifically, the following ASCA Ethical Standards are addressed by the content in this chapter:

A Responsibility to Students

A.1 Supporting Student Development

- A.1.e. Are concerned with students' academic, career, and social/emotional needs and encourage each student's maximum development.
- A.1.h. Provide effective, responsive interventions to address student needs.
- A.1.i. Consider the involvement of support networks, wraparound services, and educational teams needed to best serve students.

A.3 Comprehensive Data-Informed Program

- A.3.d. Use data to determine needed interventions, which are then delivered to help close the information, attainment, achievement, and opportunity gaps.

A.7 Group Work

- A.7.a. Facilitate short-term groups to address students' academic, career, and/or social/emotional issues.
- A.7.d. Use data to measure member needs to establish well-defined expectations of group members.
- A.7.g. Facilitate groups from the framework of evidence-based or research-based practices.
- A.7.i. Measure the outcomes of group participation (process, perception, and outcome data).

B Responsibilities to Parents/Guardians, School, and Self

B.2 Responsibilities to the School

- B.2.e. Collaborate with appropriate officials to remove barriers that may impede the effectiveness of the school or the school counseling program.
- B.2.q. Collaborate as needed to provide optimum services with other professionals such as special educators, school nurses, school social workers, school psychologists, college counselors/ admissions officers, physical therapists, occupational therapists, speech pathologists, administrators.

Resources

Websites

Links to the following can be found on our eresource at www.routledge.com/ 9781138501614.

- What Works Clearing House.
- Collaborative for Academic, Social and Emotional Learning.
- Fredrickson Center for School Counseling Outcome Research and Evaluation.
- Positive Behavioral Interventions and Supports Technical Assistance Center-Tier 2.
- Student Success Skills.
- SAIG curriculum.

Further Reading

Everett, S., Sugai, G., Fallon, L., Simonsen, B., & O'Keefe, B. (2011). *School-wide tier II interventions: Check In-Check Out getting started workbook.* Center on Positive Behavioral Interventions and Supports, Center for Behavioral Education and Research, University of Connecticut.

Hatch, T., Kruger, A., & Pablo, N. (2019). *Hatching tier two and three interventions in your elementary school counseling program: Implementing core curriculum and other tier one activities.* Thousand Oaks, CA: Corwin Press.

Teaching Activity 1: Request for Assistance Assessment

Whether or not your school has a request for assistance system, it is important to establish a process that allows teachers to elicit support for a struggling student to get the support they need in a timely manner. First, review the Tier 2 *Request for Assistance* template illustrated in Figure 5.3. Next, review the *Request for Assistance* form your school uses and compare your school's form to the template in Figure 5.3. Based on this comparison, make a note of any improvements you would like to make. Then develop action steps to create, improve, or implement the components of a *Request for Assistance* form based on the areas in need of improvement. Finally, answer the following questions to reflect on your *Request for Assistance* process:

1   Is the *Request for Assistance* process at your school effective and efficient? If so, what makes it work so well? If not, what specific steps can you take to improve the process?

2   Do all staff know how to access the *Request for Assistance* form? Is the form accessible? Do all staff know what to do with the form after completing it? Do all staff know what happens after the form is delivered to the Tier 2 team? If you answered no to any of these questions, what specific steps can you take to improve the process?

Teaching Activity 2: Tier 2 Intervention Organizing Matrix

The purpose of this activity is to take inventory of current interventions within the school. Activity 2 can help Tier 2 teams make decisions to continue using effective evidence-based interventions, and to discontinue or modify interventions that are not impacting students and are instead taking up valuable staff time and resources.

1   First, use Table 5.3 and list all of the current Tier 2 interventions being implemented in your school in the first column. This list can be thought of as an inventory, whereby you write down what you already have. Because the implementation of the MTSS framework is a school-wide approach involving multiple staff and stakeholders, include Tier 2 interventions that are implemented by anyone in the school, including the school counselor.

2   Next, record the number of students that can participate in the intervention at any one time. This helps determine if the intervention is designed for a targeted small group (i.e., Tier 2) instead of a classroom of students (i.e., Tier 1 school-wide) or individual student (i.e., Tier 3); as well as the number of students that can be recommended for the intervention.

3   In the third column, record the person responsible for implementing the intervention. This helps determine personnel capacity, expertise of available staff members, and allows the Tier 2 team to see who is involved in Tier 2 interventions in the school.

4   Next, record the function of behavior that the intervention is intended to address. The idea is to have interventions for each of the major functions of student behavior previously discussed in this chapter. Keep in mind that some interventions may address more than one function of behavior.

5   Finally, indicate if the intervention is evidence-based by checking the "Yes", "No", or "Not sure" box in the final column. The Tier 2 team may need to review relevant literature or websites, or consult with a district administrator or university partner to determine if an intervention is evidence-based. Given that there are a number of readily accessible evidence-based interventions, the idea is that if an intervention is marked "No" or "Not sure", the intervention should not be used until there is evidence that the intervention is effective for students.

Table 5.3 Intervention checklist

Tier 2 Intervention	Capacity (# of students)	Who Implements Intervention?	Function of Behavior	Is Intervention Evidence-Based?
			Obtain/Access Peer Attention	☐ Yes ☐ No ☐ Not sure
			Obtain/Access Adult Attention	☐ Yes ☐ No ☐ Not sure
			Obtain/Access Preferred Activity	☐ Yes ☐ No ☐ Not sure
			Obtain/Access Object, Tangible Material	☐ Yes ☐ No ☐ Not sure
			Escape/Avoid Social Interaction/ Attention	☐ Yes ☐ No ☐ Not sure
			Escape/Avoid Task or activity	☐ Yes ☐ No ☐ Not sure
			Escape/Avoid Tangible Material	☐ Yes ☐ No ☐ Not sure

Used and modified with permission from Olsen, J., 2017 (source: the Author). California State University Long Beach.

Multiple Choice Questions

1   **Based on the key functions of a Tier 2 team, which of the following school personnel should be regularly included on the Tier 2 team?**

    a   Administrator, school counselor, general education teacher, special education teacher, academic interventionist, behavior interventionist.
    b   Meeting facilitator, administrator, school counselor, general education teacher, special education teacher, academic interventionist.
    c   Meeting facilitator, administrator, school counselor, general education teacher, special education teacher, academic interventionist, office manager.
    d   Administrator, school counselor, general education teacher, special education teacher, behavior interventionist.

2   **What three types of data were highlighted in the chapter that can be used to identify students in need of Tier 2 supports?**

    a   Hallway observation data, parent survey data, office discipline referral (ODR) data.
    b   Suspension data, classroom observation data, teacher survey data.
    c   School-wide screener data, office discipline referral (ODR) data, request for assistance data.
    d   School-wide screener data, office discipline referral (ODR) data, functional behavioral assessment (FBA) data.

3   **What strategies can be used to align Tier 2 interventions with students' needs?**

    a   Gut feelings.
    b   Ask what interventions the staff like and use those interventions.
    c   Identify evidence-based interventions.
    d   Brief functional assessment.
    e   c and d.

4   **What are the typical categories for the function of students' behaviors?**

    a   Fight or flight.
    b   Obtain/access or escape/avoid.
    c   Attention and memory.
    d   Knowledge and skill.

5   **Which of the following strategies would increase the cultural responsiveness of the Tier 2 process?**

    a   Involve families in making interventions align with their culture.
    b   Ask a resident living near the school to be on the Tier 2 team.
    c   Disaggregate academic and discipline data by ethnicity.
    d   Review Tier 2 data once a year to determine student outcomes.
    e   a and c.
    f   a and d.

Answers: Q1 a, Q2 c, Q3 e, Q4 b, Q5 e.

References

Algozzine, B., Barrett, S., Eber, L., George, H., Horner, R., Lewis, T., . . . Sugai, G. (2014). *School-wide PBIS Tiered Fidelity Inventory*. OSEP Technical Assistance Center on Positive Behavioral Interventions and Supports, U.S. Department of Education's Office of Special Education Programs (OSEP) and the Office of Elementary and Secondary Education (OESE). Retrieved from: www.pbis.org.

American School Counselor Association (ASCA) (2011). *ASCA position statements: The school counselor and the identification, prevention, and intervention of behaviors that are harmful and place students at-risk.* Alexandria, VA: Author.

American School Counselor Association (ASCA) (2012). The *ASCA National Model: A framework for school counseling programs* (3rd Ed.). Alexandria, VA: Author.

American School Counselor Association (ASCA) (2016). *ASCA ethical standards for school counselors.* Alexandria, VA: Author.

American School Counselor Association (ASCA) (2018). *ASCA position statements: The school counselor and Multi-Tiered Systems of Supports.* Alexandria, VA: Author.

Anderson, C. M., & Borgmeier, C. (2010). Tier II interventions within the framework of school-wide positive behavior support: Essential features for design, implementation, and maintenance. *Behavior Analysis in Practice, 3*(1), 33–45.

Bain, S. F. (2012). School counselors: A review of contemporary issues. *Research in Higher Education Journal, 18.* Retrieved from: https://eric.ed.gov/?id=EJ1064655.

Bal, A. (2015). *Culturally responsive Positive Behavioral Interventions and Supports.* WCER Working Paper No. 2015-9. Retrieved from: https://wcer.wisc.edu/docs/working-papers/Working_Paper_No_2015_09.pdf.

Bal, A., & Perzigian, A. T. (2013). Evidence-based interventions for immigrant students experiencing behavioral and academic problems: A systematic review of the literature. *Education & Treatment of Children, 36*(4), 5–28.

Barrett, S., Eber, L., & Weist, M. (Eds) (2013). *Advancing education effectiveness: Interconnecting school mental health and school-wide positive support.* U.S. Department of Education's Office of Special Education Programs (OSEP) Center for Positive Behavioral Interventions and Supports. Retrieved from: www.pbis.org/common/cms/files/Current%20Topics/Final-Monograph.pdf.

Belser, C. T., Shillingford, M. A., & Joe, J. R. (2016). The ASCA model and a Multi-Tiered System of Supports: A framework to support students of color with problem behavior. *The Professional Counselor, 6*(3), 251–262.

Berger, C. (2013). Bringing out the brilliance: A counseling intervention for underachieving students. *Professional School Counseling, 17*(1), 86–96.

Betters-Bubon, J., Brunner, T., & Kansteiner, A. (2016). Success for all? The role of the school counselor in creating and sustaining culturally responsive positive behavior intervention and supports programs. *The Professional Counselor, 6*(3), 263–277.

Betters-Bubon, J., & Donohue, P. (2016). Professional capacity building for school counselors through school-wide positive behavior interventions and supports implementation. *Journal of School Counseling, 14*(3), 1–35. Retrieved from: http://jsc.montana.edu/articles/v14n3.pdf.

Boneshefski, M. J., & Runge, T. J. (2014). Addressing disproportionate discipline practices within a school-wide Positive Behavioral Intervention and Supports framework: A practical guide for calculating and using disproportionality rates. *Journal of Positive Behavior Interventions, 16*(3), 149–158, doi:10.1177/1098300713484064.

Bradley, R., Danielson, L., & Doolittle, J. (2007). Responsiveness to intervention: 1997 to 2007. *Teaching Exceptional Children, 39*(5), 8–12.

Bruce, A. M., Getch, Y. Q., & Ziomek-Daigle, J. (2009). Closing the gap: A group counseling approach to improve test performance of African-American students. *Professional School Counseling, 12*(6), 450–457, doi:10.5330/PSC.n.2010-12.450.

Bruhn, A., Lane, K., & Hirsch, S. (2014). A review of Tier 2 interventions conducted within multi-tiered models of behavioral prevention. *Journal of Emotional and Behavioral Disorders, 22*(3) 171–189, doi:10.1177/1063426613476092.

Bruhn, A. L., Woods-Groves, S., Fernando, J., Taehoon, C., & Troughton, L. (2017). Evaluating technology-based self-monitoring as a Tier 2 intervention across middle school settings. *Behavioral Disorders, 42*(3), 119–131, doi:10.1177/0198742917691534.

Campbell, A., Rodriguez, B. J., Anderson, C., & Barnes, A. (2013). Effects of a Tier 2 intervention on classroom disruptive behavior and academic engagement. *Journal of Curriculum and Instruction, 7*(1), 32–54.

Cartledge, G., & Kourea, L. (2008). Culturally responsive classrooms for culturally diverse students with and at risk for disabilities. *Exceptional Children, 74*(3), 351–371.

Cheney, D., Lynass, L., Flower, A., Waugh, M., Iwaszuk, W., Mielenz, C., & Hawken, L. (2010). The check, connect, and expect program: A targeted, Tier 2 intervention in the schoolwide positive behavior support model. *Preventing School Failure, 54*, 152–158.

Cheney, D. A., Stage, S. A., Hawken, L. S., Lynass, L., Mielenz, C., & Waugh, M. (2009). A 2-year outcome study of the check, connect, and expect intervention for students at risk for severe behavior problems. *Journal of Emotional and Behavioral Disorders, 17*(4), 226–243.

Cressey, J. M., Whitcomb, S. A., McGilvray-Rivet, S. J., Morrison, R. J., & Shander-Reynolds, K. J. (2015). Handling PBIS with care: Scaling up to school-wide implementation. *Professional School Counseling, 18*(1), 90–99.

Crone, D. A., Hawken, L. S., & Horner, R. H. (2010). *Responding to problem behavior in schools: The behavior education program.* New York: Guilford Press.

Curtis, R., Van Horne, J. W., Robertson, P., & Karvonen, M. (2010). Outcomes of a school-wide positive behavioral support program. *Professional School Counseling, 13*(3), 159–164.

Davis, B. G. (2009). *Tools for teaching.* Hoboken, NJ: John Wiley & Sons.

Debnam, K. J., Pas, E. T., & Bradshaw, C. P. (2012). Secondary and tertiary support systems in schools implementing school-wide positive behavioral interventions and supports: A preliminary descriptive analysis. *Journal of Positive Behavior Interventions, 14*(3), 142–152.

Debnam, K. J., Pas, E. T., & Bradshaw, C. P. (2013). Factors influencing staff perceptions of administrator support for Tier 2 and 3 interventions: A multilevel perspective. *Journal of Emotional and Behavioral Disorders, 21*(2), 116–126.

Donohue, P., Goodman-Scott, E., & Betters-Bubon, J. (2016). Using universal screening for early identification of students at risk: A case example from the field. *Professional School Counseling, 19*(1), 133–143.

Drummond, T. (1994). *The student risk screening scale (SRSS).* Grants Pass, OR: Josephine County Mental Health Program.

Duarte, D., & Hatch, T. (2015). Successful implementation of a federally funded violence prevention elementary school counseling program: Results bring sustainability. *Professional School Counseling, 18*(1), 71–81.

Everett, S., Sugai, G., Fallon, L., Simonsen, B., & O'Keefe, B. (2011). *School-wide tier II interventions: Check In-Check Out getting started workbook.* Center on Positive Behavioral Interventions and Supports, Center for Behavioral Education and Research, University of Connecticut.

Falco, L. D., Crethar, H., & Bauman, S. (2008). Skill-builders: Improving middle school students' self-beliefs for learning mathematics. *Professional School Counseling, 11*(4), 229–235.

Filter, K. J., McKenna, M. K., Benedict, E. A., Horner, R. H., Todd, A. W., & Watson, J. (2007). Check In/Check Out: A post-hoc evaluation of an efficient, secondary-level targeted intervention for reducing problem behaviors in schools. *Education and Treatment of Children, 30*(1), 69–84.

Garbacz, S. A., McIntosh, K., Eagle, J. W., Dowd-Eagle, S. E., Hirano, K. A., & Ruppert, T. (2016). Family engagement within schoolwide Positive Behavioral Interventions and Supports. *Preventing School Failure, 60*(1), 60–69.

Gerrity, D. A., & DeLucia-Waack, J. L. (2007). Effectiveness of groups in the schools. *Journal for Specialists in Group Work, 32*(1), 97–106.

Gerzel-Short, L., & Wilkins, E. A. (2009). Response to intervention: Helping all students learn. *Kappa Delta Pi Record, 45*(3), 106–110.

Goforth, A. N., Nichols, L. M., Stanick, C. F., Shindorf, Z. R., & Holter, O. (2017). School-based considerations for supporting Arab American youths' mental health. *Contemporary School Psychology, 21*(3), 191–200.

Goodman-Scott, E. (2014). Maximizing school counselors' efforts by implementing school-wide Positive Behavioral Interventions and Supports: A case study from the field. *Professional School Counseling, 17*, 111–119.

Goodman-Scott, E., Betters-Bubon, J., & Donohue, P. (2016). Aligning Comprehensive School Counseling Programs and Positive Behavioral Interventions and Supports to maximize school counselors' efforts. *Professional School Counseling, 19*(1), 57–67, doi:10.5330/1096-2409-19.1.57.

Grothaus, T. (2013). School counselors serving students with disruptive behavior disorders. *Professional School Counseling, 16*, 245–255.

Gruman, D. H., & Hoelzen, B. (2011). Determining responsiveness to school counseling interventions using behavioral observations. *Professional School Counseling, 14*(3), 183–190.

Hawken, L. S., Bundock, K., Barrett, C. A., Eber, L., Breen, K., & Phillips, D. (2015). Large-scale implementation of Check-In, Check-Out: A descriptive study. *Canadian Journal of School Psychology, 30*(4), 304–319.

Horner, R. H., Sugai, G., & Anderson, C. M. (2010). Examining the evidence base for school-wide positive behavior support. *Focus on Exceptionality, 42*(8), 1–14.

Hoyle, C. G., Marshall, K. J., & Yell, M. L. (2011). Positive behavior supports: Tier 2 interventions in middle schools. *Preventing School Failure, 55*, 164–170.

Hunter, K. K., Chenier, J. S., & Gresham, F. M. (2014). Evaluation of Check In/Check Out for students with internalizing behavior problems. *Journal of Emotional and Behavioral Disorders, 22*(3), 135–148, doi:10.1177/1063426613476091.

Irvin, L. K., Horner, R. H., Ingram, K., Todd, A. W., Sugai, G., Sampson, N. K., & Boland, J. B. (2006). Using office discipline referral data for decision making about student behavior in elementary and middle schools: An empirical evaluation of validity. *Journal of Positive Behavior Interventions, 8*, 10–23.

Irvin, L. K., Tobin, T. J., Sprague, J. R., Sugai, G., & Vincent, C. G. (2004). Validity of office discipline referral measures as indices of school-wide behavioral status and effects of school-wide behavioral interventions. *Journal of Positive Behavior Interventions, 6*, 131–147.

Kayler, M. S., & Sherman, J. (2009). At-risk ninth-grade students: A psychoeducational group approach to increase study skills and grade point averages. *Professional School Counseling, 12*(6), 434–439.

Lane, K. L., Cantwell, E. D., Common, E. A., Oakes, W. P., Menzies, H. M., Schatschneider, C., & Lambert, W. (2017). Psychometric evidence of SRSS-IE scores in middle and high schools. *Journal of Emotional & Behavioral Disorders, 25*(4), 233–245, doi:10.1177/1063426616670862.

Lane, K. L., Capizzi, A. M., Fisher, M. H., & Ennis, R. P. (2012). Secondary prevention efforts at the middle school level: An application of the behavior education program. *Education and Treatment of Children, 35*(1), 51–90.

Lemberger, M. E., & Clemens, E. V. (2012). Connectedness and self-regulation as constructs of the Student Success Skills program in inner-city African American elementary school students. *Journal of Counseling & Development, 90*(4), 450–458.

Leverson, M., Smith, K., McIntosh, K., Rose, J., & Pinkelman, S. (2016). *PBIS cultural responsiveness guide: Resources for trainers and coaches.* PBIS OSEP Technical Assistance Center on Positive Behavioral Interventions and Supports. Eugene, OR: University of Oregon. Available from: www.pbis.org.

Loman, S. L., & Horner, R. H. (2014). Examining the efficacy of a basic functional behavior assessment training package for school personnel. *Journal of Positive Behavior Interventions, 16*(1), 18–30.

Maggin, D. M., Zurheide, J., Pickett, K. C., & Baillie, S. J. (2015). A systematic evidence review of the Check-In/Check-Out program for reducing student challenging behaviors. *Journal of Positive Behavior Interventions, 17*, 197–208.

Malott, K. M., Paone, T. R., Humphreys, K., & Martinez, T. (2010). Use of group counseling to address ethnic identity development: Application with adolescents of Mexican descent. *Professional School Counseling, 13*(5), 257–267.

March, R. E., & Horner, R. H. (2002). Feasibility and contributions of functional behavioral assessment in schools. *Journal of Emotional and Behavioral Disorders, 10*(3), 158–170.

March, R. E., Homer, R. H., Lewis-Palmer, T., Brown, D., Crone, D., Todd, A. W., & Carr, E. G. (2000). *Functional assessment checklist: Teachers and staff (FACTS).* Eugene, OR: Educational and Community Supports.

Marchant, M., Anderson, D. H., Caldarella, P., Fisher, A., Young, B. J., & Young, K. R. (2009). Schoolwide screening and programs of positive behavior support: Informing universal interventions. *Preventing School Failure, 53*(3), 131–144.

Martens, K., & Andreen, K. (2013). School counselors' involvement with a school-wide positive behavior support intervention: Addressing student behavior issues in a proactive and positive manner. *Professional School Counseling, 16*, 313–322.

McCormac, M. E. (2015). Preventing and responding to bullying: An elementary school's 4-year journey. *Professional School Counseling, 18*(1), 1–14.

McGinnis, E., & Goldstein, P. (2003). *Skillstreaming in early childhood: New strategies and perspectives for teaching prosocial skills.* Champaign, IL: Research Press.

McIntosh, K., Barnes, A., Eliason, B., & Morris, K. (2014). *Using discipline data within SWPBIS to identify and address disproportionality: A guide for school teams.* Positive Behavioral Interventions and Supports OSEP Technical Assistance Center. Eugene, OR: University of Oregon. Retrieved from: www.pbis.org/school/equity-pbis.

McIntosh, K., Borgmeier, C., Anderson, C. M., Horner, R. H., Rodriguez, B. J., & Tobin, T. J. (2008). Technical adequacy of the functional assessment checklist: Teachers and staff (FACTS) FBA Interview measure. *Journal of Positive Behavior Interventions, 10*(1), 33–45.

McIntosh, K., Brown, J. A., & Borgmeier, C. J. (2008). Validity of functional behavior assessment within an RTI framework: Evidence and future directions. *Assessment for Effective Intervention, 34,* 6–14.

McIntosh, K., Campbell, A. L., Carter, D. R., & Dickey, C. R. (2009a). Differential effects of a Tier two behavior intervention based on function of problem behavior. *Journal of Positive Behavior Interventions, 11*(2), 82–93, doi:10.1177/1098300708319127.

McIntosh, K., Campbell, A. L., Carter, D. R., & Zumbo, B. D. (2009b). Concurrent validity of office discipline referrals and cut points used in schoolwide positive behavior support. *Behavioral Disorders, 34,* 100–113.

McIntosh, K., Frank, J. L., & Spaulding, S. A. (2010). Establishing research-based trajectories of office discipline referrals for individual students. *School Psychology Review, 39*(3), 380–394.

McIntosh, K., & Goodman, S. (2016). *Integrated Multi-Tiered Systems of Support: Blending RTI and PBIS.* New York: Guilford Publications.

Miller, L. M., Dufrene, B. A., Joe, O. D., Tingstrom, D., & Filce, H. (2015a). Self-monitoring as a viable fading option in Check-In/Check-Out. *Journal of School Psychology, 53,* 121–135.

Miller, L. M., Dufrene, B. A., Sterling, H. E., Olmi, D. J., & Bachmayer, E. (2015b). The effects of Check-In/Check-Out on problem behavior and academic engagement in elementary school students. *Journal of Positive Behavior Interventions, 17*(1), 28–38.

Miller, M., Fenty, N., Scott, T., & Park, K. (2011). An examination of social skills instruction in the context of small-group reading. *Remedial and Special Education, 32*(5), 371–381, doi:10.1177/0741932510362240.

Mitchell, B. S., Stormont, M., & Gage, N. A. (2011). Tier two interventions implemented within the context of a tiered prevention framework. *Behavioral Disorders, 36*(4), 241–261.

Ockerman, M. S., Mason, E. M., & Hollenbeck, A. F. (2012). Integrating RTI with school counseling programs: Being a proactive professional school counselor. *Journal of School Counseling, 10*(15), 1–37. Retrieved from: http://files.eric.ed.gov/fulltext/EJ978870.pdf.

Ohrt, J. H., Lambie, G. W., & Ieva, K. P. (2009). Supporting Latino and African-American students in advanced placement courses: A school counseling program's approach. *Professional School Counseling, 13*(1), 59–63.

Ohrt, J., Webster, L., & De La Garza, M. (2014) The effects of a success skills group on adolescents' self-regulation, self-esteem, and perceived learning competence. *Professional School Counseling, 18*(1), 169–178.

OSEP Technical Assistance Center on Positive Behavioral Interventions and Supports (2015). *Positive Behavioral Interventions and Supports (PBIS) implementation blueprint: Part 1 – Foundations and supporting information.* U.S. Department of Education's Office of Special Education Programs (OSEP). Eugene, OR: University of Oregon. Retrieved from: www.pbis.org.

Pas, T. T., Bradshaw, C. P., & Mitchell, M. (2011). Examining the validity of office discipline referrals as an indicator of student behavior problems. *Psychology in the Schools, 48*(6), 541–555, doi:10.1002/pits.20577.

Preciado, J. A., Horner, R. H., & Baker, S. K. (2009). Using a function-based approach to decrease problem behaviors and increase academic engagement for Latino English Language Learners. *Journal of Special Education, 42*(4), 227–240, doi:10.1177/0022466907313350.

Ratts, M. J., & Hutchins, A. M. (2009). ACA advocacy competencies: Social justice advocacy at the client/student level. *Journal of Counseling & Development, 87*(3), 269–275.

Ratts, M. J., Singh, A. A., Nassar-McMillan, S., Butler, S. K., & McCullough, J. R. (2016). Multicultural and social justice counseling competencies: Guidelines for the counseling profession. *Journal of Multicultural Counseling & Development, 44*(1), 28–48, doi:10.1002/jmcd.12035.

Rose, J., & Steen, S. (2015). The Achieving Success Everyday group counseling model: Fostering resiliency in middle school students. *Professional School Counseling, 18*(1), 28–37.

Ross, S. W., Romer, N., & Horner, R. H. (2012). Teacher well-being and the implementation of school-wide Positive Behavior Interventions and Supports. *Journal of Positive Behavior Interventions, 14*(2), 118–128.

Ryan, T., Kaffenberger, C. J., & Carroll, A. G. (2011). Response to intervention: An opportunity for school counselor leadership. *Professional School Counseling, 14*(3), 211–221, doi:10.5330/PSC.n.2011-14.211.

Sailor, W., Dunlap, G., Sugai, G., & Horner, R. (2009). *Handbook of positive behavior support.* New York: Springer.

Schellenberg, R., & Grothaus, T. (2011). Using culturally competent responsive services to improve student achievement and behavior. *Professional School Counseling, 14*(3), 222–230, doi: 2156759X1101400306.

Scott, T. M., Alter, P. J., Rosenberg, M., & Borgmeier, C. (2010). Decision-making in secondary and tertiary interventions of school-wide systems of positive behavior support. *Education & Treatment of Children, 33*(4), 513–535.

Scott, T. M., & Martinek, G. (2006). Coaching positive behavior support in school settings: Tactics and data-based decision making. *Journal of Positive Behavior Interventions, 8*(3), 165–173.

Sheridan, B. A., MacDonald, D. A., Donlon, M., McGovern, K., & Friedman, H. (2011). Evaluation of a social skills program based on social learning theory, implemented in a school setting. *Psychological Reports, 108*(2), 420–436, doi:10.2466/10.11.17.PR0.108.2.420-436.

Sherrod, M., Getch, Y. Q., & Ziomek-Daigle, J. (2009). The impact of positive behavior support to decrease discipline referrals with elementary students. *Professional School Counseling, 12*(6), 421–427.

Shi, Q., & Steen, S. (2012). Using the Achieving Success Everyday (ASE) group model to promote self-esteem and academic achievement for English as a Second Language (ESL) students. *Professional School Counseling, 16*, 63–70, doi:10.5330/PSC.n.2012-16.63.

Simonsen, B., Myers, D., & Briere, D. (2011). Comparing a behavioral Check-In/Check-Out (CICO) intervention to standard practice in an urban middle school setting using an experimental group design. *Journal of Positive Behavior Interventions, 13*(1), 31–48, doi:10.1177/1098300709359026.

Sink, C. A. (2009). School counselors as accountability leaders: Another call for action. *Professional School Counseling, 13*(2), 68–74.

Sink, C. A., Edwards, C. N., & Eppler, C. (2012). *School based group counseling.* Belmont, CA: Brooks/Cole.

Sink, C. A., & Ockerman, M. S. (2016). School counselors and a Multi-Tiered System of Supports: Cultivating systemic change and equitable outcomes. *The Professional Counselor, 6*(3), v–ix.

Smith, H. M., Evans-McCleon, T. N., Urbanski, B., & Justice, C. (2015). Check In/Check Out intervention with peer monitoring for a student with emotional-behavioral difficulties. *Journal of Counseling & Development, 23*, 451–459, doi:10.1002/jcad.12043.

Stage, S. A., Cheney, D., Lynass, L., Mielenz, C., & Flower, A. (2012). Three validity studies of the daily progress report in relationship to the check, connect, and expect intervention. *Journal of Positive Behavior Interventions, 14*(3), 181–191, doi:10.1177/1098300712438942.

Steen, S. (2011). Academic and personal development through group work: An exploratory study. *The Journal for Specialists in Group Work, 36*(2), 129–143.

Sugai, G., & Horner, R. (2006). A promising approach for expanding and sustaining school-wide positive behavior support. *School Psychology Review, 35*, 245–259.

Sugai, G., Horner, R., Dunlap, G., Hieneman, M., Lewis, T., Nelson, C., Scott, T., . . . Ruef, M. (2000). Applying positive behavior support and functional behavioral assessment in schools. *Journal of Positive Behavior Interventions, 2*(3), 131–143.

Sugai, G., Sprague, J. R., Horner, R., & Walker, H. M. (2000). Preventing school violence: The use of office discipline referrals to assess and monitor school-wide discipline interventions. *Journal of Emotional and Behavioral Disorders, 8*, 94–101.

Tobin, T. J., & Sugai, G. M. (1999). Using sixth-grade school records to predict school violence, chronic discipline problems, and high school outcomes. *Journal of Emotional and Behavioral Disorders, 7*, 40–53.

Tobin, T. J., Sugai, G., & Colvin, G. (1996). Patterns in middle school discipline records. *Journal of Emotional and Behavioral Disorders, 4*, 82–94.

Todd, A. W., Campbell, A. L., Meyer, G. G., & Horner, R. H. (2008). The effects of a targeted intervention to reduce problem behaviors: Elementary school implementation of Check In-Check Out. *Journal of Positive Behavior Interventions, 10*(1), 46–55.

Turnbull, A., Edmonson, H., Griggs, P., Wickham, D., Sailor, W., Freeman, R., & Warren, J. (2002). A blueprint for school-wide positive behavior support: Implementation of three components. *Exceptional Children, 68*, 377–402.

Turtura, J. E., Anderson, C. M., & Boyd, R. J. (2014). Addressing task avoidance in middle school students: Academic behavior check-in/check-out. *Journal of Positive Behavior Interventions, 16*(3), 159–167, doi:10.1177/1098300713484063.

Uehara, D. (2005). Diversity in the classroom: Implications for school counselors. *Multicultural Perspectives, 7*(4), 46–53.

Walker, B. A. (2010). Effective schoolwide screening to identify students at risk for social and behavioral problems. *Intervention in School and Clinic, 46*(2), 104–110.

Warren, J. M., & Robinson, G. (2015). Addressing barriers to effective RTI through school counselor consultation: A social justice approach. *Electronic Journal for Inclusive Education, 3*(4).

White, N. J., & Dixon-Rayle, A. (2007). Strong teens: A school-based small group experience for African American males. *Journal for Specialists in Group Work, 32*(2), 178–189.

Wyatt, S. (2009). The brotherhood: Empowering adolescent African-American males toward excellence. *Professional School Counseling, 12*(6), 463–470.

Yong, M., & Cheney, D. A. (2013). Essential features of Tier 2 social-behavioral interventions. *Psychology in the Schools, 50*(8), 844–861.

Ziomek-Daigle, J., Goodman-Scott, E., Cavin, J., & Donohue, P. (2016). Integrating a Multi-Tiered System of Support with comprehensive school counseling programs. *The Professional Counselor, 6*(3), 220–232.

6 Tier 3

Specialized Services for Students with Intensive Needs

Jolie Ziomek-Daigle, Jason Cavin, Jennifer Diaz, Brent Henderson, and Alexandra Huguelet

Introduction

Students with increased behavioral or social/emotional needs can benefit from Tier 3 services or interventions offered through Multi-Tiered Systems of Support (MTSS), such as Positive Behavioral Interventions and Supports (PBIS) and Response to Intervention (RTI). School counselors are integral to this process and can assist students with elevated needs by providing direct services as *interveners* (e.g., providing counseling) and indirect services as *supporters* (e.g., consulting with school staff), and fulfill these roles as part of a Comprehensive School Counseling Program (CSCP; Ziomek-Daigle, Goodman-Scott, Cavin, & Donohue, 2016). In this chapter, we provide an overview of the school counselor's role in MTSS and background information on Tier 3 supports and interventions. We include Functional Behavioral Assessment/Behavior Intervention Plans (FBA/BIP) and specific interventions such as individual and small-group counseling, evidence-based practices, and wraparound services. We conclude the chapter by discussing using data in Tier 3 supports. Additionally, throughout the chapter we include cultural and ethical considerations, as well as case studies to help readers apply content to practice.

The School Counselor's Role in MTSS

As emphasized throughout this book, school counselors can be a critical part of the multidisciplinary leadership team that designs school-wide programming for MTSS (Betters-Bubon, Brunner, & Kansteiner, 2016; Cowan, Vaillancourt, Rossen, & Pollitt, 2013; Ziomek-Daigle et al., 2016). For school counselors, being an integral part of the MTSS team is a natural fit (Goodman-Scott, 2014; Goodman-Scott, Betters-Bubon, & Donohue, 2016; Ockerman, Patrikakou, & Hollenbeck, 2015; Ziomek-Daigle, et al., 2016) as school counselors are uniquely qualified to not only work with students, but also with faculty, staff, parents, and community stakeholders (Goodman-Scott et al., 2016; Ockerman et al., 2015). School counselors are encouraged through the ASCA National Model to develop CSCPs that are driven by student data and based on standards in academic, career, and social/emotional development, and that are equitable for *all* students (ASCA, 2012). As discussed in Chapter 2, school counselors also understand the importance of responding to and enhancing student social/emotional competence, as psychological wellness influences academic achievement and career/post-secondary awareness and success. Thus, MTSS is a natural fit with CSCPs. Hallmarks of both MTSS and CSCPs include that they are preventative in nature, culturally responsive, grounded in a collaborative systems approach, serve all students through tiered supports, and attend to both academic and mental health/behavioral student needs. Overall, MTSS, through the integration of PBIS and RTI, addresses the total student: both their academic and mental health/behavioral needs.

Due to their specialized training, school counselors are also uniquely qualified to take the lead in the identification of culturally competent interventions associated with MTSS. In fact, ASCA released a revised position statement on the school counselor's role, which includes, "advocating for equitable education for all students and working to remove systemic barriers" (ASCA, 2018, p. 1). This, of course, starts with CSCPs that engage all stakeholders, benefit all students equitably, and extends to the interventions school counselors implement within their CSCP and MTSS. As the MTSS supports increase through the tiers (see Chapter 1), school counselors can monitor approaches or interventions utilized with their students to ensure fidelity in delivery and outcomes (Betters-Bubon et al., 2016).

Tier 3: Background Information

For the reasons previously described, we devote our chapter to the role school counselors play in working with students who need Tier 3 academic and behavioral support. Counselors will provide and/or facilitate services for youth who have the most significant needs (e.g., the 5–10% of students who do not respond to Universal/Tier 1 and Tier 2 interventions). It is estimated that one in four students are managing mental health conditions such as anxiety, depression, and behavioral disorders (Macklem, 2011). Therefore, undoubtedly, school counselors will be integral in being the liaison to services, supports, and resources. Within strong MTSS, less than 5% of the school population will need, and be eligible for, Tier 3 services (Cowan et al., 2013); however, those who do need the support may have complex and challenging needs. In the next section, we will discuss Tier 3 services and the role of the school counselor in providing these supports and/or collaborating with key stakeholders.

Why Tier 3 Supports?

Issues of school safety, violence prevention, and management of serious student behavior have prompted educators and counselors to explore the use of research and evidence-based practices with students who have elevated needs, such as those with mental health conditions and/or behavioral disabilities. Many of the Tier 3 evidence-based practices are a direct result of school attempts to manage disruptive student behavior, enhance the classroom environment, and provide elevated, supportive services to students with complex needs (Scott & Eber, 2003). Additionally, educational reform prompted educators to develop evidence-based frameworks to better identify and support struggling learners (see Chapter 10 for more information on evidence-based practices).

What Are Tier 3 Supports?

Students requiring Tier 3 support need more frequent and intense interventions and interactions than those offered at Tier 2 to address specific behavioral and academic needs. As mentioned previously, it is estimated that 5% of students receive or are in need of Tier 3 services. These types of interventions should be chosen and designed based on the results of an FBA, which we will discuss in detail in this chapter. For example, an intervention used to address students' academics and behavioral needs would be pullout instruction (Ockerman, Mason, & Hollenbeck, 2012) whereas an intervention to address student behavior might be an intensive behavior plan.

One hallmark of Tier 3 or tertiary systems is the focus on integrated systems, collaboration with key stakeholders, and the use of research and evidence-based practices, and, all the while, data is continuously being collected and analyzed for progress (Scott & Eber, 2003; Ziomek-Daigle, et al., 2016). Students who are identified for Tier 3 supports have needs that are complex as previous interventions have not proved successful, and key stakeholders need to be involved in the assessment, data collection, and services offered. This tier necessitates "the widest range of perspectives from among the widest range of systems and stakeholders" (Scott & Eber, 2003, p. 133).

The MTSS is designed to address disproportionality, which is the over or underrepresentation of groups of students in different activities or categories. For example, students of color, males, those from the lower or working class, those on free or reduced lunch are often the casualties of disproportionality with high suspension and behavioral referral rates (Kashi, 2008). The preventative-focused approach of MTSS provides direct teaching of expected academics and behaviors, as well as opportunities for more specific instruction through small group and individualized supports, which makes it a promising practice to address disproportionality. An expectation of MTSS is change at the systemic level (e.g. classroom, school, district, community) to help students make more desirable choices and offer the most effective interventions (Scott & Eber, 2003). More recent attention on social-emotional programming, restorative justice initiatives, and the use of culturally relevant counseling practices (e.g., trauma-informed care) further address disproportionality. School counselors are positioned to advocate for all students having access to these programs and that students of color and other underserved populations are not disproportionally referred for Tier 3 interventions (ASCA, 2012; Betters-Bubon et al., 2016; Warren & Robinson, 2015).

Who Provides Tier 3 Supports?

Many individuals are involved in the implementation of Tier 3 services, including teachers, administrators, school counselors, school psychologists, school social workers, allied school and community-based mental health providers, physical therapists, and speech therapists. Tier 3 services include indirect and direct supports to students. School counselors might have a coordinating role in Tier 3; to gather wraparound services and secure releases for individual providers and to coordinate allied professionals to provide counseling in and out of the schools. School counselors can provide supports indirectly by collaborating with key stakeholders and allied professionals, or providing direction in a student crisis. School counselors may also have a role in providing more direct supports. Specifically, school counselors may deliver Tier 3 supports such as individual counseling and group counseling on a time-limited basis. Additionally, school counselors are uniquely trained to provide interventions via direct services in the classrooms, through small groups or on an individual basis (Ziomek-Daigle, et al., 2016). It should be noted that school counselors will need to examine their role and/or involvement within Tier 3 MTSS. Thus, their role may depend on the school setting, levels served, and many contextual considerations. Ockerman et al. (2012) suggest finding a balance between the MTSS team member and intervener, keeping in mind that school counselors can provide reports related to progress monitoring but also carry a high student load.

How Are Tier 3 Supports Provided?

School counselors will often encounter students who are not responding to Tier 2 supports or who are identified from universal screening (see Chapter 7) and are in need of more intensive, durable services. Despite the individualized nature of Tier 3 interventions, not all Tier 3 interventions are implemented individually or target individual students. As outlined by ASCA (2018), Tier 3 interventions can take the form of small-group or individual counseling on a time-limited basis. Berkeley, Bender, Peaster, and Saunders (2009) discuss that a few states (e.g., Utah, Louisiana, and West Virginia) provide both group and individual counseling at the Tier 3 level, while some states only provide group counseling (e.g., Arizona, Pennsylvania, Delaware, Nebraska, and Kansas) and others only provide individual interventions (e.g., Florida, Ohio, Washington, and Oregon).

School counselors may deliver individual counseling on a time-limited basis or may refer to allied mental health professionals in the community, such as licensed professional counselors, psychologists, marriage and family therapists, and social workers. In some cases, there can also be a referral made for the student to receive special education services after the implementation of Tier 3 services (Kashi, 2008; Sherrod, Getch, & Ziomek-Daigle, 2009). This process can vary from state to state, with some states making special education referrals after the implementation of Tier 3 interventions and other states making the referrals before. For example, in some school districts in the state of Georgia, Tier 4 was added to the Pyramid of Interventions as the final step in a special education determination or, in some school districts, it offers an approach to more individualized services. Please see Figure 6.1.

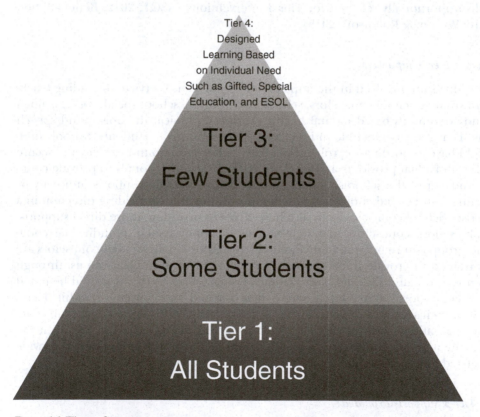

Figure 6.1 Tiers of support.

How Do You Plan for Tier 3 Interventions?

Most of the planning for the Tier 3 supports will be done by the MTSS leadership team. The MTSS teams will look different across schools; however, most teams will include an administrator, school counselor, social worker, school psychologist, special education coordinator, and teacher representatives. The role and responsibilities of each member of the MTSS team should be clearly defined and understood. Who collects the data? Who is the point person for progress monitoring? Who provides the intervention? Who facilitates the meetings? As stated earlier in the chapter, school counselors may move across the roles of intervener, facilitator, and supporter, and each school will have their own unique MTSS composition.

Tier 3 interventions should be agreed upon by stakeholders to be beneficial for students (Bal, Thorius, & Kozleski, 2012). Within the Tier 3 process, school counselors are trained to examine behavioral norms and interventions through a cultural lens. Specifically, within the Tier 3 referral process, school counselors can ask critical questions to ensure a "problem behavior" is in need of intervention. Questions such as:

- Are the problems this student is experiencing due to cultural differences between the teacher(s) and the student?
- Is the behavior the student is demonstrating the result of any oppression, racism, or prejudice the student or the student's family have experienced?

The answers to these questions are critical in understanding academic, social, and/or emotional difficulties students experience in school, particularly when they have reached a level of intervention that is singularly focused, individualized, and where family involvement is crucial.

The following case study challenges the readers to consider cultural competence when serving on the three MTSS teams and advocating for students.

A White, female, 1st grade teacher suggests one of her students needs additional MTSS services for impulsivity, anger outbursts, and a lack of motivation to complete work. This student is a Black male and lives with his mom who is single and working two shifts to support her three children. During the last MTSS meeting, the teacher requests the team develop a behavioral plan or at least begin to track his occurrences of noncompliance and disruption. She shares in the meeting that she "just doesn't understand these students whose parents aren't involved in school and students who lack manners." She complains that she has reached out to the mother via e-mail but has received no response, and that the student constantly interrupts her during lessons, never uses an inside voice, and is always trying to 'show out' in her classroom, even after multiple Tier 2 interventions.

How could the culture of the family and the culture of the teacher impact this process? Could it be impacting the student's review in the MTSS process?

What aspects of this student's behavior could be related to culture or at least life circumstances?

Imagine how you would handle the conversation with this teacher. How could her cultural identity impact the way she sees this student?

How could the counselor discuss the appropriateness of a behavioral plan for this student?

The MTSS team utilizes three critical pieces of information when creating a plan for a student in need of Tier 3 services: (a) data that identifies the need for the intensive intervention, such as universal screening data, attendance, behavior reports, or a FBA; (b) schedules and lesson plans that detail the implementation of the intervention; and (c) a description of the plan to monitor the program's fidelity (Debnam, Pas, & Bradshaw, 2012). We focus on the first part of this process, the FBA, in the following section and then move to specific interventions and data tools.

Functional Behavioral Assessment/Behavior Intervention Plan (FBA/BIP)

An FBA should be completed when stakeholders recognize a need for Tier 3 interventions. Unlike the brief FBA described in Chapter 5, an intensive FBA is a combination

Functional Assessment Checklist for Teachers and Staff (FACTS-Part A)

Step 1 Student/ Grade: ______________ Date: ______________
Interviewer: ______________ Respondent(s): ______________

Step 2 **Student Profile:** Please identify at least three strengths or contributions the student brings to school.
____
____

Step 3 **Problem Behavior(s): Identify problem behaviors**

___ Tardy	___ Fight/physical Aggression	___ Disruptive	___ Theft
___ Unresponsive	___ Inappropriate Language	___ Insubordination	___ Vandalism
___ Withdrawn	___ Verbal Harassment	___ Work not done	___ Other ______
	___ Verbally Inappropriate	___ Self-injury	

Describe problem behavior: ______________

Step 4 **Identifying Routines: Where, When and With Whom Problem Behaviors are Most Likely.**

Schedule (Times)	Activity	Likelihood of Problem Behavior	Specific Problem Behavior
		Low High 1 2 3 4 5 6	
		1 2 3 4 5 6	
		1 2 3 4 5 6	
		1 2 3 4 5 6	
		1 2 3 4 5 6	
		1 2 3 4 5 6	
		1 2 3 4 5 6	
		1 2 3 4 5 6	
		1 2 3 4 5 6	
		1 2 3 4 5 6	
		1 2 3 4 5 6	

Step 5 **Select 1-3 Routines for further assessment: Select routines based on (a) similarity of activities (conditions) with ratings of 4, 5 or 6 and (b) similarity of problem behavior(s). Complete the FACTS-Part B for each routine identified.**

Figure 6.2 Sample FBA.

Functional Assessment Checklist for Teachers and Staff (FACTS-Part A) by R. E. March, R. H. Horner, T. Lewis-Palmer, D. Brown, D. A. Crone, A. W. Todd, & Carr, E. (2000). Functional Assessment Checklist for Teachers and Staff (FACTS). Eugene, OR: University of Oregon.

of procedures that gather data about possible events that might predict or maintain a student's behavior and it is designed to help school staff understand the root cause of behavior. A Behavior Intervention Plan (BIP) is a series of specific steps educators take to facilitate change in student behavior. To facilitate the FBA/BIP process, school counselors may need additional professional training or might choose to work directly with those with more specific training, such as school psychologists or special education teachers.

What Is the Process for Developing an FBA/BIP?

The FBA process includes an assessment of a targeted student behavior, including any antecedents that increase the occurrence of the behavior(s), and any consequences that result from the occurrence. Both direct and indirect methods are used to complete the FBA process. School staff directly observe the student in the classroom and record data to determine the targeted behavior. Examples of targeted behaviors include hitting, interrupting, work refusal, and disruption. In addition, staff interview teachers, parents, and the student and compare the answers to find common links/themes. Staff then analyze the direct and indirect assessment information to determine the function of the behavior. For example, a student might hit others when frustrated with the academic requirements; thus, the function of the behavior would be to escape work. Additional functions that might be identified include gaining or avoiding the following: peers or adult attention, sensory input, or a particular task/activity. An excellent resource that can be used to create the FBA is the Functional Assessment Checklist for Teachers and Staff (FACTS; March, Horner, Lewis-Palmer, Brown, Crone, Todd, & Carr, 2000; see Figure 6.2).

The FACTS is one type of assessment that can guide the FBA/BIP process, in addition to many others listed on the PBIS.org (e.g., Competing Pathway analysis, Functional Behavioral Assessment Behavior Support Plan (F-BSP) Protocol; www.pbis.org). The MTSS leadership team members overseeing Tier 3 and the FBA/BIP process should decide on the assessment and process that best meets their students' needs, as well as their school's/district's resources. Such decisions are highly individualized. For instance, the FACTS may be used for Tier 2 supports in one school (see Chapter 5), or Tier 3 supports in another, depending on the needs and circumstances.

One parent's experience with the FBA process is described below.

My son is very bright, has ADHD, anxiety, and a few other issues. His grades are exceptionally strong, despite him not participating in class and having a hard time completing classwork. Although we have a 504 plan and related accommodations in place this school year, we have seen a lot more struggles.

Our associate principal called me recently, suggesting the school completes an FBA assessment on my son to get more information on his struggles. I filled out a parental questionnaire, the school psychologist interviewed my son, and the teachers collected data. It was a long process. The results were put into bar graphs, pie charts, and percentages. We then got together as a team (me, my son's teachers, and the school psychologist, counselor, and associate principal). I learned a lot about my son's behavior, such as the most frequent times of the day he struggles, when he is more engaged, etc. It was really quite amazing to be able to look at the data and see when his mind starts to shift.

(continued)

(continued)

Also, we determined triggers that we weren't able to pinpoint before. We also have a Behavior Intervention Plan (BIP) for next year. I can honestly say that this was the first time I felt good when I left a 504 meeting. I know that we won't see a 100% turn around immediately; changes and progress will take time, but this is a start. If your child is struggling in school with behavior issues related to ADHD, and possibly other diagnosed behavior problems, I suggest you also ask about the FBA/BIP process.

What do you notice about the FBA/BIP process?

What changes do you notice in the parent's perception of the FBA/BIP process?

How can this practice strengthen the relationship between parents and schools?

The FBA guides the process of creating a BIP. The BIP includes specific goals for the reduction of target behaviors and implementation of replacement behaviors through specific interventions. The plan often specifies who will deliver the interventions, methods for measuring progress, and possible ways to reinforce new behaviors (see Figure 6.3 for a sample BIP). Data from these interventions are compiled and analyzed to determine the effectiveness of the plan and adjustments can be made as needed. When goals are mastered, there should be periodic maintenance checks to ensure the continued implementation of the behavior interventions.

Take a moment and search online (e.g., a Google search) for different types of FBAs. Pair with a peer and share what you learned from the review and what additional questions you have.

Daily Progress Report (DPR)

Quite frequently, BIPs will include Daily Progress Reports (DPR) that teachers complete throughout the day. Students will carry these throughout the day and have teachers, including specials or connections teachers, provide feedback on specific behaviors that were identified through the FBA process. More intensive and individualized than the Check-in/ Check-out process described in Chapter 5, DPRs allow students to receive specific and continuous feedback and reinforcement on the targeted behaviors (See Figure 6.4).

A middle school MTSS team, including school counselors, teachers, and administration, recently met to review Monica's progress in Tier 2 supports. Monica is a Latina, female, 6th grade student with a high number of absences and discipline referrals. The majority of her discipline referrals are for physical aggression. Monica has been receiving CICO, a Tier 2 intervention, implemented by the student's homeroom teacher, Ms. Flores. Each morning, the student and the teacher review the behavior expectations for the day and set a goal. The student then collects feedback from her teachers about progress towards those goals throughout the day. At the end of the day, Monica and Ms. Flores review the results and Ms. Flores acknowledges and encourages Monica's efforts.

After implementing and collecting data on CICO for six weeks, the MTSS team analyzed the data and found that, unfortunately, Monica's attendance had not improved and her discipline referrals increased. Because the CICO intervention with the specific student was not effective, the MTSS team decided to provide Monica with Tier 3 supports and initiated the FBA/BIP process to determine the triggers of Monica's physical aggression at school.

The FBA showed that Monica's aggressive behaviors occurred in her two-hour block period with Ms. Sims, her Science teacher. Observational data showed that the aggressive behaviors occur when there is idle time and Ms. Sims usually responds to Monica with a verbal reprimand, ignoring her, or praising another student. Thus, the FBA analysis showed that Monica gained teacher attention approximately every five minutes during idle class time. This attention seemed to exacerbate the situation, with Monica demonstrating aggressive behavior as a means of gaining attention and control. The BIP plan outlined ways to teach Monica new behaviors (e.g. asking for help and direct instruction during idle time). In addition, it outlined how Ms. Sims could provide increased opportunities for Monica to learn the new behaviors, respond positively to her efforts, and provide consistency in her responses. Monica was also included in a Tier 3 small-group intervention focused on these skills, which was led by the school counselor. The team decided to collect data through the use of frequency charts, noting number of behaviors (both targeted and direct), number of observations, and when teacher interventions took place.

How was data used in this case study?

How did the use of data inform decision making?

What are some other ways Ms. Sims can provide support to Monica?

What Is the School Counselor's Role in the FBA/BIP Process?

The FBA/BIP process will be conducted by school staff who have received specialized training, which may be the school counselor, special education teachers, social workers, school psychologists, or a behavioral interventionist. Regardless of who conducts the FBA, school counselors can work closely with other school staff as part of the multidisciplinary team to offer teachers behavioral consultation regarding implementing the BIP. This might include meeting with teachers to develop behavior goals for groups or individual students. In addition, when adhering to the BIP, school counselors could complete observations in the classroom to assess teacher/student interaction. Based on the information recorded, school counselors could work collaboratively with teachers to develop an individualized intervention.

What Are the Cultural Considerations of the FBA/BIP Process?

Research suggests that behavioral approaches, such as an FBA/BIP and associated DPR, may be effective cross-culturally (Leverson, Smith, McIntosh, Rose, & Pinkelman, 2016; Stage, Cheney, Lynass, Mielenz, & Flower, 2012). At the same time, these programs are based on the use of behavior analysis and reinforcement systems where students' behavior sheets are marked throughout the day with points for displaying desired behaviors.

Behavior Intervention Plan

Student Information	Name/Grade:		Date:
BIP Team Members:			
Problem Behavior: • *Inappropriate behaviors* • *Known antecedents* • *Environmental concerns related to behavior*			
Replacement Behavior: • *What is expected of the student?*			
Method of Teaching Replacement Behavior And By Whom: • *How will we teach the desired behavior and who will teach it?*	☐ Direct instruction, by:_____ ☐ Small Group Support by: _____ Topic/Evidence Based Program for group:_____ ☐ Behavior contract, by:_____ ☐ Re-teaching of behavioral expectations, by:_____ ☐ Providing cues/prompts/reminders, by:_____ ☐ Modeling, by:_____ ☐ Use of mentor(s),by:_____ ☐ Other_____, by:_____		
Accommodations: • *What help will we give the student to help him/her succeed?*	**Accommodations to assist the student:** ☐ Clear, concise directions ☐ Frequent prompts ☐ Frequent breaks ☐ Teacher/staff proximity ☐ Private Reminders ☐ Modify assignments ☐ Review rules & expectation ☐ Alternate recess ☐ Cooling off period ☐ Regular contact with parents/guardians ☐ Predictable routine ☐ Preferential seating ☐ Specifically define limits ☐ Provide highly-structured setting ☐ Other_____		**Who will for provide the accommodation?**
Method of Measuring Progress: • *How will we know if it's working or not?*	☐ Direct observation ☐ Daily/Weekly behavior sheet ☐ Self-monitoring ☐ Number of discipline referrals ☐ Other:_____		
Length of behavior plan	☐ ____		
Positive Consequences for Appropriate Behavior • *What will help reinforce positive behavior?*	☐ Verbal praise ☐ Earned privileges ☐ Tangible rewards ☐ Immediate feedback ☐ Free time ☐ Computer time ☐ Positive call or note home ☐ Positive visit to office ☐ Other: _____		
Negative Consequences For Inappropriate Behavior: • *What happens if student does not behave?*	☐ Send to office/Office Discipline Referral (ODR) ☐ Escort to another area/Time Out ☐ Loss of privileges ☐ Phone call home ☐ Detention ☐ In-school suspension ☐ Out-of-school suspension ☐ Other: _____		

Figure 6.3 Sample Behavior Intervention Plan.

Used with permission from J. Betters-Bubon.

Name:_____ Date:_____	Behavior #1:			Behavior #2:			Behavior #3:		
Literacy	1	2	3	1	2	3	1	2	3
Related Arts	1	2	3	1	2	3	1	2	3
Recess/Lunch	1	2	3	1	2	3	1	2	3
Math	1	2	3	1	2	3	1	2	3
Science	1	2	3	1	2	3	1	2	3
Total Points= **Points Possible = 45**	Today:_____%			Goal:_____%			Goal Achieved: Y N		
Rating Scale: 3 = Excellent	**2 = Mixed/Somewhat**					**1 = Will Try Harder**			
Parent signature:									

Figure 6.4 Daily Progress Report (DPR).

As mentioned previously, teachers lacking cultural competence could do grave harm to students' education and motivation if they only examine students' behaviors through unchecked biases and positions of privilege. However, school counselors have opportunities to offer insight in this situation. School counselors should keep in mind that target behaviors, or goals on DPRs, written in generic terms, can be confusing or unclear to the adults (Ziomek-Daigle & Cavin, 2015). For example, target behaviors such as "Show Respect for Classmates" or "Keep Hands to Self" can be very vague and even misleading. For students, "showing respect" may have a very different meaning at home than at school. In addition, sometimes cultural games that students may play in their neighborhood or homes (e.g., roasting, playing the dozens, snap) can seem disrespectful to teachers expecting students to treat one another with "respect," as defined by the teacher and/or school. Therefore, definitions of target or desired behaviors should be described in observable, measurable, and distinctive terms that are not value-laden (Bal, 2016). Also, all adults that take part in the evaluation of a student's behavior need to be trained on which behaviors are targeted. Student behaviors will not improve if the expectations are not written explicitly and the teachers and school staff are unclear of the expectations for the DPRs. As such, school counselors can and should be involved in examining Tier 3 interventions to ensure cultural fit.

Tier 3 Interventions

Now that we've outlined background information on the FBA process, we will discuss possible Tier 3 interventions. Tier 3 interventions target a number of skill areas, including academic, social/emotional, and behavioral skills. Specifically, Tier 3 interventions can be provided for students who need more intensive services than those offered in Tier 1 and Tier 2 (e.g., classroom lessons; CICO, small-group math intervention). The next section will present specific examples of Tier 3 interventions. Specifically, we describe evidence-based practices (EBPs), including broad approaches (e.g., individual counseling, push in academic instruction) and research-based programs and curricula (e.g., The Coping Cat Curriculum; the Reading Rockets Curriculum).

Individual or Small-Group Counseling

Tier 3 interventions include small-group and individual counseling. When provided by the school counselor these should be delivered on a time-limited basis (e.g., three to five sessions, based on school/setting context). For example, school counselors may facilitate small-group counseling for students needing Tier 3 support in the areas of academic, social, and/or behavioral interventions. School counselors have utilized evidence-based programs within small groups to help students better manage social skills, relationships and conflict, anxiety, and academic improvement with positive outcomes (Sherrod, Getch, & Ziomek-Daigle, 2009). The MTSS team may recommend a student receive a certain number of sessions of individual counseling before further evaluation or data collection occurs. In the same vein, an Individualized Education Program (IEP) may stipulate that a student with disabilities receives weekly (e.g., four to six weekly sessions) individual counseling to manage test anxiety, social phobia, coping skills, social skills, and so forth. School counselors can offer these sessions as direct services within a CSCP, complying with the recommendations of the IEP, as long as the sessions are time limited and are not considered long-term therapy (ASCA, 2018). Though ASCA does not recommend school counselors function as therapists with weekly appointments, school counselors are trained to work with students individually and, thus, can be a part of Tier 3 interventions, either directly or indirectly (e.g., collaboration and consultation). For students requiring longer-term intensive academic, social, and/or behavioral supports through individual school-based counseling, we suggest that this counseling is conducted by a school or community-based mental health provider with an appropriate caseload for such work, who then collaborates and consults with the MTSS leadership team, including the school counselor. Alternatively, the MTSS leadership team may also refer students with chronic mental health needs to local mental health settings and providers, such as Licensed Professional Counselors (LPCs), school family therapists, and other allied professionals. In fact, much research is now focused on the integration of school-based mental health for students in need of Tier 3 supports (see Barrett, Eber, and Weist, 2013, for a comprehensive overview).

Evidence-Based Practice (EBP)

Whether offered in an individual or group setting, the focus of intervention within Tier 3 should be grounded in evidence-based approaches. As described in Chapter 10, EBP, such as counseling approaches or specific curricula, are those grounded in research that has been demonstrated to affect student social/emotional or academic development (see Chapter 10 for definitions and additional information). For example, several counseling theories have strong research support and have provided evidence or outcomes related to behavior change (e.g. CBT, play therapy). Play therapy in schools is a viable research-based intervention that has shown effectiveness for students demonstrating greater need for individual services. Specifically, Winburn, Gilstrap, and Perryman (2017) offered play therapy as a research-based program that is multiculturally sensitive and relevant, due to the fact that play is a voluntary action and viewed as universal across cultures. Reality therapy is another approach that is appropriate for students in need of Tier 3 services. Sunawan and Xiong (2016) discussed the benefits of using reality therapy in developing effective achievement goals with students. Haskins and Appling (2017) present an integrative relational cultural theory and reality therapy approach to counseling diverse youth as both theories examine behaviors within the context of relationships and offer empowerment through relational support. This integrative approach is ideal for school counselors who are serving students through Tier 3 supports.

In addition to specific counseling approaches, school counselors can also use structured curriculum in individual or small-group settings to support students who are in need of Tier 3 intervention. Table 6.1 summarizes examples of Tier 3 EBP, which includes both specific programs and broad approaches.

Culturally Relevant Tier 3 Interventions

The question is often raised of whether EBPs and specific evidence-based curricula can be used with youth in general, and specifically with culturally diverse youth, if the interventions have not been validated with those populations. Research studies are inconclusive, with some citing that adapting interventions for specific populations can increase effectiveness and others concluding that changing an intervention could alter the original treatment effectiveness (Ngo, Langley, Kataoka, Nadeem, Escudero, & Stein, 2008). As counseling professionals who understand research and cultural relevancy, school counselors can offer their expertise and examine the programs to ensure interventions work for our student populations. For illustrative purposes we describe one such evidence-based program next.

CBITS

The Cognitive-Behavioral Intervention for Trauma in Schools (CBITS) is an evidence-based program delivered through a small group or on an individual basis in the school setting. This intervention helps participants reduce symptoms of post-traumatic stress disorder such as depression and behavioral problems. The CBITS was originally developed for youth of color and immigrant youth who were exposed to trauma (Jaycox, 2004). Participants learn social and coping skills via cognitive-behavioral techniques, including cognitive restructuring, exposure, psychoeducation, and meditation (see Table 6.2 for a modified summary of sessions). The intervention is appropriate for students in 5th–12th grade.

Research findings suggest that CBITS participants who completed the program reported a reduction in post-traumatic stress and depressive symptoms (Ngo et al., 2008). The CBITS program is culturally responsive in its delivery and encourages counselors to embed culturally relevant material to increase participant engagement and program meaningfulness. One CBITS treatment component includes social problem-solving. The researchers suggest including aspects of spiritual coping such as prayer, meditation, and meeting with a religious leader (Ngo et al., 2008). These specific strategies of spiritual coping are important components in ethnic culture and context and can aid the problem-solving process. The trauma narrative is another CBITS treatment component and participants are encouraged to create a rap, song, poem, or graphic novel about a traumatic event and its ending.

How can you use culturally responsive interventions to meet the needs of students receiving Tier 3 supports?

Are you aware of any interventions that might not meet the needs of all students?

How can you learn more about possible Tier 3 interventions?

Table 6.1 Tier 3 evidence-based practices

EBP	Focus	Format	Outcomes
Second Step Violence Prevention Program	Reduction in impulsive and aggressive behavior through the improvement of social skills	Classroom guidance and small group	Reduce aggression in students and behavioral referrals. Also promote a more positive school climate (Zyromski & Mariani, 2016). Reduced aggressive behavior, reduced behavioral referrals, bullying incidents. Increase in neutral or pro-social behaviors in playground and cafeteria settings. Improved academic achievement and effort (Carey, Dimmitt, Hatch, Lapan, & Whiston, 2008).
Functional family therapy, multi-systemic therapy, and parent management programs	Oppositional defiant disorder, conduct disorder, and attentive deficit disorders	Family therapy	Improved behavior, reduced criminal charges (Eder & Whiston, 2006).
Coping Cat Program	Anxiety disorders such as generalized anxiety, separation anxiety, and social phobia	Small-group and individual counseling. Cognitive-behavioral, manual-based program. Parents are involved in treatment and are trained to be coaches. Uses modeling, exposure, role play, relaxation, and in vivo experiences	Decrease in anxiety, fear, negative thoughts, and depressive symptoms, and improved coping skills (Hourigan, Settipani, Southam-Gerow, & Kendall, 2012).
Anger Coping Program	Anger management	Small-group and based on the cognitive-behavioral approach	Reduces aggressive and disruptive behaviors in students with excessive behavioral referrals. (Larson & Lochman, 2011).
Trauma-focused cognitive-behavioral therapy	Trauma/crisis	Small group	Reduction in reactions to PTSD, depressive symptoms, and behavior disruptions (Macklem, 2011).

Intervention	Focus	Delivery	Description / Outcomes
Family-based interventions, family counseling, parent involvement	Academic improvement, student motivation	Family counseling	Increases student achievement, attendance, graduation rates, and post-secondary enrollment. Also, increase in student motivation and classroom behavior. See the Families and Schools Together (FAST) program (Kratochwill, McDonald, Levin, Scalia, & Coover, 2009).
Play therapy	Behavior, building relationships, aggression, coping skills	Individual or small-group counseling	Nondirective approaches may be helpful in building the therapeutic alliance, expressing emotion, and building communication skills. Students may benefit with more directive approaches if they need specific behavior improvement such as reducing aggression toward others or coping skills (Winburn, Gilstrap, and Perryman, 2017).
Aggression Replacement Training (ART)	Aggression and anti-social behavior	Small group	Changes in prosocial skills, anger management, and moral reasoning (Gundersen & Svardal, 2006).
Cognitive Behavioral Interventions for Trauma in Schools (CBITS)	Trauma	Small group	Changes in cognition, stress, or trauma exposure, learns relaxation and social problem solving (Ngo, Langley, Kataoka, Nadeem, Escudero, & Stein, 2008).
Check & Connect	School disengagement	Individual	Improves attendance and engagement (Christenson & Reschly, 2010).
Wraparound	Serious emotional and behavioral difficulties	Team-based approach that creates individualized intervention plan	Improves disciplinary outcomes and GPA. Fewer emotional and behavioral problems (Bruns & Suter, 2010).

Table 6.2 CBITS lessons

Session 1	Introductions
Session 2	Common reactions to trauma, relaxation
1–3 Individual Sessions	Imaginal Exposure to Traumatic Event (Between group sessions 2 and 6)
Session 3	Thoughts and feelings
Session 4	Combatting negative thoughts (hot seat)
Sessions 6, 7	Exposure to trauma through imagination, writing, drawing
Session 8	Introduction to social problem solving
Session 9	Practice with problems solving and hot seat
Session 10	Planning/graduation

Wraparound

In addition to CBITS, another specific Tier 3 intervention is wraparound. Wraparound is a process where the student, their family, and any other individual who is influential in the student's life (e.g., mentor, case manager, probation officer) collaboratively develops a plan to assist students in achieving their future goals (e.g., temporary housing or summer employment) or behavior management (aggression, anti-social behavior) (Suter & Bruns, 2009). The most important piece of the wraparound process is the input received from the student and family members. The wraparound team notes goals and creates the best possible path and plan for the student to achieve those goals. The plan takes place across all areas of the student's life including home, school, and the community, and should be revisited frequently to ensure that the student's goals have not changed and the path is still viable.

WHY WRAPAROUND?

Wraparound support, rooted in mental health reform and child welfare, is a coordinated system of care and a community-based approach "to providing comprehensive, integrated services through multiple professionals and agencies, in collaboration with families" (Eber, Hyde, & Suter, 2011; Scott & Eber, 2003, p. 13). Emerging during the 1980s as part of social work and child welfare programs for individuals with extreme emotional and behavioral disorders, wraparound has been widely used in implementing systems of care models by designing individualized and flexible services and interventions for youth and families (Eber & Nelson, 1997). Wraparound is an excellent example of a best practice that involves integral individuals and systems in students' lives as it can be focused on prevention (e.g., recommendation of a half-day treatment program vs inpatient) or intervention (e.g. family counseling, respite care for the student during extended school breaks or weekends). Tenets of wraparound services are similar to the hallmarks of CSCPs. Elements of both include: addressing issues through cultural competence, data/outcome-driven decision making, essential involvement from stakeholders, and collaborative inter-professional teaming and consultation (Ziomek-Daigle et al., 2016).

IS WRAPAROUND SUPPORTED BY RESEARCH?

The wraparound approach has been found to be effective for students with complex emotional and behavioral problems and schools are ideal settings for interagency collaboration and individualized care (Epstein, Nordness, Gallagher, Nelson, Lewis, & Schrepf, 2005). Positive outcomes of the wraparound approach include improvement in living situations, health care access, academic progress, mental health, resiliency, and juvenile justice-related outcomes (Suter & Bruns, 2009). Using wraparound is especially relevant with transitional-aged youth (i.e., ages 17–25) as this is the age when youth "age out" of foster care and juvenile justice programming, move from youth to adult social services, and is often when special education services terminate. Furthermore, transitional-age youth appear to have the highest rates of both psychiatric and substance use problems, with rates of mental illness as high as 28% (Epstein et al., 2005). The high prevalence and severity rates of psychiatric and substance use disorders in this age group underscore the need for intervention for this vulnerable population.

Do an internet search for "Wraparound Integrity Tool" and view the various scales used to assess the wraparound process. Some items include:

- Meet with family
- Meet with key team members
- Develop strengths list
- Identify natural supports
- Gather baseline data
- Develop needs assessment
- Assign priorities to team members
- Develop function-based positive behavior support plan
- Identify community resources
- Address transition.

WHO IS INVOLVED IN WRAPAROUND?

Wraparound is a team-based service planning and coordination process that blends home, school, and community interventions. As a culturally competent and strengths-based approach, the wraparound process values family voice and choice, and addresses the complex needs of the student rather than focusing attention on one individualized problem, such as chronic absenteeism or problematic behavior (Suter & Bruns, 2009). This "holistic prevention tool" utilizes a systems framework to address multiple areas in a child's life and actively involves family and community entities (West-Olatunji, Frazier, & Kelley, 2011, p. 224). Thus, the team should include school, community, and family representatives.

WRAPAROUND PROCESS

According to Eber, Hyde, and Suter (2011), there are four distinct phases of wraparound that a team works through to help a student be successful. During Phase 1, *Engagement and Team Development*, relationships are built among team members, student, and family. A team facilitator explains the process and engages the family in dialogue regarding process, concerns, and potential members of the team. The team identifies student baseline strengths and conducts a needs assessment within this initial phase (Eber et al., 2011).

Within Phase 2, *Initial Plan Development*, the team discusses quality-of-life issues, specific strategies that might address these issues, and defines team member roles. During Phase 3, *Plan Implementation*, both natural supports (e.g., childcare) and evidence-based interventions (e.g., FBA) are identified and team members work with support personnel (e.g., teachers) who are stakeholders in ensuring the plan is successful (Eber et al., 2011). The final phase, *Plan Completion and Transition,* includes progress monitoring with more natural supports (e.g., referral to family counseling). Students' functioning is continuously monitored and assessed (Eber & Nelson, 1997). We have included a case study below to illustrate the wraparound process.

Brad is a 17-year-old high school student in foster care. He has been with his current family for the past four years. Throughout Brad's senior year, his behaviors at home and at school have intensified resulting in an increase in discipline referrals and suspensions. The school year is coming to an end and Brad will be graduating in a few months. The MTSS team has been providing Brad with Tier 2 supports, such as CICO and a community mentor, and his behavioral referrals have only slightly decreased. Because of the possible upcoming transition out of foster care and graduation, the MTSS team has decided to provide Brad with more intensified individualized Tier 3 supports to ensure he has support through this transition during the rest of the school year.

The MTSS team decides to develop a wraparound plan. As part of Phase 1, they expand the team to include other stakeholders in Brad's life, including his foster parents, homeroom teacher, school counselor, school-based mentor, Child Protective Services case worker, and the college/career transition coach. The team is facilitated by the school counselor. As part of Phase 2, they collaboratively established a plan with specific goals to support Brad during the transition from high school. This plan includes on-going family counseling with a licensed professional counselor, and dual enrollment opportunities at the local technical college. In Phase 3, the team implements the family counseling intervention to help Brad develop positive coping skills to lessen problematic behaviors at home and at school, and to facilitate enrollment at the technical college. In Phase 3, the team assists Brad in his post-secondary plans and upcoming transition out of foster care. The team meets every two weeks to review Brad's behavioral and achievement progress monitoring data. Through progress monitoring, the team recognized the wraparound plan to be effective in assisting Brad and his family through the transitions of graduation and enrollment in a post-secondary institution. As part of Phase 4, the team discussed interagency coordination that would allow the most natural and pragmatic supports to continue for Brad, including family counseling, connections to community supports, and career counseling. With these supports in place, Brad continued to live with his foster parents while completing a two-year community college program.

Look again at the wraparound integrity tool you found from your previous search.

What elements of wraparound were in place?

What could the team have done to strengthen the approach?

With a clear understanding of Tier 3 supports including small-group and individual counseling, programs that are rooted in evidence-based practices, and wraparound, we will now move on to ways to use data in the delivery of Tier 3 supports, one hallmark of MTSS.

Use of Data in Tier 3

As outlined by various researchers and in Chapter 9 of this book, practitioners use data to determine the effectiveness and reliability of MTSS interventions (Betters-Bubon et al., 2016; Ockerman et al., 2012; Ziomek-Daigle et al., 2016). Not only do Tier 3 interventions need to benefit the student, but data should also support the success with which the interventions are applied in other situations, such as other classrooms or at home (see the FBA section above). When working with students who need Tier 3 interventions, first and foremost it is important to track the implementation of the interventions to ensure that all students are receiving the correct level of services. Recommending students for Tier 3 interventions should be supported by student data which show the need for support at this level (Ockerman et al., 2012; Patrikakou, Ockerman, & Hollenbeck, 2016; Ryan, Kaffenberger, & Carroll, 2011). Data can also determine if a particular intervention is working. For example, if an intervention is meant to decrease the number of discipline referrals for a student and the data shows that no decrease has occurred, the situation must be re-evaluated and another intervention put in its place. Goals should be reviewed periodically to ensure they are still appropriate for a student. Finally, outcomes must be tracked so that results can be recorded and used to support the future implementation with students as needed. A quick Google search or visit to the PBIS World website provides a number of intervention-tracking resources. See Figure 6.5 and the Resources section at the end of the chapter.

Second, from budgetary and personnel standpoints, it is important that interventions are effective. The outcomes of the interventions have to support the use of financial and human resources to justify implementing MTSS (Betters-Bubon et al., 2016). Data which supports the implementation of services can sometimes lead to increased funding for services and other types of services being made available to school systems for use with students.

Finally, school counselors can play an important role in this process. The ASCA Ethical Standards (2016) provide unwavering support for school counselors as connoisseurs of data; making sure that student data has been reviewed and analyzed before placing

DATA												Monthly Totals
Behavior 1												
Behavior 2												
Behavior 3												
Behavior 4												
Behavior 5												
Intervention 1												
Intervention 2												
Intervention 3												
Intervention 4												
Intervention 5												

Figure 6.5 Progress monitoring tool.

students in more restrictive environments. Through active engagement in this process, school counselors can build a repertoire of preventative initiatives and interventions that can be helpful in preventing and identifying problem behaviors and concerns before they reach the secondary (Tier 2) or tertiary (Tier 3) stages (Scott & Eber, 2003).

Are There Assessment Systems Specific to Tier 3 Supports?

To assess the effectiveness of Tier 3 interventions, researchers found that MTSS teams utilize the Individual Students Systems Evaluation Tool (I-SSET) as a useful way to gather data for continuous program improvement (Debnam et al., 2012). The I-SSET documents the process and procedures of Tier 2 and 3 interventions, and measures the effectiveness of commonly used interventions such as CICO, small-group counseling, and time-limited individual counseling. The tool includes 35 items and three focus areas (foundations, targeted interventions, and individualized interventions) with a summary score (Anderson et al., 2011). External evaluators conduct the I-SSET in three–four hours, conducting interviews with school stakeholders, such as administrators and staff members, and reviewing procedures and outcomes of systems. Other assessments that can be used to assess the fidelity of Tier 3 include the Tiered Fidelity Inventory (TFI), Monitoring Advanced Tiers Tool (MATT) and the Benchmarks for Advanced Tiers (BAT). More information on these tools can be found at www.pbis assessments.org.

Conclusion

Beginning in kindergarten and extending through high school, Multi-Tiered Systems of Support, like PBIS and RTI, provide opportunities for school counselors to collaborate with their students, families, faculty, and community to meet the needs of all students. In this chapter, we presented information on Tier 3 supports including the FBA/BIP processes, individual counseling, small-group counseling, evidence-based programs and curriculums, and wraparound support. Further, we discussed data collection at Tier 3 along with cultural and ethical considerations for school counselors to fully engage in the process. The central themes in Tier 3, including coordination of intensive individualized/group intervention, and specific examples of Tier 3 interventions were interwoven throughout the chapter. Whether school counselors are providing direct or indirect intervention for students at the Tier 3 level of support, the school counselor's role is critical and engaged in the process.

For more information and a school counselor's perspective on *Tier 3: Specialized Services for Students with Intensive Needs* please see Chapter 12 "Voices from the Field," Voices 1, 6, 9, and 10.

ASCA Ethical Standards

Ethical considerations are important when data is used to recommend Tier 3 interventions to target specific students' behavior and academic success (Ockerman, et al., 2012). As members of the MTSS team in their school, counselors can examine potential areas where students might be negatively impacted by an intervention (ASCA, 2018; Betters-Bubon et al., 2016; Goodman-Scott, 2014; Goodman-Scott et al., 2016; Ockerman et al., 2012; Ryan et al., 2011; Sink, 2016; Ziomek-Daigle et al., 2016). With an understanding of equitable data use, school counselors can advocate on students' behalf. School counselors, equipped to recognize data misuse, use the ethical standards to initiate and guide conversations to ensure an equitable resolution for the student.

When thinking about a school's implementation of Tier 3 programming, the following list of ethical standards pertain, related to data, equity, and access (ASCA, 2016). Specifically, school counselors:

A   Responsibility to Students

    A.1   Supporting Student Development

- A.1.a. Have a primary obligation to the students, who are to be treated with dignity and respect as unique individuals.
- A.1.e. Are concerned with students' academic, career, and social/emotional needs and encourage each student's maximum development.
- A.1.h. Provide effective, responsive interventions to address student needs.
- A.1.i. Consider the involvement of support networks, wraparound services, and educational teams needed to best serve students.

    A.6   Appropriate Referrals and Advocacy

- A.6.a. Collaborate with all relevant stakeholders, including students, educators, and parents/guardians when student assistance is needed, including the identification of early warning signs of student distress.

    A.10   Underserved and At-Risk Populations

- A.10.c. Identify resources needed to optimize education.
- A.10.f. Advocate for the equal right and access to free, appropriate public education for all youth, in which students are not stigmatized or isolated based on their housing status, disability, foster care, special education status, mental health, or any other exceptionality or special need.

B   Responsibilities to Parents/Guardians, School and Self

    B.1   Responsibilities to Parents/Guardians

- B.1.a. Recognize that providing services to minors in a school setting requires school counselors to collaborate with students' parents/guardians as appropriate.

    B.2   Responsibilities to the School

- B.2.a. Develop and maintain professional relationships and systems of communication with faculty, staff, and administrators to support students.
- B.2.k. Affirm the abilities of and advocate for the learning needs of all students. School counselors support the provision of appropriate accommodations and accessibility.
- B.2.o. Promote equity and access for all students through the use of community resources.

Resources

Websites

Links to the following can be found on our eresource at www.routledge.com/ 9781138501614.

- What is Tier 3 PBIS?
- Tier 3 Supports, Tools, Presentations, Publications, and Training.
- PBIS World Tier 3.
- Center on Response to Intervention.
- Attendance Works.
- What is an FBA?
- FBA Case Study.

Teaching Activity 1

Directions: As school counselors are often in the role of consultant and collaborator, prepare an agenda and role play a wraparound meeting to address a student with significant behavior issues. What norms will you set for the meeting? What is the goal of the meeting? Remember to first discuss the student's strengths before exploring concerns. Who will be at the table? Use the sample agenda below as a start:

Sample Agenda – Wrap Around Meeting for Alex A.

1   Introductions – what role do you play in Alex's school day?
2   Current levels of progress – how is he doing in your class/intervention group?
3   Strengths – what does Alex enjoy? What is he excelling at?
4   Immediate areas of concern – what is the most pressing issue to address to ensure that Alex is as available for learning as possible? What goal(s) are we working toward?
5   Intervention planning – what interventions will be used? By whom? How often? To achieve what goal? How will progress be monitored?
6   Communication plan – How will progress be communicated to stakeholders?
7   Next meeting – When will we meet next?

Consider:

- What makes a meeting efficient, effective, and successful overall?
- How does a wraparound team handle disagreement or differing opinions?
- When should a meeting be tabled?

Teaching Activity 2

Directions: The goal of this activity is to understand the collaborative process of conducting an Functional Behavioral Assessment.

1   First, search online to find a video of a FBA/BIP process. Make a note of the discrete tasks involved.
2   As a school counselor, what roles could you have in this process?

3 Consider the following questions: how is the BIP developed? Who communicates the plan to the student? To the parent? To classroom teachers? What do you think makes a FBA/BIP successful?

Multiple Choice Questions

1 **What percentage of the student population will need and be eligible for Tier 3 services?**

   a 90% or more.
   b 50%.
   c 25%.
   d Less than 10%.

2 **What is not one of the hallmarks of tertiary systems?**

   a A focus on integrated systems.
   b Occasionally using data to make decisions.
   c Collaboration with key stakeholders.
   d The use of research and evidence-based practices.

3 **Which program is an evidence-based curriculum developed for youth experiencing anxiety?**

   a Second Step Violence Prevention Program.
   b Trauma-Focused Cognitive Behavior Therapy (TF-CBT).
   c Coping Cat Program (CCP).
   d Anger Coping Program (ACP).

4 **Wraparound is conceptualized as a team-based service planning and coordination process that blends:**

   a Only home and school interventions.
   b Home, school, and community interventions.
   c Just school and community interventions.
   d All of the above.

5 **A FBA identifies the purpose of behavior and guides the process of creating a Behavior Intervention Plan (BIP). The BIP includes which of the following?**

   a A list of consequences for the student's misbehavior.
   b Specific goals for the reduction of target behaviors and implementation of replacement behaviors through specific interventions.
   c Academic goals and interventions.
   d All of the above.

Answers: Q1 d, Q2 b, Q3 c, Q4 b, Q5 a.

References

American School Counselor Association (ASCA) (2012). *The ASCA National Model: A framework for school counseling programs* (3rd Ed.). Alexandria, VA: Author.

American School Counselor Association (ASCA) (2016). *ASCA ethical standards for school counselors.* Alexandria, VA: Author. Retrieved from: www.schoolcounselor.org/asca/media/asca/Ethics/EthicalStandards2016.pdf.

American School Counselor Association (ASCA) (2018). *The school counselor and Multitiered Systems of Support.* American School Counselor Association Position Statement. Retrieved from: www.schoolcounselor.org/asca/media/asca/PositionStatements/PS_MultitieredSupportSystem.pdf.

Anderson, C. M., Lewis-Palmer, T., Todd, A. W., Horner, R. H., Sugai, G., & Sampson, N. K. (2011). *Individual Student Systems Evaluation Tool.* Eugene, OR: Educational and Community Supports, University of Oregon. Retrieved from: www.pbis.org/common/cms/files/pbisresources/ISSET_TOOL_v2.8_February_2011.pdf.

Bal, A. (2016). From intervention to innovation: A cultural-historical approach to the racialization of school discipline. *Interchange, 47*(4), 409–427.

Bal, A., Thorius, K., & Kozleski, E. (2012). Culturally responsive positive behavioral support matters. Tempe, AZ: The Equity Alliance. Retrieved from: www.equityallianceatasu.org/sites/default/files/CRPBIS_Matters.pdf.

Barrett, S., Eber, L., & Weist, M. (2013). *Advancing education effectiveness: Interconnecting school mental health and school-wide positive behavior support.* Eugene, OR: Educational and Community Supports, University of Oregon. Retrieved from: www.pbis.org/common/cms/files/Current%20Topics/Final-Monograph.pdf.

Berkeley, S., Bender, W. N., Peaster, L. G., & Saunders L. (2009). Implementation of response to intervention: A snapshot of progress. *Journal of Learning Disabilities, 42*(1), 85–95.

Betters-Bubon, J., Brunner, T., & Kansteiner, A. (2016). Success for all? The role of the school counselor in creating and sustaining culturally responsive PBIS programs. *The Professional Counselor, 6*(3), 263–277.

Bruns, E. J., & Suter, J. C. (2010). Summary of the wraparound evidence base. In E. J. Bruns & J. S. Walker (Eds), *The resource guide to wraparound.* Portland, OR: National Wraparound Initiative.

Carey, J. C., Dimmitt, C., Hatch, T. A., Lapan, R. T., & Whiston, S. C. (2008). Report of the national panel for evidence-based school counseling: Outcome research coding protocol and evaluation of student success skills and second step. *Professional School Counseling, 11*(3), doi: 2156759X0801100306.

Christenson, S. L., & Reschly, A. L. (2010). Check & Connect: Enhancing school completion through student engagement. In B. Doll, W. Pfohl, & J. Yoon (Eds), *Handbook of youth prevention science* (pp. 327–348). New York: Routledge.

Cowan, K., Vaillancourt, K., Rossen, E., & Pollitt, K. (2013). *A framework for safe and successful schools* [Brief]. Bethesda, MD: National Association of School Psychologists. Retrieved from: www.nasponline.org/schoolsafetyframework.

Debnam, K. J., Pas, E. T., & Bradshaw, C. P. (2012). Secondary and tertiary support systems in schools implementing school-wide positive behavioral interventions and support: A preliminary descriptive analysis. *Journal of Positive Behavior Interventions, 14*(3), 142–152, doi: 10.1177/10983007/2436844.

Eber, L., Hyde, K., & Suter, J. C. (2011). Integrating wraparound into a schoolwide system of positive behavior supports. *Journal of Child Family Studies, 20,* 783–790.

Eber, L., & Nelson, C. M. (1997). School-based wraparound for students with emotional and behavioral challenges. *Exceptional Children, 63*(4), 539–555.

Eder, K. C., & Whiston, S. C. (2006). Does psychotherapy help some students? An overview of psychotherapy outcome research. *Professional School Counseling,* 9(5), doi: 2156759X0500900504.

Epstein, M. H., Nordness, P. D., Gallagher, K., Nelson, J. R., Lewis, L., & Schrepf, S. (2005). School as the entry point: Assessing adherence to the basic tenets of the wraparound approach. *Behavioral Disorders, 30*(2), 85–93.

Goodman-Scott, E. (2014). Maximizing school counselors' efforts by implementing school-wide positive behavioral interventions and supports: A case study from the field. *Professional School Counseling, 17*(1), 111–119, doi:10.5330/prsc.17.1.518021r2x6821660.

Goodman-Scott, E., Betters-Bubon, J., & Donohue, P. (2016). Aligning Comprehensive School Counseling Programs and Positive Behavioral Interventions and Supports to maximize school counselors' efforts. *Professional School Counseling, 19*(1), 57–67, doi/pdf/10.5330/1096-2409-19.1.57.

Gundersen, K., & Svartdal, F. (2006). Aggression replacement training in Norway: Outcome evaluation of 11 Norwegian student projects. *Scandinavian Journal of Educational Research, 50*(1), 63–81.

Haskins, N., & Appling, B. (2017). Relational-cultural theory and reality therapy: A culturally responsive integrative framework. *Journal of Counseling & Development, 95*(1), 87–99, doi: 10.1002/jcad.12120.

Hourigan, S. E., Settipani, C. A., Southam-Gerow, M. A., & Kendall, P. C. (2012). Coping cat: A cognitive-behavioral treatment for childhood anxiety disorders. In A. Rubin (Ed.), *Programs and interventions for maltreated children and families at risk* (pp. 91–104). Hoboken, NJ: John Wiley & Sons.

Jaycox, L. (2004). *Cognitive-behavioral intervention for trauma in schools: Training manual.* Longmont, CO: Sopris West Educational Services.

Kashi, T. L. (2008). Response to intervention as a suggested generalized approach to improving minority AYP scores. *Rural Special Education Quarterly, 27*, 37–40.

Kratochwill, T. R., McDonald, L., Levin, J. R., Scalia, P. A., & Coover, G. (2009). Families and schools together: An experimental study of multi-family support groups for children at risk. *Journal of School Psychology, 47*(4), 245–265.

Larson, J., & Lochman, J. E. (2011). *Helping school children cope with anger: A cognitive-behavioral intervention* (2nd Ed.). New York: Guilford Press.

Leverson, M., Smith, K., McIntosh, K., Rose, J., & Pinkelman, S. (2016). *PBIS cultural responsiveness field guide.* Department of Education's Office of Special Education Programs (OSEP) and the Office of Elementary and Secondary Education (OESE), OSEP Technical Assistance Center. Retrieved from: www.pbis.org/Common/Cms/files/pbisresources/PBIS%20Cultural%20Responsiveness%20Field%20Guide.pdf.

Macklem, G. L. (2011). *Evidence-based school mental health services: Affect education, emotion regulation training, and cognitive behavioral therapy.* New York: Springer.

March, R. E., Horner, R. H., Lewis-Palmer, T., Brown, D., Crone, D. A., Todd, A. W., & Carr, E. (2000). *Functional Assessment Checklist for Teachers and Staff* (FACTS). Eugene, OR: University of Oregon.

Ngo, V., Langley, A., Kataoka, S. H., Nadeem, E., Escudero, P., & Stein, B. D. (2008). Providing evidence-based practice to ethnically diverse youths: Examples from the Cognitive Behavioral Intervention for Trauma in Schools (CBITS) program. *Journal of the American Academy of Child & Adolescent Psychiatry, 47*, 858–862.

Ockerman, M. S., Mason, E. C. M., & Hollenbeck, A. F. (2012). Integrating RTI with school counseling programs: Being a proactive professional school counselor. *Journal of School Counseling, 10*(15), 1–37.

Ockerman, M. S., Patrikakou, E., & Hollenbeck, A. F. (2015). Preparation of school counselors and response to intervention: A profession at the crossroads. *The Journal of Counselor Preparation and Supervision, 7*(3), 161–184. Retrieved from: http://dx.doi.org/10.7729/73.1106.

Patrikakou, E., Ockerman, M. S., & Hollenbeck, A. F. (2016). Needs and contradictions of a changing field: Evidence from a national response to intervention implementation study. *The Professional Counselor, 6*(3), 233–250.

Ryan, T., Kaffenberger, C. J., & Carroll, A. G. (2011). Response to intervention: An opportunity for school counselor leadership. *Professional School Counseling, 14*(3), 211–221.

Scott, T. M., & Eber, L. (2003). Functional assessment and wraparound as systemic school processes: Primary, secondary, and tertiary systems examples. *Journal of Positive Behavior Interventions, 5*(3), 131–143.

Sherrod, M. D., Getch, Y. Q., & Ziomek-Daigle, J. (2009). The impact of positive behavioral support to decrease discipline referrals with elementary students. *Professional School Counseling, 12*, 421–424.

Sink, C. A. (2016). Incorporating a Multi-Tiered System of Supports into school counselor preparation. *The Professional Counselor, 6*(3), 203–219, doi:10.15241/cs.6.3.203.

Stage, S., Cheney, D., Lynass, L., Mielenz, C., & Flower, A. (2012). 3 validity studies of the daily progress report in relationship to the check, connect and expect intervention. *Journal of Positive Behavior Interventions, 14*(3), 181–191, doi: 10.1177/1098300712438942.

Sunawan, S., & Xiong, J. (2016). An application model of reality therapy to develop effective achievement goals in tier 3 intervention. *International Education Studies, 9*(10), 16–26, doi: 10.5539/ies.v9n10p16.

Suter, J. C., & Bruns, E. J. (2009). Effectiveness of the wraparound process for children with emotional and behavioral disorders: A meta-analysis. *Clinical Child and Family Psychology Review, 12*(4), 336–351.

Warren, J. M., & Robinson, G. (2015). Addressing barriers to effective RTI through school counselor consultation: A social justice approach. *Electronic Journal for Inclusive Education, 3*(4), 1–27.

West-Olatunji, C., Frazier, K. N., & Kelley, E. (2011). Wraparound counseling: An ecosystemic approach to working with economically disadvantaged students in urban school settings. *Journal of Humanistic Counseling, 50*(2), 222–237.

Winburn, A., Gilstrap, D., & Perryman, M. (2017). Treating the tiers: Play therapy responds to intervention in the schools. *International Journal of Play Therapy, 26*(1), 1–11, doi: 10.1037/pla0000041.

Ziomek-Daigle, J., & Cavin, J. (2015). Shaping youth and families through positive behavior support: A call for counselors. *The Family Journal, 23,* 386–373, doi:10.1177/1066480715601106.

Ziomek-Daigle, J., Goodman-Scott, E., Cavin, J., & Donohue, P. (2016). Integrating a Multi-Tiered System of Supports with Comprehensive School Counseling Programs. *The Professional Counselor, 6*(3), 220–232, doi:10.15241/jzd.6.3.220.

Zyromski, B., & Mariani, M. A. (2016). *Facilitating evidence-based, data-driven school counseling: A manual for practice.* Thousand Oaks, CA: Corwin Press.

7 Universal Screening to Support MTSS

Peg Donohue

Introduction

How do school counselors know which students are in need of intervention? With large caseloads and multi-faceted roles, school counselors must determine which students require an intentional and targeted intervention and which students simply need a brief session to steer them back on track. In our field, we want to ensure that no students fall through the proverbial crack. This might be the quiet student who becomes increasingly isolated, posts angry or threatening statements and images on social media, or seeks distance from their family. How would we know this student might need mental health intervention? What if we miss the "red flags?" What if we fail to recognize that a student is internalizing their pain and they plan to hurt themselves or others?

In light of increasing incidents of violence in schools, school counselors and school staff need a systematic and effective way to identify students and implement interventions. In this chapter I describe universal screening (US), the practice of assessing all students to identify barriers to learning, including the rationale for implementation, how US fits within Multi-Tiered Systems of Support (MTSS), the eight steps involved, and the school counselor's corresponding role. In addition, I explore the benefits and challenges involved in screening students for mental health, behavioral, and social/emotional concerns.

Emergent Mental Health Concerns

Research shows that one out of seven students in schools in the U.S. have a diagnosable mental health disorder before the age of eight (Perou et al., 2013), and nearly one in five 9–17 year olds has a diagnosable psychiatric disorder (Tyler, Hulkower, & Kaminski, 2017). In fact, during any given year, approximately 13–20% of students aged 3–17 will be diagnosed with a mental health disorder, which has been on the rise since 1994 (Perou et al., 2013). The National Institute of Health indicates that approximately one in four adults has a mental health disorder. Unfortunately, significant barriers exist for families seeking access to mental and behavioral health treatment in our country. For example, estimates suggest that only 15% to 25% of children with mental/behavioral health disorders undergo treatment (Martini, Hilt, & Marx, 2012). O'Connell, Boat, and Warner (2009) advise that "a 2– to 4–year window may exist between initial presentation of symptoms in youth and the development of a disorder, suggesting an opportunity to intervene before problems become more serious in children" (p. 37). The initial onset of most mental illnesses is between the ages of 7 and 11 (Kessler, Berglund, Demler, Jin, Merikangas, & Walters, 2005); many mental illnesses surface before a young person leaves high school (Lenzenweger, Lane, Loranger, & Kessler, 2007). Thus, an important window of opportunity exists during which we can identify K-12 students who need mental health support and provide interventions that teach essential lifelong coping strategies, enabling them to be more available for learning.

Unfortunately, there are many cases where students have struggled with mental health concerns alone because they weren't recognized or weren't on any staff member's "radar." Often, school staff wait for teacher referrals, or student failure, before helping students access necessary services. Why is this the case? First, the referral process for assessing an individual's mental health often mirrors the academic referral process. A student must show significant deficiency and undergo a lengthy battery of tests to determine intervention. Second, teachers-in-training lack sufficient coursework to confidently identify and refer students' mental health problems (Tilly, 2008). Finally, school staff are more apt to notice students who externalize their struggles than those who internalize their pain. Research indicates that students with internalizing concerns, such as anxiety, depression, suicide, social withdrawal, difficulty sleeping, and trauma are less likely to be identified and treated in the schools than students demonstrating externalizing behaviors (i.e., aggression, defiance, etc.; Bradshaw, Buckley, & Ialongo, 2008; Forns, Abad, & Kirchner, 2011; Gonzalez, Monzon, Solis, Jaycox, & Langley, 2016; Weist et al., 2018). A 2008 study found that while 75% of students with externalizing behaviors were identified for related services, only 40% of students with internalizing behaviors were identified and treated (Bradshaw et al., 2008). Universal screening increases the likelihood of identifying youth with internalizing behaviors early (Weist et al., 2018) because we know that even students who achieve academically might be internalizing or struggling inwardly. Intervention science suggests that identifying individuals at an early age is an effective practice to ensure healthy academic, emotional, and behavioral development. Further, while educators may more easily identify students with externalizing behaviors, they may not know the underlying cause. Hence, conducting US helps us better understand the sources of students' behaviors (Weist et al., 2018).

School counselors seek to meet the needs of *all* students as they design and implement Comprehensive School Counseling Programs (CSCPs) and MTSS. We can better achieve this goal by implementing reforms which place the same emphasis on identifying students with mental health, behavioral, and social/emotional challenges, as we do for identifying students whose literacy and numeracy skills are below grade level. Next, I will describe how school counselors and MTSS teams can approximate this balance through US.

Universal Screening

Each fall, PreK-12 students across the country file down to the nurse's office for vision and hearing screenings. Every year, students complete academic benchmark tests to determine their academic strengths and needs. Why do school staff organize these annual rituals? Because we know that students who have a visual or auditory impediment are not 100% ready to learn. Thankfully, these barriers can be addressed through an intervention (e.g., glasses, a hearing aid, etc.). As a result of these screenings, schools contact students' families and often parents/guardians follow up with a specialist to address the concern. There is no controversy. No one is upset. Parents/guardians are often thankful that their children will have the supports that allow them to keep up with their peers academically and socially. Similarly, universal screening (US) of mental health, behavioral, and social/emotional concerns help to identify student concerns that may inhibit school performance.

Universal screening, or US, is "the systematic assessment of *all* children within a given class, grade, school building, or school district on academic and/or social-emotional indicators that the school personnel and community have agreed are important" (Ikeda, Nessen, & Witt, 2008, p. 113). The official policy statement from Mental Health America (Nguyen, Davis, Counts, & Fritze, 2016) explains "early identification, accurate diagnosis, and effective treatment of mental health or substance use conditions in school-aged young people can alleviate enormous suffering and heartbreak and help young people to benefit from their education and to lead productive lives" (p. 1). The overall goal of US is to identify childhood mental health problems preventatively, before the behaviors merit a parent or teacher referral for services (Severson, Walker, Hope-Doolittle, Kratochwill, & Gresham, 2007).

Recommendations for US

Several sources avidly recommend and support US. First, the Individuals with Disabilities Education Act (IDEA, 2004), which governs special education services, indicates that educational teams are responsible for identifying students in need of all services (i.e., speech and language, special education, occupational therapy, counseling, etc.). This part of the federal law called "Child-Find" indicates that "school district personnel have the legal responsibility to ensure that all children within their jurisdiction, birth to 21, regardless of the severity of their disability, and who need special education and related services are identified, located, and evaluated" (IDEA, 2004). Related services can include universally screening every student for mental health, behavioral, and social/emotional concerns that can impede student access to the general education curriculum.

In addition to the federal government, a number of organizations and commissions have specifically recommended US for mental health. After the tragic events of April 1999 when two teens entered Columbine High School in Littleton, Colorado, killing 12 and ending their own lives, then President George W. Bush established the President's New Freedom Commission on Mental Health (Hogan, 2003). The President directed the Commission to identify policies that could be implemented by federal, state, and local governments to optimize the utility of existing resources, improve collaborative efforts to provide treatments and services, and advance efforts to ensure community integration for adults with a serious mental illness and children with a serious emotional disturbance. The commission recommended all schools in the U.S. develop programs to implement US for mental health. That same year, the U.S. President's Commission on Excellence in Special Education called for the use of US in schools.

In 2009 the National Association of School Psychologists, the National Research Council, and the Institute of Medicine endorsed US in schools. The American Pediatric Association endorsed regular mental health and substance abuse screening during well-child visits as a way of addressing emergent mental health concerns in 2010. Finally, after the tragic school shooting in Newton, Connecticut, where 20 first graders and 6 educators lost their lives, several organizations, including the American School Counseling Association (ASCA), collaborated on *A Framework for Safe and Successful Schools* (Cowan, Vaillancourt, Rossen, & Pollitt, 2013), endorsing MTSS. Relatedly, a report filed by the Connecticut Office of the Child Advocate in 2014 identified "missed opportunities" to support Adam Lanza throughout his development. In fact, the very first recommendation from this report was the implementation of US to provide early identification and intervention for children with maladaptive or violent behavior: "systems must facilitate and financially support universal screening for behavioral health and developmental impairments for children ages birth to 21" (Office of the Child Advocate, 2014, p. 9).

More recently, Humphrey and Wigelsworth (2016) indicated the need for universal school-based mental health screening for students in grades 6–12. They cited the following benefits of US: (a) no at-risk child goes unidentified; (b) US provides useful baseline data that can assist with allocating resources and designing interventions and preventative programming; (c) US is cost effective—it is less expensive to address emergent issues rather than clinical levels of distress (Humphrey & Wigelsworth, 2016).

Finally, in 2017, the Ohio Positive Behavior Intervention and Support Network published a handbook on implementing US in schools, giving districts a blueprint for implementing US within MTSS.

Universal Screening and MTSS

As mentioned in previous chapters, MTSS is an approach for systematically supporting students' academic, social, emotional, and behavioral development, and is widely implemented throughout the country. For instance, as of 2016, 45 states implement Response to Intervention (RTI; Patrikakou, Ockerman, & Hollenbeck, 2016) while nearly 26,000 schools nationwide implement Positive Behavioral Interventions and Supports (PBIS; PBIS, 2018; see Chapters 1 and 2 for more information).

Currently, US is a central component of RTI, to screen all students for academics. Specifically, all students are exposed to high quality literacy and numeracy instruction (Tier 1). Those who do not meet standards on benchmark assessments receive targeted small-group academic interventions (Tier 2); those who are not successful after six to eight weeks of small-group intervention are referred to more intensive interventions (Tier 3), which may involve an increased frequency of intervention, as well as a 1:1 or 1:3 interventionists to student ratio (Vincent, Sprague, Pavel, Tobin, & Gau, 2015). Students who are still not able to master essential concepts in literacy and numeracy after engagement in Tier 3 intervention may be referred for special education testing. Similarly, PBIS relies on several methods for identifying students in need of Tier 2 or Tier 3 supports, such as office discipline referrals, failing grades, absences, etc. Thus, schools implementing MTSS are universally screening all students for academics and for some (limited) behavioral indicators.

However, while MTSS is widely implemented throughout the country, and despite the plethora of strong recommendations for universally screening for mental health, behavioral, and social/emotional factors, few schools utilize this strategy. For instance, researchers conducted a national study of 450 elementary, middle, and high school district officials from a broad range of American cities with differing socioeconomic levels. Only 12% of participants reported adopting US in their schools (Bruhn, Woods-Groves, & Huddle, 2014).

To strengthen MTSS implementation, US should be used to screen for a variety of characteristics: academics, physical and mental health, behavioral, and social/emotional skills. Expanding US to encompass mental health, behavioral, and social/emotional components ensures that all aspects of a child's development are addressed during their K-12 years. There has been growing research regarding the benefits of US. In one recent study, researchers found that utilizing a US process within MTSS led to a 180% increase in students identified with behavioral/mental health concerns (Splett et al., 2018). Overall, US fits well within the structure of MTSS, providing a mechanism to identify and address students' needs.

Universal Screening and CSCPs

School counselors design, implement, and continuously improve their CSCP (e.g., the ASCA National Model) to meet students' academic, career, and social/emotional concerns (ASCA, 2012). Within a CSCP, the ASCA position statement on MTSS recommends that, "school counselors must provide school-based prevention and universal interventions and targeted interventions for students with mental health and behavioral health concerns" (ASCA, 2018, p. 1). To deliver targeted interventions, students with elevated needs must first be identified. One strategy for identification is US, which not only provides a framework for identifying students, but also a way to directly and indirectly serve students through a CSCP. Thus, US can be situated within CSCPs. Before describing the specific role of the school counselor in US, I will first describe US implementation.

The Process of Implementing US

Initiating a US program to identify students with emergent mental health concerns takes a great deal of thoughtful planning and team work. While these eight steps may look a little different in every school or district, following a structured team process will best ensure effectiveness (Center for School Mental Health, 2018). I will describe each step and provide related examples.

Step 1: Foundation: Assemble a Team and Get Buy-In

Step 2: Clarify Goals and Purpose

Step 3: Resources and Logistics

Step 4: Select Screening Tool

Step 5: Decide on Consent

Step 6: Data Collection, Administration, Follow-Up

Step 7: Services/Interventions

Step 8: Continued Assessment

Step 1: Foundation: Assemble a Team and Get Buy-In

The first step in US is assembling a multidisciplinary team specific to US (e.g., US team) that is situated within the greater MTSS leadership team. The MTSS team is a larger team that oversees the comprehensive implementation of tiered supports. The multi-disciplinary US team can include school-based mental health providers, (e.g., school counselors, school social workers, school psychologists), general education and special education teachers, at least one administrator, a community-based mental health pro-vider, and family representation. Thus, the school counselor is one member of the US team, and not solely responsible for US. Next, school psychologists are critical members of the team who oversee the assessment process, due to their expertise in psychological assessment. Thus, to be in compliance with state and federal special education laws, a school psychologist must be available to conduct educational testing in order to deter-mine eligibility for specialized instruction (Fagan, 2003). In addition, social workers, school family therapists, general educators, and special educators also provide impor-tant perspectives on effective assessment and intervention. Likewise, administrators are key contributors to the US team since they are responsible for school operations and resources. It is also important to include community-based mental health providers as team members or consultants, to gain their expertise and ready them for a potential increase in counseling referrals. Finally, having a family member on the team ensures that parent/guardian perceptions of the screening program are prioritized.

After selecting the US team, this team must gain buy-in from key stakeholders. Specifically, the team can do an intensive review of key data that might lend credence

Table 7.1 Students in grades 9–12 identified with clinical levels of anxiety prior to universal screening

Year	Total	Percent of Population	Males	Females	Percent with 504 plans
2013–2014	29	8%	20	9	50%
2014–2015	37	11%	15	22	57%
2015–2016	40	11%	19	21	65%
2016–2017	48	14%	22	26	77%
2017–2018	57	16%	27	30	81%

to the need for US. For instance, one school district had data showing increasing student absences. The US team utilized this attendance data to highlight a need for US and explained to administrators how US could assist the school to better understand the underlying needs of absentee students, thus gaining administrator buy-in. Correspondingly, it is recommended that the US team assess key priorities of the school/district, and discuss related data, to gain buy-in from stakeholders and key decision-makers. Further, using data to gain buy-in can also clarify the goals or purpose of US, discussed next.

Step 2: Clarify Goals and Purpose

The US team must clarify their unique goals and purpose for conducting US, which guides implementation. While one school district may begin a US program to address the high number of students in emotional distress, another district may desire to teach healthy coping skills to mitigate high anxiety. Thus, the US team tracks data in order to develop the rationale, purpose, and goals for US, which also increases stakeholder buy-in, as discussed previously. As a result, this second step of US is closely intertwined with the first step, as communicating the purpose, goals, and rationale of US may garner stakeholder buy-in.

The US team can analyze MTSS data, such as discipline referrals, academics, attendance records, and previous intervention data, as well as perception data from staff, students, and family members (e.g., what do these stakeholders perceive as the biggest student challenges in the school?). With this data the US team can identify trends and, thus, goals and purpose.

For example, in Table 7.1 a US high school team noted an increase in both the number of students with diagnosed anxiety and the demand for 504 plans to address anxiety throughout their feeder elementary and middle schools. By looking at a five-year trend in the data, the US team convinced the elementary and middle schools to join them in screening for anxiety to support early prevention and intervention efforts.

Next, and throughout this chapter, I'll discuss the US process in my previous district, Shoretown Public Schools (a pseudonym).

Shoretown Public Schools

In the four-year period prior to implementing US, we saw a significant increase in the number of students diagnosed with anxiety and a startling rise in the number of students who were referred to mobile crisis services because of suicidal ideation. By monitoring these data points, we were able to gain buy-in and provide a clear rationale for our interest in piloting a US program in our district, as well as specific goals and purpose. Stakeholders including administrators, teachers, parents, and school board members supported the proposal to pilot a US program to address the increase in significant mental health concerns.

Step 3: Resources and Logistics

Universal screening requires considerable pre-planning during which the team must carefully consider necessary resources and logistics to successfully navigate implementation. It is important to note that the first three steps of the US process may happen fluidly and together, as gaining school/district buy-in may be contingent upon available resources, such as time and money.

Please see the following list of questions to examine when considering implementing US in your school or district.

- Who should be on the US team? Which staff should be involved in implementation? How should they be trained?
- What are we screening for?
- Which students are screened? How often are they screened?
- What screening assessment(s) do we use?
- What resources (financial and time) do we have available to implement US?
- How do we notify parents/guardians and gain their consent? Should we request passive or active consent?
- What liability issues should we consider?
- How will we document the process and results of US?
- What is the optimal timeline for implementation?
- What available follow-up services do we have for our students?

As you can see, there is much to consider before implementing US. I will address many of these questions in the following sections. However, there are two topics I will address first: time and legal issues.

Time

When planning for US generally, the MTSS team must consider the time that many team members will spend on US administration, data analysis, and parent/guardian communication. Planning, implementing, and coordinating interventions will also require a significant time commitment. In order to best support US, it is recommended that school staff, such as school counselors, have manageable recommended student caseloads (e.g., for school counselors, 1:250).

Legal Issues

Any time educators collect sensitive data about students, concerns about confidentiality and liability arise. Before implementing US, the US team should consult district policies, state, and federal laws. The team must also decide on logistics such as how to confidentially store and report US data. It is recommended that US teams consult with school district legal counsel prior to beginning the US process.

Shoretown Public Schools

The US team was led by the Director of Pupil Personnel Services; she championed this effort as a way of supporting district goals to identify students in need of services and to provide effective and efficient evidence-based interventions. Also, the US team included the school counselors and school psychologists for all participating schools, as well as outside agencies and pediatricians. We wanted to have expertise, buy-in, and awareness from outside providers in case we did not have sufficient district resources to meet students' identified mental health needs. Teachers and parents/guardians were also essential team players in planning. We spent an entire school year preparing to pilot US for 3rd, 6th, and 9th grade students. We selected students in these transition years because we had the greatest concerns about our students who were moving from educational levels. We could not have moved forward with our US program unless we were fully prepared with resources and logistics.

Step 4: Select Screening Tool

The US team bases important decisions on the needs of the school/district, as well as on a variety of other impactful factors. Most importantly, they must be in accord about the pressing concerns for which they are most interested in screening (e.g., depression, anxiety, etc.). In this section, I'll discuss the different types of screeners, including screening for resiliency, then additional factors such as psychometric properties and cost.

First, when considering US, there are a number of potential screeners to choose from. Please see Table 7.2 below, which lists commonly used screeners you and your team might find helpful.

Also, to note, many schools use resiliency scales. Parents/guardians who are wary of mental health assessments may be more amenable to resilience screeners, which focus on coping with adversity, seeking assistance, etc. These screeners provide data to guide both prevention and intervention. For instance, researchers recently examined the use of school-based screeners for the early identification of students at risk for high levels of truancy (Wroblewski, Dowdy, Sharkey, & Kyung Kim, 2019). They found that social and emotional screeners identified students' strengths in self-awareness, self-management, social awareness, relationship skills, and decision-making skills. Three psychometrically sound and widely used resiliency scales include: the Connor-Davidson Resilience Scale (CD-RISC; Connor & Davidson, 2003); Academic Resilience Scale (ARS-30; Cassidy, 2016); Brief Resilience Scale (Smith et al., 2008). For a more complete list, please see Windle, Bennett, and Noyes (2011).

Who Completes the Screeners?

Regardless of the screening measure chosen, screening data can be collected in several ways, including student self-report, parent inventories, and teacher inventories. Whether screeners are completed by students, parents, or teachers, it's important to clearly explain the screener, the purpose of administration, and the plan for addressing the data derived from the screener.

SELF-REPORTS

Self-reports are the gold standard in US, as asking students directly provides the most reliable data regarding their behavior, cognitions, and mental health. Students may decipher

Table 7.2 Commonly used behavioral and mental health universal screeners

Name	Age Levels	Description
Systematic Screener for Behavior Disorders (SSBD), 2004	3–12 Years	Teacher evaluation report. Screener identifies top three internalizers and externalizers in class.
Strengths and Difficulties Questionnaire (SDQ), 2002	4–17 Years	Teacher, parent, or student evaluation. 25-item screener measures internalizing, externalizing, and prosocial behaviors.
Social Skills Improvement System (SSIS) Rating Scales, 2008	3–18 Years	Teacher, parent, or student evaluation. Screener measures social skills, problem behaviors (e.g., externalizing, internalizing), and academic competence.
Behavior Assessment System for Children 3: Behavior and Emotion Screening System (BASC-3 BESS), 2015	3–18 Years	Teacher, parent, or student evaluation. 25–30-item screener measures internalizing and externalizing behaviors, school problems, and adaptive skills.
Beck Youth Inventories, Second Edition (BYI-2), 2005	7–18 Years	Self-reported evaluation. 20-item screener measures emotional and social impairment. Five inventories.
Revised Children's and Adolescent Depression Scale (RCADS)	8–18 Years	Self-reported evaluation. 47-item screener measures separation anxiety disorder, social phobia, generalized anxiety disorder, panic disorder, obsessive compulsive disorder, and major depressive disorder, total anxiety scale, and a total internalizing scale.
Generalized Anxiety Disorder 7-item (GAD-7)	11–17 Years	Self-reported evaluation. Screener measures mild, moderate, and severe anxiety. Identifies students in need of further testing and intervention.
Patient Health Questionnaire (PHQ 9)	11–17 Years	Self-reported evaluation. Screener measures presence and severity of depression.
Car, Relax, Alone, Forget, Friends, Trouble (CRAFFT)	12–18 Years	Self-reported evaluation. Six-item screener identifies adolescents for high risk alcohol and other drug use disorders simultaneously.
Behavior Intervention and Monitoring Assessment System (BIMAS)	5–18 Years	Self-reported evaluation. 34-item screener measures social, emotional and behavioral functioning in children and adolescents, ages 5–18.

that specific answers may lead to a referral. For some, this is a welcome relief (e.g., "someone finally asked me") while for others, it may feel intrusive. It is important to consider that students may engage in social desirability, which means they answer in ways they think they *should* answer instead of in a manner that is accurate. Screeners must be carefully chosen when considering students' chronological and developmental age. To that end, each screening administrator should be provided with the same developmentally appropriate script to be read to students prior to administering the screener. In addition, school staff should be aware that answering screening questions may possibly trigger some students struggling with personal and familial issues.

PARENT INVENTORIES

Parent inventories can be helpful, especially for children who are pre-literate. Some schools may choose to administer a US to parents at an evening parent program to ensure greater participation. Others send hard copies of protocols home. Of course, all efforts should be made to translate the parent inventory into all native languages represented in the school.

TEACHER INVENTORIES

Teacher inventories include those that rely on teacher identification and observation of symptoms or behaviors. Many are brief, such as the BASC-2 and BESS, which take teachers about 10 minutes per student to complete. Teacher screening scales tend to be most accurate when teachers work in a self-contained setting (grades PreK–5 generally speaking). The task of completing a screener on a student who spends only 45 minutes in a teacher's classroom daily is more difficult. However, team discussion can be helpful in this instance.

Psychometric Properties

As with any assessment, a screener must undergo rigorous examination to determine if it is valid and reliable. The validity of a screener is defined by its accuracy in identifying students with the presenting issue or concern, or measuring what it purports to measure. Reliability is the degree to which a screener produces stable and consistent results. Thus, the same results occurring in the screener would be given repeatedly. While well-meaning US team members might suggest creating a screener from scratch or making changes to an existing screener, unfortunately these approaches will not yield reliable and valid data. The team must select a screener with sound validity and reliability properties in order to move forward with US in their school or district.

Cost

The school/district will need financial resources to implement US. Costs may include purchasing instruments, testing software, protocols, staff training, clerical support, and so forth. Some instruments involve cost per protocol or per administration, whereas others with web-based assessment include licensing fees. Computer-based assessments require well-maintained computers and site licenses. Many protocols are available at a reduced rate when large quantities are administered. For instance, one district was able to put screening tools on an internal server so that they could get student screening data in real time. Students who demonstrated need were contacted within 24 hours and received support in seven days or less. Expediting this process can be efficient and cost-effective. In addition, many on-line assessment systems such as AIMSweb have a built-in screening feature. An annual site license is necessary for AIMS-web and the like. Many screening tools can be used free of charge.

Shoretown Public Schools

In our school, the school psychologist played an important role in selecting and discussing potential screeners. Based on our district-wide data trends, there was an increased number of high school students with anxiety and depression, and we wanted to screen specifically for these concerns. We first looked at screeners we were already using in the school district, due to familiarity with the assessment, including reliability and validity, staff training requirements, as well as cost and time. Since we often used the full BASC to assess students for special education services, we investigated this assessment as a potential screener. We found that the BASC-2 or BESS is a commonly used screener related to the BASC (Kamphaus & Reynolds, 2007). It was developed as a school-wide screening tool for children in grades Pre-K–12 and identifies behavioral and emotional strengths and weaknesses by looking at externalizing behaviors (e.g., acting out), internalizing behaviors (e.g., withdrawing), and adaptive skills (e.g., social and self-care skills). With only 30 questions, it is relatively easy to administer. The screener was also inexpensive to administer and could be completed using a computer, thus assuring we could get our results quickly.

Next, our school team investigated potential instruments that screened for anxiety and depression. As a team, we only considered assessments that were psychometrically reliable and valid.

We looked at screening questions, considering both teacher inventories and self-reports. Our school psychologists discussed the validity, reliability, and purpose of each screener. We noted screeners we are already using in our district such as the BASC. We wanted a student self-report that could be completed in under 10 minutes. We were careful to select a screener which had inclusive and developmentally appropriate language. Weighing all these factors, we settled on the 30-question BASC-2.

While Shoretown Public Schools decided to use one screener across the district, another district preferred to employ a more complex approach: enlisting a variety of screeners, across many grade levels, at different times during the school year. See Figure 7.1 below, illustrating the screeners used to identify students in grades 3–12. Specifically, the teachers completed the Strengths and Difficulties Questionnaire (SDQ) for the youngest students in grades 3 and 4, and they also screened for anxiety and depression by using the Revised Children's Anxiety and Depression Scale (RCADS). The Generalized Anxiety Disorder 7-item (GAD-7) was used to screen students in 9–12th grade for interfering levels of anxiety. They also used the Patient Health Questionnaire (PHQ-9) to measure the frequency of depressive episodes and severity of the depression for this age group. Last, the CRAFFT screener assessed for alcohol and drug use and related behaviors. Overall, each school can individualize their approach to screening, whether utilizing one screener or several.

Grade	Anxiety	Depression	Substance Use	Global Scale
3				SDQ
4				SDQ
5	RCADS	RCADS		
6	RCADS	RCADS		
7	RCADS	RCADS	CRAFFT	
8	RCADS	RCADS		
9	GAD-7	PHQ-9	CRAFFT	SDQ
10	GAD-7	PHQ-9		SDQ
11	GAD-7	PHQ-9		SDQ
12	GAD-7	PHQ-9		SDQ

Figure 7.1 Sample universal screening plan.

(Source: the Author.)

Step 5: Decide on Consent

Given the delicate nature of US, parents must be adequately informed during every step of the process. Thus, schools should decide on the type of consent needed. Popular in US process is the use of passive consent, which means that families are contacted, often through several means, and asked to contact the school if they want their child withdrawn from the screening. Thus, without parent contact, the school will assume that parents/guardians give consent for their child's screening. For example, in one district, the screening process was posted on the website, emailed home to parents, and communicated via automatic phone call. In addition, they held informational meetings, provided links to all screeners on their website, and provided hard copies of protocols in the school's main office. Also, when communicating about US, staff normalized the US process, such as comparing it with academic benchmark screening or vision tests.

Step 6: Data Collection, Administration, Follow-Up

Once the US team has consent, they must decide how to administer the screener.

Timeline

It is recommended that screeners are administered more than once per year to gain data on students at multiple times, as a screener is simply a snapshot of a child on a given day (Lane, Oakes, & Menzies, 2010). In addition, teacher-completed screeners should be conducted only after they have time to adequately observe and interact with their students. Thus, a team may decide to screen in October, February, and May in schools with a 10-month school year (see Table 7.3). Data collected in October can be utilized to identify students with elevated needs, form intervention groups, and refer students to outside mental health providers. Data collected in February may provide preliminary data about the effectiveness of intervention and highlight students who were not identified in the first round of screening. Finally, some districts may opt to screen a third time in May,

Table 7.3 Optimal procedural timeline for initial universal screening program in schools

Month	Action Taken
Spring (year prior)	Select screener, plan communication, inform stakeholders, secure resources.
September	Finalize planning of logistics for US administration.
October	Administer screener.
October (days immediately following screening)	Identify students with immediate needs to support within 24 hours. Create small-group intervention to start within five school days.
October to February	Facilitate small-group instruction; meet with students individually; address widespread concerns via classroom guidance (e.g., test-taking anxiety). Progress monitor.
February	Re-administer screener.
February (days immediately following screening)	Identify students with immediate needs to support within 24 hours. Create small-group intervention to start within five school days. Integrate students from first round of screening who continue to need support into new intervention groups.
May	Plan for fall screening program.

which could give further information about the effectiveness of interventions as a whole, as well as providing valuable insights for plans in the subsequent school year.

Also, when planning the timeline for data collection, administration, and follow-up, US team members should consider piloting their US process. Thus, it is advisable to start with a small sample such as a classroom or grade level. Initial challenges can be more easily addressed on a small scale, rather than school-wide.

Other timing considerations when administering US include that some middle and high schools found success administering screeners during regularly scheduled advising periods. In addition, one district worked collectively to screen at each school on separate mornings, to have sufficient numbers of professionals available, and to ensure standardization of administration.

Educating and Informing School Staff

Before administering the screener, the US team should provide professional development to school staff, to provide them with background information on the screening process as well as to increase their capacity to identify warning signs of emotional distress. In addition, given the sensitive nature of screening results, it's essential to develop a clear policy regarding how, when, and to whom results are shared, consulting the school district's legal counsel. For instance, based on FERPA (the Family Educational Rights and Privacy Act), as well as state and district policy, do teachers and other school staff have the right to know the results of the screening process?

Staff Training to Administer

To ensure consistency and for ethical and appropriate practices, staff administering screeners must be trained in the appropriate protocols. Relatedly, master's-level US team members (e.g., school psychologists, school counselors, etc.) should administer screeners. It is suggested that staff administering screeners follow scripts and procedures to ensure standardized administration across students.

Scoring

Each screener has specific cut-off scores which inform results (e.g., elevated levels of anxiety). Once students are identified by the results of the screener, staff should follow previously determined protocol for communicating with parents/guardians and the student, as well as referring/providing services.

Students with high risks should receive immediate follow-up, such as same-day services (Center for School Mental Health, 2018). Before administering screeners, the US team must have referral sources in place, such as informing local crisis centers and community service boards of screening dates, ensuring streamlined referrals. Students with critical concerns should meet with a school-based mental health professional (school counselors, school psychologists, school social workers, etc.) within 24 hours of screening. As a result, it is best to conduct screenings early in the week so that team members have enough time to meet with students directly after screening.

Sharing Results with Parents/Guardians

After identifying students with elevated needs, parents/guardians should be contacted directly. For instance, members of the US team, such as school-based mental health professionals, could inform parents/guardians by telephone and then follow-up by sending letters. This provides both the US team member and the parent/guardian with ample time to exchange information, answer questions, and partner to begin planning an effective on-site or off-site intervention plan.

Shoretown Public Schools: Sharing Results with Parents

We agreed that the best way to inform parents of students who had elevated or highly elevated scores would be to call home. We reached each parent/guardian by phone prior to mailing out result letters. These calls gave school counselors the opportunity to make a personal contact with parents and to offer to partner with them to ensure their child got assistance.

A school counselor recounted a call with a parent:

> The third parent I called gave a response I likely will never forget. When I told her that I was calling because her son came out elevated for possible depression or anxiety on the recent universal screening, she immediately replied, 'I am so glad you called me. He is my oldest and I have been worried. I wasn't sure if it was the normal ups and downs of adolescence, or if it was something more. I was going to call you. Now I know I should have trusted my mother's intuition. I will take him to see his pediatrician. They have a good rapport. If he tells my son to talk to someone about what is going on with him, he'll do it. So, thank you!'

Step 7: Services/Interventions

Once students are identified as having elevated needs through US, it is imperative that services are suggested. For instance, Weist et al. (2018) suggested several strategies to identify and meet the needs of students with internalizing concerns. Specifically,

(a) screening procedures that increase the likelihood of early identification of these problems; (b) Tier 1 supports that make schools more predictable, consistent, positive, and safe learning environments; (c) Tier 2 supports that improve the structure, instruction, reward, and feedback for students who need a modest level of increased assistance to be successful; and (d) Tier 3 supports that allow individualized and evidence-based assessment and intervention across social, emotional, behavioral, and academic domains. (Weist et al., 2018, p. 10)

Students who are identified through US can receive a range of services, including strengthened Tier 1 supports, as well as school and/or community-based supports at the Tier 2 (group) or Tier 3 (individual) level, depending on student needs (please see Chapters 5 and 6 on Tier 2 and 3 interventions, respectively). Further, supports should be evidence-based (such as those recommended in Chapter 10). Strong Kids and Strong Teens (Harlacher & Merrell, 2010), Coping Cats (Albano & Kendall, 2002), and Taking Action (Stark & Kendall, 1996) are three evidence-based programs worth exploring.

In order to have a meaningful school-based US process, adequate mental health supports and interventionists must be available to all students. Further, many districts who utilize US find that there is a tremendous disconnect between their students' mental health needs and the services they have available. Many students, especially those in underserved communities, have less access to quality school and community-based mental health professionals than their counterparts in more affluent areas (Allen, Balfour, Bell, & Marmot, 2014). Thus, US teams must prepare to provide counseling referrals, ensuring that all identified students can have access to services. As such, it is essential to align with community mental health providers and pediatricians before

Table 7.4 Review of middle school students' academic, social/emotional, behavioral, and attendance data

Student #	Tier 1 – no intervention			1 no concerns	1 ODR	1
	Tier 2 – small-group intervention			2 elevated	2–4 ODR	2–4
	Tier 3 – intensive small-group intervention			3 highly elevated	5 or more ODR	5 or more
	Math tiered support	*Reading tiered support*	*Writing tiered support*	*BASC-2s*	*Office disciplinary referrals*	*Days absent as of 12/1*
111	1	2	2	1	1	5
222	1	1	3	3	5	4
333	3	3	2	2	5	5
444	1	1	1	1	2	2
555	2	2	2	3	5	7
666	1	3	3	2	1	6
777	3	2	2	2	7	9
888	3	1	1	2	9	5
999	2	3	3	3	11	1
1010	2	3	3	2	3	4

screening. Also, some schools and districts have secured grants and partnerships, enabling community-based mental health providers to provide services at the school. Last, US data is an excellent tool for advocating for additional school counselors, school social workers, school psychologists, and school-based mental health clinicians.

Table 7.4 below illustrates how a middle school team might look at their screening data to see where the greatest need for group and individual intervention exists.

In addition to providing student supports, US teams can also facilitate psychoeducation and resources to parents/guardians. Please see the example below describing how one school held parent presentations on student anxiety.

Shoretown Public Schools: Parent Support Groups

After two years of US, school counselors and school psychologists planned a very successful parent program on anxiety. The following year it was offered three times with excellent attendance at each. Parents listen to presentations by therapists who provided successful counseling to clients with anxiety. Parents shared resources and strategies with one another. Most importantly, they learned that they were not alone in their struggle to parent a child with anxiety.

Step 8: Continued Assessment

Once a screener has been administered and scored, and students are receiving services, the US team continues to meet to reflect on the US process and plan for future steps. Hence, US is an iterative, or on-going, cyclical process. For instance, the team may discuss the effectiveness of the screener: did they gather useful data? Were there challenges to administration or scoring, such as false positives or false negatives? How did the data guide intervention? How did US compare with previous practices of identifying and serving students with elevated needs? For instance, identifying students with internalizing behaviors may be of particular interest, as students who were not "on the school's radar" prior to screening are often the most vulnerable.

Another aspect of continued assessment involves teaming with stakeholders such as parents/guardians, teachers, and community-based mental health providers. The US team should be confident that student data was shared in an appropriate and timely manner. Often this is an area that must be addressed in the initial rounds of screening. Finally, the assessment team must ensure that intervention plans were aligned with identified needs. Progress monitoring for individual students should be reviewed to identify areas of growth.

Shoretown Public Schools: Data Analysis

Once all parents were notified, the US team met to conference about the students identified through the screeners. Those who had sufficient supports previously in place outside of school support (according to their parent/guardian) were monitored. The remaining students were considered for both group and individual interventions, depending on need. Some were able to join groups that were already formed. For others, we created groups. It was clear that we needed to utilize a pre- and post-test to ensure that the intervention was meeting the student needs.

Considerations with US Screening Data

As you can see, the US process lends itself to a team-based approach that results in US data that can be used in a myriad of ways to inform school practice. In this section, I describe how to use US data alongside academic and discipline data to inform interventions, monitor progress, and finally to suggest changes in practice and staffing.

Combine US Data with Academic and Discipline Data

The US team can consider and align US data with other forms of data, focusing on students' social/emotional, behavioral, and academic development, thus assessing the whole child. Reviewing this data together allows the US team to consider trends over time and look for correlations between behavior and emotional well-being. This enables school staff to recognize the interconnectedness of student variables, such as how absences can impact academic achievement. Table 7.4 exemplifies this approach, as a more complete picture of a student emerges when we look at their literacy, numeracy, and behavioral screeners alongside disciplinary and attendance data. Specifically, student data is coded based on students' level of needed supports (e.g., green = requiring only Tier 1; yellow = requiring Tier 2; red = requiring Tier 3 supports). Coding the data according to the three tiers helps the US team review the data quickly and efficiently. Further, this format facilitates avenues for interventionists responsible for establishing Tier 2 groups and provides sufficient data to understand the student from multiple vantage points simultaneously.

School-Specific Data

Universal screening data can also assist school staff as they address the root cause of increased mental health concerns specific to their school community. For example, the US team can review a specific concern by looking at composite scores across all students from a given screener. For example, school counselors in one district utilized US data from the Revised Children's Anxiety and Depression Scale (RCADS) and found that between 11% and 14% of students in grades 5–8 had elevated scores for anxiety and depression (see Table 7.5). A quick glance revealed that a coordinated response was needed to address this level of depression and anxiety. As such, the corresponding US team examined the root cause of the depression and anxiety, which included the prevalence of substance use and suicide in their district. This information gave the team and collaborating partners the information they needed to effectively and efficiently address student needs.

Progress Monitoring

When examining US data, it is helpful to look at the same group of students across time to determine whether interventions are working. For instance, the BASC2 screener might be used to identify the number of students who score in the elevated or highly elevated range for depression. A community mental health partner might then provide further assessment (e.g., the complete BASC) and intervention to students with the highest needs while the MTSS team provides Tier 1 wellness initiatives. School-wide screening data would then be collected in the spring to assess progress. While US data should not be used to monitor progress for a specific student, as that is not the purpose, regular review of school-level data makes it possible to identify trends in rates of students with concerns over time. Figures 7.2 and 7.3 show how a school district demonstrated the benefits of their US initiative. The rate of students reporting the severe and moderate levels of depression on the PHQ-9 (Patient Health Questionnaire-9) decreased steadily between

Table 7.5 RCADS average grades 5–8

RCADS	Student Population	%	Total Elevated Scores (At Risk + Clinical)
Total Sample	2,125	100%	
Grade 5	474	22.31%	
No Concern	407	85.6%	
At-Risk	21	**4.43%**	14.4%
Clinical Concern	46	**9.70%**	
Grade 6	521	24.52%	
No Concern	453	86.95%	
At-Risk	23	**4.41**	13.05%
Clinical Concern	45	**8.64%**	
Grade 7	571	26.87%	
No Concern	505	88.44%	
At-Risk	19	**3.33%**	11.56%
Clinical Concern	47	**8.23%**	
Grade 8	559	26.31%	
No Concern	483	86.40%	
At-Risk	27	**4.83%**	13.06%
Clinical Concern	49	**8.77%**	
			Grades 5–8 AVG= 13.04%

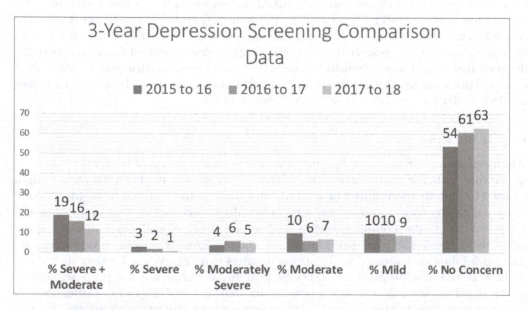

Figure 7.2 Three-year depression screening comparison data.

(Source: the Author.)

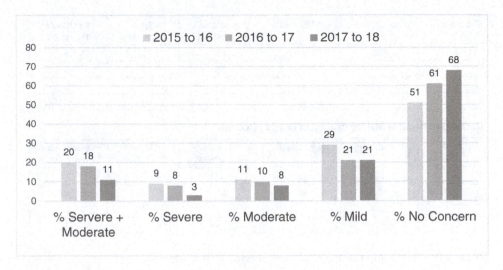

Figure 7.3 Three-year anxiety screening comparison data.

(Source: the Author.)

the fall of 2015 and spring of 2018. The same can be said of the trend for self-reporting anxiety. Sharing this type of data with key stakeholders (e.g., school administrators and board members) ensures that screening efforts will continue to receive the financial and human resources necessary to sustain and possibly expand the program, which I discuss in the next section.

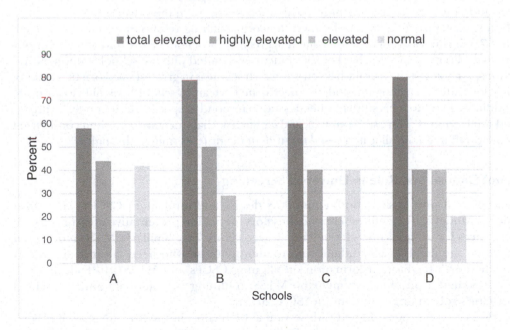

Figure 7.4 District BASC2 data by school.

(Source: the Author.)

2 0 1 6	School	Population	% Elevated	# School Psychologists	# School Counselors	# Behavior Therapists
	A	500	54	1.5	2	.5
	B	500	25	1.5	2	.5
	C	500	36	1.5	2	.5
	D	500	20	1.5	2	.5

Data-based decision making to allocate or add resources

2 0 1 7	School	Population	% Elevated	# School Psychologists	# School Counselors	# Behavior Therapists
	A	500	54	2	3	2
	B	500	25	1.5	2	.5
	C	500	36	2	3	2
	D	500	20	1.5	2	.5

Figure 7.5 Data-based decision making to allocate mental health services.

(Source: the Author.)

Allocation of Resources Based on US Data

Perhaps one of the best uses of school-wide US data is the allocation or addition of mental health and staffing resources. In looking at Figure 7.4, we can see that School A has the largest number of students who are Elevated or Extremely Elevated on the BASC-2. While only one measure, it is a good indicator that additional resources should be dispatched to that site. The administrator and US team should also look at critical school data such as rates of non-attendance, academic failure, office discipline referrals, suspension, expulsions, and graduation rates to confirm which school(s) are in the greatest need.

In a similar way, US data can be used to allocate staffing resources to schools in need. Figure 7.5 illustrates district BASC2 data disaggregated by school before and after US implementation. Previously each school of 500 students was staffed with two school counselors and a school psychologist. Based on what you see, which school is in greatest need of a third school counselor? After evaluating the students' needs, the US team at school A was able to advocate for additional staff to meet students' needs so as to respond to specific student needs with targeted interventions. Thus, staff can look at data, such as that in Figure 7.5, when considering how new staff might be allocated based on student needs (determined through US).

School Counselors' Role in Universal Screening

As mentioned previously, school counselors design and implement CSCPs. The ASCA National Model (2012) guides school counselors to include preventative measures for all and services for students with elevated needs (see Figure 7.6). Similarly, MTSS is designed to address the needs of all students and to identify those who need additional support (see Chapter 2 for more information on aligning CSCPs and MTSS). In fact, in 2018, ASCA updated a position statement on MTSS, outlining the rationale and the school counselor's role in implementation (ASCA, 2018).

Universal screening is aligned with several key concepts in the ASCA National Model. Creating a system of US fits within the Delivery System of ASCA National Model, in providing direct student services, such as counseling, and indirect student services, such as collaboration and consultation with other stakeholders, such as the US team. Finally, US

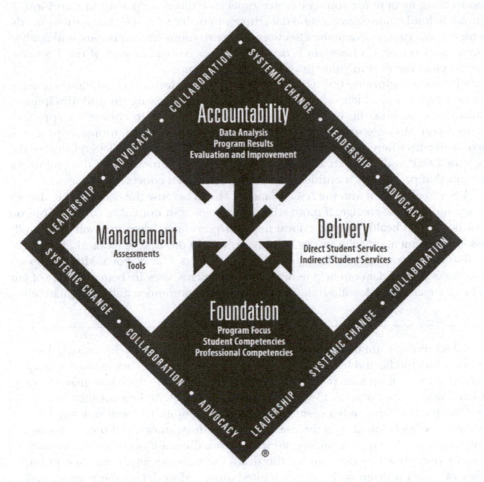

Figure 7.6 The ASCA National Model.

Reprinted from *ASCA National Model: A framework for school counseling programs* (3rd Ed.), by the American School Counselor Association, 2012, Alexandria, VA: Author. Copyright 2012. Reprinted with permission.

provides additional data that school counselors can use in their advocacy and work on systemic change. I'll discuss each in turn starting with direct services.

Universal screening helps school counselors utilize data to better implement direct services to students. Without clear data assessing student behavior, mental health status, and social/emotional competencies, school counselors must use perception data or guess work to develop groups and provide intervention. Using data to identify and support students early in their academic journey is in keeping with the ASCA National Model, focusing on prevention. As previously stated, the data collected through US provides the US leadership team members, such as school counselors, with vital information that can be used to design individual and group interventions. Identifying trends in the data supports school counselors' efforts to develop effective and relevant school counseling core curriculum taught to all students as a Tier 1 intervention. For example, one district identified a rise in the number of 8th grade students who were scoring in the elevated or highly elevated range for anxiety during the fall term. School counselors from both the middle school and high school worked with all students and parents to identify ways to combat anxiety and practice self-care. Parent evenings were planned to share information and strategies about addressing anxiety for younger teens, especially those preparing to transition to high school. School counselors must be data-driven in order to determine student needs, close achievement gaps, evaluate the effectiveness of programs/interventions, and analyze outcome data. A robust US program is driven by data. As such, as part of the US team, school counselors use data to guide programmatic decisions.

Next, school counselors are trained in effective collaboration and consultation to serve students as a supporter, which is also echoed in their work serving on multidisciplinary leadership teams such as the US team. This team collaborates to choose an appropriate screener, consults on scoring and services, provides intervention, monitors progress, and makes referrals when necessary. Thus, implementing US within MTSS reinforces the alignment of CSCP and MTSS to assist school counselors as a member of the multidisciplinary team that proactively identifies students with elevated concerns.

Lastly, US is in alignment with the ASCA National Model because the data generated leads to advocacy and systemic change. If more school counselors can normalize conversations on mental or behavioral health and the critical need for prevention, then they will successfully help de-stigmatize mental health in our country. In education, if we measure it, it matters. It's clear that school counselors believe mental health matters. Our National Model supports student wellness and US data can help us determine if students' lives are better because of our CSCP. The case example below illustrates the importance of prevention and de-stigmatization.

Universal screening team members examined the rate of emergency psychological service calls at the middle and high school over a three-year period. They noticed a sharp rise in the number of students presenting with suicidal ideation, which had grown from 1% (4 or 5 students per year) to 4% (16–18 students per year). At the same time, the district discovered that the number of students who were chronically absent (missing 18 or more days of school) was also on the rise. By tracking those students who were missing school, it became clear that identifying students before the point of crisis was necessary. Like many districts across the country, this district was also seeing an increase in the number of students diagnosed with generalized anxiety disorder, as the number had doubled during the previous two years. As a result, these students' families were seeking services to help their child to be more successful, which were primarily 504 plans. The district team found themselves wondering how many other students were suffering in silence. In this scenario school counselors could get involved to track data and implement US as a preventative approach to meet the needs of students and families.

In sum, advocating for US is a valuable use of school counselors' time. Once fully functional, US data can demonstrate both successes and gaps in the direct services (teaching school counseling core curriculum, individual and group counseling) delivered as part of their CSCP. The use of US helps school counselors, as part of a multidisciplinary team, create a clear and effective system to identify and intervene with students who struggle with mental health concerns, or in their academic, social, or emotional development.

Benefits to Implementing US

There are many positives to expending time and energy in creating an effective and efficient US system in a school or district. First, all students are screened. Over time, with appropriate intervention, US should reduce the number of students needing interventions.

In this way, no students fall through the cracks. Second, the data collected can serve as a baseline for monitoring progress for a school or district. As stated before, this data can help educational leaders allocate and/or increase services.

Third, districts have reported that US has been correlated with cost savings over time. It is easier and less expensive to intervene when an emergent mental health concern is present (Dowdy, Ritchey, & Kamphaus, 2010; Lane et al., 2010). We know that our best chance of making a lasting impact with students is early identification and intervention. Determining and providing intervention to 3rd graders with specific social and emotional challenges is much easier to accomplish and has more lasting results than waiting for a child to fail socially in middle school or engage in juvenile delinquency or substance abuse in high school.

Fourth, US increases teacher and parent awareness of and sensitivity to the impact of mental illness on their students' social, emotional, behavioral, and academic growth. The stigma attached to mental health or mental illness is deeply engrained in many facets of our society. Students and parents who see mental health screeners used in the school will come to expect this feedback just as they are accustomed to having their vision and hearing checked.

Finally, implementing and sustaining US promotes professional collaboration. School-based multidisciplinary US teams meet a myriad of student and family needs when they work together to both identify needs and implement evidence-based interventions. When teams use screeners and interventions backed by research, their efforts yield the best possible outcomes. An administrator from a local school describes the positive outcomes below.

> There were three important outcomes of introducing universal screening in our district: (a) we identified kids we didn't know needed help; (b) we introduced mental health into the general educators' conversation in a concrete and understandable way; (c) we encouraged our school-based mental health teams to work even more collaboratively to identify and meet the needs of students. These are things we have been trying to do, with limited success, for years! (School Administrator)

Challenges to Implementing US

In addition to the positive outcomes of US, there are very real concerns and constraints. Research suggests limitations include a lack of awareness about US, limited time and financial support, and concerns about providing the necessary interventions when administering screeners (Chafouleas, Kilgus, & Wallach, 2010). Further roadblocks to screening are community acceptance, families' right to privacy, family concerns about stigmatization, and potential misidentification of students (Chafouleas et al., 2010). In this section, I describe a number of these challenges, including stigma, availability of services, and cultural considerations.

Stigmatization

As mentioned previously, the stigma associated with mental health persists. Many well-meaning administrators and parents feel uncomfortable confronting issues related to mental illness. Seeing schools as exclusively places of learning rather than communities where children develop in all ways can limit efforts to embrace mental health as an integral component of overall health. It is essential to provide professional development for teachers when piloting and sustaining a US program. Additionally, concerns about parental consent procedures and confidentiality exist when considering adopting US. However, informing parents, teachers, school board members, and administrators about the ration-ale and implementation of US and subsequent interventions is essential to beginning a successful US program. Only then can stigma be alleviated.

Limited Services

Many schools or districts are reluctant to initiate US because of concerns about meeting the student needs identified by the screener. This presents a real ethical question, espe-cially for schools located in rural areas with few mental health professionals within driving distance. Worse yet, administrators worry that there will be an excessive number of false positives, opening them up to lawsuits and other unpleasant parental interactions.

Cultural Biases

Another constraint may be the availability of culturally relevant instruments coupled with the strong distrust of "airing one's dirty laundry." Seeking mental health services is taboo in many cultures. Parents often resist "labeling" of their children and are concerned that the process will lead to pressure to medicate their child if a diagnosis is derived after additional testing. Knowing one's community and the cultures represented is a signifi-cant asset throughout the process of implementation. Since a myriad of screeners exist, this knowledge helps the team select one that is culturally appropriate. Overall, though several constraints exist regarding US, with ample pre-planning, including staff training and revised protocol, schools and districts can work through many of them. Ultimately, weighing the benefits and challenges of US is dependent on each school and district.

Special Considerations

Not all mental health screening should be approached in the same way. In the final section of this chapter, I focus on two approaches that require special consideration—screening for trauma and suicidal ideation.

Screening for Trauma

As more and more schools take a trauma-informed approach to teaching and learning, school counselors must develop a clear understanding of the process of screening for trauma. Trauma is defined as the response to an event that involves actual or perceived threat to oneself or others through death, serious injury, or violation of the body, which results in feelings of intense fear and/or powerlessness (Butler et al., 2009). Traumatic events can include accidents, child abuse and neglect, domestic violence, community vio-lence, sexual assault, natural disasters, medical illness, parent/caregiver death, hostage situations, inconsistent parenting due to mental health issues, incarceration of a parent, war (deployment of parent), terrorism, and other man-made disasters.

Recent research indicates that young children can reliably recount their post-traumatic stress symptoms (Gonzalez et al., 2016). Thus, early screening for trauma can facilitate interventions that mitigate the impact of trauma on a child's academic, social, and emo-tional development. However, despite the fact that 66% of all students report one or more traumatic or adverse experiences during their school-age years (Gonzalez et al., 2016; Kataoka, Zhang, and Wells, 2002), very few schools systematically screen for trauma. Instituting a trauma screener gives stakeholders a better understanding of the extent and severity of trauma exposure, as well as students' resiliency after these experiences. This information provides school leaders and US teams with the vital information necessary to plan for cohorts of children with high trauma exposure, and to take an informed school-wide approach to programs like restorative practices.

In US for trauma, parents should give active consent, despite the likelihood of a lower response rate. Additionally, parents should be informed about the instrument, the purpose of the screener, and the interventions planned for students who score in the elevated range (Eklund, Rossen, Koriakin, Chafouleas, & Resnick, 2018). Developmentally appropriate screening methods must be used so that children can easily understand questions. When parents are informed that the school makes all efforts to be sensitive to students who have withstood trauma, they are more likely to partner with the school to support the healing process.

Screening for Suicide

High school and college-age students are at the greatest risk for depression and suicide. In 2014, suicide was the tenth leading cause of death in the U.S., claiming the lives of more than 44,000 people (Curtin, Warner, & Hedegaard, 2016). Among youth, the statistics are even more concerning: suicide was the third leading cause of death among individuals between the ages of 10 and 14, and the second leading cause of death among individuals between the ages of 15 and 34 (Curtin et al., 2016). Screening for suicide requires specific skills, experience, and resources in order to discern a child's mental state effectively, efficiently, and expeditiously. The following case study outlines one example.

In recent years, there have been more than twice as many suicides as homicides in the U.S. Minnesota high school counselor Anne Erickson decided to take action, due to the increased rates of suicide at her school. Erickson and her school-based mental health team decided to screen for suicide and depression; they selected the *Reynolds Adolescent Depression Scale* (2nd Ed.) (Reynolds, 2004). This screener was appealing because it was brief (30 questions) and had high reliability and validity with adolescents. With an eighth-grade reading level, the screener was deemed accessible to students and did not include controversial questions (Erickson & Abel, 2013). In addition to screening, school counselors implemented classroom lessons through health class to all 9th and 10th graders about the signs of depression and suicide, and provided strategies to teens regarding steps to take if a friend was feeling suicidal. They invited speakers from local community organizations to discuss available services.

Thus, this screening process was a collaborative effort between the school counselor, health teacher, and school psychologist. The school-based team also developed a partnership with a free medical clinic in the community to ensure that students could get support 24 hours a day. The results were impressive. Over a ten-year period, there was a significant decrease in reported depression (> 50% decrease amongst 12th graders) and a sizable reduction in suicide attempts (75% decrease in 9th grade). Students reported feeling more open to discussing mental health and reporting their own challenges and those of their peers. Over the span of 10 years, Erickson and her team reached out to multiple families and only one refused services. In this respect, implementing US can and has saved lives.

How did the school counselor involve others in the screening process?

What additional considerations are imperative when doing this type of US?

Conclusion

Understanding the landscape of our students' mental health is a significant step forward for our profession. Weist, Rubin, Moore, Adelsheim, & Wrobel (2007) remind us that:

> When implemented with appropriate family, school, and community involvement, mental health screening in schools has the potential to be a cornerstone of a transformed mental health system. Screening, as part of a coordinated and comprehensive school mental health program, complements the mission of schools, identifies youth in need, links them to effective services, and contributes to positive educational outcomes valued by families, schools, and communities. (p. 58)

The purpose of this chapter was to provide school counselors with an overview of integrating universal screening into MTSS and CSCP programs. I have focused on the eight steps necessary to implement US and highlight four main summary points below:

1   20% of US students have mental health concerns, and are thus unavailable for learning.
2   Universal screening is a key component of MTSS.
3   The process of implementing US is unique to each district.
4   Identifying students with mental health, social/emotional, and behavioral needs is an essential school counselor activity.

Universal identification of students in need of academic remediation has long been a "go to" strategy for U.S. public schools. However, screening for behavior and mental health

Figure 7.7 Stand up to stigma.

concerns such as depression and anxiety requires a paradigm shift for educators, including careful planning and training. Any time we provide content-rich and effective professional development for our school community, we help build our collective capacity to support students more comprehensively. Simply screening for disorders will not give our school-based mental health teams a complete picture of students' well-being. Similarly, we no longer look for academic shortcomings, but we try to build upon a student's assets.

Armed with this US data, school counselors can help make lasting, effective, and systemic change. School counselors are uniquely positioned to advocate for creating a system of US that fits the emergent needs in their schools or districts. Further, school counselors are keenly aware of the benefits of collaborating with other school-based mental health professionals and stakeholders to maximize efforts, and identify and facilitate services to students in need of support. Most importantly, school counselors who champion US are also working to eliminate the stigma that surrounds mental health. Simply put, mental health is health. And universal screening is a proactive, preventative strategy for promoting students' health, particularly their mental health, promoting the academic, career, and social/emotional success of every student.

For more information and a school counselor's perspective on *Universal Screening to Support MTSS* please see Chapter 12 "Voices from the Field," Voices 6 and 10.

ASCA Ethical Standards

There are multiple ASCA Code of Ethics standards that guide implementation of US. These include those that focus on confidentiality, student and parent rights, appropriate referrals, student records, evaluation, and sharing information with other professionals. First, if we identify students with emergent mental health needs, we must have the school and community resources to help students with elevated scores. This likely involves a systemic coordination of care with a district team of mental health providers and community agencies. Second, we must consider how to communicate with parents prior to screening, whether the support post-screener will be school provided or "parent provided." Finally, the time that lapses between identifying students and implementing interventions must be as short as possible.

Third, if the data is collected, it must be used for its intended purpose. Ethical implementation of universal screening must safeguard against false positives. A false positive would entail a screener which shows a student is heightened when, in reality, they are not. This could be due to an error in the screening software, human error, or untruthful responses to the screener questions. In any case, school counselors who suspect a student's score is a false positive must take steps to validate the score or re-administer the screener. Finally, universal screeners for social, emotional, or behavioral health may need to be followed up with additional assessment. Just as an eye doctor would need to do further testing to identify the nature and degree of visual impairment, so a school psychologist or community therapist would need to do additional assessments to understand the true nature of the concern. The following list includes other ethical considerations when implementing US. Specifically, school counselors:

A Responsibility to Students

A.2 Confidentiality.

- A.2.f. Recognize their primary ethical obligation for confidentiality is to the students but balance that obligation with an understanding of parents'/ guardians' legal and inherent rights to be the guiding voice in their children's lives. School counselors understand the need to balance students' ethical rights to make choices, their capacity to give consent or assent, and parental or familial legal rights and responsibilities to make decisions on their child's behalf.

A.6   Appropriate Referrals and Advocacy

- A.6.a. Collaborate with all relevant stakeholders, including students, educators, and parents/guardians when student assistance is needed, including the identification of early warning signs of student distress.
- A.6.b. Provide a list of resources for outside agencies and resources in their community to student(s) and parents/guardians when students need or request additional support. School counselors provide multiple referral options or the district's vetted list and are careful not to indicate an endorsement or preference for one counselor or practice. School counselors encourage parents to interview outside professionals to make a personal decision regarding the best source of assistance for their student.
- A.6.c. Connect students with services provided through the local school district and community agencies and remain aware of state laws and local district policies related to students with special needs, including limits to confidentiality and notification to authorities as appropriate.

A.12   Student Records

- A.12.a. Abide by the Family Educational Rights and Privacy Act (FERPA), which defines who has access to students' educational records and allows parents the right to review and challenge perceived inaccuracies in their child's records.

A.13   Evaluation, Assessment and Interpretation

- A.13.a. Use only valid and reliable tests and assessments with concern for bias and cultural sensitivity.
- A.13.b. Adhere to all professional standards when selecting, administering, and interpreting assessment measures and only utilize assessment measures that are within the scope of practice for school counselors and for which they are licensed, certified, and competent.
- A.13.c. Are mindful of confidentiality guidelines when utilizing paper or electronic evaluative or assessment instruments and programs.
- A.13.d. Consider the student's developmental age, language skills, and level of competence when determining the appropriateness of an assessment.
- A.13.e. Use multiple data points when possible to provide students and families with accurate, objective, and concise information to promote students' well-being.
- A.13.f. Provide interpretation of the nature, purposes, results, and potential impact of assessment/evaluation measures in language the students and parents/guardians can understand.
- A.13.g. Monitor the use of assessment results and interpretations and take reasonable steps to prevent others from misusing the information.
- A.13.h. Use caution when utilizing assessment techniques, making evaluations, and interpreting the performance of populations not represented in the norm group on which an instrument is standardized.

B Responsibilities to Parents/Guardians, School and Self

B.1 Responsibilities to Parents/Guardians

- B.1.a. Recognize that providing services to minors in a school setting requires school counselors to collaborate with students' parents/guardians as appropriate.

B.2 Responsibilities to the School

- B.2.q. Collaborate as needed to provide optimum services with other professionals such as special educators, school nurses, school social workers, school psychologists, college counselors/admissions officers, physical therapists, occupational therapists, speech pathologists, administrators.

Resources

For Further Reading

Eklund, K., Rossen, E., Koriakin, T., Chafouleas, S. M., & Resnick, C. (2018). A systematic review of trauma screening measures for children and adolescents. *School Psychology Quarterly*, *33*(1), 30.

Lane, K. L., Menzies, H. M., Oakes, W. P., & Kalberg, J. R. (2011). *Systematic screenings of behavior to support instruction: From preschool to high school*. New York: Guilford Press.

Weist, M. D., Evans, S. W., & Lever, N. A. (Eds) (2008). *Handbook of school mental health: Advancing practice and research*. Heidelberg: Springer Science & Business Media.

Windle, G., Bennett, K. M., & Noyes, J. (2011). A methodological review of resilience measurement scales. *Health and Quality of Life Outcomes*, *9*(1), 8.

Websites

Links to the following can be found on our eresource at: www.routledge.com/9781138501614.

- Instructional video.
- Free assessment measures.
- Center for School Mental Health.
- Universal screening manuals.
- Center for School Mental Health (2018). *School mental health screening playbook: Best practices and tips from the field.*
- Colorado Framework for School Behavioral Health Services Universal Screening Toolkit.
- Ohio PBIS *School-wide universal screening for behavioral and mental health issues: Implementation guidance.*

Teaching Activity 1

Directions: Think about a school in which you are currently working or interning. Please consider:

Part A: What are the most prevalent presenting problems for students? What barriers to learning are school counselors prioritizing and attempting to address? What data determines each of these needs? What could be a potential screener to address each of these needs? What would be the best way to administer the screener(s)?

Part B: How you would present this information to your school administration. What benefits and challenges could you address? Create three–four PowerPoint slides for this potential presentation.

Teaching Activity 2

Directions: Explore the National Association of School Psychologists (NASP) website for potential screeners. Identify three that address a particular issue (e.g., anxiety, depression, or substance abuse). Next, interview a school psychologist to find out what screeners they recommend using to address that same concern, and why.

Multiple Choice Questions

1 **School-based mental health teams who desire to design and implement universal screening should include:**

   a   School counselors.
   b   Parents.
   c   Teachers.
   d   Administrators.
   e   All of the above.

2 **Selecting a screener should be a quick and easy process.**

   a   True.
   b   False.

3 **It's ok to delay scoring a universal screener until additional staff are hired to provide group counseling.**

   a   True.
   b   False.

4 **If my colleagues want to create our own universal screener, I should support that idea.**

   a   True.
   b   False.

5 **Most schools resist implementing universal screening because:**

   a   District administrators are afraid it will lead to lawsuits.
   b   It costs a lot of money.
   c   They don't know if they will have enough resources to meet students' needs.
   d   Teachers are hesitant to fill out questionnaires about children truthfully because it might label a child forever.
   e   All of the above.

Answers: Q1 e, Q2 b, Q3 b, Q4 b, Q5 c.

References

Albano, A. M., & Kendall, P. C. (2002). Cognitive behavioural therapy for children and adolescents with anxiety disorders: Clinical research advances. *International Review of Psychiatry, 14*(2), 129–134.

Allen, J., Balfour, R., Bell, R., & Marmot, M. (2014). Social determinants of mental health. *International Review of Psychiatry, 26*(4), 392–407.

American School Counselor Association (ASCA) (2012). *ASCA National Model: A framework for school counseling programs.* American School Counselor Association. Alexandria, VA: Author.

American School Counselor Association (ASCA) (2018). The school counselor and multi-tiered systems of support. ASCA position statements. Alexandria, VA: Author. Retrieved from: www.schoolcounselor.org/asca/media/asca/PositionStatements/PS_MultitieredSupportSystem.pdf.

Bradshaw, C. P., Buckley, J. A., & Ialongo, N. S. (2008). School-based service utilization among urban children with early onset educational and mental health problems: The squeaky wheel phenomenon. *School Psychology Quarterly, 23*(2), 169.

Bruhn, A. L., Woods-Groves, S., & Huddle, S. (2014). A preliminary investigation of emotional and behavioral screening practices in K–12 schools. *Education and Treatment of Children, 37*(4), 611–634.

Butler, L. D., Koopman, C., Azarow, J., Blasey, C. M., Magdalene, J. C., DiMiceli, S., . . . & Kraemer, H. C. (2009). Psychosocial predictors of resilience after the September 11, 2001 terrorist attacks. *The Journal of Nervous and Mental Disease, 197*(4), 266–273.

Cassidy, S. (2016). The Academic Resilience Scale (ARS-30): A new multidimensional construct measure. *Frontiers in Psychology, 7,* 1787.

Center for School Mental Health (2018). School Mental Health Screening Playbook: Best Practices and Tips from the Field. Baltimore MD: University of Maryland School of Medicine. Retrieved from: http://csmh.umaryland.edu/media/SOM/Microsites/CSMH/docs/Reports/School-Mental-Health-Screening-Playbook.pdf.

Chafouleas, S. M., Kilgus, S. P., & Wallach, N. (2010). Ethical dilemmas in school-based behavioral screening. *Assessment for Effective Intervention, 35*(4), 245–252.

Connor, K. M., & Davidson, J. R. (2003). Development of a new resilience scale: The Connor-Davidson resilience scale (CD-RISC). *Depression and Anxiety, 18*(2), 76–82.

Cowan, K. C., Vaillancourt, K. I., Rossen, E. & Pollitt, K. (2013). *A framework for safe and successful schools* [(Brief]. Bethesda, MD: National Association of School Psychologists.

Curtin, S. C., Warner, M., & Hedegaard, H. (2016). *Increase in suicide in the United States, 1999–2014.* National Center for Health Statistics Brief, April. Hyattsville, MD: National Center for Health Statistics.

Dowdy, E., Ritchey, K. & Kamphaus. R. (2010). School-based screening: A population-based approach to inform and monitor children's mental health needs. *School Mental Health, 2*(4), 1–11, doi:10.1007/s12310-010-9036-3.

Eklund, K., Rossen, E., Koriakin, T., Chafouleas, S. M., & Resnick, C. (2018). A systematic review of trauma screening measures for children and adolescents. *School Psychology Quarterly, 33*(1), 30.

Erickson, A., & Abel, N. (2013). A high school counselor's leadership in providing school-wide screenings for depression and enhancing suicide awareness. *Professional School Counseling, 16*(5), 283–289.

Fagan, T. K. (2003). School psychology. In W. C. Borman, D. R. Ilgen, & R. J. Klimoski (Eds), *Handbook of psychology: Industrial and organizational psychology* (Vol. 12, pp. 413–429). Hoboken, NJ: John Wiley & Sons Inc.

Forns, M., Abad, J., & Kirchner, T. (2011). Internalizing and externalizing problems. In *Encyclopedia of adolescence* (pp. 1464–1469). New York: Springer.

Gonzalez, A., Monzon, N., Solis, D., Jaycox, L., & Langley, A. K. (2016). Trauma exposure in elementary school children: Description of screening procedures, level of exposure, and post-traumatic stress symptoms. *School Mental Health, 8*(1), 77–88.

Harlacher, J. E., & Merrell, K. W. (2010). Social and emotional learning as a universal level of student support: Evaluating the follow-up effect of strong kids on social and emotional outcomes. *Journal of Applied School Psychology, 26*(3), 212–229.

Hogan, M. F. (2003). New Freedom Commission report: The president's New Freedom Commission: recommendations to transform mental health care in America. *Psychiatric Services, 54*(11), 1467–1474.

Humphrey, N., & Wigelsworth, M. (2016). Making the case for universal school-based mental health screening. *Emotional and Behavioural Difficulties, 21*(1), 22–42.

Ikeda, M., Nessen, E., and Witt, J. (2008). Best practices in universal screening. *Best Practices in School Psychology, 5*, 103–114.

Individuals with Disabilities Education Act (IDEA), 20 U.S.C. § 1400 (2004).

Kamphaus, R. W., & Reynolds, C. R. (2007). *Behavioral & emotional screening system.* New York: NCS Pearson.

Kataoka, S., Zhang, L., & Wells, K. (2002). Unmet need for mental health care among U.S. children: Variation by ethnicity and insurance status. *American Journal of Psychiatry, 159*(9), 1548–1555.

Kessler, R. C., Berglund, P., Demler, O., Jin, R., Merikangas, K. R., & Walters, E. E. (2005). Lifetime prevalence and age-of-onset distributions of DSM-IV disorders in the National Comorbidity Survey Replication. *Archives of General Psychiatry, 62*(6), 593–602.

Lane, K. L., Menzies, H. M., Oakes, W. P., & Kalberg, J. R. (2011). *Systematic screenings of behavior to support instruction: From preschool to high school.* New York: Guilford Press.

Lane, K. L., Oakes, W. P., & Menzies, H. M. (2010). Systematic screenings to prevent the development of learning and behavior problems: Considerations for practitioners, researchers, and policy makers. *Journal of Disabilities Policy Studies, 21*, 160–172.

Lenzenweger, M. F., Lane, M. C., Loranger, A. W., & Kessler, R. C. (2007). DSM-IV personality disorders in the National Comorbidity Survey Replication. *Biological Psychiatry, 62*(6), 553–564.

Martini, R., Hilt. R., Marx, L., Chenven, M., Naylor, M., Sarvet, B., & Ptakowski, K. K. (2012). *Best principles for integration of child psychiatry into the pediatric health home.* Washington, DC: American Academy of Child & Adolescent Psychiatry. Retrieved from: www.aacap.org/App_Themes/ AACAP/docs/clinical_practice_center/systems_of_care/best_principles_for_integration_of_ child_psychiatry_into_the_pediatric_health_home_2012.pdf.

Nguyen, T., Davis, K., Counts, N., & Fritze, D. (2016). *Prevention and early intervention B4Stage4: The state of mental health in America, 2016.* Retrieved from Mental Health America website: www. mentalhealthamerica.net/sites/default/files/2016%20MH%20in%20America%20FINAL%20 SPOTLIGHT.pdf.

O'Connell, M. E., Boat, T., & Warner, K. E. (2009). *Preventing mental, emotional, and behavioral disorders among young people: Progress and possibilities.* Committee on the Prevention of Mental Disorders and Substance Abuse Among Children, Youth, and Young Adults: Research Advances and Promising Interventions, National Research Council and Institute of Medicine.

Office of the Child Advocate (2014). *Shooting at Sandy Hook Elementary School: Report of the office of the child advocate.* Hartford, CT: Author. Retrieved from: www.ct.gov/oca/lib/oca/sandyhook11212014.pdf.

Patrikakou, E., Ockerman, M. S., & Hollenbeck, A. F. (2016). Needs and contradictions of a changing field: Evidence from a national response to intervention implementation study. *The Professional Counselor, 6*(3), 233–250, doi:10.15241/ep.6.3.233.

Perou, R., Bitsko, R. H., Blumberg, S. J., Pastor, P., Ghandour, R. M., Gfroerer, J. C., . . . & Parks, S. E. (2013). Mental health surveillance among children—United States, 2005–2011. *MMWR Surveillance Summaries, 62*(Suppl 2), 1–35.

Positive Behavioral Interventions and Supports (PBIS) (2018). *Implementing PBIS.* Eugene, OR: University of Oregon. Retrieved from: www.pbis.org.

Reynolds, W. M. (2004). *Reynolds adolescent depression scale – 2.* Odessa, FL: Psychological Assessment Resources.

Severson, H. H., Walker, H. M., Hope-Doolittle, J., Kratochwill, T. R., & Gresham, F. M. (2007). Proactive, early screening to detect behaviorally at-risk students: Issues, approaches, emerging innovations, and professional practices. *Journal of School Psychology, 45*(2), 193–223.

Smith, B. W., Dalen, J., Wiggins, K., Tooley, E., Christopher, P., & Bernard, J. (2008). The brief resilience scale: Assessing the ability to bounce back. *International Journal of Behavioral Medicine, 15*(3), 194–200.

Splett, J. W., Trainor, K. M., Raborn, A., Halliday-Boykins, C. A., Garzona, M. E., Dongo, M. D., & Weist, M. D. (2018). Comparison of universal mental health screening to students already receiving intervention in a multitiered system of support. *Behavioral Disorders, 43*(3), 344–356.

Stark, K. D., & Kendall, P. C. (1996). *Treating depressed children: Therapist manual for Taking Action.* Ardmore, PA: Workbook Publications, Inc.

Tilly, W. D. (2008). The evolution of school psychology to science-based practice: Problem solving and the three-tiered model. In A. Thomas & J. Grimes (Eds), *Best practices in school psychology V* (pp. 17–36). Bethesda, MD: National Association of School Psychologists.

Tyler, E., Hulkower, R., & Kaminski, J. (2017). *Behavioral health integration in pediatric primary care: Considerations and opportunities for policymakers, planners, and providers.* New York: The Millbank Quarterly, The Millbank Memorial Fund.

Vincent, C. G., Sprague, J. R., Pavel, M., Tobin, T. J., & Gau, J. M. (2015). Effectiveness of school-wide positive behavior interventions and supports in reducing racially inequitable disciplinary exclusion. In D. J. Losen (Ed.), *Closing the school discipline gap: Equitable remedies for excessive exclusion* (pp. 207–221). New York: Teachers College Press.

Weist, M. D., Eber, L., Horner, R., Splett, J., Putnam, R., Barrett, S., . . . & Hoover, S. (2018). Improving Multitiered Systems of Support for students with "internalizing" emotional/behavioral problems. *Journal of Positive Behavior Interventions, 20*(3), doi: 1098300717753832.

Weist, M. D., Rubin, M., Moore, E., Adelsheim, S., & Wrobel, G. (2007). Mental health screening in schools. *Journal of School Health, 77*(2), 53–58.

Windle, G., Bennett, K. M., & Noyes, J. (2011). A methodological review of resilience measurement scales. *Health and Quality of Life Outcomes, 9*, 1–18.

Wroblewski, A. P., Dowdy, E., Sharkey, J. D., & Kyung Kim, E. (2019). Social-Emotional screening to predict truancy severity: Recommendations for educators. *Journal of Positive Behavior Interventions, 21*, 19–29, doi:1098300718768773.

8 School Counselors Consulting and Collaborating Within MTSS

Blaire Cholewa and Kathleen C. Laundy

Introduction

The quotes abound when talking about the importance of teamwork and collaboration in any endeavor. It is no different when thinking about Multi-Tiered Systems of Support (MTSS) in schools. The enactment of an effective MTSS requires coordinated, systemic, and sustained effort among various stakeholders in each school system and the communities which support them. An important rule of thumb is to remember that none of those who support student achievement functions in a vacuum as a solo provider. With the growth of multidisciplinary MTSS initiatives across the U.S., the importance of consultation and collaboration skills cannot be overstated.

As school counselors, we can harness the expertise of stakeholders using consultation and collaboration to enhance the educational experiences and success of PK-12 students (ASCA, 2012; Gysbers & Henderson, 2012). We provide critical services through our work with parents/guardians, administrators, teachers, school psychologists, licensed counselors, social workers, family therapists, and other team members to promote student achievement and resilience at individual, classroom, and school levels (Erford, 2015).

Historically, the U.S. educational system addressed student needs through individually-based assessments and interventions. In recent years, more systemic approaches have emerged to address broader variables that affect student achievement and resiliency, such as school bullying and violence. Earlier chapters have addressed the recent development of systemic MTSS initiatives such as Response to Intervention (RTI) and Positive Behavioral Intervention and Supports (PBIS), as broad-based ways to support all students. For instance, Tier 1, or universal supports are preventatively provided to all students (see Chapters 3 and 4), Tier 2 supports are small-group supports given to some students (see Chapter 5), and last, Tier 3, or targeted supports are given to students with the highest needs, which are typically chronic, complex, and on-going (see Chapter 6). Collaboration and consultation are essential to developing an effective system of tiered supports.

As Sugai and colleagues mentioned in Chapter 1, the MTSS leadership team must have the "authority, schedule, resources, and incentives to develop, implement, and monitor MTSS" (see page 16). Key stakeholders from all professionals in the community should be invited to be part of the MTSS leadership team. This leadership team includes school administrators and other school staff (such as the school counselor), and is comprised of overlapping members across the three tiers. A Tier 1 team designs sound preventative systems for all students. A smaller subset of the Tier 1 team is comprised of a Tier 2 team and a Tier 3 team. These teams develop systems to identify students in need of extra support in a myriad of areas of academics, behavior, social/emotional competencies, and other student outcomes such as attendance. These three teams will be discussed in greater depth later.

In this chapter, we will address consultation and collaboration as effective ways for school counselors to meet both individualized and systemic initiatives in schools. Further, we will discuss the key aspects of consultation and collaboration and will then provide examples of what they look like in the context of a MTSS. We will also talk about MTSS leadership teams, interventions, cultural, and diversity implications, and relevant ethical standards.

Consultation and Collaboration: Two Sides of the Same Coin?

> School counselors are advocates, leaders, *collaborators*, and *consultants* who create systemic change by providing equitable educational access and success by connecting their school counseling programs to the district's mission and improvement plans. (Preamble of the ASCA Code of Ethics, 2016)

Consultation and collaboration are two complementary yet theoretically different services. They are often used interchangeably and/or discussed in tandem in both literature and practice. As such, it is easy to get confused about their meaning. Here we will outline their theoretical differences to provide clarity about the ways in which they can be utilized. The key with both consultation and collaboration in school counseling and MTSS is the fact that they are often indirect services, in contrast to direct service to students. Consequently, the school counselor works actively with other adult stakeholders to impact the functioning of an individual student, group of students, classroom, or school system.

Consultation

Although collaboration is probably the more familiar term, we will start by describing consultation as it is a bit more specific. According to Dinkmeyer, Carlson, and Michel (2016), consultation usually involves three parties: the consultant, the consultee, and the student(s) or problem, and is thus often referred to as a triadic process (see Figure 8.1). In schools, the consultant helps the consultee to better work with students or address a problem. The consultee could be an individual (e.g., a parent, teacher, administrator), a group (e.g., a team of teachers), or a system (e.g., a classroom or school). For example, the fifth-grade teachers in your school (consultee) may approach you (consultant) to get help managing conflict that is occurring among the girls in their classes. After gaining a full understanding of the problem, you could work with the teachers to help them develop some strategies to address the conflict. Once the teachers implement the strategies, you could circle back and evaluate the progress.

The beauty of such consultation is that by school counselors helping the teachers with this issue, not only will the situation with the girls be resolved, but the teachers will be more equipped to handle a similar type of problem in the future (Brown, Przywansky, & Schulte, 2011; Cholewa, Goodman-Scott, Thomas, & Cook, 2017). Thus, consultation with teachers can be a very time-efficient strategy because the intervention can impact each of the students in the teacher's class as well as future students, given the teacher's evolved attitude and skill set. The same is true when consulting with other stakeholders, such as caregivers, nurses, administrators, etc. Within MTSS, consultation can equip stakeholders to design and implement Tier 1, Tier 2, and Tier 3 interventions. For example, a high school counselor may consult with administration to implement a week-long, Tier 1, school-wide initiative around dating violence awareness. The school counselor could help the administrator frame the initiative in a way

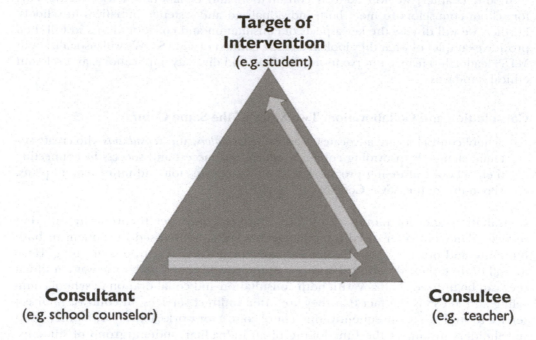

Figure 8.1 Triadic process of consultation.

(Source: the Authors.)

that is developmentally appropriate and might then facilitate communication among the students through a core school counseling lesson.

In reading about consultation, did you notice where the action lies? Consultation is distinct in that it is the consultee who enacts the intervention to work with the student(s) to address the problem (Kampwirth, 2006). The consultant helps with the development of the plan and intervention as well as enhancing consultee attitudes and skills that will aid them in working more effectively. Ultimately, the action and power is incumbent on the consultee to enact (Brown et al., 2011; Dinkmeyer et al., 2016). That is not to say that the relationship is a hierarchical one, where the consultant is viewed as the all-knowing expert. Rather, many counseling scholars emphasize the significance of an equal, egalitarian relationship between the consultant and the consultee (Dinkmeyer et al., 2016: Kampwirth, 2006). It is important to note that at times the consultation process may ultimately transition from the school counselor's indirect service to a direct service with the student(s) of concern (e.g., in Tier 2 or Tier 3 interventions), should the consultee and school counselor deem it necessary.

Consultation Stages

There are numerous models of consultation, including behavioral, mental health, process, theoretically based, etc. Across these models are a common set of activities that take place (Brown et al., 2011). For this chapter, we have taken Brown et al.'s (2011) eight stages and simplified them into the six stages that are most relevant for school counselors (see Table 8.1 below). We also highlight some of the critical knowledge, skills, and attitudes needed to effectively navigate each stage.

Table 8.1 Six stages of consultation

Consultation Stages
1   Initiate consulting relationship
2   Define the problem and set goals
3   Select strategy/intervention
4   Implement strategy/intervention
5   Evaluate
6   Terminate

Note: Adapted from Brown, Przywansky, and Schulte (2011).

Initiate Consulting Relationship

As school counselors, the first crucial step is the initiation of the consulting relationship. Much like in the counseling relationships, consultants need to be able to develop relationships that are characterized by mutual trust and respect, as well as confidentiality (Dinkmeyer et al., 2016). Teachers report the importance of good relationships and open communication in their consultations with school counselors (Cholewa et al., 2017). The consultee must be honest in their views and feel heard and understood by the consultant (Brown et al., 2011; Cholewa et al., 2017; Parsons & Kahn, 2005), while also understanding the roles of both the consultant and the consultee.

Hopefully, you will already have built relationships with teachers and other allied professionals (e.g., school psychologists, social workers, family therapists, and administration) within your school. Within these relationships, role structuring is important as a stakeholder may want you as the consultant to just "fix it" yourself, rather than seeing themselves as active in the process. Helping them understand the non-hierarchical, triadic process will set up the structure for empowering consultation initiatives to move forward.

Define the Problem and Set Goals

The importance of adequately defining the problem cannot be overstated. The last thing you want is to enact a thoughtful plan that ultimately does nothing to improve the situation because it is addressing the wrong problem (Brown et al., 2011). Therefore, taking time to skillfully draw out the consultee's concerns and the history and background of these concerns, to determine what has been tried previously to address these concerns, and to identify specific behaviors and examples, will be especially helpful. A thorough definition can then help determine what specific goals and objectives the consultant and consultee are working to develop. A question to ask is "What would it look like if the problem was no longer a problem?" (Parsons & Kahn, 2005). This allows the consultee to outline what will be specifically observed if the problem is resolved. For example, having a goal of students getting along better with others is probably too vague. Instead, you would want to help the consultee outline specific behaviors, such as being able to sit at the lunch table with peers without an argument breaking out.

Select Strategy/Intervention

Upon defining the area of concern and setting specific goals, the consultant and consultee work together to determine the steps and strategies to be implemented to achieve that goal (Brown et al., 2011). This process includes the mutual exploration of multiple potential strategies and interventions. Here is where you can use your knowledge and skills related to child development, relationship building, multiculturalism, etc. to brainstorm alongside the consultee. Ultimately, however, the consultee decides amongst the alternatives in accordance with his/her skill level and the resources available in the school (Brown et al., 2011). Once a strategy or intervention is selected, it must be implemented through careful and thoughtful planning, considering potential pitfalls and problems that may arise (Brown et al., 2011).

Implement Strategy/Intervention

Depending on the concern and the intricacy of the intervention, the consultee may need frequent contact (e.g., in person, phone, email) to aid in the implementation of the plan and to utilize the consultant's feedback to make modifications as necessary. For example, if it is determined that a student receiving Tier 3 supports needs to be on a behavior modification plan, the teachers may need the school counselor's (or another member of the MTSS team's) support to implement the plan and navigate the pitfalls that may arise.

Evaluate

Next, the consultant and consultee need to take time to evaluate the process of strategy implementation, as well as the actual outcome(s) of the intervention, to determine if their goals were reached (Brown et al., 2011). If the goals were not reached, the consultant and consultee may need to examine (1) how the strategy was implemented to ensure it was implemented as intended, (2) explore other intervention alternatives, and/or (3) revisit the problem definition and goals. As a result, modifications may be made and/or new strategies implemented and evaluated until the goal is reached.

Terminate

Finally, upon achieving the desired outcome, during termination the consultant and consultee summarize the success, discuss how it was accomplished, and what can be applied to future situations (Brown et al., 2011; Parsons & Kahn, 2005). Of course, in schools a relationship continues, but the "official" consultation period is over, until something else arises.

In summary, you can see that consultation is a triadic relationship in which the consultant works closely with a consultee stakeholder to help and/or better serve a student or group of students. Hopefully in the process, the consultee becomes increasingly equipped with the knowledge and skills to respond to future concerns. As the action lies within the hands of the consultee, the consultant–consultee relationship is critical. The consultation process relies on the six stages outlined in the preceding paragraphs. The process begins with the relationship and builds on the strengths and autonomy of the consultee as the problem is defined, interventions are brainstormed, implemented and evaluated. Keeping these stages in mind will help build your consultation skills when working with other stakeholders in schools.

What stage of the consultation process would be the most difficult for you?

How can you help yourself feel better equipped to enact that stage?

You might be thinking, "Okay, but what would consultation steps look like in real life?" Let's take the case of Adrian, a kindergarten student who was discussed in the Tier 2 MTSS team because of behavioral outbursts and class disruption. Initially, he participated in a Tier 2 group focusing on emotional regulation. However, the amplification of his behaviors grew to include throwing chairs and running from the classroom, which necessitated Tier 3 evaluation and intervention. After thoughtful consideration, the team decided that part of the Tier 3 supports would include school counselor–teacher consultation between Maria (school counselor) and Katiya (kindergarten teacher). While Maria and Katiya had met and talked about a few students in passing, they had never worked closely before. Therefore, initially Maria spent time listening to and validating Katiya's feelings of frustration and helplessness.

Next, they began to discuss in detail what Katiya was experiencing with Adrian. Maria asked Katiya to explain what Adrian's problematic behaviors sounded and looked like in the classroom and helped her identify instances when the problematic behaviors did (e.g., transitions, unstructured time) and did not arise (e.g., when connected with peers or Katiya). Katiya articulated that she was aiming for Adrian to be able to initially transition from carpet time or learning stations back to his desk without a behavioral outburst 80% of the time. With that as the goal, Katiya and Maria spent time brainstorming various interventions and techniques that might be successful. Ultimately, they decided that they would institute two interventions: a count-down for transitions was instituted that included Katiya specifically getting at Adrian's eye level for major transitions to communicate the time left for the first-time warning, then using successive count-downs to be given orally. Given Adrian's predisposed pattern of exhibiting more appropriate behavior when with his peers, Katiya and Maria identified one of her male students to be Adrian's buddy to help him with transitions.

After three days, Maria checked in with Katiya and, while there was some improvement, the breakdowns were still plentiful. While meeting with the Tier 3 MTSS team, they realized they had not provided enough scaffolding for Adrian's buddy and that Katiya was struggling to remember to provide Adrian with count-downs. They came up with a plan to talk with Adrian's buddy and then put a visual reminder in Katiya's room to help her remember to provide the count-downs for Adrian. A week later, Maria again checked in and they discussed what was working and decided that, while progress was being made (75% successful transitions), Adrian might also benefit from check-ins with Maria, as the school counselor, and/or individual mental health counseling with an outside agency.

Because of Katiya and Adrian's tremendous progress, Maria terminated the formal consultation meetings, but of course reminded Katiya of her availability. They continued contact as Maria provided Katiya with updates on the individual counseling sessions. Maria also provided Katiya with specific language about the emotional regulation work she was doing with Adrian, so that Katiya could utilize the same language in class. Within two and a half months, Adrian was doing much better and having only sporadic outbursts (i.e., once every two to three weeks).

What would you do if a consultee chose not implement the team's suggested strategies?

What would you do if a student resists your interventions?

Collaboration

Collaboration can be conceptualized a bit more broadly than consultation, in that it involves more interactive and reciprocal dynamics. It typically consists of a relationship between two or more parties to reach common goals (Erford, 2015; Friend & Cook, 2013). In the case of MTSS and school counseling, the goal is to support the academic and social/emotional development of all students.

Shared Responsibility

The distinction from consultation is that the parties involved in collaboration have shared responsibility for the implementation of the interventions (Brown et al., 2011; Dougherty, 2014; Kampwirth, 2006). One example of this might be a school counselor working with an 11th grade English teacher to design and deliver curricular materials about writing the personal statement of a student's college applications. Another might be to participate regularly in MTSS leadership team meetings to track and support a student's progress on their 504 plan. The communication skills mentioned in the consultation section are relevant for collaboration as well. The distinction is the reciprocity of communication among the members of the collaboration team.

Shared Leadership

Within collaboration you are working with the other parties to not only address the issue at hand, but to also build working relationships among members of that collaboration team (Brown et al., 2011). At times, this may mean striving to align the goals of the various participants who are all working together on a decided goal (Kania & Kramer, 2013). Collaboration may be short term, focusing on just the immediate issue at hand, or more long term, such as working for systems change such as a more positive school climate (Brown et al., 2011). When working within MTSS, both short- and long-term collaborations are relevant, as can be seen in the example below.

The school-based mental health professionals (one school counselor, Max, one school psychologist, Lilian, and one social worker, Leslie) from a rural school district in the northeast worked with each other and with surrounding agencies to support student achievement. To better observe, collaborate, and plan, they meet together monthly in the mornings before school to accommodate all participants and to collaborate. Upon examining the school district and town's demographic data, it became evident that there was an influx of new immigrant families from Syria. As a result, they brought these findings to the MTSS leadership team, of which they were all members. One 5th grade boy, Kadan, presented to the middle school MTSS team with extreme shyness, he struggled to learn English, and his parents reported to the school counselor that he was reluctant to come to school. The MTSS team decided to address Kadan's reluctance by using positive support with him and his family to encourage his attendance.

First, the Tier 2 MTSS team collaborated to institute weekly Tier 2 groups, co-led by the school counselor Max and the school social worker Leslie. During this group, Kadan and other middle school students from dual language families were paired with English speaking peers to play board games. The groups were held during the students' lunch period. Max and Leslie took turns positively reinforcing the children's attempts to speak and cooperate with each other. During the initial six-week period, Max and Leslie documented that most of the immigrant children were observed speaking more often in the group. Most students who participated in the group responded favorably to the positive encouragement provided by the staff co-leaders.

Kadan, however, did not show as much progress as others in his group. At the next MTSS meeting the team decided to gather more information. Thus, Leslie learned from Kadan's willing family that he previously survived a military attack while at school in Syria, losing two close friends. As a result, the MTSS team referred Kadan to a licensed professional counselor (LPC) in the community, who diagnosed Kadan with PTSD and began individual counseling with him. Max and the LPC worked collaboratively to create a treatment plan for Kadan, with Max implementing the school portion of the plan. After six weeks of individual counseling with the LPC, and continued group counseling at school, Kadan's grades began to improve and he showed significant progress in both overcoming his shyness and showing more active class contribution. Although he was by nature a shy boy, by the end of that school year Kadan's social comfort and school achievement improved considerably. The school district developed a specialized summer school program for Kadan and other children who had immigrated to the district to assist them in reaching grade level performance. The collaborative activities by his MTSS team and outside providers also gave Kadan and his family the support to help him better assimilate to his new culture while addressing his concerns using a trauma-informed approach.

What stands out to you about the collaborative relationships in this case study?

What skills would you bring into collaborative relationships?

Types of Collaboration

Collaborations can be complex, as the example above suggests. However, they can be simple. For example, the ASCA National Model (2012) indicates that collaboration can include such activities as resource sharing, giving joint presentations with other stakeholders, and developing advisory councils or other groups focused on a specific task (e.g., the MTSS team).

Collaborations may start modestly, then evolve into more extensive collaborations over time. For instance, one school district recognized a need to better coordinate the collaboration efforts among existing school and community professionals who provided MTSS services to students. The Special Education Director of that school system first organized a district-wide monthly group that she called the Collaborative Services Team (CST). Membership included school counselors, school family therapists, school psychologists, school social workers, allied physical and occupational therapists, and community mental health staff. Topics for the discussion group

(continued)

(continued)

initially included current community issues and needs that were identified by the group such as changes to mandated reporting protocols.

Over time, the CST membership began requesting opportunities to address more specific information about diagnosis, disabilities and systemic MTSS service provision across the elementary, middle, and high school in that town. One important result was that as more efficient consultation and collaboration developed, better wraparound services were established for students and families. School and agency leaders began to address service and personnel needs to boost student achievement in that town. Professional relationships were strengthened and school climate in that town became more positive. The short-term collaboration efforts of this CST evolved into valuable and productive long-term collaborations for the town. A second result was the implementation of universal screening for emergent mental health concerns such as anxiety and depression. For more information about universal screening, see Chapter 7.

Each town and school district have unique needs, and such needs vary significantly across school settings and levels. But if collaborative relationships are built among the school and agency staff, more efficient MTSS can be developed. For instance, the term "invisible needs" includes those barriers to learning that are not immediately apparent at first glance. Students with "invisible needs" (such as Kadan who immigrated to the U.S. from Syria in the second case study) are more likely to be recognized and serviced by collaborative wraparound care. Further, the supportive MTSS services that school counselors and allied professional staff provide becomes more comprehensive and effective.

What are some "invisible needs" you have identified in students at your school that might be met by MTSS?

What might that intervention be and with whom would you collaborate to begin that process?

MTSS Leadership Team Consultation and Collaboration

Now that we have described consultation and collaboration, it is important to examine the key stakeholders that may make up the MTSS leadership team within a school, as these are the primary providers school counselors collaborate with to effectively implement MTSS. In this chapter, we want to emphasize the importance of creating strong MTSS leadership teams who are adequately trained to maximize educational effectiveness. Some MTSS leadership team members will participate in all three teams (Tier 1, Tier 2, and Tier 3 leadership teams) in order to avoid siloed thinking and increase interconnectedness of student support via MTSS. Please see Table 8.2 for more details on these three interconnected teams.

To provide an example and expand on the table, a school counselor and speech/language pathologist, as members of a Tier 2 MTSS team, might collaborate to provide social skills groups for students using an evidence-based program. As such, the school counselor may communicate these actions to both the Tier 1 and Tier 3 teams to maintain communication across teams. Note that MTSS teams vary considerably across rural,

Table 8.2 MTSS leadership teams

Definition: A MTSS leadership team is a multidisciplinary task group, made up of professionals from varying training backgrounds whose complementary roles and functions overlap, with the aim to plan and facilitate MTSS implementation in their school.

Many school-based MTSS leadership teams include school counselors, school psychologists, administrators, teachers, special educators, and interventionists. The *goals* of the MTSS leadership team are to work collaboratively to both promote a positive, productive, and safe learning environment for all students as well as to define and address all barriers/constraints that arise for students, educators, and families (see Chapter 1 for more information). The collaborative approach of the MTSS leadership team can increase the team's collective capacity to serve students in a more effective and innovative manner. The *objective* of the MTSS leadership team is to meet regularly to review student data in order to design/implement evidence-based practices and interventions that account for individual's challenges while fostering academic, behavioral, and social/emotional competence for all students.

Sample MTSS Leadership Team Tasks

Tier 1	Tier 2	Tier 3
1 Coordinate and support universal preventative program 2 Review school-level data monthly 3 Coordinate universal screening program 4 Select behavioral and social/emotional learning curriculum	1 Meet biweekly to review student-level data and determine intervention effectiveness 2 Plan and implement/oversee targeted intervention groups 3 Plan and implement/ oversee professional development based on concrete, identifiable needs (e.g., executive functioning, self-management, etc.) for educators and paraeducators	1 Meet with wraparound service providers to review student progress and plan intervention 2 Provide/oversee 1:1 services as needed 3 Vet community services for future referral and collaboration
Sample Members (8–10 members): School Counselors School Psychologists Administrators School Social Worker School Family Therapists** General Educators Special Educators Interventionists Others (as needed or available)*	Sample Members (5–6 members): School Counselor(s) School Psychologist Administrators School Social Worker School Family Therapist** General Educators Special Educators Interventionists	Sample Members (varies): School Counselor School Psychologist School Social Worker School Family Therapist** Designated Educators Administration Outside supports (e.g., LPC, as needed) Wraparound Coordinator

Notes:

*Team composition will vary based on availability, resources, and expertise.

**Very few states currently credential MFTs to work in schools, though this is evolving (School-based Marriage Family Therapists).

urban, and suburban settings, as well as at elementary, middle, and high school levels. It is important to know the composition of MTSS teams in your schools and districts in order to best join and practice effectively with your school.

As stated in Table 8.2, MTSS leadership teams are comprised of many school-based professionals. One of the most important members of the team is a school-based administrator, such as the principal or assistant principal. Administrators' active engagement and support is an essential element of successful MTSS implementation and sustainability, as they oversee the vision and operations of the school, including funding, professional development, initiatives, resources, and so forth. Though the MTSS leadership team is not based on a hierarchical model, these teams need the backing of the administration to successfully plan and implement MTSS school-wide and targeted initiatives. Next, other key stakeholders with whom school counselors collaborate and consult are allied school-based mental health professionals which we will now describe in more detail.

Overlapping Roles of School-Based Mental Health Professionals

Figure 8.2 below portrays the overlapping roles of school-based mental health professionals: school counselors, school psychologists, school social workers, and school family therapists. However, just as there is significant variety in the graduate training of these professionals, there also can be variability in their specific skill sets. The roles of each school-based mental health professional can also evolve over time, depending upon the talents, resources, and constraints of each school system, as well as normal attrition. In the next section, we will describe the roles of these school-based mental health professionals in more depth, including their necessary redundancies.

All school-based mental health professionals are trained to provide some similar services to support student achievement in schools, in a context we call "necessary redundancies" (Laundy, 2015). The skill sets of school-based mental health professionals equip them to provide some form of individual and group counseling and services to students. In addition, these professionals are all prepared to work on crisis intervention teams and are often a part of the MTSS leadership team (see Table 8.2 above). The school-based

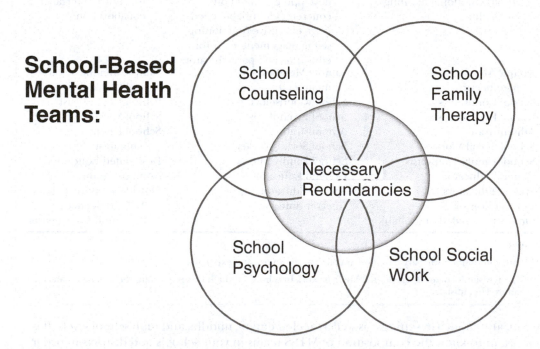

Figure 8.2 School-based mental health professionals.

mental health professionals provide direct and indirect interventions such as participating in IEPs and 504 plans, and are part of multidisciplinary teams, data collection, and interpretation and planning. Many engage in joint training and professional development coursework as well. For the most effective collaborations to occur, it is important for all school-based mental health providers to learn about the specific skill sets of each other in their school, as each has a core set of skills. Below we describe key multidisciplinary members of the MTSS and other school-based teams.

School Counselors

School counselors implement proactive, preventative, Comprehensive School Counseling Programs, examining and utilizing data to drive programming and deliver direct and indirect services (ASCA, 2012). With regards to delivery, school counselors facilitate core curriculum to every student as a Tier 1 support, such as classroom lessons and school-wide initiatives (ASCA, 2012; see Chapters 3 and 4). In collaboration with other school-based mental health professionals, they assist in determining students with elevated needs and in the implementation of Tier 2 and Tier 3 interventions (as outlined in Chapters 5 and 6). They conduct a range of other roles to serve students across the three tiers, including helping to interpret school testing and assessment measures (along with school psychologists, social workers, and family therapists), preparing students for post-secondary planning, and of course participating on multidisciplinary teams. Please see other chapters of this text for more information about the scope of school counselor skills and competencies in relation to MTSS (e.g., Chapter 2).

School Psychologists

School psychologists are traditionally trained in individual cognitive and achievement assessment of student needs and strengths, and they have been part of school-based multidisciplinary teams for over 50 years. They evaluate the eligibility for special education and other support services. Because of their psychometric training, school psychologists often take the lead in analyzing school data in MTSS meetings (e.g., Functional Behavioral Assessments [FBA]), as well as helping to make referrals and coordinating school and community support for students. Data from the FBA is used by the team to create a Behavioral Intervention Plan (BIP). For more on this process see Chapters 5 and 6.

School Social Workers

School social workers are historically the individuals who link up student needs with resources within the school and community to support achievement. They have been school-certified since the 1970s. They too are skilled in obtaining social/emotional histories, helping provide links between school, home, and community, and mobilizing resources to assist student learning needs. Many schools employ school social workers to support families who are experiencing economic challenges, transitions, and new referrals to special education. School social workers help educate parents about how to best support their children's education.

School Family Therapists

School family therapists, now certified in a handful of states, are school-based professionals grounded in systemic thinking. Through their systems lens, they collect developmental histories and assess and treat the mental health of students and families. They are especially skilled at developing collaborative relationships and participating in systemic initiatives to support student learning. School family therapists are also specifically trained to work in the schools to enlist family support for student planning, and to help schools collaborate with outside mental health and social agencies on behalf of the students and families they service. As you look at Table 8.2, you will notice that school family therapists can provide services for students throughout the three tiers. In a similar vein, many schools/districts are partnering with community mental health providers (e.g., LPCs, LCSWs) to provide individual and group counseling in schools.

Because school counselors, school psychologists, social workers, and school family therapists are all trained in building relationships and conducting groups, such collaborative partnerships can strengthen the sustainability of MTSS leadership teams. Their historic and professional lenses may differ, but the "necessary redundancies" of their training make them natural consultative and collaborative partners. Further, what makes MTSS leadership teams effective are both the knowledge and the communication skills of all members. Such skills are embedded in consultation and collaboration expertise, where effective relationships can be developed to "get the job done." In other words, effective multidisciplinary teams "play well in the sand box" with each other to achieve the goals of the MTSS approach.

The Role of the School Counselor on MTSS Leadership Teams

As integral members of the MTSS team, school counselors are in a strong position to provide consultative and collaborative leadership to the MTSS leadership team (Goodman-Scott, Betters-Bubon, & Donohue, 2016). Because they are trained in the use of data and data-based decision making, they can be invaluable to the MTSS team when it comes to collecting data about school and community demographics, student needs, and helping the team to monitor the progress of interventions, particularly in Tiers 2 and 3. Furthermore, with their expertise in consultation, collaboration, and group dynamics, school counselors can help their MTSS leadership teams to be more active and effective.

School counselors are well-trained professionals that can lead, support and/or advocate for their MTSS teams and initiatives. We recommend school counselors actively seek consultative and collaborative opportunities with other school professionals with whom they work. Aligning with like-minded school leaders and allied school-based mental health professionals helps to make such teamwork more possible. And addressing school initiatives "for the long haul" makes the success of those school team initiatives more possible. It fosters sustainability, particularly as school systems face the inevitability of staff attrition.

In a similar vein, building collaborative relationships can take school counselors time and persistence, and may take a circuitous path. We have seen initiatives begin and thrive, then falter, when a key school leader, such as an administrator, resigns or is transferred to another system. Often, even when schools are making strong progress, MTSS leadership teams need time to regroup and assess the possibilities of MTSS initiatives when a key team member leaves. School counselors may find it helpful to remember that the fruits of good consultation and collaboration are often best realized over a long period of time, rather than in a typical school year.

What do you see as school counselors' strengths and skills that can be harnessed on multidisciplinary teams?

What strengths do you have personally that would be beneficial to a team?

Using Data and Selecting Interventions on MTSS Leadership Teams

As you have seen throughout this textbook, there are numerous Tier 1, Tier 2, and Tier 3 interventions that can readily be implemented to positively impact the school, smaller groups of students, and/or individual students (see Chapters 3 through 6). Given the numerous options, MTSS leadership teams have the important task of selecting appropriate interventions through collaborative data-based decision making. In making such selections, the MTSS leadership team members consider school data and individual student data. For instance, with regard to school data, the MTSS leadership team may collect data about graduation rates, student dropout rates, ethnic and social variables, happenings in the community such as school violence, etc., with the goal of designing MTSS initiatives that more fully meet the needs and promote the healthy functioning of all students in their system. For the individual student data, it is important to get a full account of the student's presenting concerns, as the data and issues of concern drive the intervention selection. For example, the MTSS leadership team initially determines if the concern at hand necessitates Tier 1, Tier 2, and/or Tier 3 intervention. Once that is decided, the team collaborates to determine which specific interventions are best aligned and would lead to success. Team members must weigh out the strengths and weaknesses of the student, not to mention the school's resources and the personnel's capacity to enact the intervention.

When considering interventions for a student in need of Tier 2 or Tier 3 services, it is important that the MTSS team match the intervention to the function of the student's behavior, and identify the underlying root cause. Experts in the field of applied behavioral analysis concur that at the root of behavior is typically the student's desire to escape, avoid, or gain access to something, be it attention, reward, discomfort, etc. (Hansen, Wills, Kamps & Greenwood, 2014). Thus, for example, in PBIS, a Check-in/Check-out intervention may not be successful for a student whose function of behavior is escape, but may be more successful for a student whose function is attention seeking (Hoyle, Marshall, & Yell, 2011). The MTSS team carefully considers the information they have about the issue of concern for particular students when collaborating to choose an intervention.

This is where having numerous perspectives can be both advantageous and a challenge. Each member of the MTSS leadership team brings both their personal and professional orientation, and thus their ways of viewing each situation. The multidisciplinary nature of the team allows for multiple perspectives about assessment and intervention, which may necessitate extra time to come to consensus.

Similar to step five of the consultation process outlined earlier, as members of MTSS teams, school counselors must monitor and evaluate the interventions. In doing so, school counselors examine data, which is at the foundation of all MTSS work. For instance, if a Tier 2 MTSS team decided on a reading intervention for a group of students in need of Tier 2 supports, it would be important to monitor the students' reading proficiency to determine progress. The hope is that after a six-week Tier 2 intervention, students would no longer need Tier 2 services. However, as we know, progress may not always happen immediately and may require multiple interventions. If we do not monitor the interventions and the students' progress closely, resources may be expended without student gains. We will share more about data in Chapter 9. Overall, the Tier 2 MTSS team's data monitoring underlies much of their important work.

Navigating Difficulties on MTSS Teams

You might be thinking "How can so many professions operate collaboratively and efficiently in school settings?" Often, constraints occur in schools that hinder the ability to consult and collaborate. There are three major constraints to effective multidisciplinary consultation and collaboration in schools.

The first constraint is the *inherent difference between disciplines*. As one of my (first author) supervisors once said, having several different mental health professions makes it, at times, confusing to fully appreciate the unique and overlapping skills of each discipline. Similarly, MTSS leadership teams may also vary considerably, based on each system's specific needs and resources. This constraint means that initially it can be difficult to discern how to consult and collaborate fully with fellow MTSS leadership team members. How does one then learn the scope of practice for each profession? We invite the posture of "cultural humility" (Hernandez-Wolfe & McDowell, 2014), that carries respectful curiosity about the cultural dynamics of a system such as a school. Cultural awareness and "humility" encourages more rich consultation and collaboration among school counselors and teachers, administrators, and other professionals by recognizing the internal policies, roles, services, and relationships within schools.

The second constraint involves the *shift from linear to systemic thinking*. Often we hear feedback in schools such as: "I teach math, not behavior," or "I don't have time for differentiation." It is a curious paradox that the more graduate training one receives, often the less familiar one becomes with the training of other similar professions. Increased graduate training can run the risk of creating siloes, and schools do have histories of linear, individually-oriented traditions. But the past few decades have provided many systemic opportunities to support student achievement through MTSS. These initiatives invite professionals to look more broadly at the variables that support student success, and to engage actively in consultation and collaboration with other school professionals, to learn how integral these can be to student success. As graduate students and school counselors, you likely have training and supervisory support to ask questions and engage with the initiatives at your school. We encourage you to utilize that supervision to learn about how MTSS operates in your setting. Become active learners as quickly as you can, in order to discover consultation and collaborative opportunities at your school.

While operating with "cultural humility" and trying to break out of siloes are integral steps, you may still face problems and conflicts when collaborating and consulting with a variety of stakeholders on multidisciplinary teams. It is important to prepare yourself to work with that teacher that asserts, "I teach math, not behavior" or that staff member that asks, "you want me to collect what kind of data?" It is here that you rely on your counseling skills training. One cannot underestimate the power of paraphrasing, reflections of feelings, and open-ended questions. You can use what emerges from active listening to answer the question, "Why is this individual hesitant or resistant?" Is it habit, strength, insecurity, labor intensity, poor planning/delivery, or skill deficits (Kampwirth, 2006)? Much like in counseling, your conceptualization will guide how you proceed.

Once you get to the crux of an individual's hesitancy, you can then address them as needed. This might include adjusting a Tier 1, Tier 2, or Tier 3 plan, providing encouragement and ideas, acknowledging effort, inquiring, or by providing support through resources and preparations (Kampwirth, 2006). It can be helpful to remember that, 99 out of 100 times, stakeholders want what is best for students. Thus, allow this to serve as a unifying factor, as well as a motivator, to keep an open mind and work collaboratively.

The third constraint involves the very real *challenge of funding for school counseling and other allied professionals*. The resulting competition for jobs is real and frustrating, and resources in schools are often challenged and curtailed. The competing interest in funding for preventive screening, support services, and school safety has only intensified as school violence has escalated in this country (Cowan et al., 2013).

We believe that consultation and collaboration enhance our ability to support student learning and healthy functioning. We urge you to learn as much as you can about the broader systemic issues in your school community. One way is through advocacy. Join your local, state, and national support organizations, and attend school and legislative meetings that address support for student success initiatives. Where they exist, join and participate in multidisciplinary advocacy groups in your local and regional areas.

Cultural and Diversity Implications in Consultation and Collaboration

As we consider consultation and collaboration, the cultural and diversity implications are of paramount importance. To begin, we must reflect on our own cultural backgrounds and heritage. Hernandez-Wolfe and McDowell (2014) describe three aspects of cultural diversity that are important to consider in the helping fields, namely cultural equity, cultural humility, and intersectionality. Cultural equity refers to the importance of examining one's own experience with privilege and marginalization in relation to others. This recognition highlights the importance of thinking deliberately about your own personal advantages and how power differentials can operate as you enter school systems (Hernandez-Wolfe & McDowell, 2014). Cultural humility relates to curiosity about the unique cultural features of the system one enters, and implies an ongoing posture of respect for the participants in that system rather than resting on the perceived comforts of stereotyping. Intersectionality refers to the many axes of identity, where all of us are situated across systems of privilege and oppression, including gender, race, social class, sexual orientation, and religion (Hernandez-Wolfe & McDowell, 2014). We must consider the aspects of the identity of those with whom we work, both stakeholders and students.

School can be a very difficult place for our students from backgrounds that differ from the dominant culture of the school. Variables such as socioeconomic status, differential abilities, gender identity, languages spoken, ethnicity, and power and privilege all affect school culture. In the U.S., the teacher workforce predominantly consists of Caucasian females (U.S. Department of Education, 2016) and scholars note that the culture of schools aligns with white middle-class values (e.g., Gay, 2010). Some literature suggests that students from groups whose culture does not align with the norms, values, and knowledge espoused by the school may experience a cultural disconnection between home and school (Gay, 2010; Nieto & Bode, 2016), which can result in psychological distress (Cholewa & West-Olatunji, 2008).

As members of the MTSS leadership team, utilizing consultation and collaboration, we can work with various school stakeholders, particularly teachers and administrators, to improve the educational experiences of students from marginalized groups (Amatea & West-Olatunji, 2007). From the outset, when MTSS is being developed within the schools, we must consider culture and engage families as we develop policies and expectations (Bal, Thorius, & Kozleski, 2012). Culturally relevant MTSS practices include elements focused on the staff's cultural self-awareness and knowledge, equity-focused outcomes, evidence-based practices in alignment with students' culture, and decision-making that incorporates culture (Betters-Bubon, Brunner, & Kansteiner, 2016). For additional discussion of cultural relevancy in MTSS, see Chapter 11.

The MTSS leadership team needs to critically examine the school's data and corresponding school-wide processes to ensure that certain groups of students (or teachers) are not being inequitably advantaged over others. As school counselors, you can consider bringing in the ASCA Model's (2012) School Data Profile (see Chapter 9 of this text and p. 66 of the 2012 ASCA Model) as a way of examining school data for equity gaps. For example, does the data reflect that certain student groups are disproportionately being retained or dropping out? Similarly, within MTSS (RTI or PBIS, specifically), are certain groups of students more likely to be identified/referred for Tier 2 and Tier 3 services as a result of school staff biases? Upon identifying such practices, the MTSS leadership team may need to collaborate with administrators to fully explore the intricacies and systems underlying such equity gaps, and ultimately determine ways to rectify the problem. For example, numerous research studies suggest that Black/African American and Latino students, as well as students from low-income backgrounds, are disproportionately referred for special education and receive disproportionate exclusionary discipline (e.g., Noltemeyer, Ward, & Mcloughlin, 2015; Skiba et al., 2011). Consequently, you may find similar trends in your schools.

Researchers suggest some of this disproportionality may relate to the disconnection between home and school mentioned above. However, there are promising results related to culturally responsive educational practices and academic outcomes (see Aronson & Laughter, 2016, for a review of the literature), and disciplinary outcomes (e.g., Gregory, Allen, Mikami, Hafen, & Pianta, 2014). As such, this is an important area on which school counselors and allied school-based mental health professionals on the MTSS leadership team can consult with teachers, if such practices are lacking at their school. Culturally responsive practices are best described as "using the cultural knowledge, prior experiences, frames of reference, and performance styles of ethnically diverse students to make learning encounters more relevant and effective for them. It teaches to and through the strengths of these students" (Gay, 2010, p. 31). The case study below will help you consider implications of cultural responsivity in collaboration and consultation.

One university placed both school counselor and school family therapy graduate students in an urban K-8 school for their internship experience. The graduate students noticed that middle school teachers repeatedly referred several of the same students and even referred to them as "frequent flyers." Most of the teachers were female, young, and from Caucasian ancestry. The students, some of whom were children of Latino, African, and Caribbean-American families, would request bathroom breaks during class, then walk around the building and engage in conflicts with students and teachers. Teachers expressed fear and anger about these behaviors. School staff invited the graduate students to collaborate with them during their weekly team meetings to address the situation.

The interns suggested working with the teachers to help resolve the cultural discomfort and perceived differences between the staff and student backgrounds. Thus, the interns started consultation groups for teachers during weekly professional development time. After addressing their cultural discomfort, over the course of the year, the teachers' behavior towards these students became more insightful and informed. Teachers and students became better equipped to manage the conflict, Tier 2 groups were established with students, and, as a result, disciplinary referrals and suspension rates diminished, and the "frequent flyer" rates went down.

How can collaboration and consultation impact cultural responsiveness of individuals and school systems?

This idea of cultural responsiveness is not new to us as counselors, as we are ethically bound to practice with cultural competence (ASCA, 2016) and have received multicultural training. With our own multicultural knowledge and skill base, we are poised to not only advocate for culturally responsive practices, but to consult and collaborate with teachers, assisting in their successful implementation of culturally responsive practices. As shown in the above example, we can harness our own multicultural expertise to work with teachers through school-wide professional development or small-group professional development on cultural self-awareness and cultural responsiveness. This may entail serving as a cultural bridge, helping to counter deficit views teachers may have about students, demonstrating how to build on families' strengths and knowledge (Amatea & West-Olatunji, 2007). Furthermore, we can work with individual teachers to help enhance their awareness, knowledge, and skills in working with their students, helping them to contextualize culturally based behavior and develop culturally responsive interventions.

Conclusion

This chapter traced the evolving role and impact that school counselors bring to MTSS leadership teams. Specifically, this chapter outlined critical skills in consultation and collaboration that equip school counselors to support student achievement and well-being through both indirect consultation interventions with school staff and through system-wide direct collaborative initiatives.

American education has witnessed the historical shift from providing special education services to boost individual student achievement to developing MTSS across broader systemic layers of school culture. School counselors actively employ consultation and collaboration skills to help support teachers and educational teams across these tiers in culturally sensitive ways. This chapter defined and illustrated how consultation and collaboration skills can be utilized, and the roles that school counselors on MTSS leadership teams play to support educational success for all students.

In this chapter we introduced MTSS leadership team members, including school-based administrators, as well as school counselors, school psychologists, school social workers, and school family therapists. Further, we addressed how school counselors collaboratively work with the MTSS leadership team and allied school professionals to boost student achievement. We emphasized the collective power of consultation and collaboration in the MTSS team to illustrate how important these skills are to both students and educators. Consultation and collaboration skills give school counselors and other allied school professionals the "power to empower" when on the MTSS leadership team.

Finally, we summarized the cultural and ethical considerations necessary for school counselors to successfully function in education. School systems widely differ across settings (i.e., urban, suburban, rural) as well as educational levels (i.e., elementary, middle, high). The MTSS leadership team composition and roles also vary according to school district needs and resources. School counselors use vital consultation and collaboration skills to ethically design the best fit for their skill set and the school system they serve.

It is precisely the strength of healthy collaborative MTSS leadership teams that helps to ensure the sustainability of these important system-wide MTSS initiatives. The multidisciplinary school-based relationships are built over time and help empower teams to grow and thrive, even in the event of loss of key team members. Effective MTSS frameworks that are initiated, grown, and sustained over time are the ones that employ relevant data and, through healthy consultation and collaboration, design and implement effective and measurable initiatives to help all students succeed.

For more information and school counselors' perspectives on *Consulting and Collaborating Within MTSS*, please see Chapter 12 "Voices from the Field," voices 1, 3, 6, 7, and 9.

ASCA Ethical Standards

As school counselors consult and collaborate within the MTSS team and other stakeholders, they must keep in mind a number of ethical standards. Many of the ethical standards listed below highlight that ethical school counseling practice involves communicating, collaborating, and consulting with families, faculty, administrators, and mental health and allied professionals. Participating on MTSS teams falls within our ethical responsibility.

Consultation and collaboration require that school counselors carefully navigate issues of maintaining and protecting students' confidentiality in the process (see Section A.2). School counselors may know a lot of information about a student and his/her family, and/or the presenting situation, given their previous work with the student. Yet, making the determination about what information to convey to members of the MTSS teams can be difficult. The standing practice promoted within ASCA's position statement on confidentiality (ASCA, 2014) is that school counselors disclose the student's or their family's private information on a need-to-know basis, and if sharing the information would be of benefit to the student. Thus, school counselors thoughtfully consider the consequences to the student if such information is shared and whether the benefits outweigh the costs. Given the nature of MTSS teams, we recommend that school counselors become familiar with their own and other professionals' ethical standards as they work on school teams.

This ethical responsibility with regard to confidentiality becomes increasingly complicated given our work with minors in schools (Stone, 2013). Not only are our actions governed by ASCA's ethical code, but they are also governed by the Family Educational Rights and Privacy Act (FERPA), which is a federal law administered by the U.S. Department of Education's Family Policy Compliance Office (USDOE/FPCO, 2015). The Family Educational Rights and Privacy Act relates to the disclosure of identifiable information coming from students' educational records. The law gives parents of students under 18 the right to access their students' educational record, of which school counseling records may be a part (see Stone, 2013).

Finally, information in students' educational records cannot be disclosed without consent of the parent (if the student is a minor). However, the exception is that information can be shared with school officials with legitimate education interest (LEI; Stone, 2013). Thus, school officials can access the student record if doing so relates to their job description, or performing tasks related to student's education or discipline, or to provide the student with services such as counseling (Stone, 2013).

In summary, within our ASCA Code of Ethics (2016), we are ethically bound to collaborate and consult with various stakeholders both inside and outside of the school. As we do so, we must consider our ethical standards related to confidentiality, while simultaneously taking into account educational laws such as FERPA. Although traversing these complex situations can be arduous at times, it can be rewarding to work with individuals across multiple disciplines in a combined effort to promote student success. The following ASCA Ethical Standards are addressed by the content in this chapter. Specifically, school counselors:

A   Responsibility to Students

A.1   Supporting Student Development

- A.1.i. Consider the involvement of support networks, wraparound services, and educational teams needed to best serve students.

A.2   Confidentiality

- A.2.a. Promote awareness of school counselors' ethical standards and legal mandates regarding confidentiality and the appropriate rationale and procedures for disclosure of student data and information to school staff.
- A.2.f. Recognize their primary ethical obligation for confidentiality is to the students but balance that obligation with an understanding of parents'/guardians' legal and inherent rights to be the guiding voice in their children's lives. School

counselors understand the need to balance students' ethical rights to make choices, their capacity to give consent or assent, and parental or familial legal rights and responsibilities to make decisions on their child's behalf.

- A.2.h. Protect the confidentiality of students' records and release personal data in accordance with prescribed federal and state laws and school policies including the laws within the Family Education Rights and Privacy Act (FERPA). Student information stored and transmitted electronically is treated with the same care as traditional student records. Recognize the vulnerability of confidentiality in electronic communications and only transmit sensitive information electronically in a way that is untraceable to students' identity.
- A.2.j. Protect the confidentiality of students' records and release personal data in accordance with prescribed federal and state laws and school board policies.

A.3　Comprehensive Data-Informed Program

- A.3.a. Collaborate with administration, teachers, staff, and decision makers around school-improvement goals.

A.6　Appropriate Referrals and Advocacy

- A.6.a Collaborate with all relevant stakeholders, including students, educators, and parents/guardians when student assistance is needed, including the identification of early warning signs of student distress.
- A.6.f. Attempt to establish a collaborative relationship with outside service providers to best serve students. Request a release of information signed by the student and/or parents/guardians before attempting to collaborate with the student's external provider.

A.12　Student Records

- A.12.a. Abide by the Family Educational Rights and Privacy Act (FERPA), which defines who has access to students' educational records and allows parents the right to review and challenge perceived inaccuracies in their child's records.

B　Responsibility to Parents/Guardians, School, and School Staff

B.2　Responsibilities to the School

- B.2.a. Develop and maintain professional relationships and systems of communication with faculty, staff, and administrators to support students.
- B.2.f. Provide support, consultation, and mentoring to professionals in need of assistance when in the scope of the school counselor's role.
- B.2.q. Collaborate as needed to provide optimum services with other professionals such as special educators, school nurses, school social workers, school psychologists, college counselors/admission officers, physical therapists, occupational therapists, speech pathologists, administrators.

Resources

Further Reading

Cowan, K. C., Vaillancourt, K. I., Rossen, E. & Pollitt, K. (2013). *A framework for safe and successful schools* [(Brief]. Bethesda, MD: National Association of School Psychologists. Retrieved from: www.nasponline.org.

Fine, M. J., & Carlson, C. (Eds) (1992). *Handbook of family–school interventions: A systems perspective.* Boston, MA: Allyn & Bacon.

Gerrard, B., & Soriano, M. (Eds) (2013). *School-based family counseling: Transforming family–school relationships.* Lexington, KY: Institute for School-Based Family Counseling.

Laundy, K. C. (2015). *Building school-based collaborative mental health teams: A systems approach to student achievement.* Camp Hill, PA: The Practice Institute.

McIntosh, K., & Goodman, S. (2016). *Integrated Multi-Tiered Systems of Support: Blending RTI and PBIS.* New York: The Guilford Press.

Websites

Links to the following can be found on our eresource at www.routledge.com/ 9781138501614.

- Worksheets, outlines, and samples of letters to be used when consulting with parents and teachers on behavior or academic problems.
- Missouri Comprehensive School Counseling Program Responsive Services: Consultation Guide.

Teaching Activity

Directions: Consider each of these collaboration scenarios. Discuss your course of action for each with your small group or in your written response:

1   How would you respond if a teacher, who did not qualify as someone that "need[ed] to know," asked you a question about a student's personal information? Consider how you would protect the student's confidentiality but still maintain your relationship with the teacher.
2   What steps would you and your (actual or hypothetical) MTSS leadership team take to prepare for a group of 50 students in grades 5–8 immigrating from Syria after experiencing significant traumatic events? Consider the Tier 1, 2, and 3 needs of the students.
3   Investigate the referral forms used by teachers in elementary, middle, or high schools. The form should include key background information about the student's strengths, presenting concerns, and previous interventions implemented. Bring a copy of the referral form to class. Be prepared to share with a small group and discuss which forms you think are both comprehensive and easy to use. Finally, as a team, create a referral form with the best elements of each.

Multiple Choice Questions

1   **What is the unique difference between consultation and collaboration?**

   a   The egalitarian relationship.
   b   The individual who implements the intervention.
   c   The individuals participating.
   d   Collaboration consists of more than two people.

2   **Which of the following is NOT true of the problem definition/goal-setting stage of consultation?**

    a   The goal might be developed before the problem is defined.

    b   The consultee's experience is validated.

    c   Review interventions that have been attempted already.

    d   Identify target behaviors.

3   **Which of the following is true regarding FERPA?**

    a   FERPA is an ethical standard related to students' educational records.

    b   It is a law related to educational records but varies based on the state.

    c   This law states that parents/guardians of minors can have full access to their student's educational record.

    d   According to FERPA, parents always have to give written consent for school officials to access their student's file.

4   **What is the most valuable contribution of consultation and collaboration to school MTSS teams?**

    a   School personnel get along better with students.

    b   School personnel get along better with each other.

    c   More effective and sustainable initiatives can be developed in schools.

    d   Parents better understand the plans made for their children by school teams.

5   **What is a major difference between current MTSS initiatives and more traditional special service provision in schools?**

    a   Traditional special services offer a wider range of services to students than MTSS.

    b   The current MTSS approach offers services to a wider range of students than traditional special services.

    c   The success of traditional special services is harder to measure.

    d   Current MTSS services take longer to implement than traditional special services.

Answers: Q1 b, Q2 a, Q3 c, Q4 c, Q5 b.

References

Amatea, E., & West-Olatunji, C. (2007). Joining the conversation about educating our poorest children: Emerging leadership roles for school counselors in high poverty schools. *Professional School Counseling, 11*, 81–89.

American School Counselor Association (ASCA) (2012). *ASCA National Model: A framework for school counseling programs* (3rd Ed). Alexandria, VA: Author.

American School Counselor Association (ASCA) (2014). *The school counselor and confidentiality. ASCA position statement.* Alexandria, VA: Author. Retrieved from: www.schoolcounselor.org/asca/media/asca/PositionStatements/PS_Confidentiality.p.

American School Counselor Association (ASCA) (2016). *Ethical standards for school counselors.* Alexandria, VA: Author.

Aronson, B., & Laughter, J. (2016). The theory and practice of culturally relevant education: A synthesis of research across content areas. *Review of Educational Research, 86*, 163–206.

Bal, A., Thorius, K., & Kozleski, E. B. (2012). *Culturally responsive positive behavioral support matters.* Tempe, AZ: The Equity Alliance. Retrieved from: www.equityallianceatasu.org/sites/default/files/CRPBIS_Matters.pdf.

Betters-Bubon, J., Brunner, T., & Kansteiner, A. (2016). Success for all? The role of the school counselor in creating and sustaining culturally responsive positive behavior interventions and supports programs. *The Professional Counselor, 6,* 263–277.

Brown, D., Pryzwansky, W. B., & Schulte, A. C. (2011). *Psychological consultation and collaboration: Introduction to theory and practice* (7th Ed.). New York: Pearson.

Cholewa, B., Goodman-Scott, E., Thomas, A., & Cook, J. (2017). Teachers' perceptions and experiences consulting with school counselors: A qualitative study. *Professional School Counseling, 20,* 77–88.

Cholewa, B., & West-Olatunji, C. (2008). Exploring the relationship among cultural discontinuity, psychological distress, and academic outcomes with low-income, culturally diverse students. *Professional School Counseling, 12,* 54–61.

Cowan, K. C., Vaillancourt, K., Rossen, E., & Pollitt, K. (2013). *A framework for safe and successful schools* [Brief]. Bethesda, MD: National Association of School Psychologists.

Dinkmeyer, J., Carlson, J., & Michel, R. (2016). *Consultation: Creating school-based interventions* (4th Ed.). New York: Routledge.

Dougherty, M. (2014). *Psychological consultation and collaboration in school and community settings* (6th Ed). Belmont, CA: Brooks/Cole.

Erford, B. (2015). Consultation, collaboration and encouraging parental involvement. In B. Erford (Ed.), *Transforming the school counseling profession* (4th Ed., pp. 303–324). Upper Saddle River, NJ: Pearson.

Friend, M. & Cooke, L. (2013). *Interactions collaboration skills for school professionals* (7th Ed). Boston, MA: Pearson.

Gay, G. (2010). *Culturally responsive teaching: Theory, research, and practice* (2nd Ed.). New York: Teachers College Press.

Goodman-Scott, E., Betters-Bubon, J., & Donohue, P. (2016). Aligning Comprehensive School Counseling Programs and Positive Behavioral Interventions and Supports to maximize school counselors' efforts. *Professional School Counseling, 19,* 57–67.

Gregory, A., Allen, J. P., Mikami, A. Y., Hafen, C. A., & Pianta, R. (2014). Eliminating the racial disparity in classroom exclusionary discipline. *Journal of Applied Research on Children, 5*(2), 1–22.

Gysbers, N. C., & Henderson, P. (2012). *Developing and managing your school guidance and counseling program* (5th Ed.). Alexandria, VA: American Counseling Association.

Hansen, B. D., Wills, H. P., Kamps, D. M., & Greenwood, C. R. (2014). The effects of function-based self-management interventions on student behavior. *Journal of Emotional and Behavioral Disorders, 22*(3), 149–159.

Hernandez-Wolfe, P., & McDowell, T. (2014). Bridging complex identities with cultural equity and humility in systemic supervision. In T.C. Todd and C. L. Storm (Eds), *The complete systemic supervisor: Context, philosophy and pragmatics* (2nd Ed.). New York: John Wiley & Sons, Ltd.

Hoyle, C., Marshall, K., & Yell, M. (2011). Positive behavior supports: Tier 2 interventions in middle schools. *Preventing School Failure, 55,* 164–170.

Kampwirth, T. (2006). *Collaborative consultation in the schools: Effective practices for students with learning and behavior problems* (3rd Ed). Upper Saddle River, NJ: Pearson.

Kania, J., & Kramer, M. (2013). *Embracing emergence: How collective impact addresses complexity.* Stanford Social Innovation Review. Stanford, CA: Stanford University.

Laundy, K. C. (2015). *Building school-based collaborative mental health teams: A systems approach to student achievement.* Camp Hill, PA: The Practice Institute.

Nieto, S. & Bode, P. (2016). *Affirming diversity: The sociopolitical context of multicultural education* (6th Ed). New York: Allyn & Bacon.

Noltemeyer, A. L., Ward, R. M., & Mcloughlin, C. (2015). Relationship between school suspension and student outcomes: A meta-analysis. *School Psychology Review, 44,* 224–240, doi:10.17105/spr-14-0008.1.

Parsons, R., & Kahn, W. (2005). *The school counselor as consultant: An integrated model for school-based consultation.* Belmont, CA: Brooks/Cole.

Skiba, R. J., Horner, R. H., Chung, C. G., Rausch, M. K., May, S. L., & Tobin, T. (2011). Race is not neutral: A national investigation of African American and Latino disproportionality in school discipline. *School Psychology Review, 40*, 85–107.

Stone, C. (2013). *School counseling principles: Ethics and law* (3rd Ed.). Alexandria, VA: American School Counselor Association.

U.S. Department of Education, Family Policy Compliance Office (USDOE/FPCO) (2015). *Family Educational Rights and Privacy Act* (FERPA). Washington, DC: Author. Retrieved from: www2. ed.gov/policy/gen/guid/fpco/ferpa/index.html.

U.S. Department of Education, Office of Planning, Evaluation and Policy Development (2016). *The state of racial diversity in the educator workforce.* Washington, DC: Author. Retrieved from: www2. ed.gov/rschstat/eval/highered/racial-diversity/state-racial-diversity-workforce.pdf.

9 Using Data in MTSS to Demonstrate How School Counselors Make a Difference

Julia V. Taylor and Melanie Burgess

Introduction

Why is data collection and analysis important? How do school counselors collect meaningful data and make sense of it? How do school counselors measure the impact of their work? When I began my graduate program, many school counselors-in-training had a downright terrified look on their face once we began to discuss data and accountability measures. Sure, they appreciated that evidence-based practices should be used, that advocacy is a central tenet of school counseling, and that measuring growth and progress is critical to the success and legitimacy of Comprehensive School Counseling Programs (CSCPs); however, once the word data was introduced, our anxiety increased. I recall hearing phrases such as, "We are school counselors, not statisticians," "I hate doing math," or, jokingly, "Can't we measure progress by the number of high-fives we receive from students?"

Data can be powerful, exciting, and meaningful. Data can also be overwhelming and scary, especially for those who do not understand it or know how to harness its power. In alignment with the American School Counselor Association (ASCA) National Model, school counselors need to show how their CSCPs impact student outcomes. Likewise, Multi-Tiered Systems of Support (MTSS) affect student outcomes. Data from your CSCP and MTSS can be an essential tool to better understand how to maximize your efforts to become more effective and to better meet the needs of your school community.

Throughout this chapter, we aim to introduce the importance of data, including different types of data and data tools/assessments you can readily use to collect, organize, and analyze data from your CSCP. Similarly, we will introduce you to common MTSS data collection tools, as data from both CSCP and MTSS greatly influence school counseling decisions. We will focus on how data can be used to drive your CSCP and MTSS framework, to evaluate the effectiveness of your programs, and to advocate for your students. Within this chapter, we will outline Root Cause Analysis as a specific data analytic tool to help you identify and diagnose achievement and equity gap concerns in your schools. Lastly, we discuss ethical implications of using data and practical applications of data usage throughout. So, without further ado, let's dive into the fascinating world of data.

When you think about data collection and analysis, how do you feel? Is your feeling positive (I love numbers!) or negative (I failed math)?

Where did this association stem from and, if it is negative, what are a few positive affirmations you can say to yourself to encourage a growth mindset?

The Importance of Data in CSCPs and MTSS

Since the inception of the ASCA National Model in 2002, school counselors have been charged with answering the question "How are students different as a result of your work?" The ASCA National Model provides a counseling framework, shifting from a service to a comprehensive program to meet the academic, social/emotional, and postsecondary needs of all students. A CSCP is driven by student data and reflects a rigorous curriculum designed to promote academic success (ASCA, 2012).

Moreover, as mentioned in previous chapters, MTSS is a framework comprised of Response to Intervention (RTI), systems focusing on student academics, and Positive Behavior Intervention Supports (PBIS) focusing on student behavior. Similar to CSCPs, MTSS is driven by data to determine student needs; incorporating school-wide, classroom, small-group, and/or individual evidence-based prevention and intervention, and emphasizing a systemic approach. As you can read in Chapter 2 and elsewhere in the book, there is much overlap between CSCPs and MTSS frameworks. Aligning MTSS with your CSCP will undoubtedly boost data collection and assessment opportunities, therefore optimizing your effectiveness in your school (Goodman-Scott & Grothaus, 2017). Before delving further into the alignment of these systems, we first will provide an overview of different types of data that are utilized within both.

Types of Data

There are three essential types of data that should inform your CSCP and MTSS: (1) Process, (2) Perception, and (3) Outcome.

Process Data

Process data provide information regarding the number of students that participated in a school counseling program or intervention, along with a description of the activity. For example, small-group counseling, core curriculum lesson plans, school counseling events, and/or individual counseling (Kaffenberger & Young, 2013). Process data can also include the number of students who have experienced an MTSS universal lesson or specific Tier 2/3 intervention.

Perception Data

Perception data provide information about students' attitudes, skills, or perceived knowledge. Perception data is often collected in small groups, core curriculum lessons, and large-group activities through surveys, pre/post-tests, or other methods (Kaffenberger & Young, 2013). Administrators often request perception data from school counselors in the form of a semester or end-of-year report related to specific CSCP activities. Additionally, the MTSS team may collect perception data. For example, the team might

Table 9.1 Examples of process data

Elementary School	29 third graders participated in a small group during the 2017–2018 school year.
Middle School	372 seventh graders received Signs of Suicide training, and 36 students requested to follow up with a school counselor.
High School	248 juniors and seniors attended a career cafe session during the 2017–2018 school year.

Table 9.2 Examples of perception data

Elementary School	72% of fifth grade students reported being cyberbullied by a peer.
Middle School	97% of seventh grade students who received mindfulness lessons for six weeks reported a decrease in stress.
High School	84% of ninth grade students who participated in a study skills group believed they were better prepared for quizzes and tests.

construct a pre/post-test asking for students' or parents' input on perceptions of school climate. Another example of perception data includes the MTSS team completing the Self-Assessment Survey (SAS; Sugai, Horner, & Todd, 2000). The SAS asks all staff to provide input (perceptions) on how well PBIS systems are in place around the school. A final example might include the MTSS team doing the School-wide Evaluation Tool (SET; Horner et al., 2004), in which students and staff are asked about knowledge of PBIS universal expectations and acknowledgments. The results from both would then be used by the MTSS leadership team to plan for additional systems/programming.

Outcome Data

While there are a variety of existing data sources, some of the most highly prioritized data are outcome data focused on student outcomes. Outcome data report the impact or outcome of a targeted intervention, such as student achievement (e.g., grades, course enrollment, SAT scores), attendance, and behavior (e.g., office discipline referrals [ODRs], suspension rates; Kaffenberger & Young, 2013). Outcome data are often shared with stakeholders (grant funders, teachers, administrators, parents, etc.) and can be used to identify the need to maintain, intensify, or discard a program. Outcome data is often utilized by MTSS teams in the form of school-level achievement reports, ODRs (broken down by grade, location, time of day, etc.), as well as attendance, school completion rates, etc. (please see examples later in the chapter, such as Figures 9.3–9.6). These types of data are particularly useful for school-level programming. In fact, the MTSS leadership team examines academic and behavioral data on a monthly basis to look for patterns and student needs. As outcome data are especially prioritized in school counseling, utilizing MTSS-gathered and analyzed outcome data to guide a CSCP can help school counselors be more efficient and effective. To be sure, school counselors are encouraged to answer the question "How are students different as a result of our work?" by creating school counseling program goals to impact student outcome data. We will take a closer look at MTSS/CSCP program and data alignment in the next section.

Table 9.3 Examples of outcome data

Elementary School	80% of identified fourth grade students who participated in the "Peace Club" moved from "not-proficient" to "proficient" under the citizenship category on their second quarter report card.
Middle School	Referrals for bullying decreased by 35% after school counselors provided upstander lessons to all seventh graders, and met individually with students referred two or more times for bullying behavior.
High School	Minority students taking the Advanced Placement (AP) exam increased by 28% after school counselors utilized small-group counseling and provided AP Exam study books and additional resources to identified students.

MTSS and CSCP Alignment

School counselors fulfill an essential role in schools, which is why they are often in high demand from students, staff, parents, and administrators. While feeling pulled in many directions, sometimes the last thing they need is another task to add to the pile. The beauty of MTSS and CSCPs is the tremendous overlap between the two, which encourages both to be integrated and, in turn, can strengthen both frameworks and increase efficiency (Ziomek-Daigle, Goodman-Scott, Cavin, & Donohue, 2016; Goodman-Scott, Betters-Bubon, & Donohue, 2016). In fact, ASCA proposes that school counselors align their CSCP with MTSS to enhance student achievement and behavior (ASCA, 2018), which can start by using data. For example, due to the *Every Student Succeeds Act*, schools are required to collect yearly school climate data, regardless of whether they have an active MTSS program (ASCD, 2015). Moreover, MTSS trainers emphasize the importance of beginning department, team, and district-wide meetings with discussion of data. In addition, collection and discussion of data are already infused into many aspects of the school counseling role. Since school counselors are already called to be leaders in the school who design and implement data-driven CSCPs, MTSS is often seen as appealing because it is rooted in data collection, monitoring, and data-driven decision making (Ziomek-Daigle et al., 2016). Both MTSS and CSCPs involve prevention, using evidence-based practices, advocating for systemic change, equity, and creating a positive school climate, all of which stem from consistent collection and analysis of student and school data.

Next, we will provide examples of CSCP-MTSS alignment. A school counselor's CSCP might involve prevention through implementing an evidence-based bullying prevention curriculum. This can also be understood through the MTSS lens as a school-wide evidence-based bullying prevention program provided as a universal/Tier I intervention. In both instances, the school counselor would use data to determine whether the program is effective, to monitor progress, and track student outcomes to see trends in bullying-related ODRs and suspensions. The bullying prevention curriculum could be implemented in classrooms by the school counselor as a part of the CSCP core curriculum classroom lessons, whereas all school staff would be involved in the universal/Tier 1 school-wide implementation of the bullying prevention curriculum (e.g., school-wide assemblies, announcements, posters) as part of a larger MTSS initiative. Aligning both the CSCP and MTSS frameworks allow the school counselor to offer multi-layered systems of support that include classroom curriculum, individual and group counseling, prevention, interventions, and wraparound services, while collecting and tracking student data (Ziomek-Daigle et al., 2016; Goodman-Scott, 2014; Goodman-Scott et al., 2016).

As we previously mentioned, MTSS teams and school counselors utilize a lot of the same data to inform their frameworks. The MTSS teams regularly collect and analyze outcome data, including student achievement, attendance, and behavior, to guide MTSS activity and school-wide goals, whereas one of the hallmarks of a CSCP, such as the ASCA National Model (2012), is the use of data to show how students are different as a result of the school counseling program. Thus, the MTSS team collects and analyzes data and school counselors also collect data that can simultaneously inform their CSCP and MTSS frameworks.

For example, as described by authors (e.g., Betters-Bubon & Donohue, 2016; Ziomek-Daigle et al., 2016), a MTSS team may learn that ODRs are negatively impacting their school climate and leading to missed class time. As a result, the MTSS team can observe trends in ODRs regarding frequency, type of behavior, location, grade level, day of the week, and time of the year, and create a school-wide goal to lower ODRs. As a collaborative member of the team, school counselors aid in the MTSS data-analysis process and create school counseling program goals to assist the MTSS efforts to lower ODRs. Further, school counselors can use MTSS data to complete ASCA Closing the Gap action plans, as well as use pre-existing MTSS school data to determine which students need Tier 2 or 3 interventions. Finally, school counselors may find it extremely advantageous to use one of the many tools within MTSS data collection (e.g., SWIS, which will be discussed later in the chapter) to import existing CSCP data into the school counseling program, or export MTSS data to inform the CSCP.

Similarly, MTSS teams can utilize school-counselor-specific data. For instance, school counselors often conduct Tier 1 needs assessments or collect small-group perception data to inform their CSCPs. This data may be used by the MTSS team to assess universal needs and create school and program goals. In a specific example, a student needs assessment might indicate a high number of students who are struggling with anxiety. Working with the school counselor, the MTSS team may implement universal lessons on anxiety strategies.

Both frameworks align with one another, inform one another, and enhance the credibility of one another (Goodman-Scott et al., 2016). To be sure, school counselors who are on the MTSS team are often better informed on school-wide data trends and thus better equipped to positively impact student outcomes (Goodman-Scott & Grothaus, 2017). Furthermore, MTSS leaders are great people to recruit as school counseling advisory council members, to reciprocally inform CSCPs. Further, previous research showed that school counselors who aligned MTSS with their existing CSCP saw no change in the amount of time they allocated to specific school counseling tasks (Cressey, Whitcomb, McGilvray-Rivet, Morrison, & Shander-Reynolds, 2015). And, as demonstrated by Cressey and colleagues (2015), MTSS can be an efficient use of time.

Think about situations that would require a Tier 1, Tier 2, and Tier 3 intervention.

Based on the information you just read, what steps would you use to decide who to target and/or what data to use within each of the Tiers?

The following case study illustrates how a school counselor can utilize the various types of data within their CSCP/MTSS programs.

Andrea is a school counselor at an elementary school in the southeast region. She is on her school's MTSS team and collaborates often with her administration about school-wide data. The MTSS team reviewed the ODR data and noted an increased number of office discipline referrals for first grade students compared with other grade levels and previous data. The team agreed that Andrea would review each of the identified first graders' report cards. In doing so, she noticed many students had difficulty with self-control. She discussed this with the MTSS team and decided to target and work on self-control and emotional regulation with all first grade students during the second quarter.

Andrea collaborated with the teachers and implemented weekly *Second Step* lessons. She collected perception data from teachers and students using a survey that targeted skills aligned with the *Second Step* program, including self-control. She delivered the survey at the mid-point and end of the lessons. Andrea's goal for the identified students included improving self-control as indicated on the *Demonstrates Self-Control* grade on the report card.

At the end of the second quarter, Andrea brought the data to the MTSS team to examine the behavioral and report-card data again. They identified four students who received more than three ODRs and four who did not improve their self-control score on the report card. She decided to design a Tier 2 intervention for these students in the form of an eight-week small group, which she'd implement during the third quarter. Since Andrea is a registered yoga teacher, she designed a group using mindfulness and emotional regulation skills that included a physical yoga practice focused on improving self-control (Harper, 2010; Williamson, 2012). Prior to the group starting, Andrea collected perception data from each student, teacher, and guardian, and also monitored these students' office referrals throughout.

By the end of the third quarter, seven out of eight students receiving the small group intervention reduced their office visits and 47% of the identified students raised their grade from a 2 to a 3 or 4 on the *Demonstrates Self-Control* section of their report card. After Andrea analyzed the data, she created bar graphs to share with the MTSS team, her administration, and other educational stakeholders to show how students are different as a result of the intervention. The bar graphs below represent outcome data for office referrals at the individual and whole-school level. No bar represents a zero-point value, meaning no students were referred to the office.

What do you notice about the collaborative approach to data use in this case study?

How did Andrea work in collaboration with the MTSS team to impact student outcomes?

How did Andrea and the MTSS team use data to show that the intervention was effective?

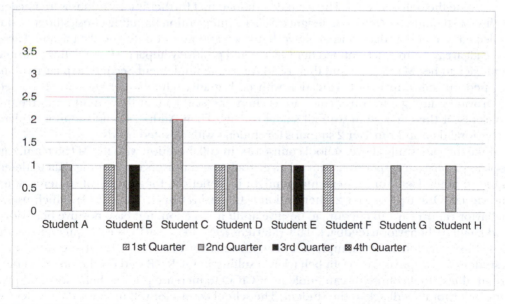

Figure 9.1 Individual student outcome data for behavior-related office visits.
(Source: the Authors.)

(continued)

(continued)

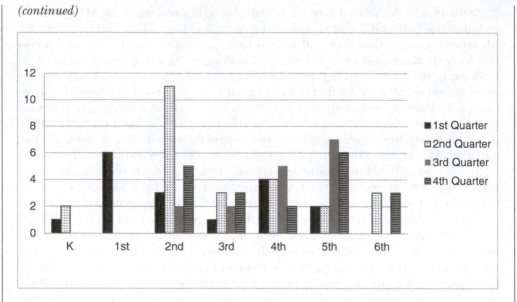

Figure 9.2 Grade level outcome data for behavior-related office visits for all students.
(Source: the Authors.)

As you can see, Andrea, in collaboration with the MTSS team, used process, perception, and outcome data to inform Tier 1 and Tier 2 interventions with students. First, the team examined ODRs (outcome data) to determine the need for focusing on self-control. After Andrea delivered self-control lessons for *all* first graders, she brought the data to the team to reexamine the outcome data. The team determined that further interventions were needed with *some* students. Andrea then designed a Tier 2 intervention targeting at-risk students, she collected perception data, and analyzed both perception and outcome data again. These were all areas Andrea determined her CSCP could positively impact. She took this information back to her MTSS team and they asked Andrea to implement Second Step curriculum focused on self-control and regulation with each grade, school-wide. She was also asked to provide training and consultation to teachers and staff so that they could reinforce the concepts of the curriculum with all students daily. Then Andrea would monitor student behavioral data and run Tier 2 supports for students with elevated needs.

Like the case study above, school counselors, in collaboration with the MTSS team, can look at patterns in suspensions, attendance, grades, and universal screening data to determine whether Tier 2 or 3 interventions might be beneficial for a group of students or an individual. One type of Tier 2 intervention is Check-in/Check-out (CICO), which uses a behavior report card to encourage positive adult interaction, increase positive behaviors, and facilitate behavioral feedback daily (Martens & Andreen, 2013; see Chapter 5 for additional information). For example, the school counselor may notice recurring issues with a student's disruptive classroom behavior, resulting in ODRs. Based on the observed data trend, the school counselor can implement CICO to increase positive behaviors and provide behavioral feedback to the student. The school counselor will monitor data collected from the daily CICO report cards to make data-based decisions on whether to modify or discontinue this Tier 2 intervention. Assessing, organizing, and evaluating school data in these ways might seem like a difficult task; however, there are PBIS data tools and assessments that can help, as well as collaborating with the MTSS team.

Data and Program Planning

Beyond student-level intervention, school profile data can be used to create program and school-level changes. School profiles provide specific outcome data to help school counselors identify potential focus areas and program goals (Kaffenberger & Young, 2013). You can locate your school profile (also known as a school report card) on your state's Department of Education website. School profiles typically list student demographics, state test scores, discipline data, attendance data, college and career readiness data, and trends in academic decline or growth. As the English language idiom goes, "A picture is worth a thousand words." The teaching activity located at the end of this chapter will guide you in this process. School profile data portray a detailed image of each school and help school counselors ask important questions such as:

- What data should I examine?
- How do I know the problem is really a problem?
- How do I decide if the problem is within my locus of control or sphere of influence?
- Once I know there is a problem, what should I do next?

Figures 9.3–9.6 show publically available high school graduation rates for a large suburban high school (total enrollment: 1,400; 78% White, 5% Hispanic, 7% Black, 6% Asian, 4% multi-racial; 10% of students have a disability; and 14% are economically disadvantaged).

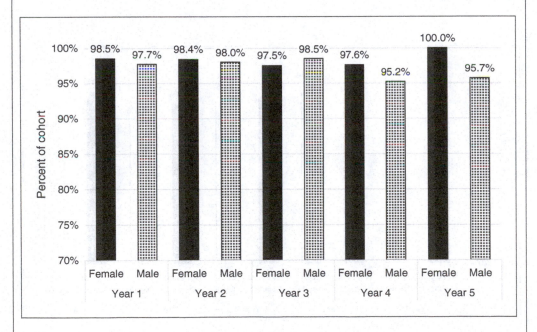

Figure 9.3 Sample high school completion rate by gender.

(Source: the Authors.)

(continued)

(continued)

What do you notice about trends across different groups?

How might you approach your work to improve graduation rates?

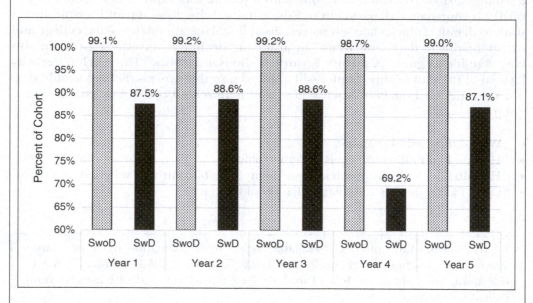

Figure 9.4 Sample high school completion rate by disability status.

(Source: the Authors.)

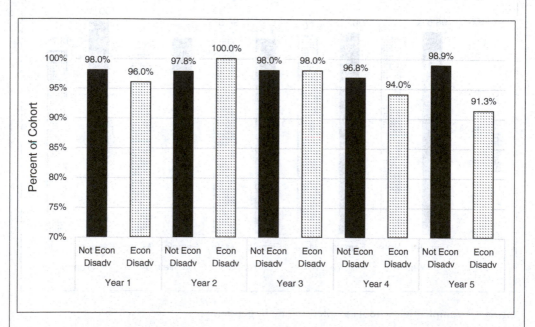

Figure 9.5 Sample high school completion rate by economic disadvantage.

(Source: the Authors.)

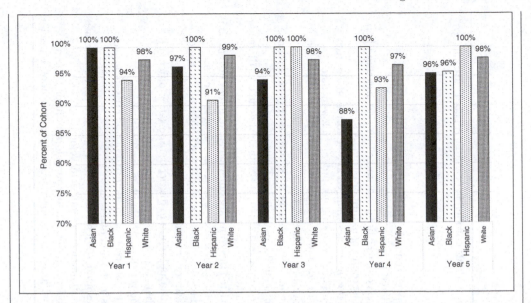

Figure 9.6 Sample high school completion rate by ethnicity.

(Source: the Authors.)

These are difficult questions to answer. One helpful way to diagnosis potential achievement and equity gaps in outcome data is to conduct a Root Cause Analysis (RCA; Rooney & Heuvel, 2004).

Root Cause Analysis (RCA)

A RCA is a data analysis procedure used to identify what happened, how the problem happened, and why the problem happened. In education, RCA involves an examination and analysis of data to determine commonalities and underlying factors that impact student achievement (James-Ward, Frey, & Fisher, 2012). To guide school improvement goals, school leaders often access outcome data (attendance, behavior, and achievement) and perception data (classroom observations, performance evaluations, school climate surveys, staff morale, etc.) to determine specific areas to target. Similarly, school counselors use school improvement goals to identify potential areas they can impact.

Root Cause Analysis assumes there are three reasons a problem could occur: (1) a physical condition (i.e., too many students in a classroom); (2) a human condition (i.e., a teacher has poor classroom management and sends students to the office too much); and/or (3) an organizational condition (i.e., we have always had a zero-tolerance policy to send home students who violate the dress code) (MindTools, n.d.). In order to identify how to solve a problem, RCA guides school leaders through five steps: (1) identify the problem; (2) collect data; (3) identify possible causal factors; (4) identify root causes, and (5) recommend interventions and solutions. Table 9.4 is an example of RCA in a high school setting.

Without performing a RCA, would the aforementioned problems continue to occur? It is vital that school counselors drill down and disaggregate data to determine a root cause in order to prevent the problems from reoccurring. In addition, RCA helps school counselors to determine if they are able to intervene and/or impact the situation. For instance, school

Table 9.4 RCA in a high school setting

Step One	Identify the Problem	What is happening?	65% of ninth and tenth grade students enrolled in year-long Algebra I are failing.

Step One	Identify the Problem	What is happening?	65% of ninth and tenth grade students enrolled in year-long Algebra I are failing.
Step Two	Collect Data	What proof do you have that there is a problem? How long has the problem been a problem? What else is happening because of the problem?	• Student report cards. • End-of-grade exams. • Students have been underperforming in this class for three years. • Graduation rates have declined. • Many students on this bus receive free breakfast, and either skip breakfast when they are late, or eat breakfast resulting in further tardiness.
Step Three	Identify Possible Causal Factors	What led to the problem? Why is the problem continuing? What other problems are occurring as a result?	• The problem began when the bus routes changed in an effort for the district to save on fuel costs. The bus begins picking up students in low-income neighborhoods at 5:45am. In addition, the bus is often late due to city traffic. • Many students enrolled in year-long Algebra I ride the impacted bus routes. • School counselors and administration do not have control over the bus routes. • Students are not able to enroll in Biology without Algebra I. • Students have to repeat the course and are in class with freshmen, thus there are decreases in student motivation.
Step Four	Identify Root Causes	What is the real reason the problem occurred/is occurring?	• Students who ride the impacted bus route are often late, and, if they miss the bus, many do not have transportation to school causing chronic absenteeism. • Tardiness and absenteeism result in missed material that is difficult for students to comprehend without classroom instruction.
Step Five	Recommend Interventions/ Solutions	What can be done to ensure the problem does not occur again? How will a solution be implemented? Who will be responsible? Are there risks?	• Provide student outcome data and report to district transportation office and request the bus route be changed. • Move core classes, including year-long Algebra I, to another time. • Allow students on this bus to eat breakfast in their first period class so they are able to eat and do not miss instruction time. • Until the bus situation is resolved, students are likely to still be tardy and/or miss school, which will continue to impact academic achievement. • Administration responsible for logistics, school counselors monitor student progress, teachers report progress directly to student's alphabet school counselor.

counselors could meet individually with each student failing year-long Algebra I to increase motivation, but it would not likely impact their achievement due to the fact they are missing valuable class time. A second example pertains to an examination of 32 students who have missed five or more days of school. If 14 of the 32 students had suffered from the flu and previously never had an attendance problem, it would be pointless for a school counselor to conjure up an intervention for those students. This situation is out of the school counselor's locus of control. However, it would be worthwhile to use RCA to determine why the other 18 students have missed five or more days, and how the school counseling program can intervene and prevent future recurrences. The following case study provides an overview on how a school counselor can utilize RCA at a large high school.

Rikard is the school counseling director at Park West, a large high school in the northwestern region. His school has approximately 2,400 students and each school counselor has a caseload of 400-plus students (ASCA recommends a ratio of 1:250). During the back-to-school leadership team meeting last year, Rikard's principal discussed a district-wide initiative to reduce suspensions and asked the school counseling department for help. During the previous year, 152 students missed over 450 days of school due to suspensions. In the past three years, Park West's state test scores have dropped significantly in Math and Language Arts. Consider the two scenarios outlined below.

Scenario One

Rikard shared this information with his team, and they decided to meet with the students who were suspended last year and still enrolled at Park West. They collected process data to show the administration team they had met with each individual student. At the end of the year, the school counselors were surprised to see the number of students suspended had increased by 3%.

Scenario Two

After the problem had been identified by the MTSS team, Rikard disaggregated his data by looking at the number of students suspended by grade, the number of days suspended, and the reason why they were given in- or out-of-school suspension. Through this process, he identified numerous causal factors that contributed to the number of suspensions last year.

First, Rikard noted that a large percentage of 9th graders that were suspended for disorderly conduct were from the same World History class, and many of them had never been in trouble before. He looked in his school's data system and noted countless referrals for minor infractions from that same teacher last year, and a handful already this year. In addition, he noticed a large percentage of juniors and seniors were given in-school suspension for a day after their fifth tardy (per school policy), many of which were obtained after lunch (juniors and seniors are allowed to leave campus for their 35-minute lunch period).

Rikard took his findings to the MTSS team to discuss the root causes. The 9th grade suspensions seemed to be caused by a classroom management issue in World

(continued)

(continued)

History. The 11th and 12th grade suspensions needed further examination. The MTSS team held a focus group for current seniors who were chronically tardy last year. Students reported being late due to long lines at nearby fast food restaurants and traffic getting into the junior and senior parking lots. After the MTSS team's RCA, they constructed a list of recommendations.

Rikard took their recommendations to the administration team. Due to the likelihood of this problem reoccurring with current students, they requested the principal observe the World History teacher's class and offer assistance with classroom management, and perhaps impose a lunch detention or after-school detention policy prior to sending students to the office. Since the majority of students suspended in 9th grade World History last year were no longer enrolled in this class, the team recommended they meet with individual students in 9th grade who had already received an office referral from this teacher to discuss impulse control and self-regulation to reduce the likelihood of further discipline referrals.

The MTSS team recommended administration consider revising the in-school suspension policy to revoke the off-campus privileges of those with five or more tardies. It was also recommended that the school resource officer monitor the parking lot at the end of lunch. Lastly, the MTSS team noted they were often not aware of a student's suspension until after they returned to school. The school counselors requested to be notified immediately when a student in their caseload was suspended and to make it mandatory that a student meets with their school counselor prior to returning to class.

What are your reactions to these two different versions of the same case study?

What types of data were utilized by the school counselor and MTSS team?

Reflect on the RCA process. What steps would be most difficult?

As you can see from this case study, scenario two is the most effective strategy to utilize data. Using RCA, Rikard was able to disaggregate the data to identify areas his CSCP and MTSS framework was more likely to impact, while the administration took care of areas that were out of the school counselor's control. It is essential that school counselors drill down and disaggregate data to determine which educational stakeholder is in the best position to solve a problem. In practice, your school may have a MTSS team already collecting and routinely analyzing data, similar to this case study. That data and team approach would help school counselors and administrators identify areas of concern. As a school counselor, similar to Rikard, you can take a leadership role in the process by conducting a RCA, disaggregating data that are already being collected, and supporting your MTSS team in initiatives similar to this case study.

What are the benefits of analyzing data with a RCA?

How can a RCA help school counselors design and implement stronger interventions?

SMART Goals

An additional benefit to conducting RCAs is that results can be used to design school counseling program goals, or SMART goals. The acronym SMART stands for specific, measurable, attainable, results-oriented, and time-bound (Kaffenberger & Young, 2013). SMART goals are an important component in both CSCPs and MTSS frameworks; therefore, when school counselors create SMART goals, they are completing a standard for both. School counseling program goals are meant to help school counselors narrow equity and opportunity gaps, and they are often focused on attendance, behavior, and/or academic achievement. It is recommended that school counselors review their school improvement plan to identify specific target areas the school counseling program can help (Kaffenberger & Young, 2013). Specifically, the school improvement plan should be guided by the school's MTSS, and thus influences the CSCP focus. Take a moment to complete the teaching activity at the end of the chapter to assess your knowledge of SMART goals.

MTSS Data Tools

Organizing and making sense of student and school data to drive your CSCP can certainly become daunting. Beyond that, gauging the fidelity of PBIS implementation in your school, evaluating current efforts, and targeting future annual goals, might also seem discouraging and intimidating. Fortunately, there are school-wide systems that can be of help. For example, the School-Wide Information System (SWIS) is a helpful and confidential tool that aligns with the MTSS framework to identify patterns in student behavior data and facilitate decision making (Curtis, Van Horne, Robertson, & Karvonen, 2010; Betters-Bubon & Donohue, 2016). Once school staff import student behavior data into the web-based program, clear, concise reports are generated to show behavior trends. Reports can be generated based on referrals by month, location, problem behavior, time of day, student, day of the week, grade level, staff, and ethnicity. The SWIS also compiles multi-year reports to show trends and an overall school summary. Although data can be complex, SWIS takes care of the "heavy lifting" by analyzing the data and producing relevant reports to maximize your efforts when decision making and action planning in your CSCP. If you enter a district that does not have SWIS, know that many other data systems can be modified to help organize behavioral and academic data. For example, systems like Infinite Campus and PowerSchool have updated their systems to include data analysis components.

While evaluating behavioral data is made easier through SWIS or other similar systems, assessing and monitoring the actual implementation process and fidelity of MTSS in your school is made manageable through a variety of MTSS assessments. Imagine implementing MTSS in your school and thinking, "now what?" You might have a lot of unanswered questions, such as: "Are we implementing this the way it should be implemented?" "Are we making progress towards our goals?" "What do the students/staff think about this?" "How can our MTSS framework and tiered supports be improved?" There are likely a lot of questions running through your mind. The MTSS assessments facilitate answering these questions using their reliable and evidence-based assessments (PBIS Apps, 2017).

The MTSS assessments help school staff and school teams better understand their program implementation (e.g., program strengths/weaknesses, perceptions of school climate, school risk/protective factors, and implementation fidelity). These assessment results can be used to drive your CSCP action plans, track progress, identify where modifications/more supports are needed, and gauge school staff/student

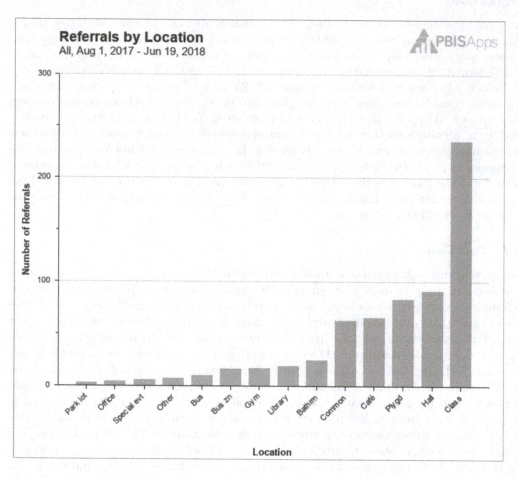

Figure 9.7 Sample SWIS report.

From SWIS (www.pbisapps.org). Reprinted with permission from Educational and Community Supports, University of Oregon.

perceptions. For example, let's go back to our earlier discussion about the implementation of a bullying prevention curriculum. School counselors, in conjunction with the MTSS team, could implement a pre/post school safety survey to identify specific areas where students feel unsafe, target those areas during program implementation, and utilize a post-survey to determine effectiveness. The MTSS assessments are available online through www.PBISassessment.org with descriptions, support materials, training resources, and scoring guides (PBIS Apps, 2017). Please see Table 9.5 below for a brief snapshot of the available assessments.

Additional tools exist to help screen students, monitor progress, identify appropriate interventions, and organize data. For instance, eduCLIMBER is a user-friendly cloud-based system where data can be imported, analyzed, and tracked to identify needs, monitor progress, and make data-based decisions based on your student's needs (eduCLIMBER, n.d.). A major goal of eduCLIMBER is to make RTI data more accessible

Table 9.5 Current PBIS assessments

Name of Assessment	Assessment Goal(s)	Who Takes It?	When Is It Taken?	Tier?
Benchmarks for Advanced Tiers (BAT)	Advanced assessment that evaluates implementation of Tier 2 and 3 support systems	PBIS coach and school team, once they consistently score 80%+ on MATT	Annually	Tier 2 and 3
Benchmarks of Quality (BoQ)	Evaluates Tier I fidelity, effectiveness, and strengths/weaknesses	PBIS coach and school team	Annually, in spring	Tier I
Early Childhood Benchmarks of Quality (ECBoQ)	Evaluates Tier I fidelity, effectiveness, and strengths/weaknesses	PBIS coach and school team	Annually	Tier I
Individual Student Systems Evaluation Tool (ISSET)	Research tool that assesses status of Tier 2 and 3 implementation	School team	Twice in the first year, then annually	Tier 2 and 3
Monitoring Advanced Tiers Tool (MATT)	Basic assessment that monitors progress of Tier 2 and 3 support systems	PBIS coach and school team	Quarterly; 3–4 times per year	Tier 2 and 3
School Climate Survey	Assesses student perceptions of school climate	Elementary: students between grades 3–5 Middle/High: students between grades 6–12	Annually or twice per year (during first 45 days and last 45 days)	Outcome tool
School Safety Survey (SSS)	Determines risk and protective factors for the school	Must be completed by a minimum of five educators: administrator, custodial staff, supervisory staff, certified staff, and office staff	Annually	Outcome tool
School-wide Evaluation Tool (SET)	Research tool completed from an "outsider's perspective" to evaluate SWPBIS implementation	Trained SET evaluator will visit school to complete assessment	Twice in the first year, then annually	Tier I
Self-Assessment Survey (SAS)	Identifies staff perceptions of PBIS implementation status	All school staff	Annually	All Tiers
Team Implementation Checklist (TIC)	Progress monitoring tool to assess Tier I implementation	School Teams	Quarterly; 3–4 times per year	Tier I
Tiered Fidelity Inventory (TFI)	Single, efficient survey that addresses SET, BoQ, TIC, SAS, BAT, and MATT elements	School system planning teams (three–eight individuals including coach, administrator, and representation from all Tier teams)	Pre-assessment; Quarterly; Annually upon reaching 70% fidelity	All Tiers

Note: PBIS Apps (2017).

and manageable. Finally, The Center on Response to Intervention has extensive charts of screening tools, progress monitoring tools, and interventions on a variety of academic areas and developmental levels (The National Center on Intensive Intervention at American Institutes for Research, n.d.).

Conclusion

Data are a meaningful and essential component of the role of a school counselor. Data provides school counselors with rich information and a variety of ways to assess, evaluate, advocate, investigate, and continuously determine if they are making a difference for students and schools, and also improving their CSCPs. Through reading this chapter, we hope you have gained insight into how data is used in school counseling, the types of data you will be collecting, and a variety of practical data tools and assessments you can incorporate into your CSCP and MTSS framework. Also, we trust you recognize the value of participating in your school's MTSS team, and how CSCPs and MTSS data can both inform and strengthen one another, therefore maximizing your efforts and time. Finally, we expect you now have ways you can use data for social justice and advocacy, particularly through using RCA. Data does not have to be overwhelming and scary, and hopefully you are ready to use the information you have learned to improve your school counseling program. To use words from Brene Brown: "Maybe stories are just data with a soul." Every story you hear, every interaction you have with a family, and each time you advocate for a student can be tied to data. Data and accountability are critical in PK-12 school counseling; therefore, go forth and use your data stories to show how students are different as a result of your work and awesome school counseling program.

For more information and a school counselor's perspective on *Using Data in MTSS to Demonstrate How School Counselors Make a Difference* please see Chapter 12 "Voices from the Field," Voices 1, 2, 4, 6, 7, 8, and 9.

ASCA Ethical Standards

The ASCA's Ethical Standards for School Counselors (2016) reflects the importance of data-driven CSCP; it is no longer an ethical option for school counselors to refrain from implementing a CSCP. Stone (2017) argues that to help students achieve the best results, school counselors must constantly examine data points. "Without disaggregated data, it is all just a guess as to whether the strategies and interventions school counselors have put into place are making a difference and advancing students" (p. 377). Using both CSCP and MTSS data can help school counselors do just that: constantly examine a range of data points, including the intentional disaggregation of data. School counseling programs that are built around the school's data provide a framework for improving outcomes for all students and it is a necessary component of the ethical and equity-minded school counselor. As you read through the following list, consider whether school counselors who do not utilize data are violating ASCA Ethical Standards.

The ASCA Ethical Standards particularly relevant to data use within comprehensive programs and MTSS include those focused on Comprehensive Data-Informed Programs (A.3). Specifically, school counselors:

A   Responsibility to Students

A.3   Comprehensive Data-Informed Programs

- A.3.a. Collaborate with administration, teachers, staff, and decision makers around school-improvement goals.
- A.3.b. Provide students with a comprehensive school counseling program that ensures equitable academic, career, and social/ emotional development opportunities for all students.
- A.3.c. Review school and student data to assess needs including, but not limited to, data on disparities that may exist related to gender, race, ethnicity, socioeconomic status, and/or other relevant classifications.
- A.3.d. Use data to determine needed interventions, which are then delivered to help close the information, attainment, achievement, and opportunity gaps.
- A.3.e. Collect process, perception, and outcome data and analyze the data to determine the progress and effectiveness of the school counseling program. School counselors ensure the school counseling program's goals and action plans are aligned with district's school improvement goals.
- A.3.f. Use data-collection tools adhering to confidentiality standards as expressed in A.2.
- A.3.g. Share data outcomes with stakeholders (ASCA, 2016).
- A.4.c. Identify gaps in college and career access and the implications of such data for addressing both intentional and unintentional biases related to college and career counseling.

B   Responsibility to Parents/Guardians, School, and the Self

B.2   Responsibility to the School

- B.2.b Design and deliver comprehensive school counseling programs that are integral to the school's academic missions; driven by student data; based on standards for academic, career, and social/emotional development; and promote and enhance the learning process for all students.

Resources

Websites

Links to the following can be found on our eresource at www.routledge.com/ 9781138501614.

- MindTools (n.d.). *Root cause analysis: Tracing a problem to its origins.* Retrieved from: www.mindtools.com/pages/article/newTMC_80.htm.
- School-Wide Information System (SWIS).

Data and Data Visualization Tools

- Canva.
- Charted.
- Google Charts.
- Infogram.

- Piktochart.
- Tableau Public.

Further Reading

Dimmitt, C., Carey, J. C., & Hatch, T. (2007). *Evidence-based school counseling: Making a difference with data-driven practices.* Thousand Oaks, CA: Corwin Press.

Hatch, T. (2014). *The use of data in school counseling: Hatching results for students, programs, and the profession.* Thousand Oaks, CA: Corwin Press.

Zyromski, B., & Mariani, M. (2016). *Facilitating evidence-based, data-driven school counseling: A manual for practice.* Thousand Oaks, CA: Corwin Press.

Teaching Activity 1

Directions: Take a moment to review your school's report card. If you are a graduate student, look at your practicum or internship site's report, or check out a local school.

1 At first glance, what does the information tell you about the school?
2 List three areas that might benefit from a school counseling intervention.
3 Next, check out prior data for the areas you selected. Do you notice any trends? If yes, what could be the potential causes?
4 If not, what could have changed from the previous year to the current year?

Teaching Activity 2

Using Table 9.6, write in the left column which goals are SMART and which goals are not.

Table 9.6 SMART or not?

	School counselors will meet with all 11th-grade students enrolled in an AP course about taking the exam.
	By May 2017, the number of 11th-grade first-generation college students enrolled in an AP course who take the AP exam will increase from 45% to 75%.
	All students with three or more suspensions in a year will reduce the number of days suspended.
	By May of 2018, seventh-grade students with three or more days of ISS in the first semester will reduce by 50%.
	By May of 2018, identified third-grade students with five or more absences in the previous school year will decrease by 25%.
	Third-grade students who are absent from school will decrease by 25% by May 2018.

Multiple Choice Questions

1 **The number of students you select for an intervention is**:

   a Perception data.
   b Process data.
   c Outcome data.
   d Root cause analysis data.

2 **By May of 2019, minority students enrolled in an AP class who take the AP exam will increase from 48% to 80%. This is an example of a:**

a PBIS intervention.
b SMART goal.
c SWIS data.
d Root Cause Analysis.

3 **A Tier I intervention directly impacts:**

a The whole school.
b Targeted at-risk students.
c Administration.
d School counselors.

4 **"95% of students who received mindfulness lessons believe it helped with test anxiety." What kind of data is this?**

a Process.
b Outcome.
c SWIS data.
d Perception.

5 **A Root Cause Analysis helps:**

a Identify the root cause of a problem.
b School counselors to drill down and disaggregate data.
c Provide meaningful interventions to students.
d All of the above.

Answers: Q1 b, Q2 b, Q3 a, Q4 d, Q5 d.

References

American School Counselor Association (ASCA) (2012). *The ASCA National Model: A framework for school counseling programs* (3rd Ed.). Alexandria, VA: Author.

American School Counselor Association (ASCA) (2016). *ASCA ethical standards for school counselors.* Alexandria, VA: Author.

American School Counselor Association (ASCA) (2018). *The professional school counselor and Multi-Tiered Systems of Support.* American School Counselor Association Position Statement. Alexandria, VA: Author. Retrieved from: www.schoolcounselor.org/asca/media/asca/PositionStatements/PS_MultitieredSupportSystem.pdf.

Association for Supervision and Curriculum Development (ASCD) (2015). *Elementary and secondary education act: Comparison of the No Child Left Behind Act to the Every Student Succeeds Act.* Alexandria, VA: Author. Retrieved from: www.ascd.org/ASCD/pdf/siteASCD/policy/ESEA_NCLB_ComparisonChart_2015.pdf.

Betters-Bubon, J., & Donohue, P. (2016). Professional capacity building for school counseling through school-wide Positive Behavioral Interventions and Supports implementation. *Journal of School Counseling, 14*(3).

Cressey, J. M., Whitcomb, S. A., McGilvray-Rivet, S. J., Morrison, R. J., & Shander-Reynolds, K. J. (2015). Handling PBIS with care: Scaling up to school-wide implementation. *Professional School Counseling, 18*(1), 90–99.

Curtis, R., Van Horne, J. W., Robertson, P., & Karvonen, M. (2010). Outcomes of a school-wide positive behavioral support program. *Professional School Counseling, 13,* 159–164.

eduCLIMBER (n.d.). *About us.* Retrieved from: www.educlimber.com/welcome/about-us.

Goodman-Scott, E. (2014). Maximizing school counselors' efforts by implementing school-wide Positive Behavioral Interventions and Supports: A case study from the field. *Professional School Counseling, 17,* 111–119.

Goodman-Scott, E., Betters-Bubon, J., & Donohue, P. (2016). Aligning Comprehensive School Counseling Programs and Positive Behavioral Interventions and Supports to maximize school counselors' efforts. *Professional School Counseling, 19,* 57–67, doi:10.5330/1096-2409-19.1.57.

Goodman-Scott, E., & Grothaus, T. (2017). Ramp and PBIS: "They definitely support one another": The results of a phenomenological study. *Professional School Counseling, 21*(1), 119–129.

Harper, J. C. (2010). Teaching yoga in urban elementary schools. *International Journal of Yoga Therapy, 20*(1), 99–109.

Horner, R. H., Todd, A. W., Lewis-Palmer, T., Irvin, L. K., Sugai, G., & Boland, J. B. (2004). The school-wide evaluation tool (SET) a research instrument for assessing school-wide positive behavior support. *Journal of Positive Behavior Interventions, 6*(1), 3–12.

James-Ward, C., Frey, N., & Fisher, D. (2012). Root cause analysis. *Principal Leadership, 13*(2), 57–61.

Kaffenberger, C., & Young, A. (2013). *Making data work* (3rd Ed.). Alexandria, VA: American School Counselor Association.

Martens, K., & Andreen, K. (2013). School counselors' involvement with a school-wide positive behavior support system: Addressing student behavior issues in a proactive and positive manner. *Professional School Counseling, 16*(5), 313–322.

MindTools (n.d.). *Root cause analysis: Tracing a problem to its origins.* London: Author. Retrieved from: www.mindtools.com/pages/article/newTMC_80.htm.

PBIS Apps (2017). *PBIS Assessment.* Eugene, OR: University of Oregon. Retrieved from: www.PBIS assessment.org.

Rooney, J. J., & Heuvel, L. N. V. (2004). Root cause analysis for beginners. *Quality Progress, 37*(7), 45–56.

Stone, C. (2017). *School counseling principles: Ethics and law* (4th Ed.). Alexandria, VA: American School Counselor Association.

Sugai, G., Horner, R. H., & Todd, A. W. (2000). *Effective behavior support: Self-assessment survey.* Eugene, OR: University of Oregon, Positive Behavioral Intervention and Supports Technical Assistance Center.

The National Center on Intensive Intervention at American Institutes for Research (n.d.). *Tool charts.* Washington, DC: Author. Retrieved from: https://intensiveintervention.org/resources/tools-charts.

Williamson, L. A. (2012). Yoga in public schools. *Teaching Tolerance, 42,* 27–28.

Ziomek-Daigle, J., Goodman-Scott, E., Cavin, J., & Donohue, P. (2016). Integrating a Multi-Tiered System of Supports with Comprehensive School Counseling Programs. *The Professional Counselor, 6*(3), 220–232, doi:10.15241/jzd.6.3.220.

10 Evidence-Based Practices Across MTSS

Melissa Mariani and Summer Perhay Kuba

Introduction

Evidence-based practice (EBP) refers to the utilization of treatments and interventions that have been field tested and proven to benefit their intended recipients. Evidence-based practices can include medicines, therapies, approaches, techniques, strategies, services, programs, and curriculum. The majority of professions now stress an EBP model and strongly encourage practitioners to adhere to and incorporate EBPs into their daily work. However, debate continues about how EBP is defined, what qualifies as EBP, and whether this framework relies too heavily on research at the expense of individual qualities which make each person/client/student unique. What gets lost in terms of both the implementer's and recipient's personal characteristics and preferences when an EBP model is followed? Does the EBP model suggest a one-size-fits-all solution ("cookbook" approach) for everyone? These are some of the questions that professionals grapple with when faced with this topic.

In this chapter, the authors will shed a positive light on the use of EBPs in school counseling. We believe that when counselors in training, practicing counselors, and counselor educators are properly educated and assisted in the EBP process, they feel more competent and are better able to execute what's asked of them. Evidence-based practice also fits well within the various roles school counselors have as interveners and coordinators of both Comprehensive School Counseling Programs (CSCPs) and Multi-Tiered Systems of Support (MTSS). However, integrating EBPs within your school programming can take time, energy, and research. Adjustment and change, though difficult, are oftentimes necessary. The question is, will you be an embracer or a resister? To quote a famous song from Disney's *Aladdin*, "Are you in or are you out?" We hope (for your sake and the sake of perpetuating this wonderful profession) that you are IN! Now, let's arm you with the tools you need to hit the ground running.

> When do you first recall hearing the term "evidence-based practice"?
>
> To what field was it related? What was your understanding of its meaning at that point?

This chapter will provide you with an understanding of EBP and a process for thinking through and acting on this approach. Next, we will provide an explanation of how and why EBP fits well with MTSS. The authors will then provide a list of recommended EBP interventions that are presently available at Tier 1, Tier 2, and Tier 3, which can be used to positively impact student outcomes. A review of several of those interventions will be expounded upon and a comprehensive summary table will be provided. Finally, a discussion of the cultural and ethical implications/considerations regarding EBPs will follow. We encourage you to stop at the reflection questions in our chapter and work through the activities offered. In doing so, our hope is that you come to understand and value how EBP has challenged our profession to grow. Finally, we encourage you to execute what was suggested and begin to document your own effectiveness as well as share your results – and if you need partners in this process, don't hesitate to reach out to a counselor educator (or two).

Evidence-Based Practice

Whether you are a graduate student, counselor educator, or practicing school counselor it's likely you've heard a lot of buzz surrounding the term "evidence-based practice" or EBP. Over the past several decades, this movement has taken the professional world by storm, impacting fields from medicine, to education, social work, and, more recently, counseling. The medical community was the first to operationalize this framework in the late 1970s and early 1980s, using the term to refer to the use of treatments supported by scientific evidence (Davies, Nutley, & Smith, 2000). Sackett and colleagues (1996) offered a commonly used definition for EBP in medicine, referring to it as the integration of three equally important factors: (1) the use of the best available research evidence, (2) clinical expertise, and (3) patient/client values and preferences. An additional consideration speaks to the soundness of the research conducted (an area we will get into later in the chapter), which oftentimes escapes most practitioners who are not regularly involved with reading and assessing research studies (Sackett, 2000). Figure 10.1 visually articulates the evidence-based practice model. Evidence-based practice has been defined as both a *belief* in incorporating the best available research findings into everyday practice and as a *process* in making informed practice decisions (Rubin, 2008; Rubin & Bellamy, 2012).

Figure 10.1 Evidence-Based Practice model.

Note: EBP = Evidence-Based Practice.

Education has gradually adopted an EBP mindset by instituting more stringent accountability standards for all. Davies (1999) suggested that evidence-based education impacts both policy and practice by (1) utilizing existing evidence, and (2) establishing new evidence where current evidence is insufficient or lacking. Where once reluctant, the majority of educators now embrace the fact that sticking to "what works" provides an added layer of effectiveness and professionalism. Documenting how students grow, change, improve, and learn based on the approaches, methods, practices, skills, and interventions one provides has become like second nature to most educators.

Evidence-based practice (EBP) is an overarching umbrella term encompassing a range of practices, such as programs, approaches, techniques, curriculum, etc. In this chapter, we use EBP only for "evidence-based practice." So as not to confuse the reader, we will then spell out references to "evidence-based programs" or "evidence-based techniques," which are types of EBPs.

A definitive example of how EBP is evident in education is the Multi-Tiered Systems of Support (MTSS) process (including Response to Intervention [RTI] and Positive Behavioral Interventions and Supports [PBIS]), which follows a step-by-step system for documenting universal screenings for behavior and academic needs, instituting scientifically supported Tier 1 programs to all students, targeting students who need additional support with Tier 2 and Tier 3 interventions, and regularly monitoring their progress (McIntosh & Goodman, 2016). Alignment at each of these three levels is visually represented in Figure 10.2, which includes serving *all* (Tier 1), *some* (Tier 2), and *few* (Tier 3) students. As you can see, school counselors are called upon to provide more intensive specific services and interventions at the various levels moving up the diagram. For example,

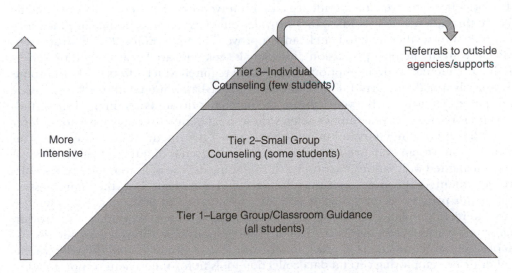

Figure 10.2 MTSS Tier alignment with school counselor approach to direct services.

Note: MTSS = Multi-Tiered Systems of Support.

if a student is struggling with test-taking skills presented during a classroom lesson (Tier 1) on "managing test anxiety," he/she can be targeted for a small-group intervention (Tier 2) to further teach and practice these skills.

Counselors, however, seem a little more hesitant to adopt EBP than professionals in other specialties, perhaps because traditionally the field has been much more "feeling focused" than "data focused." Similarly, counselors may have a history of creating their own intervention, using an "intervene and hope" approach. Another reason for resistance might lie in the fact that many counselors do not feel properly trained or prepared to critique, collect, analyze and/or discuss research. The following section outlines why counselors should consider integrating EBP into their MTSS and CSCPs.

Now that you have a better understanding of how evidence-based practice is defined and what factors need to be considered, please answer the following questions:

> How do you see each of these factors (e.g., student values, your expertise as a counselor, and the most current research out there on the topic) applying to a school counselor's job?

> Are there any additional factors that you think should be added?

Why Use EBP?

Do you recall that in Chapter 2 the authors referred to there being "no magic antidote" that exists to help us solve all of the problems we see our students experience? Well, EBPs might be our best bet to finding that solution! The reasons in support of operating from an EBP model have been well-documented (Baron, 2012; Custpec, 2004; Davies, Nutley, & Smith, 2000; Dimmitt, Carey, & Hatch, 2007; Haskins & Baron, 2011; Hoagwood, 2003–2004; Nathan & Gorman, 2007; Raines, 2008; Zyromski & Mariani, 2016). For one, proponents state that an evidence-based approach provides recipients (clients/students) with more effective care. Since evidence-based interventions have been documented as effective through scientific studies, they provide some degree of assurance to practitioners who want those they treat to benefit and improve (Mihalic & Elliot, 2015). Most often, particularly in the helping professions, individuals seek out care because they are suffering physical, mental, and/or emotional pain, so the regimen which offers the fastest route to healing is usually preferred. Furthermore, evidence-based interventions have already been "proven" to work, at the very least for the outcomes documented in published studies. Therefore, when a practitioner selects these treatments, they can have some level of confidence that the intervention is likely to impact the intended outcome area. The second reason why an evidence-based approach is preferred is that these treatments have also been aligned with various measures, offering some degree of accountability. As EBPs have documented effectiveness, a practitioner could investigate how they might assess their client's progress before, during, and after treatment and make necessary changes in the intervention plan when and if the data supports it. Published studies also provide details about various assessments and can offer suggestions regarding analysis and discussion of results and limitations. A practitioner reading these studies could then determine whether or not employing certain data collection tools fit for their client or not. In addition, once the practitioner had collected their own data, they could check this against the published research on the EBP and determine if their findings were similar.

Evidence-Based Practice in School Counseling

So when did the demand/call for EBP first emerge in school counseling? For several decades now, leaders in the field have been calling for further "outcome studies" that lend support for what school counselors do (Carey & Dimmitt, 2012; Dimmitt, Carey, & Hatch, 2007; Dimmitt, Carey, McGannon, & Henningson, 2005; Webb & Brigman, 2006; Whiston, 2002; Whiston & Sexton, 1998; Whiston, Tai, Rahardja, & Eder, 2011). Although more research is still needed, there is clear evidence to support the implementation of CSCPs, in particular the support services that school counselors offer which benefit students' academic, behavioral, emotional, personal/social, and college/career goals (Belasco, 2013; Dollarhide & Saginak, 2008; Mariani, Webb, Villares, & Brigman, 2015; Masia-Warner et al., 2016; Sink & Stroh, 2003; Sink, Akos, Turnbull, & Mvududu, 2008; Whiston & Quinby, 2009; Villares, Frain, Brigman, Webb, & Peluso, 2012). In addition, valuable research conducted by Carrell and Hoekstra (2011) indicated that adding one full time counselor to a school can have a dramatic impact on students' academic achievement and behavior, increasing boys' reading and math achievement by over one percentile point and reducing boys' and girls' disciplinary problems by 20%. School counselors who spend the majority of their time with students, providing services they are uniquely trained for, are also more satisfied in their jobs (Pyne, 2011). That being said, there is a delicate balance between holding true to the core tenets of one's profession and responding to its current demands.

Although the American School Counselor Association (ASCA) National Model outlines specific roles and responsibilities, oftentimes school counselors complain that they are inundated with paperwork, testing, and other superfluous duties which bog them down and essentially take the counseling out of their counseling positions. One remedy

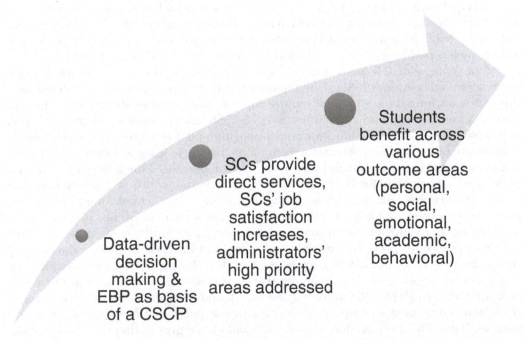

Figure 10.3 Data-based decision making and EBP process.

Note: CSCP = Comprehensive School Counseling Program; EBP = Evidence-Based Practice; SCs = school counselors.

to this professional dilemma is the marrying of data-driven decision making and the use of EBP; when school counselors have at their disposal and feel competent to implement techniques and programs that are known to be the most effective for students, and share their results with key stakeholders, accountability is fulfilled and a win-win situation happens for everyone. School counselors get to provide services they are specifically trained for, administrators see improved student outcomes of interest to them, and students benefit personally, socially, emotionally, and academically (see Figure 10.3). Therefore, practicing school counselors would benefit from an increased understanding as to the positive impact that EBPs and curricula can have on students.

EBP and Advocacy

Evidence-based practice can help validate counselors' roles in schools and assist them in advocacy efforts. In order to make this happen, however, they must resist the temptation to solely plan for, collect, analyze, and report on their daily activities. Instead, they must integrate EBP interventions within a comprehensive program to impact student outcomes. Only when this mind shift occurs can one begin to accept this new wave of thinking and action, and begin to add lasting value to the counseling field. Of course, in order to do this, counselors must also be skilled in EBP and feel competent in delivering well-supported interventions which are known to impact students across various academic, social, and career domains. To take it a step further, counselors must be provided with the proper tools to gather data (process, perception, and outcome/results; see Chapter 9) which supports their efforts.

Even with a clear picture of the impact that EBP can have on students, it can still be extremely difficult to fulfill all of the roles that school counseling demands. One of the chapter authors (Mariani) can recall how critical it was for her to connect the dots for her principal early on in her work as an elementary and middle school counselor, and show how allowing access to students to deliver EBP would further the school's goals and link to the School Improvement Plan (SIP). For instance, one year the 7th grade girls were struggling with repeated complaints of "girl problems" and "relational bullying," so the school counselor (Mariani) decided to take a two-pronged approach by implementing Student Success Skills (SSS) in all the middle school classrooms, and supplementing this with a daylong outing to an adventure ropes course with just the girls to reinforce some teamwork, trust, and communication. The SSS teaches students cognitive, social, and self-management skills but impresses upon students the importance of creating a community of caring, support, and encouragement. These lessons, followed up by the practice of applying that content in the ropes course, permitted the girls to develop new patterns of behavior and find new ways to work through their conflicts. The other chapter author (Kuba) also remembers how, at the beginning of her school-counseling career, there were a variety of administrative and testing responsibilities on her plate. It wasn't until she began to advocate for herself as a professional and for the needs of her students that she was able to "prove her worth," so to speak, and was able to move toward a more comprehensive program. It was a battle at times, but she started with her teacher colleagues by asking some of them to let her visit their classrooms to implement EBPs such as Ready to Learn (RTL), Ready for Success (RFS), and SSS. The more time she spent in classrooms implementing EBPs, the more teachers experienced the positive impact on their students. The more academic, social, and emotional growth they saw, the more the teachers began to vocalize those experiences with administrators, who then started to genuinely understand the impact an EBP-driven CSCP could have on students, teachers, and the entire school climate.

Process and Models for EBP in School Counseling

One model for school counselors, the "Model of Evidence-Based School Practice (EBP) in Counseling Practice," is offered by Dimmitt, Carey, and Hatch (2007, p. 4). These authors state that counselors must be skilled in: (1) *problem description* (knowing what needs to be addressed), (2) *outcome research use* (knowing what is likely to work), and (3) *intervention evaluation* (knowing if the intervention made a difference). Much like the visual depicted in Figure 10.1 above, these three components are all equal and necessary; where they converge represents evidence-based school counseling practice.

Now that we have discussed some advantages of EBP for you as a practicing school counselor, consider the following question:

What are some additional advantages of employing EBP for your students, teachers, administrators, parents, and the profession?

This model provides an integral framework for increasing the level of understanding counselors have regarding what is expected of them with regard to evidence-based intervention. This is described in detail in Dimmitt, Carey, and Hatch's seminal book *Evidence-based school counseling: Making a difference with data-driven practices* (2007). However, practitioners often stop because they feel uncertain about how to execute particular parts of the model. Addressing this difficulty, Zyromski and Mariani (2016) suggested a step-by-step process to help school counselors move towards EBP. That process model is shown below in Figure 10.4 (Zyromski & Mariani, 2016, p. 6). Further information on this process can be found in their book *Facilitating evidence-based, data-driven school counseling: A manual for practice* (2016).

The process suggested above moves in a clockwise direction, guiding the school counselor through four different components: (1) assessing the problem/concern (*assess*), (2) setting SMART goals (*goals*), (3) selecting appropriate evidence-based interventions (*interventions*), and (4) evaluating those interventions, reporting on those results, and using those findings to drive future programming and services (*evaluating and evolving*). Many school counselors know how to collect and review school-level data derived from their school's report card, school improvement plan, or data management system (see Chapter 9 for additional information). Furthermore, the majority are competent in setting SMART goals based on this data, as this aligns with the expectations set forth for most educators. Yet issues often arise with step 3, as many still employ interventions, lessons, and techniques that they developed personally, heard about from colleagues, or perhaps found on the internet through sites such as *Pinterest*. While these sites might offer ideas that are fun and engaging, they don't necessarily provide interventions that are research-based, which clearly demonstrates a gap in EBP.

Where do you (as a school counseling practitioner) go to access information about the interventions you provide?

How can counselor educators and researchers increase school counselors' confidence in accessing, training for, and implementing EBP interventions adequately?

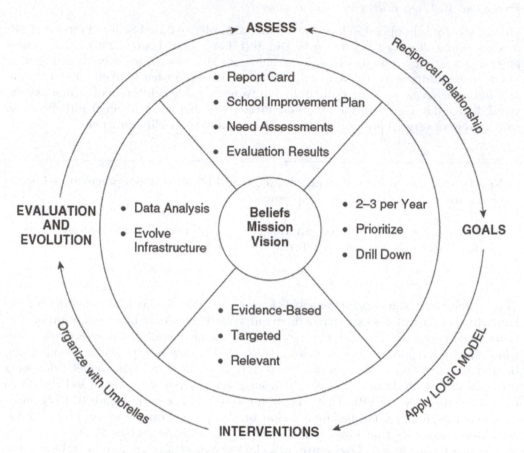

Figure 10.4 Process for building evidence-based school counseling programs.

Reprinted from *Facilitating evidence-based, data-driven school counseling* by B. Zyromski & M. Mariani, 2016. Copyright 2016 by Sage Publishing. Reprinted with permission.

For the readers' ease, the chapter authors have done this work for you. After reviewing several research-based sites that conduct systematic reviews to evaluate the salience of various EBP, we have compiled a list of these practices and programs that are available across Tier 1, 2, and 3 for you to consider. The resources used to develop these lists represent national departments, government administrations, and private organizations that many school counselors are familiar with and may refer to for program suggestions (Table 10.1). The Children Services Council (n.d.) defines an EBP as "a set of coordinated services/activities that demonstrate effectiveness [on some desired outcome] based on research" (Mihalic & Elliot, 2015). As you can see, these resource sites have rigorous standards by which they have assessed certain curriculum to be evidence-based. In addition, we also accessed The Ronald H. Fredrickson Center for School Counseling Outcome Research and Evaluation (CSCORE; www.umass.edu/schoolcounseling/index.php). The CSCORE's projects include research, program evaluation, and consultation. The CSCORE also provides professional development to school counselors and districts nationwide and, as such, is particularly relevant to the readers of this chapter.

What Does It Mean to Be "Evidence-Based"?

Before describing the EBP we have selected to include in our chapter, we first will define what it means to be "evidence-based," as a myriad of definitions exist. For instance, Drake et al. (2001) define EBP as any practice that has been established as effective through scientific research (much the same as the definition provided by others), however they add that this is established according to "a clear set of explicit criteria." This is where several authorities differ. For example, in our profession, we have several resources to guide us in the use of EBP, several of which are cited in Table 10.1, yet even these vary in what they consider "meeting standards" to qualify as an EBP, evidence-based program, or curriculum.

Next, McIntosh and Goodman (2016) included the following in their definition of "evidence-based":

(1) There must be at least two, high quality experimental studies (either group studies with random assignment to condition or experimental single-case designs); (2) these studies must be conducted by teams at different institutions (with at least one team that is not affiliated with the developers); (3) these studies must consistently document educationally meaningful, positive effects on valued outcomes without any negative side effects; and (4) there is evidence that the practice can be implemented fully by typical school personnel with typical resources. (p. 141)

In addition, these scholars offered that another level of evidence is also critical, suggesting that, "After its selection and implementation, the practice must be shown to work with the particular students who you are supporting, especially when supporting students who are culturally and linguistically diverse" (p. 141). Similarly, the What Works Clearinghouse (WWC; n.d.) offers a range of findings/categories on programs which have undergone rigorous evaluation. Those programs that earn the top two ratings adhere to the criteria listed below in Table 10.1. The WWC is considered one of the most comprehensive and leading authorities on program evaluation across disciplines.

Upon careful review of the sources detailed above, and others listed in Table 10.1, we decided to use the following criteria to determine which evidence-based practices and programs to include in the Tier 1, 2, and 3 sections/tables in this chapter. These include that the intervention: (1) could be implemented with children/adolescents in grades PK-12, (2) followed a manualized process that could be easily delivered/replicated by a qualified professional, (3) had at least two research studies conducted (at least one of these studies conducted by someone other than the developer, and (4) documented positive impacts on students' social, emotional, behavioral, and/or academic performance. With a clear definition in place we can now turn toward the specific interventions at each tier level. Each section includes a table that summarizes specific EBP within tiers. Please note that Tables 10.2 and 10.3 focus on evidence-based programs while Table 10.4 includes both practices and programs. Teaching Activity 2 (see page 292) offers a way to check your knowledge of EBP.

Tier 1 EBP

Referring again to Figure 10.2 and the alignment of MTSS with the direct services that professional school counselors provide, Tier 1 represents core curriculum. This includes classroom lessons delivered to students in a large group, whole-class setting, and school-wide programs, such as initiatives for the entire school, as a school-wide college and

Table 10.1 Resource sites used for compiling school counseling EBP Tier 1, 2, 3 lists

Evidence-Based Practice Resources	Content	EBP Definition/Criteria Used
American Group Psychotherapy Association at www.agpa.org/home/practice-resources/evidence-based-practice-in-group-psychotherapy	Group Therapy	Evidence-based practice is using the best available research, combined with clinical judgment and client preferences.
Blueprints for Healthy Youth Development *In partnership with the Annie E. Casey Foundation* University of Colorado Boulder Institute of Behavioral Science Center for the Study and Prevention of Violence, http://blueprintsprograms.com	Outcome areas related to behavior, education, emotional well-being, physical health or relationship. Interventions for individuals, peers, family, school, and community – ages 0 (infancy) to 22 (early adulthood).	**Promising programs** meet the following standards: 1 *Intervention specificity*: identified outcome, specific risk and/or protective factors targeted, population and how the intervention works to produce this change. 2 *Evaluation quality*: a minimum of (a) one high quality randomized control trial or (b) two high quality quasi-experimental evaluations. 3 *Intervention impact*: evidence from high quality evaluations indicates significant positive change in intended outcomes that can be attributed to the program and there is no evidence of harmful effects. 4 *Dissemination readiness*: The program is currently available for dissemination and has the necessary organizational capability, manuals, training, technical assistance, etc. required for implementation with fidelity. **Model programs** meet these additional standards: 1 *Evaluation quality*: A minimum of (a) two high quality randomized control trials or (b) one high quality randomized control trial plus one high quality quasi-experimental evaluation. 2 Positive intervention impact is sustained for a minimum of 12 months after the program intervention ends.
The Ronald H. Fredrickson Center for School Counseling Outcome Research and Evaluation (CSCORE), www.umass.edu/schoolcounseling/index.php.	CSCORE's projects include research, program evaluation, and consultation. CSCORE also provides professional development to school counselors and districts nationwide.	

Source	Topic	Criteria
Collaborative for Academic, Social, and Emotional Learning (CASEL) at www.casel.org. EBP summary for Preschool and Elementary SEL interventions at www.casel.org/preschool-and-elementary-edition-casel-guide. EBP summary for Middle and High School SEL interventions at www.casel.org/preschool-and-elementary-edition-casel-guide.	Social and Emotional Learning Interventions and Programs for students in PK-12.	**Inclusion criteria:** 1 At least one qualifying evaluation study on the program (with comparison group in addition to pre/post test). 2 Addresses at least one of the four set outcome domains (academic performance, positive social behavior, reduced conduct problems, and/or reduced emotional distress, SEL). 3 A significant program effect was documented on an outcome in that domain as measured by observations, school records, or ratings made by teachers, parents, or students.
Social Programs That Work by the Coalition for Evidence-Based Policy at http://evidencebasedprograms.org.	Addictions and Substance Use/Abuse, Community-Based Programs for Youth and Families.	**Top Tier:** 1 Programs shown in well-conducted randomized control trials (RCTs), carried out in typical community settings, to produce sizable, sustained effects on important outcomes. 2 Evidence includes a requirement for replication—specifically, the demonstration of such effects in two or more RCTs conducted in different implementation sites, or, alternatively, in one large multi-site RCT. 3 Such evidence provides confidence that the program would produce important effects if implemented faithfully in settings and populations similar to those in the original studies.
U.S. Department of Education, Institute for Educational Science's (IES) What Works Clearinghouse at https://ies.ed.gov/ncee/wwc.	Evaluation of Student Outcomes (Academic), K-12 Learning Assessment, Post-Secondary Transitions, Students with Special Needs, Supporting Positive Academic Outcomes (academic success, attendance, promotion, graduation), Use of Data.	Criteria Used to Determine the WWC Rating of Effectiveness (*Top Two Designations Only*) for an Intervention (WWC, n.d., p. 29) **Positive effects:** Strong evidence of a positive effect with no overriding contrary evidence. Two or more studies show statistically significant positive effects, at least one of which meets WWC group design standards without reservations. No studies show statistically significant or substantively important negative effects. **Potentially positive effects:** Evidence of a positive effect with no overriding contrary evidence. 1 At least one study shows statistically significant or substantively important positive effects. 2 Fewer or the same number of studies show indeterminate effects than show statistically significant or substantively important positive effects. 3 No studies show statistically significant or substantively important negative effects.
U. S. Substance Abuse and Mental Health Services Administration's (SAMHSA) National Registry of Evidence-Based Programs and Practices at www.nrepp.samhsa.gov/landing.aspx.	Addictions, Substance Use and Abuse, Assessment in Mental Health, Mental Health Counseling and Interventions, Wellness and Prevention.	An effective program is: 1 Rigor—the strength of the study's methodology. 2 Effect size—must be calculated and offer strength of impact on treatment group. 3 Program fidelity—if program was delivered as intended to the treatment group. 4 Conceptual framework—how clearly the components of the program are articulated.

career program, or school-wide social-emotional initiatives. As interveners and supporters, school counselors are not only charged with the implementation of these programs, but also with assisting teachers in the delivery of EBPs. Upon review of the resource sites listed in Table 10.1, the authors determined an appropriate list of evidence-based classroom school counseling core curriculum at the Tier 1 level: Second Step, Student Success Skills (SSS), Promoting Alternative Thinking Strategies (PATHS), Positive Action (PA), Responding in Peaceful and Positive Ways (RIPP), Too Good for Violence, and Too Good for Drugs. A comprehensive list of these programs is provided in Table 10.2, which includes the developer and year of publication, purchase information, grade level, delivery details, training options, intent of the program, and relevant research. We provide brief descriptions of these "go-to" Tier 1 programs below.

Second Step

Second Step is a comprehensive social-emotional learning (SEL) classroom-based program designed to address the needs of students in prekindergarten through eighth grade. Second Step was developed by the *Committee for Children* in 1985 with the most updated edition in 2017 and specifically addresses empathy, friendship skills, self-regulation, problem-solving, and emotion management. The research on Second Step is impressive, with multiple studies pointing to positive outcomes for students after lesson delivery (Edwards, Hunt, Meyers, Grogg & Jarrett, 2005; Espelage, Rose, & Polanin, 2015; Low, Cook, Smolkowski, & Buntain-Ricklefs, 2015).

Student Success Skills

Student Success Skills (SSS) is an evidence-based SEL program that was originally developed by Brigman and Campbell in 2003 with the most updated edition by Brigman and Webb in 2016. The program focuses specifically on teaching students key cognitive, social, and self-management skills that have been shown to enhance academic achievement. Over 28 studies have linked the SSS program to academic achievement and social-emotional development (Lemberger, Selig, Bowers, & Rogers, 2015; Villares, Frain, Brigman, Webb, & Peluso, 2012; Zyromski, Mariani, Kim, Lee, & Carey, 2017).

Promoting Alternative Thinking Strategies (PATHS)

Promoting Alternative Thinking Strategies (PATHS) is a SEL program focusing on conflict resolution, emotion regulation, decision-making, and empathy. It was developed in 1994 by Kusche and Greenberg and updated in 2011. PATHS was shown to be effective in improving children's emotional competence and reducing their aggression in schools. Students who participated in the PATHS program were less socially withdrawn, demonstrating higher emotional knowledge and more socially competent behavior (Kam, Greenberg & Walls, 2003; Domitrovich, Cortes, & Greenberg, 2007).

Positive Action (PA)

Positive Action (PA) is a social-emotional program for students in grades pre-kindergarten through 12th grade, developed in 1997 and updated in 2010 (Allred, 1997; Allred & Flay, 2010). The program's focus includes developing student self-concept, self-management skills, social skills, setting goals, and academic strategies. A number of evaluation outcomes include improved academic performance, reduced conduct problems, improved academic behaviors, more positive life satisfaction, lower levels of depression and anxiety, as well as positive results in self-control, prosocial peer affiliations, honesty, respect for parents, prosocial interactions, and respect for teachers (Lewis, DuBois, Bavarian, Acock, Silverthorn, Day, Ji, Vuchinich, & Flay, 2013; Guo, Wu, Smokowski, Bacallao, Evans, & Cotter, 2015; Lewis, Vuchinich, Ji, DuBois, Acock, Bavarian, & Flay, 2016).

Responding in Peaceful and Positive Ways (RIPP)

Responding in Peaceful and Positive Ways (RIPP) was developed for middle school students in response to neighborhood violence in Richmond, Virginia in 1992 with the most recent edition in 2000 (Meyer, Farrell, Northup, Kung, & Plybon, 2000). This violence prevention program is designed to teach students healthy problem-solving skills and alternatives to violence. The research on this program yielded results indicating less favorable attitudes toward violence, less physical aggression, less delinquent behavior, and higher peer support for nonviolent behavior, as well as less drug use and less frequent peer pressure to use drugs. Lower rates of aggression and victimization along with improved life satisfaction were also reported (Farrell, Valois, Meyer, & Tidwell, 2002/2003).

Strong Kids

Strong Kids was originally developed in 2010 by Kenneth Merrell to address resiliency, empathy, awareness of emotions, communication skills, goal setting, stress reduction, anger management, and to prevent anxiety, depression, and social withdrawal in kindergarten through twelfth grade students. The research conducted on Strong Kids supports improved emotional and social behavior, improved academic progress, an increase in grade point average, and a decrease in behavior referrals (Whitcomb & Merrell, 2012; Kramer, Caldarella, Young, Fischer, & Warren, 2014). Implementation of the Strong Kids program also supports a preventative approach when it comes to internalizing behaviors of at-risk students (Kramer, Caldarella, Young, Fischer, & Warren, 2014).

Too Good Programs

The final programs of interest are the Too Good programs: Too Good for Drugs (TGFD) and Too Good for Violence (TGFV). Developed by the Mendez Foundation (1995; 2013), TGFV was designed as a violence prevention program with a focus on character education, healthy beliefs, and positive social-emotional skills. The TGFD program teaches children how to resist peer pressure associated with the use of illegal drugs, alcohol, and tobacco, life skills related to problem-solving, and identification of personal values. Research supports the TGFV program in that students more frequently used personal and social skills and were more engaged in prosocial behaviors. Students displayed more positive social and resistance skills, communication skills, and emotional competency. A decrease in high risk students' use of tobacco, alcohol, binge drinking, and marijuana, and a strengthening effect on high risk students' risk and protective skills and attitudes was also reported (Hall & Bacon, 2006; Hall, Bacon & Ferron, 2013).

Tier 2 EBP

Within MTSS, Tier 2 EBP includes more intensive interventions than those in Tier 1. Often, school counselors provide these to students in a small-group (two–eight students) format as a second layer of support, knowing that students should still be provided with all

Table 10.2 Tier 1 evidence-based programs

Name of Program/ Curriculum	Developer/Year of Publication	Manual/ Materials Required? Y/N	Training Required/ Offered?	Grade Level	Delivery Details	Intent of Program	Relevant Research Articles Supporting Effectiveness
Second Step www.secondstep.org	Committee for Children (2017)	Y $199–$4,300	Webinars offered with purchase of curriculum	PreK-8	13–28 weekly lessons @ 20 minutes each depending on grade level.	Empathy, friendship skills, problem solving, emotion management.	1 **Low, S., Cook, C. R., Smolkowski, K., & Buntain-Ricklefs, J. (2015).** • Large-scale, matched, randomized-control design. • Moderated effects, with 8 out of 11 outcome variables indicating the intervention produced significant improvements in social-emotional competence and behavior for children who started the school year with skill deficits relative to peers. 2 **Espelage, D. L, Rose, C. A., & Polanin, J. R. (2015).** • Longitudinal nested-cohort design. • Significant gains in knowledge about social-emotional skills.
Student Success Skills (SSS) http://studentsuccessskills.com	Brigman & Webb (2003; 2016)	Y $75	In-person training offered (contact developer)	4–12	5 weekly lessons—45 minutes each, plus 3 monthly booster lessons.	Social and self-management skills, cognitive skills, caring relationships, encouraging classrooms, healthy habits, goal setting.	1 **Lemberger, M. E., Selig, J. P., Bowers, H., & Rogers, J. E. (2015).** • Two-level randomized design. • Significant gains in both math and reading. • Marked improvement noted in emotional control, plan and organize, as well as task completion and classmate support. 2 **Villares, E., Frain, M, Brigman, G., Webb, L., & Peluso, P. (2012).** • Two-level cluster randomized trial design. • Significant gains in both math and reading scores. 3 **Zyromski, B., Mariani, M., Kim, B., Lee, S., & Carey, J. (2017).** • One-group pre-post design. • Significant difference found between knowledge of cognition and regulation of cognition. Significant findings were found for the SESSS subscale self-regulation of arousal; students increased their ability to regulate levels of potentially debilitating arousal after participating in the SSS program.

Program	Citation	Evidence-based	Cost	Grade	Dosage	Skills addressed	Research
Promoting Alternative Thinking Strategies (PATHS) www.pathstraining.com/main	Kusche & Greenberg (1994; 2000; 2011)	Y	$475–$2,550	Training offered but not required. In-person 2-day workshop is $5,000 + reimbursement for trainer expenses. Online workshop: 1–2 participants, $650 per person; 3–4 participants, $450 per person; 5+ participants, $350 per person.	PreK-6	40–52 lessons 20–30 minutes 2–3 times per week	Conflict resolution, emotion regulation, decision-making, empathy.	**1 Crean, H. F., & Johnson, D. B. (2013).** • Cluster randomized trial. • Positive effects on student aggressive outcomes, acting out, and conduct problems. **2 Kam, C., Greenberg, M. T., & Walls, C. T. (2003).** • Quasi-experimental matched-group design. • Intervention effects were not found for all the intervention schools; however, the intervention was effective in improving children's emotional competence and reducing their aggression in school. **3 Domitrovich, C. E., Cortes, R. C., & Greenberg, M. T. (2007).** • Randomized clinical trial. • Improved emotional knowledge and more socially competent.
Positive Action (PA) www.positiveaction.net	Allred (1997), Allred & Flay (2010)	Y	$400+ for each grade level kit	Training offered but not required. On-site training for 1 day + travel ($3,600). On-line webinars and self-training workshop kits available.	PreK-12	140 15-minute lessons	Healthy self concept, self-management, social skills, setting and achieving goals, academic integration strategies provided for ELA.	**1 Lewis, K. M., DuBois, D. L., Bavarian, N., Acock, A., Silverthorn, N., Day, J., Ji, P., Vuchinich, S., & Flay, B. R. (2013).** • Cluster-randomized trial. • Favorable change over the course of the study in positive affect and life satisfaction as well as significantly lower depression and anxiety. **2 Lewis, K. M., Vuchinich, S., Ji, P., DuBois, D. L., Acock, A., Bavarian, N., Flay, B. R. (2016)** • Matched-pair, cluster-randomized controlled design. • Positive effect in self-control, prosocial peer affiliations, altruism, respect for parents and prosocial interactions as well as respect for teachers. **3 Guo, S., Wu, Q., Smokowski, P. R., Bacallao, M., Evans, C. B. R., & Cotter, K. L. (2015).** • Longitudinal design. • Statistically significant effects on self-esteem and school hassles scores. Beneficial effects on change in aggression scores but not statistically significant.

(continued)

Table 10.2 (continued)

Name of Program/ Curriculum	Developer/Year of Publication	Manual/ Materials Required? Y/N	Training Required/ Offered?	Grade Level	Delivery Details	Intent of Program	Relevant Research Articles Supporting Effectiveness
Responding in Peaceful and Positive Ways (RIPP) www.nrepp.samhsa. gov/ProgramProfile. aspx?id=129#hide-4	Meyer & Northup (1998)	Y $350/grade level. $5/student workbook. Contact supplier, Wendy Northup, at wendynorthup@ hughes.net.	Y Training offered, not required. 3-day onsite training $850/person.	6th, 7th, 8th grade	25 50-minute sessions 1x/week.	Problem-solving, healthy alternatives to violence.	**1 Farrell, A. D., Valois, R. F., Meyer, A. L., & Tidwell, R. P. (2003).** • Although not consistent across all time/measures, there were significant findings on aggression, life satisfaction, and victimization. **2 Farrell, A. D., Valois, R. F., & Meyer, A. L. (2002).** • Less favorable attitudes toward violence and higher peer support for prosocial behavior. Less frequent peer pressure to use drugs.
Strong Kids https:// strongkidsresources. com	Kenneth Merrell (2010)	Y $42.95 for each component (Strong Start, Strong Kids, Strong Teens).	Training and consultation offered but not required.	K-12	10–12 lessons depending on grade level (30–60 minutes each).	Cognitive, affective, and social functioning of students.	**1 Whitcomb, S., & Merrell, K. (2012).** • Interrupted time-series design. • Showed an increase in student knowledge about emotions and a decrease in student internalizing behaviors. **2 Kramer, T., Caldarella, P., Young, R., Fischer, L., & Warren, J. (2014).** • Quasi-experimental design. • After implementation there were decreases in students' internalizing behaviors and greater increases in prosocial behaviors for at-risk students.
Too Good Programs Too Good for Violence (TGFV) Too Good for Drugs (TGFD) www.toogoodprograms. org	Mendez Foundation (1995/2013)	Y $180–$600 depending on grade level.	Available but not required. On-site training $2,000/day + travel (1–3 days recommended).	K-12	7–12 lessons depending on grade level (30–60 minutes each).	Violence prevention, character education, healthy beliefs, social-emotional skills, life skills, values, resistance skills to negative peer pressure and the use of illegal drugs, alcohol, and tobacco.	**1 Hall, B. W., & Bacon, T. P. (2005; 2006).** • Stratified Matched RTC. • More frequent use of social skills and prosocial behavior and more positive scores in emotional competence, social, resistance, and communication skills. **2 Hall, B. W., Bacon, T. P., & Ferron, J. M. (2013).** • Stratified randomized treatment-control design. • TGFD implementation had a suppression effect on high risk students' reported 30-day use of tobacco, alcohol, binge drinking, and marijuana, and a strengthening effect on high risk students' risk and protective skills and attitudes.

Tier 1 interventions. Thus, the programs identified in this section were designed to provide a more targeted approach addressing specific needs. Table 10.3 provides a comprehensive list of Tier 2 EBPs and brief descriptions of specific programs are included below.

Student Success Skills (SSS)

The SSS small-group intervention is designed for 4th through 12th grade students who have participated in the Tier 1 SSS classroom intervention and need additional support in problem-solving and self-management skills (Brigman & Webb, 2003; 2016). The program targets cognitive and metacognitive skills, social skills, and self-management skills with a focus on goal setting, memory skills, listening, teamwork, and managing attention, motivation, and anger (Webb & Brigman, 2007). This small-group intervention has yielded student gains in both reading and math FCAT scores as well as significant gains in teacher-reported student behavior (Campbell & Brigman, 2005). There have also been significant improvements in student connectedness, metacognitive skills, and teacher-reported executive functioning (Lemberger & Clemens, 2012). Additional research support is included in Table 10.3.

Skills for Social and Academic Success (SASS)

Skills for Social and Academic Success is a small-group program that targets social anxiety and social skills, including initiating and maintaining conversations, establishing friendships, and realistic thinking (Fisher, Masia-Warner, & Klein, 2004). The program is designed for adolescents and includes two parent, two teacher, and two individual sessions. Research supports the use of SASS when working with students in small groups. Significantly lower observer-rated anxiety behaviors, social anxiety, and greater total functioning were reported, as well as lower social avoidance and distress (Masia-Warner, Klein, Dent, Fisher, Alvir, Albano, & Guardino, 2005). In one study, it was also reported that 59% of those that received the SASS intervention no longer qualified for a social phobia diagnosis (Warner, Fisher, Shrout, Rathor, & Klein, 2007). Although the program cost is quite expensive, the research supports its use in addressing anxiety and social skill deficits.

Incredible Years (IY): The Dina Dinosaur Social Skills and Problem-Solving Curriculum

Dr. Carolyn Webster-Stratton (2001) designed this program to address conduct problems in children aged three–eight years old. The weekly two-hour group sessions focus on social competence, conflict management, emotional literacy, anger management, and peer interactions. Although there is a plethora of research studies conducted on the IY curriculum, there is limited research on the Dina Dinosaur Social Skills and Problem-Solving Curriculum. Research suggests that after implementation, children displayed less aggression at school and even fewer externalizing problems at home. The students also displayed more positive behavior with peers and were able to manage conflict more appropriately than those in the control group (Webster-Stratton, Reid, & Hammond, 2001).

Coping Cat

Coping Cat is a cognitive behavioral intervention that helps children between the ages of 8 and 13 recognize anxious thoughts and develop strategies to cope with anxiety-filled situations. Coping Cat was developed in 1985 by Kendall and Hedtke with the most recent update in 2006. Coping Cat can be implemented in small groups or individually and includes 16 sessions. Research suggests a reduction in anxiety among children after implementation of the Coping Cat program (McNally Keehn, Lincoln, Brown, & Chavira, 2013; Starrenburg, Kuijpers, Kleinjan, Hutschemaekers, & Engels, 2016; 2017).

WhyTry

WhyTry was developed by Christian Moore in 2008 as a resiliency education program. It was designed specifically to improve behavior, enhance motivation, diminish academic challenges, reduce truancy, and prevent violent behavior. It was developed as a small-group curriculum for students in kindergarten through 12th grade where each lesson allows the student to personalize real-life situations as they work through a problem-solving approach (Alvarez & Anderson-Ketchmark, 2009). The research suggests a decrease in negative behavior toward peers, an improvement in motivation to succeed, and a decrease in the number of discipline referrals (Alvarez & Anderson-Ketchmark, 2009; Wilhite & Bullock, 2012).

Each of the EBPs listed above are small-group programs that promote students' social and emotional competence and provide opportunities for practice. There is at least one carefully conducted evaluation that documents positive impacts on student behavior, social-emotional development, and/or academic performance. However, the majority of these Tier 2 evidence-based programs come with high price tags, outdated research, and/or limited research conducted by an independent researcher. The need for more evidence-based options at the Tier 2 level is evident.

Tier 3 EBP

Tier 3 represents even more intensive interventions than those listed in Tables 10.2 and 10.3. These interventions are typically provided to a small percentage of the student population to offer social, emotional, academic, and/or behavioral support and are often provided on an individual basis. In this section readers will find a description of the specific approaches and interventions for students at highest risk, as well as a summary of the selected interventions for Tier 3 listed in Table 10.4.

Due to time constraints and large caseloads, school counselors are often limited in their ability to provide extensive long-term individual counseling to students. More often than not, brief counseling strategies/techniques are selected. When more intense and pervasive issues are present, counselors make a referral to an outside agency. Although most school counselors are not trained to provide intensive long-term therapy, they are equipped with knowledge and skills in how to utilize solution-focused brief therapy (SFBT), cognitive behavioral (CBT), and motivational interview (MI) techniques with students. The SFBT, CBT, and MI techniques are each well-established "go-to" approaches for school counselors yet they differ greatly from the manualized programs described above in Tier 1 and Tier 2. These counseling approaches are not considered "manualized" interventions but are evidence-based and used as part of a comprehensive program when working individually with students. In the school setting, five–eight individual sessions are appropriate and these specific approaches have been shown to be the most effective way to help students develop the skills necessary to be successful academically, socially, and emotionally. Specific information about each approach is outlined below.

Solution-Focused Brief Therapy (SFBT)

Solution-focused brief therapy was developed by de Shazar and Berg in the 1980s to help individual or small groups of students develop resiliency and problem-solving skills. The

Table 10.3 Tier 2 evidence-based programs

Name of Program/ Curriculum	Developer/Year of Publication	Manual/Materials Required? Y/N	Training Required/ Offered? Y/N	Grade Level	Delivery Details	Intent of Program	Relevant Research Articles Supporting Effectiveness
Student Success Skills (SSS) http:// studentsuccessskills. com	Brigman & Webb (2003; 2016)	Y $75	In-person training offered (contact developer).	4–12	8 45-minute lessons, 1 booster lesson that can be repeated.	Social problem solving, self-management skills.	1 **Campbell, C. A., & Brigman, G. (2005).** • Randomized Control Trial/Pre-post Control Group Design. • 240 5th and 6th graders participated in pre-test–post-test control group design with randomization. ANCOVA used to evaluate FCAT reading and math data and gains reported in reading and math achievement (0.002) between treatment and comparison groups overall, and 0.051 for reading scores. Gains in teacher-rated behavior showed significance of 0.051. 2 **Lemberger, M. E., & Clemens, E. V. (2012).** • Randomized Control Trial. • 53 (treatment) and 47 (comparison) African-American inner-city 4th and 5th grade students in a pre/post design. • Small effect size in student self-report of school support between the control and treatment groups. • Large effect size was found for differences in student report of metacognitive skills between the control and treatment groups. • MANOVA revealed significant difference in teacher report of students' executive functioning.

(continued)

Table 10.3 (continued)

Name of Program/ Curriculum	Developer/Year of Publication	Manual/Materials Required? Y/N	Training Required/ Offered? Y/N	Grade Level	Delivery Details	Intent of Program	Relevant Research Articles Supporting Effectiveness
Skills for Social and Academic Success (SASS)	Dr. Carrie Masia-Warner (Assistant Professor of Psychiatry, NYU Child Study Center), Fisher, Masia-Warner, & Klein (2004)	Manual available at NYU Child Study Center $1,600. For more information contact Child Trends, Stephen Russ, (240) 223-9382, sruss@childtrends.org or Child Trends DataBank, David Murphy, Senior Research Scientist, (240) 223-9207, childtrendsdatabank@childtrends.org	N/A	Adolescents	12 40-minute group sessions; 2 booster lessons; 2 individual sessions (15 minutes); 4 weekend events; 2 parent meetings (45 minutes), 2 teacher trainings (45 minutes).	Social anxiety; social skills (initiating conversations, maintaining conversations and establishing friendships, listening and remembering, and assertiveness training).	**1 Warner, C. M., Fisher, P. H., Shrout, P. E., Rathor, S., & Klein, R. G. (2007).** • Randomized Control Trial. • 36 female students aged 14–16 were randomized. There were clinically significant improvements. 59% of the SASS group no longer qualified for a diagnosis of social phobia versus 0% of the attention control. **2 Masia-Warner, C., Klein, R. G., Dent, H. C., Fisher, P. H., Alvir, J., Albano, A. M., & Guardino, M. (2005).** • Random Control Trial. • SASS (n = 18) or wait-list control group (n = 17). Pre-test and post-test collection on anxiety/mood disorders, social phobic disorders, depression, and loneliness through self-report, parent report, and observer report. Treatment group had significantly lower observer-rated anxiety disorders, social phobic disorder, social anxiety, and total functioning. • Significantly lower self-reported social avoidance and distress, significantly lower parent-reported social avoidance and distress in treatment group.

Program	Author (year)	Cost / Materials	Training	Age Range	Sessions	Focus	Rating	Research
Incredible Years (IY) The Dina Dinosaur Social Skills and Problem-Solving Curriculum www.incredibleyears.com	Carolyn Webster-Stratton, PhD (2001)	Materials $1,375; additional costs for extra teacher books and DVDs.	Y $550/day for 3-day training + travel; ongoing consultation for $175/hour.	Ages 3–8 years	18–22 weekly 2-hour sessions.	Conduct problems, social competence, conflict management, emotional literacy, anger management, positive peer interactions.	1	**Webster-Stratton, C., Reid, J., & Hammond, M. (2001)** • Randomized Control Trial, pre/post design. ANOVA revealed significant reduction in conduct problems in the treatment group and significant increases in conduct problems in the control group.
Coping Cat www.workbookpublishing.com	Kendall & Hedtke (1985; 2006)	Manual $24, workbook $26.95.	Training is optional.	Ages 8–13	16 sessions (3 segments)	Anxiety.	1 2	**Starrenburg, M. L. A v., Kuijpers, R. C. W. M., Kleinjan, M., Hutschemaekers, G. J. M., & Engels, R. C. M. E. (2017; 2016).** • Randomized Controlled Trial. • Lower levels of anxiety reported. **McNally Keehn, R. H., Lincoln, A. J., Brown, M. Z., & Chavira, D. A. (2013).** • Randomized Control Trial. • Evidence of a reduction of anxiety in children with autism.
WhyTry www.whytry.org	Christian Moore (2008)	$599/year with annual renewal of $99.	2-day training offered but not required. $550/person; includes curriculum.	K-12	10 units with a variety of lessons within each (60 minutes).	Violence prevention, academic success, truancy reduction, resilience education.	1	**Wilhite, S., & Bullock, L. (2012).** • Mixed Method Design. • Significant decrease in the number of disciplinary referrals and several areas on the behavioral rating scales. Improvements also noted in regards to social stress, anxiety, sense of inadequacy, somatization, and internalization of problems.

focus on present and future goal setting can be utilized at all grade levels. Research suggests gains in grade point average, a more positive impact on student academic ability as well as less frequent emotional difficulty (Daki & Savage, 2010; Newsome, 2004).

Cognitive Behavioral Therapy (CBT)

In the 1960s, Aaron Beck founded CBT for implementation with individuals suffering with depression, anxiety, trauma, and difficulties with problem-solving. However, CBT is now used when addressing all types of concerns and when working with adults and children of all ages including students in an educational setting (Bernstein, Layne, Egan, & Tennison, 2005; Fazzio-Griffith & Ballard, 2014). Cognitive Behavioral Therapy implementation at the individual level was associated with improvements in childhood anxiety as well as a significant reduction in social anxiety among adolescents (Bernstein et al., 2005; Warner, Fisher, Shrout, Rathor, & Klein, 2007). The research supports CBT as an effective individual approach in working with students in an educational setting.

Motivational Interviewing (MI)

Motivational Interviewing (MI), a person-centered counseling approach often used to address clients/students who are ambivalent to change, was first introduced in 1983 by William Miller, a clinical psychologist (Paul, 2017). Later, in 1991, both William Miller and Stephen Rollnick took MI even further, elaborated on these fundamental concepts and developed a specific approach to utilize in a counseling setting (Paul, 2017; Rollnick, Kaplan, & Rutschman, 2016). Their goal was to not only motivate students but to change student attitudes and behaviors to help them develop a more positive outlook on life (Paul, 2017; Rollnick, Kaplan, & Rutschman, 2016). Motivational Interviewing was ultimately designed to help students recognize that a change needs to be made by drawing out what motivates them intrinsically (North, 2017). Lisa Sheldon (2010) went even further and outlined MI by using two acronyms, OARS and FRAMES: OARS refers to open-ended questions, affirmations, reflective listening, and summary statements, while FRAMES refers to feedback, responsibility, advice, menu, empathy, and self-efficacy. Through the use of OARS and FRAMES, school counselors can open the door to communication while also guiding students as they are setting short- and long-term goals for themselves. Positive changes in student behavior, higher grades, and significant improvements in classroom participation after the implementation of MI were found (Strait, Smith, McQuillin, Terry, Swan, & Malone, 2012). If school counselors are able to practice MI, students will begin to recognize the potential within themselves (North, 2017).

FIRST STEP Next

FIRST STEP Next was designed to address emotional regulation and antisocial and aggressive behavior among children in grades pre-K through 2nd grade and was originally developed by Dr. Hill Walker in 1998, with the most recent revision in 2015. Research suggests that student behavior and social skills improved based on parent/teacher ratings, while other research points to gains in prosocial and adaptive behavior (Walker, Seeley, Small, Severson, Graham, Feil, Serna, Golly, & Forness, 2009; Sumi, Woodbridge, Javitz, Thornton, Wagner, Rouspil, Yu, Seeley, Walker, Golly, Small, Feil, & Severson, 2013).

The Tier 3 evidence-based approaches covered in this section are for students who are struggling most and in greatest need of individualized support. The selected programs have research backing their effectiveness with students PK-12.

Table 10.4 Tier 3 evidence-based programs

Name of Program/ Curriculum	Developer/Year of Publication	Manual/ Materials Required? Y/N	Training Required/ Offered? Y/N	Grade Level	Delivery Details	Intent of Program	Relevant Research Articles Supporting Effectiveness
Solution-Focused Brief Therapy (SFBT) www.sfbta.org/about_sfbt.html	De Shazer & Berg (1997)	N/A	Counselor training program.	All	5 to 8 45-minute sessions.	Goal-directed resiliency, present and future focus.	1 Newsome, W. S. (2004). • Quasi-Experimental Design (N=52). • Increased mean grade scores. 2 Daki, J., & Savage, R. S. (2010). • Randomized Control Trial. • Improved reading/literacy skills.
Cognitive Behavioral Therapy (CBT) https://beckinstitute.org/about-beck	Beck (1960s)	N/A	Counselor training program.	All	Varies.	Depression, anxiety, trauma, problem-solving.	1 Masia-Warner, C., Fisher, P. H., Shrout, P. E., Rathor, S., & Klein, R. G. (2007). • Attention Control Trial. • Reduction in social anxiety among adolescents.
Motivational Interviewing (MI)	William Miller (1983) William Miller & Stephen Rollnick (1991)	N/A	Counselor training program.	All	Varies.	Individuals ambivalent to change.	1 Strait, G. G., Smith, B. H., McQuillin, S., Terry, J., Swan, S., & Malone, P. (2012). • Randomized Trial. • Positive changes in student behavior, significant improvements in classroom participation and improved grades.
FIRST STEP Next https://pacificnwpublish.com/products/FIRST-STEP-Next.html	Hill M. Walker, PhD. 1998—First Step to Success. 2015—FIRST STEP Next.	$485	Training guide included in purchase.	PreK-2	50–60 hours over 3 month timeframe	Emotional regulation, address antisocial or aggressive behavior.	1 Sumi, W. C., Woodbridge, M. W., Javitz, H. S., Thornton, S. P., Wagner, M., Rouspil, K., Yu, J. W., Seeley, J. R., Walker, H. M., Golly, A., Small, J. W., Feil, H. G., & Severson, H. H. (2013; 2012). • Randomized Control Trial. • Improved social skills as well as adaptive behaviors. 2 Walker, H. M., Seeley, J. R., Small, J., Severson, H. H., Graham, B. A., Feil, E. G., Serna, L., Golly, A., & Forness, S. R. (2009) • Randomized Controlled Trial. • Pre-post teacher parent/teacher ratings of student behavior and social skills showed significant improvement in both.

Now that you have reviewed each tier and possible programs that can be implemented in your CSCP, list the program/interventions you currently use at each tier and consider:

Are they evidence-based?

If not, which one(s) could you incorporate that are relevant to the needs of your students and your school-counseling program?

Cultural Implications

We live in an ever-changing world where the term diversity continues to expand to include all the qualities that make our students unique as individuals; diversity can also describe the overlapping commonalities of a group that differentiate it from the larger, mainstream population. It's easy to say that school counselors should learn and practice culturally relevant strategies, but the question still remains, "Is there ample research available when determining the effectiveness of EBP in regards to racial diversity?" The answer, unfortunately, is "no." This should then make us reflect on how our CSCPs truly meet the ASCA Ethical Standards for School Counselors (2016), and if we are effectively meeting the needs of all of our students. In order to best address student issues, school counselors need to be aware of what constitutes an evidence-based program/practice, and whether that program or practice would be relevant and applicable to their student population.

Conclusion

Today, professional school counselors are faced with increased demands which require them to wear multiple hats and juggle many tasks, one of the most stressful of which is demonstrating accountability by linking school counseling interventions and services to measurable changes, improvements, and outcomes in their students. Our teachers, parents, and administrators say: "Are students better, happier, more successful as a result of the things you are doing? Show me!" The literature supports using various EBPs across the continuum of three tiers: Tier 1, Tier 2, and Tier 3. However, the challenge remains accessing it, understanding it, becoming adequately trained, and feeling competent in the use of these EBPs, in order to competently assess their delivery and student outcomes. This chapter provided an overview of EBP and offered a convincing argument as to why school counselors and counselor educators should embrace this mindset. We offered a host of programs/approaches to assist school counselors when selecting and delivering EBPs across the three tiers to meet the needs of *all*, *some*, and *few* students. Our intent is that you use this chapter to begin your own EBP journey! And, as we asked at the start, "Are you in or out?"; our hope is that we've made it a bit easier for you to say, "I'm in!"

For more information and a school counselor's perspective on *Evidence-Based Practices Across MTSS* please see Chapter 12 "Voices from the Field," Voices 1, 6, and 9.

ASCA Ethical Standards

The need to choose appropriate evidence-based practices and interventions within a Comprehensive School Counseling Program is reinforced by the American School

Counselor Association (ASCA, 2016). The use of EBPs should ensure that all students are provided with equitable opportunity and outcomes. Further, the ASCA requirements signify how the knowledge, use, and incorporation of sound research-based practices, which are proven to be a "good fit" for the population being targeted, are central to what counselors are expected to know and do. These standards provide a guide for school counselors as they choose interventions, at each tiered level, that best meet the needs of their specific population of students. Specifically, according to ASCA, school counselors:

A Responsibility to Students

A.1 Supporting Student Development

- A.1.e. Are concerned with students' academic, career, and social/emotional needs and encourage each student's maximum development.
- A.1.h. Provide effective, responsive interventions to address student needs.

A.3 Comprehensive Data-Informed Program

- A.3.b. Provide students with a Comprehensive School Counseling Program that ensures equitable academic, career, and social/emotional development opportunities for all students.
- A.3.c. Review student and school data to assess needs including, but not limited to, data on disparities that may exist related to gender, race, ethnicity, socio-economic status, and and/other relevant classifications.
- A.3.d. Use data to determine needed interventions, which are then delivered to help close the information, attainment, achievement, and opportunity gaps.
- A.3.e. Collect process, perception, and outcome data and analyze the data to determine the progress and effectiveness of the school counseling program. School counselors ensure the school counseling program's goals and action plans are aligned with district's school improvement goals.

B Responsibilities to Parents/Guardians, School and the Self

B.2 Responsibilities to the School

- B.2.m. Promote cultural competence to help create a safer, more inclusive school environment.

B.3 Responsibilities to Self

- B.3.k. Work toward a school climate that embraces diversity and promotes academic, career, and social/emotional development for all students.

Teaching Activity 1

Review a policy document related to your area of professional practice (i.e., a copy of your job/position description).

1 Does the policy document include any mention of EBP, the use of data, accountability, effective practice, student outcomes?
2 What are your reactions to this?

Teaching Activity 2

The Professional Counselor is a peer-reviewed, open access, electronic journal provided by the National Board of Certified Counselors (NBCC). Review the research article: Mariani, M., Webb, L., Villares, E., & Brigman, G. (2015). Effect of participation in Student Success Skills on prosocial and bullying behavior. *Professional Counselor, 5*(3), 341–353, which was written by one of the chapter authors and is accessible online. Assess the information about the Student Success Skills (SSS) classroom program (see www.studentsuccessskills.com).

1   Does this intervention meet the four criteria designated by the authors as qualifying as evidence-based?

Resources

Further Reading

Children's Services Council (n.d.). *The journey to evidence-based programming.* Children's Services Council of Palm Beach County. Retrieved from: www.cscpbc.org.

Collaborative for Academic, Social and Emotional Learning (2013). *Effective social and emotional learning programs: Preschool and elementary school edition.* Chicago, IL: Author. Retrieved from: www.casel.org/guide/programs.

Substance Abuse and Mental Health Services Administration (SAMHSA) (2017). SAMHSA's National Registry of Evidence-based Programs and Practices (NREPP). Rockville, MD: Author. Retrieved from: www.samhsa.gov/nrepp.

U.S. Department of Education, Institute of Education Sciences, & National Center for Education Evaluation and Regional Assistance (2003). *Identifying and implementing education practices supported by rigorous evidence: A user friendly guide.* Retrieved from: https://ies.ed.gov/ncee/pubs/evidence_based/evidence_based.asp.

Multiple Choice Questions

1   **Which of the following defines "evidence-based practice"?**

    a   Any practice that has been established as effective through scientific research.
    b   Any intervention offered at the Tier 1, Tier 2, and Tier 3 level.
    c   Manualized programs implemented by school counselors.
    d   All of the above.

2   **When delineating between Tier 1, Tier 2, and Tier 3 interventions, which tier offers the most proactive and preventative approach to a Comprehensive School Counseling Program.**

    a   Tier 1.
    b   Tier 2.
    c   Tier 3.
    d   All of the above.

3   **Zyromski and Mariani (2016) suggested that school counselors follow which of the following steps when working towards developing an evidence-based school counseling program:**

a   Assess the problem.
b   Set SMART goals.
c   Select appropriate evidence-based interventions.
d   Evaluate interventions and report findings.
e   All of the above.

4   **When aligning the MTSS approach with school counselor practice, Tier 2 relates to the following direct service area:**

a   Individual counseling.
b   Small-group counseling.
c   Classroom guidance/large-group counseling.
d   None of the above.

5   **The EBP Model offered by Sackett and colleagues (1996) integrates which of the following factors:**

a   Clinical expertise.
b   Patient/client values and preferences.
c   The use of the best available research evidence.
d   All of the above.

Answers: Q1 a, Q2 a, Q3 e, Q4 b, Q5 d.

References

Allred, C. (1997). *The Positive Action Program.* Twin Falls, IN: Positive Action, Inc.

Allred, C., & Flay, B. (2010). *The Positive Action Program.* Twin Falls, IN: Positive Action, Inc.

Alvarez, M. E., & Anderson-Ketchmark, C. (2009). Review of an evidence-based school social work intervention: WhyTry. *Children & Schools, 31*(1), 59–61.

American School Counselor Association (ASCA) (2016). ASCA ethical standards for school counselors. Alexandria, VA: Author. Retrieved from: www.schoolcounselor.org/asca/media/asca/Ethics/EthicalStandards2016.pdf.

Baron, J. (2012). Applying evidence to social programs. *Econonmix.* Retrieved from: http://coalition4evidence.org/468-2/publications.

Beck, A. T. (1967). *Depression: Clinical, experimental, and theoretical aspects.* Philadelphia, PA: University of Pennsylvania Press.

Belasco, A. S. (2013). Creating college opportunity: School counselors and their influence on post-secondary enrollment. *Research in Higher Education, 54*(7), 781–804.

Bernstein, G. A., Layne, A. E., Egan, E. A., & Tennison, D. M. (2005). School-based interventions for anxious children. *Journal of the American Academy of Child & Adolescent Psychiatry, 44*(11), 1118–1127.

Brigman, G., & Webb, L. (2003; 2016). *Student Success Skills.* Boca Raton, FL: Atlantic Education Consultants.

Campbell, C. A., & Brigman, G. (2005). Closing the achievement gap: A structured approach to group counseling. *Journal for Specialists in Group Work, 30*(1), 67–82, doi:10.1080/01933920590908705.

Carey, J., & Dimmitt, C. (2012). School counseling and student outcomes: Summary of six statewide studies. *Professional School Counseling, 16*(2), 146, doi.org/10.1086/605768.

Carrell, S. E., & Hoekstra, M. (January 28, 2011). *Are school counselors a cost-effective education input?* Available at SSRN: https://ssrn.com/abstract=1629868 or dx.doi.org/10.2139/ssrn.1629868.

Children's Services Council (n.d). *The journey to evidence-based programming.* Palm Beach, FL: Children's Services Council of Palm Beach County. Retrieved from: www.cscpbc.org.

Committee for Children (1985; 2017). *Second Step: Skills for social and academic success.* Seattle, WA: Author. Retrieved from: www.cfchildren.org/second-step.aspx.

Crean, H. F., & Johnson, D. B. (2013). Promoting alternative thinking strategies (PATHS) and elementary school aged children's aggression: Results from a cluster randomized trial. *American Journal of Community Psychology, 52*(1), 56–72, doi:10.1007/s10464-013-9576-4.

Custpec, P. A. (2004). Bridging the research-to-practice gap: Evidence-based education. *Centerscope, 2*(2), 1–8.

Daki, J., & Savage, R. S. (2010). Solution-focused brief therapy: Impacts on academic and emotional difficulties. *The Journal of Educational Research, 103*(5), 309–326, doi:10.1080/00220670903383127.

Davies, H. T. O., Nutley, S. M., & Smith, P. C. (Eds) (2000). *What works? Evidence-based policy and practice in the public services.* Bristol: Policy Press.

Davies, P. (1999). What is evidence-based education? *British Journal of Educational Studies, 47*(2), 108–121. Retrieved from: www.jstor.org/stable/3122195.

De Shazer, S., & Berg, I. K. (1997). 'What works?' Remarks on research aspects of solution-focused brief therapy. *Journal of Family Therapy, 19*(2), 121–124.

Dimmitt, C. L., Carey, J. C., & Hatch, P. A. (2007). *Evidence-based school counseling: Making a difference with data-driven practices.* Thousand Oaks, CA: Corwin Press.

Dimmitt, C., Carey, J., McGannon, W., & Henningson, I. (2005). Identifying a school counseling research agenda: A Delphi study. *Counselor Education and Supervision, 44*, 214–228.

Dollarhide, C. T., & Saginak, K. A. (2008). *Comprehensive school counseling programs: K-12 delivery systems in action.* Boston, MA: Allyn and Bacon.

Domitrovich, C. E., Cortes, R. C., & Greenberg, M. T. (2007). Improving young children's social and emotional competence: A randomized trial of the preschool "PATHS" curriculum. *The Journal of Primary Prevention, 28*(2), 67–91, doi:10.1007/s10935-007-0081-0.

Drake, R. E., Goldman, H., Leff, H. S., Lehman, A. F., Dixon, L., Mueser, K. T., & Torrey, W. C. (2001). Implementing evidence-based practices in routine mental health service settings. *Psychiatric Services, 52*, 179–182.

Edwards, D., Hunt, M. H., Meyers, J., Grogg, K. R., & Jarrett, O. (2005). Acceptability and student outcomes of a violence prevention curriculum. *The Journal of Primary Prevention*, (5), 401–418.

Espelage, D. L., Rose, C. A., & Polanin, J. R. (2015). Social-emotional learning program to reduce bullying, fighting, and victimization among middle school students with disabilities. *Remedial and Special Education, 36*(5), 299–311, doi:10.1177/0741932514564564.

Farrell, A. D., Valois, R. F., & Meyer, A. L. (2002). Evaluation of the RIPP-6 violence prevention program at a rural middle school. *American Journal of Health Education, 33*(3), 167–172.

Farrell, A. D., Valois, R. F., Meyer, A. L., & Tidwell, R. P. (2002; 2003). Impact of the RIPP violence prevention program on rural middle school students. *The Journal of Primary Prevention, 24*(2), 143–167, doi:10.1023/A:1025992328395.

Fazzio-Griffith, L. J., & Ballard, M. B. (2014). Cognitive behavioral play therapy techniques in school-based group counseling: Assisting students in the development of social skills. *Vistas Online, 18*, 1–14. Retrieved from: www.counseling.org/knowledge-center/vistas.

Fisher, P. H., Masia-Warner, C., & Klein, R. G. (2004). Skills for Social and Academic Success: A school-based intervention for social anxiety disorder in adolescents. *Clinical Child and Family Psychology Review, 7*(4), 241–249.

Guo, S., Wu, Q., Smokowski, P. R., Bacallao, M., Evans, C. B. R., & Cotter, K. L. (2015). A longitudinal evaluation of the positive action program in a low-income, racially diverse, rural county: Effects on self-esteem, school hassles, aggression, and internalizing symptoms. *Journal of Youth and Adolescence, 44*(12), 2337–2358, doi:10.1007/s10964-015-0358-1.

Hall, B., & Bacon, T. (2006). Building a foundation against violence. *Journal of School Violence, 4*(4), 63–83, doi:10.1300/J202v04n04_05.

Hall, B. W., Bacon, T. P., & Ferron, J. M. (2013). Randomized controlled evaluation of the too good for drugs prevention program: Impact on adolescents at different risk levels for drug use. *Journal of Drug Education, 43*(3), 277–300, doi:10.2190/DE.43.3.e.

Haskins, R., & Baron, J. (2011). *Building the connection between policy and evidence: The Obama evidence-based initiatives.* London, UK: NESTA. Retrieved from: http://coalition4evidence.org/wp-content/uploads/2011/09/Haskins-Baron-paper-on-fed-evid-based-initiatives-2011.pdf.

Hoagwood, K. (2004). Evidence-based practice in child and adolescent mental health: Its meaning, application, and limitations. *Emotional and Behavioral Disorders in Youth, 7–8,* 24–26.

Kam, C., Greenberg, M. T., & Walls, C. T. (2003). Examining the role of implementation quality in school-based prevention using the PATHS curriculum. *Prevention Science, 4*(1), 55–63, doi:10.10 23/A:1021786811186.

Kendall, P. C., & Hedtke, K. A. (1985; 2006). *The Coping Cat Program Workbook.* Ardmore, PA: Workbook Publishing.

Kramer, T., Caldarella, P., Young, R., Fischer, L., & Warren, J. (2014). Implementing Strong Kids school-wide to reduce internalizing behaviors and increase prosocial behaviors. *Education and Treatment of Children, 37*(4), 659–680, doi:10.1353/etc.2014.0031.

Kusche, C. A., & Greenberg, M. T. (1994; 2011). *The PATHS Curriculum.* Seattle, WA: Developmental Research and Programs.

Lemberger, M. E., & Clemens, E. V. (2012). Connectedness and self-regulation as constructs of the student success skills program in inner-city African American elementary school students. *Journal of Counseling & Development, 90*(4), 450–458, doi:10.1002/j.1556-6676.2012.00056.x.

Lemberger, M. E., Selig, J. P., Bowers, H., & Rogers, J. E. (2015). The influence of the Student Success Skills program on the executive functioning skills, feelings of connectedness, and academic achievement in a predominately Hispanic, low-income middle school district. *Journal of Counseling and Development, 93*(1), 25–37, doi: 10.1002/j.1556-6676.2015.00178.x.

Lewis, K. M., DuBois, D. L., Bavarian, N., Acock, A., Silverthorn, N., Day, J., Ji, P., Vuchinich, S., & Flay, B. R. (2013). Effects of positive action on the emotional health of urban youth: A cluster-randomized trial. *The Journal of Adolescent Health: Official Publication of the Society for Adolescent Medicine, 53*(6), 706–711, doi:10.1016/j.jadohealth.2013.06.012.

Lewis, K. M., Vuchinich, S., Ji, P., DuBois, D. L., Acock, A., Bavarian, N., & Flay, B. R. (2016). Effects of the Positive Action Program on indicators of positive youth development among urban youth. *Applied Developmental Science, 20*(1), 16, doi:10.1080/10888691.2015.1039123.

Low, S., Cook, C. R., Smolkowski, K., & Buntain-Ricklefs, J. (2015). Promoting social-emotional competence: An evaluation of the elementary version of Second Step. *Journal of School Psychology, 53*(6), 463.

Mariani, M., Webb, L., Villares, E., & Brigman, G. (2015). Effects of participation in student success skills on pro-social and bullying behavior. *The Professional Counselor, 5*(3), 341–353. Retrieved from: http://tpcjournal.nbcc.org/effect-of-participation-in-student-success-skills-on-prosocial-and-bullying-behavior.

Masia-Warner, C., Colognori, D., Brice, C., Herzig, K., Mufson, L., Lynch, C., Reiss, P. T., Petkova, E., Fox, J., Moceri, D., Ryan, J., & Klein, R. G. (2016). Can school counselors deliver cognitive-behavioral treatment for social anxiety effectively? A randomized controlled trial. *Journal of Child Psychology and Psychiatry, 57*(11), 1229–1238, dx.doi.org/10.1111/jcpp.12550. Retrieved from: www.researchgate.net/publication/299381138.

Masia-Warner, C., Fisher, P. H., Shrout, P. E., Rathor, S., & Klein, R. G. (2007). Treating adolescents with social anxiety disorder in school: An attention control trial. *Journal of Child Psychology and Psychiatry, 48,* 676–686.

Masia-Warner, C., Klein, R. G., Dent, H. C., Fisher, P. H., Alvir, J., Albano, A. M., & Guardino, M. (2005). School-based intervention for adolescents with social anxiety disorder: Results of a controlled study. *Journal of Abnormal Child Psychology, 33*(6), 707–722.

McIntosh, K., & Goodman, S. (2016). *Integrated Multitiered Systems of Support: Blending RTI and PBIS.* New York, NY: Guilford Press.

McNally Keehn, R. H., Lincoln, A. J., Brown, M. Z., & Chavira, D. A. (2013). The Coping Cat program for children with anxiety and autism spectrum disorder: A pilot randomized controlled trial. *Journal of Autism and Developmental Disorders, 43*(1), 57–67, doi:10.1007/s10803-012-1541-9.

Mendez Foundation (1995; 2013). *Too Good for Drugs.* Tampa, FL: C.E. Mendez Foundation, Inc.

Mendez Foundation (1995; 2013). *Too Good for Violence.* Tampa, FL: C.E. Mendez Foundation, Inc.

Merrell, K. W., & Gueldner, B. A. (2010). *Social and emotional learning in the classroom: Promoting mental health and academic success.* New York: Guilford Press.

Meyer, A. L., Farrell, A., Northup, W., Kung, E., & Plybon, L. (2000). *Promoting nonviolence in early adolescence: Responding in peaceful and positive ways.* New York: Plenum Publishers.

Meyer, A., Northup, W., & Plybon, L. (1998). Responding in Peaceful and Positive Ways (RIPP): A violence prevention booster for seventh graders. Unpublished manuscript.

Mihalic, S. F., & Elliott, D. S. (2015). Evidence-based programs registry: Blueprints for Healthy Youth Development. *Evaluation and Program Planning, 48,* 124–131.

Miller, W. R. (1983). Motivational interviewing with problem drinkers. *Behavioural and Cognitive Psychotherapy, 11*(2), 147–172.

Miller, W., & Rollnick, N. (1991). *Motivational Interviewing: Preparing people to change addictive behavior.* New York: Guilford Press.

Moore, C. (2008). *The WhyTry program.* Salt Lake City, UT: WhyTry.

Nathan, P. E., & Gorman, J. M. (2007). *A guide to treatments that work* (3rd Ed.). New York: Oxford University Press.

Newsome, W. S. (2004). Solution-focused brief therapy groupwork with at-risk junior high school students: Enhancing the bottom line. *Research on Social Work Practice, 14*(5), 336–343, doi:10.1177/1049731503262134.

North, R. A. (2017). *Motivational interviewing for school counselors.* San Bernardino, CA: Reagan A. North.

Paul, H. A. (2017). Motivational interviewing in schools: Conversations to improve behavior and learning, by S. Rollnick, S. G. Kaplan, & R. Rutschman. *Child & Family Behavior Therapy, 39*(2), 155, doi:10.1080/07317107.2017.1307682.

Pyne, J. R. (2011). Comprehensive School Counseling Programs, job satisfaction, and the ASCA National Model. *Professional School Counseling, 15*(2), 88–97.

Raines, J. C. (2008). *Evidence-based practice in school mental health.* New York: Oxford University Press.

Rollnick, S., Kaplan, S., & Rutschman, R. (2016). *Motivational interviewing in schools: Conversations to improve behavior and learning.* New York: The Guilford Press.

Rubin, A. (2008). *Practitioner's guide to using research for evidence-based practice.* Hoboken, NJ: John Wiley & Sons.

Rubin, A., & Bellamy, J. (2012). *Practitioner's guide to using research for evidence-based practice* (2nd Ed.). Hoboken, NJ: John Wiley & Sons.

Sackett, D. L., Straus, S. E., Richardson, W. S., Rosenberg, W., & Hayes, R. B. (2000). *Evidence-based medicine: How to practice and teach EBM* (2nd Ed.). New York: Churchill Livingstone.

Sackett, D. L., Rosenburg, W. M. C., Muir Gray, J. A., Haynes, R. B., & Richardson, W. S. (1996). Evidence-based medicine: What it is and what it isn't. *British Medical Journal, 312,* 71–72.

Sheldon, L. A. (2010). Using motivational interviewing to help your students. *The NEA Higher Education Journal,* 152–157.

Sink, C. A., Akos, P. A., Turnbull, R. J., & Mvududu, N. (2008). An investigation of Comprehensive School Counseling Programs in Washington state middle schools. *Professional School Counseling, 12,* 43–53.

Sink, C. A., & Stroh, H. R. (2003). Raising achievement test scores of early elementary school students through Comprehensive School Counseling Programs. *Professional School Counseling, 6,* 350–364.

Starrenburg, M. L. A. v., Kuijpers, R. C. W. M., Kleinjan, M., Hutschemaekers, G. J. M., & Engels, R. C. M. E. (2016; 2017). Effectiveness of a cognitive behavioral therapy-based indicated prevention program for children with elevated anxiety levels: A randomized controlled trial. *Prevention Science, 18*(1), 31–39, doi:10.1007/s11121-016-0725-5.

Strait, G. G., Smith, B. H., McQuillin, S., Terry, J., Swan, S., & Malone, P. S. (2012). A randomized trial of motivational interviewing to improve middle school students' academic performance. *Journal of Community Psychology, 40*(8), 1032–1039.

Substance Abuse and Mental Health Services Administration (SAMHSA) (2017). SAMHSA's National Registry of Evidence-based Programs and Practices (NREPP). Rockville, MD: Author. Retrieved from: www.samhsa.gov/nrepp.

Sumi, W. C., Woodbridge, M. W., Javitz, H. S., Thornton, S. P., Wagner, M., Rouspil, K., Yu, J. W., Seeley, J. R., Walker, H. M., Golly, A., Small, J. W., Feil, H. G., & Severson, H. H. (2013).

Assessing the effectiveness of First Step to Success: Are short-term results the first step to long-term behavioral improvements? *Journal of Emotional and Behavioral Disorders, 21*(1), 66–78, doi:10.1177/1063426611429571.

Villares, E., Frain, M., Brigman, G., Webb, L., & Peluso, P. (2012). The impact of Student Success Skills on standardized test scores: A meta-analysis. *Counseling Outcome Research and Evaluation, 3*(1), 3–16, dx.doi.org/2150137811434041.

Walker, H., Stiller, B., Coughlin, C., Golly, A., Sprick, M., & Feil, E. (1998; 2015). *FIRST STEP Next.* Eugene, OR: Pacific Northwest Publishing.

Walker, H. M., Seeley, J. R., Small, J., Severson, H. H., Graham, B. A., Feil, E. G., Serna, L., Golly, A., & Forness, S. R. (2009). A randomized controlled trial of the First Step to Success early intervention: Demonstration of program efficacy outcomes in a diverse, urban school district. *Journal of Emotional and Behavioral Disorders, 17*(4), 197–212, doi:10.1177/1063426609341645.

Warner, C. M., Fisher, P. H., Shrout, P. E., Rathor, S., & Klein, R. G. (2007). Treating adolescents with social anxiety disorder in school: An attention control trial. *Journal of Child Psychology & Psychiatry, 48*(7), 676–686, doi:10.1111/j.1469-7610.2007.01737.x.

Webb, L., & Brigman, G. (2006). Student success skills: Tools and strategies for improved academic and social outcomes. *Professional School Counseling, 10*(2), 112–120.

Webb, L., & Brigman, G. A. (2007). Student success skills: A structured group intervention for school counselors. *The Journal for Specialists in Group Work, 32*(2), 190–201, doi:10.1080/019339 20701227257.

Webster-Stratton, C. (2001). *Incredible Years: The Dina Dinosaur Social Skills and Problem-Solving Curriculum.* Seattle, WA: The Incredible Years, INC.

Webster-Stratton, C., Reid, J., & Hammond, M. (2001). Social skills and problem-solving training for children with early-onset conduct problems: Who benefits? *Journal of Child Psychology and Psychiatry and Allied Disciplines,* (7), 943–952.

What Works Clearinghouse (WWC) (n.d.). *Procedures and standards handbook Version 3.* Washington, DC: Institute of Education Sciences.

Whiston, S. C. (2002). Response to the past, present, and future of school counseling: Raising some issues. *Professional School Counseling, 5,* 148–155.

Whiston, S. C., & Quinby, R. F. (2009). Review of school counseling outcome research. *Psychology in the Schools, 46*(3), 267–272.

Whiston, S. C., & Sexton, T. L. (1998). A review of school counseling outcome research: Implications for practice. *Journal of Counseling & Development, 76,* 412–426.

Whiston, S. C., Tai, W. L., Rahardja, D., & Eder, K. (2011). School counseling outcome: A meta-analytic examination of interventions. *Journal of Counseling & Development, 89*(1), 37–55, dx.doi.org/10.1002/j.1556-6678.2011.tb00059.x.

Whitcomb, S. A., & Merrell, K. W. (2012). Understanding implementation and effectiveness of Strong Start K-2 on social-emotional behavior. *Early Childhood Education Journal, 40*(1), 63–71, doi:10.1007/s10643-011-0490-9.

Wilhite, S., & Bullock, L. I. (2012). Effects of the WhyTry social skills program on students with emotional and/or behavioral problems in an alternative school. *Emotional & Behavioural Difficulties, 17*(2), 175–194, doi:10.1080/13632752.2012.675135.

Zyromski, B., & Mariani, M. A. (2016). *Facilitating evidence-based, data-driven school counseling: A manual for practice.* Thousand Oaks, CA: Corwin Press.

Zyromski, B., Mariani, M., Kim, B., Lee, S., & Carey, J. (2017). The impact of Student Success Skills on students' metacognitive functioning in a naturalistic school setting. *The Professional Counselor, 7*(1), 33–44, doi:10.15241/bz.7.1.33.

11 Culturally Responsive MTSS
Advocating for Equity for Every Student

Jennifer Betters-Bubon, Holly Kortemeier, and Stephanie Smith-Durkin

Introduction

According to Dewey, "the purpose of education has always been to everyone, in essence, the same—to give the young the things they need in order to develop in an orderly, sequential way into members of society" (1934, p. 12). As members of school communities, school counselors influence students' academic, social-emotional, and career development through Comprehensive School Counseling Programs (CSCPs). Specifically, school counselors examine school-wide achievement and opportunity gaps and then provide prevention and intervention assistance to impact these gaps. Thus, we are in the business of educating all students, instilling skills and knowledge that will allow them to succeed in our world. In a similar way, successful MTSS should meet the needs of all students across all three tiers of support, serving all students through Tier 1 universal curriculum and support, some students through Tier 2 academic and behavioral interventions, and few students through Tier 3 intensive services. All approaches should infuse culturally responsive practices to combat disproportionality in school discipline and educational access, while also creating effective and equitable learning environments. This requires attention to the student demographics and cultural context of each particular school. In this chapter, we outline the importance of being culturally responsive throughout all tiers of MTSS and school counselors' related roles as advocates and change agents regarding equity in CSCP and MTSS implementation. We will first discuss educational trends, both the challenges and inequities, then, second, we will provide an overview of culture in education, including culturally responsive practices and culturally responsive school counseling. Finally, we discuss how to infuse cultural responsivity into MTSS and the critical role the school counselor plays in this process.

Educational Challenges and Inequities

Educators face numerous challenges each and every day. Inequitable public funding models have led to vast differences in resources between our rural, urban, and suburban schools (Darling-Hammond, 2007). Daily realities are affected by teacher shortages, students' growing mental health needs, and a plethora of initiatives related to increasing student achievement. We also face very real challenges in student outcomes. Some students are succeeding and some students are not, as evidenced by the clear and extensive academic and discipline gaps. Black, Latino, and Native American students have lower academic achievement outcomes (e.g., SAT/ACT Scores, enrollment in AP courses, etc.) compared with their White and Asian peers in school districts across the United States (Figures 11.1 and 11.2; The Annie E. Casey Foundation, 2017).

As school counselors, we see the discipline gap being played out in our schools (Bryan, Day-Vines, Griffin, & Moore-Thomas, 2012). We see the students who get sent to the office, know the students who struggle with determining their future career and life goals,

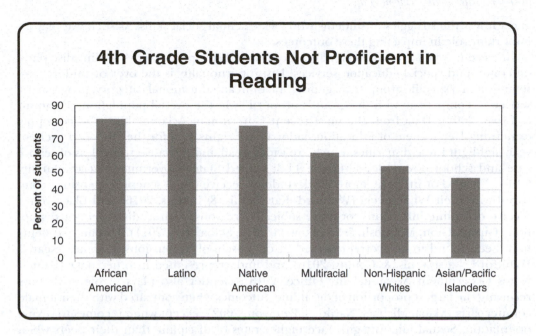

Figure 11.1 Academic achievement across student groups.

Adapted from *2017 KIDS COUNT data book: State trends in child well-being* by The Annie E. Casey Foundation, 2017. Copyright 2017 by The Annie E. Casey Foundation.

Note: "Not proficient in reading" is the percentage of fourth-grade public school students who did not reach the proficient level in reading as measured by the National Assessment of Educational Progress (NAEP).

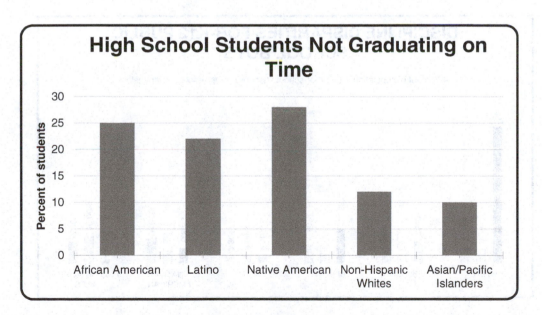

Figure 11.2 Four-year graduation rates across student groups.

Adapted from *2017 KIDS COUNT data book: State trends in child well-being* by The Annie E. Casey Foundation, 2017. Copyright 2017 by The Annie E. Casey Foundation.

Note: "Not graduating on time" is the percentage of an entering freshman class not graduating in four years.

and witness the struggles of students who lack essential social skills. As such, we play an important role in impacting these outcomes.

In recent years, researchers have identified disproportionality within discipline outcomes and special education services. Disproportionality is the over or underrepresentation of a specific group (e.g., gender, race) in an educational category, program, or service in comparison with the group's proportion in the overall population (Donovan & Cross, 2002). Data from the most recent Government Accountability Office report examining Department of Education national civil rights data for the 2013–2014 school year highlight these disparities, which are widespread and pervasive regardless of school type and school poverty level (Figure 11.3; United States Government Accountability Office, 2018). For instance, more Black students receive out-of-school suspensions compared with their White peers (Whitford, Katsiyannis, & Counts, 2016) and Black youth receive discipline infractions for more subjective reasons, such as disrespect or disruption (Girvan, Gion, McIntosh, & Smolkowski, 2017; Skiba et al., 2011). Hispanic students have been found to be overrepresented in out-of-school suspensions in some research (Whitford, Katsiyannis, & Counts, 2016) and underrepresented in other data (United States Government Accountability Office, 2018). Gender also plays a role, with boys receiving the largest proportion of discipline outcomes when compared with their female counterparts (Skiba, Michael, Nardo, & Peterson, 2002), except when it comes to sexual orientation. Sexual minority girls face higher rates of discipline than their peers when compared with sexual minority boys (Mittleman, 2018). This inequity extends beyond discipline to the services students receive in schools, namely with regard to special education. The students most affected by disproportionality tend to be low income, Black, and Native American youth within the high-incidence disability categories (e.g., emotional and behavioral disorders, learning disabilities, intellectual disability, and speech and language impairments; Kramarczuk Voulgarides, Fergus, & King Thorius, 2017).

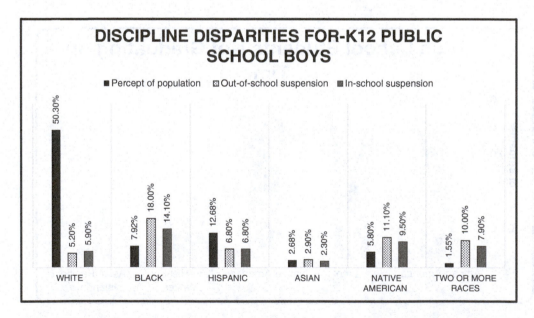

Figure 11.3 Discipline data.

Adapted from *K-12 Education: Discipline disparities for Black students, boys, and students with disabilities* by the United States Government Accountability Office, 2018. Copyright 2018 by the United States Government.

What does this ultimately mean? Students' ability to succeed in school predicts future societal outcomes, with research suggesting that discipline at school can be a student's first point of entry into the school-to-prison pipeline (Irby, 2014; McIntosh, Girvan, Horner, & Smolkowski, 2014). Further, we know the discipline gap is linked to the achievement gap (Gregory, Skiba, & Noguera, 2010) and that high school completion rates and subsequent college-going reflects disproportionality. For example, the high school dropout rate in 2016 was 5.9% for all students and 4.6% for White students, 6.5% for Black students, and 9.2% for Hispanic students (U.S. Department of Commerce, 2016). Further, from 2003 to 2015, the percentage of Asian students and White students who enrolled in college immediately following their high school graduation was consistently higher than the percentage of Black students and Hispanic students. Notably, the percentage of Hispanic students who enrolled in post-secondary education steadily increased in the same time frame (National Center for Education Statistics, 2018).

As you can see from the trends previously described, there are alarming inequities across education, which highlight the need for school counselor awareness and action as they directly and indirectly serve students, through both CSCP and MTSS implementation. Additionally, as school counselors, we have access to provide services to all (Tier 1), some (Tier 2), and few (Tier 3) students, in order to help all students achieve equitable outcomes. Integrating culturally responsive practices into MTSS and CSCP can be a key to changing the data as previously described (e.g., McKinney, Bartholomew, & Gray, 2010) and students' outcomes. In the next section, we will focus a bit more on the role of culture in education systems more generally, as well as providing an overview of culturally responsive educational and counseling practices that can be designed to meet the needs of all students.

Culture and Education

Culture is an individual's ability, gender, sexual orientation, language, race, ethnicity, socioeconomic status, and spirituality (Schellenberg & Grothaus, 2009). Culture is also the learned traditions, principles, and behaviors that are shared by members of the same group (Onwuegbuzie & Frels, 2016). As our society becomes increasingly diverse, we must become more knowledgeable about a multitude of cultures, norms, values, and communication styles, especially those of the stakeholders within our school communities. This extends to aspects of culture outside of race and ethnicity as culture encompasses socioeconomic status, gender, religion, ability, sexuality, language, and trauma history. Using this information, we are better equipped to create a school environment in which all students achieve.

Today, we recognize the importance and need for culturally responsive educational practices, focusing on culturally responsive pedagogy, a term first developed by pioneering scholar Gloria Ladson-Billings (1995). Culturally responsive pedagogy, which is the theory and practice of teaching, focuses on collective empowerment, academic success, cultural competence, and critical consciousness. To effectively implement culturally responsive pedagogy, educators must develop a critical awareness of their roles as agents of change, maintain high expectations for all students, use student-centered and content-driven curriculum, and build meaningful relationships with students, staff, families, and communities (Farinde-Wu, Glover, & Williams, 2017). We use the term *educators* in this section and throughout when referring to all individuals who work in schools, including school counselors.

What Are Culturally Responsive Practices?

Within the educational literature, many terms have been used to describe culturally responsive practices, including "culturally responsible, culture compatible, culturally appropriate, culturally congruent, culturally relevant, and multicultural education" (Harmon, 2012, p. 12). Culturally responsive practices are infused in multiple ways in a variety of school settings for the primary purpose of ensuring an equitable educational experience for all. Cultural responsiveness includes (a) providing all students with effective instruction and adequate resources for learning, (b) using students' cultures and experiences to help them build bridges between their lives and their learning, (c) holding high expectations for all students, and (d) demonstrating care and respect for students (Klingner et al., 2005; Leverson, Smith, McIntosh, Rose, & Pinkelman, 2016). The advancement of culturally responsive practices has been possible only after decades of advocacy, reform, and support. Next, we will describe culturally responsive practices in regards to schools and school counseling.

Culturally Responsive Schools

Educators around the country work to create, implement, and evaluate culturally responsive practices; similarly, researchers have pointed to the following key features of such culturally responsive approaches in schools (Sullivan, 2012; Villegas and Lucas, 2002):

- build relationships with students;
- affirm diversity;
- develop sociocultural consciousness;
- engage in critical reflection;
- promote change in practices and policies;
- commit to ongoing professional learning;
- acknowledge learning needs of all students.

At the core of culturally responsive practice is the idea of *relationship*. To truly be culturally responsive, educators must get to know their students by developing personal connections and a solid foundation of trust and respect. Educators who *affirm diversity* acknowledge, respect, and value differences amongst students, staff, families, and community members. Every student, staff member, family, and community has a unique and complex history and experience that must be recognized and validated. Next, *developing a sociocultural consciousness* requires educators to understand that individuals are influenced by their environment and that context plays a role in behavior. This awareness helps educators avoid ethnocentrism, which occurs when individuals use their own culture as a lens through which to view, and subsequently judge, the cultures of others. School staff members who engage in *critical reflection* consider how one's own culture affects his or her attitude, beliefs, values, behavior, and interpersonal interactions. In order to promote change, educators must support and take ownership of *justifiable change in practices and policies*, especially when inequities are present. Being aware of the impact of school policy on students and being supportive of change that leads to better outcomes for students is critical. Similarly, to reach higher levels of cultural responsiveness, educators must also be *lifelong learners*; they must stay up to date on recent research, sustain their curiosity, and continue to learn about their profession. Lastly, it is important to acquire an *understanding of the diverse learning needs of students*, including the teaching methods that are most effective and the assistance that is most beneficial.

"No significant learning can occur without a significant relationship" (James P. Comer).

As a school counselor, what is your role in helping facilitate positive relationships between students and staff?

What successes or challenges have you had developing relationships with students who are different than you (e.g., race, gender, ethnicity, sexual orientation)?

How can you balance the need for relationships with maintaining high expectations for all students?

Culturally Responsive School Counseling

As you read the section above, you may have considered the connection between culturally responsive education and school counselors' roles. The field of counseling is grounded in multicultural wellness and awareness. For example, Ratts, Singh, Nassar-McMillan, Butler, and McCullough (2015) offer an important framework that can assist counselors in their work with clients (Figure 11.4). The figure outlines the different layers that lead to multicultural and social justice competence: (1) counselor self-awareness, (2) client worldview, (3) counseling relationship, and (4) counseling and advocacy interventions. This relates to the systemic approach described in Chapter 3, focusing on counselor cultural awareness of self and client worldview within the construction of effective counseling relationships and interventions. School counselors are well positioned to encourage culturally responsive strategies within the complex systems in which they work.

Further, ASCA (2015) encourages culturally competent school counselors to work with school and community stakeholders to establish inclusive environments promoting the academic, social/emotional, and career well-being of all students, regardless of background. School counselors are trained and ethically bound to be *culturally competent*, having engaged in assessment of their own identity, recognition of personal biases, and reflection of cultural differences. Finally, school counselors can use their roles as advocates, leaders, and collaborators to create systemic change in schools to meet the social/emotional, academic, and career needs of all students. Culturally competent school counselors foster cultural pluralism and are committed to creating inclusive school communities.

Examine the seven key elements of culturally responsive practice.

What knowledge, skills, or attitudes acquired in your preparation overlap with these elements?

How do you see yourself utilizing your knowledge, skills, and attitudes to create a culturally responsive school environment?

While the suggestions for school counseling cultural responsiveness may feel overwhelming, we have good news! School counselors have frameworks to organize culturally

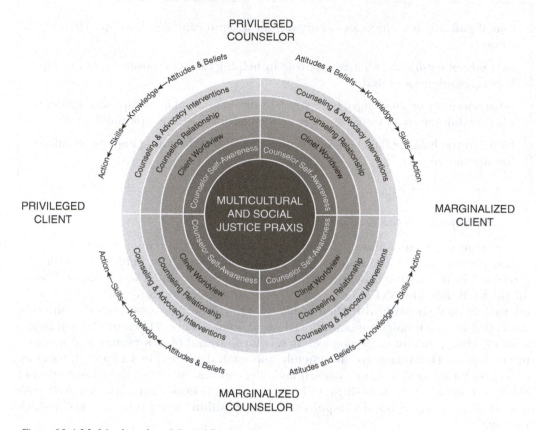

Figure 11.4 Multicultural and Social Justice Counseling Competencies.

From *Multicultural and Social Justice Counseling Competencies* by M. J. Ratts, A. A. Singh, S. Nassar-McMillan, S. K. Butler, & J. R. McCullough. Alexandria, VA: American Counseling Association. Retrieved from: www. counseling.org/docs/default-source/competencies/multicultural-and-social-justice-counseling-competencies. pdf?sfvrsn=8573422c_20. Copyright 2015 by The Multicultural Counseling Competencies Revisions Committee. Reprinted with permission.

responsive efforts. They implement CSCPs to serve the needs of all students and can align these programs with school-wide MTSS (Belser, Shillingford, & Joe, 2016; Goodman-Scott, Betters-Bubon, & Donohue, 2016). Further, school counselors can integrate culturally responsive practices within these systems of support to impact student academic achievement and promote student social/emotional and career development (ASCA, 2018; ASCA, 2015; Bemark & Chung, 2008; Robinson & Roksa, 2016). Culturally competent school counselors utilize school-wide, student-based data to make informed decisions to create universal culturally supportive school climates (Betters-Bubon, Brunner, & Kansteiner, 2016). For example, after disaggregating data collected by their high school, a school counselor may note that 90% of White students are pursuing post-secondary education compared with 71% of African American students and 66% of Hispanic students. This counselor could then examine the root cause of this discrepancy, such as evaluating the academic and career planning process, noting participation across multiple subgroups. Then, the school counselor could collaborate with stakeholders to remedy the situation, such as leading difficult conversations about participation rates, and asking students and parents questions about improving the process.

School counselors are poised to serve as school leaders, infusing cultural responsiveness within their school's MTSS. In the next section, we describe how to fully develop culturally responsive MTSS with a specific focus on how you, the school counselor, can use your knowledge and skills in this work.

Culturally Responsive MTSS

As described in the initial chapters of this book, MTSS encompass both Response to Intervention (RTI) and Positive Behavioral Interventions and Supports (PBIS). Response to Intervention is a multi-tiered approach to providing students with needed academic supports, while PBIS is traditionally known for focusing on student behavior (McIntosh & Goodman, 2016). Recently, the field has begun to address cultural responsiveness within MTSS (e.g., Bal, 2018; Bal, Kozleski, Schrader, Rodriguez, & Pelton, 2014; Fallon, O'Keeffe, & Sugai, 2012; Hernández Finch, 2012; Sugai, O'Keeffe, & Fallon, 2012; Swain-Bradway, Loman, & Vincent, 2014). To be culturally responsive, MTSS must be context-specific and grounded in the needs of the students and community. In addition, cultural responsiveness must be embedded throughout the systems. Our focus is on how school counselors can ensure MTSS implementation is culturally responsive and effective.

As you have read in Chapter 1, outcomes, systems, practices, and data are the foundation of effective MTSS. School counselors are tasked with building academic and behavioral systems in our schools (e.g., problem-solving teams), in which we utilize effective teaching and intervention practices (e.g., small-group counseling). The systems and practices should be guided by the use of data and should lead to more positive academic and behavioral outcomes for students. It is important to note the interconnection between these four elements: a change in practice may influence and be influenced by data, which would lead to changes in outcomes, and so forth.

Consider the importance of outcomes, systems, practices, and data in MTSS.

How do these elements relate to CSCPs? Specifically: what outcomes do school counselors try to impact? What systems do they put in place? What practices do they engage in? What data do they use?

Vincent, Randall, Cartledge, Tobin, and Swain-Bradway (2011; Figure 11.5) have a helpful framework that highlights how to explicitly include cultural responsiveness in elements of MTSS. Their model describes how to intentionally incorporate cultural knowledge, relevance, validity, and equity into the four elements (outcomes, systems, practices, and data) of MTSS previously described. Next, we will look at the culturally responsive components in Vincent and colleagues' (2011) model a bit more closely before moving on to specific examples. As we do so, consider the ways in which these culturally responsive components may be integrated in CSCP.

Cultural equity refers to a focus on social justice for all students, regardless of background. Multi-Tiered Systems of Support should create positive outcomes for all students, and we must examine who succeeds in our schools on a continual basis. Culturally equitable outcomes can only be achieved when many perspectives are included when implementing school-wide initiatives such as MTSS and CSCPs. *Cultural knowledge* is knowing features of specific cultures or ethnic groups whereas *cultural self-awareness* focuses on understanding of self as a cultural being. For MTSS to be culturally responsive, school staff must know students, their backgrounds, and engage in ongoing professional development on topics related to cultural biases. *Cultural relevance* means that we teach students in culturally responsive ways while *cultural validation* means that we make culture visible in the school. Within MTSS, we must know our students and families, help them see their cultures in the school, while engaging in critical reflection about which values and behaviors are expected and taught within the school system. *Cultural validity* involves being sound in our decision making and, within schools, ensuring the data used to make decisions is valid. This includes examining a variety of data sources, and our policies and procedures in light of this data, to make decisions about how and what we teach.

Overall, aspects of culture must be woven into the practices that we implement and the systems we build in schools. We must utilize data in such a way as to identify systems and practices that may not be meeting the needs of students across different cultural backgrounds. Only then can we expect equitable outcomes for students and families. Now that we have examined cultural equity, knowledge, relevance, and validity, we return to Figure 11.5 and focus on examples that integrate these into the outcomes, systems, practices, and data of culturally responsive MTSS. Throughout we will highlight the critical role the school counselor plays in integrating cultural responsivity into both MTSS and CSCPs.

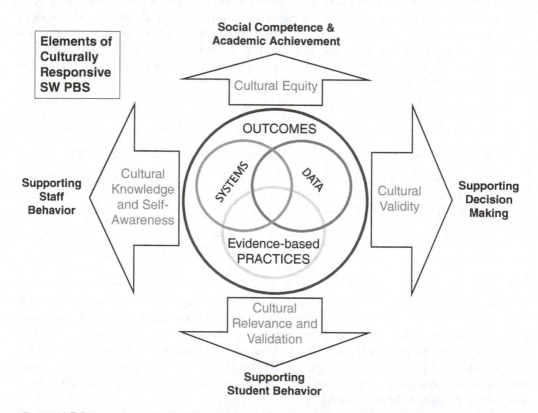

Figure 11.5 Integrating school-wide positive behavior support and culturally responsive practices.

Reprinted from "Toward a conceptual integration of cultural responsiveness and schoolwide positive behavior support" by C. G. Vincent, C. Randall, G. Cartledge, T. J. Tobin, & J. Swain-Bradway, 2011, *Journal of Positive Behavior Interventions, 13*(4), 219–229. Copyright 2011 by Sage Publishing.

As a school counselor, how do you integrate culture into the school initiatives and events?

What are some things school counselors can do to support staff and students who do not see anyone from their same race, religion, ethnicity, or sexual identity in the school building?

Culturally Responsive Outcomes

The overall outcome of MTSS must focus on cultural equity rather than equality, which is demonstrated in Figure 11.6. The first picture shows *equality* as all students are given *the same support*: some students will lose out on watching the game as the supports do not allow them to see over the fence. The second picture represents *equity* as students are given *what they need*: each student now has access to the game because each was given needed supports. To take this one step further, in education we can go beyond providing students with additional supports, to examine and modify the existing system so that *all students have access*. Our belief is that through effective culturally responsive MTSS, we can remove systemic barriers that impact student success.

Tia has been a school counselor for several years, at a school with strong MTSS implementation. She has noticed a trend in bullying and harassment reports. In recent years, data shows an increase in bullying and harassment of students from LGBTQ backgrounds. She looks to school board policy and the school handbook and cannot find any policy that speaks specifically to discriminatory behavior to this group. She approaches the MTSS team to discuss ways in which to approach this inequity.

What are your reactions to this case study, particularly the outcome data?

What potential next steps can you recommend to Tia and the MTSS team?

Unfortunately, the systems existing in schools do not always value, nor are they based on, the removal of barriers for student success. For example, we know PBIS show promise in positively impacting a variety of educational outcomes, including office discipline referrals (Flannery, Fenning, Kato, & McIntosh, 2014) and school climate outcomes (Bradshaw, Koth, Thornton, & Leaf, 2009); however, these programs have not always led to reductions in disparate discipline outcomes for ethnic minority youth (Vincent & Tobin, 2011; Vincent, Swain-Bradway, Tobin, & May, 2011). However, recent case studies reflect that consistent implementation of culturally responsive instruction within a MTSS framework can lead to equitable results (McIntosh, Ellwood, McCall, & Girvan, 2018). Culturally responsive MTSS, then, must reinforce the belief that *all students can excel in school*. Specifically:

Culturally responsive educational systems are grounded in the beliefs that all culturally and linguistically diverse students can excel in academic endeavors when their culture, language, heritage, and experiences are valued and used to facilitate their learning and development, and they are provided access to high quality teachers, programs, and resources. (Klingner, et al., 200, p. 8)

To ensure the outcomes are focused on equity, culturally responsive approaches should be infused throughout the implementation of MTSS. This includes the intentional examination of cultural context and learning history of students, families, faculty, and community members (Bal, 2018; Sugai, O'Keeffe, & Fallon, 2012). The PBIS OSEP Technical Assistance Center created a field guide to help integrate equity efforts into PBIS implementation (Leverson, Smith, McIntosh, Rose, & Pinkelman, 2016). Many of these ideas and practices can be integrated to create equitable MTSS. As such, we will refer to different aspects of this guide throughout the next section (please see the Resources section at the end of the chapter). This guide suggests that rather than augmenting existing MTSS efforts with culturally responsive approaches in an additive manner, cultural responsivity starts with a clear intentional vision for outcomes. Table 11.1 outlines ways to integrate cultural responsiveness throughout MTSS, highlighting school counselors' corresponding roles.

Ryhan is a school counselor in a rural school district. While diversity of skin color is limited in the school population, diversity in social class abounds. As the organizer of her CSCP and a member of the MTSS, she wants to promote self-awareness in staff.

To better help staff understand students and families, Ryhan helps organize a back-to-school event in the community center in the low-income neighborhood rather than at the school. Ryhan knows that interacting with families on neutral territory diminishes the power difference that parents (especially those from low social class) can feel when interacting with staff. She involves key parents from the community to assist in the planning of the event to gain buy in and help spread the word. Parents felt empowered and 95% indicated they would attend another event on Ryhan's event evaluation.

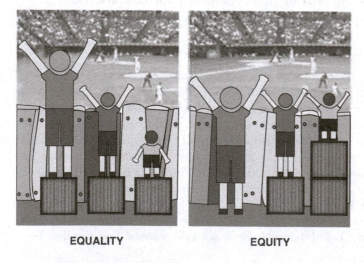

EQUALITY   **EQUITY**

Figure 11.6 Equity and equality.

From *The evolution of an accidental meme* by C. Froehle, 2016. Retrieved from: https://medium.com/@CRA1G/the-evolution-of-an-accidental-meme-ddc4e139e0e4. Reprinted with permission.

Table 11.1 Culturally responsive MTSS elements

MTSS Outcomes Focused on Cultural Equity	School Counselor Role
District and school policies focused on equity. High and achievable expectations that are considerate of context and culture.	Advocate for district- and school-level policies that reflect the needs of the school/community population.

MTSS Systems Grounded in Staff Cultural Knowledge/Self-Awareness	
• Professional development on the culture of students and families. • Active involvement of families in system development. • Commitment among staff to engage in difficult conversations. • Culturally responsive discipline procedures are in place. • The role of explicit and implicit bias in school discipline processes and academic support is examined.	• Utilize cultural self-awareness assessments with school staff and students. • Provide opportunities for teachers to learn about student cultures/families. • Include parents and community members on MTSS, equity, and CSCP teams. • Create and lead professional development on the role that bias plays in schools. • Take an active role in the school climate/discipline committee.

MTSS Practices That Lead to Cultural Relevance and Validation	
• Behavioral expectations and academic content are taught in ways that reflect student experience. • Positive interaction and high expectations highlighted in schools. • Cultural diversity affirmed in the school.	• Ensure behavioral expectations and school counseling curriculum are taught in culturally responsive ways. • Highlight cultures of the students in universal practices and events. • Assist teachers in the evaluation of their classrooms to ensure culturally responsive practices are in place.

MTSS Data-Based Decision Making Grounded in Cultural Validity	
• Academic and behavioral data is disaggregated and reviewed regularly. • Interventions targeted to impact disproportionate outcomes. • Culturally responsive tools are utilized in the problem solving/decision making processes. • CR-PBIS and CR-RTI instruments are used to assess fidelity.	• Regularly examine and disaggregate data from CSCP and school-wide. • Regularly drill down into data; conduct Root Cause Analysis to determine possible reasons for disproportionality in data. • Conduct CSCP and Tier 2/3 interventions (e.g., small groups) that impact disproportionate outcomes. • Monitor fidelity of MTSS implementation across all tiers.

Note: See also: Sugai, O'Keeffe, & Fallon, 2012; McIntosh, Girvan, Horner, & Smolkowski, 2014.

School Counselor Role in MTSS/CSCP Outcomes

To truly create inclusive school and community environments, ASCA advises school counselors to advocate for student equity and access to opportunities, as well as help low-income and culturally diverse students and their families overcome systems of oppression and social injustice that may hinder student achievement (ASCA, 2015). For example, school counselors, alongside the MTSS leadership team, can examine state testing and dropout rates for students in the district and look for potential equity issues that impact these outcomes, such as disproportionate discipline referrals, access to transportation to and from school, etc. Further, the ASCA School Counselor and Equity for All Students Position Statement (2012) encourages school counselors to recognize student differences and advocate for equitable treatment to rid schools of obstacles that can hinder the development and achievement of our students. Again, along with the MTSS team, we need to promote school policies that encourage the academic achievement of all students, regardless of demographics, such as gender, income, social class, ethnicity, sexual orientation, ability, religion, language, or trauma history (ASCA, 2012; ASCA, 2016a; ASCA 2016b). Culturally responsive systems, then, are created to support these policies and vision. We describe how to create systems grounded in these outcomes in the next section.

Culturally Responsive Systems

While Chapter 3 of this book focused on creating systems of support within Tier 1, our focus will include a focus on integrating cultural responsiveness across all tiers. Culturally responsive school and system-level change must include input from school and community stakeholders. For example, the MTSS leadership team should include multiple perspectives from different school professionals (e.g., support staff, general education teachers, special education teachers, specialist teachers, administration, students, etc.) as well as families and the community. Without diverse voices, MTSS practices may accentuate the dominant culture in the school to the exclusion of many students and families. For example, Fraczek (2010) documented the experiences of non-native English speakers in a PBIS middle school, noting that students felt they needed to fit into a predominantly White culture that was emphasized through the use of PBIS.

How do you engage multiple perspectives in systems change? Some schools have had success utilizing 'Learning Labs', equity teams, and other parent involvement efforts (Bal et al., 2014; Bal, Thorien, & Kozleski, 2012; Kourea, Lo, & Owens, 2016). Learning Labs include a regular time and space in which parents, community members, and those traditionally marginalized from school-based decisions engage in dialogue and collaboration with school staff and researchers (Bal et al., 2014). The groups define the goals, the overarching cause of disproportionality, and how to best change faulty systems in the school. Integrating these types of opportunities for family engagement can enhance educators' understanding, while creating a space for the voices of all stakeholders involved in students' lives (Bal et al., 2012). This approach has been found successful across levels, including high school (Bal, Afacan, & Cakir, 2018). This approach requires intentional engagement and inclusion of families, and the PBIS network published a parent engagement document outlining specific ways to create meaningful family involvement (see Weist, Garbacz, Lane, & Kincaid, 2017 and the Resources section). For successful family–school partnerships to occur, school staff must approach families with openness and authenticity, honoring the norms and culture of the community, presuming positive intentions while building sincere, honest, and genuine relationships (Garbacz, Witte, & Houck, 2017). Doing this necessarily requires cultural knowledge and self-awareness, which we discuss more fully next.

In what ways can school staff establish culturally responsive family–school partnerships to support school-wide systems?

What are strategies that work to engage families? What might get in the way of true partnership?

Cultural Knowledge

One way to impact the cultural responsiveness of a system is by increasing staff cultural knowledge. School staff cannot effectively suggest or provide impactful counseling and educational interventions without first understanding the student and his or her world (i.e., culture). Attending courses, training, and professional development can help school staff expand cultural knowledge, understand new terminology, and gain insight into the values of specific groups. Beyond training, school staff must get to know students and their families, as well as the surrounding school community. One strategy that some schools are embracing is the use of home visits. While once reserved for specialized school staff (e.g., school counselors, school social workers), home visits by teachers have led to increased home–school connection for students (Garbacz et al., 2017). Acknowledging the diversity that exists within the school is one of the first steps to create a culturally inclusive system of support.

Cultural Self-Awareness

Fostering cultural self-awareness within and among staff is key to working with students from diverse backgrounds. In fact, it is often the first step in helping staff develop relationships with students who are different from them. Implicit or unconscious bias, the unconscious attitudes or stereotypes that affect our actions and decisions (Greenwald & Banaji, 1995; Staats, 2014), is a critical concept that has recently been brought to the forefront of education research. Unconscious bias often impacts how school staff perceive and interpret behavior, which then leads to cultural misunderstandings and subsequent 'discipline' problems. For example, teachers may misinterpret overlapping speech, often known as the 'call-response' pattern within African American communities, as being disruptive (Weinstein, Tomlinson-Clarke, & Curran, 2004). A student might then be sent to the office, which situates the problem within the student rather than within the system. Additionally, a wide array of research has begun to examine 'vulnerable decision points' that may influence which students may need interventions (Girvan et al., 2017; McIntosh, Girvan, Horner, & Smolkowski, 2014; Smolkowski, Girvan, McIntosh, Nese, & Horner, 2016). Only through examination of our own mindsets can we recognize how our own cultural views impact these many decision points and, ultimately, student outcomes.

The School Counselor Role in MTSS /CSCP Systems

School counselors can promote cultural knowledge and awareness through CSCP and MTSS implementation. For example, school counselors are well versed in creating needs assessments and thus might include questions about student and family culture. For example, questions could include: "What language do you speak at home?" "List three of your family traditions," and "How is your home culture similar or different from the school culture?" The results could then be used within the CSCP and MTSS frameworks.

A needs assessment could lead to new knowledge about different cultures in the school, which then could assist the MTSS team and the school counseling program create a welcoming, inclusive, and affirmative school environment (ASCA, 2015; Schellenberg & Grothaus, 2009).

With knowledge and training in sociocultural concepts, school counselors can provide in-service training and workshops to school staff regarding bias, cultural practices, and educational equity. In addition, we can lead difficult conversations about race with staff, family, and students. For example, research suggests that "addressing racial disparities requires addressing race" (Carter, Skiba, Arredondo, & Pollock, 2017, p. 12). With a background in group process, school counselors can help facilitate these conversations. For example, we can facilitate staff participation in a Privilege Walk that focuses on social class, difference, and privilege. Finally, we can bring disaggregated data to meetings and encourage reflective conversations about which students are succeeding and which are being left behind, and the reasons for the discrepancies.

School counselors can and must walk alongside our teachers in self-awareness activities. That means we must engage in our own self-assessments, do a 'gut-check' and explore personal beliefs and implicit biases regarding working with diverse populations (ASCA, 2015). If we do not identify our own biases, we may end up practicing "colorblind school counseling" or counseling practices that ignore student racial, ethnic, and cultural differences (Smith, Geroski, & Tyler, 2014). Individuals who use colorblind counseling techniques may think "I don't see color" when working with others from diverse backgrounds, believing that he or she is being open, fair, and accepting with students (Smith et al., 2014). This inaccurate and harmful practice promotes equal, rather than equitable, treatment of students and reinforces subtle racism, microaggressions, and bias. Please refer to Table 11.1 for additional ways to impact culturally responsive systems.

Think for a moment about a school you know well and reflect on the following questions:

Is there a shared responsibility for educating all students?

Are there opportunities for professional development focused on cultural knowledge and self-awareness?

Are teachers and school staff forming collaborative relationships with diverse students and families?

Are staff taking a truly expansive view of diversity (e.g., beyond skin color)?

Is there a clear process in place for addressing instances of racial slurs, disproportionality, and cultural insensitivity within behavioral systems?

By answering yes to the previous questions, school counselors can be confident that universal systems are culturally responsive.

Culturally Responsive Practices

We have described how to create systems of support that focus on equitable outcomes. Culturally responsive MTSS must also include specific practices that ensure students' cultures are validated and teaching approaches are culturally relevant. These practices are directly related to the description of culturally relevant practices described earlier in the chapter, in that they should (a) include a cultural lens for viewing behavioral norms and academic learning, (b) minimize cultural mismatches in behavioral expectations and academic instruction, and (c) affirm the diversity found within the school environment (Banks & Obiakor, 2015; Xu & Drame, 2008). In other words, we must look at what we teach both in terms of academics and behavior to ensure that there is common ground and understanding of all, while acknowledging the diversity of our students and families.

How do we create culturally responsive practices? First, and as mentioned previously, we need to know the students and families in the school community. Second, we need to understand what instructional and behavioral practices work (which are evidence-based) and find out who they work for and in what contexts (Cunningham & Fitzgerald, 1996). Third, we need to analyze if the practices we are utilizing are aligned with the backgrounds and beliefs of our students and families. Let's look at an example to clarify. Typical PBIS programs focus on the creation of a common set of universal school-wide expectations. This practice is known to have a positive impact on school climate. At the same time, these expectations must be culturally and contextually relevant and align with the student population, which can only happen via input from a diverse group of school staff, family, and community members. For instance, a school in Canada with a large Indigenous population did just that. They created the Golden Rules (*Have Positive Goals, Respect Yourself, Respect Others, Respect Your School and the Environment,* and *Ask for Help when You Need It*) in conjunction with the elders and community members to honor the diverse students and the community in which the school was situated (McIntosh, Moniz, Craft, Golby, & Steinwand-Deschambeault, 2014). The school team went beyond knowing the students and community to include their beliefs and voices in the creation of the school expectations and subsequent practices. Figure 11.7 shows another example of a school that incorporated the voices of the community. In this case the school expectations were created with Apsaalooke community and tribal members. The first teaching activity at the end of this chapter allows you further time to examine school expectations.

The practices used to teach the school-wide behavioral expectations should build on prior knowledge, be meaningful, culturally relevant, and take into consideration both student and teacher characteristics (García & Ortiz, 2008). Some MTSS teams have students help create lesson plans, raps, and school videos to communicate the values and expectations to all students. Other schools have included parent voices in the teaching process. For example, Kourea et al. (2016) interviewed African American parents to get examples of behavioral expectations that teachers then wove into their classroom lessons, thus integrating students' lived experiences into the school. The *PBIS cultural responsiveness field guide* contains many other helpful examples of how to teach specific behavioral expectations, define classroom procedures, and provide feedback/acknowledgment that are culturally responsive and inclusive of different voice (Leverson et al., 2016). Additionally, research has found that staff who use culturally responsive proactive practices are able to "get ahead" of negative behavior and provide school-wide consistency (Goodman-Scott, Hays, & Cholewa, 2018).

Finally, all school-to-home communication related to the school expectations and MTSS in general should be in families' native languages to promote family engagement. School counselors and other school staff should consider inclusive ways of engaging in parent communication, whether via text, personal phone messages, or home visits (Betters-Bubon & Schultz, 2018). Having translators available during school conferences, meetings (i.e., IEP, 504), and other events helps to bridge the cultural gap that often exists between schools and families.

Figure 11.7 Culturally responsive school expectations.

Reprinted with permission from the Apsaalooke Community and Mr. Jason Cummins, tribal member and Crow Agency Public School Principal.

The School Counselor Role in MTSS/CSCP Practices

School counselors can do many things to ensure that diversity is affirmed and celebrated in the school environment as part of both MTSS and their CSCP; several examples are listed above. In addition, first and foremost, school counselors can take the lead in helping all understand diversity. For example, as part of a universal strategy to teach students about culture, a school counselor could conduct 1st grade classroom lessons on the different types of families. A high school counselor might collaborate with the health teacher to show the film *Babies* in the 9th grade health class, as they simultaneously complete a sex education course. Facilitating a discussion after the movie could help students process their thoughts and feelings regarding cultural observations they noticed within the film, as well as awareness of their own culture. Likewise, school counselors can critically assess different Tier 1 programs to ensure cultural relevance. For example, we can facilitate thoughtful discourse with school staff and families about school expectations and beliefs about behavior, e.g., what does respect mean to us? To our students and families? (For example, Betters-Bubon et al., 2016.) When coordinating a career day, school counselors should be mindful to include a diverse range of occupations and to invite community members who represent the entire student population, as well as representation from a range of education levels, social class memberships, genders, racial/ethnic identities, etc. For instance, invite professionals from all 16 career clusters who have different post-secondary education, who work in different neighborhoods, and who are from diverse backgrounds. This could help expose students to a variety of professions held by a range of individuals. As a result, students may learn beneficial skills and validate their cultural identities, particularly from having community members with cultural similarities visibly present within the school building.

Further, school counselors can consult with teachers to create culturally responsive classrooms. A number of forms are listed in the chapter's Resources section, and each allows the teacher to assess his or her classroom in terms of culturally responsive practices. For example, the Double Check Assessment (Hershfeldt et al., 2009) asks teachers to rate their reflective thinking about children and their group membership (e.g., "I understand culture and why it is important") and reflection (e.g., "I encourage positive interactions"). This assessment goes beyond awareness to facilitate reflection on effective communication (e.g., "I consistently communicate high expectations"), connection to curriculum ("My instruction contains exemplars from the backgrounds of my students"), and sensitivity to student's culture ("recognize students' social and political consciousness"). School counselors can then work with teachers to create more culturally inclusive classroom practices through the collaborative and consultative relationships.

Culturally Responsive Data Analysis

Culturally responsive MTSS include data analysis that leads to culturally valid decision-making. This means MTSS leadership teams must disaggregate data, such as academic, discipline, and college/career data, to determine which students are succeeding and which students are being left behind. Chapter 9 outlines effective data use in MTSS and CSCP, so our focus in this chapter is on the assurance that decisions are valid and based on the related equitable outcomes. One excellent resource is *Using data within SWPBIS to identify and address disproportionality: A guide for school teams* (McIntosh et al., 2014). This manual offers a four-step process by which to analyze outcome, system, practice, and interventions. The steps include: (1) Problem Identification, (2) Problem Analysis, (3) Plan Implementation, and (4) Plan Evaluation. Within culturally responsive approaches, MTSS teams must first examine whether a problem exists, analyze the level at which the problem occurs, determine a way to intervene, and then evaluate the actions.

Within each step, MTSS teams should assess outcomes for disproportionality. One easy way to do this is to disaggregate data by different subgroups (e.g., ethnicity, gender, grade level, etc.) and compare that with the population in a school. To further analyze the data, Risk Indexes and Risk Ratios can be used. The Risk Index determines the percent of the group that receives a certain outcome, while the Risk Ratio compares the index with a comparison group. A Risk Ratio of greater than 1 suggests a group is overrepresented in a given category, while less than 1 suggests underrepresentation. Many excellent tools have been created that allow teams to enter information about their student population and academic/behavioral data, and then calculates Risk Indices and Ratios (see: www.wisconsinpbisnetwork.org/educators/pbis-in-action/risk-ratio.html; Green et al., 2015). Also, please review the second teaching activity at the end of this chapter and the associated figures and analysis questions.

In addition to examining disproportionality, data analysis must also consider the fidelity of MTSS implementation. Again, Chapter 9 provides a comprehensive overview of the tools that individuals can use to assess how well the systems and structures within

MTSS are functioning (e.g., MATT, SAS). In addition, it is important to utilize tools that help school staff consider both culture and equity. For example, the Midwest PBIS network created a culturally responsive schoolwide Self-Assessment (www.midwestpbis. org/materials/special-topics/equity). This tool helps the MTSS team examine how culture is integrated into and across the tiers of support. For example, for items such as "Tier 1 team membership is representative of the cultural groups of the school and community" and "Use evidence-based practices that are effective for use with staff and students from varied cultural backgrounds," the team will indicate *in place, partially in place* or *not in place*. A second tool, the Modified Tiered Fidelity Inventory Walkthrough Tool, published by Leverson, Smith, McIntosh, Rose and Pinkelman (2016), includes a walkthrough of the school to assess staff and student understanding of the school rules and acknowledgment system. The focus is on including a representative group of students and staff.

The School Counselor Role in MTSS/CSCP Data Analysis

School counselors are trained and ready to facilitate culturally responsive conversations around school data. School counselors can utilize existing discipline and achievement data to examine areas of need and possible disparities based on student demographics (e.g., race/ethnicity, sexual orientation, SES, gender identity, and disability status; Carter et al., 2017).

School counselors are also ready to facilitate difficult conversations related to students who do not respond to universal/Tier 1 academic and behavioral supports. For example, sometimes educators' focus can rest solely on student behaviors, rather than focusing on the teacher behavior and/or overall classroom environment (Harris-Murri, King, & Rostenberg, 2006). Culturally valid decisions must include sociocultural factors (e.g., student cultural and linguistic backgrounds, teacher background) that impact a student's academic or behavioral success. For instance, García and Ortiz (2008) suggest that when assessing a student for a potential learning disability, we might examine factors such as teacher qualifications, aspects of instruction, as well as student characteristics (see Table 11.2). As such, decision making moves beyond a focus on the student level to include environmental factors that might impact student success.

School counselors can help assess the relevance of the chosen interventions by utilizing cultural responsiveness checklists within the intervention planning process. This includes asking questions about how the student's family has been involved, and

Table 11.2 Additional factors that influence learning or behavioral problems in school

Teacher	Qualifications, experience, track record, teaching style, expectations, perceptions, instruction, and behavioral management.
Instruction	Motivation, sequence instruction (teacher, reteach, teach prerequisite skills), language of instruction, effective teaching behaviors, coordination with other programs.
Evaluation of Instruction	Standards, ongoing data collection, modification based on evaluation, staff development.
Exposure to Curriculum	Continuity of exposure, domains, scope and sequence, students' entry level, basic skills, higher cognitive skills, mastery, practice.
Student	Experiential background, language proficiency, cultural characteristics, cognitive/learning style, socioeconomic status, locus of control, modes of communication, self-concept, motivation.

Note: Adapted from García & Ortiz (2008).

whether extenuating circumstances may be impacting the student (e.g., trauma, life stressors, absences, student language, SES, etc.). School counselors can speak to the intersection of trauma and cultural responsiveness to help problem-solving teams to see the full picture of students' lives. The Resource list at the end of the chapter includes checklists/assessments school counselors can present within the problem-solving process to ensure that culture is adequately discussed and that culturally valid decisions are made.

Case Study

The following case study brings together many elements that relate to the creation of culturally responsive MTSS and CSCPs.

Karen is a middle school counselor in a suburban school of 500 students that is becoming increasingly diverse. The suburb had a population of approximately 10,000 residents. The student demographics included 50% Caucasian, 28% Hispanic, 10% African American, 10% Native American and 2% Asian American.

Culturally Responsive Outcomes

As part of her CSCP, Karen disaggregated discipline data and noted a disproportionately high number of Hispanic and African American students who were referred for office discipline referrals (ODRs). This data was particularly striking for students in 6th grade. Prior to 6th grade, students whose primary language is Spanish were in two-way immersion programs. The district had not yet extended that program to the middle school setting. Also, when examining district outcome data from the local high school, Karen saw inequitable academic outcomes for student graduation rate. Please see the figures below for data on both referrals and graduation trends.

Culturally Responsive Systems

Karen had a strong CSCP in place and was integral in the creation of a MTSS leadership committee at her school. The leadership team included school representatives such as classroom teachers, special teachers (e.g., music), support staff (e.g., educational and classroom assistants), special education teachers, student support staff (e.g., psychologist, social worker), administrators, along with family and community representatives. The team included members that mirrored the school demographics, meeting on a monthly basis to discuss data, student behaviour, and school-wide supports. The school counselor led a 6th grade leadership group and discussed decisions/ideas with them as well.

Culturally Responsive Data

Karen shared the discipline and referral data during the MTSS leadership team meeting; the team examined the disproportionate outcomes. To better understand

(continued)

(continued)

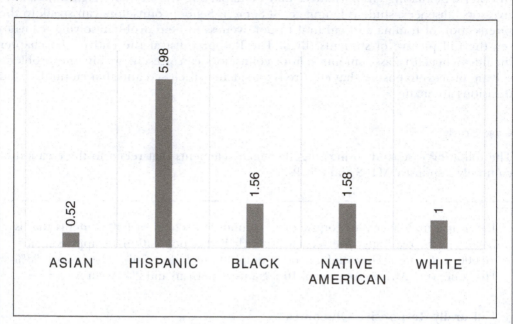

Figure 11.8 Risk Ratio for office discipline referrals
(Source: the Author.)

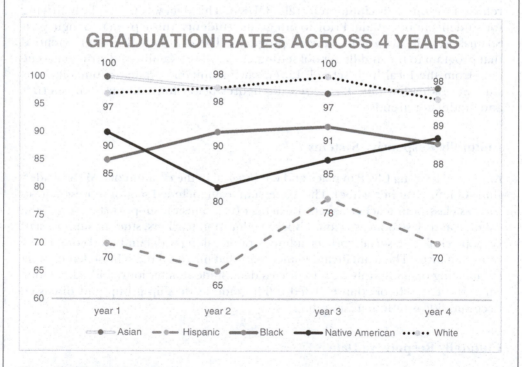

Figure 11.9 Graduation rates
(Source: the Author.)

the root cause behind the disproportionality in the referrals and graduation rates, the team decided to engage in learning more about the nature of the problem (see the list below), after which they created a plan outlining what practices they wanted to implement to address the problems.

- Surveying staff about behavioral expectations.
- Talking to focus groups of students about behavioral expectations as well as academic/career expectations and outcomes.
- Informally and formally talking with families about behavior and future career planning and expectations.
- Observing 6th grade classrooms/hallways/lunches.
- Meeting with high school counselors/school staff to discuss graduation trends and drop-out rates across all student groups.

Culturally Responsive Practices

Only after having a full understanding of the problem did the staff move forward with implementing practices. They decided that their interventions needed to take place at the system and individual levels to include:

- Re-teaching school expectations and reinforcing positive behavior more consistently across the building, and starting with 6th graders; more posters in the 6th grade hallway outlining expectations.
- Relationship building in 6th grade classrooms, focused on those between students and between students and staff; the team created lessons that teachers could deliver during their advisory periods.
- Staff development on developmental and cultural needs of adolescents, including culturally responsive classroom practices (e.g., student voice and choice, opportunities to respond).
- Student counseling groups for students with consistent records of classroom difficulty—focused on emotion regulation.
- More focused academic and career planning conferences with Hispanic families. Some of these took place in the neighborhood center closer to where many parents lived.

The changes did not happen overnight. In fact, the changes in practice were implemented over a two-month period. The MTSS leadership team collected data throughout the process, monitoring ODR data after the lessons and expectations were taught, and they found a significant reduction. Staff were able to provide feedback on their learning after the staff development presentation. The school counselor collected pre/post data from students who were involved in the small group. Many members of the school community, including staff, students, and families, were involved in the problem-solving and solution-finding process. Without a MTSS, these interventions would have not been as easy to implement. Without a team, the problem-solving process would not have happened.

(continued)

(continued)

As you consider the case study, which aspects of the systemic change process would have been most difficult for you?

How can you challenge yourself and your future colleagues to see the big picture and create systems that support all students?

What's one small thing you think you can do right now that will make the greatest impact?

Conclusion

School counselors can serve as leaders, advocates, and collaborators in creating culturally responsive MTSS and CSCPs to best impact student outcomes. Multi-Tiered Systems of Support is an intentional approach grounded in cultural equity. As such, culturally competent school counselors must challenge the status quo, make necessary school-wide changes to benefit all students (Bemark & Chung, 2005), and, through advocacy, eliminate classroom, school, and/or district policies impeding educational equity. With the understanding of the impact a student's culture has on his or her academic and behavioral performance, school counselors can work to create culturally relevant practices (e.g., school-wide expectations, discipline responses). In conjunction with administrators and MTSS leadership teams, they equip staff with necessary knowledge about their cultures and students' cultures, while ensuring that decisions made at the systems level are examined with a cultural lens. They utilize data to impact the achievement and opportunity gap, all while building relationships.

Students come to us with various academic, mental, and social/emotional needs. This chapter focused on specific ways in which you, as a current or future school counselor, can create systems of support that meet the needs of *all* students. With intentional focus on creating culturally responsive systems, school counselors can ensure they are fulfilling the purpose of education. While there is much work to be done, have hope: research suggests that school administrators and staff feel ready to take on the integration of culturally responsive efforts (Avant, 2016; Fallon, O'Keeffe, Gage, & Sugai, 2015). Only through these efforts can we be sure that the words of John Dewey are realized, that we "give the young the things they need in order to develop in an orderly, sequential way into members of society" (1934, p. 12).

For more information and a school counselor's perspective on *Culturally Responsive MTSS: Advocating for Equity for Every Student* please see Chapter 12 "Voices from the Field," Voices 1, 6, and 8.

ASCA Ethical Standards

School counselors have an ethical obligation to create school-wide systemic change by removing student barriers to success. This means that school counselors are well versed in cultural responsiveness and how to integrate it into MTSS and CSCP. With training in social-cultural topics, school counselors are situated to provide leadership in the difficult conversations that can take place around issues related to diversity, discrimination, and disproportionality. In addition, the role school counselors hold in the school allows them to create positive and meaningful relationships with parents, helping them to engage in their child's education and participate in the CSCP/MTSS system planning. Further, school counselors can serve as models to all staff on how to treat all students, regardless of background, in equitable ways. They can utilize culturally inclusive language and ensure that all students have opportunity and access in the school system. In particular, the most recent ASCA Ethical Standards (2016c) outline a number of ethical imperatives that align with culturally responsive practice. Specifically, school counselors:

A   Responsibility to Students

A.1 Supporting Student Development

- A.1.a. Have a primary obligation to the students, who are to be treated with dignity and respect as unique individuals.
- A.1.f. Respect students' and families' values, beliefs, sexual orientation, gender identification/expression and cultural background and exercise great care to avoid imposing personal beliefs or values rooted in one's religion, culture, or ethnicity.

A.10 Underserved and At-Risk Populations

- A.10.a. Strive to contribute to a safe, respectful, nondiscriminatory school environment in which all members of the school community demonstrate respect and civility.
- A.10.d. Collaborate with parents/guardians, when appropriate, to establish communication to ensure students' needs are met.
- A.10.e. Understand students have the right to be treated in a manner consistent with their gender identity and to be free from any form of discipline, harassment, or discrimination on their gender identity or gender expression.

B   Responsibilities to Parents/Guardians, School, and Self

B.1   Responsibilities to Parents/Guardians

- Respect the rights and responsibilities of custodial and noncustodial parents/guardians and, as appropriate, establish a collaborative relationship with parents/guardians to facilitate students' maximum development.

B.2 Responsibilities to the School

- B.2.d. Provide leadership to create systemic change to enhance the school.
- B.2.e. Collaborate with appropriate officials to remove barriers that may impede the effectiveness of the school or the school counseling program.
- B.2.i. Advocate for equitable school counseling program policies and practices for all students and stakeholders.
- B.2.j Strive to use translators who have been vetted or reviewed and bilingual/multilingual school counseling program materials representing languages used by families in the school community.
- B.2.k. Affirm the abilities of and advocate for the learning needs of all students. School counselors support the provision of appropriate accommodations and accessibility.

- B.2.m. Promote cultural competence to help create a safer more inclusive school environment.
- B.2.o. Promote equity and access for all students through the use of community resources.
- B.2.p. Use culturally inclusive language in all forms of communication.
- B.2.q. Collaborate as needed to provide optimum services with other professionals such as special educators, school nurses, school social workers, school psychologists, college counselors/ admissions officers, physical therapists, occupational therapists, speech pathologists, administrators.

Resources

Further Reading

Grothaus, T., & Johnson, K. F. (2012). *Making diversity work: Creating culturally competent school counseling programs.* Alexandria, VA: American School Counselor Association.

Hammond, Z. (2015). *Culturally responsive teaching & the brain.* Thousand Oaks, CA: Sage.

McIntosh, K., Barnes, A., Eliason, B. & Morris, K. (2014). *Using discipline data within SWPBIS to identify and address disproportionality: A guide for school teams.* Technical Assistance Center on Positive Behavioral Interventions and Supports (funded by the Office of Special Education Programs, U.S. Department of Education). Eugene, OR: University of Oregon. Retrieved from: www.pbis.org/Common/Cms/files/pbisresources/PBIS_Disproportionality_Data_Guidebook.pdf.

Singleton, G. E. & Linton, C. (2006). *Courageous conversations about race.* Thousand Oaks, CA: Corwin Press.

Wisconsin RTI Center/Wisconsin Department of Public Instruction (2017). *Wisconsin's framework for equitable Multi-Level Systems of Support.* Retrieved from: www.wisconsinrticenter.org/assets/files/resources/1516404144_2018%20RtI%20WI%20Framework%20for%20Equitable%20Multi%20Level%20Systems2_compressed.pdf.

Wisconsin RTI Center/Wisconsin PBIS Network (n.d.). *Equitable classroom practices self-assessment.* Retrieved from: www.wisconsinrticenter.org/assets/files/Universal%20Reading/Day%203/3.04%20Equitable%20Classroom%20Practices%20Self%20Assessment.pdf.

Websites

Links to the following can be found on our eresource at www.routledge.com/9781138501614.

- Checklist for culturally responsive practices.
- Equity resources.
- Building culturally responsive systems resources.
- PBIS resources for equity.
- Multi-Tiered Systems of Support for English Learners.

Teaching Activity 1

Do an internet search to find typical school rules and expectations. Once you find them discuss the rules in small groups and answer the following:

1   What values are generally emphasized?
2   Are the rules and expectations communicated in a positive, culturally responsive language?
3   What behaviors are considered as positive or negative? Are these reflective of a particular group of individuals?
4   How will you know that you have developed school-wide expectations that are culturally meaningful for all students and their communities?
5   How do you ensure that behavioral expectations are taught in ways that are culturally connected?

Teaching Activity 2

Consider the following scenario: Tige is a school counselor in a district with an enrollment of 1,600 students. He examines the Risk Ratio data for suspensions and reading scores and brings them to the Tier 1 MTSS team for analysis. After examining Figures 11.10 and 11.11, discuss the questions below.

What does the disaggregated data say about students?

Is implementation of MTSS benefitting all groups of students (gender, ethnicity, race, SES) equally?

Based on what you know about creating systems of support, how would you drill deeper to evaluate the potential cause (think back to the Root Cause Analysis described in Chapter 9)? How can the school counselor work as part of the MTSS team to implement interventions across the tiers?

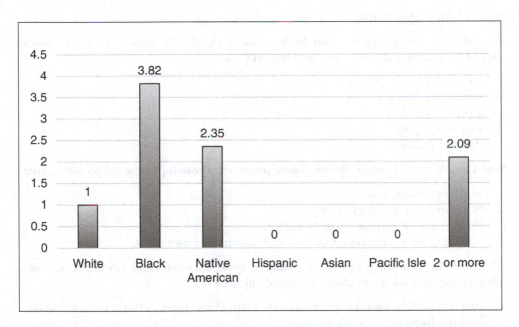

Figure 11.10 Sample Risk Ratio data for student suspension.

Adapted from "Risk Ratio calculator" by the Wisconsin PBIS network. Retrieved from: www.wisconsinpbis network.org/educators/pbis-in-action/risk-ratio.html.

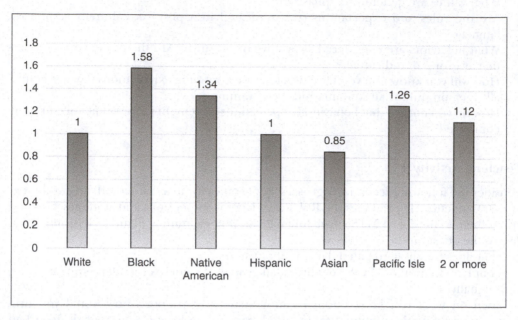

Figure 11.11 Sample Risk Ratio data for student reading assessment.

Adapted from "Risk Ratio calculator" by the Wisconsin PBIS network. Retrieved from: www.wisconsinpbis network.org/educators/pbis-in-action/risk-ratio.html.

Multiple Choice Questions

1   **According to the model created by Vincent et al. (2011), which of the following should be intentionally incorporated into MTSS?**

    a   Cultural knowledge.
    b   Cultural relevance.
    c   Cultural validity.
    d   Cultural equity.
    e   All of the above.

2   **When implementing culturally responsive practices, whose input should be considered?**

    a   Only staff members.
    b   Students and staff members.
    c   Students, staff members, and families.
    d   Students, staff members, families, and community members.

3   **Which of the following strategies would be most effective and culturally sensitive when trying to learn more about students' culture?**

    a   Ask the student and their parents to tell you about their culture, their traditions, and the holidays they celebrate.
    b   Google students' cultures and read online articles about people from that culture.
    c   Regularly interact with the students and ask them typical non-invasive questions about their experiences at appropriate times.
    d   Consult with one of your friends who has the same culture as your students and ask them many questions about their upbringing.

4   **A group of students, who identify as sexual minorities, enter your office and are upset with a teacher who used a derogatory word during class when referring to individuals who do not identify as heterosexual. What would the best approach be to solve the situation?**

    a   Tell the students that there is nothing that can be changed as the teacher is tenured and has worked in the school for many years.

    b   Tell an administrator about the situation and let him or her handle it.

    c   Hold a meeting with the teacher and students and mediate their conversation so that understanding on both sides can be sought.

    d   Excuse those students from that teacher's class for the remainder of the week.

5   **Disproportionality:**

    a   Is not a problem in public schools today.

    b   Is a problem in public but not private schools.

    c   Refers to over/under representation of a group of students in discipline categories.

    d   Is the over- or under-representation of a specific group (e.g., gender, race) in an educational category, program, or service in comparison with the group's proportion in the overall population.

Answers: Q1 e, Q2 d, Q3 a, Q4 c, Q5 d.

References

American School Counselor Association (ASCA) (2012). *ASCA position statement: The school counselor and equity for all students.* Alexandria, VA: Author. Retrieved on August 15, 2007 from: www.schoolcounselor.org.

American School Counselor Association (ASCA) (2015). *ASCA position statement: The school counselor and cultural diversity.* Alexandria, VA: Author. Retrieved on August 15, 2007 from: www.schoolcounselor.org.

American School Counselor Association (ASCA) (2016a). *The school counselor and LGBTQ youth.* Alexandria, VA: Author. Retrieved August 31, 2017 from: www.schoolcounselor.org.

American School Counselor Association (ASCA) (2016b). *The school counselor and transgender/gender-nonconforming youth.* Alexandria, VA: Author. Retrieved August 31, 2017 from: www.schoolcounselor.org.

American School Counselor Association (ASCA) (2016c). *ASCA ethical standards for school counselors.* Alexandria, VA: Author.

American School Counselor Association (ASCA) (2018). *ASCA position statement: The school counselor and multitiered system of supports.* Alexandria, VA: Author. Retrieved on August 12, 2018 from: www.schoolcounselor.org.

Avant, D. W. (2016). Using Response To Intervention/Multi-Tiered Systems of Supports to promote social justice in schools. *Journal for Multicultural Education, 10*(4), 507–520.

Bal, A. (2018). Culturally responsive Positive Behavioral Interventions and Supports: A process–oriented framework for systemic transformation. *Review of Education, Pedagogy, and Cultural Studies, 40*(2), 144–174, doi: 10.1080/10714413.2017.1417579.

Bal, A., Afacan, K., & Cakir, H. I. (2018). Culturally responsive school discipline: Implementing Learning Lab at a high school for systemic transformation. *American Educational Research Journal, 55*(5), 1–44, doi.org/10.3102/0002831218768796.

Bal, A., Kozleski, E. B., Schrader, E. M., Rodriguez, E. M., & Pelton, S. (2014). Systemic transformation from the ground–up using Learning Lab to design culturally responsive schoolwide positive behavioral supports. *Remedial and Special Education, 35*(6), 327–339, dx.doi: 10.1177/0741932514536995.

Bal, A., Thorien, K., & Kozleski, E. (2012). Culturally responsive Positive Behavior Support matters. *What Matters brief.* Tempe, AZ: The Equity Alliance at Arizona State University. Retrieved from: www.equityallianceatasu.org/sites/default/files/CRPBIS_Matters.pdf.

Banks, T., & Obiakor, F. E. (2015). Culturally responsive positive behavior supports: Considerations for practice. *Journal of Education and Training Studies, 3*(2), 83–90, doi.org/10.11114/jets.v3i2.636.

Belser, C. T., Shillingford, M. A., & Joe, J. R. (2016). The ASCA model and a Multi-Tiered System of Supports: A framework to support students of color with problem behavior. *The Professional Counselor, 6,* 251–262, doi: 10.15241/cb.6.3.251.

Bemark, F., & Chung, R. C.-Y. (2005). Advocacy as a critical role for urban school counselors: Working toward equity and social justice. *Professional School Counseling, 8*(3), 196–202.

Bemark, F., & Chung, R. C.-Y. (2008). New professional roles and advocacy strategies for school counselors: A multicultural/social justice perspective to move beyond the nice counselor syndrome. *Journal of Counseling & Development, 86,* 372–381, doi.org/10.1002/j.1556-6678.2008.tb00522.x.

Betters-Bubon, J., Brunner, T., & Kansteiner, A. (2016). Success for all? The role of the school counselor in creating and sustaining culturally responsive PBIS programs. *The Professional Counselor, 6*(3), 263–277, doi: 10.15241/jbb.6.3.263.

Betters-Bubon, J., & Schultz, J. (2018). School counselors as social justice leaders: An innovative school-family-community based partnership with Latino students and families. *Professional School Counseling, 21*(1b), 1–11, doi: 10.1177/2156759X18773601.

Bradshaw, C. P., Koth, C. W., Thornton, L. A., & Leaf, P. J. (2009). Altering school climate through school-wide Positive Behavioral Interventions and Supports: Findings from a group-randomized effectiveness trial. *Prevention Science, 10*(2), 100, doi.org/10.1007/s11121-008-0114-9.

Bryan, J., Day-Vines, N. L., Griffin, D., & Moore-Thomas, C. (2012). The disproportionality dilemma: Patterns of teacher referrals to school counselors for disruptive behavior. *Journal of Counseling & Development, 90*(2), 177–190.

Carter, P. L., Skiba, R., Arredondo, M. I., & Pollock, M. (2017). You can't fix what you don't look at: Acknowledging race in addressing racial discipline disparities. *Urban Education, 52*(2), 207–235, doi.org/10.1177/0042085916660350.

Cunningham, J. W., & Fitzgerald, J. (1996). Epistemology and reading. *Reading Research Quarterly, 31*(1), 36–60.

Darling-Hammond, L. (2007). Third annual Brown lecture in education research—The flat earth and education: How America's commitment to equity will determine our future. *Educational Researcher, 36*(6), 318–334, dx.doi.org/10.3102/0013189X07308253.

Dewey, J. (1934). Individual psychology and education. *The Philosopher, 12*(1), 1–6.

Donovan, S., & Cross, C. (2002). *Minority students in special and gifted education.* Washington, DC: National Academy.

Fallon, L. M., O'Keeffe, B. V., Gage, N. A., & Sugai, G. (2015). Brief report: Assessing attitudes toward culturally and contextually relevant schoolwide positive behavior support strategies. *Behavioral Disorders, 40*(4), 251–260, doi.org/10.17988/0198-7429-40.4.251.

Fallon, L. M., O'Keeffe, B. V., & Sugai, G. (2012). Consideration of culture and context in school-wide positive behavior support: A review of current literature. *Journal of Positive Behavior Interventions, 14*(4), 209–219, dx.doi.org/10.1177/1098300712442242.

Farinde-Wu, A., Glover, C. P., & Williams, N. N. (2017). It's not hard work; it's heart work: Strategies of effective, award-winning culturally responsive teachers. *Urban Review: Issues and Ideas in Public Education, 49*(2), 279–299, doi.org/10.1007/s11256-017-0401-5.

Flannery, K. B., Fenning, P., Kato, M. M., & McIntosh, K. (2014). Effects of school-wide Positive Behavioral Interventions and Supports and fidelity of implementation on problem behavior in high schools. *School Psychology Quarterly, 29*(2), 111–124, dx.doi.org/10.1037/spq0000039.

Fraczek, M. (2010). Perpetuating a culture of White behavior: The experiences of non-native speaking Hispanic students in a PBIS school (Doctoral dissertation, Boston College University Libraries). Retrieved from ProQuest Dissertations and Theses (3397846).

Froehle, C. (2016, April 14). *The evolution of an accidental meme.* Retrieved from: https://medium.com/@CRA1G/the-evolution-of-an-accidental-meme-ddc4e139e0e4#.6sim0it5w.

Garbacz, S. A., Witte, A. L., & Houck, S. N. (2017). Family engagement foundations: Supporting children and families. In M. D. Weist, S. A. Garbacz, K. L. Lane, & D. Kincaid (Eds), *Aligning and integrating family engagement in Positive Behavioral Interventions and Supports (PBIS): Concepts and strategies for families and schools in key contexts.* Center for Positive Behavioral Interventions and Supports (funded by the Office of Special Education Programs, U.S. Department of Education). Eugene, OR: University of Oregon Press. Retrieved from: www.pbis.org/Common/Cms/files/pbisresources/Family%20Engagement%20in%20PBIS.pdf.

García, S. B., & Ortiz, A. A. (2008). A framework for culturally and linguistically responsive design of response-to-intervention models. *Multiple Voices For Ethnically Diverse Exceptional Learners, 11*(1), 24–41.

Girvan, E. J., Gion, C., McIntosh, K., & Smolkowski, K. (2017). The relative contribution of subjective office referrals to racial disproportionality in school discipline. *School Psychology Quarterly, 32*(3), 392–404, dx.doi.org/10.1037/spq0000178.

Goodman-Scott, E., Betters-Bubon, J., & Donohue, P. (2016). Aligning Comprehensive School Counseling Programs and Positive Behavioral Interventions and Supports to maximize school counselors' efforts. *Professional School Counseling, 19*, 57–67.

Goodman-Scott, E., Hays, D. G., & Cholewa, B. (2018). "It takes a village:" A case study of Positive Behavioral Interventions and Supports implementation in an exemplary middle school. *The Urban Review, 50*(1), 97–122, doi:10.1007/s11256-017-0431-z.

Green, A. L., Nese, R. N. T., McIntosh, K., Nishioka, V., Eliason, B., & Canizal Delabra, A. (2015). *Key elements of policies to address discipline disproportionality: A guide for district and school teams.* OSEP Technical Assistance Center on Positive Behavioral Interventions and Supports (funded by the Office of Special Education Programs, U.S. Department of Education). Eugene, OR: University of Oregon. Retrieved from: www.pbis.org/Common/Cms/files/pbisresources/PBIS%20Disproportionality%20Policy%20Guidebook%202016-7-24.pdf.

Greenwald, A. G., & Banaji, M. R. (1995). Implicit social cognition: Attitudes, self-esteem, and stereotypes. *Psychological Review, 102*(1), 4–27.

Gregory, A., Skiba, R. J., & Noguera, P. A. (2010). The achievement gap and the discipline gap: Two sides of the same coin? *Educational Researcher, 39*(1), 59–68, doi.org/10.3102/0013189X09357621.

Harmon, D. A. (2012). Culturally responsive teaching through a historical lens: Will history repeat itself? *Interdisciplinary Journal of Teaching & Learning, 2*(1), 12–22.

Harris-Murri, N., King, K., & Rostenberg, D. (2006). Reducing disproportionate minority representation in special education programs for students with emotional disturbances: Toward a culturally responsive response to intervention model. *Education and Treatment of Children, 29*, 779–799.

Hernández Finch, M. E. (2012). Special considerations with response to intervention and instruction for students with diverse backgrounds. *Psychology in the Schools, 49*(3), 285–296, doi.org/10.1002/pits.21597.

Hershfeldt, P. A., Sechrest, R., Pell, K. L., Rosenberg, M. S., Bradshaw, C. P., & Leaf, P. J. (2009). Double-Check: A framework of cultural responsiveness applied to classroom behavior. *TEACHING Exceptional Children Plus, 6*(2), Article 5. Retrieved from: www.jhsph.edu/research/centers-and-institutes/center-for-prevention-of-youth-violence/field_reports/Article.pdf.

Irby, D. (2014). Trouble at school: Understanding school discipline systems as nets of social control. *Equity & Excellence in Education, 47*(4), 513–530, dx.doi.org/10.1080/10665684.2014.958963.

Klingner, J. K., Artiles, A. J., Kozleski, E., Harry, B., Zion, S., Tate, W., Durán, G. Z., & Riley, D. (2005). Addressing the disproportionate representation of culturally and linguistically diverse students in special education through culturally responsive educational systems. *Education Policy Analysis Archives, 13*(38), 1–40. Retrieved August 30, 2017 from: http://epaa.asu.edu/epaa/v13n38.

Kourea, L., Lo, Y. Y., & Owens, T. L. (2016). Using parental input from Black families to increase cultural responsiveness for teaching SWPBS expectations. *Behavioral Disorders, 41*(4), 226–240, doi.org/10.17988/bedi-41-04-226-240.1.

Kramarczuk Voulgarides, C., Fergus, E., & King Thorius, K. (2017). Pursuing equity: Disproportionality in special education and the reframing of technical solutions to address systemic inequities. *Review of Research in Education, 41*(1), 61–87, doi.org/10.3102/00917 32X16686947.

Ladson-Billings, G. (1995). But that's just good teaching! The case for culturally relevant pedagogy. *Theory Into Practice, 34*(3), 159–165, dx.doi.org/10.1080/00405849509543675.

Leverson, M., Smith, K., McIntosh, K., Rose, J., & Pinkelman, S. (2016). *PBIS cultural responsiveness field guide: Resources for trainers and coaches.* OSEP Technical Assistance Center on Positive Behavioral Interventions and Supports (funded by the Office of Special Education Programs, U.S. Department of Education). Eugene, OR: University of Oregon. Available from: www.pbis.org.

McIntosh, K., Ellwood, K., McCall, L., & Girvan, E. (2018). Using discipline data to enhance equity in school discipline. *Intervention in School and Clinic, 53*(3), 146–152.

McIntosh, K., Girvan, E. J., Horner, R. H., & Smolkowski, K. (2014). Education not incarceration: A conceptual model for reducing racial and ethnic disproportionality in school discipline. *Journal of Applied Research on Children: Informing Policy for Children at Risk, 5*(2), 4.

McIntosh, K., Girvan, E. J., Horner, R. H., Smolkowski, K., & Sugai, G. (2014). *Recommendations for addressing discipline disproportionality in education.* OSEP Technical Assistance Center on Positive Behavioral Interventions and Supports (funded by the Office of Special Education Programs, U.S. Department of Education). Eugene, OR: University of Oregon. Retrieved from: https://nces.ed.gov/nationsreportcard/pubs/studies/2009455.aspx.

McIntosh, K., & Goodman, S. (2016). *Integrated Multi-Tiered Systems of Support: Blending RTI and PBIS.* New York: Guilford.

McIntosh, K., Moniz, C., Craft, C. B., Golby, R., & Steinwand-Deschambeault, T. (2014). Implementing school-wide Positive Behavioural Interventions and Supports to better meet the needs of Indigenous students. *Canadian Journal of School Psychology, 29*(3), 236–257, http://dx.doi.org/10.1177/0829573514542217.

McKinney, E., Bartholomew, C., & Gray, L. (2010). RTI and SWPBIS: Confronting the problem of disproportionality. *Communique, 38*(6), 227–238.

Mittleman, J. (2018). Sexual orientation and school discipline: New evidence from a population-based sample. *Educational Researcher, 47*, 181–190.

National Center for Education Statistics (2018). Immediate college enrollment rate. Washington, DC: Author. Retrieved on May 6, 2018 from: https://nces.ed.gov/programs/coe/indicator_cpa.asp.

Onwuegbuzie, A. J., & Frels, R. (2016). *Seven steps to a comprehensive literature review: A multimodal and cultural approach.* London: Sage.

Ratts, M. J., Singh, A. A., Nassar-McMillan, S., Butler, S. K., & McCullough, J. R. (2015). *Multicultural and Social Justice Counseling Competencies.* Alexandria, VA: American Counseling Association. Retrieved from: www.counseling.org/docs/default-source/competencies/multicultural-and-social-justice-counseling-competencies.pdf?sfvrsn=20.

Robinson, K., & Roksa, J. (2016). Counselors, information, and high school college-going culture: Inequities in the college application process. *Research in Higher Education, 57*(7), 845–868, doi: 10.1007/s11162-016-9406-2.

Schellenberg, R., & Grothaus, T. (2009). Promoting cultural responsiveness and closing the achievement gap with standards blending. *Professional School Counseling, 12*, 440–449.

Skiba, R. J., Horner, R. H., Chung, C. G., Rausch, M. K., May, S. L., & Tobin, T. (2011). Race is not neutral: A national investigation of African American and Latino disproportionality in school discipline. *School Psychology Review, 40*(1), 85.

Skiba, R. J., Michael, R. S., Nardo, A. C., & Peterson, R. L. (2002). The color of discipline: Sources of racial and gender disproportionality in school punishment. *The Urban Review, 34*(4), 317–342.

Smith, L. C., Geroski, A. M., & Tyler, K. B. (2014). Abandoning colorblind practice in school counseling. *Journal of School Counseling, 12*, 1–31.

Smolkowski, K., Girvan, E. J., McIntosh, K., Nese, R. N., & Horner, R. H. (2016). Vulnerable decision points for disproportionate office discipline referrals: Comparisons of discipline for African American and White elementary school students. *Behavioral Disorders, 41*(4), 178–195, doi.org/10.17988/bedi-41-04-178-195.1.

Staats, C. (2014). *Implicit racial bias and school discipline disparities: Exploring the connection.* Columbus, OH: Kirwan Institute for the Study of Race and Ethnicity. Retrieved from: http://kirwan institute.osu.edu/wp-content/uploads/2014/05/ki-ib-argument-piece03.pdf.

Sugai, G., O'Keeffe, B. V., & Fallon, L. M. (2012). A contextual consideration of culture and schoolwide positive behavior support. *Journal of Positive Behavior Interventions, 14,* 197–208, doi. org/10.1177/1098300711426334.

Sullivan, A. L. (2012). Culturally responsive practice. In A. L. Noltemeyer & C. S. McLoughlin (Eds), *Disproportionality in education and special education* (pp. 181–198). Springfield, IL: Charles C. Thomas, Publisher.

Swain-Bradway, J., Loman, S. L., & Vincent, C. G. (2014). Systematically addressing discipline disproportionality through the application of a school-wide framework. *Multiple Voices for Ethnically Diverse Exceptional Learners, 14*(1), 3–17.

The Annie E. Casey Foundation (2017). *2017 KIDS COUNT data book: State trends in child well-being.* Baltimore, MD: Author. Retrieved from: www.aecf.org/resources/2017-kids-count-data-book.

U.S. Department of Commerce (2016). *Census Bureau Current Population Survey (CPS), October, 1967 through 2015* [data file]. Washington, DC: Author. Retrieved from: https://nces.ed.gov/programs/digest/d16/tables/dt16_219.70.asp?current=yes.

United States Government Accountability Office (2018). *K-12 Education: Discipline disparities for Black students, boys, and students with disabilities* (Report No. GAO-18-258). Washington DC: Author. Retrieved from: www.gao.gov/products/GAO-18-258.

Villegas, A. M., & Lucas, T. (2002). Preparing culturally responsive teachers: Rethinking the curriculum. *Journal of Teacher Education, 53*(20), 20–32, doi.org/10.1177/0022487102053001003.

Vincent, C. G., Randall, C., Cartledge, G., Tobin, T. J., & Swain-Bradway, J. (2011). Toward a conceptual integration of cultural responsiveness and schoolwide positive behavior support. *Journal of Positive Behavior Interventions, 13*(4), 219–229, dx.doi.org/10.1177/1098300711399765.

Vincent, C. G., Swain-Bradway, J., Tobin, T. J., & May, S. (2011). Disciplinary referrals for culturally and linguistically diverse students with and without disabilities: Patterns resulting from school-wide positive behavior support. *Exceptionality, 19*(3), 175–190, dx.doi.org/10.1080/09362835.2011.579936.

Vincent, C. G., & Tobin, T. J. (2011). The relationship between implementation of school-wide positive behavior support (SWPBS) and disciplinary exclusion of students from various ethnic backgrounds with and without disabilities. *Journal of Emotional and Behavioral Disorders, 19*(4), 217–232, doi.org/10.1177/1063426610377329.

Weinstein, C. S., Tomlinson-Clarke, S., & Curran, M. (2004). Toward a conception of culturally responsive classroom management. *Journal of Teacher Education, 55*(1), 25–38.

Weist, M. D., Garbacz, S. A., Lane, K. L., & Kincaid, D. (2017). *Aligning and integrating family engagement in Positive Behavioral Interventions and Supports (PBIS): Concepts and strategies for families and schools in key contexts.* Center for Positive Behavioral Interventions and Supports (funded by the Office of Special Education Programs, U.S. Department of Education). Eugene, OR: University of Oregon Press. Retrieved from: www.pbis.org/Common/Cms/files/pbisresources/Family%20Engagement%20in%20PBIS.pdf.

Whitford, D. K., Katsiyannis, A., & Counts, J. (2016). Discriminatory discipline: Trends and issues. *NASSP Bulletin, 100*(2), 117–135, doi.org/10.1177/0192636516677340.

Xu, Y., & Drame, E. (2008). Culturally appropriate context: Unlocking the potential of response to intervention for English language learners. *Early Childhood Education Journal, 35*(4), 305–311, doi.org/10.1007/s10643-007-0213-4.

12 Voices from the Field

At the heart of MTSS are the school staff who design and implement systems that help them to serve the students in their schools. Their passion for working smarter (not harder) is central to their success, in order to provide a quality education in a positive environment. Thus, we have devoted this chapter to school counselors' firsthand accounts of designing and implementing MTSS in their schools. Each author has volunteered to share their perspective on the benefits and challenges to approaching their work utilizing the three tiers of intervention, and the reasons that their team elected to move to this systemic approach. We also have one school counselor who speaks specifically to universal mental health screening within the context of MTSS; you can find his contribution at the end of this chapter. Our intent is to demonstrate the lived experience of school counselors implementing MTSS in elementary, middle, and high schools in urban, suburban, and rural school districts in the U.S. We hope reading their stories will help inform your work as a school counselor as you develop and support MTSS to benefit your students and school community.

VOICE 1

Katie: Elementary School Counselor, Illinois

Why Did Your School Elect to Implement PBIS/MTSS?

I work at a K-8 school in an urban setting with 900 students in grades preschool through eighth grade. Collectively, between our student body and families, our school population speaks at least 25 different languages and we have a large population of recent immigrants from all over the world. Around 94% of our students receive free or reduced lunch. I am the only counselor in my school so I service students in all grade levels. My school had been implementing PBIS/MTSS when I started as a school counselor. We continued because *it gave staff a common language to speak to students*, and established school-wide behavior expectations for all locations of the building.

How Has It Impacted Your Work/Role as a School Counselor?

The PBIS/MTSS have impacted my role as a counselor because *I now view all of the counseling work I do through the three-tiered model*. I attended a district professional development where we sorted our counseling services into the 3 Tier Model below, according to the American School Counselor Association Domains (academic, social/emotional, career).

Tier 1 Implementation/Sustainability

As I mentioned, the school had a solid foundation for PBIS/MTSS. *The PBIS/MTSS team had already developed many Tier 1 strategies, establishing school-wide behavior expectations for different locations of the school and an incentive program to reward students following the stated behavior expectations.* Additionally, the team regularly reviewed school-wide data to determine focus areas of the school climate and culture. For example, the team would examine which locations of the school had the most discipline referrals to determine if school routines should be retaught or modified to decrease behavior incidents.

As the school counselor, I am the coordinator of the Tier 1 PBIS/MTSS team. My responsibilities include assigning meeting roles to members (facilitator, note taker, motivator, and time keeper), relaying meeting information to our school administration, and helping the PBIS/MTSS team determine our school year focus based on our district culture/climate assessment and our school's social/emotional level rating. As the only counselor in the school, almost every task I complete related to PBIS/MTSS is a team effort and includes a high level of collaboration with other staff in the building. We are lucky to have a team of talented teachers and dedicated administrators and try to assign tasks based on team members' areas of strength.

Each year, our PBIS/MTSS team gives a *Staff Refresher Presentation* during the beginning of the year professional development. The purpose of this is to introduce new staff members to our school-wide expectations and systems, and present relevant school culture and climate data points to staff. We also have a PBIS/MTSS Kick-Off Assembly for students within the first weeks of school to teach our school-wide expectations and our incentive program. Teachers on the committee and myself design the format and content, and lead these school-wide kick-off assemblies (we have three divided up by grades). Throughout the year, we have PBIS/MTSS "spirit weeks" to reinforce the school-wide expectations. Each day during spirit week aligns with an expectation. For example, to highlight our school's value of "citizenship" we have a pajama day with a slogan of "Great citizens dream big."

Another Tier 1 intervention I implement is a Community Resource Fair for families. We host the fair twice a year—during our Back to School Bash in September and during our Parent–Teacher Conference Night in April. *We invite multiple agencies in our neighborhood that can provide resources to our families. The agencies provide support or assistance in the areas of medical support, academic tutoring, immigration help, legal assistance, and mental health.*

Tier 2 Implementation/Sustainability

As the school counselor, I also take a leadership role in establishing and maintaining Tier 2 group counseling interventions. I collaborate with the school social worker and school psychologist to determine the types of small groups. We examine students' needs based on school-wide data and conversations with staff members including teachers, administrators, and recess monitors. Once we decide what Tier 2 group interventions to implement, we provide pre-surveys and pretests for the teachers to complete on involved students, which give us knowledge of students' skills. We also send home consent forms to families which explain the intervention. The social worker and I planned and co-facilitated each group session. Following the group, we had teachers complete post-surveys on student skills and then compared the pre- and post-data to measure student progress. In addition, I reviewed the attendance and grades of each student who participated in a Tier 2 group to document growth. Groups were all research-based interventions; our school district provided training and curriculum for these groups.

Tier 3 Implementation/Sustainability

Our main Tier 3 social/emotional support is provided by an outside agency. *Community therapists come to our school three–four days per week to provide individual therapy to students* that have been recommended by teachers. *As the school counselor, I serve as the liaison between the community counseling agency and our staff and families.* I help staff members determine which students would be appropriate candidates for counseling and assist them with filling out the referral forms. I ensure that the community therapists have a confidential space in our school building to meet with students. I meet regularly with the outside agency to discuss the progress of the students and discuss any other logistics. I also refer families to different community agencies including food pantries, family therapy centers, immigration resources, and medical clinics.

What Outcomes Have You Noticed?

A key benefit of implementing PBIS/MTSS at the Tier 1 level is that it establishes school-wide behavior expectations. *Any staff member can speak to any student in the school using a common language about positive behavior* in the hallways, bathrooms, cafeteria, playground, and lunchroom. Additionally, PBIS/MTSS at Tier 1 gives our staff chances to reward and praise our students. Our school has "CARES Cards" that staff members can give to students when they are "caught" following the school-wide expectations. Students can redeem these cards for prizes in their classrooms and at our end of the year "CARES Fair." These positive interactions happen not only between the homeroom teacher and their students, but also with security guards, enrichment teachers, clerks, and other staff and students. Staff members are encouraged to give students specific praise using the language of the behavior matrix such as "thank you for walking in line at Volume 0." Students feel acknowledged and happy when they are rewarded with a CARES Card. There are also no "surprises" on how students should behave in different settings of the building since students are familiar with expectations. This past school year our school was rewarded with an "Exemplary" Social/Emotional Learning Status by our district. Implementing PBIS/MTSS was a crucial element leading to this status.

There are positive outcomes with the Tier 2 work we do as well. I work with a co-leader to facilitate Tier 2 group counseling interventions including Social Skills Group Intervention (SS Grin) and Structured Psychotherapy for Adolescents Responding to Chronic Stress (SPARCS). The district offered training, curriculum, and supplies in these research-based interventions. We share results from the groups with our administrators and personnel from the district who rate our school's Social/Emotional Learning (SEL) Status on our School Report Card. Ratings on a School Report Card for SEL Status range from Emerging to Exemplary. We categorize the results from counseling groups according to BAG Data: Behavior, Attendance, and Grades. For example, Figures 12.1 and 12.2 show outcome data from our Social Skills Group Intervention with students in 3rd and 4th grade. We had a SS Grin group in the fall and spring, and each were co-ed, utilizing The Social Skills Achieved Learning Questionnaire (ALQ) as a teacher pre- and post-test measure. See Figures 12.1 and 12.2 for behavior and academic results from students who participated in SS Grin.

The two graphs below (Figure 12.3 and Figure 12.4) show data from our SPARCS Group Intervention completed with 6th and 7th grade students. The group was co-ed and met for 16 sessions. The first graph shows student attendance with number of absences from each semester. The second graph shows the math grades from 2nd to 4th quarter for students who participated in SPARCS.

How Did You Handle the Challenges You Encountered with Implementation?

Two of the most significant challenges of implementing MTSS are lack of time and availability of mental health professionals to collaborate with. I am the only counselor for approximately 900 students in preschool through eighth grade. At our school, we have a social worker assigned 2.5 days per week and a psychologist assigned 2 days per week. Many Tier 2

Outcome Data – SS Grin (3rd & 4th): Behavior

ALQ for Social Skills

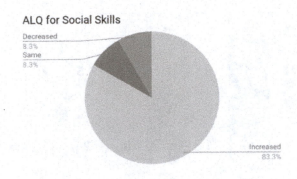

Decreased
8.3%
Same
8.3%

Increased
83.3%

Achieved Learning
Questionnaire
for Social Skills
(Higher is better)

- Completed by Teacher

- 10/12 students who participated in SS
  Grin Groups during SY 16-17
  increased their score on the ALQ
  (teacher reported increased social
  skills)

Figure 12.1 Elementary school behavior outcome data.

Outcome Data – SS Grin (3rd & 4th): Academics

Reading Grades for SS Grin Students

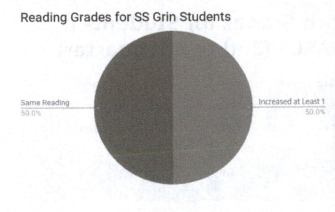

Same Reading
50.0%

Increased at Least 1
50.0%

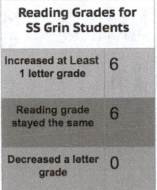

Reading Grades for SS Grin Students	
Increased at Least 1 letter grade	6
Reading grade stayed the same	6
Decreased a letter grade	0

Figure 12.2 Elementary school academic outcome data.

counseling groups require two clinicians to lead them, so we have to schedule all of our group sessions and schedule planning meetings on days that they are present in the building. As a school counselor, I maintain a detailed daily on-line calendar that I use to track my time and share this with the administrators. I have my entire day scheduled with lessons and meetings in an effort to have a proactive counseling program. Many times, there is a type of mental health crisis in our building that needs the attention of a school clinician. *On the days I am the only mental health professional in the building, I have to stop my pre-planned MTSS-related activities and attend to the crisis.* This happens several times per year. For example, last school year I completed over 20 risk assessments for students, which usually take the entire school day. This affects the fidelity of the implementation of MTSS interventions because they are not implemented consistently.

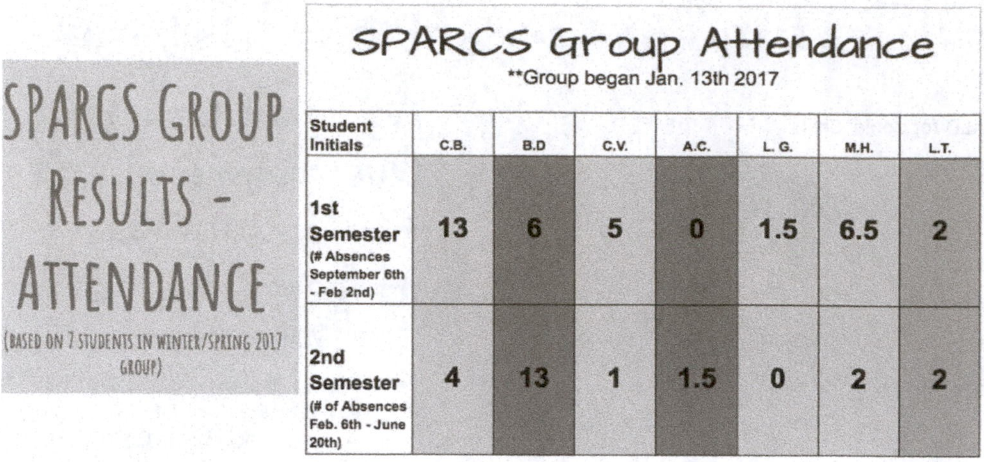

SPARCS GROUP RESULTS - ATTENDANCE

(BASED ON 7 STUDENTS IN WINTER/SPRING 2017 GROUP)

SPARCS Group Attendance
**Group began Jan. 13th 2017

Student Initials	C.B.	B.D	C.V.	A.C.	L. G.	M.H.	L.T.
1st Semester (# Absences September 6th - Feb 2nd)	13	6	5	0	1.5	6.5	2
2nd Semester (# of Absences Feb. 6th - June 20th)	4	13	1	1.5	0	2	2

Figure 12.3 Elementary school SPARCS group attendance data.

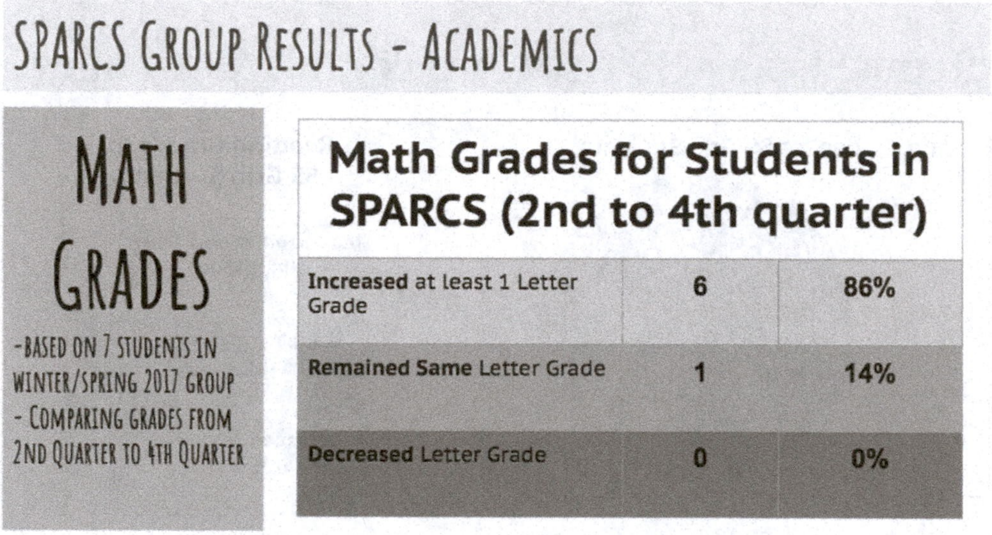

SPARCS GROUP RESULTS - ACADEMICS

MATH GRADES

-BASED ON 7 STUDENTS IN WINTER/SPRING 2017 GROUP
- COMPARING GRADES FROM 2ND QUARTER TO 4TH QUARTER

Math Grades for Students in SPARCS (2nd to 4th quarter)

Increased at least 1 Letter Grade	6	86%
Remained Same Letter Grade	1	14%
Decreased Letter Grade	0	0%

Figure 12.4 Elementary school academic outcome data.

VOICE 2

Renee: Elementary School Counselor, Montana

Why Did Your School Elect to Implement PBIS/MTSS?

The state of Montana mandated that any school wishing to continue with Comprehensive School and Community Treatment (CSCT) services must have implementation of a school-wide positive behavior and supports program. The CSCT is an on-site school-based mental health program provided by outside agencies and funded by Medicaid or private insurance. The mandate came as a result of the need for more appropriate referrals for these programs. Rather than making referrals for students with behavior problems, the state leadership wanted assurance that we would approach barriers to learning in different ways so that students with true mental health needs would be served through CSCT.

Our school administration resisted implementation of what we call Montana Behavioral Initiative (MBI; another phrase for PBIS/MTSS), until the state issued this mandate for health services.

What Outcomes Have You Noticed?

The most positive outcome for me as a school counselor has been that now our entire MBI team and staff recognize the need for positive behavioral supports. Those supports are no longer relegated only to the counseling program, as in the past. We have a universal language for students and staff and *all* are held accountable for safety, respect, and responsibility. *The PBIS/MTSS has also given validation to what I have been doing for over a decade in the school counseling program. The staff understand why I run new student groups (Tier 2 intervention) and give out a Respect Award (recognition for positive behavior).* It has given context to everything we do as school counselors. The special education teacher in our school recently attended her first PBIS/MTSS conference and her first response was, "Wow, it totally makes me appreciate what you (the school counselor) have been doing all these years!"

How Has It Impacted Your Work/Role as a School Counselor?

Now school counselors aren't the only ones responsible for the emotional well-being of the students. After attending training, staff understand how important it is to treat each student with dignity and respect, and realize this is expected. But it hasn't always been that way. Teachers were allowed to bully students and use intimidation tactics to "make" the students behave. This, of course, put me at odds with teachers who did that! Everyone is on the same page now with regard to communicating respectfully and it feels like we are much more of a team.

One of the hardest things for me to implement regarding the ASCA National Model was the data piece. This was in many ways because our school was not "data conscious." I have had a new Principal every two to three years, and each one had a different system for tracking discipline, and some didn't track at all. There was no consistency. The PBIS/MTSS has empowered us to develop systems that will exist regardless of who is the administrator, thus enabling us to use data consistently.

I have also seen that the adoption of PBIS/MTSS has empowered not only the school counselors but other staff members to be leaders in different areas. It feels less autocratic and more democratic. This has created a much more creative and positive work environment and I think everyone is doing a better job as an educator as a result.

What Advice Would You Give Pre-Service School Counselors About PBIS/MTSS as They Prepare to Enter the Workforce and Collaborate on School-Wide Efforts?

Embrace it! It makes so much sense and is a wonderful compliment to the ASCA National Model. When everyone is using data, serving all kids, and being intentional about providing supports for each student, you have a great school! Also, be a leader in PBIS/MTSS efforts and promote it in your school. You are the heart of the program and are providing supports within all three tiers, so you should be a strong voice in the effort.

VOICE 3

Rebecca: Elementary School Counselor, North Carolina

Why Did Your School Elect to Implement PBIS/MTSS?

I first began my work in RTI (Response to Intervention) in the early 2000s as a school counselor at a large urban elementary school. I was the Student Support Team (SST) coordinator for my school and the district disseminated information about RTI through the SST. At the beginning, SST was reliant on the classroom teacher to refer students for areas of need. If a teacher didn't like doing paperwork, or felt they knew what was best for the child, a student might get overlooked by the team. At the end of the school year, we created a list of students who might need support the following year. We called this a "watch list" and grade-level Professional Learning Communities (PLCs) would check in on their "watch list" monthly to make sure students were making adequate growth. As our team worked to improve our academic processes, we realized that our behavior processes needed some work.

The SST group worked with our PBIS/MTSS group to create a Behavior Support Team (BST). The PBIS/MTSS group had created a solid foundation for Tier 1 behavioral support in our building. We taught school-wide rules and bi-annual lessons on expectations, such as showing videos and skits to teach expected behaviors in different areas of the school. In addition, we had a school-wide system where classes could earn compliments for positive behavior around the building.

We also needed to look at interventions. We created a functional BST referral form where teachers would describe the behavior and the functions of behavior. The teacher was required to meet with the counselor for a consultation before going to the BST. Once at the BST, the team would have already reviewed the referral to maximize problem solving. On the BST *we had representation from K-2, 3–5, a specialist teacher, along with the counselor, psychologist, and social worker.* Because the ideas came from other teachers, the referring teacher was more open to implementing the ideas.

Copies of the behavior plan created in the meeting were given to any teacher who worked with that student and kept on file in the counselor's office. We also asked that teachers call parents before and after the meeting to keep them informed on the interventions.

What Outcomes Have You Noticed?

We were able to decrease behavior referrals to the office overall and create a more positive school climate, which was reflected in our state working conditions survey and student surveys. One of our primary goals was to decrease the number of minor behavior referrals from one year to the next. We targeted students who received minor referrals for the same behavior four or more times. Over time, we saw a reduction in those targeted behaviors. As the counselor, we are often viewed as the "behavior experts" in our buildings. However, some counselors have very little training or expertise in behavior. I took a Functional Behavioral Assessment/Behavior Intervention Planning (FBA/BIP) class in graduate school as an elective and it was extremely helpful in my work. The benefits for students and teachers were evident.

How Has It Impacted Your Work/Role as a School Counselor?

One unintended benefit of the collaboration between the PBIS/MTSS, SST, and BST teams was that it allowed the school counselors to create effective action plans based on data. We focused on students with office discipline referrals (ODRs). We met with a student after the second time they received an ODR and created a behavior plan with the

My Weekly Chart

Name_____   Week of_____

Behavior	Monday	Tuesday	Wednesday	Thursday	Friday
Staying in my seat	☺ 😐 ☹	☺ 😐 ☹	☺ 😐 ☹	☺ 😐 ☹	☺ 😐 ☹
Keeping my hands and feet to myself	☺ 😐 ☹	☺ 😐 ☹	☺ 😐 ☹	☺ 😐 ☹	☺ 😐 ☹
Following directions	☺ 😐 ☹	☺ 😐 ☹	☺ 😐 ☹	☺ 😐 ☹	☺ 😐 ☹
Completing my work	☺ 😐 ☹	☺ 😐 ☹	☺ 😐 ☹	☺ 😐 ☹	☺ 😐 ☹
Overall	☺ 😐 ☹	☺ 😐 ☹	☺ 😐 ☹	☺ 😐 ☹	☺ 😐 ☹
Notes					

Parent signature_____ Date _____

Figure 12.5 Sample elementary behavior tracking form.

student (see Figure 12.5). We then incorporated the student into our Check-in/Check-out system and monitored their behavior daily. Our goal was to prevent students from getting additional ODRs. One year, 89% of targeted students had four or fewer ODRs in the school year.

What Advice Would You Give Pre-Service School Counselors About PBIS/MTSS as They Prepare to Enter the Workforce and Collaborate on School-Wide Efforts?

As our district implements MTSS, we see the connection between behavior and academics getting stronger. I now work in central office and am a part of a behavior collaborative where we look at what the district is doing to support behavior at all three tiers. We have created resources that support schools in finding professional learning opportunities and curriculum. I am excited about the focus that we have as a district on social emotional learning and supporting the whole child.

VOICE 4

Holly: Elementary School Counselor, Maryland

Why Did Your School Elect to Implement PBIS/MTSS?

My diverse suburban elementary school of 700 students had seen a steady increase in office referrals over several years. When a new principal arrived, she came from a school that had implemented PBIS/MTSS. When she surveyed the staff about their concerns and what they wanted changed, negative student behaviors and the increasing number of referrals were near the top of the list. She laid the groundwork for PBIS/MTSS by first using standardized classroom expectations. That consensus-building on expected student behaviors became our behavior matrix, and the rest fell into place much more easily.

What Outcomes Have You Noticed?

For many years the data showed a sharp decline in ODRs, especially within the first three years of implementation. We had a lot of success with adding a minor referral form that addressed behaviors without students leaving the classroom and missing instruction. There was also a change in the climate and culture of the building. *Staff members bought into the idea of focusing on the positive; when students made a mistake, they reminded and re-taught students about the school expectations.* It took a little while for some staff members who had been at the school for decades to shift from addressing negative behaviors to reinforcing positive behaviors, but most have now embraced that change.

There was also a shift for parents. My school is the only one in the cluster to implement PBIS/MTSS and it is located in a highly competitive part of the county where there is statistically a much lower rate of academic referrals. It took a while for parents to stop comparing how different teachers or grade levels implemented PBIS/MTSS. They became more accepting when their children came home with stories about how their positive behaviors were acknowledged and how they had earned rewards. Within five years, *I had several parents ask me how they could utilize this type of PBIS/MTSS system at home, sometimes at their child's request!*

Positive Behavioral Interventions and Supports/Multi-Tiered Systems of Support is an on-going process. For instance, an increase in our student population has meant that our ODRs have risen again, and we need to refocus on teaching Tier 1 practices to all students and staff.

How Has It Impacted Your Work/Role as a School Counselor?

I was recruited early in the process to help with PBIS/MTSS implementation. The school climate changed in many positive ways that also facilitated my work as the sole school counselor for all 700 students. With time, the school building became a place that was calm, consistent, and positive. *Everyone knew what the expectations were for every part of the building. That made it easier for me to walk into any classroom, the cafeteria, the playground, and arrival/dismissal areas and utilize the same system of positive reinforcement.* It also provided access to a team of educators that represent all grade levels and student support providers with the PBIS/MTSS committee. Within this committee, we focus on hard data and staff perceptions about social/emotional/behavioral needs and we have the power to address them.

What Advice Would You Give Pre-Service School Counselors About PBIS/MTSS as They Prepare to Enter the Workforce and Collaborate on School-Wide Efforts?

It is vital for a new counselor to know how many years PBIS/MTSS has been implemented, the perceived success of the systems, and the level of knowledge and support from the administration. They should understand that most school districts focus of the academic side of MTSS (e.g., RTI). It is very likely that new school counselors are stepping into a situation in which the counselor "owned" PBIS/MTSS and did much of the work.

In their first year, school counselors should use their lack of knowledge about the school, staff, and students to their advantage! Build shared leadership capabilities by making sure the PBIS/MTSS committee represents a cross-section of the entire building and includes other stakeholders where possible. Rotate roles on the committee and give each member meaningful responsibilities. Get training on the systems used to collect the data and see how it ties in to the system used by the rest of the school. Use a fidelity inventory to have staff self-reflect on what they need to improve and use a similar form for yourself. But the best source of information is the students. Ask students what the rules and expectations are and find out what happens when they follow them! The school counselors should also be willing to share their data with district leadership. *Each year I create a trifold displaying our key data for our superintendent and school board.* Teams like ours are rewarded for our collaborative efforts to make positive change. The reward funds are used to purchase paper to print our good reward tickets! It feels great to be recognized in a large district like ours with 83,000 students.

VOICE 5

Jeannie: Middle School Counselor, Florida

Why Did Your School Elect to Implement PBIS/MTSS?

The year we started, we had a new principal who was looking for something to help with the student behavior issues. My assistant principal and I were doing research on RTI for behavior and learned about PBIS/MTSS. There was a district initiative to provide training and support at pilot schools. Although all the pilot schools had been previously chosen, my principal insisted that our school was included, and we got basic training for our team.

What Outcomes Have You Noticed?

We saw a significant decrease of 12% in our school discipline referrals from year 1 to year 2 as we adopted and implemented our behavioral expectations. However, progress has been inconsistent because of multiple administration changes. Some have been supportive of PBIS/MTSS and others have not.

How Has It Impacted Your Work/Role as a School Counselor?

The PBIS/MTSS made my job easier, as it fits perfectly with teaching social/emotional competencies to students. With PBIS/MTSS, expected behaviors are explained, taught, practiced, and retaught throughout the campus. It made managing my classroom lessons much easier too. I did not have to remember dozens of different classroom rules or feel I was disciplining a class. I only needed to remind students of the school rule for the given behavior. Whether it was for calling out or being unkind to a classmate, I could remind them by saying the P in PAWS means Perform Personal Best. I would ask the students, "Are you performing your personal best right now?" I liked that we focused on the same expectations and we used a common vocabulary as a school. I would go on the morning news every day and review the expectations for different areas on our campus from our behavior matrix (e.g., "This week we are talking about the S in PAWS, 'Show respect.' When you show respect in the classroom you raise your hand and wait to be called on, wait quietly for the teacher's help, and use materials correctly").

How Did You Handle the Challenges You Encountered with Implementation?

Because this was something supported by my administration, the initial implementation was not a problem. However, it was time consuming to create materials and train teachers. Some teachers balked because they did not accept this new approach, but *administrative support and expectations for implementation and faculty training were key.* Difficulties occurred a few years into implementation when our administrators changed. Each year we got further from the original implementation team and with every administrative change the program got weaker. There was not the original commitment, understanding of need, and level of support required to continue a robust program. When a new administration came in and saw things were working, they didn't understand what we had done to get there. As a result, the administration either severely pared down the yearly training or eliminated it altogether.

What Advice Would You Give Pre-Service School Counselors About PBIS/MTSS as They Prepare to Enter the Workforce and Collaborate on School-Wide Efforts?

- *Learn all you can about PBIS/MTSS*, understand how it relates to your role as a school counselor and how it will not only enhance and complement everything that you do, but also what your teachers do.
- When students know the behavioral expectations, and are confident in the consistent implementation of those expectations, *teaching time increases and so does student engagement and achievement.*
- *Be prepared to invest in training teachers and training students.* The first week of school should be spent teaching, practicing, and re-teaching your school's behavioral expectations; *it will pay off in the long term.*
- *Follow up after initial implementation.* There is work to be done every year, and year after year. Review your discipline, achievement, and attendance data to help your administration and staff see the difference. There is maintenance with any system and if you don't keep it up the system will crash.
- *You must have administrative support* and at least 80% of your faculty supporting you. Collect the discipline data every quarter and show them how PBIS/MTSS is making a difference in your school.
- *PBIS/MTSS takes time and consistency.* If people say it's not working they are not being consistent.
- *Involve parents* early on with the behavioral expectations. Show them how they are being used at school and they can also be used at home.

VOICE 6

Peg: Former Middle School Counselor, Connecticut

Why Did Your School Elect to Implement PBIS/MTSS?

Prior to my career as a counselor educator, *I was a middle school counselor for 16 years. I served as a site coordinator of our PBIS/MTSS implementation for three years.* We decided to formally embrace PBIS/MTSS after a few years of developing Tier 1 interventions to address student behavior. Though we had some initial success, we struggled to create strong Tier 2 and Tier 3 interventions.

Our team consisted of general educators, special educators, a para professional, our assistant principal, our school psychologist, and our school counselors. *We wrote a grant to secure three years of funding which would cover training, technical assistance, access to the School-Wide Information System (SWIS)* and coverage for substitutes on training days.

What Outcomes Have You Noticed?

We saw dramatic changes in our students' behaviors. The drop in office discipline referrals (ODRs) was close to 70%. This attracted the attention of the State Department of Education. They asked what we were doing that led to these changes. We told them that we were doing our best to implement PBIS/MTSS with fidelity. There were several outcomes that have had lasting impact. First, *with the reduction of ODRs, our administrators were able to be freed up to be the curricular leaders we needed*—especially with the advent of the Common Core. Second, our students who started with PBIS/MTSS on their first day of middle school moved through the grade levels with the understanding that there would be clear behavioral expectations in every aspect of their school day (bus ride, hallways, classroom, cafeteria, auditorium, etc.). While it was most challenging to implement with the 8th graders, once the students who started middle school with PBIS/MTSS matriculated to 8th grade it became easier for their teachers to have high expectations for their behavior.

How Did You Handle the Challenges You Encountered with Implementation?

Like most PBIS/MTSS teams, we faced challenges. The first time PBIS/MTSS was brought up to the staff, the well-meaning presenter shared images of what PBIS/MTSS looks like in elementary school. Our middle school teachers were turned off by one of the rewards highlighted: a dancing dinosaur in the cafeteria! That was unfortunate and set us back. By the time we got the grant, most were more open to PBIS/MTSS as a staff. We still met resistance amongst staff and parents. As we know, PBIS/MTSS is about adult behavior as well as student behavior. *We spent time working with teachers on ways to emphasize and celebrate positive behavior instead of harping on negative behavior. We encouraged the 4:1 rule.* This rule suggests that for every correction, give students four statements of specific praise (e.g., "I like the way you encouraged your group to keep working to find a solution even though they were getting discouraged."). There were also parents who questioned our new "behavior program" and felt that it was too stringent. In the long run, we saw better results for students academically, socially, and emotionally. The school climate was enhanced and teachers seemed less stressed when students were meeting behavioral expectations.

As we reflected, we came to understand that approaching PBIS/MTSS specifically and teaching in general in a culturally relevant way was an area of growth for us. We visited other schools with more diverse populations where PBIS/MTSS was being implemented. We sought out culturally relevant PBIS/MTSS training and made sure to include diverse perspectives on our implementation team.

Fortunately, *we had district-level support for PBIS/MTSS implementation.* We are a small district with one elementary, middle, and high school. Both the middle and high school received the same grant to implement PBIS/MTSS. Efforts to involve the elementary school were not initially successful, but the two schools partnered as they implemented PBIS/MTSS as best as they could. District leaders were interested in our progress and supported the development of our teams.

In addition to the 70% reduction of ODR, we were able to quantify an increase in our school climate surveys for both teachers and students. *More students felt safer and more welcomed in schools. Teachers felt better supported when it came to behavior con-*

Table 12.1 Behavior matrix for core school counseling lessons

	When the School Counselor is Talking	*When a Student is Talking*	*When We Are Working in Groups*
Be Safe	Ask questions.	Sit quietly in your seat.	Welcome everyone's ideas and perspectives.
Be Respectful	Practice active listening.	Practice active listening.	Practice active listening. Acknowledge everyone's contributions.
Be Responsible	Follow directions.	Raise your hand to speak.	Complete assigned tasks.

cerns. Most importantly, the focus on creating positive classroom environments and clear behavioral expectations made way for a significant increase in instructional time and gave teachers, school counselors, and administrators greater capacity by addressing behavior.

Although I am not sure about everyone on my team, I would implement PBIS/MTSS all over again. Two significant benefits I received from PBIS/MTSS were the rich training and the experience of making systemic change in a large school. *The SWIS data we collected gave us a clear picture of our behavioral "hot spots" and the times of days when most ODRs occurred.* We had success implementing Check-in/Check-out (CICO; see Figure 12.6) and used several evidence-based curricula (e.g., Strong Kids and Coping Cats) as a centerpiece to our Tier 2 intervention groups. Overall, I felt as though implementing PBIS/MTSS was a win–win. Our students' behavior improved, teachers engaged with students in a more positive manner, and those of us who embraced our training were able to improve our capacity as change makers, interventionists, and behavioral experts.

We were also able to respond to district-wide needs. After a year where we saw an increase in calls to mobile crisis for students who were at extreme levels of emotional distress, we met to consider options. Because we were implementing MTSS and looking at data regularly, we decided to explore universal screening (US) for emergent mental health concerns. In 2013, shortly after the tragic shooting at Sandy Hook Elementary School, we started US in our district. This data remains important today as the team plans for services, staffing, and interventions.

CHECK IN CHECK OUT POINT SHEET

Points Possible _____
Points Received _____
% of Points _____
Goal Met _____

2 – Great Job!
1 – So, so
0 – Doesn't meet goal

Name: _____
Date: ___ / ___ / ___

GOALS:

Target Behaviors	MATH	SOCIAL STUDIES	SPECIALS	RECESS	LANGUAGE ARTS	SCIENCE
Respectful	2 1 0	2 1 0	2 1 0	2 1 0	2 1 0	2 1 0
Responsible	2 1 0	2 1 0	2 1 0	2 1 0	2 1 0	2 1 0
Safe	2 1 0	2 1 0	2 1 0	2 1 0	2 1 0	2 1 0

Parent Signature:_____

Figure 12.6 Sample Check-in/Check-out (CICO) point sheet.

What Advice Would You Give Pre-Service School Counselors About PBIS/MTSS as They Prepare to Enter the Workforce and Collaborate on School-Wide Efforts?

I think pre-service school counselors should make all efforts to do their fieldwork in a school which is successfully implementing PBIS/MTSS. It is one thing to read about PBIS/MTSS or even see a video. Working in a school that is implementing it is an essential thing to experience. The lived experience is always the best teacher. I would encourage pre-service school counselors to be patient about the implementation process. There are stops and starts in implementation: there is hardly a straight line. As one administrator said, PBIS/MTSS is like building the plane while it is flying.

In addition, I think *administrators need to know how essential their affirmation is for the health and effectiveness of PBIS/MTSS implementation.* They must support all stakeholders—parents, community members, coaches, bus drivers, teachers, student support team members. Most importantly, school administrators need to advocate for school counselors to be available to support PBIS/MTSS implementation. Too many school counselors have caseloads that exceed the ASCA recommended ratio of 1:250. Some have non-counselor duties assigned to them (e.g., creating the master schedule and overseeing standardized testing). Both of these constraints hinder a school counselor's availability to support PBIS/MTSS implementation. School counselors are uniquely prepared to assist with systems change and to support the development of effective interventions which promote their students' academic, social, and emotional development.

VOICE 7

Hennessey: Middle School Counselor, New York

Why Did Your School Elect to Implement PBIS/MTSS?

We began to implement PBIS/MTSS during the 2007–2008 school year. At that time, we were experiencing increased discipline referrals specifically surrounding insubordination, verbal, and physical fights. We were interested in exploring a systemic approach which could help to decrease referrals and improve our school climate. I was a member of the team charged with implementation of PBIS/MTSS at the middle school level. Our team consisted of two counselors, three teachers, and our assistant principal. We received professional development in the MTSS framework, which included an academic component (RTI) and a behavioral component (PBIS).

We began the initial implementation of PBIS/MTSS by reviewing discipline referrals from the previous year. We identified areas that were "hot spots" in our building. These included unstructured time in the hallways, cafeteria, bathrooms, and on the bus. We then looked at the content of each referral to brainstorm what types of behaviors we wanted to target for intervention. We began with a broad look at trends and moved towards individual students. We identified the following student outcome measures: attendance, grades, and individual numbers of referrals.

What Advice Would You Give Pre-Service School Counselors About PBIS/MTSS as They Prepare to Enter the Workforce and Collaborate on School-Wide Efforts?

Our biggest challenge was buy-in from the staff. The PBIS/MTSS was brand new and felt like "another initiative" in the ever-changing world of public education. Our team left the professional development sessions with such a sense of optimism, but we also knew we needed the teachers to be excited. *We needed staff to buy-in to create a successful roll-out that would ultimately improve the climate of the building.*

We very strategically chose members of the initial team; teachers who were considered leaders in the building according to the other staff. These may not necessarily have been our instructional leaders or department chairs, but teachers with a loud voice who could help to empower the rest of the staff to embrace PBIS/MTSS. Today, our middle school has a well-established PBIS/MTSS program—the program is run by two coordinators who are teachers.

The most salient piece of advice I can give new counselors is two-fold: *(1) work diligently in laying the groundwork for developing a cohesive, cross-disciplinary PBIS/MTSS team, and (2) work equally as diligently to make sure your program is data-driven. A counselor's most valued asset is their ability to view the greater school community through a systemic lens and foster relationships with all stakeholders:* students, families, teachers, and administrators. *This skill set is a counselor's superpower;* counselors are in the optimal position to advocate for PBIS/MTSS through these relationships. Some examples might include presenting data to administrators from similar schools that have already implemented PBIS/MTSS, attending a Board of Education meeting and presenting PBIS/MTSS to the community, and meeting with teachers to together develop interventions that fall under the umbrella of PBIS/MTSS. Through our work (and my guess is we aren't alone) *we discovered that we were already implementing a lot of PBIS/MTSS practices, we just needed to label them.*

My second piece of advice surrounds data-driven practices. Be proactive in exploring the trends in your district: discipline, attendance, grading practices. Work with the PBIS/MTSS team to set realistic goals while advocating for increased support around the factors we know impact educational success: poverty, crime, attachment, as well as drug and alcohol use. Use the data in your district and your community to build systemic PBIS/MTSS supports that truly benefit all students, especially those in the most difficult situations. And most importantly, don't do any of it alone! Collaborate with staff and more importantly students! Use your superpower to enable students to find their superpowers and make change—ultimately it is their school!

VOICE 8

Jacob: Former Elementary and High School Counselor, Washington and North Carolina

Why Did Your School Elect to Implement PBIS/MTSS?

When our school first started implementing MTSS, the district served over 19,000 students across 32 schools. To fulfill the district commitment of equity in education, high expectations for all, and partnering with families to ensure all students achieve their potential, *MTSS implementation began to create a social culture that contributes to students' academic success.* Elementary schools were the first to be trained in MTSS, followed by middle and high schools, and a district coach supported implementation. Our school was particularly excited to implement MTSS because we needed a systematic framework to address the social, behavioral, and academic needs of all our students. *Given the ethnic, socio-economic, and language diversity of our students, we also needed a framework that focused on data-based decision making, evidence-based practices, and culturally responsive interventions.* Overall, our staff saw PBIS/MTSS implementation as an opportunity to change the culture of our school, and create a safe, predictable, and productive learning environment.

What Outcomes Have You Noticed?

As a school counselor, I noticed significant outcomes as a result of MTSS implementation. The first thing you noticed walking into our school was the clear and consistent expectations for all students. Students know what is expected of them and what it takes to be successful, and staff consistently reinforce expectations by taking advantage of teachable moments rather that reacting with discipline. *Our school began to feel like a respectful and fun place to be because the students, their families, and our staff collaborated to implement MTSS and make it work within our context.* Another outcome was the establishment of academic and behavior-focused teams. We developed a team with skilled staff dedicated to analyzing academic data, coordinating tiered academic interventions, and monitoring student progress. In collaboration with this team, we developed a Tier 1 school-wide team that met monthly, a Tier 2 team that met bi-weekly, and a Tier 3 team that met every week to focus on student behavior. Later, *these teams became more and more integrated to focus on academics and behavior simultaneously.* These teams built our staff's capacity to collect and analyze student data, and use that data to make decisions about how to best support all of our students.

The impact of our improved school culture and the establishment of systems to provide students with academic and behavioral interventions were evident in our school-wide data. We demonstrated academic gains and reduced problem behavior each year of MTSS implementation; and continue to maintain these results. For example, in the first year of MTSS implementation, the average referrals per day during the last month of the school year (when things can get very hectic!) was above four. During the fifth year of MTSS implementation, the average referrals per day during that same month was less than one.

How Has It Impacted Your Work/Role as a School Counselor?

Implementing MTSS revolutionized my work as a school counselor. First and foremost, *it expanded my reach.* I was able to have a direct and indirect impact on more students because *I was not the only one in the school analyzing student data regularly,* using data to determine needs and make decisions, and evaluating systems and practices to ensure effectiveness. *My time was used more effectively because I didn't have to do everything;* I coordinated the Tier 2 team and was part of other MTSS teams, but we also had teachers, administrators, and support staff on these teams and involved in academic and behavioral interventions happening throughout the school. *Being a part of MTSS implementation also increased my visibility as a school counselor and gave me opportunities to advocate for students as a leader in the school.* More and more, *I was seen by staff as an integral part of students' academic, social, and behavioral success* because they observed my contributions to MTSS teams. In addition, when school staff analyzed our school-wide data, they saw the impact of the services and interventions I provided. Overall, MTSS systems and practices improved the implementation of my school counseling program and I contributed knowledge and skills to the MTSS implementation process.

How Did You Handle the Challenges You Encountered with Implementation?

We certainly experienced challenges during MTSS implementation. To handle those challenges we kept coming back to our systems, fidelity of implementation, and training. Developing and documenting systems (e.g., procedures for collecting and reporting data, process for providing Tier 2 interventions, schedule for teaching expectations) was a continual process. But *whenever we felt disjointed as a staff, we looked back at our systems to see if we were thinking preventatively,* documenting our actions, so everyone was on the same page, and making sure that students, families, and staff had a voice in what we were doing.

We also focused on fidelity of implementation. Often times, when faced with data indicating a lack of student progress, we used the many available tools to check if we were doing what we said we would do, in the way we said we would do it. When we faced challenges with implementation, checking fidelity and making adjustments to get back on track was very helpful. In the end, some of the challenges we faced were also related to a lack of knowledge or skills as new MTSS implementers. To address this challenge, we established a regular professional development schedule that I was included in as a school counselor. This professional development included building-level supports, district sponsored training, state-level conferences, and, in some cases, trips to other schools to see exemplars.

What Advice Would You Give Pre-Service School Counselors About PBIS/MTSS as They Prepare to Enter the Workforce and Collaborate on School-Wide Efforts?

Pre-service school counselors have a tremendous opportunity. They are being trained at a time when the ASCA National Model is well established and MTSS is being implemented in thousands of schools across the U.S. My advice to pre-service school counselors is to *learn about the core concepts of MTSS, but also think about how you can align your school counseling program with MTSS.* I encourage pre-service school counselors to seek out practicum and internship experiences where schools are implementing Comprehensive School Counseling Programs aligned with the ASCA National Model and MTSS. This bridges the connection between theory and practice. I also encourage pre-service school counselors to attend training and conferences during their programs to get exposure to MTSS content outside of the school counseling preparation program. These experiences give pre-service school counselors the opportunity to connect with professionals aligning school counseling programs with MTSS and to receive training from experts in the field.

VOICE 9

Brenda: School Counseling District Supervisor, Nebraska

Why Did Your School Elect to Implement PBIS/MTSS?

With an enrollment of approximately 42,000 students, our school district is Nebraska's second largest school district. Prior to becoming a district administrator six years ago, I was a high school counselor at three different high schools (one rural school and two suburban) for 24 years. In my current role, I work with 88 school counselors and 36 school social workers who serve 60 schools/programs. We are in our fifth year of implementation of PBIS/MTSS and throughout we have worked to delineate the roles of school counselors, school social workers, and school psychologists in PBIS/MTSS.

As PBIS/MTSS becomes more deeply integrated into our district, we have the opportunity to consider not only which students need intervention, but which school professional might be best suited to provide that intervention. Our school counselors, school social workers, and school psychologists (we refer to them collectively as "school-based mental health team members") are all integral to facilitating and coordinating interventions. Our challenge is to maximize the unique contribution of each school-based mental health team member, in order to create a system that provides the best possible service to students. In order to begin this process our district leadership team reviewed the needs of students in our schools, the roles within PBIS/MTSS that would be best filled by a school-based mental health team member, and the models of best practice from professional associations.

After identifying student needs and how we would support those needs in our PBIS/ MTSS model, we looked at the practice models from the American School Counselor

Association, the School Social Work Association of America, and the National Association of School Psychologists, which provide excellent guidance and advocacy for appropriate roles that these professionals play in a school. Information from these associations reflects the current status of the profession as well as promoting the advancement of ideal roles. Our review of student needs and the practice models from each association shows overlap in a number of areas. For example, each model indicates that school-based mental health team members provide direct supports to students in multiple settings, consult with staff and parents, use data to inform decisions, provide referrals to community resources, and serve on systems teams. Our next steps were then to align each with specific roles and interventions in PBIS/MTSS.

The foundation of PBIS/MTSS is Tier 1 (universal) supports for students. Teaching students about school-wide expectations within various environments such as the classroom, hallway, cafeteria, or playground is the responsibility of all staff in the building and helps to prevent difficulties from developing. In our district, the Second Step social/emotional learning curriculum is taught by classroom teachers in grades preK-5 and again in 6th and 7th grades by teachers in specific subjects. Students who attend schools with school counselors receive additional classroom lessons related to academic, career, and social/emotional development by their school counselor, who provides large-group lessons intended for building skills in all students.

Students who need more support move to Tier 2 (secondary) interventions that begin with Check-in/Check-out (CICO). Students whose needs are not met through CICO participate in a Cognitive Behavioral Interventions for Trauma in Schools (CBITS)/Bounce Back Group. Any of the school-based mental health team members in a building might coordinate interventions at Tier 2, such as determining participants for an intervention and monitoring data about the efficacy of the intervention. Thus, we will facilitate CBITS/Bounce Back Groups focused on problem-solving, social skills, and academic success, and teach other staff how to facilitate some of these skill-building groups.

As students "move up the triangle" to supports at Tier 3 (tertiary) and their needs become more individualized, the expertise of the school psychologist is especially important. School psychologists conduct Functional Behavior Assessments and participate in writing Behavior Intervention Plans for students. Students who experience mental health crises themselves, or within their families, benefit from the assistance of the school social worker whose expertise in connecting school, family, and community is essential.

Each team member can bring valuable insights that help the MTSS teams create and sustain a positive school climate within a building. Their talents, however, are likely to be especially helpful when they are members of the school or systems teams that are aligned to their area of specialization.

What Outcomes Have You Noticed?

A key component of PBIS/MTSS includes the examination of data on student behavior and performance prior to and following interventions. Each team member in the building participates in the process of collecting and analyzing data. An effective system of data collection helps us better identify student needs. In fact, wanting to prevent students from "falling through the cracks" is a driving force behind implementing PBIS/MTSS. A less obvious, but equally important, consideration is that an effective data tracking system helps us all to avoid "over-serving" some students or assigning students to a higher level of support than might be required to address their needs.

Through PBIS/MTSS, we were able to systematize the way that students enter and exit interventions. This allows us to minimize the time spent meeting about individual students ("admiring the problem") and more time providing students with direct services and monitoring their response to those interventions. *The ASCA National Model recommends that 80% of the school counselor's time be spent on direct services to students and robust data systems within PBIS/MTSS help to achieve this.*

One example includes data from our CBITS/Bounce Back Groups, which is co-facilitated by the school counselor and the school social worker.

Report from Cognitive Behavioral Interventions for Trauma in Schools

CBITS/Bounce Back Groups

Cognitive Behavioral Interventions for Trauma in Schools (CBITS)/Bounce Back Groups were conducted with 70 students in at least eight elementary schools, three middle schools, and one high school. In at least one school, multiple groups were conducted during the school year. Students who participate in CBITS/Bounce Back tend to be the most mobile and their families at times relocate without much notice. This means that some students who start the group are unable to complete it and it makes it impossible to have both the pre- and post-intervention symptom screening checklists scores. *Of the 37 students on which we have data from the pre- and post-intervention administration of a trauma-symptom checklist, the data indicated that 32 (86%) of students were experiencing fewer distressing symptoms by the end of the intervention.*

In terms of academic and behavioral change, in the high school group four of the five participants had *fewer failing grades at the end of the group* and many elementary students were able to *better manage their behaviors in the classroom.* Some students were able to maintain improved behavior for several weeks after the end of the group.

The majority of the students participating in CBITS/Bounce Back report enjoying the group and gaining positive results from it. Students frequently commented that they were able to use skills learned in group (such as how to control their emotions and calm down) outside of the group and that they found support from others in the group.

This coming year we are working on a project with a professor from a local university, the Intentional Small Group (ISG), that includes screening tools that will help us track perception data. We are putting together curriculum that includes lessons from Second Step (www.secondstep.org), Skillstreaming, and Overcoming Obstacles.

How Has It Impacted Your Work/Role as a School Counselor?

School counselors serve mainly on the Tier 1 and early Tier 2 teams. As educators with a mental health focus, they teach important skills to all students in classroom, small-group, and individual settings. School counselors are often the first school-based mental health team members to recognize that a student is struggling and provide early interventions to students who need a little more.

In our district, school social workers serve mainly in Tier 2 and Tier 3. They sometimes overlap with school counselors in working with Tier 2 by co-running groups (e.g., emotional regulation, coping with divorce/loss, etc.). Their emphasis is mostly in the upper Tier 2 area with mental health and trauma-informed groups. School social workers provide specialized supports for students and families who are experiencing barriers to success that may be related to mental health concerns at Tier 3. Serving on Tier 2 and Tier 3 teams fits their role well.

School psychologists have expertise in individual assessment of academic, behavioral, and mental health needs. Their skills are maximized in upper Tier 2 and Tier 3 when formal individualized plans (such as Student Assistance Plans, Behavior Intervention Plans, 504 Plans, or Individualized Education Plans) are needed to support students who have not been successful with interventions at lower levels. In addition, many school psychologists possess skills in data gathering and coordinate the data collection system for PBIS/MTSS.

While this model is a starting point, our school-based mental health team members are certainly not limited to the roles outlined above [Editor note: these roles are outlined in greater depth in Chapter 8 on collaboration and consultation]. The needs of students and the staffing levels of school-based mental health team members in a building often determine which professional will implement a specific intervention at a given time. Defining their roles helps us determine who the "experts" are in a certain intervention and who should take the lead in implementation. We include all school-based mental health team members in training about all interventions so that they each understand and support the intervention even when they are not leading it.

How Did You Handle the Challenges You Encountered with Implementation?

Some things that helped: talking, listening, explaining, clarifying, talking, listening, explaining, clarifying . . . ! We had all of our school-based mental health team members (counselors, social workers, psychologists) and at times our community mental health therapists participate in joint training on specific pieces of PBIS/MTSS—especially Tier 2 since that's where the most overlap in roles occurs (Check-in/Check-out, SAIG, Mental Health Focused Small Groups, CBITS/Bounce Back, etc.). We are still working on this— in fact we will be training all of our counselors and social workers to do FBAs starting this school year (formerly only the school psychologists did these). We had some staff who were "early adopters" demonstrate what they were doing for others also. That is helpful too. In fact, *one person agreed to have her small group video-recorded to show her reinforcing the school-wide expectations throughout the [counseling] group. It was impactful when we showed that it really can be done!* We sent some clinicians to the National Forum also so they could get a better picture of the concept of MTSS and PBIS.

It's a work in progress but those were some things that helped!

What Advice Would You Give Pre-Service School Counselors About PBIS/MTSS as They Prepare to Enter the Workforce and Collaborate on School-Wide Efforts?

- *School-based mental health team members are valuable professionals who contribute to creating and maintaining a positive school climate that fosters success for each student. Delineating the roles of these professionals will help your team* to intentionally align the unique skills of our clinicians so that we may effectively meet the needs of students at all tiers in PBIS/MTSS. It is important to identify the specific roles of each school-based mental health team member and work together to meet students' diverse needs.
- When implementing a direct intervention with students, *collect data throughout that intervention to determine its effectiveness.*
- Agree ahead of time how the team will identify students in need of interventions, what type of intervention will be used, and how to analyze the data.
- Decide how movement from one tier to another will happen (e.g., who needs it, what do they need, and how are they doing).

VOICE 10

Universal Mental Health Screening Within MTSS.

John: Director of School Counseling, Massachusetts

Why Did You and Your Team Explore Universal Mental Health Screening as Part of Your MTSS Implementation?

Our motivation was to understand and support the whole student. We wanted a richer understanding of the function of a student's behavior. We are explicitly teaching Social and Emotional Learning (SEL) competencies as we explicitly teach behavior. Our goal is to provide integrated interventions that address the whole student's needs. We needed screening to make that happen.

We had so many students with unmet needs, and we wanted to find a more proactive way to identify them before they experienced a crisis. We also sought to understand the overarching needs of the district related to mental health. This is why I got into the field, and I was surprised at the lack of mental health services available to students at the outset of my career. My district has pushed to make mental health a focus of our Comprehensive School Counseling Program. It is less about providing one type of intervention or another. Rather, we need to provide an integrated intervention that is informed by understanding the root of each student's complex needs, and providing related services to meet those varied needs.

You Mentioned That You Had Some Mentoring to Establish Universal Screening in Your District. What Did That Look Like?

We met with professors from the University of Maryland at the Center for School Mental Health, gathered information about their work, and applied to be a part of their grant opportunity, which really set the stage for our work to establish a quality and sustainable comprehensive school mental health system. This collaboration led to the work we have been doing related to universal screening.

What was Your First Step?

When working with the Center for School Mental Health, we conducted a local needs assessment, which targeted areas for improvement, in order to direct our work. One of those areas was universal screening, so we began to consider what it would mean to introduce this practice to our school district. The Center for School Mental Health gave us a great deal of support, training, resources, and technical assistance, and taught us how to make decisions that were best for our district using a quality improvement model. We also had the opportunity to learn from other school districts who were also afforded this grant opportunity.

What Were Your Goals?

Our goals changed throughout the program. However, the most important things we accomplished were:

- Establishing universal screening in grades 3–12 to support early identification and prevention.
- Establishing formal agreements backed by a memorandum of understanding with local mental health agencies to augment the services offered through the schools. Thus, we were able to put community-based mental health services in place for our students.
- Establishing a tiered system of mental health services and supports, including SEL instruction, group and individual counseling using evidence-based practices.

- Scaling up our use of evidence-based practices, particularly cognitive behavioral therapy.
- Redefining the role of school counselors and school psychologists and empowering them to engage in evidence-based counseling with their students.

How Do the Tiers of Support Work in Your School?

At Tier 1, we teach and model SEL competencies for all students. These competencies are explicitly taught in health classes by school counselors and health teachers, and SEL is integrated into the classroom in order to leverage the whole faculty in our prevention approach. In addition to instruction related to the SEL competencies, we have also worked to model trauma-sensitive practices that can be integrated in the classroom. After conducting an SEL needs assessment, we selected three age-appropriate SEL curricula: Second Step (elementary), Social Thinking (elementary/middle school) and Facing History and Ourselves (high school). The SEL curriculum is delivered through an advisory program, and we are always seeking new curriculum to supplement our practices and to address the most pressing concerns identified through needs assessments. This approach gives us the opportunity to do important prevention work.

In Tier 2, we have developed targeted SEL instruction, models of group counseling, and behavior plans. Our goal is to help students feel like they are not alone in their struggles. We hope to reduce stigma and to provide healthy role models.

In Tier 3, we provide both one-on-one counseling services and wraparound services. Usually students with Tier 3 needs have a diagnosed mental health concern. We sometimes collaborate with specialized community-based clinicians to augment the school counselor's work and to ensure the appropriate wraparound services are offered to meet the student's needs completely.

What Were Your First Steps in Implementing Universal Screening in Your District?

Two years ago, we began out small. We started with one student and a single measure. We have since ramped it up to five measures which are administered in grades 3–12. By starting small we could get a clear sense of what we wanted to screen for and who we wanted to screen. For example, we administer the CRAFFT substance abuse screener in both 7th and 9th grade. Research shows that most students begin experimenting in 8th grade. The 7th grade screener essentially serves as a baseline so we can identify 9th graders who have begun to use at dangerously high levels.

How Do You Select Interventions for Your Students?

It is less about providing one type of intervention or another. Rather, we need to provide an integrated intervention that is informed by an understanding of the complex needs of each student and generates from an integrated system that accounts for those varied needs.

What Is Your Long-Range Vision for Your School District as It Relates to Universal Screening?

We are continuing to pilot use of different screening tools that can help us understand our population more comprehensively. As we compile the results from these varied assessments, our hope is to paint a clearer picture of how best we can support our entire population and each individual student. We would like to engage families and teachers in the screening process more as we grow. Having multiple perspectives to draw from will only serve to give credence to the data that we use and aid in our understanding of the presentation of issues in a variety of contexts.

Concluding Thoughts

In this book we outlined strategies to strengthen school counseling programs through CSCP–MTSS alignment, including school counselors as leaders, advocates, collaborators, and culturally responsive systemic change agents in this alignment, serving students both directly and indirectly, as well as the use of data and evidence-based practices. We suggest that this alignment helps school counselors work more efficiently and centrally in their school, as well as to serve students with complex and diverse needs. In this last section of the book, we provide final thoughts and look ahead to the future.

From our time in the K-12 schools, we editors remember being inundated with the latest and greatest strategy, program, or approach that we were asked to use with students. Every year there were new initiatives, and often they were piled on top of those initiated the previous year. We still see this today: there are always new trends in K-12 education. As this book goes to print, we are seeing certain topics that are receiving increased attention in K-12 education: mental health, social/emotional learning, serving un-documented students, college and career readiness/access, mindfulness, and a renewed focus on school safety, preventing school violence, and trauma-informed care. As we see educational trends come and go, how does MTSS fit into this ebb and flow? Is MTSS one more approach that will come and go with the times? We don't think so, and here is why.

First, similar to CSCPs, MTSS is a framework for offering services. Thus, while there are central components to the MTSS framework (see Chapter 1), and the CSCP framework (see Chapter 2), the implementation of these frameworks is modified to fit the unique needs of each school. Thus, MTSS is not *one more initiative*, rather, we believe it is a framework to capture the trends that come and go in education. For instance, although MTSS has been in existence for nearly 20 years, the framework has been used to implement various educational priorities and trends.

For example, there has been a recent renewed call to address the mental health of youth given significant gaps in services (Kauffman & Badar, 2018; Hoover, 2018). Schools are primary places where students can receive mental health services (Atkins, Cappella, Shernoff, Mehta, & Gustafson, 2017) and MTSS can integrate mental health-specific universal prevention and targeted intervention to help youth who face barriers accessing these services outside of school (Sanchez, Cornacchio, Poznanski, Golik, Chou, & Comer, 2018). Relatedly, universal mental health screening can be used within MTSS to preventatively identify students with mental health needs (Weist, Garbacz, Lane, & Kincaid, 2017). In a similar vein, MTSS can integrate trauma-informed care into existing systems of support (Chafouleas et al., 2016) as well as organize college and career activities (Hatch, Duarte, & De Gregorio, 2018; Morningstar, Lombardi, & Test, 2018), and school violence initiatives, including the systematic identification of students at risk for initiating this school violence (Katsiyannis, Whitford, & Ennis, 2018). Finally the MTSS framework has been effective to organize multi-tiered interventions for topics especially relevant to school counselors including bullying (Nickerson, 2017), Social Emotional Learning/Social Skills (Cook, Frye, Slemrod, Lyon, Renshaw, & Zhang, 2015), and restorative practices (Smith et al., 2018; Wang & Lee, 2018). In addition, research is just now extending beyond the school walls to include the promise of MTSS partnerships with community and mental health agencies that allow for greater prevention and provision of services for students with elevated needs (Barnett, Eber, & Weist, 2013; Hoover, Sapere, Lang, Nadeem, Dean, & Vona, 2018; Reinke, Thompson, Herman et al., 2018). Overall, research is focused on how educators and counselors can examine these important and timely topics within the context of a three-tiered MTSS approach.

Second, MTSS has been backed by tremendous research (see Chapter 2 for a brief overview) and federal funding. Researchers continue to highlight the benefits of MTSS. For example, PBIS has been shown to impact student behavioral and academic outcomes (Kim, McIntosh, Mercer, & Nese, 2018) and create stronger atmospheres of professional trust/climate among staff (Houchens, Zhang, Davis, Niu, Chon, & Miller, 2017). In addition, programs have successfully integrated culture into MTSS across all school levels, including high school (Bal, Afacan, & Cakir, 2018). Finally, according to Avant (2016), effective implementation of MTSS can foster a sense of equity and social justice in school communities. Due to the continued research documenting effectiveness, as well as the national support for and implementation of MTSS (McIntosh & Goodman, 2016), we believe this is a framework that can and will continue to evolve within the landscape of ever-changing educational trends.

As mentioned throughout the book, school counselors face a myriad of challenges. School counselors face large ratios (Glander, 2017) as well as job descriptions that include a number of competing demands that compete with directly serving students. For over 15 years the ASCA National Model has helped clarify the school counselor role and professional identity, and, more generally, CSCPs have been in existence for several decades. Similar to MTSS, CSCPs are vibrant evolving frameworks that can be modified based on the needs of each school, and can include important educational trends. Thus, it benefits school counselors to align themselves with appropriate educational initiatives, especially initiatives that share overlapping goals and can strengthen CSCP implementation. This collaboration enhances school counselors' ability to implement their program and serve students. Further, aligning CSCPs with prioritized educational efforts enables school counselors to advocate for their work by demonstrating to stakeholders how a school counselor fits within schools' central mission, vision, and work.

Throughout any systemic change, we must remember our purpose. Most students need some form of support as they journey from K–12. Approaching academic and behavioral needs with strong classroom instruction and prevention in Tier 1, evidence-based small-group interventions in Tier 2, and highly collaborative teams in Tier 3 is an effective approach to ensure student success. It is imperative that school counselors recognize the need for systems change and take a leadership role in implementation to positively impact outcomes for all students.

In sum, we live in a fast-paced, constantly changing global society. Though we don't know what new K-12 educational approaches will be upon us next, we do believe that both CSCPs and MTSS are two frameworks that are equipped to include a diverse array of future educational trends, just as they have evolved so far.

To you, our readers: as pre-service and practicing school counselors, as well as school counseling leaders, supervisors, and faculty, we hope this book has been helpful. We hope you have gained knowledge on and strategies regarding the CSCP–MTSS alignment. But, most importantly, we hope you have gained the confidence to take that first step: to investigate this alignment on your own. Though future educational trends remain unknown, we climb the staircase of the future one step at a time. As you consider how to best serve your students, schools, and communities now and in the future, we encourage you to take your journey one step at a time, using the best practices and research available. And we encourage you to maintain hope, flexibility, and faith so you can continue assessing and adapting to the future. As we look toward the future of CSCPs, MTSS, and education, we highlight the following quote by the revolutionary civil rights leader Dr. Martin Luther King Jr.: "Faith is taking the first step even when you don't see the whole staircase." Good luck with your next step.

References

Atkins, M. S., Cappella, E., Shernoff, E. S., Mehta, T. G., & Gustafson, E. L. (2017). Schooling and children's mental health: Realigning resources to reduce disparities and advance public health. *Annual Review of Clinical Psychology, 13*, 123–147.

Avant, D. W. (2016). Using Response To Intervention/Multi-Tiered Systems of Supports to promote social justice in schools. *Journal for Multicultural Education, 10*(4), 507–520.

Bal, A., Afacan, K., & Cakir, H. I. (2018). Culturally responsive school discipline: Implementing Learning Lab at a high school for systemic transformation. *American Educational Research Journal, 55*(5), 1–44, doi.org/10.3102/0002831218768796.

Barnett, S., Eber, L., & Weist, M. (2013). *Advancing education effectiveness: Interconnecting school mental health and school-wide positive behavior support.* Eugene, OR: University of Oregon: Retrieved from: www.pbis.org/common/cms/files/Current%20Topics/Final-Monograph.pdf.

Begeny, J. C. (2018). An overview of internationalization and its relevance for school and educational psychology. *Psychology in the Schools, 55*, 897–907.

Chafouleas, S. M., Johnson, A. H., Overstreet, S., & Santos, N. M. (2016). Toward a blueprint for trauma-informed service delivery in schools. *School Mental Health, 8*, 144–162, doi: 10.1007/s12310-015-9166-8.

Cook, C. R., Frye, M., Slemrod, T., Lyon, A. R., Renshaw, T. L., & Zhang, Y. (2015). An integrated approach to universal prevention: Independent and combined effects of PBIS and SEL on youths' mental health. *School Psychology Quarterly, 30*(2), 166–183.

Glander, M. (2017). *Selected statistics from the public elementary and secondary education universe: School year 2015–2016.* Washington, DC: National Center for Education Statistics. Retrieved from: https://nces.ed.gov/pubs2018/2018052.pdf.

Hatch, T., Duarte, D., & De Gregorio, L. K. (2018). *Elementary school counseling: Implementing core curriculum and other tier one activities.* Thousand Oaks, CA: Sage Publications.

Hoover, S. (2018). When we know better, we don't always do better: Facilitating the research to practice and policy gap in school mental health. *School Mental Health, 10*(2), 190–198.

Hoover, S. A., Sapere, H., Lang, J. M., Nadeem, E., Dean, K. L., & Vona, P. (2018). Statewide implementation of an evidence-based trauma intervention in schools. *School Psychology Quarterly, 33*(1), 44–53, dx.doi.org/10.1037/spq0000248.

Houchens, G. W., Zhang, J., Davis, K., Niu, C., Chon, K. H., & Miller, S. (2017). The impact of Positive Behavior Interventions and Supports on teachers' perceptions of teaching conditions and student achievement. *Journal of Positive Behavior Interventions, 19*(3), 168–179.

Katsiyannis, A., Whitford, D. K., & Ennis, R. P. (2018). Historical examination of United States intentional mass school shootings in the 20th and 21st centuries: Implications for students, schools, and society. *Journal of Child and Family Studies, 27*, 1–12.

Kauffman, J. M., & Badar, J. (2018). *The scandalous neglect of children's mental health: What schools can do.* Abingdon: Routledge.

Kim, J., McIntosh, K., Mercer, S. H., & Nese, R. N. (2018). Longitudinal associations between SWPBIS fidelity of implementation and behavior and academic outcomes. *Behavioral Disorders, 43*(3), 357–369.

McIntosh, K., & Goodman, S. (2016). *Integrated Multi-Tiered Systems of Support: Blending RTI and PBIS.* New York: Guilford.

McIntosh, K. M., Mercer, S. H., Nese, R. N., Strickland-Cohen, K., Kittelman, A., Hoselton, R., & Horner, R. H. (2018). Factors predicting sustained implementation of a universal behavior support framework. *Educational Researcher, 47*, 307–316.

Morningstar, M. E., Lombardi, A., & Test, D. (2018). Including college and career readiness within a Multitiered Systems of Support framework. *AERA Open, 4*(1), 1–11.

Nickerson, A. B. (2017). Preventing and intervening with bullying in schools: A framework for evidence-based practice. *School Mental Health, 11*, 1–14.

Reinke, W. M., Thompson, A., Herman, K. C., Holmes, S., Owens, S., Cohen, D., . . . & Copeland, C. (2018.) The County Schools Mental Health Coalition: A model for community-level impact. *School Mental Health 10*, 173–180, doi.org/10.1007/s12310-017-9227-2.

Sanchez, A. L., Cornacchio, D., Poznanski, B., Golik, A. M., Chou, T., & Comer, J. S. (2018). The effectiveness of school-based mental health services for elementary-aged children: A meta-analysis. *Journal of the American Academy of Child & Adolescent Psychiatry, 57*(3), 153–165.

Smith, L. C., Garnett, B. R., Herbert, A., Grudev, N., Vogel, J., Keefner, W., . . . & Baker, T. (2018). The hand of professional school counseling meets the glove of restorative practices: A call to the profession. *Professional School Counseling, 21*(1), 1–10, doi: 2156759X18761899.

Sugai, G., Simonsen, B., Salle, T. L., & Freeman, J. (2017). Promoting school-wide social skills. In P. Strumley (Ed.), *The Wiley handbook of violence and aggression* (Vol. 3, pp. 1283–1295). Hoboken, NJ: Wiley-Blackwell.

Wang, E. L., & Lee, E. (2018). The use of responsive circles in schools: An exploratory study. *Journal of Positive Behavior and Interventions* [online publication], doi.org/10.1177/1098300718793428.

Weist, M. D., Garbacz, S. A., Lane, K. L., & Kincaid, D. (2017). *Aligning and integrating family engagement in Positive Behavioral Interventions and Supports (PBIS): Concepts and strategies for families and schools in key contexts.* Center for Positive Behavioral Interventions and Supports (funded by the Office of Special Education Programs, U.S. Department of Education). Eugene, OR: University of Oregon Press. Retrieved from: www.pbis.org/Common/Cms/files/pbisresources/Family%20Engagement%20in%20PBIS.pdf.

Index

Note: References in *italics* are to figures, those in **bold** to tables.

504 plan 169–170, **194**, 210, 228, 233, 313, 349; team **48**

academic achievement 4, 72, **86**, 163, **176**, **205**; across student groups *299*; 310; and CSCP 31, 33–34; and cultural equity *306*; and evidence-based practice 9, 278; and school counselor role 271
academic content 4, 109, **309**
accountability 73, 92–93; in the ASCA National Model 33–34; cycle *89*; and evidence-based practice 269–270
achievement gap 32, 34, 41, 152, 210; 298; and discipline gap 301; and MTSS alignment 152; *see also* academic achievement
acknowledgement 8, **15**, 74, 106, 248; staff 17; student 37
Action plan 259, 336; in MTSS **13**, **15**, 18–19, 22; in school counseling 34, 51, 85, 250
administrators 30–31; 40; 62, 64, 165; annual agreement 35; collaboration with 234, 237; consultation with 223; and data 138, 247–248; role on teams **13**, 17, 134–135, 167, 193; 222, *231*, 231–232; and universal screening 211–212; *see also* team, leadership
advocacy 237, 246, 262, 320, 347; in aligned programs 41, *43*, 44, *46–47*; and ASCA National Model 32–33; and culturally responsive practice 302–304; and evidence-based practice 272; in Tier 2 133, 135–137; and universal screening 209–210; using data 143, 151–152
American School Counselor Association (ASCA) 55, 62
American School Counselor Association (ASCA) National Model 31–34, 247, 271, 335, 348; collaboration 229; and data 249, 335; and evaluation 125, 151; and MTSS integration 2, 40–41, *43*, 246, 353; Tier 1 100, *108*; Tier 2 142–143, 148; Tier 3 163; and universal screening 208–210
American School Counselor Association (ASCA) position statement *see* position statement

anxiety 12, **14**, 164, 209–210, 230, 250; assessment of 169, 190; **194**, **200**, 205, *207*; tiered intervention 279, **281**; Tier 2 intervention 283, **286–287**; Tier 3 intervention 174, *176*; 288; **289**; and school counselor role 124, 246; and universal screening 196–197, **197**, 199, 202, 204, 209
assessment systems 182
assessment *see* data
attendance *14*, 20, 39, *47*, 52, 77, 229, 257, 331; interventions 79, 168, 171, *177*, 184, 332, *334*; *see also* data

behavior change 11, 66, 143, 174
behavior science 6
Behavior intervention plan (BIP) **15**, 58, 163, *168*, 169–172, 336; *see also* Functional Behavior Analysis (FBA)
benchmark test 39, 190, 192, 200
bias 237; cultural 173, 212, 303, 306, 312; implicit *309*, 311; *see also* culture
Bronfenbrenner, U. 64, 70, 72, 90, 93; bioecological systems theory 65–68, *66*
bullying 7, 50–51, **76**, **83**, 106–107, 117; data *248*; evidence-based practice 176, 272; intervention and prevention 149, 249, 259, 307

Car, Relax, Alone, Forget, Friends, Trouble (CRAFFT) **197**, 199, *200*, 351
Center for School Counseling Outcome Research and Evaluation (CSCORE) 55, 88, 103, 128, 274, **276**
Center for School Mental Health 193, 217, 350
Check-in/Check-out (CICO) 15, 38, **48**, 52, 235, 252; decision-making guidelines 151–152; in practice 170–171, 180, 342, 347; point sheet *342*; Tier 2 process 146–148
classroom management 4, 6, 74, 115, 257–258; and classroom dynamics 123; strategies 117–122
closing the gap 48, 142; Action Plan 51
coaching 17–18, **21**, 22
Cognitive Behavioral Therapy (CBT) 15, 284, 288, **289**

collaboration 30, 41, 228–229, 331, 336, 345, 350; and alignment 41–44; in ASCA National Model 31–33; case study 250–252; culturally responsive 38, 237–238, 310; definition of 228; difficulties 235–237; and MTSS team 230–232; in Tier 1 73, 85, 122–124; in Tier 2 135–136, 151; in Tier 3 164; school counselor role **47–49**; types 229–230; *see also* consultation

Collaborative for Academic, Social, and Emotional Learning (CASEL) 107, 128, **277**, 292

college and career: activities 101; data 103, 253; fairs 48; readiness 20, 31, 33, 352

community resources 179, 215, 331, 347

Comprehensive School Counseling Program (CSCP) 1, 20, **21**, **23**, 267, 304; culture 308, 310–316; data 34, 87–88, 246–248; 271; history 30–31; mission statements **86**; and MTSS alignment 40–45, 85, 249–252; Tier 1 73, 78, 80, 100; Tier 2 145, 148; Tier 3 174; and universal screening 192–193; *see also* ASCA National Model

consultation 4, 34, *42*, **47–48**; culturally responsive 237–238; definition 223–224; difficulties 235–237; example 252, 336; and MTSS team 230–232; stages 224–227; in Tier 1 73, 85, 87, 109, 122–124; in Tier 3 53, 171, 178; triadic process *224*; *see also* collaboration

continuum 6, 12, **15**, **21**, 36, **40**; -based approach 5, 40–41, 63; of behavior strategies *7*, *118*; of practice **15**; of school-wide practice *8*, 8

Coping Cat 174, **176**, 203, 283–284, **287**, 342

crisis **49**; response 34, *42*, **46**, 53; team 47, 232

culture: in decision making **20**, 139, 167; definition of 301; family 134, 310; school 44, **47–49**, 74, 133, 237; student *72*, 116, 175, 229; systems 39, 68, 89; *see also* cultural; culturally responsive

cultural: self-awareness 237, *306*, **309**, 311; equity *306*, 307, *308*, **309**; knowledge *306*, **309**, 311, 312; relevance *306*, **309**, 314; validation *306*

culturally responsive 39, **40**, 41, 307–308, **309**; data analysis 315–316; outcomes 307; PBS 306; practices 238–239, 301–302, 304, 312–314; school counseling 303–305; school expectations 314; schools 302–303; strategies 50; systems 307, 310; Tier 1 supports 101; Tier 2 supports 134, 139, 146, 152; Tier 3 supports 175; *see also* culture

Cognitive-Behavioral Intervention for Trauma in Schools (CBITS) **48**, 175, **177**, 178, 347–349

Daily Progress Report (DPR) 147–148, 170–171, 173

data 246–247, 335; accountability cycle *89*; and the ASCA National Model 31–34; academic 32, 151, 205, 259, *334*, 345;

baseline 191; culturally relevant 305–306, *306*; disaggregation of 139, 258, 262, 312, 315; and evaluation 19; and evidence-based practice 39, 87–88, *274*; leadership team use *231*; legal issues 195; observation 171; program planning 253–255; in RTI 4, 262; school counselor use in MTSS 44, *46*, 142–143, 234, 249–252, 316, 344; and selecting interventions 235, 347; and intervention effectiveness 149, 349; in Tier 1 102–107; in Tier 2 138–140; in Tier 3 168–169, 181–182; *see also* data types; data-based decision making; office discipline referral (ODR); progress monitoring

data, attendance 31, 34, 50, 88, 106, 194, *203*, 208, *334*

data, behavioral 134, 140, 248, 252, 259

data, discipline 54, 139, 205, *300*, 317, 340

data, outcome 34, 51–52, 103–104, 106–107, 142, 248–249, *248*, 251–252, 252, *253–255*; 307, 317–318, 332

data, perception 194, 247–248, *248*, 250–251, 348

data, process 247, *247*, 257

data, school-wide *14–15*, 50, *82*, 304, 331, 345

data-based decision making 3, 18, 24, **309**, 344; and advocacy 151–152; in CICO 151; and evidence-based practice *271*, 272; and mental health services *208*; and MTSS leadership team 234–235; school counselor role 15, 252; Tier 2 134–136, *137*, 150

data-based system *13*

data tools 168; MTSS 259–262; *see also* School Wide Information System (SWIS)

depression **49**, 51, 164, 175, 199, 213; data *200*, 205–206, *206*; intervention 175, 279, **281**, **286**, 288, **289**; screening tools **197**; and suicide 213

differentiation 88, 113, 129, 236; instruction 4, 78, 115–116

Direct Instruction 4, 9–11, 22, 149, 171, *172*

discipline 31, 51, 238, 298, 300–301, **309**, 345; gap 298, 301; procedures 74, 99, 139; *see also* data; office discipline referral

disproportionality 51, 165, 238, 298, **309**, 310, 312; and data analysis 315, 319; in discipline 34, 300–301; in special education 300–301

ecological 101; models, 33, 62, 64–65; *see also* Bronfenbrenner; Lerner; systems theory

eduCLIMBER 260, 262

equality 307–308

equity 305–309; and data use 237

Ethical Standards 23, 54, 240; collaboration 239; data 262; culture 290, 320–321; and evidence- based practice 290; Tier 1 91, 126; Tier 2 142; Tier 3 153, 181–182; and universal screening 215

evaluation 125; intervention evaluation 273; performance evaluation 34; program evaluation 274; tools 88, 182, 248

Every Student Succeeds Act (ESSA) 249
evidence-based practice (EBP) 9, 267–268;
    and advocacy 272; definition 275; process
    and models 273–274; in school counseling
    271; Tier 1 82–83, 87–88, 275–279; Tier 2
    145–146, 279–284; Tier 3 174–177, 284–289;
    why use 270
executive functioning 50, **231**, 283, **285**
externalizing 103, 138, 190, 283

Functional Assessment Checklist: Teachers
    and Staff (FACTS) 144, 168–169; *see also*
    Functional Behavior Assessment
FERPA 201, 216, 240–241
FIRST STEP Next 288–289
flipped classroom 115
Functional Behavior Assessment (FBA) 53;
    brief 143–145; cultural considerations 171,
    173; process for developing 168–170; *see also*
    Behavior Intervention Plan
funding 17–18, 181

gratitude journaling 84

implementation 16; fidelity of 2, 5, 8; phases
    of 11, 18–20; research on 11–12; school
    counselor role 20–22
Incredible Years (IY) 283, 287
Individual Education Plan (IEP) 3, 174, 233
Individuals with Disabilities Act (IDEA) 3, 191
internalizing 103, 138, 190, 202, 208
intervention: individual 166; organizing 150,
    154; planning 66–77, 71; small group 33,
    36, 51, 148–149; targeted 36–37, 145; Tier 1
    50–51, 66, 80–84; Tier 2 51–52; Tier 3 52–53;
    universal screening 51, 99, 103, 109, 138

learning objectives 107
Lerner, R. 68–72; *see also* Bronfenbrenner;
    systems theory
lesson plans 107–108; academic content 109;
    behavioral content 109–110; determining
    format 113; template 108

matrix: behavior 74, **75–77**, 332, 337, 339, **341**;
    intervention organizer 154; teaching *10*, 11,
    13, 51, 113, **117**
mental health 19, 33–34, 42, 51, 163–164, 174,
    189–190; stigma 211–212
mental illness: stigmatization 211–212
Mindsets and Behaviors 34, 63, 100; and
    academic content standards 109; and
    behavioral standards 110, 117; and data use
    87–88, 103–104; learning objectives 107; in
    Tier 1 73, 80–81, 85, 100, **101**; and school
    improvement 106
Motivational Interviewing (MI) 288
multidisciplinary teams 2, 233–234, 236; *see also*
    team, leadership

National Model *see* ASCA National Model
needs assessment 102–103; sample 104–105

Office Discipline Referral (ODR) 50–51,
    138–139, *140*, 142, **203**, 248–249, 319, 338;
    case study 250–252, 317–318, 336; reduction
    in 340–341; *see also* data
outcome data *see* data, outcome
outcome measures 150, 343

parent 93, 200, 211, 213, 331; education 124
perception data *see* data, perception
policy 17–18
position statement, ASCA 41, 90, 142, 164, 192,
    208, 240, 310
Positive Action (PA) 278–279
Positive Behavior Intervention and Supports
    (PBIS) 36–37; and assessment 182, 261
prevention 5–6, 38
process data *see* data, process
progress monitoring 181, 205–206
Promoting Alternative Thinking Strategies
    (PATHS) 278

ratio 146, 192, 257, 343; and data *323*, *324*; risk
    ratio 315, *318*
recognized ASCA Model Programs (RAMP) 43
referrals 335; academic 193–194, 338;
    behavior 138, 336, 151, 170–171; case
    study 180, 250–251, 257–258, 317–319;
    cultural implications 238, *318*; ethical
    standards 183, 215–216, 241; evidence-
    based practices **176**, **287**; implementation
    331, 335, 337, 340, 343, 345, 347;
    school counselors' role 210, 310; school
    psychologists 233; team 202–203; tiered
    model **46–48**, 53, 166
relationship 41, 67–71, **76–77**, 118, 179, 224,
    228, 234, 239; culturally responsive 302–303,
    319; ethical standards 24, 91, 128, 183, 241,
    321; with teachers 4, 121–3, 225; Tier 2 52
request for assistance: template 138–142, *141*
resiliency scale 196
Response to Intervention (RTI) 4, 29, 35, *42*,
    53, 62, **86**, 163, 247; culturally responsive
    305; implementation 336; screening and
    assessment 192, 262; Tier 1 99
Responding in Peaceful and Positive Ways (RIPP)
    278–279; evidence-based programs **282**
restorative practices 51, 213, 353, 355
reward 24, **83**, 97, 203, 235, 331–332, 338–339, 341
Root Cause Analysis (RCA) 246, 255, 263–266,
    309, 323

Second Step **83**, **176**, 278; case study 250, 252;
    interventions 149; programs 50, **280**
school-based mental health teams 204, 211, 213,
    215, 347–349; overlapping roles 232–234;
    screening 191; *see also* team, leadership
school climate 37, 52, 63, 74, 87, 114, 228,
    248–249; culturally responsive 304, 313;
    ethical standards 55; evidence-based
    practices 176; implementation 331, 341
school culture *see* culture
school data profile 51, 237, 253

school family therapist 174, 193, 229, **231**; overlapping roles 232–234

school–home communication 134, 313

school psychologist 8, 191, 193, 196; collaboration 229; ethical standards 24; implementation 331, 346–347; leadership **231**; overlapping roles 232–234; role 199, 349; screening 213; tiered models 53, 134, 165, 167, 169

school social worker 24, 134, 149, 165–167, 193, **231**; ethical standards 153; implementation 331, 346–349; leadership 228–229, 231; overlapping roles 232–234

School-Wide Information System (SWIS) 259, 263, 340

screener 100, 138; choosing 199; cost 198–199; parent inventory 198; psychometric properties 198; scoring 202; self-report 196–198; teacher inventory 198; types 196, **197**; *see also* universal screening

self-assessment 22, **23**, 34; data 248, **261**, 312, 316; evidence-based programs 88

self-regulation **14**, 159–160, 258, 278, 295; evidence-based programs **280**

Skills for Social and Academic Success (SASS) 283, **286**, 293–294

Skillstreaming 149, 160, 348

small group intervention 33, 36, 51, **148–150**, 150, 171, 251, 283, 353; evidence base 146, 270; school counselors' role 143; screening 192, **201**, **203**; *see also* intervention

SMART goals 80, **259**, 273, 293; evidence base 87

Social Academic Intervention Group (SAIG) **145**, 148–149

Social and Emotional Learning (SEL) 33, **49**, 58, 107, 128, 154, 219, **277**, 292, 295; implementation 347, 350; leadership **231**

social justice 41, **46**, 162, 188, 262, 354; counseling competencies 152, 160, 303–304, *304*, 328; cultural and diversity implications 89–90, 152, 303–305; equity 30; school communities 95, 325, 353

solution-focused brief therapy (SFBT) 284, **289**, 294, 296

staff development 27, 57, 124, **316**, 319

Strong Kids 203, 219, 279, **282**, 295, 342

Student Success Skills 50, 81, 98, 85, 145, 149, 154, 295; advocacy 272; evidence-based program 72, **83**, 278, **280**, 283, **285**

suicide 114, 190, 205, 213, 219; awareness 131; training 247

sustainability 16, 18–19, 158, 232, 234, 239–241, 330–331

systems theory 33, 39, 64, 78, 87, 92, 95; *see also* Bronfenbrenner; Lerner

team, leadership 8, 33, 38, 53, 228; composition **13**, 17, 222–223, 23–31, 310; data use 235–236, 248, 257, 315; difficulties 235–237; executive functions 17–19, *48*;

guiding questions **20**; implementation demonstrations 19–20; tasks **231**; implementation functions 16, 18–19; overlapping roles 232–234; school counselor role **21**; shared 228; Tier 1 **14–15**, 101, 103, 106, 109; Tier 3 163, 167, 169, 174; and universal screening 209–210; *see also* consultation and collaboration

Too Good Programs 278–279; for drugs (TGFD) 279; for violence (TGFV) 279; evidence base **282**

training 30, 66, 102, 171, 198, 332; case study 252; concerns 190; cultural knowledge 31; ethical standards 23, 127, 238, 320; evidence base **177**; implementation functions 17–19, **21**, 148; overlapping roles 232–233; presenting 121; program 149; school counselor role in MTSS/CSCP systems **21**, 44–45, 49, 312, 346; 335–6, 339, 341–2, 349; school counselors 164, 169, 236, 246, 349; solution-focused brief therapy (SFBT) **285–287**, **289**; staff 201; teaming functions 22; Tier 1 **280–282**; Tier 2 134–136, 140, 142, 144

trauma 80; cognitive-behavioral intervention for trauma in schools (CBITS) 175, 347–348; concerns 190; evidence-based practices **176–178**, **289**; screening for 212–213; Tier 2 **48**; *see also* CBITS

universal screening 138, 142–143; benefits 205, 210–211; challenges 211–212; consent 200, 211, 213; data collection 200–201; interventions 202, 204; legal considerations 191, 195, 201; parents/guardians 202, 204; process steps 193; recommendations 191–192; resource allocation 208; school counselor role 208–210; suicide 213; team 193–194, 196, 199; timeline 201; training and 198, 201, 212; trauma 212–213; *see also* screener

universal supports 8, 19, 35–36, 38, *42*, 62, 99–101, 103, 222; academic content 109; implementation 347; interventions 203; sample *100*; school counselor role 316; school-wide 114

Values-in-Action 81

violence 189, 222; programs 279, **282**, **287**; resources **276**; screening for 212, school 235–236; Tier 1 **83**, 223, 278; Tier 3 164, **176**

Well-Being Therapy (WBT) 84

What Works Clearinghouse (WWC) 56; evidence-based practice 87, 275; resources 128, **277**

WhyTry 284; evidence base **287**

wraparound 37, 182, 230, 351; case study 180; ethical standards 153, 183, 240; evidence base 177; logistics 179; process 179; rational 178; research 178–179; services 249; support **47**; Tier 3 52–53, 63, 163, 165

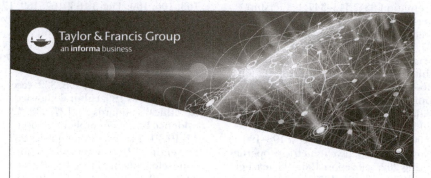